THE ROAD TO
MONTICELLO

THE ROAD TO
MONTICELLO

THE LIFE AND MIND OF

Thomas Jefferson

KEVIN J. HAYES

OXFORD
UNIVERSITY PRESS

OXFORD
UNIVERSITY PRESS

Oxford University Press, Inc., publishes works that further
Oxford University's objective of excellence
in research, scholarship, and education.

Oxford   New York
Auckland   Cape Town   Dar es Salaam   Hong Kong   Karachi
Kuala Lumpur   Madrid   Melbourne   Mexico City   Nairobi
New Delhi   Shanghai   Taipei   Toronto

With offices in
Argentina   Austria   Brazil   Chile   Czech Republic   France   Greece
Guatemala   Hungary   Italy   Japan   Poland   Portugal   Singapore
South Korea   Switzerland   Thailand   Turkey   Ukraine   Vietnam

Copyright © 2008 by Oxford University Press, Inc.

Published by Oxford University Press, Inc.
198 Madison Avenue, New York, New York, 10016

www.oup.com

Library of Congress Cataloging-in-Publication Data
Hayes, Kevin J.
The road to Monticello : the life and mind of Thomas Jefferson / by Kevin J. Hayes.
p. cm.
Includes bibliographical references.
ISBN 978-0-19-530758-0
1. Jefferson, Thomas, 1743–1826—Books and reading.   2. Jefferson, Thomas, 1743–1826—
Literary art.   3. Jefferson, Thomas, 1743–1826—Notebooks, sketchbooks, etc.
4. Jefferson, Thomas, 1743–1826—Influence.   5. Presidents—United States—Biography.
6. Monticello (Va.)—History.   7. United States—Intellectual life—1783–1865.   I. Title.
E332.2.H395   2007
973.4'6092—dc22   2007005039

Image on title page appears courtesy of the Thomas Jefferson Foundation

3 5 7 9 8 6 4 2

Printed in the United States of America
on acid-free paper

For my parents

CONTENTS

PART I: THE EDUCATION OF THOMAS JEFFERSON

1. Fire! — 1
2. A Boy and His Books — 15
3. A Correct, Classical Scholar — 30
4. William and Mary — 43
5. The Williamsburg Circle — 57
6. The Limits of English Law — 73
7. A Shelf of Notebooks — 86
8. Becoming a Burgess — 102

PART II: FAMILY AND NATION

9. Domestic Life and Literary Pursuits — 117
10. Rude Bard of the North — 133
11. *A Summary View of the Rights of British America* — 147
12. The Pen and the Tomahawk — 161
13. *The Declaration of Independence* — 174
14. The Book Culture of Philadelphia and Williamsburg, Contrasted — 191
15. Of Law and Learning — 207
16. Lines of Communication — 220
17. *Notes on the State of Virginia* — 233
18. The Narrow House — 247
19. An American Odyssey — 260

PART III: OUR MAN IN PARIS

20. Bookman in Paris   275
21. Talking about Literature   293
22. London Town   309
23. Summer of '86   326
24. An Inquisitive Journey through France and Italy   340
25. A Tour through Holland and the Rhine Valley   355
26. Last Days in Paris   369

PART IV: SERVANT OF THE PEOPLE

27. The Young Idea   383
28. *The Anas*   404
29. Letters from a Virginia Farmer   418
30. The Vice President and the Printed Word   432
31. The First Inaugural Address   449
32. The Wall of Separation   461
33. "Life of Captain Lewis"   478
34. The President as Patron of Literature   495

PART V: MONTICELLO

35. Return to Monticello   515
36. Letters to an Old Friend   532
37. The Library of Congress   546
38. The Retirement Library   564
39. *The Life and Morals of Jesus of Nazareth*   581
40. *The Autobiography*   595
41. The University of Virginia from Dream to Reality   613
42. The Life and Soul of the University   628

Acknowledgments   645
An Essay on Sources   647
Notes   655
Index   711

PART I

THE EDUCATION OF THOMAS JEFFERSON

CHAPTER I

Fire!

Fire! The word struck fear into every homeowner in colonial America. In a land where homes were shingled with wood, heated by wood, and lit with candles, fires were inevitable. All a person could do was to take some modest precautions and then try not to worry about the damage an errant spark might cause. There is no evidence to indicate that Thomas Jefferson, the youthful master of the family plantation in the Virginia Piedmont known as Shadwell, was worried about the mansion house there when he left home one February afternoon in 1770 to conduct some business in nearby Charlottesville. Already he had been master of Shadwell for half his life, since the death of his father, Peter Jefferson, thirteen years earlier. Having left the property countless times before, occasionally for months at a stretch, he had no reason to be more concerned this day than any other.

But during his brief absence, the house caught fire. The blaze spread quickly, and the house was soon engulfed. Both the building and its contents were almost completely consumed. The *Virginia Gazette* reported that Jefferson's home "burnt to the ground with all his furniture, books, papers, &c." He was less concerned with the furniture or the *et cetera*: the loss of his books and papers pained him much more. Family tradition tells what happened next. From Shadwell a slave was dispatched to locate Jefferson and inform him of the disaster. Once he told him what had happened, Jefferson had but one question: what about the books? The answer he received was disturbing. No, the man informed him, none of the books had survived.[1]

Though this anecdote may not indicate precisely what happened that day, it has the ring of truth. The story conveys something expressed in many different ways over the course of his life: Jefferson was a man with a profound love of books. Both the *Virginia Gazette* report and this traditional anecdote suggest that he lost his entire library; other accounts of the fire hint that some books had survived. In his own writings, Jefferson mentioned the incident multiple times. Into his copy of that year's almanac, which doubled as his daily memorandum book, he inscribed a laconic note: "Lost all my papers accts. etc. by fire."[2] Appearing among other legal notations rather than within his day-to-day accounts, this note confirms the loss of his legal papers. It does not mean he lost all his papers. Many of the separate notebooks he started before 1770 do survive. This *et cetera* may refer to his books, but there's no way to tell.

His correspondence sheds some light on the true extent of his loss. Writing the Reverend James Ogilvie, who had visited Shadwell earlier, Jefferson explained, "Since you left us I was unlucky enough to lose the house in which we lived, and in which all its contents were consumed. A very few books, two or three beds etc. were with difficulty saved from the flames."[3] Familiar with the contents of the house, Ogilvie could appreciate what his friend had lost.

A letter to another friend, John Page, describes the damage in slightly more detail. Jefferson lamented: "My late loss may perhaps have reached you by this time, I mean the loss of my mother's house by fire, and in it, of every paper I had in the world, and almost every book. On a reasonable estimate I calculate the cost of the books burned to have been £200. sterling. Would to god it had been the money; then had it never cost me a sigh!"[4] Jefferson's preference for books over money places him among the cadre of true book lovers.

Since this lament occurs in a letter to Page, however, it must be read with a raised eyebrow. The two had become close friends in their teens while classmates at the College of William and Mary. When they were apart, they often amused each other by exchanging cleverly crafted letters. Though overshadowed in literary history by his correspondence with John Adams, Jefferson's letters to Page represent some of his finest belletristic writing. They show him using a variety of literary and rhetorical devices, including hyperbole. For example, his earliest known letter to Page, written on Christmas 1762, begins, "This very day, to others the day of greatest mirth and jollity, sees me overwhelmed with more and greater misfortunes than have befallen a descendant of Adam for these thousand years past I am sure; and perhaps, after excepting Job, since the creation of the world."[5]

Describing personal events to Page, Jefferson typically exaggerated them to tell a better story. Before concluding each letter, he would lay bare his exaggerations to reveal what had really happened and how he truly felt. The letter describing the Shadwell fire is no exception. Early in its text Jefferson stated that he had lost almost every book he owned, but toward its end he elaborated the extent of the destruction in greater detail: "To make the loss more sensible it fell principally on my books of common law, of which I have but one left, at that time lent out. Of papers too of every kind I am utterly destitute. All of these, whether public or private, of business or of amusement have perished in the flames."[6] These remarks verify the loss of manuscript material but qualify the loss of books, implying that some books in other subjects escaped the blaze.

Beyond the loss of books, the loss of private papers "of amusement" is also regrettable. Except for his letters to Page and a few other friends, nothing of a belletristic nature in Jefferson's possession before 1770 survives. Later he admitted that he had been guilty of writing some doggerel in his youth, but no specimens of his early poetry survive. The absence of such pleasure-writing keeps the portrait of young Jefferson in the shadows.

The loss of so much manuscript material by fire gave Jefferson an object lesson in the value of the printed word. When documents exist in unique manuscript copies, they and the ideas they contain are always in danger of destruction. Discussing the importance of preserving the laws of Virginia and considering the ease with which unique manuscripts could be destroyed, Jefferson observed:

> All the care I can take of them will not preserve them from the worm, from the natural decay of the paper, from the accidents of fire, or those of removal, when it is necessary for any public purpose.... Our experience has proved to us that a single copy, or a few, deposited in MS. in the public offices, cannot be relied on for any great length of time. The ravages of fire and of ferocious enemies have had but too much part in producing the very loss we now deplore. How many of the precious works of antiquity were lost, while they existed only in manuscript? Has there ever been one lost since the art of printing has rendered it practicable to multiply and disperse copies? This leads us then to the only means of preserving those remains of our laws now under consideration, that is, a multiplication of printed copies.[7]

Print can help preserve and perpetuate the written word. Works that are printed and widely disseminated not only influence the thought and actions of mankind, but also ensure the survival of the written word and therefore make it possible that the ideas those words contain can continue to influence the thought and actions of mankind. In the age of mechanical reproduction, there seems no reason not to make multiple copies of important documents to guard against fire and other forms of destruction.

Recognizing that unique manuscripts could be lost by pure chance, Jefferson understood that pure chance determined their survival, too. Documents that escape conflagration become the stuff of history. Though Jefferson preserved an extraordinary quantity of his personal manuscripts, he did not preserve everything. Entering public life shortly before witnessing the birth of a new nation and becoming a central player in its drama, he foresaw that his papers, regardless how personal, would also become a part of history.

Consequently, he destroyed many of his most personal papers, including the complete set of letters he and his wife exchanged during their courtship and throughout their marriage, a correspondence that, in terms of literary quality, may have exceeded the letters he wrote either Adams or Page. Jefferson carefully guarded his personal life: he was unwilling to leave the destruction of documents to chance. Though he kept much, he destroyed what he wanted to destroy, leaving a record that is quite full in terms of his professional and public life, but murky when it comes to his personal life.

Discerning which of Jefferson's books survived the Shadwell fire and which perished is difficult. The survivors became part of the great library Jefferson assembled over the next four decades and ultimately sold to the federal government in 1815 to replace the first Congressional library, which itself was destroyed by fire during the War of 1812. Jefferson's personal collection thus formed the core of the Library of Congress, which, in turn, suffered further destruction in 1851, when the U.S. Capitol, where the books were housed, caught fire. Many of those volumes that managed to survive the 1770 fire at Shadwell did not survive the 1851 fire at Washington.

Hundreds of books printed before 1770 survive with evidence of Jefferson's ownership, but seldom do these survivors divulge whether he acquired them before 1770. Though Jefferson inscribed unique marks of ownership in his books, rarely did he date his inscriptions. Over time, he changed the way he inscribed his books, so differences among the survivors can help approximate the dates he acquired some of them.

No surviving book is more useful for dating Jefferson's marks of ownership than the 1752 Oxford edition of the *Book of Common Prayer* that he inherited from his father.[8] The front flyleaf is inscribed:

Peter Jefferson
30th April 1753

This prayer book is listed as part of the estate inventory prepared after Peter Jefferson's death when his older son inherited it with the rest of his father's books. Once the volume entered his possession, Thomas inscribed its title page with the following:

Ex Libris
Thomae Jefferson

Fourteen years old when his father died, young Jefferson showed his age, and something of his personality, with this inscription. The latinization of his Christian name reveals his boyhood love of the classical languages. The inscription seemed jejune in retrospect. He regretted it and later defaced the book's title page in a half-hearted attempt to obscure the inscription.

Jefferson ultimately devised a simple, yet elegant way of marking his books, which he continued using throughout his life. At a time when other members of the Virginia gentry showed off their books by adorning them with specially commissioned, engraved armorial bookplates, Jefferson used a scarcely noticeable method to identify his. Given the democratic values that formed the core of his political philosophy, it is understandable that he eschewed the aristocratic pretensions that armorial bookplates embodied.

Just because he never used a bookplate does not mean he never thought about using one. As he rebuilt his personal library after the Shadwell fire, he asked friend and fellow Virginian Thomas Adams, then living in England and working in the mercantile trade, to see if he could locate the Jefferson coat of arms. The letter containing this request has been quoted as proof of Jefferson's curiosity about his family lineage. Since the letter was written as he was busy rebuilding his library, the request may have had a more pragmatic purpose: Jefferson was considering an engraved armorial bookplate. Even as he asked Adams to locate the family crest, he did not disguise his condescension toward the whole idea: "Search the Herald's office for the arms of my family. I have what I have been told were the family arms, but on what authority I know not. It is possible there may be none. If so I would with your assistance become a purchaser, having Sterne's word for it that a coat of arms may be purchased as cheap as any other coat."[9]

Laurence Sterne was one of Jefferson's favorite authors. Five years before the Shadwell fire, Jefferson had acquired a two-volume edition of Sterne's popular devotional work, *The Sermons of Mr. Yorick*.[10] In his two most lasting books—*The Life and Opinions of Tristram Shandy* and

A Sentimental Journey through France and Italy—Sterne makes brief, satirical comments about heraldry. In his correspondence, Jefferson alluded to *Tristram Shandy* as early as 1766.[11] But he had a different work in mind as he made this remark to Thomas Adams. Jefferson's editors have yet to identify the allusion, but he was thinking about *A Political Romance*, the controversial pamphlet Sterne published in 1759. The pamphlet was so controversial that its publication was suppressed. Nearly the entire printing was burned: only a few copies escaped the flames. From one surviving copy, *A Political Romance* was reprinted in the collected edition of his works published the year after Sterne's death. Jefferson's allusion to it shows how deeply his attention to Sterne went and indicates another title that had been in his Shadwell library, the five-volume edition of *The Works of Laurence Sterne* published in 1769.

Telling his correspondent to search the Herald's office, Jefferson had in mind the scene in Sterne's political allegory where a parson searches the parish register and discovers an important piece of information about a watch-coat that represented his position, which he was attempting to secure by inheritance for his young son: "The great watch-coat was purchased and given, above two hundred years ago, by the lord of the manor, to this parish-church, to the sole use and behoof of the poor sextons thereof, and their successors for ever, to be worn by them respectively in winterly cold nights in ringing *complines*, *passing-bells*, *etc.*"[12] Sterne's political allegory emphasizes how patently absurd were the ingrained traditions of inheritance and established laws of entail that limited inheritance to specific persons. Working to establish a democracy in the coming years, Jefferson would fight hard to eliminate such ideas about inheritance.

Nowhere in *A Political Romance* or, for that matter, in any of his published writings does Sterne use the phrase Jefferson attributes to him: "A coat of arms may be purchased as cheap as any other coat." The saying is Jefferson's, and it offers a sample of how his mind worked. Recognizing a similarity between Sterne's fictional coat and a tradition of inheritance that privileged wealth over virtue and talent, Jefferson associated the two in a pithy and memorable phrase.

Ultimately, he decided against using an ostentatious armorial bookplate. Instead, Jefferson marked his books with a few strokes of the pen. In his day, printers commonly placed consecutive alphabetical characters at the bottom of the first page of every gathering of leaves in a book. The term "signature" not only referred to the character printed on the first leaf of each gathering, but also became synonymous with the individual gatherings. Jefferson used these signatures as the basis for his marks of ownership: he placed a cursive T preceding the printed J on the first page of the J-signature, and a cursive J after the printed T on the first page of the T-signature.

Jefferson was not the only one who coded his books in this manner. Philip Bliss, the Oxford antiquary, similarly marked the B- and P-signatures of his books with manuscript P's and B's.[13] A few collectors who subsequently acquired volumes from Jefferson's library appreciated his system of identifying his books so much that they, too, inscribed the signatures of their books similarly.

These signature inscriptions do more than serve as a discreet way of identifying a book's owner. Whereas armorial bookplates pasted inside the front cover and autographs on the title page and flyleaf adorn a book's periphery, signature inscriptions like Jefferson's are embedded deeply within each book. They give the impression of a book owner who is intensely engaged with the books he owns. Jefferson's marks of ownership graphically symbolize a central fact of his life: his personal identity was inextricably tied to his books.

In addition to its defaced title-page inscription, Jefferson's copy of the *Book of Common Prayer* also contains these signature inscriptions. Once he devised the new method of initialing the first page of the J- and T-gatherings, he marked his prayer book in this manner and then tried to efface the title-page inscription. Books Jefferson acquired a few years after he inherited his father's *Book of Common Prayer* contain no title-page inscriptions in his hand. Clearly, he abandoned this early method in favor of inscribing the J- and T-signatures.

With the books he acquired throughout his adult life, he continued the practice of inscribing the J- and T-signatures—though late in life he did make a small alteration. For his retirement library, which he started assembling upon selling his great library to Congress, he quit using cursive and began inscribing his T's and J's in block capitals—a deliberate effort to distinguish his retirement library from the collection he had sold to Congress.[14]

Because Jefferson stopped inscribing the title pages of his books before the Shadwell fire, surviving books containing title-page inscriptions in his hand must have been in his possession already and, therefore, had escaped the conflagration. But these few survivors add only a modest amount of information regarding his early intellectual development.

His copy of Bishop Thomas Wilson's *Short and Plain Instruction for the Better Understanding of the Lord's Supper*, for example, survives with the title-page inscription "Ex Libris Thomae Jefferson." The fact of his ownership of this book hardly distinguishes Jefferson from his peers:

nearly all Anglican youth of his generation used such works while studying for their catechism. Bishop Wilson's was among the best—readers appreciated the "elegant simplicity of its language, and its unaffected piety."[15] Although designing his work for young communicants, Wilson did not talk down to them. He approached his subject with a serious attitude and a scholarly air. Presenting the order for administering the Lord's Supper, for instance, Wilson supplied both the order and accompanying explanations in parallel columns, a technique Jefferson appreciated and would use himself in his legal and scholarly writing.

Other surviving volumes with similarly inscribed title pages show that Jefferson accumulated books useful for his study of Latin and Greek. A copy of Basil Kennett's *Antiquities of Rome* suggests that his intense study of Latin was prompting a general interest in the history and culture of ancient Rome. Similarly, his copy of John Potter's two-volume *Antiquities of Greece* supplied much information about Greek art, culture, and civilization. Potter's work also contained many well-executed engravings. Both volumes had handsomely rubricated title pages, which Jefferson made his own by inscribing his name on them.

Beyond a few title-page inscriptions, documentary evidence regarding the contents of the Shadwell library is spotty at best. By one estimate it contained three or four hundred volumes, and by another, five hundred.[16] No complete inventory of its contents survives. Three partial lists do: (1) a list of the titles in Peter Jefferson's library that forms a part of his detailed estate inventory, (2) a list of books Thomas Jefferson either purchased from or had bound by the offices of the *Virginia Gazette* in 1764 and 1765, and (3) an invoice of several books he received in one particular shipment from a London bookseller in 1769.[17] The manuscript notebooks that survived the Shadwell fire offer a handful of additional clues regarding the books in Jefferson's possession.

Surviving volumes, combined with the scant documentary evidence, do permit some surmises regarding the general contents of the Shadwell library. History and law were well represented. Jefferson owned numerous books of both ancient and modern history written in both ancient and modern languages. His fairly extensive law collection included manuals of criminal procedure, civil procedure, and equity pleading; compilations of laws and statutes, including the most up-to-date collections of Virginia laws and older collections of English statutes; reports of cases; collections of trials; and books of forms.

His library also contained a number of belletristic works: essays by Joseph Addison, whom Jefferson ranked among the most eloquent writers in the English language; several editions of periodical essays; the collected works of many English poets from Mark Akenside to Edward Young, including a handsomely bound and gilt folio edition of John Milton's *Works*; and a few novels, too. In addition to Sterne's collected works, Jefferson owned an English translation of Salomon Gessner's popular novel, *The Death of Abel*, the most widely known work of German literature in colonial America.

Though he prided himself on his knowledge of classical languages, Jefferson enjoyed current English translations of classical works, too. Shelved among his books at Shadwell were an English translation of *The Commentaries of the Emperor Marcus Antoninus* and *Thoughts of Cicero*, a compilation of extracts from the great Roman orator and philosopher treating a variety of different subjects: conscience, eloquence, friendship, old age, passion, religion, and wisdom.

Published in an attractive duodecimo format, *Thoughts of Cicero* suited the hand as well as the eye. Besides being a convenient reference, it was also a good tool for learning languages: its text was printed in Latin and French in parallel columns on the even pages and English on the odd pages. The heavily annotated English text gave Jefferson much additional miscellaneous information, updating Cicero's ideas with quotations from prominent eighteenth-century thinkers such as Francis Hutcheson and John Locke. Over the ensuing decades, Jefferson would add many more polyglot editions of classic texts to his library.

As testament to his wide-ranging religious, legal, and cultural interests, he also owned a copy of the Qur'an, specifically, George Sale's English translation, *The Koran, Commonly Called the Alcoran of Mohammed*. Being, as Muslims believe, the revealed word of God, the Qur'an not only constitutes the sacred scripture of the Islamic faith, but also forms the supreme source of Islamic law. Reading the Qur'an helped Jefferson broaden his legal studies. The Qur'an also helped him continue studying the history of religion. His curiosity about Islam is consistent with his curiosity regarding how traditional religious customs and beliefs are passed from one culture to another.[18]

Jefferson also owned many practical works for home and garden, including *The Theory and Practice of Gardening*, John James's English version of the influential work of landscape gardening and architecture by Antoine-Joseph Dézallier d'Argenville. More than merely translating the French text, James had reworked it to suit English climate, English flora, and English tastes.[19] This work helped determine the direction British pleasure gardens took during the eighteenth century. It would shape Jefferson's theories of gardening, too.

The library at Shadwell contained books about homes as well as gardens, including James Gibbs's *Rules for Drawing the Several Parts of Architecture*. Though heavily influenced by Palladian architecture, Gibbs was not a strict Palladian. He disliked being held to any particular style and incorporated elements of the Italian baroque and ideas from Christopher Wren as part of his architectural designs.[20] Gibbs's aesthetic, which emphasized intuitive feelings over taste, significantly influenced Jefferson's aesthetic, not just in terms of architecture but also in terms of art and literature.

Other volumes in the Shadwell library treated the domestic arts. For example, his father's copy of William Ellis's *London and Country Brewer* became one of several books about brewing beer he would own. More a connoisseur of fine wines than a beer drinker, Jefferson nevertheless developed expertise as a brewer. He brewed malt liquor to serve at his table, and he believed in the healthful properties of drinking porter, which he called "peculiarly salutary for your stomach."[21]

Perhaps no other work in the Shadwell library was more important in terms of Jefferson's intellectual development than one by Sir Francis Bacon. When he had his copy of Bacon rebound in Williamsburg during the mid-1760s, the clerk at the printing office identified the volume in his daybook as a folio titled "Bacon's Philosophy." This short title stood for *The Advancement of Learning*, a work that exerted a profound influence on Jefferson. He considered Bacon one of the three greatest minds in history, along with Sir Isaac Newton and John Locke. Jefferson eventually adapted the faculties of the mind Bacon posited in *The Advancement of Learning*—memory, reason, and imagination—to organize his books. The three major groups into which Jefferson subdivided his library—history, philosophy, and fine arts—directly correspond to Bacon's faculties of the mind.

In contrast to the heartfelt emotions Jefferson expressed at the loss of his books and papers in the Shadwell fire, his lack of emotion at the loss of the mansion house stands out in bold relief. The letter he wrote Page about the fire identifies the structure as "my mother's house" and conveys little regret at its loss. Jefferson's description of the house reveals his characteristic precision. Technically, the house was his mother's. Peter Jefferson had willed it to his wife, so she was the legal owner. The house was hers in spirit, too.

When Peter Jefferson had married Jane Randolph in October 1739, he was already intending to build a plantation in the Virginia Piedmont. He had acquired land there sometime before their marriage. During their early years together, Peter and Jane Jefferson lived at Fine Creek, where their first two daughters were born, Jane in 1740 and Mary the following year. Sister Jane would become a special favorite of young Thomas, who fondly remembered her singing psalms to him. After Mary's birth, Peter Jefferson relocated his family to the Piedmont plantation, which he named Shadwell, in honor of his wife, who had been born in Shadwell parish, London. Here Thomas Jefferson was born on April 2, 1743, or, reckoned by the new-style calendar, April 13, 1743. The following year Mrs. Jefferson gave birth to Elizabeth.

Then a part of Goochland County, the area containing Thomas's birthplace would become a part of Albemarle County when Goochland was partitioned. Peter Jefferson began building Shadwell on the north side of the Rivanna River in much the same way other contemporary Virginia plantations were built. Their first home, the one in which Thomas was born, was built using local materials and erected on a stone foundation. A passel of outbuildings were constructed on the premises. Once Peter Jefferson had established himself sufficiently, he turned his attention to the task of constructing the mansion house, which was erected during the early to mid 1750s.[22]

The term "mansion house" may be an overstatement. When it was constructed, Shadwell lacked the grandeur of the best Tidewater mansions, yet Peter Jefferson's house became the finest in the region upon its completion. At his death in 1757, Shadwell contained a substantial group of buildings. After the fire, the family relocated to one of the smaller ones, likely the original home in which Thomas had been born.

During his boyhood, Thomas spent less time at Shadwell than he spent elsewhere. When he was two years old, his father's good friend William Randolph of Tuckahoe, died unexpectedly. Randolph's will named Peter Jefferson executor. A codicil contained the unusual request that his friend take charge of both his plantation and the education of his children. Given his diligence and profound sense of responsibility, Peter Jefferson complied with Randolph's dying wish and removed his own family to Tuckahoe.

Thomas's early memories, therefore, are associated with Tuckahoe, not Shadwell. Here, Martha, his fourth sister, was born. Jane Jefferson would give birth to five more children, three surviving into adulthood: Lucy, Anna Scott, and Randolph. Twelve years younger than his older brother, Randolph Jefferson remains a shadowy presence in Thomas's life. Peter did not bring his growing family back to Shadwell for several years. By the time he did, he had already arranged to board young Thomas with a local minister, where the boy could attend school. After his father's death, Thomas did not remain at Shadwell but went to study at another small local school. Through his adolescence and teenage years, therefore, he spent relatively little time at Shadwell.

His fondest memories of Shadwell were not of the fine home his father built but of the surrounding woods: its outdoors, not its indoors. Here he learned tracking, trailing, and hunting. Even when he became more engaged with the world of books during his teenage years, his studies would often take him outdoors for purposes of exercise and contemplation. The pursuit of knowledge, after all, required the same kind of personal discipline as the pursuit of physical fitness. As Jefferson observed, "The faculties of the mind, like the members of the body, are strengthened and improved by exercise."[23] On horseback or afoot, young Jefferson found that his outdoor excursions often led him to a peak on his father's property located along the ridge of the Southwest Mountains. He would eventually christen it Monticello.

Describing Monticello a decade and a half after he had begun building his home there, Jefferson captured the place in all of its natural beauty. This description occurs in his renowned "Dialogue between My Head and My Heart," which he wrote as part of a letter to Maria Cosway. Since she was a painter, Jefferson, speaking from the Heart, depicted his home as an ideal place for her to develop her landscape painting. He wrote: "And our own dear Monticello, where has nature spread so rich a mantle under the eye? Mountains, forests, rocks, rivers. With what majesty do we there ride above the storms! How sublime to look down into the workhouse of nature, to see her clouds, hail, snow, thunder, all fabricated at our feet! And the glorious Sun, when rising as if out of a distant water, just gilding the tops of the mountains, and giving life to all nature."[24]

Though he recognized the mountain's natural beauty when he was in his teens, there is no telling precisely when Jefferson began to consider building a home at its top. The idea likely occurred to him before he gave much thought to practical considerations. How, perchance, would a person obtain water on a mountaintop?

Among the books he inherited from his father was one by the influential British landscape gardener Stephen Switzer. This work's influence on Jefferson has yet to be gauged—mainly because his ownership of it has yet to be noticed. The book perished in the fire at Shadwell. The nearly illegible manuscript title listed in Peter Jefferson's estate inventory has so far escaped identification, but the book was *Ichnographia Rustica, or, The Nobleman, Gentleman, and Gardener's Recreation*. In this work, Switzer provided a detailed set of "rules for laying out a country estate." The aesthetic he exemplified is similar to the aesthetic that eighteenth-century poets advocated. Landscaping their country estates, Switzer's readers were told to follow nature.[25]

Switzer devoted a chapter to the subject of choosing a location for a country seat. He praised homes having good views but identified three basic needs to solve before building a home at a lofty location: wood, water, and proper soil. Sufficient wood and proper soil may have been worth considering in the modest elevations of England, but both were plentiful in Virginia. Water presented Jefferson the only real physical difficulty. Considering the spectacular views Monticello offered and the psychological benefits derived from them, Jefferson decided that building atop the mountain was worth whatever difficulties locating a good source of water presented. As Switzer observed, "A high Scituation has indeed one Consideration to recommend it, as is like to overballance a Thousand Advantages in other Scituations, I mean its Height, and by Consequences the Nobleness of the View, and the Clearness of the Air."

If Jefferson had not made up his mind to build on Monticello already, what Switzer had to say next surely convinced him:

Those Places being such as will clear and relax the Passages of the Head and Breast, and such from which we view the beautiful Scenes of Nature, and like the great Philosopher from his Eminence in Philosophy, (tho' not with the same kind of Satisfaction) see the busie World acting their several Parts of their Labour and Toil below, fills the Mind with immense Idea's, and makes the World below us as our own.[26]

Visiting a decade after construction had begun, the Chevalier de Chastellux recorded his impressions of Monticello. His words capture Jefferson's personal explanation as to why he decided to build atop the mountain, an explanation reflecting Switzer's influence. Chastellux wrote that Jefferson's "house stands pre-eminent in these retirements; it was himself who built it and preferred this situation; for although he possessed considerable property in the neighbourhood, there was nothing to prevent him from fixing his residence wherever he thought proper. But it was a debt nature owed to a philosopher and a man of taste, that in his own possessions he should find a spot where he might best study and enjoy her ... and it seemed as if from his youth he had placed his mind, as he has done his house, on an elevated situation, from which he might contemplate the universe."[27]

When Shadwell caught fire, Jefferson had already begun building at Monticello. The fact that he would possess a great new home of his own design located at a place of his own choosing no doubt mitigated the sense of loss he may have felt with the destruction of the mansion house at Shadwell. Though construction had not progressed far enough to make the place habitable, in his mind's eye he could see it completed, from the outside as well as from within. In terms of Jefferson's personal development, the Shadwell fire came at a propitious time: the building of Monticello and the rebuilding of his library would occur simultaneously. He saw each as an outward reflection of his personality and imagined both on a grand scale.

Completed or not, Monticello held great symbolic value for Thomas Jefferson. Beyond its importance as an architectural landmark, it remains valuable as a symbol of his mind. For him, Monticello represented a retreat from public life. When he was there, he could indulge himself in the pleasures of scholarship and family. When his public responsibilities kept him away from home, he could imaginatively return to Monticello.

Though Jefferson's patriotism and his dedication to liberty and justice, not to mention his ambition, drew him to politics and government, his personal and intellectual inclinations made him seek sanctuary in a home of his own design, a place where he could pursue his interests in art, music, science, and literature. Contemplating his experiences after his retirement from public office, he observed, "The whole of my life ... has been a war with my natural tastes, feelings and wishes. Domestic life and literary pursuits, were my first and my latest inclinations, circumstances and not my desires led me to the path I have trod."[28]

Both before and after it was completed, Monticello represented in Jefferson's mind an ideal place to which he could always return. The story of his life is a story of a man whose profound commitment to the public welfare compelled him to a life of leadership yet who always longed for an ideal world where he could enjoy the life of the mind.

CHAPTER 2

A Boy and His Books

The chapman was a familiar figure along the byways of colonial America. With a pack on his back filled with a variety of inexpensive goods both useful and entertaining, the chapman crisscrossed the colonies selling his wares. Men and women, boys and girls, all came to know the chapman and eagerly anticipated his visits. Among his wares, he usually kept a stock of books. They were known not only as Chapman's books, but also as "little books," "small books," or, regardless of their largely fictional nature, "small histories." Some people just called them "histories." The most ambitious chapmen stocked a good selection of titles. Chapbook texts popular in eighteenth-century America included *Dr. Faustus*, *The Famous History of the Seven Champions of Christendom*, *The History of Fortunatus*, *The History of Parismus*, *The History of Tom Thumb*, *Jack the Giant Killer*, *Reynard the Fox*, *Valentin and Orson*, and *The Wise Men of Gotham*. These entertaining storybooks captured the attention of numerous young readers in colonial America—Thomas Jefferson included.

Though often printed thousands at a time, few of these chapbooks survive. None survive with evidence of Jefferson's ownership. If he saved any beyond his childhood, then they perished in the Shadwell fire. Chances are they did not last that long. They may have lasted long enough for his younger sisters Elizabeth and Martha to read once their precocious brother had outgrown them. Usually, chapbooks were read and read and read again until they fell apart, at which time they became so much waste paper: tinder for fires, wrapping paper for dried goods, or, quite frankly, lavatory paper.

Jefferson's later correspondence offers a clue to his earliest childhood reading. Writing to Maria Cosway after she had returned to England while he remained in Paris, Jefferson imagined a fanciful way for them to be together:

I wish they had formed us like the birds of the air, able to fly where we please. I would have exchanged for this many of the boasted preeminences of man. I was so unlucky when very young, as to read the history of Fortunatus. He had a cap of such virtues that when he put it on his head, and wished himself anywhere, he was there. I have been all my life sighing for this cap. Yet if I had it, I question if I should use it but once. I should wish myself with you, and not wish myself away again.[1]

As his reference to the work suggests, *The History of Fortunatus* told a fantastic tale about an adventurous man who acquired an inexhaustible purse and a magic cap that not only made him invisible but also transported him anywhere he wished to go. The work was so widely known that Fortunatus's purse and cap had become proverbial.[2]

The sigh Jefferson let escape in the letter to Maria Cosway is an obvious affectation meant to endear her, yet it also signals how fondly he remembered reading *Fortunatus*, a work he would continue to recall. In response to an American correspondent who had written to relay information about his family, Jefferson replied from Paris:

The distance to which I am removed renders that kind of intelligence more interesting, more welcome, as it seems to have given a keener edge to all the friendly affections of the mind. Time, absence, and comparison render my own country much dearer, and give a lustre to all it contains which I did not before know that it merited. Fortunatus's wishing cap was always the object of my desire, but never so much as lately. With it I should soon be seated at your fireside to enjoy the society of yourself and family.[3]

Jefferson's surviving correspondence also alludes to *The History of Tom Thumb*.[4] His familiarity with the tales of Fortunatus and Tom Thumb make likely his familiarity with many of the day's other chapbook stories, but it is impossible to know which ones he read as a child. Suffice it to say that his well-known preference for small-format books stretches back to his earliest reading.

Jefferson and John Page were almost exact contemporaries—the two had been born within a few days of one another—and Page's boyhood experience reading these little books resembles Jefferson's attention to Fortunatus. Page became quite fond of reading at a young age. Remembering what he read prior to entering a Latin grammar school at the age of nine, he recalled "the little amusing and instructing books" his grandmother had given him. After entering this school, he initially found the study of Latin difficult because it interrupted his "delightful reading of Histories and Novels."[5]

These little books cast a spell over their young readers they found difficult to break. Chapbook stories revealed strange new worlds— strange not only because they were fantastic but also because they described places where the ordinary rules of society did not apply. Chapbooks fired the imaginations of young colonial American readers and allowed them to picture worlds very different from their own.

When Thomas was five, his father placed him at an English school. Jefferson's autobiography is the sole authority for this information; most agree that he attended the school conducted at Tuckahoe and studied with the Randolph children. Here, he improved his reading proficiency with Aesop's *Fables* and *Robinson Crusoe*, works that many children in colonial America read around this same age. Jefferson later purchased some books of fables for Polly Randolph, a member of the family's next generation, when she was six years old. Another time he bought a copy of *Robinson Crusoe* for a different young member of the Randolph family. Jefferson came to know both works well, and they would remain lifelong favorites, especially Aesop's *Fables*. He would eventually acquire several editions of Aesop in Greek, sometimes with Latin translations and usually with learned commentary. Outlining a program of Native American education, he emphasized the importance of teaching Indians how to read English and specifically mentioned two books the reading Indians he knew particularly enjoyed: Aesop's *Fables* and *Robinson Crusoe*.[6]

The numerous references to Aesop's *Fables* in his correspondence display the lifelong influence the work had on Jefferson. Serving as a member of Congress during the early 1780s and having to cope with several contentious legislators, he appreciated a letter from his friend Francis Hopkinson, who had sent him the latest science news from Philadelphia's intellectual world. Responding to Hopkinson, Jefferson commented, "In truth amidst this eternal surfeit of politics wherein one subject succeeds another like Aesop's feast of tongues a small entremêt of philosophy is relieving."[7] These words reflect a sentiment that frequently recurs in Jefferson's correspondence. For much of his adult life, politics would provide the main course while philosophy—the term then incorporated all the sciences—offered a temporarily diverting side dish.

In this letter to Hopkinson, Jefferson alluded to an episode from one of the fabulous lives of Aesop, which prefaced contemporary collections of Aesop's fables. As the story goes, Aesop's master, the philosopher Xanthus, having invited his disciples home for dinner, ordered Aesop to serve a fine, savory meal. Aesop served tongue as the first course, for which the

disciples praised Xanthus, finding tongue a dish appropriate to philosophical discourse. When Aesop brought the second course—another
tongue dish—the disciples, at first taken aback, finally approved the dish,
for they realized that one tongue could sharpen another. When Aesop
brought out more tongue for the third course, the disciples could think of
nothing good to say about it. Xanthus threatened to beat Aesop, who
proceeded to explain the propriety of his culinary choice: every doctrine
and all philosophy are established and propagated by the tongue.

The next day Xanthus planned another dinner for his disciples.
Hoping to avoid the fiasco of the previous day, he ordered Aesop to
prepare the worst meal he could. Aesop served exactly the same dishes.
Asked for an explanation, he responded that nothing could be worse
than the tongue. Men perished and cities were destroyed by rumors the
tongue spreads; in short, nothing propagated evil more than the tongue.

It is not difficult to understand why this anecdote stayed with Jefferson: the literal and figurative connotations of the word "tongue"
would remain significant to him throughout his life. While emphasizing
the tongue's physicality, the anecdote also uses the word abstractly to
represent the entire process of communication. Both literally and figuratively, the tongue serves as the conduit through which ideas are con-
verted into words. Being the physical organ that makes speech possible,
the tongue had become a synonym for language and been extended to
connote the written word. Whenever Jefferson wished to deepen his
study of any particular subject, he sought to learn the language most
pertinent to his studies. For him, the study of different tongues would be
a lifelong pursuit.

He remembered other fables of Aesop's, especially those that were
useful as political allegories, like the one about the miller, his son, and
their ass. By trying to please everyone, the miller ends up pleasing no one
and loses his ass in the bargain.[8] Elsewhere Jefferson referred to the fable
in which wolves negotiate a peace treaty with some sheep, stipulating
only that the sheep give up their dogs. As soon as the sheep meet the
terms of the treaty, the wolves devour them. When some Federalist
opponents expressed a desire for a monarchical form of government,
Jefferson compared them to Aesop's frogs, which implore Jupiter to send
them a king. Jupiter eventually chooses as their king a heron, which eats
up all its amphibious subjects.[9]

Jefferson also appreciated Aesop's fable about the old man and his sons.
Nearing his death, the old man asks his sons to bring him a bundle of
slender rods. As requested, one son brings him the bundle, and the old
man hands it to each son in turn and asks them to break the rods that had

been bound together. None can do so. Next, the father asks them to break the rods one by one. They easily break every rod. "My sons," the old man tells them, "if you are all of the same mind, then no one can do you any harm, no matter how great his power. But if your intentions differ from one another, then what happened to the single rods is what will happen to each of you!" During the summer of 1776, as members of the Continental Congress were designing a seal for the United States of America, Jefferson recalled Aesop's fable and suggested that instead of a coat of arms, a more appropriate emblem for the United States of America would be an image of the father presenting the bundle of rods to his sons.

As an adolescent, Jefferson also encountered a poem from Thomas White's *Little Book for Little Children*.[10] He remembered lines from it all his life and recalled them in a letter to his granddaughter Cornelia a half century later:

> I've seen the sea all in a blaze of fire
> I've seen a house high as the moon and higher
> I've seen the sun at twelve oclock at night
> I've seen the man who saw this wondrous sight.

These lines present paradoxes intended to force younger readers to study their geography and discover where in the world these contradictory phenomena could possibly occur. Such paradoxes encouraged adolescents to use their brains to solve difficult problems.

In 1752 Jefferson entered the Latin grammar school run by the Reverend William Douglas, rector of St. James-Northam Parish in Goochland County. Born in Scotland in 1708, Douglas, by his own account, was educated "in the learned Languages, Geography, Mathematics and Chronology." He subsequently attended the College of Glasgow for two years, where he studied ethics, logic, metaphysics, and other branches of philosophy. Leaving Glasgow, he attend the College of Edinburgh, where he studied church history, divinity, French, Hebrew, moral philosophy, and physics.[11]

Douglas worked as a private tutor in Virginia during the mid-1740s. Late that decade he returned to Great Britain to be ordained. On October 5, 1749, the Reverend Mr. William Douglas received the King's bounty for Virginia, which meant that he obtained the passage money provided to clergymen licensed by the Bishop of London to serve in the colonies. Back in Virginia in 1750, Douglas assumed the rectorship at Goochland, which had been vacated upon the death of the Reverend Anthony Gavin the previous year.[12]

Besides teaching Jefferson the fundamentals of ancient and modern languages, Douglas likely inculcated his young pupil in matters of conduct. Biographical evidence, though scant, suggests Douglas's concern for the piety of the children in his charge. His messages to his nieces are filled with advice to read good books and to achieve happiness through industry, frugality, and careful planning. From Douglas's viewpoint, Philip Doddridge's *Sermons to Young Persons* offered ideal advice for the coming generation. His knowledge of books extended well beyond such works of popular piety, however. He owned a fairly extensive personal library: at his death it was valued at £150. Though his executors did not inventory the titles it contained, its recorded value indicates a substantial collection.[13]

The single best record of Douglas's personality and his intellectual predilections is the record book he kept during the course of his career as rector of St. James-Northam Parish and maintained after leaving the parish in 1777. This detailed record of births, baptisms, marriages, and deaths represents a model of record-keeping and is more thorough than any similar Virginia records of the time. He went so far as to note the maiden names of mothers when their children were born or baptized. Remarkably, he often recorded slave marriages and christenings, too. The Douglas register forms a major contribution to American genealogical literature.

It is difficult to assess how Douglas's record-keeping manifested itself in his teaching methods. On one hand, the register may indicate that he took his pastoral duties more seriously than his role as a teacher. On the other, the register embodies a level of meticulousness Douglas demanded of himself and may have demanded from his students. As an adult, Jefferson himself would develop a reputation as a meticulous record-keeper.

Among the births and deaths of his parishioners, Douglas also included references to the deaths of many literary figures. Though no inventory of his library survives, the names of authors mentioned in the register indicate the cast of his mind. Names of the founders and leaders of the Protestant Reformation confirm Douglas's dedication to his faith. He also mentioned many widely read devotional authors: Richard Baxter, Presbyterian divine and prolific author; Isaac Watts, best remembered as a hymnist but also a prolific author of popular schoolbooks; John Scott, whom Douglas identified as the author of a book titled *The Christian Life*; John Tillotson, whom Douglas included in a list of "several renowned old worthys famous for their holy useful writings and zeal for the reformation"; and William Wollaston, the author of *The Religion of Nature Delineated* and "an eminent Writer" in Douglas's words. Jefferson would not share his teacher's opinion of this last author. He later referred to the philosophy underlying Wollaston's work as a whimsical theory of moral principles.[14]

Douglas's list of worthies is not restricted to authors of divinity. He recorded the death of Grotius: "Aug: 28. 1645—Grotius died 71: 4 months—his age. 'Be serious' was his last advice." Recording Grotius's death date a second time in the register, Douglas referred to him as "the great statesman and scholar." He also listed the death dates of John Gay, "the famous poet"; John Locke, "the Philosopher"; and Sir Isaac Newton. The entries he made after Jefferson had left his school include the following: "Aug: 25 1776—Mr. Da: Hume the Historian died a meer sceptist."

These names convey Douglas's knowledge of an array of subjects from political philosophy to *belles lettres* to history and science. Douglas's hodgepodge of names from Western intellectual history indicates a quirky curiosity about the ideas they represent and the fame their words and ideas brought them. Taken together, these various names form a collective *memento mori*. Regardless how great their ideas or how wide their fame, all met their earthly end.

In addition to inculcating piety in young Jefferson and teaching him the fundamentals of Latin grammar, his teacher may have exposed him to other intellectual currents. At Glasgow Douglas had studied with Gershom Carmichael, who introduced his students to the names of Locke and Grotius and the ideas they represented. Carmichael not only incorporated their thought in both his lectures and writings, but also pioneered a new approach to moral philosophy prefiguring subsequent intellectual developments that flourished with the Scottish Enlightenment. Most important, he propagated an innovative approach to the study of natural law.

Carmichael is best known for his annotations and supplements to the Glasgow edition of Samuel Pufendorf's *De Officio Hominis et Civis*. This annotated edition was adopted as a textbook by contemporary professors, and it became standard reading in moral philosophy courses through the mid-eighteenth century. Francis Hutcheson, to name Carmichael's most distinguished pupil, found his edition even more useful than Pufendorf's original.[15] There is no telling precisely how much Carmichael influenced Douglas in the matter of natural law or, in turn, how much Douglas influenced Jefferson, but the possibilities are intriguing. The subject of natural law would profoundly shape Jefferson's thought; his exposure to such ideas could have come as early as his adolescence.

Regardless of his teacher's miscellaneous knowledge, Jefferson was unimpressed with his linguistic accomplishments. Remembering his adolescent education, he called Douglas "a superficial Latinist" who was even "less instructed in Greek."[16] Despite his small Latin and less Greek, Douglas managed to teach his eager student the rudiments of these languages, which then served as a basis for learning French. Jefferson would sustain a profound love of Latin and Greek and would continue to devote a portion of his leisure time to the study of the classical tongues throughout his life.

Though previous biographers have taken Jefferson at his word and downplayed Douglas's influence on him, the animosity Jefferson expressed toward his teacher seems unduly harsh. It is important to note that his critique is directed only toward Douglas's linguistic abilities, not his overall scholarly accomplishments. Other evidence suggests that Douglas was a good teacher. Recommending him for Holy Orders to the Bishop of London, William Dawson, the commissary of Virginia—the highest ranking official of the Anglican Church in the colony—stated that Douglas had "behaved himself exceedingly well in the Office of a private Tutor."[17]

Jefferson left little indication regarding what books he read either at the English school or at Douglas's, but the evidence shows that during his schooldays he was starting to assemble his first library. Peter Jefferson's accounts indicate payment for several books for his son during the time he boarded with Douglas.[18] Though these accounts list no titles, there were certain basic texts that formed an essential part of the curriculum.

Later references to basic schoolbooks in Jefferson's writings may offer a clue to what he read during his adolescence. His letters show him overseeing the education of his nephews during the 1770s and 1780s after the unexpected death of his best friend and brother-in-law, Dabney Carr, who had married his younger sister Martha. One letter mentions some specific works Jefferson found suitable for the three Carr boys that may indicate books he read himself as part of his own education.[19]

The boys, aged eight, ten, and twelve at the time of Jefferson's letter, received an education at the hands of their uncle that closely parallels the one he had received. Peter, the oldest, was reading Virgil and would soon begin studying French. Dabney Junior, the youngest, was concentrating on English, but Jefferson hoped he would be ready for Latin within the next year or so. His educational plan must have worked, because Dabney Carr, Jr., became a learned man who would later distinguish himself as a prominent Virginia jurist during the early nineteenth century. Ten-year-old Samuel, with his uncle's help, was making it through his grammar and had made it halfway through his Cordery.

By Cordery, Jefferson meant the colloquies of the sixteenth-century Genevan schoolmaster Maturin Cordier. Designed as a Latin conversation manual for beginning students, Cordier's *Colloquia* went through countless editions from the sixteenth into the nineteenth century. Many thousands of Corderies were imported into British North America during the colonial era, and the work is listed in numerous Virginia library inventories from the period. During the eighteenth century, selected editions, generally consisting of precisely one hundred colloquies, became more popular than the complete work, which contained more than double that number. At the same time Jefferson was studying with Douglas, John Page was reading his Cordery at the grammar school of the College of William and Mary, the use of which was mandated by statute: "Because nothing contributes so much to the Learning of Languages, as dayly Dialogues, and familiar Speaking together, in the Languages they are learning; let the Master therefore take Care that out of the Colloquies of Corderius and Erasmus, and Others, who have employed their Labours this Way, the Scholars may learn aptly to express their Meaning to each other."[20] In combination with other basic works, the Cordery gave students a working vocabulary sufficient to allow them to read Latin prose and verse without having to run to the dictionary to look up every other word.

Jefferson's literary commonplace book indicates the books he turned to next, after mastering the fundamentals of Latin. The earliest entries in the commonplace book date from the last two years he spent at Douglas's school. Planning its contents before making any entries, Jefferson allotted space for quoting passages from Virgil, Horace, and Ovid. Though the planned entries from Virgil are missing, the commonplace book contains several Latin quotations from Horace's *Odes* and *Satires* and Ovid's *Heroides*.[21]

One of the most striking Latin entries from Horace that Jefferson made in his commonplace book can be translated as, "O rural home: when shall I behold you! When shall I be able, now with books of the ancients, now with sleep and idle hours, to quaff sweet forgetfulness of life's cares!" This entry, inscribed by Jefferson in his adolescence, anticipates a sentiment he would echo time and again over the course of his political career. Copying this passage from Horace, he may have anticipated his enduring love of books and learning as well as the responsibilities that would take him from his studies for long periods of time.

Jefferson acquired Greek more slowly than Latin. After learning to read Latin verse, he was still mastering the fundamentals of Greek orthography, diction, and syntax. Conventionally, French was introduced after Greek but was generally acquired more rapidly. A copy of *Rerum Romanorum Epitome*, Florus's synopsis of Roman history in a

French and Latin parallel text edition, survives among Jefferson's books at the Library of Congress with his early title-page inscription. This edition of Florus offered him a useful methodology. Parallel text editions not only facilitated language acquisition, but also let their readers compare the relationship between language and meaning.

At some point in his education, Jefferson turned to Fénelon's *Les Aventures de Télémaque*, a late-seventeenth-century fictional work that formed part of the education of nearly everyone who learned French in eighteenth-century America.[22] Recommending several French books to Peter Carr, who was just starting to study the language, Jefferson placed *Télémaque* first. Written for Fénelon's pupil, the young Duke of Burgundy, this didactic novel narrates the adventures of Ulysses' son and, in so doing, offers a pleasant guide to leadership to help the young duke.

This work, too, may have exerted an influence on Jefferson's nascent political thought. It not only emphasized the responsibilities rulers have to their subjects, but also affirmed the congruence between the government of man and the harmony of nature. Fénelon articulated similar ideas in *Télémaque* that could be found in other works Jefferson read in his boyhood. Asked what man is free, young Telemachus responds that man is free only when fear and desire have no sway over him and when he is subject only to reason and the gods.[23] Ideas Jefferson was encountering in his reading were starting to recur and coalesce. They would keep doing so as his education continued.

Another French book Jefferson owned also dates from this period, Charles Drelincourt's *Les Consolations de l'Ame Fidèle, Contre les Frateurs de la Mort* or, as it was known in its English translation, *The Christian's Defense against the Fears of Death*. Jefferson's copy, which survives at the Library of Congress, is missing its title page. Apparently, the title page was already gone by the time it came into his hands. His inscription, which appears on the first page of the book's dedication, suggests that he acquired the volume in his teens. An inscription on the book's flyleaf, also in Jefferson's hand, details it provenance:

> The gift of
> Mrs Rachael Gavin widow of the revd Anthony Gavin, a Spaniard, author of the Master key to Popery and Rector of Saint James's Northam parish, Goochland Virginia, to Th: Jefferson.

These words reveal Jefferson's cognizance of the Reverend Gavin's reputation as both author and clergyman. Some years after publishing his virulent anti-Catholic treatise, *A Master-Key to Popery*, Gavin had received the King's bounty for Virginia. He preached briefly in Henrico Parish before taking the position in St. James-Northam Parish. After his death in 1749, his wife, Rachel, inherited his property, including his books.[24]

Though neither of Jefferson's inscriptions in his copy of Drelincourt's *Consolations* is dated, he likely received the book in 1757. The work is one of a number of popular books designed to help readers cope with death. William Sherlock's *Practical Discourse Concerning Death* was better known in colonial Virginia, but copies of Drelincourt, mostly in English translation, were not unusual. Drelincourt's *Consolations* had a fine contemporary reputation. Daniel Defoe, in his short story "A Relation of the Apparition of Mrs. Veal," called it the best book on the subject ever written; its author "had the clearest notions of death and of the future state of any who had handled that subject."[25] A prefatory note to the English translation of Drelincourt's text suggests that the book made an ideal present for the bereaved, an aspect of it that helps date Jefferson's acquisition. The custom of giving appropriate books as funeral presents was a well-established tradition in colonial America by the time Peter Jefferson died on August 17, 1757.[26]

Peter Jefferson's death was not unanticipated. Though only forty-nine, he had been quite ill throughout the summer months. Starting the last week of June, Dr. Thomas Walker, friend, neighbor, and family physician, was making professional visits to Shadwell on an increasingly frequent basis. In July, Peter felt concerned enough about the state of his health to make a will. Around the time of his father's death, Thomas broke off his studies with Douglas to return to Shadwell.

No firsthand accounts of Peter Jefferson's funeral survive, but his *Book of Common Prayer*, which details the actions that should be taken and the words that must be spoken during the burial of the dead, functions as a record of the event in retrospect. As the ceremony neared its end, the coffin was lowered into the grave and those in attendance cast earth upon the coffin.

"Forasmuch as it hath pleased Almighty God of his great mercy to take unto himself the soul of our dear brother here departed," the priest intoned, "we therefore commit his body to the ground; earth to earth, ashes to ashes, dust to dust, in sure and certain hope of the resurrection to eternal life, through our Lord Jesus Christ, who shall change our vile body, that it may be like unto his glorious body, according to the mighty working, whereby he is able to subdue all things to himself."

Thomas Jefferson retained fond memories of his father throughout his life, but he remembered him more for his strength and judgment than for his intellect. Trained as a surveyor, Peter Jefferson had not had a great deal of formal education, yet he had made an effort to acquire a modicum of literary refinement. Thomas later expressed pride in his father's curiosity and desire for knowledge. Being, in his son's words, "eager after information, he read much and improved himself." In his will, Peter stipulated that Thomas would receive "my books, mathematical instruments, and my cherry tree desk and bookcase." Peter Jefferson's library, though slight by the impressive standards set by well-to-do gentlemen in Tidewater Virginia, was one of the largest in Albemarle County then, though it contained fewer than fifty volumes.[27]

The library Thomas Jefferson inherited from his father formed a curious collection of practical and pleasurable works. He received the few law books his father had owned, the most substantial being *A Collection of Proceedings and Trials against State Prisoners* by the prolific historical writer Thomas Salmon. Apparently the work did not survive the fire at Shadwell, but Jefferson later acquired another copy of Salmon's *Collection*—from his father-in-law. With complete editions of *The Spectator*, *The Tatler*, and *The Guardian* and a three-volume edition of Joseph Addison's *Miscellaneous Works*, Peter Jefferson's collection was rich in belletristic essays. As a popularizer of many current philosophical ideas, Addison gave Thomas Jefferson a solid foundation upon which he could build a superstructure of knowledge.

His father's library also included some influential works of history, travel, and geography, including John Ogilby's important compilation, *America*, a good portion of which is devoted to the story of the exploration and settling of Virginia. This, along with his father's copy of *Laws of Virginia*, constitute the first known items of Virginiana Thomas Jefferson acquired for his library. Throughout his life he would keep collecting books about Virginia and eventually assemble a fine collection of Virginiana.[28] Alas, Ogilby would not be part of it. His father's copy of Ogilby's *America* did not survive the fire at Shadwell, and Jefferson's subsequent correspondence reflects the loss. Finding a copy of the work listed in a bookseller's catalogue many years later, he tried to purchase it but was unsuccessful. Despite his best efforts, he never could replace his father's copy of Ogilby's *America*.

Two works from his father's collection were well known throughout colonial America, Paul de Rapin-Thoyras's *History of England* and Lord Anson's *Voyage*. Thomas inherited a two-volume folio edition of Nicolas Tindal's translation of Rapin's *History of England* and also Tindal's two-volume sequel to it, which continued the story of England to the accession of King George II. Rapin's *History* introduced Jefferson, and many others of his generation, to Whig history. Most important, the work affirmed the Saxon roots of liberal democracy and the idea that Saxon kings could not change the laws or levy taxes at their will.[29]

Peter Jefferson's copy of *The History of England* perished in the Shadwell fire, too, but his son eventually replaced it with a ten-volume edition in the original French. One visitor to Monticello noticed this edition of Rapin in Jefferson's library and recorded what Jefferson said about it: "Rapin was here in French, though very rare in that language. Mr. Jefferson said that after all it was still the best history of England, for Hume's tory principles are to him insupportable." Once the French edition went to the Library of Congress with the rest of his books, Jefferson acquired another copy of Tindal's English translation, the fifteen-volume octavo edition published in the late 1720s and early 1730s. Toward the end of his life, he reiterated his opinion of Rapin, asserting that "of England there is as yet no general history so faithful as Rapin's."[30]

Travel literature added much excitement to Jefferson's boyhood reading. First published at a time when the novel was making a significant impact on the literary marketplace, George Anson's *Voyage Round the World* provided contemporary readers with a nonfiction alternative that contained as much action and pathos as any novel.[31] It brought the war between England and Spain alive, set it on a world stage, and gave readers an insider's view of the strategies involved in sea battles. Anson's stories of death, privation, suffering, and perseverance were touching, and his frequent references to latitudes and out-of-the-way places allowed readers to follow his route as he circumnavigated the globe.

"When young," Jefferson wrote, "I was passionately fond of reading books of history, and travels."[32] Anson's *Voyage* fed this youthful passion and helped it endure. In the organizational scheme Jefferson later devised for his library, voyages and travels would be subsumed under the general category of "Geography." His copy of Anson's *Voyage*—either this or a replacement copy—would take its place in his library next to a universal gazetteer.[33]

The white spaces in the copy of the *Book of Common Prayer* Thomas Jefferson inherited from his father presented a convenient place for keeping vital family records—births, deaths, marriages. Jefferson's family records reveal a level of meticulousness reminiscent of his teacher's. The relative permanence of the *Book of Common Prayer* made sure these family records would last. It is not coincidence that this prayer book survived while so many other books perished in the fire at Shadwell.

Though the vital records within the book's covers remain important to Jefferson family history, the other inscriptions Thomas made in the volume are more pertinent to the story of his literary and intellectual growth. To the tenth verse of Psalm 10—"The days of our age are threescore years and ten, and though men be strong that they come to fourscore years: yet is their strength then but labour and sorrow; so soon passeth it away, and we are gone"—he supplied a footnote in Greek from the first book of Herodotus. Roughly translated it means: "For I set the limit of man's life at seventy years."

Brief as it is, this note reveals much about its author. For one thing, it shows Jefferson's scholarly bent. Learned annotations were characteristic of well-respected editions of classic texts. This annotation reveals a student in the process of replicating the efforts of his scholarly progenitors. The note also shows Jefferson's interest in comparing similar ideas emanating from different cultures, a comparative impulse that recurs through much of his scholarly writings. Authors from both the Greek and Judeo-Christian traditions, Jefferson noticed, set the term of man's life at threescore years and ten. The similar diction between the different texts may suggest a possible influence. Marginal comments in Jefferson's hand in other surviving books present many similar comparisons.

A more substantial note in his hand occurs later in the *Book of Common Prayer*, which was bound with a copy of the psalms by Nicholas Brady and Nahum Tate, *A New Version of the Psalms of David, Fitted to the Tunes Used in Churches*. Adjacent to verses 9 and 10 of Brady and Tate's metrical rendering of Psalm 18, Jefferson inscribed the corresponding passage from an earlier metrical English version of the psalms, that of Thomas Sternhold. Like the Herodotus note, this, too, shows the hand of a scholar, one who takes seriously the translation of texts from one language to another.

This marginal annotation implies an aesthetic preference on Jefferson's part, too. The Brady and Tate version reads:

> He left the beauteous Realms of Light,
> whilst Heav'n bow'd down its awful Head;
> Beneath his Feet substantial Night
>   was, like a sable Carpet, spread.
> The Chariot of the King of Kings,
>   which active Troops of Angels drew,
> On a strong Tempest's rapid Wings,
>   with most amazing Swiftness, flew.

The Sternhold version, as inscribed by Jefferson, reads:

The Lord descended from above
And bowed the heav'ns most high
And underneath his feet he cast
The darkness of the sky
On Cherubim and Seraphim
Full roially he rode
And on the wings of mighty winds
Came flying all abroad.

One crucial difference between the two involves the metrical form. The Brady and Tate version is written in iambic tetrameter, whereas the Sternhold version is written in the traditional ballad stanza form: alternating lines of iambic tetrameter and iambic trimeter. Sternhold had a pragmatic reason for structuring his psalms as ballads: he wished to turn people away from vulgar ballads and toward loftier forms of expression. Sternhold's version is also marked by a much greater simplicity in terms of diction and imagery. Drafting their version, Brady and Tate used consciously poetic diction and a variety of poetic devices, including personification and simile.

Jefferson's marginal inscription suggests a possible preference for the more folksy, down-to-earth psalms of Thomas Sternhold over the more refined versions of Brady and Tate. In "Thoughts on English Prosody," his fullest piece of literary criticism, Jefferson reiterated his preference for English psalms written in traditional ballad stanzas. And in a letter to John Adams, he stated that Sternhold, at least in this instance, rises to the "sublimity of his original, and expresses the majesty of God descending on the earth, in terms not unworthy of the subject."[34]

Regardless of the numerous inscriptions Thomas Jefferson made in his copy of the *Book of Common Prayer*, his father's flyleaf autograph may have been the book's most important inscription to him. A book formerly in the possession of a loved one and inscribed by him takes on the power of a talisman. There are few more powerful reminders of a person's existence than handwriting. The traditional identification rhymes people inscribed on their flyleafs during the eighteenth century reinforced the importance of a book as a personal, yet permanent object.[35] Book ownership guarantees a kind of immortality. Once the book owner is dead and buried, he will live on as long as others have the opportunity to read the book he had kept for a lifetime. Peter Jefferson's cherry bookcase was a handsome relic, yet Thomas appreciated the books he inherited far more. A father lives on in the books he leaves to his son.

CHAPTER 3

A Correct, Classical Scholar

As much as the books he inherited meant to Thomas Jefferson, they were no substitute for the father he had lost. He took his father's death hard and, for a time, felt helpless without him. Years later he told his grandson, Thomas Jefferson Randolph: "When I recollect that at 14. years of age, the whole care and direction of my self was thrown on my self entirely, without a relation or friend qualified to advise or guide me, and recollect the various sorts of bad company with which I associated from time to time, I am astonished I did not turn off with some of them, and become as worthless to society as they were."[1] Without Peter Jefferson's guidance, his son's upbringing was consigned to committee. The men who formed the group of Thomas's guardians and the executors of his father's estate included Peter Randolph, his mother's cousin; John Harvie, a family friend and business associate who would serve as the estate's working executor; and Dr. Thomas Walker, neighbor and family physician.

Dismissing both relatives and friends as unqualified, Jefferson seems hard on his guardians, but his dismissal cannot be taken too literally. Written to inculcate a sense of self-sufficiency in a grandson, Jefferson's words should not be interpreted as an indictment of his guardians, all of whom were intelligent, ambitious, and generally well read. Dr. Walker, for instance, exemplified many qualities Jefferson admired. Though a professional man, he devoted considerable effort exploring the western parts of Virginia. You can tell a man by the books in his library. The inventory of Walker's library reveals his knowledge of such authors as William Shakespeare and Jonathan Swift.[2] In other words, Dr. Walker combined the fortitude and vision of a western explorer with the professionalism of his calling and the refinement of a man of letters.

His guardians sent him to study with one of the finest classical scholars in Virginia, the Reverend James Maury, whom Jefferson succinctly characterized as "a correct classical scholar," an epithet suggesting that Maury could provide the proper classical education that seemed beyond the capacity of his former teacher, William Douglas. Exactly five months after his father's death, Thomas left Shadwell to live and learn with Maury, whose school has been called one of the finest private schools in the colonial South.[3]

Jefferson's new teacher had come from a devout Huguenot family. Matthew Maury and Mary Anne Fontaine had immigrated to Virginia when their son was in short pants. James Maury enjoyed telling friends how he and his family had come to Virginia. The Reverend Jonathan Boucher warmly remembered the way he told his personal history: "Mr. Maury was of French parents; begotten, as he used to tell, in France, born at sea, reared in England, and educated in America."[4] As recorded by Boucher, Maury's tale is colorful yet not entirely accurate; he was born in Dublin in April 1718. The following year his parents brought him to Virginia and settled in King William County, where his uncle, the Reverend Francis Fontaine, was serving as rector of St. Margaret's Parish.

Maury attended the College of William and Mary in the late 1730s, where he ingratiated himself to James Blair, president of the college and commissary of Virginia. Blair found Maury "an ingenious young man" and a generally excellent student, proficient "in the study of Latin and Greek authors" and knowledgeable of "some systems of philosophy and divinity."[5] He earned the commissary's favor to such an extent that Blair presented him with a copy of his four-volume edition of sermons selected from those he had delivered over the course of his lengthy career as a clergyman, *Our Saviour's Divine Sermon on the Mount...Explained.* Maury's copy of this work, which survives at the University of Virginia, is inscribed: "James Maury Willm and Mary Coll. March 17. 1740. The gift of the Reverd. James Blair, Commissary of Virginia &c." Possibly through Maury's influence, Christ's "Sermon on the Mount" became one of Jefferson's favorite biblical texts. In July Blair appointed Maury usher of the grammar school at William and Mary, a position that also involved overseeing the college library. By early 1742, Maury had decided to sail to London to take Holy Orders.

Blair wrote a letter of recommendation to the Bishop of London, whose diocese included Virginia. Since the Anglican church refused to give Virginia its own bishop, all local men wishing to serve as ordained Anglican ministers in Virginia had to make the arduous trip to London to take Holy Orders. The inconvenience rankled colonial church leaders— none moreso than Commissary Blair, who believed Virginia should have its own bishop and who very much wanted to be the first Bishop of

Virginia. In his letter of recommendation Blair praised Maury's classical education yet expressed uncertainty regarding the depth of his professional knowledge. After stating that Maury had studied some systems of divinity, Blair wrote, "I confess as to this last I could have wished he had spent more time in it before he had presented himself for holy orders, that his judgment might be better settled in the serious study of the Holy Scriptures and other books both of practical and polemical Divinity."[6]

Despite Blair's misgivings, Maury was ordained by the Bishop of London, received the King's Bounty in June 1742, and returned to Virginia.[7] He first preached in King William County and eventually became rector of Fredericksville Parish in Louisa County, where he remained until his death in 1769. Whatever shortcomings Maury may have had in terms of his knowledge of divinity when his career started, he made up for them over its course. The author of his obituary in the *Virginia Gazette* observed, "It might have been hard to say whether he was more to be admired as a learned man or reverenced as a good man."[8]

In 1743 Maury wed Mary Walker, niece to Dr. Thomas Walker. Overall, she bore him thirteen children, twelve of whom survived into adulthood. By the middle of the 1750s, Maury, in part to support his growing family, acquired a plantation of his own near the estate of Mary's uncle. Writing to one correspondent, he described the location of his home as follows: "I am planted about two miles to the northeast of Walker's under the South West Mountains in Louisa, close by one of the head springs of the main northern branch of Pamunkey, which runs through my grounds—a very wholesome, fertile, and pleasant situation, where, I thank God, I enjoy more blessings and comforts than I deserve."[9] To supplement his income as preacher and planter, Maury took on the role of teacher.

When Jefferson arrived at Maury's school in January 1758, he was something of a weedy youth, tall and slim with a shock of sandy red hair. His classmates included Dabney Carr and James Maury, Jr. A few years later James Madison, not the future president of the United States but the future president of the College of William and Mary, entered Maury's school. Jefferson's surviving comments about his school chums suggest that they formed a close-knit group of friends and compatriots who enjoyed exercise in the open air as much, if not more, than they enjoyed their bookish studies.

In a character sketch—a literary genre at which Jefferson excelled—he spoke highly of Dabney Carr. His description indicates the moral and intellectual caliber of his childhood friend and Jefferson's devotion to Carr:

His character was of a high order. A spotless integrity, sound judgment, handsome imagination, enriched by education and reading, quick and clear in his conceptions, of correct and ready elocution, impressing every hearer with the sincerity of the heart from which it flowed. His firmness was inflexible in whatever he thought was right: but when no moral principle stood in the way, never had man more the milk of human kindness, of indulgence, of softness, of pleasantry of conversation and conduct.[10]

Writing in 1812 to James Maury, Jr., then serving as U.S. Consul to Liverpool, Jefferson addressed him as "My dear and ancient friend and classmate" and imagined what might happen were they to reunite: "We would beguile our lingering hours with talking over our youthful exploits, our hunts on Peter's mountain, with a long train of *et cetera*, in addition, and feel, by recollection at least, a momentary flash of youth. Reviewing the course of a long and sufficiently successful life, I find in no portion of it happier moments than those were."[11]

Peter Jefferson had taught his son the value of fresh air and vigorous exercise, and Thomas's good health and longevity were due in part to his daily exercise regime. Small of stature, Maury lacked Peter Jefferson's athleticism, but he did not discourage the athletic pursuits of his students. Recognizing the importance of physical fitness, he advocated the healthfulness of the Piedmont in comparison to Tidewater Virginia: "Persons who have been either born in the mountainous country hereabouts, or resided in it long enough to acquire what we call a mountain constitution, on their removal to the flatter lands and the large rivers, are infallibly unhealthy there, however healthy and robust they used to be here, so that, in the course of a few years, an athletic habit degenerates and dwindles into one valetudinary and cachectic."[12] Elsewhere Maury observed, "A sound mind in a sound body, with a competent share of the comforts of life, is doubtless the highest pitch of happiness to which a reasonable man could aspire."[13] His most prominent student would often express similar sentiments.

Though his school generally provided a good atmosphere for learning, Maury was occasionally distracted from the life of the mind. He grumbled about the Two-Penny Act. Passed the same year Jefferson began attending his school, this legislation fixed the parsons' salaries at two pence per pound of tobacco and effectively reduced their salary by two-thirds. By no means alone in his dissatisfaction with the Virginia legislature, Maury would become the central figure in the Parson's Cause, as the issue came to be called. He apparently did not let his politics get in the way of his teaching, at least not very much. Jefferson vaguely remembered Maury inveighing against the Two-Penny Act but otherwise scarcely remembered the Parson's Cause.[14]

Maury owned a substantial library that offered his students opportunities for further study. The person who inventoried his estate counted four hundred volumes, excluding pamphlets. The few volumes that survive with evidence of Maury's ownership reveal his interests in divinity and history, but the absence of a detailed catalogue makes it impossible to determine how his personal library may have influenced Jefferson's thought. During the time he studied with Maury, Jefferson continued to augment his own personal library. The surviving accounts of guardian John Harvie indicate that in late 1759, Jefferson received a substantial shipment of books.[15] These accounts do not mention specific titles, however.

A catalogue of Dabney Carr's personal library, which survives as part of his estate inventory, offers the best evidence regarding the books Jefferson read while studying with Maury.[16] Carr's inventory lists numerous schoolbooks. Since Carr died before any of his children reached the age for formal schooling, the schoolbook titles listed in his inventory represent those he read in his youth and, therefore, those Jefferson read, too.

The classical authors and titles in Carr's inventory provide a good indication of the Latin and Greek curricula at Maury's school. Carr's inventory suggests that Maury had his students reading complete texts in Latin while they were still mastering the fundamentals of Greek. Latin authors and works listed include Cicero's *De Officiis* and *Orationes*, a collection of Horace's verse, Cornelius Nepos's *De Vita Excellentium Imperatorum*, Ovid's *Epistolae*, Quintilian, and Virgil's *Opera*. Discussing suitable reading for schoolchildren many years later, Jefferson suggested, "Nothing would interest them more than such works as Cornelius Nepos."[17] Nepos gave Jefferson and his fellow students an inspiring collection of patriotic biographies detailing the lives of Greek and Roman soldiers.

Greek is represented by more basic works: a Greek grammar, a Greek dictionary, and a Greek Testament. Jefferson fondly remembered studying his Greek grammar as a schoolboy. Francis Walker Gilmer, who befriended him in the early nineteenth century, recorded an anecdote Jefferson related about his behavior at school in comparison with that of his classmates: "Even when at school he used to be seen with his Greek Grammar in his hand while his comrades were enjoying relaxation in the interval of school hours."[18]

The Carr inventory also suggests that he and Jefferson studied French. Given Maury's personal background, it makes sense that he taught his students French. Whoever inventoried Carr's estate, however, could not read French or, at least, lacked the patience to list each of the French titles. The inventory lists only one French work separately, Charles Rollin's four-volume *De la Manière d'Enseigner et d'Étudier les Belles-Lettres* or *The Method of Teaching and Studying the Belles Lettres*. Rollin's work emphasizes the importance of learning French and advocates an open-minded, humanist approach to the study of literature. Rollin stressed the importance of cultivating the teacher–student relationship, an idea Maury took to heart.

The remaining French books Carr owned are listed simply as five French books. Though the inventory provides no additional clues to identify these books, other evidence permits the identification of one. J. D. Matthieu's *Dialogues Rustiques*, a fundamental work designed for learning how to speak French, survives among Jefferson's books at the Library of Congress. Its vellum covers besoiled, its pages bethumbed, the inside cover of this book nonetheless bears a clearly legible inscription: "Dabney Carr son Livre."

Other titles in Carr's library indicate that Maury taught a wide variety of subjects. One such title is Robert Dodsley's *Preceptor*, which James Boswell called "one of the most valuable books for the improvement of young minds that has appeared in any language."[19] Dodsley outlined a general course of education covering such topics as astronomy, chronology, commerce, drawing, ethics, geography, geometry, history, logic, manners, natural history, poetry, reading, rhetoric, and writing. Additional schoolbooks Carr owned taught more specific subjects: Nicolas Lenglet Dufresnoy's *Geography for Children: or A Short and Easy Method of Teaching and Learning Geography*, Isaac Watts's *Logick: or, The Right Use of Reason in the Enquiry after Truth*, and Benjamin Martin's *Philosophical Grammar*, which contains introductory information regarding cosmology, geology, meteorology, physical anthropology, and physics. Maury's correspondence verifies his interest in natural history and geology, and evidence shows that he once sent his brother-in-law fossil specimens he had found near his home.

Whereas the list of Dabney Carr's schoolbooks provides an indication of the specific authors and subjects he and his classmates read at school, Maury's correspondence describes his general ideas about education and thus establishes the theoretical framework underlying the education Jefferson, Carr, Madison, and others received from him. Written on one hundred half sheets of paper in the form of a letter to Jonathan Boucher, Maury's "Dissertation on Education" refutes Boucher's defense of classical learning and provides an educational program specifically designed for the needs of Virginia's youth.[20]

One modern reader has called Maury's "Dissertation on Education" the "most significant cultural document dealing with the colonial society of the Chesapeake."[21] Important in terms of understanding Jefferson's early biography, Maury's educational theory takes on additional importance given that one of his students would become president of the College of William and Mary and another would significantly shape educational policy during his political career and later establish the University of Virginia.

What shows most vividly in Maury's opening paragraph is his profound dedication to teaching. Central to his theory is the idea that a classical education is not essential to a good education. There are some whose education should be grounded in the classics: "An Acquaintance with the Languages, antiently spoken in Greece and Italy, is necessary, absolutely necessary, for those, who wish to make any reputable Figure in Divinity, Medicine or Law." In other words, all students with professional careers in mind needed to study Latin and Greek. Furthermore, those destined for positions of leadership "to which the Privilege of Birth, the Voice of their Country, or the Choice of their Prince may call them" should have a classical foundation. Also, the well-to-do gentleman "whose Opulence places him far above the perplexing Pursuits and sordid Cares, in which Persons of inferior Fortunes are usually engaged" will benefit from a good classical education because his wealth and position will permit him to indulge himself "in the Enjoyment of that calm Retreat from the Bustle of the World, of that studious Leisure and Philosophic Repose, which furnish him with the happiest Opportunities, not barely of making transient Visits to, but even fixing his Residence within, those sacred Recesses, sequestered Seats and classic Grounds, which are the Muses' favourite Haunts; a Repose, a Leisure, a Retreat, which nought, but his Countries pressing Calls, on some great Emergencies, has a Right to break in upon or interrupt."[22] Maury's words describe an ideal Jefferson used to guide his own life. Wanting very much to haunt the sequestered seats and classic grounds Maury described, Jefferson denied himself such pleasures to answer his country's pressing calls.

Since the situation of young Virginia gentlemen differed from that of the English, Maury argued, their education should differ. There were some subjects Virginia gentlemen must learn as children: arithmetic, chronology, eloquence, English grammar, geography, history, law, reading, and rhetoric. He recommended no specific textbooks in this letter, but his list of useful subjects resembles the list of topics Dodsley covered in *The Preceptor*.

Unlike the English gentleman, the Virginian born into wealth could not simply relax and enjoy his legacy—he had to keep working to sustain his family's wealth. The demands of learning a business, Maury held, precluded the time necessary to acquire a classical education. He insisted that the European educational model did not apply in the New World, and he offered a homely, though bookish analogy to stress his point: "Because the Genius of our People, their Way of Life, their Circumstances in Point of Fortune, the Customs and Manners and Humors of the Country, difference us in so many important Respects from Europeans, that a Plan of Education, however judiciously adapted to these last, would no more fit us, than an Almanac, calculated for the Latitude of London, would that of Williamsburg."[23]

Becoming a scholar took considerable effort. The pathway to classical knowledge was "rough and difficult." Temporarily switching to direct address, Maury's letter sounds like a teacher's advice to his students: "The Obstacles that are to be surmounted, before you can reach your Journey's End, are, believe me, far from chimerical and imaginary."[24] For those few Virginia students with the time and desire to study the classical languages, Maury provided some specific pedagogical recommendations.

He suggested storytelling as an excellent way for students to practice language skills. Children "who have but just learned to speak plain, relate Occurrences, which tho' trivial in themselves, are yet to the little Historians interesting and affecting; will hence naturally conclude Nothing better calculated at once to exercise their Memories and enrich their Understandings, than neat, plain, succinct, affecting Narration."[25] Under Maury's tutelage, it would seem, Jefferson not only developed his language skills but also developed his storytelling ability.

Some contemporary educators thought that teaching multiple languages simultaneously would overburden students' minds. Maury disagreed: "The Memories of Children must be exercised, in Order to improve them. And exercising them to a certain Degree will improve and strengthen them. But, to perplex and overcharge, and to give them moderate and due Exercise, are two Things as different, as exhilarating the Spirits with a temperate Glass, and drowning them in Excess and Debauch. That is salutary and beneficial, this hurtful and ruinous."[26] Furthermore, variety could facilitate the study of language. To the human mind, Maury argued, "nothing is more irksome, than an unvaried Prospect, than a uniform Sameness of Employment, and a dull tedious Round of undiversified Exercises."[27] In short, variety is essential to a good education.

Maury's viewpoint is remarkably similar to educational advice Jefferson would utter. To a law student under his charge, he recommended studying many different subjects beyond the scope of his law books: "The carrying on several studies at a time is attended with advantage. Variety relieves the mind, as well as the eye, palled with too long attention to a single object. But with both, transitions from one object to another may be so frequent and transitory as to leave no impression. The mean is therefore to be steered, and a competent space of time allotted to each branch of study."[28]

Though Maury says little in his "Dissertation on Education" regarding the specific curriculum, the few authors he does mention Jefferson came to know well. Maury critiqued the "empty and vociferous Pulpit-declaimer" whom the vulgar masses elevated above "an Atterbury, a Tillotson, or a Sherlock."[29] These three names refer to the day's most widely known and well-respected Anglican divines. Early American interest in Archbishop John Tillotson crossed colonial and denominational boundaries: his sermons were read from Puritan New England to Anglican Virginia.[30] Tillotson possessed a literary eloquence that helped shape eighteenth-century prose style, too. Jefferson had a three-volume folio edition of Tillotson's *Works* in his library, which also contained Francis Atterbury's *Sermons and Discourses* and the 1744 Williamsburg edition of William Sherlock's *Practical Discourse Concerning Death*.

In terms of classical authors, Maury saved his highest praise for Cicero, whom he called "Reason's great Highpriest and Interpreter." Jefferson would share this opinion. The epithets he would use to describe Cicero resemble Maury's. Jefferson said that when it came to matters of literary style Cicero was "the first master in the world."[31]

The extracts from Cicero in Jefferson's literary commonplace book date from the time he studied with Maury. Mainly they come from the *Tusculan Disputations*, in which Cicero grappled with the problems of death, grief, fear, and passion and attempted to discern the essence of happiness. Indebted to the Stoics, Cicero concluded that philosophy alone let man cope with the pain, affliction, and death he must face. Jefferson's excerpts from the work reveal his affinity with Cicero's thought. Encountering the *Tusculan Disputations* shortly after his father's death, he recognized the work's lasting relevance. Cicero's words offered salve to his grief. Jefferson was impressed with the ideas he read and the eloquence with which they were conveyed. His appreciation of the work affirms his discriminating literary tastes, too. Classical scholars consider the *Tusculan Disputations* one of the most majestic and beautiful works of Latin prose ever written.

Jefferson internalized ideas Cicero expressed in the *Tusculan Disputations*, and they became a part of his thought. In a letter to a friend a few years later he made a statement strongly reminiscent of Cicero: "The most fortunate of us all in our journey through life frequently meet with calamities and misfortunes which may greatly afflict us: and to fortify our minds against the attacks of these calamities and misfortunes should be one of the principal studies and endeavors of our lives."[32] Jefferson continued to admire the *Tusculan Disputations* and sought additional copies of the work in elegant, small-format editions. In his retirement library, he had two copies, an octavo in the Latin original and a pocket-sized French translation.

In the sixteenth chapter of the *Tusculan Disputations*, Cicero reconciled the state of the soul after death with the material world. He granted the existence of souls yet questioned the behavior of those people who conjure up the souls of the dead. They "wish the phantoms to speak and this cannot take place without tongue and palate, or without a formed throat and chest and lungs in active working."[33] Into his literary commonplace book Jefferson transcribed this passage in its Latin original. Cicero's distinction between spirit and matter reminded Jefferson that no longer could his father speak to him.

One reason Maury gave for rendering the study of classical languages unnecessary is that the discipline of learning the intricacies of grammar need not require the study of Latin and Greek. Such discipline could be achieved by studying the English language. Maury's letter contains an excellent appreciation of English, which he called "a Language as copious and nervous, as significant and expressive, as numerous and musical, nay, to my own Ears, as inchanting as any that was ever spoken by any of the different Families of the Earth."[34] Many years later, Jefferson would write a similar appreciation of English. Compared to French, the expressive possibilities of which he greatly appreciated, "the English language is founded on a broader base, native and adopted, and capable, with the like freedom of employing its materials, of becoming superior to that in copiousness and euphony."[35]

Maury not only advocated the powers of the English language, but exemplified them in his own writing. Boucher, despite his differing pedagogical views, called his friend "a singularly ingenious and worthy man" and praised his literary style: "His particular and great merit was the command of a fine style. It would have been difficult for him not to write with propriety, force and elegance." Maury's surviving sermons reveal his careful diction, clear organization, and detailed knowledge of scripture.[36] In addition, the numerous literary references they contain show the breadth of his reading and his recognition of the relevance of modern English literature.

The correspondence Maury left behind provides another good indication of the personality, reading tastes, and literary style of Jefferson's teacher. In one letter to an uncle, for instance, Maury describes with energy and enthusiasm the natural advantages of the Virginia countryside. He makes speculations regarding the commercial possibilities of the region, the expanse of the Mississippi Basin, and the possibility that Virginia could be connected to the Pacific Ocean via the waterways of North America.

In terms of both its magnitude and the enthusiasm of its author, Maury's description anticipates the "Rivers" chapter of Jefferson's *Notes on the State of Virginia*. Taking delight in his speculations, Maury incorporated an indigenous adjective—*canoeable*—and devoted much space defining what the word meant. Jefferson would come to share his teacher's fondness for neologisms. The introduction of new words, Jefferson believed, improved the English language, making it both dynamic and beautiful.[37]

Maury's description also reveals his classical knowledge. Two canoes lashed together draw only a few inches of water but "move down a current with great velocity, and leave the waterman nothing but Palinurus's task to perform when going downwards,"[38] alluding to the helmsman Palinurus from *The Aeneid*. Though displaying his knowledge of classical literature, Maury's erudition rests lightly on his words, which remain playful and unassuming.

To support his argument regarding the natural resources of North America, Maury cited information from Daniel Coxe's *Description of the English Province of Carolana*. He apologized for his inaccuracies because he was citing the book from memory: "I have read a History of the travels of an Indian towards those regions, as well as those of Mr. Cox, the reports of the natives to both of them as to the large canoes are so similar, that I perhaps may confound one with the other. Mr. Cox's book, I imagine, is very scarce. I know of but one copy in this colony, of which I had an accidental, and therefore a cursory view, about four years ago."[39] Bringing the letter to a close, Maury mentions that the copy of Coxe he had seen was the one owned by Colonel Joshua Fry.

The Indian whom Maury mentioned, best known by the name Moncacht-Apé, purportedly traveled throughout North America and found a waterway linking the Mississippi with the Pacific. The story first appeared in Dumont's *Mémoires de la Louisiane*, where Maury likely encountered it. Three decades before Dumont, Coxe's *Carolana* anticipated the story of Moncacht-Apé in much of its geographical detail. Since Maury read Coxe's *Carolana* at Fry's home, he suspected that the book had incited Fry's scheme to cross the Alleghenies and discover a waterway to the Pacific, a scheme abandoned with the onset of the French and Indian War. The war prompted Maury to take caution sending this letter. He instructed his messenger to throw the letter overboard in case of danger. Maury may have exaggerated the danger, yet he obviously relished the thrill of intrigue. He kept apprised of the war through its duration and later acquired a copy of the Dublin edition of William Livingston's account of the war, *Review of the Military Operations in North America*.

Maury's letter shows the different ways books could be used, all of which anticipate ways Jefferson would use his. Books of history, geography, and travel gave readers information regarding what was known and what had been accomplished, yet they also let them dream: to imagine the unknown and to foresee what could be accomplished. Books in colonial Virginia also functioned as social capital. Bookmen in colonial Virginia not only knew their own collections, but also familiarized themselves with their friends' and neighbors' libraries. A fine collection of books gave its owner great status in the region. A home with a superior library became a locus for interested, intelligent Virginians. Sharing a private library with houseguests became a part of Virginia hospitality.

Advocated in his pedagogical theory and exemplified in his own writings, Maury's appreciation of the power of the English language follows a trajectory in Anglo-American literary culture that begins with *Paradise Lost*. Milton's decision to write his great poem in English instead of Latin reflects his enthusiasm for his native language. Evidence suggests that Jefferson was reading Milton under Maury's tutelage, too. Entries in his commonplace book written around the time he spent with Maury contain numerous quotations from *Paradise Lost*.[40] From the first book of the poem, for instance, Jefferson copied the following:

> —What tho the Field be lost?
> All is not lost; the unconquerable Will,
> And Study of Revenge, immortal Hate
> And Courage never to submit or yield.

These lines come from a speech by Satan, who, having just been thrown from Heaven, is attempting to rouse his minions to action. Jefferson clearly appreciated these words of rebellion and bravado. He would remember them all his life. In a letter he wrote a half century later, he found these same lines from *Paradise Lost* appropriate and quoted them again.[41]

Though Maury enhanced Jefferson's appreciation of the English language, he was fueling flames kindled by Jefferson's boyhood reading of belletristic essays in his father's library. Maury's most important contribution to Jefferson's education remains the classical knowledge he gave him. In a letter to Joseph Priestley, Jefferson ably conveyed his love of ancient languages:

> I think the Greeks and Romans have left us the purest models which exist of fine composition, whether we examine them as works of reason, or of style and fancy; and to them we probably owe these characteristics of modern composition. I know of no composition of any other antient people which merits the least regard as a model for its matter or style. To all this I add that to read the Latin and Greek authors in their original is a sublime luxury; and I deem luxury in science to be at least as justifiable as in architecture, painting, gardening or the other arts. I enjoy Homer in his own language infinitely beyond Pope's translation of him, and both beyond the dull narrative of the same events by Dares Phrygius; and it is an innocent enjoyment.[42]

Conveying a preference for classical Greek and modern English verse over the pre-Homeric history of the Trojan War attributed to Dares of Phyrigia, Jefferson revealed his belief that when it came to literature, quality superseded genre. It is better to read good poetry than bad history. His preference indicates the enduring impact of his teacher, the Reverend James Maury. By the time Jefferson left Maury, the same epithet he applied to his teacher could be applied to Jefferson himself: he had become a correct, classical scholar.

CHAPTER 4

William and Mary

C hristmas 1759 found Jefferson at the home of Nathaniel West Dandridge, where, coincidentally, Patrick Henry was also spending the holiday. The two had never met. Jefferson was sixteen, Henry twenty-three. Henry was at an unsettled time in his life. He had tried being a shopkeeper and a farmer but failed in both pursuits. Yet to realize his true calling as a lawyer, he may have started reading law this holiday season. If so, he told Jefferson nothing about it. Regardless, Henry refused to let his professional uncertainty dampen his holiday spirits. Jefferson found him dancing, fiddling, and regaling others with fanciful tales.

The serious-minded Jefferson regretted Henry's apparent inability to participate in the intellectual conversations that were taking place among those gathered at the Dandridges that Christmas. Among their well-educated guests, the talk frequently turned to the sciences, but Henry showed little knowledge of them. Jefferson gave him the benefit of the doubt, surmising that the occasion of the holidays "prevented his engaging in any conversation which might give the measure either of his mind or information."[1]

Seven years younger than Henry, Jefferson, too, was at an unsettled time in his life. After Christmas he visited Chatsworth, the stately manor of Peter Randolph, his mother's cousin and his guardian. A congenial host and a good mentor, Randolph made time for a frank talk with his guest about his educational plans. As Jefferson understood the situation, he had two possible choices. On one hand, he could stay in the mountains and continue his classical education privately; on the other, he could relocate to Williamsburg and begin attending the College of William and Mary. During their conversation, Randolph expressed hope that Jefferson would attend William and Mary and tried to persuade him that doing so would be to his advantage. Randolph made a good case: Jefferson was convinced. Before packing his bags and his books, however, he needed to secure John Harvie's permission.

Leaving Chatsworth, he returned to Shadwell, put pen to paper, and outlined his reasons for wanting to attend William and Mary in a carefully worded letter to Harvie. Dated January 14, 1760, this is Jefferson's earliest known letter, and it reveals that its author was already capable of formulating a brief but persuasive argument. In the manner of a classical oration, the letter describes the problem with the status quo: "In the first place as long as I stay at the Mountains the Loss of one fourth of my Time is inevitable, by Company's coming here and detaining me from School." Jefferson followed this statement of the problem with an advantage that would accrue were he to attend college: "And likewise my Absence will in great Measure put a Stop to so much Company, and by that Means lessen the Expences of the Estate in House-Keeping."[2]

Three months shy of his seventeenth birthday, Jefferson was unwilling to assume the mantle of country gentleman and head of the estate, a position that carried with it much responsibility. The tradition of Southern hospitality was already well ingrained in eighteenth-century Virginia society. Staying at Shadwell, he had no choice save to play host to whomever might visit. Shutting himself indoors with his books was not an option. Far from being a place to retreat from society, the colonial Virginia home was a place to welcome it. Oftentimes a pleasure, hospitality could be a burden, especially for a bookish young man more intent on opening books than throwing open his doors. Whether pleasure or burden, hospitality was an obligation, and Jefferson, like it or not, was the head of the household at Shadwell and therefore compelled to uphold the social customs the position demanded.

Continuing his argument in the letter to Harvie, he supplied another important advantage that would result from attending William and Mary. Living in Williamsburg would bring him much closer to men in power, potential acquaintances who could advance his career regardless which direction it might take: "And on the other Hand by going to the College I shall get a more universal Acquaintance, which may hereafter be serviceable to me." Williamsburg lacked the appearance of a seat of colonial power to more urbane visitors; British traveler-novelist Edward Kimber called it "a most wretched contriv'd Affair for the Capital of a Country, being near three Miles from the Sea, in a bad Situation."[3] Still, it was the place where the governor lived in a handsome home known as the Governor's Palace, where the two legislative branches—the Virginia Council and the House of Burgesses—met, where the General Court convened, and where young men from many of Virginia's most well-to-do families attended college.

William and Mary had been founded in 1693, but wealthy Virginia planters remained prejudiced against the college during the early decades of its existence. They believed that the only way for their sons to obtain a good education was for them to attend Oxford or Cambridge and, if destined for the legal profession, the Inns of Court. By sending their sons to England, however, Virginia parents were putting them at risk. Maria Byrd, the widow of William Byrd II, for instance, considered sending her only son to England to complete his education, and even began planning the trip, but ultimately decided against it. As she wrote a friend, "I thought again he would certainly get the Small-Pox, which is most terrible fatal to those who are born in America, and that I should be accessory to his Death."[4] Many colonial Virginia parents, on the other hand, decided the benefits of an English education outweighed the potential risks and shipped their more-than-willing sons across the ocean.

Toward the mid-eighteenth century, Virginia planters began questioning the value of a British education yet sometimes remained unconvinced of the value of William and Mary. Making his will in 1745, William Randolph, for one, stipulated his educational plans for his son: "And my will further is that my son, Thomas Mann Randolph, shall not be educated at the College of William and Mary in Virginia, nor sent to England on any account whatever, but my executors shall keep a private tutor for his education."[5] Because Randolph chose Peter Jefferson as his principle executor, he obviously put greater stock in the judgment of a loyal and trustworthy friend than in the uncertain influences his son might encounter in college either at home or abroad.

Though the curriculum did not change drastically, over time attitudes toward the kind of education that William and Mary could provide became increasingly positive. Undergraduate students continued to take classes in two main branches of learning, moral philosophy and natural philosophy, and classes continued to be taught primarily by ordained Anglican ministers. What did change was Virginians' attitude toward the land where they made their homes: they came to appreciate their local college for many of the same reasons colonial Americans generally came to appreciate their unique society.

Preference for William and Mary increased as more and more young men who had been sent to England for their education returned to Virginia with a number of bad habits yet without visible intellectual improvement. Originally, John Page's father had planned to send him to England for his education but changed his mind because "several

Virginians, about this time, had returned from that place (where we were told learning alone existed) so inconceivably illiterate, and also corrupted and vicious, that he swore no son of his should ever go there, in quest of an education."[6] Instead, he enrolled his son in the grammar school at William and Mary. Upon finishing his course of studies at the grammar school, John remained at William and Mary and entered the undergraduate program the same time Jefferson did.

Later in the century Jefferson became one of the most strident advocates of a local, American education over a European one. He often articulated his confidence in the American educational system. His stay in Paris during the 1780s confirmed the superiority of an American education to his mind. In a letter to Walker Maury, who had followed in the footsteps of his father, the Reverend James Maury, and became both minister and teacher, Jefferson wrote, "Of all the errors which can possibly be committed in the education of youth, that of sending them to Europe is the most fatal. I see clearly that no American should come to Europe under 30 years of age: and he who does, will lose in science, in virtue, in health and in happiness, for which manners are a poor compensation."[7]

Jefferson continued thinking about the subject and further developed his ideas in a letter to John Bannister, Jr. Written the same year as the letter to Walker Maury, this letter constitutes one of the most spirited defenses of American education ever written. Jefferson enumerated the disadvantages of a European education at length:

> Let us view the disadvantages of sending a youth to Europe. To enumerate them all, would require a volume. I will select a few. If he goes to England he learns drinking, horse racing and boxing. These are the peculiarities of English education. The following circumstances are common to education in that and the other countries of Europe. He acquires a fondness for European luxury and dissipation and a contempt for the simplicity of his own country; he is fascinated with the privileges of the European aristocrats, and sees with abhorrence the lovely equality which the poor enjoys with the rich in his own country: he contracts a partiality for aristocracy or monarchy; he forms foreign friendships which will never be useful to him, and loses the seasons of life for forming in his own country those friendships which of all others are the most faithful and permanent.[8]

This last idea, that an American education will allow the student to form useful, life-long friendships, echoes one of the original arguments Jefferson made in the letter to John Harvie. Concluding his comments to Bannister, he recommended: "Cast your eye over America: who are the men of most learning, of most eloquence, most beloved by their country and most trusted and promoted by them? They are those who have been educated among them, and whose manners, morals and habits are perfectly homogenous with those of the country."[9]

Jefferson concluded his argument to Harvie by projecting how William and Mary would affect his personal education: "I suppose I can pursue my Studies in the Greek and Latin as well there as here, and likewise learn something of the Mathematics." This, the only comment in the letter regarding possible areas of study, suggests that Jefferson did not put much stock in the college's curriculum. He was primarily interested in continuing his linguistic studies, but William and Mary offered no advanced courses in the ancient languages, which were taught only in the grammar school.

Detailing the admission process to the undergraduate program at William and Mary, the college statutes stipulated that applicants should be tested to determine "whether they have made due progress in their *Latin* and *Greek*.... And let no Blockhead or lazy Fellow in his Studies be elected."[10] Because students were expected to have a reading knowledge of Latin and Greek before they started working toward bachelor's degrees, the study of languages was not part of the undergraduate curriculum. Whatever additional linguistic studies Jefferson wished to pursue, he would pursue on his own. In the letter to Harvie, he appears intent on continuing the educational program in classical learning he had developed with James Maury's help regardless what coursework the college might offer. Jefferson was looking for a quiet place where he could study without being disturbed, where he could free himself from the social demands placed on him at Shadwell. His willingness to learn more about mathematics comes as an afterthought to his main argument.

He made a good case: Harvie was convinced and gave his consent. Two months later, Jefferson left Shadwell for Williamsburg. Travelers' accounts provide a good indication of how Williamsburg appeared around the time of his arrival. A Frenchman visiting Virginia called William and Mary a very fine college that made a grand appearance. Elaborating his general description of Williamsburg, this traveler interjected some irony as he noticed that while Bruton Parish Church, where Jefferson attended services, was on one side of the Duke of Gloucester Street, the powder magazine was right across the street.[11]

Andrew Burnaby, a British traveler who had arrived in Williamsburg shortly before Jefferson, penned a good description of the city. Burnaby found it "regularly laid out in parallel streets, intersected by others at right angles" with "a handsome square in the center, through which runs the principal street, one of the most spacious in North America, three quarters of a mile in length, and above a hundred feet wide. At the opposite ends of this street are two public buildings, the college and the capitol: and although the houses are of wood, covered with shingles, and but indifferently built, the whole makes a handsome appearance."[12]

Impressed with the Duke of Gloucester Street, Burnaby remained condescending toward the city as a whole. His negativity is understandable. After all, he saw Williamsburg with the eyes of a worldly traveler. Depicting Williamsburg after he had become a little more urbane, Jefferson would describe its buildings in a similar manner. Yet, as a new college student, he saw it differently: Williamsburg was the largest and finest city he had ever seen.

On Tuesday, March 25, Thomas Jefferson matriculated at William and Mary. The detailed weather records from the period kept by Francis Fauquier, lieutenant governor of Virginia, and appended to Burnaby's *Travels* indicate that the skies were a little cloudy as Jefferson headed to class that day, but warmer weather appeared imminent. The northeast winds that had brought snow a few days earlier had now shifted to the southeast, and the temperature would climb into the fifties early this afternoon. In short, it was the kind of pleasant spring day that might render study difficult for a less serious college student, but not for young Jefferson.

William and Mary was divided into four schools: the Grammar School; the Philosophy School, which provided the undergraduate education leading to the baccalaureate; the Divinity School, which offered the college's only graduate training; and the Indian School, which, with marginal success, sought to educate Native American youth. The Philosophy School had two professors: one took charge of moral philosophy, while the other taught natural philosophy. The statutes of the college— updated just two years before Jefferson matriculated—included such subjects as physics, metaphysics, and mathematics under the general rubric of natural philosophy.

The biggest change made when the statutes were revised involved the amount of time required to earn a bachelor's degree. Formerly, it had taken only two years. In order to align William and Mary more closely with Oxford and Cambridge, the college administrators, known collectively as the board of visitors, raised the degree requirement to four years. The change did not necessarily mean that students received a more extensive education. Instead, it meant that more students left the college without taking a degree.

William and Mary had experienced a significant faculty turnover two years before Jefferson's arrival. In 1758, new masters were installed in the Grammar and Philosophy Schools. Goronwy Owen had become Master of the Grammar School. This name may mean little to students of American literature, but Owen is a major figure in the literary history of Wales. The poetry he began writing in the early 1750s marked the revival of traditional Welsh verse forms. In 1755 he became secretary of the Cymmrodorion Society of London, which encouraged other Welsh poets to continue the revival. Owen dreamed of writing a Welsh epic in the manner of Milton yet never fulfilled the dream.

An ordained minister in the Church of England, he had less success in his professional career than in his avocation as poet. Unable to find a place in Wales, he worked in a series of positions as curate and school-master in England, receiving little respect or remuneration. His fondness for drink did not help his professional career. When the fairly lucrative position at William and Mary became available in 1757, Owen obtained the post and arranged passage for himself and his family. Sadly, his wife and one of his three children died on the voyage, and Owen reached Williamsburg a sad and broken man.

As a student in the Philosophy School, Jefferson did not take courses with Owen, but he could have become acquainted with him. Owen had been John Page's teacher in the Grammar School; once Page was promoted to the Philosophy School and became Jefferson's good friend and classmate, he may have introduced him to Owen. Jefferson traced his ancestral roots back to Wales. Given this heritage and his growing interest in the study of languages, he was poised to make the acquaintance of a leading authority of classical Welsh verse. An entry in Jefferson's legal commonplace book, written a half dozen years later, reveals his ongoing interest in the Welsh language. He noted a case from Robert Raymond's *Reports of Cases Argued and Adjudged in the Courts of King's Bench and Common Pleas*, in which the propriety of the Welsh language in British courts of law came under dispute.

An expert linguist, Owen had a fine personal library that included nearly two hundred volumes, most quite old and in such languages as French, Greek, Hebrew, Latin, and Welch. Owen's Welsh books included a number of devotional manuals, Theophilus Evans's history of the early Welsh church, and John Davies's dictionary, *Antiquae Linguae Britannicae*. A standard through much of the seventeenth century, Davies's work was ultimately surpassed by Thomas Jones's dictionary, *The British Language in Its Lustre; or, A Copious Dictionary of Welsh and English*. Even as he compiled an extensive Welsh vocabulary, Jones reflected a sense of nostalgia for the language, which seemed to be passing into the realm of ancient tongues.[13] Eventually, a copy of Jones's Welsh dictionary would find its way to the shelves of Jefferson's library.

The same year Goronwy Owen became head of the grammar school at William and Mary, the Reverend Jacob Rowe began serving as Professor of Moral Philosophy, taking over the position from Richard Graham, who had been dismissed earlier. More important, William Small assumed the position as Professor of Natural Philosophy. Rowe had received an excellent education, having earned his M.A. from Trinity College, Cambridge, in 1755. He was ordained by the Bishop of London and may have served as a chaplain in the Royal Navy before coming to William and Mary. During his first year at the college, he established a reputation for his outspokenness. As a clergyman, he was among those parsons displeased with the Two-Penny Act and was unafraid to make his displeasure public. Joking that some burgesses should be hanged for passing the Act, Rowe declared that he would deny the sacraments to any burgess who voted in its favor. His words provoked their ire, and the House of Burgesses forced him to apologize for such untoward remarks.

Less that six months after Jefferson matriculated, further indiscretions on Professor Rowe's part prompted his departure from the college. Rowe's irascible nature and Owen's drink-induced lapses in judgment prompted the two professors to play leading roles in a riot between the college students and the young men of Williamsburg. Required by the college statutes to be exemplary in terms of learning, morality, observance of discipline, orderliness, piety, prudence, and sobriety, Rowe and Owen had clearly violated the conditions of their employment. Rowe was summarily dismissed; Owen was allowed to resign and subsequently became rector of St. Andrew's Parish in Brunswick County in southern Virginia, where he remained until his death in 1769. Rowe left no lasting impression on Jefferson, whose reminiscences of his college days make no mention of him.

William Small was a different story. Born in Scotland in 1734, Small graduated with his M.A. from Marischal College, Aberdeen, in 1755. Little is known of his whereabouts from the time of graduation until three years later, when he found himself in Virginia. He subscribed his oath as Professor of Natural Philosophy at William and Mary on October 19, 1758. With no one to replace Rowe after his dismissal, Small also assumed the responsibilities of the Professor of Moral Philosophy. Jefferson makes his attitude toward this development clear in the pages of his autobiography: "Fortunately the Philosophical chair became vacant soon after my arrival at college, and he was appointed to fill it per interim: and he was the first who ever gave in that college regular lectures in Ethics, Rhetoric and Belles lettres."[14] Filling both positions, Small was able to reshape the undergraduate curriculum and influence his pupils profoundly.

Jefferson's comments suggest that Small changed not only what subjects were taught but also how those subjects were taught. He introduced the lecture system to William and Mary, a system of instruction he had learned at Aberdeen from some of the leading figures in the Scottish Enlightenment. Remembering Small many years later, Jefferson wrote: "He was Professor of Mathematics at William and Mary, and, for some time, was in the philosophical chair. He first introduced into both schools rational and elevated courses of study, and, from an extraordinary conjunction of eloquence and logic, was enabled to communicate them to the students with great effect."[15]

Teaching both branches of study, Small saw no need to keep them distinct. He exposed students to new subjects and encouraged them to think about how knowledge was categorized and codified. The college statutes required the Professor of Moral Philosophy to teach "Rhetorick, Logick, and Ethicks." Fulfilling the responsibilities of the position, Small, as Jefferson said, taught "Ethics, Rhetoric and Belles lettres."[16] Jefferson was not saying that Small quit teaching logic; he was saying that Small had broadened the curriculum to include more modern subjects. Happily, the college statutes gave Small the latitude to alter the curriculum as he saw fit. Recognizing the longstanding overreliance on Aristotelian thought in traditional European college curricula, those who drafted the statutes for William and Mary left it to the board of visitors and the instructors to determine "what Systems of Logick, Physicks, Ethicks, and Mathematicks they think fit."[17] This provision gave Small the opportunity to expand the natural philosophy curriculum significantly.

As Professor of Moral Philosophy, Small may have deemphasized the teaching of ethics, if the preferences Jefferson later conveyed are any indication. Enumerating several topics of study in an admonitory letter to Peter Carr, Jefferson wrote: "Moral philosophy. I think it lost time to attend lectures in this branch. He who made us would have been a pitiful bungler if he had made the rules of our moral conduct a matter of science." With this advice, Jefferson was not recommending against the study of moral philosophy, but rather suggesting that the subject should be studied differently from the sciences. In pedagogical terms, lectures greatly aided the study of science and mathematics, as Jefferson's classroom experience with Professor Small confirmed. Alternatively, reading, combined with contemplation and the exercise of reason, provided the best way to understand moral philosophy. "In this branch therefore," Jefferson told Carr, "read good books because they will encourage as well

William Small, by unknown artist. (The Assay Office, Birmingham, England)

as direct your feelings."[18] There is one way to reconcile what Jefferson says in this letter regarding how to learn moral philosophy with the list of general subjects he remembered Small teaching: Small taught *belles lettres* as a way of teaching moral philosophy.

Of all the possible subjects Small may have taught his pupils as Professor of Moral Philosophy, logic seems most certain. At Marischal College, he had studied under William Duncan, the author of *Elements of Logick*, a widely used logic textbook of the time. Duncan's work originally appeared as part of the second volume of Robert Dodsley's *Preceptor*. Retaining the major divisions of classical logic, Duncan sought to accommodate recent trends in Scottish common-sense philosophy, an approach Jefferson found amenable. Modern-day rhetoricians have noticed that the patterns of logic Duncan outlined in *Elements of Logick* recur frequently in Jefferson's public and private writings.[19]

Despite his knowledge of moral philosophy, Small was more at home in the realm of natural philosophy, a category of learning that basically encompassed what is now termed the sciences. A brilliant scientist in his own right, Small opened his students' minds to a vast array of scientific discoveries. Remembering the education he received at William and

Mary, John Page recalled what subjects Small taught and how the professor had influenced him. Before Small had introduced him to the sciences, Page's primary interest was history, but with Small's help, "Natural and experimental Philosophy, Mechanics, and, in short, every branch of the Mathematics, particularly Algebra, and Geometry, warmly engaged my attention, till they led me on to Astronomy, to which after I had left College, till some time after I was married, I devoted my time."[20] This description of Small's personal influence is no hyperbole. In 1769, Page became involved with one of the greatest cooperative scientific endeavors of the era—the observation of the transit of Venus. He also helped found the Virginia Society for the Promotion of Useful Knowledge in 1772 and became its president two years later. Furthermore, he was elected to the most prestigious scientific body on the continent, the American Philosophical Society.

Jefferson, too, remembered learning mathematics and astronomy from Small, knowledge that stuck with him throughout his life, even though he could not always devote as much attention to it as he wished. Involved with the Reverend James Madison in observing the eclipse of 1811, Jefferson wrote, "I have been for some time rubbing up my mathematics from the rust contracted by fifty years' pursuits of a different kind. And thanks to the good foundation laid at college by my old master and friend Small, I am doing it with a delight and success beyond my expectation."[21] Jefferson's gratitude toward Small was genuine, but his assertion that fifty years had passed since he had used the mathematics Small had taught him can hardly be believed. Throughout his life, he had had numerous opportunities to apply his mathematical knowledge and often took advantage of these.

At William and Mary, Jefferson learned calculus with William Emerson's *Doctrine of Fluxions*—"the book I used at College" he called it.[22] His correspondence makes reference to the work several times. When faced with intricate mathematical problems while separated from his library, Jefferson regretted being without his copy of Emerson's *Fluxions*. Most important, he would use the work to help create his greatest agricultural invention, the Moldboard of Least Resistance. Jefferson's knowledge of higher mathematics helped him design the curvature of the moldboard in such a way that it let a plough turn over furrows with much greater facility than previously possible.[23]

A note Jefferson made in his 1772 *Virginia Almanack* confirms that Small also taught mechanics and hints that he used another of Emerson's textbooks, *The Principles of Mechanics*. Starting from Newton's basic laws of motion, Emerson described pumps, simple steam engines, waterwheels, and many other practical devices. The numerous engraved plates that Emerson included greatly contributed to the book's usefulness.[24] Though taking Emerson as his starting point, Small did not feel bound to follow his text slavishly. He added his own ideas and modifications as he adapted Emerson's *Mechanics*. Remembering what he had learned in college a decade later, Jefferson compared a "*water mill* on Small's plan" with a "*Spiral mill* from Emerson's mechanics."[25] Jefferson applied what he had learned in college by constructing models of the two mills in order to compare their efficiency.

Beyond what can be gleaned from incidental references among the papers of Page and Jefferson or conjectured from library inventories of Small's other students, the specific science curriculum they and their classmates received from him during the early 1760s has otherwise escaped historical record. The circle of scientific friends Small developed and the range of scientific interests he displayed upon his return to Great Britain later that decade reveal his understanding of nearly every known branch of scientific inquiry. He already had an excellent knowledge of medicine. Within a year after his return to Great Britain in the mid-1760s, he arranged for a medical degree from Aberdeen. He subsequently established a practice in Birmingham, where he became the center of a group of leading scientists and literati known as the Lunar Circle: Matthew Boulton, Erasmus Darwin, Thomas Day, Richard Lovell Edgeworth, James Keir, John Roebuck, James Watt, and Josiah Wedgwood.

Small assisted Boulton and Watt with their steam-engine research. He conferred with Roebuck regarding the production of alkali. He experimented with chemistry and metallurgy. He imagined possible ways to alter the world's climate. He experimented with optics and devised technical improvements for the telescope and microscope. He patented a new way of constructing timepieces. He gave thought to ways of improving agricultural machinery. He collected botanical specimens. And he even corresponded with Benjamin Franklin regarding a cure for the common cold.

Praising his teacher, Jefferson suggested that Small gave him the knowledge that fixed his destiny. Though effusive, this praise for Small is not unique. The prominent men who came to know him in Great Britain similarly honored him. Erasmus Darwin, who made Small his "favourite friend," found him unequaled in terms of his "strength of Reasoning, quickness of Invention, Learning in the Discoveries of other men, and Integrity of Heart." James Keir called him "a gentleman of very uncommon merit...who to the most extensive, various, and accurate knowledge in the sciences, in literature, and in life, joined engaging manners, a most exact conduct, a liberality of sentiment, and an enlightened humanity." Richard Lovell Edgeworth stated that Small was "esteemed by all who knew him, and by all who were admitted to his friendship beloved with no common enthusiasm."[26]

Jefferson, too, experienced Small's integrity of heart, enlightened humanity, and enthusiastic friendship. In his autobiography, he explained how quickly their friendship blossomed and how deep went its roots. Small had "a happy talent of communication correct and gentlemanly manners, and an enlarged and liberal mind. He, most happily for me, became soon attached to me and made me his daily companion when not engaged in the school; and from his conversation I got my first views of the expansion of science and of the system of things in which we are placed."[27] It is not hard to imagine the daily conversations between Small and Jefferson. Their talks could have occurred in any of a number of different locations: up and down the Duke of Gloucester Street; across the tables at the Raleigh Tavern or the coffeehouse; amidst the college's meager laboratory equipment, which Small took great pains to improve; or in Small's modestly furnished apartment at the college.

In addition to his powers of communication, Small also had excellent powers of observation. Testing the capacity of human sight, Erasmus Darwin used Small as an experimental subject and found his eyesight exceptional. He was "capable of the most patient and most accurate observation." After a number of independent trials, Small never lost sight of the smallest object with either of his eyes. Both literally and figuratively, Small helped his students see the world in new ways. "To his enlightened and affectionate guidance of my studies while at college," Jefferson wrote, "I am indebted for everything."[28]

Small likely shared his library with Jefferson, too. William and Mary had its own library, but it was woefully inadequate. After fire had destroyed the earlier college library in 1705, the collection had been rebuilt largely with donations from clergyman and philanthropists. In 1734, the Virginia legislature imposed a tax on imported liquor and earmarked its revenues for library books for the college. Subsequent fires during the nineteenth century ravaged the library's collections, destroying nearly all of its books and almost all the evidence of its contents.[29] Such evidence, had it survived, would contribute little toward understanding Jefferson's education. Undergraduates traditionally did not have library privileges. Small could have helped Jefferson access the books in the college library, but his personal collection was more up-to-date and more pertinent to his student's interests than the school library's holdings.

Jefferson's Williamsburg education extended beyond the printed word. When the Cherokee chief Ostenaco came to Williamsburg in the spring of 1762 at the head of a large band of Cherokee, he toured the college, met the governor, and made plans to visit London to meet King George III. The evening before his departure, Ostenaco delivered a moving oration to his people. Jefferson was present for this great speech and remembered it all his life. A half century later he recalled, "I was in his camp when he made his great farewell oration to his people, the evening before his departure for England. The moon was in full splendor, and to her he seemed to address himself in his prayers for his own safety on the voyage, and that of his people during his absence. His sounding voice, distinct articulation, animated action, and the solemn silence of his people at their several fires, filled me with awe and veneration, altho' I did not understand a word he uttered."[30] Jefferson became fascinated with Indian oratory and subsequently devoted much effort collecting information about Indian languages. His encounter with Ostenaco, like so many of his early encounters in Williamsburg, helped shape ideas he would hold for a lifetime.

The education Jefferson received at William and Mary greatly surpassed his expectations. All he really hoped for was a little knowledge of mathematics. Instead, what he received was a thorough grounding in the field of modern scientific inquiry. He also made some longtime friends, the most important being John Page. Comments Jefferson made in his correspondence once both had left college reveal how close they had become. Upon expressing in a letter some philosophical ideas regarding man's place in the universe, Jefferson confessed to Page, "I almost imagined myself in Williamsburgh talking to you in our old unreserved way." Making additional reflections in another letter, he characterized these remarks as "a continuation of the many conversations we have had on subjects of this kind."[31] Their intimate discussions at college allowed both men to test their knowledge and rehearse new ideas as they occurred. The experience gave them memories they would cherish throughout their lives.

Page recalled that in their college days Jefferson preferred the life of the mind to social gatherings. Talking about the time they spent together at William and Mary, Page admitted, "I was too sociable, and fond of the conversation of my friends, to study as Mr. Jefferson did, who could tear himself away from his dearest friends, to fly to his studies."[32] Page's words suggest that Jefferson successfully accomplished in Williamsburg what he had difficulty accomplishing at Shadwell: Becoming a college student, he transformed social intercourse from a matter of obligation to a matter of choice. When he wished, he could enjoy social gatherings. When he did not, he could devote time to his books.

CHAPTER 5

The Williamsburg Circle

Thomas Jefferson left William and Mary on April 25, 1762, without taking a degree. Under the old requirements, he had already attended college long enough to earn his baccalaureate. Under the new ones, he was only half finished. He saw no reason to continue. Richard Graham, dismissed as Professor of Natural Philosophy three years earlier, had been reappointed to the faculty in mid-1761, this time as Professor of Moral Philosophy. Despite Graham's learning—he had an M.A. from Oxford—he made little impression on Jefferson, who much preferred William Small as Professor of Moral Philosophy. Deciding to leave college, Jefferson saw that getting an education was more important than earning a degree. He believed that a good education extends beyond the walls of a classroom.

He would keep learning from Professor Small whether or not he stayed in college. Their friendship would endure, and their almost daily conversations would continue while both remained in Williamsburg. The education he had received from Small already went beyond moral and natural philosophy. For one thing, Jefferson was learning much about proper social conduct from his teacher. With his gentlemanly manners, Small functioned as a kind of walking conduct manual for his student, whose subsequent reputation for courtesy and good manners owes much to William Small.[1]

Jefferson left college mainly because he had decided to read law under George Wythe (pronounced "with"). He was indebted to Small for introducing him to Wythe, who had a reputation as the finest legal mind in Virginia. Wythe was an excellent teacher, too. Unlike so many other contemporary lawyers who used their students to do the clerical chores they would prefer not to do, Wythe proved to be a sensitive and caring mentor. Finding him a kindred spirit, Jefferson considered Wythe his second father.

Other Virginia lawyers surpassed him in oratorical ability; Wythe established his legal reputation through painstaking case preparation. The same could be said about Jefferson's abilities as an attorney. Though he would study eloquence in an effort to hone his oratorical skills, he, too, would distinguish himself as a lawyer by the written word, not the spoken.[2]

In addition to setting a professional example for Jefferson's legal training, Wythe represented the well-rounded man of letters. An aficionado of English verse, he was also an expert in the sciences, especially mathematics. Largely self-taught, Wythe was an excellent classicist, too. Andrew Burnaby, who met him during his time in Virginia, singled Wythe out among all Virginians and praised his "perfect knowledge of the Greek language, which was taught him by his mother in the back woods."[3]

Characterizing Wythe's personality, Jefferson found a classical reference useful: "No man ever left behind him a character more venerated than George Wythe. His virtue was of the purest tint; his integrity inflexible, and his justice exact; of warm patriotism, and, devoted as he was to liberty, and the natural and equal rights of man, he might truly be called the Cato of his country, without the avarice of the Roman, for a more disinterested person never lived."[4] Wythe made his classical learning part of his everyday life. He often peppered his conversations and correspondence with appropriate Latin mottos. His erudition allowed Jefferson to continue his pursuit of ancient tongues even as he began studying law.

Jefferson gradually realized that the study of law and languages went hand in hand. Knowledge of Latin was essential for reading such fundamental works as Justinian's *Institutes*, the compilation of Roman civil law that formed the basis for virtually every legal system throughout Europe. He continued to believe that lawyers should read Latin and regretted that its knowledge was falling from use. When American jurist Thomas Cooper presented him a copy of his annotated English translation, *The Institutes of Justinian*, in the early nineteenth century, Jefferson thanked him but interjected a sardonic comment on the state of legal education in America: "Your edition will be very useful to our lawyers, some of whom will need the translation as well as the notes."[5]

The study of other archaic languages facilitated the study of English law. In Britain, Anglo-Norman had remained the language of court and Parliament into the sixteenth century. Though it slowly fell from use, legal proceedings and treatises continued to be published in Law French, as it was called, into the eighteenth century, when its use was finally abolished by statute. Young men training for the bar in the eighteenth century still needed to know Law French to read many of the most fundamental treatises in English law.

George Wythe (1876), by John Ferguson Weir, after John Trumbull. (Independence National Historical Park)

Knowledge of Anglo-Saxon let serious students extend their expertise in English law further back in time. Jefferson traced his interest in Anglo-Saxon to his law student days. Reading John Fortescue-Aland's edition of Sir John Fortescue's *Difference between an Absolute and Limited Monarchy, as It More Particularly Regards the English Constitution*, Jefferson recognized the value of Anglo-Saxon for understanding legal terminology. In his introductory essay, Fortescue-Aland also suggested that knowledge of Anglo-Saxon was important for the well-rounded gentleman. The days of the week, for example, took their names from Anglo-Saxon. It would be unbecoming a man of letters to use words derived from Anglo-Saxon on a daily basis without knowing their origins. Furthermore, knowledge of Anglo-Saxon helps people better understand the etymology of many current English words. Words derived from Anglo-Saxon often convey their meanings more precisely than those derived from Greek or Latin.[6]

Fortescue-Aland's edition of his kinsman's work confirms the value of learning Anglo-Saxon. His annotations gloss the origins of numerous words used in the text. Placing a dagger adjacent to the word *gastful*, for instance, he noted that the word came from the Anglo-Saxon word for spirit or ghost: "So the Words, *Gastly*, or *Gastful*, in our Tongue, came to signify any thing that look'd frightful, as a Ghost, Spirit, or Apparition is said to do. From thence comes the usual Expression in the West of *England*, when a Man appears affrighted, that he is *agast*."[7]

Inspired, Jefferson began studying Anglo-Saxon using *The Rudiments of Grammar for the English-Saxon Tongue*, an elementary textbook by Elizabeth Elstob, the woman who took Jonathan Swift to task for his ignorance of Anglo-Saxon. Elstob's work remains important to literary history. She emphasized the profound influence Anglo-Saxon had on the development of English literature.[8] Jefferson would deepen his study of Anglo-Saxon with many other scholarly works. The footnotes to *Difference between an Absolute and Limited Monarchy* name several standard reference works, and Fortescue-Aland also included a thorough bibliography. Jefferson would acquire many of the listed titles for his personal library, including several by George Hickes, whom he would call "the great Restorer of the A.-S. dialect from the oblivion into which it was fast falling."[9] Chasing down the references in *Difference between an Absolute and Limited Monarchy* to deepen his knowledge, Jefferson engaged in a pattern of scholarly behavior he would frequently repeat.

His study of law and languages by no means hindered his interests in other fields of knowledge. His mentors in Williamsburg encouraged him to diversify his studies as much as possible. Jefferson would frequently join Small and Wythe as they met Lieutenant Governor Francis Fauquier at the Governor's Palace for dinner and pleasant intellectual discourse. He appreciated the Governor's Palace more from the inside than the out. He found its interior both "spacious and commodious."[10]

Fauquier exemplified the well-rounded gentleman whom his contemporaries called amiable, enlightened, generous, good-natured, and sensible. He was a man of science who appreciated literature and culture and who enjoyed sharing his interests in an atmosphere of conviviality that combined intellectual conversation with good food and drink. In recognition of his accomplishments as a scientist, he had been made a Fellow of the Royal Society (F.R.S.) in 1753. When proposed for membership the year before, he was identified as a "Gentleman of great merit, well versed in Philosophical and Mathematical inquiries, and a great promoter of usefull Learning, and the Advancement of Natural Knowledge."[11]

The lieutenant governor's library reveals both his personality and his intellect. Though Fauquier had left much of his personal library in England, the books he brought with him formed a tasteful and well-chosen collection. His Virginia library contained works written in a variety of fields—*belles lettres*, biography, history, poetry, philosophy. The gem of the collection may have been a two-volume edition of *Observations on Man*, David Hartley's pioneering psychological study, which ingeniously applied the theory of association to explain the workings of the mind. Fauquier's was a presentation copy from Hartley himself.[12] Despite the personal value of this presentation copy, Fauquier did not safeguard it as a keepsake. Rather, he loaned this and other books to Virginia friends curious to read them. His willingness to loan books from his personal library affirms Fauquier's generosity and his desire to encourage the progress of knowledge.

There may be no better evidence of Fauquier's personality than a contribution he made to the *Philosophical Transactions* of the Royal Society. Titled "An Account of an Extraordinary Storm of Hail in Virginia," the article relates an event from July 1758, the month after he arrived in Williamsburg to serve as lieutenant governor. Fauquier's powers of description bring the experience alive. The second Sunday of the month, about four that afternoon, thunder sounded and lightning flashed. Dark clouds passed over Williamsburg from the northwest. "The hailstones, or rather pieces of ice, were most of them of an oblong square form; many of them an inch and half long, and about three fourths of an inch wide and deep; and from one side of most of them there proceeded sharp spikes, protuberant at least half an inch." He gathered as many hailstones as he could and used them to make ice cream and to cool his wine—he especially enjoyed hock and madeira. The number and size of the hailstones were sufficient to last through Monday night and thus to let him keep his wine chilled for a second day in the middle of a hot Williamsburg summer.[13]

Recalling the dinner gatherings at the Governor's Palace during Fauquier's term of office, Jefferson said that he had never "heard more good sense, more rational and philosophical conversations, than in all my life besides. They were truly Attic societies. The Governor was musical also, and a good performer, and associated me with two or three other amateurs in his weekly concerts."[14] Fauquier, who knew Händel personally, owned two violins, a viola, and two cellos and could play them all. The social contacts Jefferson established around the governor's dinner table exposed him to a much broader base of knowledge than his college coursework had and did so in a pleasant and convivial way.

Save for Jefferson's appreciative comments, little additional evidence survives to document what may have transpired during these frequent dinners. Small likely played the same role in Williamsburg he would play in Birmingham, England. There, he formed a comfortable center around which other members of a group of intellectuals known as the Lunar Circle gathered. Largely uninterested in joining formal scientific organizations or contributing to their *Transactions* or *Proceedings*, Small contributed to the history of science by serving as a facilitator, someone who brought men of learning together and created a sociable atmosphere that made the exchange of ideas both enjoyable and productive.

Small made friends easily and created enduring personal relationships. Within a few months from the time he left Virginia and arrived in Birmingham, he became close friends with Erasmus Darwin and Matthew Boulton, both of whom relied heavily on his advice. In a letter to Boulton, Darwin made reference to "our ingenious Friend Dr. Small, from whom and from you, when I was last at Birmingham, I received Ideas that for many days occurred to me at the Intervals of the common Business of Life, with inexpressible Pleasure." Similarly, John Keir confided the results of his scientific experiments to Small within the first few months of their friendship. Thomas Day, more man of letters than man of science, gained Small's confidence and respected his judgment. Small advised Day against taking up medicine as a career and even introduced him to an attractive woman he thought would be right for him. Day took his advice: he avoided medicine and married the woman.[15]

Describing Small's role among the men of the Lunar Circle, Richard Lovell Edgeworth—the father of popular novelist and children's author Maria Edgeworth—stated, "Dr. Small formed a link which combined Mr. Boulton, Mr. Watt, Dr. Darwin, Mr. Wedgwood, Mr. Day and myself together—men of very different character but all devoted to literature and science."[16] Linking literature and science, Edgeworth's statement provides the key to understanding both the Lunar Circle of Birmingham and what can be termed Small's Williamsburg circle.

In Jefferson's day, literature and science were much more closely allied than they are now. Literature was not so narrowly defined then.

The term embraced any and all kinds of writing, including scientific discourse. Writing well and understanding science were both considered worthy attributes of the proper eighteenth-century gentleman. The finest scientists were often excellent writers, and the finest litterateurs took pride in their knowledge of science. Neither field had yet to emerge as a profession; rather, both provided avenues for gentlemanly endeavor. This was the era of the virtuoso, the educated and refined man who dabbled in the arts and sciences in the capacity of a highly skilled amateur. Much the same can be said about music. The ability to read music and play an instrument constituted another important attribute of the well-rounded gentleman. Jefferson's ability to play the violin provided an additional way for him to ingratiate himself to the music-loving lieutenant governor.

The passion for music Jefferson was developing found written expression in his commonplace book, which contains several quotations from a work best known as *The Beauties of the English Stage*, a compilation that brought together memorable passages from Renaissance through Restoration drama and arranged them topically. Jefferson commonplaced several excerpts pertaining to music, including the following lines from *The Merchant of Venice*:

> The Man who has not Music in his Soul,
> Or is not touch'd with Concord of sweet Sounds,
> Is fit for Treasons, Strategems, and Spoils,
> The Motions of his Mind are dull as Night,
> And his Affections dark as Erebus:
> Let no such Man be trusted.[17]

Copying a passage from Shakespeare that establishes an inverse relationship between music appreciation and political intrigue around the same time that the colonial governor was fueling his passion for music, Jefferson confirmed his love of music and acknowledged a parallel between musical and political harmony. As he cultivated his love of music in company with the governor, Jefferson got other ideas. Before long he was talking about going to Italy, where he might buy himself a good fiddle.

Small's Williamsburg circle was more intimate than the Lunar Circle of Birmingham, yet both functioned similarly. The circumference of each was variable and could expand to include visitors. During his visits to England, Benjamin Franklin, for example, befriended several members of Birmingham's scientific crowd, corresponded with them, and occasionally joined their social gatherings. Similarly, elite travelers passing through Virginia entered Small's Williamsburg circle. Andrew Burnaby joined the group during his stay in Williamsburg. Besides praising Wythe's classical learning in the pages of his *Travels*, Burnaby conveyed his gratitude to Fauquier for supplying the detailed weather data he appended to the book. "In Virginia," Burnaby admitted, "I have had the pleasure to know several gentlemen adorned with many virtues and accomplishments."[18] The circle widened to include Jefferson. John Page sometimes enjoyed the warmth of Professor Small and friends, too.

Small's Williamsburg group was not the only circle in which Jefferson moved during the early 1760s. With Page, he also belonged to the new generation of Virginia's elite, young people in their late teens and early twenties who enjoyed dancing and flirting, not to mention gossiping about the romantic fortunes and misfortunes of one another. Jefferson's musical ability transcended the bounds of intellect and served him well regardless of the company he kept. Leaving Williamsburg for Shadwell shortly before Christmas 1762, he made sure to bring the law books Wythe assigned him, but he also packed several pieces of music—a "half dozen new minuets"—for the purpose of providing entertainment at Shadwell and at the homes of others he might visit while away from Williamsburg.[19]

Jefferson spent that Christmas at Fairfield, the plantation of a friend who lived an easy day's ride from Shadwell. Part of Christmas Day Jefferson spent writing a long, fanciful letter to Page.[20] Exhibiting the hyperbole characteristic of their correspondence, it nonetheless articulates the differences between Jefferson's intellectual circle and his social one. The letter makes reference to Sir Edward Coke, whose multipart *Institutes* deserves its status as the first textbook of modern English common law. The first part of Coke's *Institutes*, familiarly known as *Coke upon Littleton*, contains the text of Sir Thomas Littleton's *Tenures* in Law French with commentary by Coke that sometimes becomes so elaborate that it practically usurps the text it annotates. *Coke upon Littleton* was required reading for all first-year law students. After telling Page he had brought a copy of the work with him to read during the Christmas holidays, Jefferson, speaking with tongue firmly in cheek, doubted whether he would be able to make it through this ponderous work.

"Well, Page," he sighed. "I do wish the Devil had old Coke, for I am sure I never was so tired of an old dull scoundrel in my life."

These words reflect less what Jefferson was really thinking and more what the beginning law student typically thought. In terms of both form and content, *Coke upon Littleton* was a demanding, yet essential work.

Once he came to know it, Jefferson would remark that Coke reconciled "all the decisions and opinions which were reconcilable" and rejected what was unreconcilable. "This work," he continued, "is executed with so much learning and judgment, that I do not recollect that a single position in it has ever been judicially denied. And although the work loses much of its value by its chaotic form, it may still be considered as the fundamental code of the English law." Another time Jefferson spoke of the "deep and rich mines of Coke and Littleton." Elsewhere he cautioned that Coke's opinion "is ever dangerous to neglect."[21]

For law students in Jefferson's day, reading *Coke upon Littleton* amounted to a rite of passage. Those who made it through the book not only felt a sense of accomplishment, but also earned the right to belittle students who had not completed it. Overseeing the legal education of his grandson-in-law Charles Lewis Bankhead many years later, Jefferson inflicted *Coke upon Littleton* on him. He even assigned it to Bankhead the same time of year his teacher had assigned it to him: over the Christmas holidays. With great glee, Jefferson wrote his granddaughter Anne Randolph Bankhead in late December, "Mr. Bankhead I suppose is seeking a Merry Christmas in all the wit and merriments of Coke Littleton. God send him a good deliverance."[22]

Though teachers told their law students they had to read *Coke upon Littleton*, no one told them they had to enjoy it. Complaining about the work became almost as essential to the rite of passage as reading it. Naming Coke an "old dull scoundrel" in his letter to Page, Jefferson was not expressing his true feelings. Rather, he was striking the pose of the beleaguered law student forced to read a book whose contemporary value he has difficulty discerning.

"But the old-fellows say we must read to gain knowledge and gain knowledge to make us happy and admired," Jefferson observed in the letter to Page. Continuing this literary pose, he exclaimed, "Mere jargon! Is there any such thing as happiness in this world? No: And as for admiration I am sure the man who powders most, parfumes most, embroiders most, and talks most nonsense, is most admired." Contrasting the advice of the "old fellows" with fashionable behavior, Jefferson implicitly compared his intellectual circle with his social one and questioned the value of reading the books his elders recommended. Before finishing the paragraph, however, he dropped the pose and admitted that the "old fellows" may be onto something: "Though to be candid, there are some who have too much good sense to esteem such monkey-like animals as these [the powdered, perfumed, embroidered, nonsense-talking sort], in whose formation, as the saying is, the taylors and barbers go halves with God almighty: and since these are the only persons whose esteem is worth a wish, I do not know but that upon the whole the advice of these old fellows may be worth following."[23]

In this same letter and others to follow, Jefferson struck another pose, that of the distraught young lover. He confessed to Page his love for Rebecca Burwell, the sister of a friend and college classmate. Before leaving Williamsburg that Christmas, Jefferson had become smitten with Miss Burwell. Out of town, he attempted to pitch woo by proxy. He wrote Page: "Remember me affectionately to all the young ladies of my acquaintance, particularly the Miss Burwells and Miss Potters, and tell them that though that heavy earthly part of me, my body, be absent, the better half of me, my soul, is ever with them, and that my best wishes shall ever attend them."[24] In subsequent letters to Page, Jefferson reiterated his fondness for Miss Burwell, often calling her Belinda or even αδνιλεβ—Belinda reversed and transliterated—for purposes of intrigue. Undoubtedly fond of her, Jefferson may not have been as infatuated with Rebecca Burwell as the surviving letters imply. Like the beleaguered law student, the forlorn romantic seems more of a literary persona Jefferson adopted for the amusement of himself and his correspondent than a genuine reflection of his feelings.

Jefferson wrote several letters to Page over the ensuing months but made little effort during that time to see Miss Burwell or to contact her directly. Having left Williamsburg before Christmas, he spent the first nine months of 1763 away from the city. Belinda's charms, it seems, were insufficient to bring him back any sooner. He did have a justifiable reason for staying away so long. He had planned to return in May, but hearing a rumor that smallpox was in town, he delayed his return until September.

It is disappointing to learn that Jefferson was away from the city that spring: during that time the Williamsburg circle expanded to welcome the most distinguished scientist in colonial America, Benjamin Franklin. Though Franklin's surviving papers say little about the week and a half he spent in Williamsburg, his activities here likely paralleled his activities in other places where groups of intellectuals gathered socially. Visiting Annapolis the preceding decade, for example, Franklin came in contact with the men of letters in colonial Maryland who formed the Tuesday Club. He greatly enjoyed their sprightly conversation and contributed to their bawdy repartee.[25]

In Virginia, Franklin had professional, intellectual, and social reasons for contacting Fauquier. Visiting Williamsburg in his capacity as Postmaster General gave him an official reason to meet the lieutenant governor. Furthermore, Thomas Foxcroft, Fauquier's secretary, was Franklin's deputy postmaster. Like Fauquier, Franklin, too, had been elected a Fellow of the Royal Society and thus had earned the right to place the letters F.R.S. after his name.

Franklin met William Small for the first time during this visit to Williamsburg. They became fast friends and renewed their friendship in England later that decade. There may be no better confirmation of their closeness than a question that occurs in a letter from Small to Matthew Boulton in June 1772: "Will you ask Dr. Franklin to repose himself chez moi for some time?" Jefferson's absence from Williamsburg deprived him of the opportunity to meet Franklin, about whom Jefferson would observe, "No one of the present age has made more important discoveries, nor has enriched philosophy with more, or more ingenious solutions of the phaenomena of nature."[26] Another dozen years would pass before very different circumstances would bring the two men together.

By the first week of October 1763, Jefferson had finally returned to Williamsburg. Page was out of town, but Jefferson wrote urging his friend to return as soon as possible: "The court is now at hand, which I must attend constantly, so that unless you come to town, there is little probability of my meeting with you any where else."[27] When either the Virginia legislature or the General Court met, Williamsburg, in Burnaby's words, was "crowded with the gentry of the country; on those occasions there are balls and others amusements; but as soon as the business is finished, they return to their plantations; and the town is in a manner deserted."[28] Jefferson's legal education compelled him to return before court convened, but the "balls and other amusements" also drew him back.

The Raleigh Tavern, located on the Duke of Gloucester Street between the Palace Green and the Capitol, was the most congenial place in Williamsburg. On the first floor, the tavern held a large assembly room known as the Apollo, a room that would be the site of many important political gatherings in the coming years. Here Jefferson renewed his acquaintance with Rebecca Burwell.[29] Their meeting did not go well. He wrote Page the following day:

> Last night, as merry as agreeable company and dancing with Belinda in the Apollo could make me, I never could have thought the succeeding sun would have seen me so wretched as I now am! I was prepared to say a great deal: I had dressed up in my own mind, such thoughts as occurred to me, in as moving language as I knew how, and expected to have performed in a tolerably creditable manner. But,

good God! When I had an opportunity of venting them, a few broken sentences, uttered in great disorder, and interrupted with pauses of uncommon length, were the visible marks of my strange confusion!

Allowance must be made for hyperbole, of course, but these comments do provide an early hint of Jefferson's natural shyness. He would attempt to renew his affection for Miss Burwell once or twice more in the ensuing weeks but all to no avail. Before another year would pass, she would become Mrs. Jacquelin Ambler.

Though the surviving information about Small's Williamsburg circle suggests one facet of Jefferson's personality and his correspondence with Page conveys another, the best documentary evidence of his whereabouts during the mid-1760s is found in the surviving ledgers or daybooks from the office of the *Virginia Gazette*. Joseph Royle, the newspaper's proprietor, imported a wide variety of books, and his printing office, located on the north side of the Duke of Gloucester Street, attracted any and all with literary interests. No ledgers survive for the first few years of the decade, but the daybooks for 1764 and 1765 provide a wealth of detail regarding who visited the shop and what they bought. Unlike Jefferson's letters to Page, these ledgers leave no room for hyperbole. Yet the daybooks do not entirely exclude the possibility of posing, for any wealthy Virginia planter could strike an intellectual pose by visiting the shop with friends and buying a book he did not intend to read. There is no indication that Jefferson made purchases in this manner—his pursuit of knowledge was both sincere and profound.

The first Saturday in February 1764 he visited the *Gazette* office to pick up what must have been a special order. On this day he acquired a one-volume folio edition of Johann Scapula's *Lexicon Graeco-Latinum*; Giuseppe Baretti's *Dictionary of the English and Italian Languages*; a two-volume quarto edition of Enrico Davila's *Guerre Civili Francia*, a work he appreciated for its dramatic retelling of the assassination of Henry IV at the hands of the Catholic fanatic François Ravaillac; a two-volume folio edition of Francesco Guicciardini's *Della Istoria d'Italia*; the recently published two-volume quarto edition of Machiavelli's *Opere Inedite in Prosa e in Verso*, with notes by the distinguished Italian jurist Giovanni Maria Lampredi; and *A Practical Treatise of Husbandry*, by Henri Louis Duhamel du Monceau.

This list of purchases confirms that Jefferson was pursuing his linguistic studies even as he was studying law. Scapula's sixteenth-century Greek and Latin dictionary commanded respect from all serious scholars. Philadelphia bookman James Logan, the finest classicist in colonial

America, had annotated his copy of Scapula's *Lexicon* heavily and had corrected or expanded numerous entries. Even while recognizing some errors in Scapula, Logan admitted its great scholarly value. Sending a Greek ode of his own composition to Robert Hunter, colonial governor of New York and New Jersey, Logan confessed, "I must not pretend that it is without Scapulas Assistance."[30] Jefferson would add two more editions of Scapula to his library in the coming years.

Other books he acquired from the printing office verify his interest in the classical languages. In September he purchased a copy of *Selecta Poemata Italorum*, a two-volume collection of Latin verse edited by Alexander Pope. Jefferson's surviving copy of William Cheselden's *Anatomy of the Human Body*, which he purchased in April, contains evidence that he was continuing his study of Greek. In the margin of the first page of chapter 1, "Sutures and Bones of the Cranium," he inscribed a long Greek passage from Herodotus concerning the bodies of the Persian dead on the battlefield at Plataea, where a skull was found with no sutures in it, the bone being seamless and continuous. Jefferson's annotation shows him engaged in a processing of questioning historical and scientific information: To what extent can history be brought to bear on the study of medicine? Is it the scientist's responsibility to reconcile empirical evidence with documentary evidence from the past?

Cheselden's *Anatomy* also suggests a relationship between science and art. The book is illustrated with a number of handsome plates keyed to lists naming parts of the human anatomy. One plate in the volume contains no such list, however: at the end of the chapter on muscles is a plate showing the musculature of two intertwined male figures patterned after a well-known image. The text adjacent to the plate explains that the illustration "is done after the famous statue of Herculus and Antaeus. The muscles here exhibited being all explained in the other plates, the figures are omitted to preserve the beauty of the plate." Anatomical knowledge not only helped to advance science, but also enhanced aesthetic appreciation. Before going abroad, Jefferson made a list of statuary he wanted to decorate Monticello; the list includes *Herculus and Antaeus*.

Other works Jefferson acquired that February day suggest that he was broadening his study of languages to include Italian. Baretti's *Dictionary*, the most complete Italian–English dictionary available, contains a useful Italian grammar. The presence of this dictionary on his list of purchases may suggest that Jefferson was just beginning his study of Italian, but other evidence hints that he had begun reading Italian a few years earlier. His surviving copy of *La Storia di Tom Jones*, Pietro Chiari's translation of the Henry Fielding novel, contains Jefferson's ownership inscription on the title page. The inscription is dated 1761. Reading a familiar novel in a new language offered a more amenable way to learn a language than reading weightier, unfamiliar works. Hopefully, Jefferson was not trying to learn Italian by starting with Davila, Guicciardini, and Machiavelli in the original.

Duhamel's *Husbandry* seems anomalous on this otherwise erudite list of books, but it serves as a reminder that Jefferson's ongoing prosperity depended upon the continuing success of his plantation. Despite his various intellectual interests, he well understood that he could not ignore the land that gave him his wealth. Inspired by Jethro Tull, Duhamel visited England, where he observed recent British agricultural developments. Duhamel's *Husbandry* is basically Jethro Tull rewritten for a French readership, integrating Duhamel's own extensive knowledge of French agronomy and the results of his unique agricultural experiments.[31] Around the same time Jefferson was reading Duhamel, he also acquired a copy of the 1762 edition of Jethro Tull's *Horse-Hoeing Husbandry*. Although the precise date is not known, his name inscribed upon the title page indicates that he acquired the book before the Shadwell fire. Jefferson subsequently admitted reading Jethro Tull "while I was an amateur in Agricultural science."[32]

The daybooks also show him acquiring works he needed to pursue his legal studies. As he would say, "A lawyer without books would be like a workman without tools."[33] The third week of February he visited the *Gazette* office and purchased several fundamental legal texts. *The Attorney's Practice in the Court of King's Bench* and *The Attorney's Practice in the Court of Common Pleas*, both compiled by Robert Richardson, offered considerable information regarding civil and criminal procedure. Joseph Harrison's *Accomplish'd Practiser in the High Court of Chancery* informed Jefferson about the fundamentals of equity pleading and procedure. He also considered buying a copy of the basic introduction to law known as *The Attorney's Pocket Companion* but decided against it at that time. Before another week had passed, however, he had second thoughts and sent Jupiter to the *Gazette* office to pick up a copy of the work.

Jupiter and Jefferson had been companions since boyhood. The two were born the same year, and they had grown up together. Neither could forget their master–slave relationship, yet each had come to rely on the other. Serving in the capacity of personal servant and coachman, Jupiter did his best to help his master. Occasionally absent-minded, Jefferson sometimes found himself without pocket change. Jupiter always had coin on hand to loan him. Furthermore, Jupiter was always ready and able, though not always willing, to fetch whatever articles his master needed at the moment. Time and again Jefferson sent him out for a variety of items—biscuits, bread, butter, candles, corn, eggs, pomade, soap, wig powder, anything. The information that survives about Jupiter suggests that he had made himself essential to Jefferson. After his death, Jefferson wrote that even "with all his defects, he leaves a void in my domestic arrangements which cannot be filled."[34]

Jefferson seldom sent Jupiter to the *Gazette* office to purchase books. He enjoyed that pleasure too much to give it over to a surrogate. Other members of the Williamsburg circle also frequented the *Gazette* office. Sometimes they came there together. In the ledger for one particular day, the names of Jefferson, Wythe, and Small appear adjacent to one another, suggesting that the three friends had come to the shop together. This day, Wythe and Small received letters from New York with postage due, and Jefferson bought a few quires of writing paper.[35]

None of his friends purchased as many books as Jefferson did in these years. Still, their purchases are significant for several reasons. The books Wythe bought are important not only because they indicate his personal impulses during the time he was Jefferson's teacher, but also because Wythe would bequeath his library to Jefferson. The first week of February, for example, Wythe purchased Robert Nelson's popular manual of Anglican theology, *A Companion for the Festivals and Fasts of the Church of England*. This copy of Nelson's *Festivals* came into Jefferson's possession upon Wythe's death many years later.

Small's purchases suggest possible topics of dinner conversation within the Williamsburg circle. The second week of February, for example, he bought a copy of Matthew Stewart's *Tracts, Physical and Mathematical, Containing, an Explication of Several Important Points in Physical Astronomy and a New Method for Ascertaining the Sun's Distance from the Earth, by the Theory of Gravity*. Stewart's *Tracts* was a landmark work in the study of analytic and celestial mechanics. He demonstrated his ingenuity by using geometrical proofs for theorems that had formerly been established by algebraic and analytic methods.[36] Think about the new ideas Stewart articulated and imagine the spirited discussion that went round the governor's dinner table that week.

If Jefferson felt intimidated by Stewart's ingenuity or, in more general terms, by the breadth of scientific topics discussed within Small's Williamsburg circle, he remedied deficiencies in his knowledge with John Barrow's *New and Universal Dictionary of Arts and Sciences*. The title page of this work lists the scientific topics it contains at considerable length. Its two-line epigram by John Dryden succinctly conveys the intellectual value of its contents:

Happy the Man, who, studying Nature's laws,
Thro' known Effects can trace the secret Cause.

In terms of number of volumes, Jefferson purchased more history books from the printing office in 1764 than books in any other area of study. In addition to the historical works in Italian, he acquired several significant histories in English: David Hume's *History of England*, William Robertson's *History of Scotland*, and William Stith's *History of Virginia*, a work he would consult frequently when he composed his *Notes on the State of Virginia*. Jefferson's copy of Stith, which survives at the Library of Congress, contains much marginalia in his hand. His overall attitude toward the historian was mixed. He called Stith "a man of classical learning, and very exact, but of no taste in style. He is inelegant, therefore, and his details often too minute to be tolerable, even to a native of the country, whose history he writes."[37] This critical comment indicates a standard of writing Jefferson set for himself. The historian not only must be precise, but also must possess an elegant style and a sense of proportion.

Much more than a record of who bought what, the *Virginia Gazette* daybooks occasionally register emotion. The entries for August 1764, for example, convey a twinge of sadness. Within a list of advertisements in the *Gazette* that month there occurs the following entry adjacent to the name of William Small: "Adv of Departure."[38] After a falling out with the College of William and Mary, Small had decided to return home. In September, he settled his sundry accounts at the *Gazette* office. Two months later he was in London. By early 1765, he was already becoming the center of Birmingham's Lunar Circle.

Jefferson kept in contact with his teacher after he returned to Great Britain, but his only known letter to Small is dated May 7, 1775. Remembering the refreshments that went around the governor's table, Jefferson sent his former teacher a present of three dozen bottles of well-aged madeira: "I hope you will find it fine as it came to me genuine from the island and has been kept in my own cellar eight years." Jefferson closed this letter to Small by expressing hope that "amidst public dissension private friendship may be preserved inviolate."[39] His hopes went for naught: Small had died months before his student's best wine and wishes arrived.

CHAPTER 6

The Limits of English Law

Though busy reading law and helping George Wythe prepare the cases he would argue before the General Court in the autumn of 1764, Jefferson still managed to find time for himself. On several occasions, the printing office of the *Virginia Gazette* lured him inside its doors. The first Wednesday of October, for example, he visited the *Gazette* office with several volumes to be rebound and gilt, yet not all his trips to the printing office involved purchasing books or having them bound. Sometimes he came to buy paper, other times to pay for postage or to buy sundries—pens, ink, stationary, all things concerned with the business of being a law student.

What Jefferson bought at the printing office reveals much about his personality—so does what he did not buy. Decks of playing cards were nearly always available here. Jefferson's friends and neighbors bought several decks for an evening's entertainment. Harry cards—those depicting Henry VIII—were the finest grade of playing cards. Local gamblers bought them half a dozen packs at a time; William Byrd III, the most notorious gambler in colonial Virginia, occasionally bought Harry cards a dozen packs at a time. During the period covered by the surviving daybooks, not once did Jefferson purchase playing cards at the printing office. Only blackguards played cards, he said.[1] He was not averse to games of chance: he often bet modest sums playing quoits or attending horse races. But the willingness with which many Virginia planters wagered their hard-earned fortunes on the turn of a card dismayed and disgusted him.

The books he brought to the *Gazette* office this early October day included two diverse works: William Rastell's *Collection in English of the Statutes Now in Force* and Mark Akenside's philosophical poem *The Pleasures of Imagination*.[2] Jefferson's attention to Rastell's *Statutes* is

understandable. Since its initial appearance in 1557, the work had become England's leading statutory compilation. New editions had appeared after nearly every Parliament to 1625. Containing statutes from
the Magna Charta through the reign of James I, the work took even the
most diligent students many weeks to read and analyze.[3] Given its title,
The Pleasures of Imagination would seem to offer a pleasant diversion
from the relatively irksome task of reading crowded lists of statutes
printed in black letter. It is easy to imagine Jefferson temporarily setting
aside old Black Letter to refresh himself with a little poetry.

Akenside's poem is not exactly light reading, though. *The Pleasures of
Imagination* is a highly erudite work with ramifications well beyond the
imaginative world it purports to explain. Akenside not only attempted to
integrate poetry and philosophy, he also tried to reconcile Platonic rationalism and Baconian empiricism.[4] Akenside's detailed notes reinforce
his scholarly bent: references to figures ranging from the historians and
philosophers of ancient Greece to the astronomers and mathematicians of
modern Europe crowd the back pages of his book.

Written in Miltonic blank verse, *The Pleasures of Imagination* plumbs
the poet's creative process. Introducing his topic in the opening lines, the
speaker of the poem stresses the originality of his purpose:

> Oft have the laws of each poetic strain
> The critic-verse imploy'd; yet still unsung
> Lay this prime subject, tho' importing most
> A poet's name: for fruitless is th' attempt
> By dull obedience and the curb of rules,
> For creeping toil to climb the hard ascent
> Of high Parnassus. Nature's kindling breath
> Must fire the chosen genius; nature's hand
> Must point the path...

In other words, a great poet does not compose his work simply by following the rules of poetic meter, rhyme, and diction. Rather, he must let
nature serve as guide—only by following nature can the poet scale the lofty
heights of Parnassus. Akenside's concept of nature is typical of much
eighteenth-century English verse, including the work of his better known
contemporary, Alexander Pope, whom Jefferson was also reading.

Perhaps the works of Rastell and Akenside are not as diverse as they
might seem. In absolute terms, both concern themselves with law: whereas
Rastell's *Statutes* exemplify positive law, Akenside's lengthy poem embodies the idea that man should not necessarily obey man-made rules but

instead should follow nature. When it comes to matters of either law or poetry, according to ideas that were becoming increasingly prevalent during the eighteenth century, nature should serve as guide. Ideally, positive law should jibe with natural law. Before another year would pass, Jefferson would realize how disparate the two could be. The breach between natural law and English constitutional law, as interpreted by Parliament regarding the American colonies, became so great over the following year it prompted in Jefferson's mind an intellectual crisis, a crisis requiring much study on his part before it could be resolved.

Jefferson spent the winter of 1764–65 reading law at Shadwell, but he was back in Williamsburg for the spring session of the General Court, which convened in April. Once the General Court adjourned, he stayed in town to continue his study under Wythe's supervision. During his time in Williamsburg that spring, Jefferson took the opportunity to observe the House of Burgesses in action. There was no gallery overlooking the legislative chamber, but interested parties were welcome to listen to the proceedings from the lobby doorway. Before this session ended, Jefferson would witness a seminal event in the movement toward American independence.

By late May, the Virginia Assembly was winding down, so much so that many of the burgesses were leaving town for their plantations. The last week of the month, fewer than forty members of the House were left to transact what legislative business remained. On Wednesday, May 29, 1765, a copy of the Stamp Act was introduced into the House of Burgesses. Or, in the suggestive words of Governor Fauquier, it "crept into the house."[5] A motion to consider the Act was made and passed. According to tradition, Patrick Henry drafted seven resolutions onto a blank leaf of an old law book he had on hand. He would move these resolutions the following day.

Standing in the lobby doorway Thursday as Henry presented and defended these resolutions, Jefferson heard a speech he would remember for a lifetime. Many years later, he recalled, "I write this from memory: but the impression made on me, at the time, was such as to fix the facts indelibly in my mind."[6] Even after witnessing the proceedings of the French National Assembly on a daily basis during his last year in Paris, he still thought Henry a superior orator. "Henry spoke wonderfully," Jefferson told an acquaintance. "Call it oratory or what you please, but I never heard any thing like it. He had more command over the passions than any man I ever knew; I heard all the celebrated orators of the National Assembly of France, but there was none equal to Patrick Henry."[7]

Listening to the proceedings with Jefferson was a mysterious French traveler, whose journal represents the only known contemporary account of the famous speech Henry delivered that Thursday. Reaching Williamsburg at noon, the stranger proceeded to the House of Burgesses, where he "was entertained with very strong Debates."[8] Given its relative immediacy, this French traveler's tale offers a more accurate rendering of Henry's speech than the one reconstructed by William Wirt for *Sketches of the Life and Character of Patrick Henry*. "In former times Tarquin and Julius had their Brutus, Charles had his Cromwell," Henry vociferated as his oration reached its climax. He did not doubt that "some good American would stand up, in favour of his country."

Stories of Henry's powerful speech circulated rapidly through Williamsburg and back to England. Hearing about the speech secondhand, Commissary William Robinson, for example, reported to the Bishop of London that Henry had "blazed out in a violent speech against the Authority of parliament and the King."[9]

Jefferson made several testaments to Henry's eloquence. For the most part, his surviving comments occur in three different places. A series of letters he wrote William Wirt constitute his fullest known comments. He made additional remarks in his autobiography and in conversation with Daniel Webster, who visited Monticello in 1824 and kept detailed notes of their conversation. Taken together, Jefferson's comments have largely determined how history has portrayed Henry's intellect.

While researching his *Life of Patrick Henry*, Wirt asked Jefferson to supply as much information as he could remember. Jefferson responded with a brief letter, which included a lengthy reminiscence by way of postscript, and offered further details in several follow-up letters. Wirt, whose writing idealizes Henry, did not use all the information he received— Jefferson's portrayal of him in the correspondence is occasionally quite critical. Wirt did accept Jefferson's depiction of Henry as a child of nature, someone whose knowledge and insight came not from books but from natural intuition.

Writing his autobiography after Wirt had published his life of Henry, Jefferson introduced additional comments supplementing what he had written privately to Wirt. In conversation with Webster, he portrayed Henry similarly. Consistent with one another, all three portraits seem fraught with internal contradiction. Jefferson himself admitted that his understanding of Henry's character was "of mixed aspect."[10] Though he used both great praise and harsh invective to portray Henry, his inconsistencies are not irreconcilable.

Generally speaking, Jefferson praised Henry's oratory yet critiqued his learning. Recalling the Caesar-had-his-Brutus speech, Jefferson appreciated "the splendid display of Mr. Henry's talents as a popular orator. They were great indeed," he continued, "such as I have never heard from any other man. He appeared to me to speak as Homer wrote." The comparison between Henry and Homer, one of Jefferson's favorite authors, is unusual. The Greek orator Demosthenes was a more common touchstone for describing Henry. Using a favorite epithet of the time, one contemporary Virginian, for instance, called Henry "our homespun Demosthenes." When Lord Byron characterized Henry as "the forest-born Demosthenes, / Whose thunder shook the Phillip of the seas," he was repeating an epithet that was already well established in American culture.[11]

In his first letter to Wirt on the subject, Jefferson described Henry as "the best humored man in society I almost ever knew, and the greatest orator that ever lived. He had a consumate knoledge of the human heart which directing the efforts of his eloquence enabled him to attain a degree of popularity with the people at large never perhaps equalled." In his reminiscence, Jefferson applauded his "torrents of sublime eloquence." Jefferson reinforced his impressions of Henry's oratorical ability by asserting that his "imagination was copious, poetical, sublime; but vague also. He said the strongest things in the finest language, but without logic, without arrangement, desultorily."[12] Linking the sublime quality of Henry's oratory with its vagueness, Jefferson echoed ideas from *The Pleasures of Imagination*. Akenside had argued that the imagination is stimulated by a combination of the sublime, the uncommon, and the beautiful.

The words Henry spoke had a delightful, almost hypnotic quality. Recalling times when the two faced one another in court, Jefferson explained, "When he had spoken in opposition to *my* opinion, had produced a great effect, and I myself been highly delighted and moved, I have asked myself when he ceased, 'What the Devil has he said,' and could never answer the enquiry." In conversation with Webster, Jefferson characterized Henry's eloquence as "impressive and sublime beyond what can be imagined."[13]

Throughout Jefferson's various descriptions of Henry's oratory, the word "sublime" recurs more frequently than any other. He used the same term to describe both Virginia's Natural Bridge and the poetry of Ossian, the legendary epic bard of ancient Scottish times. Henry's oratorical ability, Jefferson believed, was a natural phenomenon, capable of soaring to beautiful heights. Taken as a whole, Jefferson's comments suggest why he found Homer a more appropriate comparison than Demosthenes. Given its sublime quality, Henry's oratory more closely resembled classical epic verse than logical argument.

Describing Henry's lack of intellectual accomplishments and poor work habits in his autobiography, Jefferson called him "the laziest man in reading I ever knew." As harsh as this remark seems, Jefferson's comments to Webster regarding Henry's intellectual powers are even more absolute: "He was a man of very little knowledge of any sort, he read nothing and had no books." For proof, Jefferson offered the following anecdote: "Returning one November from Albemarle Court, he borrowed of me Hume's *Essays*, in two vols. saying he should have leisure in the winter for reading. In the Spring he returned them, and declared he had not been able to go farther than twenty or thirty pages, in the first volume."[14]

Henry's passion for the outdoors took time away from more bookish activities. He was especially fond of hunting—when the courts adjourned in the winter, according to Jefferson, Henry would lead a party of poor hunters from his neighborhood to the piney woods of Fluvanna, where he would pass weeks camping out, hunting deer, staying up into the small hours with "overseers and such like people," and cracking jokes around the campfire. He covered "all the dirt of his dress with a hunting shirt"—"the same shirt the whole time." As Jefferson depicted him, Henry was capable of sublime eloquence yet lacked the manners characteristic of Virginia's finest social circles.[15]

In his effort to understand Henry, Jefferson made use of the stage theory, a prevalent cultural theory of the day. By this theory, civilization has evolved through a series of stages. Whereas Europe had already progressed through the stages leading to the establishment of civilization, North America was experiencing cultural development at several stages simultaneously. As Jefferson portrayed him, Henry symbolized the re-creation of early ancient Greece on the American frontier. His image of Henry embodies the idea that the cultural evolution of North America recapitulated the development of Western civilization.

Jefferson's fullest articulation of this idea comes in a letter he wrote late in life:

> Let a philosophic observer commence a journey from the savages of the Rocky Mountains, eastwardly towards our sea-coast. These he would observe in the earliest stage of association living under no law but that of nature, subscribing and covering themselves with the flesh and skins of wild beasts. He would next find those on our frontiers in the pastoral state, raising domestic animals to supply the defects of hunting.

Then succeed our own semi-barbarous citizens, the pioneers of the advance of civilization, and so in his progress he would meet the gradual shades of improving man until he would reach his, as yet, most improved state in our seaport towns. This, in fact, is equivalent to a survey, in time, of the progress of man from the infancy of creation to the present day.[16]

Read with Jefferson's personal description of Henry in mind, this passage places Patrick Henry within Jefferson's scheme of the stages of development. There he is, rubbing his buckskin-clad elbows with the "semi-barbarous citizens, the pioneers of the advance of civilization."

Another phrase from this passage identifies the place of law within the development of civilization. In Jefferson's view, the westernmost inhabitants of North America live "under no law but that of nature." Implicitly, the continent's easternmost inhabitants live more fully under positive law than natural law. Situated on the frontier among the "semi-barbarous citizens," Henry was more in touch with natural law and natural rights than with Virginia's more refined citizenry.

In one letter to Wirt, Jefferson explained how Henry came to understand natural law and natural rights so well. He might have known about early Virginia charters from reading such works as William Stith's *History of Virginia*, but "no man ever more undervalued chartered titles than himself. He drew all natural rights from a purer source, the feelings of his own breast."[17] As Jefferson understood him, Henry could interpret and articulate law from the perspective of natural rights not because he was well read but because he lived much closer to nature than those who were well read.

Before Henry concluded his Caesar-had-his-Brutus speech, Speaker of the House John Robinson, whom Jefferson remembered as "an excellent man, liberal, friendly and rich," rose to interrupt him, calling his harangue treasonous. Robinson also expressed dismay with his fellow burgesses because none had seen fit to stop Henry.[18]

After the interruption, Henry rose to apologize, explaining that if he had offended the speaker, or the House, he sincerely asked their pardon. He further stated that he was willing to prove his loyalty to the crown with "the last Drop of his blood." He had meant no affront. The words he had spoken were addressed "to the Interest of his Country's Dying liberty which he had at heart, and the heat of passion might have led him to have said something more than he intended."[19] Other members of the House rose in his support, the issue died down, and the proceedings continued.

The burgesses had passed five of the resolutions by the day's end. Collectively, these resolutions emphasized the idea that representative government was the distinguishing characteristic of the British Constitution. In short, the Stamp Act threatened to topple the very principles on which English constitutional law was based. The strongest of the resolutions or, in Governor Fauquier's words, the "most offensive" passed this day stipulated that such efforts to impose power over the colonists had "a manifest Tendency to destroy British as well as American Freedom." The debate over this resolution, Jefferson recalled, was "most bloody," and it passed by a single vote.[20] When the House adjourned for the day, its members streamed from the legislative chambers still discussing the resolutions that had been passed.

"By God, I would have given five hundred guineas for a single vote!" Peyton Randolph exclaimed as he walked from the House into the adjacent lobby. One more negative would have divided the House, leaving the deciding vote to Robinson, who opposed the Virginia resolutions. Randolph's comments were recorded by Jefferson himself, who lingered in the lobby as the burgesses exited, enthralled with what was transpiring.

Randolph and the others who opposed the resolutions passed on Thursday were determined to reverse them on Friday. Hours before the House was scheduled to reconvene, Jefferson went to the legislative chambers, where he found Peter Randolph, a member of the governor's Council and a cousin of Peyton's, at the clerk's desk searching the *Journals of the House of Burgesses* for a precedent to expunge a vote. Jefferson remained with Peter Randolph until the bell rang to announce the start of the day's session.

Like Jefferson, the mysterious stranger who was visiting Williamsburg was also curious to see how the clash over these resolutions would end. He returned to the lobby, where he heard some "very hot Debates" about the stamp duties. Patrick Henry, believing his work finished, had mounted his horse Thursday night and left Williamsburg. Why, he "rode off in triumph," one observer commented. As a result, Henry was not around to defend the resolutions. The first four withstood Friday's debates, but the House carried a motion to expunge the fifth one. The removal of this single resolution did not placate Governor Fauquier, who dissolved the Assembly. Reporting the events that occurred to the Board of Trade, the governor explained that the older, more experienced members of the House "were overpowered by the Young, hot, and Giddy Members."[21]

In terms of their defiance of the crown, the resolutions that had not passed on Thursday were even bolder than those that had. In a way, it ceased to matter which ones were approved or rejected: copies of the Virginia resolutions that circulated throughout colonial America both in manuscript and in print were not limited to the approved ones. They included some or all of the rejected ones, too, and often made no distinction between which were approved and which disapproved.

The story of the dissemination of the Virginia resolutions provides a fine example of the written word superseding the spoken. Once the written resolutions began to circulate, the verbal jousting that had occurred among the Virginia burgesses the last few days in May no longer mattered. Reprinted in the *Maryland Gazette*, for instance, the various resolutions were seven. They ended with the following: "That any Person who shall, by Speaking, or Writing, assert or maintain, That any Person or Persons, other than the General Assembly of this Colony, with such Consent as aforesaid, have any Right or Authority to lay or impose any Tax whatever on the Inhabitants thereof, shall be Deemed, AN ENEMY TO THIS HIS MAJESTY'S COLONY."[22]

Circulated throughout colonial America, the resolutions steeled the resolve of the American colonists to resist the unjust laws British lawmakers were attempting to impose upon their American subjects. Before summer's end, news of the Virginia resolutions reached London. In England seeking to repeal the Stamp Act, Benjamin Franklin was endeavoring to find a more diplomatic solution. He, too, vehemently opposed the Act. He joked that he could make the Stamp Act meet his approval with a single change to its text: where the document stated the year the act would take effect—"one thousand seven hundred and sixty-five"—delete the word "one" and replace it with a "two."[23] Though generally agreeing with his fellow colonists, Franklin was still shocked to learn the actions of the Virginia burgesses. Hearing about their resolutions, he exclaimed, "The Rashness of the Assembly in Virginia is amazing!"

Governor Fauquier had a huge party planned the following Tuesday to celebrate the birthnight of King George III. Traditionally, Virginia gentlemen and ladies donned their finest silks and satins to attend the annual festivities at the Governor's Palace to honor the king—birthnight celebrations had been taking place in Virginia for years, and many considered it the foremost social event of the year. Previously, everyone who was anyone in Virginia society, Jefferson included, eagerly anticipated the annual event.

Yet almost no one in Williamsburg attended the birthnight festivities in 1765. For Virginians, the birth of a king had stopped being something to celebrate. Still in town that evening, the mysterious French traveler visited the Governor's Palace expecting to see a great deal of company. He was disappointed to find fewer than a dozen people there—so disappointed he did not even bother to stay for supper.

Episodes of violence soon erupted throughout colonial America as the colonists resisted British efforts to enforce the Stamp Act. Up and down the Atlantic coast, men formed groups known as the Sons of Liberty, who coerced the stamping officials, burned stamped paper, and incited fellow colonists to protest. Mobs in cities from Boston to Charleston rioted, attacking those who attempted to enforce the Stamp Act, removing them from their homes, and tossing their belongings into the street. In Virginia, a mob prevented the distributors from selling stamps, but Fauquier's presence forestalled any further violence. During his administration, Fauquier had established a reputation for fairness and good governance that the people respected even as they protested the royal power he represented.

In terms of Jefferson's intellectual life, the Stamp Act controversy prompted a significant crisis. He had devoted the past three years to legal study and had built a huge superstructure of knowledge on the foundations of English constitutional law. The Stamp Act threatened to destroy the foundation on which his knowledge was based. If acts of Parliament undermined the fundamental basis of English law, what law remained? If Parliament usurped the colonists' rights as Englishmen, what rights did they have? The answers to these two questions, Jefferson gradually came to realize, were natural law and natural rights.

Continuing to maintain his literary commonplace book during this period, he made many entries treating the subject of natural law. The commonplace book contains more entries from Henry St. John, Lord Bolingbroke than any other single author. Several concern natural law. Toward its end, Bolingbroke's *Philosophical Works* gathers isolated fragments of prose on several different topics. "Fragment 19" interprets marriage in relation to both natural law and positive law. Jefferson excerpted the following passage about the relationship between marriage and natural law: "'Increase and multiply' is the law of nature. The manner in which this precept shall be executed with greatest advantage to society, is the law of man."[24]

Marriage provided Jefferson with an ideal subject for contemplating the importance of natural law. It involved a legal contract binding two people together who originally come together in the most natural and necessary way. While reading Bolingbroke on the subject, he recalled something he had read in Hume's *History of England*. He set aside Bolingbroke to double-check his Hume, where he found a discussion of Henry VIII, which contained a lengthy passage about marriage and its relationship to positive and natural law.

Once he transcribed the pertinent passage, Jefferson set Hume aside and returned to where he had left off in Bolingbroke. The detour served to enhance his appreciation of Bolingbroke and prompted him to ponder the application of natural law further. Finding nothing noteworthy in "Fragment 20," he lingered over "Fragment 21," transcribing a passage that asserted the self-evident truth of the law of nature.

A vivid picture of Jefferson's reading process emerges from these entries: reading one work, he would be impressed enough with an individual passage that he would take the time to enter it into his commonplace book. The passage would remind him of another work he had read, so he would temporarily set aside the volume he was reading, rise from his chair, walk to where he shelved his volumes of history, pull down another, and linger over its contents long enough to locate the remembered passage and make a note of it. Jefferson had purchased Hume's *History* a few months earlier and obviously read it soon afterward. The commonplace book suggests that he was now familiar enough with its text to recall individual passages.

Dissatisfied with a cursory view of natural law, Jefferson, as he always did upon encountering a subject that intrigued him, yearned to read more deeply. He eventually accumulated nearly all of the fundamental treatises on the subject: Jean Jacques Burlamaqui's *Principes de Droit Naturel*; Grotius's *De Jure Belli ac Pacis*; Grotius's *Le Droit de la Guerre, et de la Paix*, as edited by Jean Barbeyrac; Frieherr von Pufendorf's *Le Droit de la Nature et des Gens*; Pufendorf's *Of the Law of Nature and Nations*; Christian Wolff's *Institutions du Droit de la Nature et des Gens* in Elie Luzac's Latin/French parallel text edition; two different editions of Emer de Vattel's *Le Droit des Gens*, which modernized the study of natural law and applied it to practical legal issues in the realm of international law; and Richard Cumberland's *Treatise of the Laws of Nature*, in both its Latin original and English translation.

This last work Jefferson found especially persuasive. Cumberland argued that natural law compelled mankind to promote the common good. He reached his conclusions without recourse to Scripture and without reference to the afterlife. The secular modernity Cumberland exemplified strongly appealed to Jefferson. Cumberland's application of recent scientific discoveries to support his system of ethics strengthened his argument among enlightened readers.[25]

To some contemporary thinkers, the growing number of treatises on natural law did not seem like a panacea. Jeremy Bentham, for one, found them vague, especially in terms of their purpose. He queried, "Are they political or ethical, historical or juridical, expository or censorial?"

Natural law was "an obscure phantom." Some treatises on the subject "seem to refer to *manners*, sometimes to *laws*; sometimes to what law *is*, sometimes to what it *ought* to be."[26] Jefferson, too, recognized that the treatises on natural law could be vague, but he devised a practical way to remedy such imprecision. Instead of relying on a single treatise, a reader could and should consult many different authors on the subject. When several works of natural law reach a consensus, as Jefferson told George Washington, then they form a powerful and convincing legal argument.[27] The marginal notations in his surviving copies of these treatises show him fulfilling the process he outlined to Washington. Encountering an aspect of natural law that caught his attention in one work, he consulted others to see what they said on the subject. Into his earlier edition of Vattel, for example, he inscribed marginal references to Wolff's *Institutions* and Burlamaqui's *Principes de Droit Naturel*.

Jefferson continued to update his knowledge of the subject throughout his life. His copy of the later edition of Vattel's *Le Droit de Gens*, which survives at the Library of Congress, shows that Jefferson cross-referenced Vattel with a subsequent work on the law of nature and nations by G. F. de Martens. Not only did he update the text by inscribing a reference to Martens within his copy of the work; he also backdated Vattel by double-checking a reference to Jean Bodin's *Six Livres de la République* and inscribing a cross-reference to book, chapter, and paragraph of Bodin in the margin. Bodin wrote of sovereign powers; Vattel wrote of laws that transcended the boundaries of sovereignty. Jefferson's annotation to his copy of Vattel's *Le Droit de Gens*, brief as it is, shows him scrupulously studying the relationship between sovereignty and international law.[28]

Of these works, few more significantly influenced his legal thinking than Pufendorf's *Of the Law of Nature and Nations*. Citing Pufendorf in *Howell vs. Netherland*, a case he argued in 1770, Jefferson summarized his understanding of natural law: "Under the law of nature all men are born free, everyone comes into the world with a right to his own person, which includes the liberty of moving and using it at his own will. This is what is called personal liberty, and is given him by the author of nature, because necessary for his own sustenance."[29] He would refine and expand his understanding of natural law in his greatest political writings over the ensuing decade.

The case of *Howell vs. Netherland* shows that Jefferson had synthesized his study of natural law to such an extent that he could now apply it in his arguments in court. By 1770, he had reconciled the intellectual crisis the Stamp Act precipitated in 1765. This same case, however, presented a crisis of another sort, one that Jefferson never completely reconciled. His client, the plaintiff, was a grandson of a white woman and a black man. Jefferson argued that the law of nature dictated that the man was free and not a slave. Yet the case of *Howell vs. Netherland* leads to further questions: If, by natural right, the grandson is free, then why not the father? Why not the grandfather? Why not all?

Intensifying his study of natural law from the mid-1760s, Jefferson discovered how to solve the unjust laws the English imposed upon the American colonies. When something as venerable as the English rule of law could be undermined by capricious laws that abused its subjects, a more just and permanent system of laws remained, natural law, which transcended any laws a political state could devise. What Mark Akenside had said about poetry, Jefferson realized, applied equally to law: nature's hand must point the path.

CHAPTER 7

A Shelf of Notebooks

The precise date Thomas Jefferson passed the bar remains a mystery. Some have suggested that he did not pass it until 1767, the year he recorded his first legal case, but he had to have passed it before then because he practiced law in the General Court of Virginia, not its lower county courts. In order to come before the bar of the General Court, a lawyer did not necessarily have to practice in the inferior courts, but he did have to hold for one year a license to practice in the inferior courts, which was granted upon passing the bar examination. Most likely Jefferson passed the bar in late 1765. The *Virginia Gazette* daybooks hint that he was studying for his examinations in early autumn, when he purchased a copy of *Grounds and Rudiments of Law and Equity*, a general survey that made an ideal study aid. The daybooks offer another clue to suggest that Jefferson's legal training was reaching a point of culmination: in addition to the various other goods he acquired from the printing office that autumn, he also purchased "1 skin Parchment."[1] Jefferson, it seems, was getting ready to hang his sheepskin.

The end of 1765 marks the end of the period covered by the surviving daybooks from the *Virginia Gazette* office. From here on, Jefferson's own voluminous records provide the chief source for much information regarding his intellectual pursuits and day-to-day activities. He continued to maintain his literary commonplace book. He also continued to study law independently, as his legal commonplace book indicates. In addition, he started a second legal commonplace book, one devoted specifically to equity law. He began other notebooks around this same time, too, all of which had the general purpose of keeping his life in order. In 1766, he took the first notes for what would become his *Garden Book*. Before another decade passed, he would start his *Farm Book*. The earliest of his memorandum books dates from 1767. His commonplace books are

86

largely products of the 1760s and 1770s, though he made a few sporadic entries in them later. The others he maintained regularly all his life. The commonplace books pertain to the life of the mind; the others pertain to his personal and business life. Yet all contribute to his literary life and show him in the process of making a written record of himself.

Though each of these various notebooks is meticulous in its own way, all lack the regularity of the daybooks from the printing office. Before leaving these invaluable records behind, let's linger over the purchases Jefferson made on Friday, October 11, 1765, one of the last days his name appears in them. He bought several different items that Friday, including six quires of mourning paper. This modest purchase recorded in a commercial ledger masks the well of emotions Jefferson was experiencing. Mourning paper was a special kind of stationery for announcing a death in the family. Each page was hand-painted with black borders to let recipients know the general purpose of the letter even before they read its text. Jane Jefferson, his big sister, had died the week before at the age of twenty-five, and now her brother faced the somber task of giving others the news.

Also that day, Jefferson bought a two-volume edition of William Shenstone's *Works* at the *Virginia Gazette* office. This purchase, too, could have been motivated by his sister's death. Shenstone, a melancholy poet, included numerous elegies, much funeral verse, and many tombstone inscriptions among his writings. In large part, Shenstone's verse articulates the theme of rural retirement, a theme that struck a chord with Jefferson.[2] Drafting his "Thoughts on English Prosody" two decades later, he incorporated the following lines from Shenstone's ballad "The Princess Elizabeth":

> Bred on plains, or born in vallies,
>   Who would bid those scenes adieu?
> Stranger to the arts of malice,
> Who would ever courts pursue?

Shenstone ultimately left London to return to Leasowes, his family estate, where he became an expert landscape gardener. The edition of *Works* Jefferson obtained this day includes "Unconnected Thoughts on Gardening," an essay that influenced his ideas on landscape gardening. Also forming a part of Shenstone's *Works* are the inscriptions for the monuments that dotted his estate. The inscription for his sister's tomb that Jefferson wrote echoes one of the memorial inscriptions at Leasowes. Following Shenstone, he wrote in Latin, but it can be translated as follows:

Ah, Joanna, best of girls.
Ah, torn away from the bloom of vigorous age.
May the earth be light upon you.
Farewell, forever and ever.[3]

After 1765, the story of Jefferson's visits to the *Virginia Gazette* office becomes more complicated, not only because less evidence survives to document his purchases but also because the following year a second *Virginia Gazette* office opened. Frustrated with the current *Gazette*'s reluctance to contradict the governor by voicing opposition to British policy in the wake of the Stamp Act, several Virginians sought to bring another printer to Williamsburg in order to establish a rival, independent newspaper. Jefferson himself took an active part in soliciting the services of Maryland printer William Rind. A longtime partner of Annapolis printer Jonas Green, Rind had helped him publish the *Maryland Gazette* for several years. In addition, Rind had been the proprietor of a large bookstore and circulating library in Annapolis.

The Virginians offered to support a new paper and invited Rind to relocate to Williamsburg. He accepted their offer and arrived with his family in late 1765 or early 1766. As Jefferson told Isaiah Thomas, "Until the beginning of our revolutionary disputes, we had but one press, and that having the whole business of the government, and no competitor for public favor, nothing disagreeable to the governor could be got into it. We procured Rind to come from Maryland to publish a free paper."[4] Rind began publishing his newspaper, also titled the *Virginia Gazette*, in May 1766, and Jefferson aggressively sought to obtain subscriptions for him. Rind's motto was "Open to All Parties, but Influenced by None."

Joseph Royle, the proprietor of the established *Virginia Gazette*, died later that year, but his *Gazette* was continued by his successors, Alexander Purdie and John Dixon. Through the next several years, therefore, a distinction must be made between the Purdie and Dixon *Virginia Gazette* and the Rind *Virginia Gazette*. Though Jefferson supported Rind's paper, he continued to buy books from Purdie and Dixon occasionally. But when he had a choice, he bought from Rind. For example, Purdie and Dixon published almanacs of their own, but Jefferson preferred Rind's *Virginia Almanack*.

Required to wait a year before starting his law practice, Jefferson had no intentions of remaining idle during that time. His relationship with Rind shows that even before he began his law practice or served in his first elected office, he was taking an active role in an effort to shape public opinion. The waiting period gave him leisure time he had not known since his boyhood and would not know again until his retirement from public office decades later. He spent the time actively engaged in a variety of pursuits. For one, he deepened his legal studies.

To that end, he maintained his legal commonplace book. The consecutively numbered entries are undated, but Jefferson seems to have made many in 1766. At the end of each entry, he carefully cited his source. He mostly commonplaced reports of cases during the mid-1760s, but he also excerpted some theoretical works. As the decade of the Stamp Act gave way to the decade of Revolution, the content of his entries shifted from legal reports to legal and political theory.[5]

Jefferson took an approach to his legal commonplace book that differed significantly from that of his literary one. Excerpting *belles lettres*, he usually transcribed passages verbatim. Occasionally he skipped intervening text between two notable passages and marked the gap with an ellipsis, but for the most part he recorded the written word as he found it. When it came to legal texts, precise wording was less important than capturing the gist of a case or an argument, so he sought to summarize legal theories and reports of cases as briefly as possible. Before long, he could reduce ideas to their essence.

Advice he gave those studying for the bar offers a good indication of Jefferson's method of keeping a legal commonplace book. When commonplacing reports of cases, he advised, enter "every case of value, condensed into the narrowest compass possible which will admit of presenting distinctly the principles of the case. This operation is doubly useful, inasmuch as it obliges the student to seek out the pith of the case, and habituates him to a condensation of thought, and to an acquisition of the most valuable of all talents, that of never using two words where one will do."[6]

To his grandson Thomas Jefferson Randolph, he described how he developed this method with his own legal commonplace book:

> At first I could shorten it very little: but after a while I was able to put a page of a book into 2. or 3. sentences, without omitting any portion of the substance. Go on therefore with courage and you will find it grows easier and easier. Besides obliging you to understand the subject, and fixing it in your memory, it will learn you the most valuable art of condensing your thoughts and expressing them in the fewest words possible. No stile of writing is so delightful as that which is all pith, which never omits a necessary word, nor uses an unnecessary one. The finest models of this existing are Sallust and Tacitus, which on that account are worthy of constant study.[7]

Primarily important for understanding the development of his legal thought, the entries are doubly useful for understanding Jefferson's literary life. The legal commonplace book shows him in metamorphosis from reader to writer. As examples of his ability to reduce arguments to their essentials, his entries in this notebook anticipate his subsequent writings. Jefferson's greatest works are masterpieces of concision. In addition, the footnotes he occasionally appended to his entries reveal his ongoing interests in *belles lettres* and his recognition of the interrelationships among different types of writing. Lawyers and poets can share ideas—they simply have different ways of expressing them.

Entry 557, one of the lengthier ones in the legal commonplace book, offers an excellent opportunity to see Jefferson's mind at work. He derived this and several subsequent entries from Lord Kames's *Historical Law Tracts*. In this pioneering work of legal history, Kames brought together several works on a variety of legal subjects, synthesizing his ideas about the historical development of the law. Each of Jefferson's entries from this volume derives from a separate tract. The first tract, "History of the Criminal Law," occupies eighty-nine octavo pages in the edition of Kames he owned. Jefferson condensed it to an amount of space that fills just over eight pages in the modern edition of the commonplace book—one-tenth its original size.[8] Never use ten words where one will do, he might have said.

Jefferson eliminated Kames's first three sentences. All concern basic principles of criminal law he knew well and did not need to repeat. His first sentence, therefore, is a paraphrase of Kames's fourth. Kames had written:

> Upon certain Actions, hurtful to others, the Stamp of *impropriety* and *wrong* is impressed in legible characters, visible to all, not excepting even the Delinquent.[9]

Jefferson wrote:

> On certain actions hurtful to others the stamp of wrong is impressed in characters legible even to the delinquent himself.

The departures he made from his source show Jefferson deliberately eliminating unnecessary words. He saw no reason to use the conjoined word pair, "*impropriety* and *wrong*"—he omitted the latinate word and kept the more straightforward and forceful Anglo-Saxon term. In the right hands, of course, such verbal pairs can be rhetorically and stylistically effective. Think of *Hamlet*—"the slings and arrows of outrageous fortune," "the whips and scorns of time." Jefferson himself would use conjoined pairs of words masterfully in his most persuasive writings.

Entry 557 reveals other ways Jefferson abbreviated his source. As part of his revision, he largely eliminated Kames's supporting examples and illustrative footnotes. At one point Kames took the Hottentots for example to verify his ideas regarding criminal behavior. Seeing no need to repeat this derogatory and racist example, Jefferson eliminated it altogether. Though he excised most of Kames's quotations from other sources, he did retain a few, those from Lucan and Homer.

Regardless of his desire for brevity, Jefferson expanded his source in several places to make reference to other texts. Copying a sentence from Kames expressing how heinous transgressions of the laws of nature prompted public indignation and elicited a public desire to punish criminals, Jefferson added a footnote, expanding Kames with two lines of Greek from Euripides' *Hecuba*. The lines can be translated, "For 'tis ever a good man's duty to succour the right, and to punish evil-doers wherever found."[10]

Brief as it is, Jefferson's footnote conveys much. Kames had asserted the universality of man's indignation toward evildoers. Enhancing Kames with an ancient Greek quotation, Jefferson verified the assertion by showing how the same idea had been expressed in a different time, place, and language. Kames had emphasized the importance of understanding law in terms of its historical development; Jefferson's footnote shows him doing just that. For him, law and literature offered different ways to codify universal values.

The same quotation from *Hecuba* occurs among numerous other Greek excerpts from Euripides in Jefferson's literary commonplace book. Chances are he did not reread Euripides to gloss Kames. More likely he consulted his literary commonplace book. The two notebooks could work in tandem. Whereas one recorded legal ideas and the other quoted passages from belletristic literature, the ideas they articulated occasionally coincided. When they did, Jefferson noticed.

Later in entry 557, he added another literary footnote. Annotating a passage discussing the practice of convicted criminals who designated substitutes to assume their debts—to suffer their punishments for them—Jefferson transcribed some twenty lines from *Paradise Lost* articulating the same idea. Milton had drawn an analogy between this legal practice and the offer the Son of God makes to his Father in order to assume the debt of the sinner, Man, and be crucified for his sins. The passage Jefferson extracted from Milton ends with Christ speaking to his Father:

> Behold me then; me for him, life for life
> I offer; on me let thine anger fall;
> Account me men ...

This Miltonic footnote fulfills the same functions as the earlier Euripides note, but it does something more: it indicates the extraordinary power of literature to exalt an idea to the realm of the sublime. Taking a legal concept and borrowing legal diction, Milton expressed the sacrifice the Son of God makes on man's behalf. Jefferson's footnote shows him doing precisely what he told John Bernard he had been doing at this time: "I was bred ... to the law; that gave me a view of the dark side of humanity. Then I read poetry to qualify it with a gaze on the bright side."[11]

Historical Law Tracts was one of several works by Kames that Jefferson was reading in the mid-1760s. About half of his equity commonplace book derives from Kames's *Principles of Equity*.[12] Often considered Kames's most important work, *Principles of Equity* contained much to allure Jefferson. Using the comparative method, Kames contrasted Scottish and English legal theory to reveal their similarities and differences. While Kames's treatment of equity law is primarily theoretical, he addressed many important practical legal issues, too.[13]

Jefferson also read Kames's *Essays on the Principles of Morality and Natural Religion* around this time, as something he wrote nearly a half century later suggests. In a letter dated 1814, he calls Lord Kames "one of the ablest of our advocates, who goes so far as to say, in his Principles of Natural religion, that a man owes no duty to which he is not urged by some impulsive feeling. This is correct if referred to the standard of general feeling in the given case, and not to the feeling of a single individual. Perhaps I may misquote him, it being fifty years since I read his book."[14] Jefferson ultimately acquired several other works by Kames, including *Elements of Criticism*, in which Kames takes an innovative approach to derive critical principles from human nature. *Elements of Criticism* influenced Jefferson's literary aesthetic significantly.[15]

The legal and equity commonplace books indicate the level of intensity and seriousness with which Jefferson approached his studies. But he did not spend the whole time between passing the bar and beginning his legal practice with his nose in a book. He also attuned himself to the rhythms of nature and maintained a regimen of vigorous outdoor exercise. His long walks through the countryside gave him ample opportunity to watch the seasons turn.

As the Virginia mountains shed their coat of snow and pushed out the year's new growth, Jefferson carefully observed the earliest wildflowers bloom. The colorful flowers were tinged with melancholy that year. According to family tradition, Jane Jefferson had first introduced her brother to the pleasures of wildflowers. Since childhood the two had often accompanied each other on walks through the woods. That spring, for the first time, he could not share his delight with his sister. Without her, he recorded the observations into a notebook that has become known as his *Garden Book*. It did not start out as such; none of the entries he made in 1766 concern gardening at all. They mention neither the flowers he planted nor the vegetables he grew. For instance, he planted strawberries this year, but nowhere in the entries he made for the year does he mention planting strawberries. He solely recorded his observations on wildflowers.[16]

Written after his sister's death, the entries for 1766 assume the quality of a poem in the carpe diem tradition. In terms of form, however, Jefferson's observations read almost like modernist verse:

Purple hyacinth begins to bloom.
Narcissus and Puckoon open.
Puckoon flowers fallen.
a bluish colored, funnel-formed flower in lowgrounds in bloom
purple flag blooms. Hyacinth and Narcissus gone.
Wild honeysuckle in our woods open.—also the Dwarf
    flag and Violets
blue flower in low grounds vanished.
the purple flag, Dwarf flag, Violet and wild
Honeysuckle still in bloom.

Each line in this passage save the last one records when blossoms either appeared or disappeared. The last records that the latest flowers to blossom remained in bloom. Perhaps Jefferson made this particular note because he could not wait until the bloom was off the honeysuckle: he was leaving on a trip through Maryland, Pennsylvania, and New York. He could tarry in Virginia no longer. Regardless, this last line does have the effect of seizing a moment in time.

If Jefferson brought a notebook with him to keep a journal of his trip north, it perished in the Shadwell fire. No evidence of a travel notebook survives. The fullest information regarding the journey comes in a letter he wrote John Page from Annapolis. Jefferson would do much more travel writing in Europe a decade and a half later. His letter to Page shows that he was already a pretty fair travel writer. His ostensible purpose for the trip was to visit Philadelphia to be inoculated against smallpox, but he also wanted to take advantage of the time before starting his law practice to see more of North America. Who could say when he might have another opportunity?

The letter to Page begins with a humorous description of his misfortunes along the road and echoes a passage from Laurence Sterne's *Tristram Shandy*, which itself echoes the storm scene from *King Lear*. Literary history is a set of nesting boxes: an allusion to one work often means an allusion to many. Personifying fortune as a mean-spirited duchess, Tristram Shandy claims that "in every stage of my life, and at every turn and corner where she could get fairly at me, the ungracious duchess has pelted me with a set of as pitiful misadventures and cross accidents as ever small Hero sustained."[17] Narrating his own experiences on the road, Jefferson observed:

> Surely never did small hero experience greater misadventures than I did on the first two or three days of my travelling. Twice did my horse run away with me and greatly endanger the breaking [of] my neck on the first day. On the second I drove two hours through as copious a rain as ever I have seen, without meeting with a single house to which I could repair for shelter. On the third in going through Pamunkey, being unacquainted with the ford, I passed through water so deep as to run over the cushion as I sat on it, and to add to the danger, at that instant one wheel mounted a rock which I am confident was as high as the axle, and rendered it necessary for me to exercise all my skill in the doctrine of gravity.[18]

Depicting himself with the seat of his pants soaking wet, Jefferson used the same kind of self-effacing humor characteristic of the finest travel writers. His reference to the doctrine of gravity contributes to the humor as it conveys the absurdity of formal learning in a precarious situation.

Jefferson followed these adventures on the road with an account of what he saw in Annapolis. His visit to the provincial capital coincided with the Maryland Assembly. Accompanied by a local acquaintance, Jefferson saw the lower house in session: "I went into the lower, sitting in an old courthouse, which, judging from its form and appearance, was built in the year one." The Maryland State House was not quite that old, but it was getting on in years. Having been built the first decade of the eighteenth century, it had become much too small for its present purpose, and the Marylanders had been neglecting its maintenance for years. Before another decade passed, it would be razed to make way for a new state house.

Approaching the chamber in which the lower house met, Jefferson was surprised "to hear as great a noise and hubbub as you will usually

observe at a publick meeting of the planters in Virginia." The appearance of the Speaker of the House, Colonel Robert Lloyd, immediately
drew his attention: "The first object which struck me after my entrance
was the figure of a little old man dressed but indifferently, with a yellow
queüe wig on, and mounted in the judge's chair." This unkempt little
man scarcely seemed like the speaker of the House.

Jefferson went on to describe both the clerk of the Assembly and the
members of the House as a whole. The clerk read a bill before the House
"with a schoolboy tone and an abrupt pause at every half dozen words."
The assemblymen or

> mob (for such was their appearance) sat covered on the justices' and
> lawyers' benches, and were divided into little clubs amusing them-
> selves in the common chit chat way. I was surprised to see them
> address the speaker without rising from their seats, and three, four,
> and five at a time without being checked. When a motion was made,
> the speaker instead of putting the question in the usual form only
> asked the gentleman whether they chose that such or such a thing
> should be done, and was answered by a yes sir, or no sir: and tho' the
> voices appeared frequently to be divided, they never would go to the
> trouble of dividing the house, but the clerk entered the resolutions,
> I supposed, as he thought proper. In short every thing seems to be
> carried without the house in general's knowing what was proposed.[19]

Years later Jefferson would write the standard work in the field of
parliamentary procedure, *A Manual of Parliamentary Practice*. This passage shows that he was already intrigued with the formal legislative
process.

His account of Annapolis ends with a description of the city, which
proved more complimentary than his depiction of the Maryland legislature. He especially enjoyed its handsome natural scenery and the
usefulness of its deepwater port—the beautiful and the practical.

When he was in Annapolis, news arrived that Parliament had re-
pealed the Stamp Act. As he told Page, people there celebrated its repeal
with verve. Similar celebrations took place in other colonial cities up and
down the seaboard. All were short-lived. Directly after repealing the
Stamp Act, Parliament passed the Declaratory Act, which gave it the
right to bind the American colonies to whatever legislation it felt necessary. Jefferson considered it a legislative sword of Damocles.

From Annapolis he traveled to Philadelphia. The city presented
an extraordinary sight for provincial eyes. Fellow Virginian William

Gregory of Fredericksburg, who visited for the first time some months earlier, had been especially impressed with the port: "I went and took a view of the Shipping. I never saw so many vessels at one time, at one Port. I dare say there may be 250 vessels that go to sea."[20] Jefferson experienced a similar sense of awe. In Philadelphia he found the most beautiful city he had ever seen, an opinion he reasserted even after he had seen London and Paris.

Jefferson also enjoyed the bookbuying opportunities the city had to offer. His activities in Philadelphia during this visit have gone undocumented, but if his subsequent behavior is any indication, he visited all of the bookstores in town and made purchases at most.

He carried with him a letter of introduction to the prominent Philadelphia physician John Morgan. The previous year, Morgan had returned to the city after being in Europe for an extended period of time. A distinguished man of science, he was also a connoisseur and collector of art. While taking the Grand Tour of Europe, he met many of the day's leading scientists and artists and collected several fine paintings and other *objets d'art*. Dr. Morgan's personal qualities and intellectual accomplishments were similar to those of Jefferson's friends in the Williamsburg circle. To Jefferson, Morgan presented a model of a successful professional man dedicated to the advancement of science and culture.

The smallpox inoculation kept Jefferson incapacitated for some days. Little else is known of his time in Philadelphia that year, but a letter he wrote some fifty years later dates his friendship with Charles Thomson from this visit to Philadelphia.[21] In terms of both intellect and ideology, Jefferson found in him a kindred spirit. During the Stamp Act crisis, Thomson had become a leader of Philadelphia's Sons of Liberty. In the coming years, he would work tirelessly to prevent the importation of British goods into Philadelphia and serve as secretary to the Continental Congress. Jefferson developed a deep and abiding respect for Thomson's mind. He would seek his help when he revised and expanded *Notes on the State of Virginia*.

Jefferson eventually left Philadelphia and traveled to New York, where he happened to lodge with Elbridge Gerry. Short and wiry, Gerry's slender frame did nothing to mask his great intellect or his passion for freedom. He was already dedicated to the cause of American liberty and would become a signer of the *Declaration of Independence*. He had recently completed his master's degree at Harvard College, where he wrote a thesis arguing the question, "Can the new prohibitory duties which made it useless for the people to engage in commerce, be evaded by them as faithful subjects?" It is easy to imagine the heated conversations about law and liberty that took place between Gerry and Jefferson early that summer. Before the month of July was out, Jefferson returned to Virginia by water.

Little evidence survives to document his activities during the second half of 1766. In February 1767 he resumed note-taking in matters concerning his garden, this time with a greater sense of purpose. He continued to record the coming and going of wildflowers that year, but these observations are interspersed with information about planting vegetables and flowers. The twentieth of that month he made the year's first garden-related entry, noting that he had sowed two beds of peas, his favorite vegetable.[22] On April 2, he sowed seeds for carnations, marigolds, pansies, violets, and yellow-flowered primrose. In addition to sowing seeds for these and many other varieties of flowers, he also planted cayenne peppers. On April 24, he recorded that the peas he had planted in February came to the table.

The notes he took show him in the process not only of cultivating his garden, they also show him in the process of learning how to garden. Unlike more scholarly fields of inquiry, gardening could not be learned solely from books. Few topics were more local in terms of the specific knowledge required. The classic British treatises on the subject might do well at Kew Gardens, but their information was of limited value in the Virginia Piedmont. To be a successful gardener, Jefferson needed local information, information that generally could be found only by word of mouth.

Starting in 1767, and continuing for many years after, he noted gardening hints he gleaned from friends and neighbors. That year, for example, he recorded a conversation he had had with a neighbor concerning how and when to plant artichokes. Later he noted conversations with two others about planting cucumbers and watermelons. After noting these conversations, he transcribed additional information about planting cucumbers from Philip Miller's *Gardener's Dictionary*, the foremost horticultural and agricultural handbook in the eighteenth century. Jefferson was obviously checking to see how his neighbor's information jibed with what his books told him. When it came to the matter of gardening, Jefferson used the printed word to ascertain the spoken.

His memorandum books, in turn, combine print and manuscript. Starting his legal career in 1767, he needed an accurate way to keep track of how the cases he accepted were proceeding. Careful record-keeping was especially important since legal cases often took years to resolve. His memorandum books not only supply details of his professional legal activities, they also document his day-to-day expenses.

Through the 1770s, he kept his memoranda in a series of interleaved almanacs. When an almanac for the coming year was published around November, Jefferson would acquire a copy and have it bound up with enough blank leaves to provide sufficient space for a year's worth of notes. The pocket-sized almanac, even after it was bulked up with blank leaves, remained portable enough to carry with him throughout the year. At the beginning of the volume, he would enter his legal notations. For his financial accounts he would turn the volume over—making the back the front—and enter his daily expenditures. The extra blank leaves at the center of each volume provided space for miscellaneous notes.

Eventually Jefferson began carrying an ivory table-book to keep his daily accounts. Although pocket-sized memorandum books made of blank leaves were part of a tradition in English letters that extended at least as far back as the sixteenth century, the use of ivory for table-books was a late-seventeenth-century innovation. Sometimes called a writing tablet, a writing table, or even simply a table, the table-book gave users a way to take notes on the fly. Fashioned from several oblong strips of ivory attached together at one end so that they could be spread out like a fan, the set of leaves could be inscribed, wiped clean, and reinscribed. Ivory table-books had many advantages over interleaved almanacs: they were reusable, durable, and waterproof. [23] Its reusability was its defining feature. Benjamin Franklin used an ivory table-book to record his plan for self-examination, staining the ivory leaves with his week-long chart in indelible red ink and using a lead pencil to mark the chart, which he would erase at week's end.

The portability and erasability of table-books made them ideal for the peripatetic man of letters. These same features intrigued Renaissance dramatists, who made creative use of them. Hamlet makes figurative and literal use of these memorandum books within the course of a single speech. The knowledge that Claudius has murdered his own brother destroys the concept of the world Hamlet has formed, and he resolves to erase his mind like a table-book:

> Yea, from the table of my memory
> I'll wipe away all trivial fond records,
> All saws of books, all forms, all pressures past
> That youth and observations copied there.

Hamlet's knowledge of Claudius's duplicity prompts him to start his table-book afresh: "O villain, villain, smiling, damned villain! My tables—meet it is I set it down / That one may smile, and smile, and be a villain!"

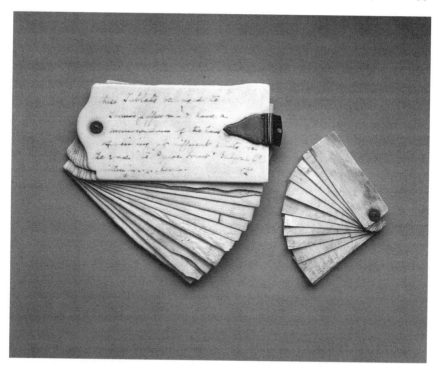

Ivory Table-Books. (Monticello, Thomas Jefferson Foundation, Inc.)

Records that Jefferson kept in his ivory table-book were less dramatic, but they did allow him to keep his life in order on a day-to-day basis. He inscribed notes, expenditures, and other quotidian details in his table-book, transferred them to his memorandum books later, and then erased the table-book to use it again.

The legal notations and financial accounts in his memorandum books are fairly bland, but the miscellaneous memoranda contain a variety of unusual topics, entered in considerably more detail than any of the day-by-day accounts. One year he used the extra space in his interleaved almanac to write a detailed, yet emotional description of Virginia's Natural Bridge, which would form the basis of his description in *Notes on the State of Virginia*. Another year he used the spare blank pages to write out some ideas about landscaping Monticello. His interleaved copy of the 1775 *Virginia Almanack* contains a transcription of the famous speech of Chief Logan. The speech greatly impressed Jefferson and would remain important to him throughout his life. He entered it when he first encountered the speech in late 1774, thus ensuring its preservation and allowing him to refer to its text whenever he wished.

Accompanying the speech in his pocket almanac is a detailed account of the circumstances in which it was delivered. After narrating the events leading to Logan's speech, Jefferson entered its complete text:

> I appeal to any white man to say if ever he entered Logan's cabbin hungry, and he gave him not meat; if ever he came cold and naked and he cloathed him not. During the course of the last long and bloody war, Logan remained idle in his cabbin, an advocate for peace. Nay such was my affection for the Whites, that my countrymen hooted as they passed by and said, "Logan is the friend of White men." I had even thought to have lived with you, but for the injuries of one man. Colo. Cresap, the last spring, in cold blood, and unprovoked, cut off all the Relations of Logan; not sparing even my women or children. There runs not a drop of my blood in the veins of any human creature. This called on me for revenge. I have sought it; I have killed many: I have fully glutted my vengeance. For my country I rejoice at the beams of peace, but do not harbor a thought that mine is the joy of fear. Logan never felt fear. He will not turn on his heel to save his life. Who is there to mourn for Logan?—Not one.[24]

Such inclusions imbue the memorandum books with a literary quality they otherwise lack. Despite the absence of artistry, Jefferson took pride in his meticulous records. Writing in the 1780s, after he had been keeping accounts for more than fifteen years, he boasted that he had kept his memorandum books "with such scrupulous fidelity that I shall not be afraid to justify them on the bed of death, and so exact that in the course of 15 years which they comprehend, I never discovered that I had made but one omission of a paiment."[25] The irony of Jefferson's financial memoranda is that though he maintained a meticulous record of his expenditures, he never balanced his accounts. He was chronically in debt yet seldom faced that fact. As his editors have explained, the records gave an artificial sense of order to Jefferson's oftentimes chaotic financial situation.[26]

His record-keeping was so meticulous that his memorandum books can function as a chronicle of where he went and how much he spent. The most niggling amounts were recorded. Though he recorded what he spent, he did not always record what he bought. When he went to the coffeehouse in Williamsburg and spent six pence on coffee, the expenditure was duly recorded. When he went to the printing office to buy books, he recorded the expenditure, but not the titles of the books. From 1767, his memorandum books provide the only information regarding his purchases from either of the *Virginia Gazette* offices. Despite his metic-ulousness, Jefferson's record of book purchases is frustratingly inade-quate.

As a record of expenditures, the accounts are most useful for doc-umenting the time Jefferson spent away from Monticello. At home in the mountains, he seldom needed to spend money. He often went several days without opening his memorandum book. Overseers kept separate account books for his plantations, but few of these survive. Though the memorandum books display his meticulous—some might say obsessive—record-keeping, they otherwise say little about his personality. Never revealing the total man, they do supply a collection of curious details that shed light on the quotidian even as they keep the corners of his mind in the dark.

Returning to Shadwell in November 1767 having successfully ap-peared before the bar of the General Court for the first time, Jefferson came home with a much greater sense of public responsibility. That same month he was elected to the vestry of Fredericksville parish, a capacity in which he would continue to serve for several years. This position marks Jefferson's official entry into local leadership. The vestry of each parish consisted of intelligent, prosperous gentlemen who collectively oversaw the welfare of their fellow parishioners. Generally characterizing Vir-ginia vestrymen, Jefferson explained that they "are well acquainted with the details and economy of private life, and they find sufficient induce-ments to execute their charge well, in their philanthropy, in the appro-bation of their neighbors, and the distinction which that gives them."[27]

As a vestryman, Jefferson gave neighbors and parishioners the op-portunity to see that the weedy youth they had known as one of the Reverend Mr. Maury's students had transformed himself into a polite, well-mannered, and well-rounded young man. His role as vestryman paved the way for his election to the House of Burgesses the following year. Henceforth, Jefferson's life would not merely be inscribed in his private notebooks—it would become a part of the annals of Virginia and of a new nation.

CHAPTER 8

Becoming a Burgess

Since starting college, Jefferson had been traveling back and forth from Shadwell to Williamsburg at least twice a year. To him Williamsburg was not only the place where he received his professional education, but also a place where he learned the social graces and developed his love of science and literature through the conviviality of friends he made there. Arriving in town a week before the spring session of General Court was scheduled to convene in 1768, he found his familiar Williamsburg world irreparably changed: his dear friend Lieutenant Governor Francis Fauquier had passed away the previous month.

His death meant not only the end of the pleasant intellectual conversation around the dinner table at the Governor's Palace that Jefferson so enjoyed, but also the end of their ensemble musical performances. Even after his death, Fauquier still contributed to the advancement of scientific inquiry in Virginia: his will stipulated that in case he died of undetermined causes, his body should be used for purposes of scientific research.[1]

Fauquier had been the ablest man to fill the role of lieutenant governor of colonial Virginia, Jefferson believed. Regardless how his friend's death affected him, he apparently did not dwell on it. The night after reaching Williamsburg that year, he attended the opening performance of William Verling's Virginia Company of Comedians at the Waller Street theater, the first of several performances he would attend there that season. Jefferson had long been an aficionado of the stage. Evidence of his previous theatergoing is sparse, but a few years earlier, after reading law at Shadwell for several months, he considered a study break in the form of an excursion to Petersburg to attend the theater there.[2]

That evening, the company performed *Douglas*, a tragedy by John Home, who was currently being touted as the Scottish Shakespeare.

Since its opening in Edinburgh the previous decade, this tragedy had been performed throughout Great Britain and had become a favorite on the London stage. Like so much other literature that appealed to Jefferson, this play incorporated themes and motifs exemplifying neoclassical thought yet anticipating Romantic ideals. While stressing the importance of civic duty and private virtue, the play derives from an old Scots ballad, takes places in the Scottish Highlands, and is overlaid with an atmosphere of brooding melancholy.[3] *Douglas* contains many of the same elements that would draw Jefferson to the poems of Ossian in the coming years.

As an afterpiece, Verling's company performed *The Honest Yorkshire-Man*, a ballad farce written and composed by Henry Carey. The title phrase represents the English prototype of the character known in America as Yankee Jonathan, a bucolic bumbler who could see through duplicity and voice universal truths despite his naiveté. Carey's Virginia audience related well to the play, which contrasts the healthy virtues of the provinces with the pomp and frivolity of the metropolis. For American colonists, some of Carey's lines resonated beyond the farcical context in which they were voiced.

Virginians who attended the theater as a diversion from their legal and business activities heard poignant phrases from Carey's pen that resembled their increasingly claustrophobic situation as colonial subjects. Henrietta Osborne, one of the most recognizable and well-liked faces on the early American stage, played Arabella, the female lead. Trapped inside her apartment with her maid, she sang words with political ramifications for her colonial audience:

> In vain you mention pleasure
> To one confin'd like me,
> Ah what is wealth or treasure,
> Compar'd to liberty.

Regardless how Jefferson took this ballad farce, witnessing a musical performance on stage, as much as he enjoyed it, was still no substitute for playing music. Governor Fauquier, the man most responsible for keeping amateur musical performance alive and well in Williamsburg, may have died, but Jefferson was not going to let the music stop. Though good-quality musical instruments were sometimes difficult to obtain, they could be found occasionally. William Pasteur, who ran the apothecary shop on the Duke of Gloucester Street, imported a variety of goods, including musical instruments. The last week in May Jefferson visited

Pasteur's shop, where he bought a new violin.[4] The frequency with which Jefferson purchased violin strings over the next few years affirms that he was continuing the musical traditions Fauquier had helped establish.

He was also augmenting his library. That spring he purchased several volumes from the library of Philip Ludwell, a prominent member of the Virginia Council who had recently passed away. Most of the titles he acquired from Ludwell's estate concern law, but one, John Toland's late-seventeenth-century work *The Militia Reformed*, gave him other ideas. Toland emphasized the value of a well-trained militia and offered some practical suggestions to keep it prepared and ready. He particularly stressed the importance of making the militia consist of men of property committed to the public good.

Before long, Jefferson would find himself in a position to test some of Toland's ideas. Within the next two years, in fact, he would be commissioned county lieutenant of the Albemarle militia, a position that entitled him to be called colonel. He accepted the responsibility of the commission, but unlike so many of his Virginia contemporaries, he eschewed the title that came with it. Never did he style himself "Colonel Jefferson."

His profession as a lawyer brought him back to Williamsburg twice yearly. The autumn of 1768 he returned in time for the next session of the General Court, which was scheduled to begin the second Monday of October. That same month, Norborne Berkeley, Baron de Botetourt, arrived to assume his position as colonial governor. Before coming to Virginia, Botetourt had had a distinguished career in business and politics in England. He served as a Member of Parliament for more than two decades before he revived the barony of Botetourt and began serving in the House of Lords. A personal friend of King George III, Lord Botetourt also served briefly as groom of the king's bedchamber. In his business activities he invested heavily in several industries in Bristol, England, including the Warmley Copper Works, which failed in 1768. The failure put Botetourt in serious financial straits, prompting him to seek the lucrative position of governor of Virginia after Fauquier's death.[5]

Botetourt's legislative experience well qualified him for the position. And unlike other governors, he was willing to reside in Virginia. Former governors had stayed in England, collecting their sizable salaries while taking little direct responsibility for colonial governance. Instead, they sent their lieutenants to Virginia to do the actual work of governing. Virginians admired Botetourt for coming to the colony himself instead of sending a lieutenant.

He made a dramatic entry into Williamsburg when he arrived at dusk on Friday, October 21, 1768. As he entered the city, members of the Virginia Council greeted their new governor and accompanied him to the capitol, where he took the oath of office. News of his arrival rapidly circulated around Williamsburg, and its citizenry sought to welcome him as best they could. The city was illuminated for the occasion, as householders placed candles in their street-facing windows. Jefferson joined the throng to welcome the new governor. His financial accounts show that he bought some extra candles this day, too.[6]

Botetourt arrived with a fair-sized personal library, which gave a good impression to those privileged enough to gain entry to the Governor's Palace during his term. The library Botetourt brought with him to Virginia, a modest but discriminating collection of more than three hundred volumes, showed his guests that he was a man of taste and refinement but by no means overly pedantic. His was not a scholar's library: his collection of ancient authors consisted mainly of books boys read in school. He had a good collection of histories, including many of the most important historical works pertaining to North America. Apparently, Botetourt had done his homework in preparation for his role as governor.[7]

His excellent collection of *belles lettres* included a number of multi-volume works by prominent French and English authors—an eight-volume French edition of Molière, Sir Thomas Hanmer's six-volume edition of Shakespeare, an eight-volume French edition of Voltaire. He also had a copy of one of Voltaire's works in English translation, *Ignorant Philosopher*. Seeing this item listed anonymously in the inventory of the governor's estate as "1 Ignorant philosopher," a nineteenth-century wit commented, "Lord Botetourt was fortunate in not having more. It would be hard to find a modern library without a dozen."[8]

Dissolving the Assembly upon taking office was standard procedure for colonial governors, and Botetourt was no exception. Upon his arrival that autumn, he dissolved the Virginia Assembly, forcing counties to hold new elections. Six months would pass before the next Assembly, time enough for him to endear himself to them. He turned himself into a patron of education: he encouraged students at William and Mary, became rector of the college, and established the Botetourt Medal to reward scholastic excellence. A statue of Governor Botetourt now stands there to commemorate his contribution to the college. His exemplary behavior earned the gratitude of the Virginia colonists. Jefferson never became close friends with Botetourt as he had with Fauquier, but he recognized the new governor's "great respectability, his character for integrity, and his general popularity."[9]

The voters of Albemarle County chose a new burgess at their spring elections: Thomas Jefferson. Now he would be going to Williamsburg not only in his professional capacity as an attorney—someone who carries out the law—but also as a legislator, someone who makes the law. Though the contemporary entries in his memorandum books make no mention of his legislative activities, they do convey a newfound, and wide-eyed, sense of excitement.

Verling's Virginia Company of Comedians had disbanded before the close of the previous year. No other acting companies came to town that season. Still, there was plenty to see in Williamsburg, and Jefferson was an anxious as anybody to see what he could. Henry Tyler, a hog farmer from Sussex County who had raised a beast weighing more than half a ton, had brought it to Williamsburg and was charging people a shilling and three pence each just to see it. Tyler had brought his hog to a fine market. Many people, Jefferson included, paid the price of admission. That hog was huge. But there was no telling precisely how huge. An "attempt was made to weigh him with a pair of steel-yards, graduated to 1200 lb.," Jefferson noted, "but he weighed more." The animal stuck in his memory and entered the pages of history when Jefferson recalled it in *Notes on the State of Virginia*.[10]

Though no live actors trod the boards of the Waller Street theater during the spring of 1769, some puppets did. Peter Gardiner, a traveling puppeteer and illusionist, brought his elaborate stage show to Williamsburg. Gardiner's puppets, four feet tall and richly dressed, seemed almost lifelike. In early April Jefferson attended Gardiner's show. That evening the puppeteer staged a performance of *The Babes in the Wood*, a theatrical adaptation of a traditional story so well known that its title characters had become proverbial.

The evening's entertainment also included a variety of other acts: "a curious view of Water Works, representing the sea, with all manner of sea monsters sporting on the waves"; indoor fireworks representing "the taking of the Havannah, with ships, forts, and batteries, continually firing"; a "curious Field of Battle, containing the Dutch, French, Prussian, and English forces, which shall regularly march and perform the different exercises to great perfection"; and a man who put his head on one chair, his feet on another, and suffered "a large rock of three hundred weight to be broke on his breast with a sledge hammer"—an early precursor to the man who catches cannonballs. Gardiner gave his audience good value; a seat in the gallery for the whole show could be had for the same price as it cost to see the giant hog. Jefferson apparently enjoyed the extravaganza—he went back twice more before the month was out.[11]

The Assembly had been something of a spectacle for Jefferson in the past. Now, instead of observing the legislative proceedings from the lobby, he would be participating in them from the floor of the House of Burgesses. On Monday, May 8, 1769, Jefferson, now twenty-six years old, joined the other burgesses gathered at the capitol. Typically, the first morning of the legislative session was filled with formalities. Soon after the burgesses assembled, Nathaniel Walthoe, clerk of the Governor's Council, delivered a message from Lord Botetourt ordering them to attend him in the Council chamber. They proceeded there and entered en masse. Wearing a handsome pale crimson, cut velvet suit, the governor was dressed to capture their attention.[12] Though no acting companies came to Virginia this spring, Botetourt's eye-catching costume let perceptive observers recognize a piece of theater when they saw it.

"Gentlemen of the House of Burgesses," the governor stated. "You must return again to your House, and immediately proceed to the Choice of a Speaker."

They made their way back to their own chambers, where they elected Peyton Randolph, one of Jefferson's old mentors, to the position of Speaker of the House. In recent years, Jefferson had encountered Randolph professionally as an attorney, and the two would continue to come in contact as America worked its way toward independence. Jefferson greatly appreciated his friend's leadership. In a character sketch of Randolph, he called him "a most excellent man; and none was ever more beloved and respected by his friends. Somewhat cold and coy towards strangers, but of the sweetest affability when ripened into acquaintance. Of attic pleasantry in conversation, always good humored and conciliatory."[13]

His assessment of Randolph's character was not entirely positive, however. Randolph was quite fat, and Jefferson, who recognized a direct relationship between a person's physical and mental condition, saw that Randolph's girth hindered his legal and intellectual activity. Continuing his character study, Jefferson wrote: "With a sound and logical head, he was well read in the law; and his opinions, when consulted, were highly regarded, presenting always a learned and sound view of the subject, but generally, too, a listlessness to go into its thorough development; for being heavy and inert in body, he was rather too indolent and careless for business, which occasioned him to get a smaller proportion of it at the bar than his abilities would otherwise have commanded."[14]

Having dispatched a message to the governor informing him that they had chosen a speaker, the burgesses awaited his response. Nathaniel Walthoe returned to the House, and the House again went to the

Council chamber. With the burgesses gathered before him, Governor Botetourt began to speak. A contemporary observer recorded that the governor's "deportment was dignified and his delivery was solemn. It was said by those who had heard and seen George III speak and act on the throne of England, that his Lordship on the throne of Virginia was true to his prototype. He spoke very slow, with long pauses."[15] Botetourt delivered to the burgesses a prepared speech officially introducing himself and expressing his hopes for an amicable legislative session.

After hearing the governor's address, the burgesses returned to the House to begin their legislative business, the first order of which was to prepare an address of their own, which would thank the governor for his remarks. Before it could be prepared, the House had to pass a formal set of resolutions outlining its general contents. Edmund Pendleton—"the ablest man in debate I have ever met with," Jefferson called him—asked the newest burgess from Albemarle county to draft the necessary resolutions.[16] In other words, Jefferson's first official responsibility as a legislator required him to apply his skills as a writer.

Regardless of his command of the English language, Jefferson remained inexperienced in the art of parliamentary procedure. After the House passed the resolutions he had drafted, it appointed him to the committee assigned to write the address. This committee included several distinguished members: Richard Bland, Richard Henry Lee, and Robert Carter Nicholas. Bland had retained Jefferson as legal counsel on several occasions, so the two were well acquainted. Given the fact that he was "profound in Constitutional lore," Bland impressed Jefferson very much. Among Virginia's legislators and politicians, Bland was, in Jefferson's words, "the most learned and logical man of those who took prominent lead in public affairs."[17] In the coming years, much the same epithet would suit Jefferson himself.

Since he had written the resolutions, the committee assigned Jefferson the task of preparing the address. Upon its completion, he presented it to the other committee members. Much to his chagrin, the committee found the address unsatisfactory. Some committee members thought it followed "too strictly the diction of the resolutions, and that their subjects were not sufficiently amplified." Jefferson prided himself on his verbal economy, but his fellow committee members let him know that, in deference to the governor, this occasion called for amplitude. Since Nicholas was most vocal in his opposition to the draft, he took the responsibility to rewrite it. As Jefferson remembered, "Mr. Nicholas chiefly objected to it, and was desired by the committee to draw one more at large which he did, with amplification enough, and it was accepted—being a young man, as well as a young member, it made on me an impression proportioned to the sensibility of that time."[18]

Despite their verbal differences, Jefferson's set of resolutions and Nicholas's address have much in common. Both thank the governor for the speech he had given to open the new Assembly, appreciate his willingness to reside in Virginia, express confidence in his abilities, and assure him that the burgesses would dutifully fulfill their responsibilities as legislators—fairly dull stuff, all in all, the kind of words any respectful legislator might say upon welcoming a new governor. Private remarks Jefferson made around that same time hold a much sharper edge. A series of maxims he inscribed in his memorandum book shortly afterward includes the following: "No liberty, no life."[19]

Eager to learn and to serve, Jefferson volunteered for much additional committee work. The opening day of the legislative session, he was appointed to the Committee of Privileges and Elections and the Committee of Propositions and Grievances. As a general rule, the work of these two committees was routine, but Jefferson found it fascinating.

Participating on the House floor differed significantly from listening from the lobby. Albemarle's newest representative quickly noticed shortcomings in his own knowledge and lapses in procedural matters within the Assembly. Having visited the Maryland Assembly three years earlier and spoofed it with the urbanity of a traveler, Jefferson had no intention of letting the Virginia Assembly become the object of humorous derision. Around the time the House of Burgesses was in session that spring, he ordered several books to supplement his knowledge.[20] This list of books shows Jefferson applying his rigorous study habits to the business of governing the colony.

One of the purchases seems a direct result of his work on the Committee of Privileges and Elections: *Determinations of the Honourable House of Commons, Concerning Elections, and All Their Incidents*. This anonymous work concerns procedural matters regarding both the elected and the electorate. Arranged into short sections discussing a variety of subjects, it essentially constitutes the do's and don'ts of running for office.

Take the subject of treating, for example. In colonial Virginia, candidates for office traditionally treated their electorate to spirits on election day. The evidence suggests that Jefferson had followed custom and treated Albemarle voters to some grog prior to his first election.[21] In *Determinations . . . Concerning Elections*, he read about the impropriety of this tradition: "No Candidate, after the Teste of the Writ, or after any Place becomes vacant, shall, by himself or any other Means on his Behalf, or at his Charge, before his Election, directly or indirectly give, present, or allow to any Person having a Vote, any Money, Meat, Drink, Entertainment, or Provision...in order to be elected."[22]

Other works covered matters of legislative assemblies, both theoretical and practical. Jefferson's list includes two works that assert the history and power of Parliament: William Petyt's *Jus Parliamentarium* and Thornagh Gurdon's *History of the High Court of Parliament, Its Antiquity, Preeminence and Authority*. Jefferson was not alone in ordering these two works to help understand and shape the colonial legislature. Philadelphia bookman Isaac Norris, Jr., for instance, ordered the same titles for the use of the Pennsylvania assembly.[23] Both authors had similar designs: Petyt and Gurdon each took the history of Parliament back to the medieval chroniclers to argue for a legally sovereign Parliament and reassert the powers of Parliament that existed before the Norman Conquest.

William Hakewill's *Modus Tenendi Parliamentum; or, The Old Manner of Holding Parliaments*, another work Jefferson ordered that spring, was compiled from the journals of the House of Commons and was designed to show how a lower house had worked and should work. Introducing his compilation, Hakewill stressed the importance of the exchange of ideas to the legislative process. He remarked, "That which is to bear the stamp of a *Law*, must be a long time a moulding: there must be previous debates, bandings of arguments, and clashings of opinions *pro and con* go before." Jefferson would cite Hakewill in *Notes on the State of Virginia* to support the idea that the law of the majority not only could be found in common law but also was "the natural law of every assembly of men, whose numbers are not fixed by any other law." Later, in *A Manual of Parliamentary Practice*, Jefferson would make numerous detailed references to Hakewill, references that verify the close attention he paid to the work.[24]

The legislative business of the Assembly remained fairly routine through the first week, but the following Tuesday, May 16, the burgesses began considering their response to the Townshend Acts and the increasingly aggressive attempts of the British to enforce them. Named for their sponsor, Charles Townshend, the Chancellor of the Exchequer, these Acts consisted of two different measures. The first called for the suspension of the New York Assembly as a means of penalizing the colony for not complying with an earlier statute regarding the quartering of British troops. The second measure imposed customs duties on glass, paint, paper, and tea. An Act passed subsequent to this measure provided for its enforcement by establishing colonial commissioners responsible for collecting the customs duties.

Previously, the Massachusetts House of Representatives had passed a resolution to send a circular letter to the other colonial legislatures urging them to oppose the Townshend duties. When news of what the Massachusetts legislators were doing reached England, British authorities instructed colonial governors to dissolve any assembly that approved the circular letter from the Massachusetts House. Parliament not only accepted this policy, but also recommended reviving an old statute allowing the government to bring anyone accused of treason to England for trial. When these issues came before the House of Burgesses, there was little question what to do: the Virginia legislators agreed to support the action of their Massachusetts counterparts. They also passed a series of resolutions stipulating that Parliament had no right to tax the colonists and that the colonists had the right to petition the king to redress their grievances. To that end, the Virginia House ordered that an address to the king be prepared and appointed a committee to draft it.

The House also ordered that copies of these resolutions be sent to the legislative bodies of the other American colonies and on Wednesday, May 17, ordered the resolutions printed. The committee presented the address to the whole House, which approved the measure. With such serious business completed, the burgesses returned to more routine matters. Minutes later Nathaniel Walthoe interrupted their proceedings with an urgent message from the governor, who commanded the attendance of the burgesses. They proceeded to the Council chamber to hear what he had to say.[25]

He made no effort to mask his anger. A contemporary observer captured the scene from the moment the burgesses entered the Council chamber. This time Governor Botetourt "was dressed in a suit of plain scarlet. The speaker advanced toward him, the members following." Imagine a group of men slowly advancing in the shape of a wedge, with the imposing figure of Peyton Randolph in the lead. At the proper distance from the governor, Randolph stopped. After a "solemn pause of a minute or two," Governor Botetourt, "with an assumed stern countenance and with considerable power, addressed the speaker and members of the house."[26]

"Mr. Speaker, and Gentlemen of the House of Burgesses," he stated. "I have heard of your Resolves, and augur ill of their Effect: You have made it my Duty to dissolve you; and you are dissolved accordingly."[27]

Suddenly, Thomas Jefferson's first term as a burgess had ended just ten days after it had begun. Some of the more experienced burgesses had suspected what the governor would do once he heard of their resolves and already knew what they would do in turn. To preserve Virginia's interests, they agreed to reconstitute themselves as an extralegislative body. They left the capitol and proceeded to the Raleigh Tavern—about a hundred paces as measured by Jefferson's lanky stride. Inside, they gathered in the spacious Apollo Room, where they formed an association and then adjourned until the next morning, when they would consider possible courses of action.

After debating different possibilities, these erstwhile burgesses ultimately drafted a set of nonimportation resolutions "in Hopes that our Example will induce the good People of this Colony to be frugal in the Use and Consumption of *British* Manufactures, and that the Merchants and Manufacturers of *Great-Britain* may, from Motives of Interest, friendship, and Justice, be engaged to exert themselves to obtain for us a Redress of those Grievances, under which the Trade and Inhabitants of *America* at present labour."[28] No longer would subscribers be able to import a variety of manufactured goods from Great Britain or articles of British manufacture from other nations. The resolutions specified a lengthy list of items, including candles, chairs, clocks, hats, jewelry, joiners' and cabinet work of all kinds, lace, looking glasses, pewter, saddles, silversmith's work of all sorts, spirits, tables, and upholstery. To this list Jefferson and the others affixed their names.

Happily, the list did not prevent its subscribers from ordering books from Great Britain. This legislative session revealed to Jefferson significant gaps in his knowledge, which he intended to remedy. Short as it was, his first term in the House of Burgesses sparked his curiosity and left him with many unanswered questions regarding legal and political theory and procedure. The books he ordered around this time show him in the process of grappling with the relationship between Great Britain and America.

The comparative approach always appealed to Jefferson. One way he sought to understand the colonists' relationship to the mother country was by examining the relationship between England and Ireland. To that end, he acquired copies of Sir William Petty's *Political Survey of Ireland* and two well-respected works by the miscellaneous writer Ferdinando Warner, *The History of Ireland* and *The History of the Rebellion and Civil Wars in Ireland*. Dissatisfied by the absence of a good general history, Warner had traveled to Ireland, acquainted himself with the Irish antiquarians, and delved into whatever primary research materials he could find. The histories resulting from his research show the respect he developed for the Irish people and their culture, although, a man of his times, Warner stopped short of condoning Irish Catholicism. Regardless, he created a reliable Irish history useful for comparing what had happened in Ireland with what was happening in America.[29]

Other works Jefferson ordered that year treat law and politics from a more general and theoretical perspective: Anthony Ellys's *Tracts of the Liberty, Spiritual and Temporal, of Protestants in England*, a work largely devoted to the topic of constitutional liberty that found other readers elsewhere in colonial America;[30] Adam Ferguson's *Essay on the History of Civil Society*, which would significantly shape Jefferson's ideas concerning man's responsibility to his fellow man; a three-volume French edition of Montesquieu's collected works; and John Locke's *Two Treatises of Government*.

All these books reached Virginia that December. Though some would perish in the fire at Shadwell the following year, their ideas remained in Jefferson's mind, where they began to meld with one another and to be applied to the unique political situation he was now facing. Combined with his ongoing attention to the study of natural law, Jefferson's study of parliamentary history and political theory gave him the basis for developing and applying his own original political thought.

Another item left off the list of goods that Virginians were forbidden from importing was musical instruments. Jefferson's accounts show that in 1769 he ordered a kind of stringed instrument very different from his violin: an Aeolian harp. Placing his order in September, he would likely receive the instrument by late spring, a time when he could throw open the windows of his home, place it lengthwise on the casement, and listen to the hauntingly beautiful music made as the wind wafted over its strings. Whereas his violin allowed Jefferson to recreate sound precisely composed and arranged by European musicians, the Aeolian harp was controlled solely by the wind. It had an unusual and irregular sound, "a soft floating witchery of sound," Samuel Coleridge called it. Beyond opening the window to let the breeze blow across it, there was no other way to control the sounds of an Aeolian harp—nature alone determined its sound. Even in music Jefferson was letting his tastes drift from the man-made and rule-governed to the natural. But he would never hear the sound of an Aeolian harp in his home at Shadwell. By the time spring came around, the mansion house there would be no more.

PART II

FAMILY AND NATION

CHAPTER 9

Domestic Life and
Literary Pursuits

Upon learning of the fire at Shadwell, Jefferson's friends were quick to respond with sympathy and offers of help. Secretary of Virginia Thomas Nelson, for one, expressed his concern and offered to lend books from his personal library. His son, Thomas Nelson, Jr., upon receiving a letter from Jefferson listing several necessary books, forwarded the request to his bookseller. George Wythe sent some publishers' catalogues and, regardless of the fire, some agricultural specimens: grapevines plus nectarine and apricot grafts.[1] Though coincidence might seem the only connection between the grafts and the book catalogues, they functioned similarly. Just as a graft can improve the quality of fruit a tree bears, books can give readers new ideas to splice onto their existing knowledge. For Jefferson, trees laden with nectarines and shelves laden with books were both symbols of the ideal life he imagined at Monticello.

The catalogues Wythe sent were issued by Foulis, the Glasgow publishing house known for its distinguished series of literary classics. Foulis editions were products of good bookmanship. Handsome yet portable volumes containing reliably edited texts, they suited Jefferson's tastes nicely. The Foulis promotional material touted its series of Greek texts for their capacity "to render the reading of the Greek Historians more convenient for Gentlemen in active life."[2] Taking advantage of his mentor's recommendations, Jefferson acquired many Foulis editions.

There is no telling precisely how many titles he ordered from the catalogues Wythe sent, but a number of Foulis editions in his library date from before 1770, including works by such classical authors as Aeschylus, Callimachus, and Epictetus. Foulis made a point of keeping titles in print; many of the books in stock during the 1770s dated from the time the Foulis brothers first went into business in the early 1740s.[3] So

Jefferson could have ordered many older editions from the catalogues he received in 1770.

He continued to appreciate the products of this press for years to come, acquiring several more Foulis editions later and also recommending them to others. Ordering a set of ancient Greek historians in Greek/Latin parallel text editions for Peter Carr in the 1780s, Jefferson stipulated that all should be in duodecimo Foulis editions.[4] Though best known for such elegant small-format editions, Foulis also published large-format works, some of which Jefferson also acquired.

The folio edition of Homer's *Iliad* may be the handsomest item the firm ever published. The cataloguer of Jefferson's library called the Foulis *Iliad* "one of the most beautiful books ever printed, so beautiful that it makes you think you can read Greek even if you can't." The Foulis *Iliad* found favor with other discriminating bookmen: Benjamin Franklin also owned a copy of it. Though Jefferson enjoyed the beauty of this edition, he appreciated it for other reasons, as well. Discussing the art of bookmaking with a correspondent, he observed, "The perfection of accuracy is to be found in the folio edition of Homer by the Foulis of Glasgow. I have understood they offered 1000 guineas for the discovery of any error in it, even of an accent, and that the reward was never claimed."[5] The perfection of accuracy: with all of his record-keeping and note-taking and measuring and calculating, Jefferson sought such accuracy himself and appreciated it in others.

Though a major inconvenience, the destructive fire at Shadwell did not really affect Jefferson's home-building plans. Informing John Page of the fire, he wrote, "If this conflagration, by which I am burned out of a home, had come before I had advanced so far in preparing another, I do not know but I might have cherished some treasonable thoughts of leaving these my native hills."[6] This statement is another of Jefferson's deliberate fictions written to please his old friend. He had no desire to exchange his native Piedmont for Tidewater. He had spent a good part of his early life shuttling back and forth between the two regions, but his heart belonged to the mountains of Virginia.

Without changing his plans, the fire did accelerate them. Preparations for building atop Monticello had begun three years earlier, when Jefferson had the initial batch of lumber prepared and ordered some window glass. He subsequently contracted with a local entrepreneur to have the top of Monticello leveled in preparation for building there. The contract stipulated that the work be completed by Christmas 1768. Slowly, the place of Jefferson's boyhood reveries was on its way to becoming his permanent home. At the time of the Shadwell fire, construction at Monticello had not advanced far enough to let him move into his new home. After the fire, he sought to make the place habitable as soon as possible. It would still take another nine months before any part of it was fit to inhabit.

By late November, the south pavilion, the first brick building at Monticello, was completed. The laconic entry Jefferson made in his almanac on Monday, November 26, 1770—"Moved to Monticello"— masks his glee. A letter to the Reverend James Ogilvie written from Jefferson's early months in his new home offers a more detailed, and charming, view of living conditions at Monticello: "I have here but one room, which, like the cobler's, serves me for parlour for kitchen and hall. I may add, for bed chamber and study too. My friends sometimes take a temperate dinner with me and then retire to look for beds elsewhere. I have hopes however of getting more elbow room this summer. But be this as may happen, whether my tenements be great or small homely or elegant they will always receive you with a hearty welcome."[7]

Jefferson's proverbial expression—"elbow room"—had long been a part of colonial American discourse. In what may be the earliest occurrence of the phrase in American literature, Thomas Morton used it in *New English Canaan* to discuss an area of land in New England he claimed was large enough to provide elbow room for hundreds of thousands of people. In the 1670s, Increase Mather critiqued New Englanders who settled far inland "without any Ministry amongst them, which is to prefer the world before the Gospel." Though such people professed the Puritan faith, they possessed "an insatiable desire after Land, and worldly Accommodations, yea, so as to forsake Churches and Ordinances, and to live like Heathen, only that so they might have Elbow-room enough in the world." In his *Histories of the Dividing Line*, William Byrd related how seventeenth-century New Englanders, "thinking they wanted Elbow-room," branched out into Connecticut.[8] To early American colonists, this proverbial phrase offered a convenient verbal formula to justify moving westward from the coastal settlements. Few words more aptly convey what has become a defining aspect of the American character, the desire for land, for spaces wide enough to permit freedom to stretch the limbs and, by extension, freedom to think and act.

As 1770 gave way to the new year, Jefferson became even more motivated to continue his building activities at Monticello—for one particular reason. With the passing of his friend Bathurst Skelton, he was beginning to see the widow Skelton in a new light. Following her husband's death, Martha Skelton had moved back to The Forest, the home of her father and stepmother, John Wayles and his wife, Elizabeth, who was the widow of Martha's brother-in-law, Reuben Skelton. In October 1770 Jefferson made his earliest known visit to The Forest.

The friendship he developed with the father facilitated his courtship with the daughter. Many years later, Jefferson characterized Wayles as "a lawyer of much practice, to which he was introduced more by his great industry, punctuality and practical readiness, than to eminence in the science of his profession. He was a most agreeable companion, full of pleasantry and good humor, and welcomed in every society."[9] Wayles owned an excellent library, which his marriage to Elizabeth Skelton had greatly enhanced. Elizabeth had inherited Reuben Skelton's fine collection of books. Jefferson admired Wayles's library, which gave them much to discuss.

Little is known about Martha or, as Jefferson often called her, Patsy or, sometimes, Patty. Since Jefferson, ever protective of their privacy, destroyed the letters they exchanged, hardly any evidence survives to document their relationship or reveal her personality. A few people who knew Martha left brief comments in their reminiscences. Former slave Isaac Jefferson, whose recollections constitute one of the most important resources for understanding the domestic life at Monticello, remembered her as small of stature yet quite pretty. Others found her sprightly and amiable. An accomplished musician, she could play the harpsichord and the pianoforte.

The destruction of their letters has also meant the loss of an important aspect of Jefferson's literary life. As a belletrist, he was at his best when writing to women. Contemporary testimony provides a slight hint of the literary quality of his letters to Martha. Mrs. Drummond, a Williamsburg woman who read one of them, said that it "bars all the Romantic, Poetical, ones I ever read." She called his writing beautiful and complimented Jefferson's "Miltonic stile."[10]

In the absence of his letters to Martha, those to other women must serve as surrogates, the fondness he expressed in them offering a rough approximation of the tenderness he conveyed to her. To Lucy Chiswell Nelson, for example, Jefferson wrote, "Fortune seems to have drawn a line of separation between us. Though often in the same neighborhood some unlucky star has still shuffled us asunder. When I count backwards the years since I had last the happiness of seeing you in this place, and recur to my own lively memory of our friendship, I am almost induced to discredit my arithmetic."[11] This he wrote to a female friend. Imagine what he wrote to the woman he loved.

Their courtship progressed significantly in the ensuing months. Before 1771 was half over, Jefferson found himself ordering a gift for her lavish enough to be a wedding present. He wrote Thomas Adams in London to request a pianoforte. Jefferson supplied some specific requirements regarding its construction: he wanted it made from solid mahogany, not veneer, and stipulated that its workmanship be "very handsome, and worthy the acceptance of a lady for whom I intend it."[12]

By midsummer, he had become so enamored of Martha that he could hardly imagine life without her. As he told a friend, "In every scheme of happiness she is placed in the fore-ground of the picture, as the principal figure. Take that away and it is no picture for me."[13] Jefferson's metaphor captures his visual sensibilities. Imagining his future happiness, he foresaw it as a beautiful painting. She eventually saw him in a similar light. She grew to love him and accepted his proposal of marriage. He took out a marriage license, and the two were wed at The Forest on January 1, 1772.

The Reverend William Coutts performed the ceremony. There was much celebrating afterward, the dances accompanied by a local fiddler. The newlyweds left The Forest in their phaeton, a light, four-wheeled open carriage drawn by a pair of horses and designed to carry two people. Jefferson preferred the phaeton over other vehicles, but it could be temperamental. They took a side trip to Shirley, the plantation of Charles Carter. They may have intended to go farther, but their phaeton broke down. The newlyweds had to stop and get their vehicle repaired before they could get back on the road again. Once the phaeton was fixed, they returned to The Forest and soon started toward Monticello.

Snow covered the land as they left her father's home. The road leading from The Forest was passable, but as the couple neared the mountains, the snow became much deeper. Jefferson told family members afterward that the inclement weather brought him and his bride to a halt eight miles from Monticello. The snow, three feet deep in places— the "deepest snow we have ever seen"—had become too much for the phaeton.[14]

The couple left the comfort of their carriage and proceeded on horseback. The trek was cold, slow-going, treacherous in spots, but romantically beautiful. They did not reach Monticello until late that evening. The house was dark and all the fires out. Irked at first, they made the best of the situation. Remembering a bottle of wine "on a shelf behind some books," Jefferson retrieved it, and soon he and his bride were making merry. Their first daughter, Martha, or Patsy, as she was known in the family, was born September 27, 1772.[15]

Mrs. Jefferson's things would not reach Monticello until the snow melted somewhat. When her personal belongings arrived, they included many books. In the family, she had a reputation as an avid reader. Only one volume among Jefferson's surviving collection contains evidence of her ownership, a copy of an English translation of Fénelon's *Adventures of Telemachus*, but other evidence suggests that she owned the kinds of books typically found on the colonial woman's bookshelf. Isaac Jefferson remembered her coming into the kitchen "with a cookery book in her hand" and reading aloud recipes for making cakes and tarts to his mother, Ursula.[16] Apparently, Mrs. Jefferson wanted to teach Ursula how to make proper English pastries. The episode shows one way print culture could interact with folk tradition.

Several books from the library of Bathurst Skelton came into Jefferson's possession through his wife. Unlike his older brother, Bathurst was no bookman. Save for a few multivolume collections of the standard eighteenth-century poets and essayists—Alexander Pope's *Works* in ten volumes, the eight-volume edition of *The Spectator*—Bathurst's collection largely consisted of textbooks from grammar school and college.

Since Bathurst Skelton had entered William and Mary in 1763, he, too, had studied with William Small. Consequently, his schoolbooks duplicated some Jefferson already owned. In other instances, they served as replacement copies for schoolbooks lost in the Shadwell fire. Jefferson unloaded the duplicates and kept the others. None of his surviving books contains evidence of Bathurst Skelton's ownership, but titles common to Skelton's estate inventory and Jefferson's great library include mathematics textbooks by several different authors and two works by James Ferguson: *Astronomy* and *Lectures of Select Subjects in Mechanics, Hydrostatics, Pneumatics and Optics*, both of which Jefferson long remembered. Three decades later he recommended Ferguson's *Astronomy* to one young man who had asked him for some bookish advice and Ferguson's *Mechanics* to another. In the late 1760s, rumors went 'round Virginia that Ferguson was planning to come to William and Mary as Professor of Natural Philosophy.[17] Perpetuating the rumor, Jefferson exclaimed, "That most famous Ferguson, who wrote on astronomy, will come, it is said, to the College of William and Mary, an excellent successor to the most excellent Small!" But Ferguson never did come, so his works served in his stead.

Jefferson's marriage also connected him to the Skipwith family. Martha's half-sister Tabitha, or Tibby, had recently married a young Virginia gentleman named Robert Skipwith. On one occasion when both men were visiting The Forest together, they talked at great length about literature and learning. Jefferson promised to help Skipwith assemble a library of his own. Afterward, Skipwith wrote to remind him of the promise. In his letter, Skipwith provided a general idea of what he wanted in a personal library, specifically, books "suited to the capacity of the common reader who understands but little of the classicks and who has not leisure for any intricate or tedious study." His letter implies that during their conversation Jefferson had been carried off by his passion for erudite scholarly books. The guidelines Skipwith provided seem intended to bring Jefferson back down to earth. Most important, Skipwith stressed that he wanted books that were "improving as well as amusing." Finally, he placed a monetary limit on the total cost of the library: five and twenty pounds sterling or, at most, thirty.[18]

But Jefferson got carried away as he assembled the list of titles for Skipwith. In terms of cost, he greatly exceeded the upper limit Skipwith stipulated. Jefferson explained, "I sat down with a design of executing your request to form a catalogue of books amounting to about 30. lib. sterl. but could by no means satisfy myself with any partial choice I could make. Thinking therefore it might be as agreeable to you, I have framed such a general collection as I think you would wish, and might in time find convenient, to procure." Jefferson had not read all the books on the list, which contains many titles he did not own. The list is as much a reflection of what Jefferson wanted to read at the moment as a recommendation to his friend. Considering Skipwith's request for a primarily belletristic library, Jefferson imagined an ideal collection of *belles lettres*, a collection he would not mind having himself.[19]

He enclosed the list with a letter to Skipwith setting forth the rationale underlying his choice of titles. Given Skipwith's request for pleasurable reading, Jefferson made the list rich in novels, including many of the most memorable ones of the century: Tobias Smollett's *Roderick Random* and *Peregrine Pickle*; Samuel Richardson's *Pamela*, *Clarissa*, and *Sir Charles Grandison*; the twelve-volume edition of Henry Fielding's *Works*, which included all of his novels; and Laurence Sterne's *Tristram Shandy*, a work Jefferson used as a touchstone for judging literary quality.

In the letter, Jefferson justified reading fiction at some length. His defense of fiction reflects the influence of another work he put on the list of recommended books, Lord Kames's *Elements of Criticism*. He synthesized Kames's critical theories to create a pithy essay on the moral utility of fiction.[20] Jefferson observed:

A little attention . . . to the nature of the human mind evinces that the entertainments of fiction are useful as well as pleasant. That they are pleasant when well written, every person feels who reads. But wherein is its utility, asks the reverend sage, big with the notion that nothing can be useful but the learned lumber of Greek and Roman reading with which his head is stored? I answer, every thing is useful which contributes to fix us in the principles and practice of virtue. When any signal act of charity or of gratitude, for instance, is presented either to our sight or imagination, we are deeply impressed with its beauty and feel a strong desire in ourselves of doing charitable and grateful acts also. On the contrary when we see or read of any atrocious deed, we are disgusted with its deformity and conceive an abhorrence of vice. Now every emotion of this kind is an exercise of our virtuous dispositions; and disposition of the mind, like limbs of the body, acquire strength by exercise. But exercise produces habit; and in the instance of which we speak, the exercise being of the moral feelings, produces a habit of thinking and acting virtuously. We never reflect whether the story we read be truth or fiction. If the painting be lively, and a tolerable picture of nature, we are thrown into a reverie, from which if we awaken it is the fault of the writer.[21]

Jefferson obscured the boundaries between fact and fiction, suggesting that a work of literature should be judged by the effect it has on the reader. Essentially, he described the ideal reading process: a good book should draw its readers into the world it creates and keep them here in an almost dreamlike state of suspension.

The examples Jefferson used to support his argument show that he had in mind not only novels but also other genres of fiction, including drama and narrative verse. He continued, "I appeal to every reader of feeling and sentiment whether the fictitious murther of Duncan by Macbeth in Shakespeare does not excite him as great horror of villainy, as the real one of Henry IV by Ravillac as related by Davila?" Jefferson was not suggesting that Skipwith read Shakespeare in lieu of Davila: the well-read gentleman need not choose between the two—as the list clarifies, he should own and read both. Elsewhere, Jefferson called Davila's *History* "one of the most entertaining books he ever read."[22] Though he had read Davila in Italian, Jefferson did not expect Skipwith to do so—he recommended Davila's *History of the Civil Wars in France* in Ellis Farneworth's English translation.

Fiction, Jefferson observed, could fulfill the purpose of teaching moral virtue better than fact. History was too uneven—few episodes in history could excite the "sympathetic emotion of virtue" at its highest level. Fiction, alternatively, could evoke a reader's sympathy because imaginary characters can be fashioned in a way real personages cannot. Fictional characters can illustrate and exemplify "every moral rule of life.

Thus a lively and lasting sense of filial duty," he continued, "is more effectually impressed on the mind of a son or daughter by reading King Lear, than by all the dry volumes of ethics and divinity that ever were written."[23]

Jefferson recommended to Skipwith the same edition of Shakespeare he owned himself: the ten-volume duodecimo edition prepared by Edward Capell and published in 1767 and 1768. The marginalia Jefferson inscribed in his copy of Capell's Shakespeare, which survives at the University of Virginia, help explain the presence of another work on his list of recommended books—Thomas Percy's *Reliques of Ancient English Poetry*—and suggest that Jefferson had been reading his Shakespeare with the eyes of a scholar during the late 1760s and early 1770s.

In his first series of ancient songs and ballads, Percy devoted the second book to ballads illustrating Shakespeare's works. Introducing this section, Percy observed, "Our great dramatic poet having occasionally quoted many ancient ballads, and even taken the plot of one, if not more, of his plays from among them, it was judged proper to preserve as many of these as could be recovered, and that they might be the more easily found, to exhibit them in one collective view." Jefferson appreciated the recovery and preservation of traditional literature. His copy of Shakespeare shows that he was reading the plays with a copy of *Reliques of Ancient English Poetry* nearby. Though Percy had collected together songs and ballads pertinent to Shakespeare in one section, Jefferson did not restrict himself to that section as he annotated his personal copy of Shakespeare. He found verbal parallels between Percy's *Reliques* and the songs and speeches in *Love's Labour's Lost*, *Measure for Measure*, *The Merry Wives of Windsor*, and *Much Ado about Nothing*. Though he specifically recommended Shakespeare's tragedies to Skipwith, Jefferson clearly enjoyed the comedies, too.

Favorably comparing *King Lear* to works of divinity, Jefferson let his animosity toward religious literature take him off track. With his reference to *Lear*, he dropped his comparison between fiction and history to compare fiction to divinity. The paucity of religious titles in the list of recommended books reinforces the skepticism toward devotional writing his comparison suggests.

Jefferson did include a category for religious books, but the fifteen titles listed under "Religion" constitute one of the most idiosyncratic lists of religious books ever compiled. Few would include the title that comes at the middle of the list—Bolingbroke's *Philosophical Works*—among a list of recommended religious books, but this particular inclusion offers the key to understanding the list as a whole. Earlier Jefferson had commonplaced a passage from Bolingbroke evaluating the New Testament as a system of ethics. Observing that collections of aphorisms culled from ancient authors had long been useful, Bolingbroke imagined a similar collection of sayings compiled from the gospel but concluded that such a compilation would be inadequate—it would form an incomplete and unconnected system of ethics. Alternatively, a compilation "from the writings of antient heathen moralists of Tully, of Seneca, of Epictetus, and others, would be more full, more entire, more coherent, and more clearly deduced from unquestionable principles of knowledge."[24]

The works Jefferson listed under religion include ones by each of the authors Bolingbroke named in this passage. From Cicero, he included the *Tusculan Disputations* and the *Offices*. He also listed *Seneca's Morals* and *Epictetus*. Only three of the titles listed under religion can really be classified as works of Christian divinity: the seven-volume edition of Laurence Sterne's *Sermons*, William Sherlock's *Practical Discourse Concerning Death*, and Sherlock's *Practical Discourse Concerning a Future Judgment*. Perhaps *Epictetus* can make some claim. Jefferson recommended that Skipwith read Epictetus in Elizabeth Carter's translation, the fullest version of his writings in English. In her critical introduction and footnotes, she compared Epictetus's thought to Christian philosophy and emphasized the superiority of Christianity. Jefferson later changed his mind about Elizabeth Carter's translation and even considered translating Epictetus himself.[25]

All of the titles in the list are organized under general subject categories in the following order:

Fine Arts
Criticism on the Fine Arts
Politics, Trade
Religion
Law
History, Ancient
History, Modern
Natural Philosophy, Natural History &c.
Miscellaneous

This, Jefferson's earliest known bibliographical scheme, lacks the underlying philosophical basis of his subsequent, more sophisticated schemes. "Fine Arts," the category containing the largest number of titles, includes novels, poetry, plays, letters, and essays. Some of the listed items suggest that he was continuing to consult the Foulis catalogues he had received from Wythe: he recommended the poems of John Dryden, John Gay, and Matthew Prior, all in duodecimo Foulis editions.

The third category, "Politicks, Trade," lists only eight titles. As Jefferson explained to Skipwith, "Of Politicks and Trade I have given you a few only of the best books, as you would probably chuse to be not unacquainted with those commercial principles which bring wealth into our country, and the constitutional security we have for the enjoiment of that wealth." Similarly, the list of law books contains only three titles because knowledge "of the minutiae of that science is not necessary for a private gentleman."[26]

Ancient history, which includes both ancient and modern authors and works, provocatively begins with the Bible. The placement of the Bible here reinforces the challenge to established religious beliefs that the books listed under religion imply. To Peter Carr, Jefferson recommended reading the Bible "as you would read Livy or Tacitus."[27] By making the Bible a work of history, Jefferson denied its status as the word of God.

The titles under natural history and philosophy cover a wide variety of scientific topics, including such up-to-date ideas as electricity, which is represented by Benjamin Franklin's *Experiments and Observations on Electricity*. Though Jefferson had yet to meet Franklin, he clearly respected his accomplishments as a scientist. Jefferson installed one of Franklin's lightning rods at Monticello. Living on a mountaintop, he was grateful for it on numerous occasions. Isaac Jefferson recorded a typical remark Thomas Jefferson made during electrical storms: "If it hadn't been for that Franklin the whole house would have gone."[28]

In closing, Jefferson downplayed the need for Skipwith to assemble such a fine personal library when he could visit Monticello as often as he wished:

> But whence the necessity of this collection? Come to the new Rowanty, from which you may reach your hand to a library formed on a more extensive plan. Separated from each other but a few paces, the possessions of each would be open to the other. A spring, centrically situated, might be the scene of every evening's joy. There we should talk over the lessons of the day, or lose them in Musick, Chess, or the merriments of our family companions. The heart thus lightened, our pillows would be soft, and health and long life would attend the happy scene.[29]

These remarks reveal the exuberant pride Jefferson took in his new home regardless how many years away from completion it was. Furthermore, his words show that his plan for a new library was integral to his plans for the new home. He clearly foresaw his home not only as a place for domestic felicity but also as a center of social interaction and intellectual discourse. During his student days, he had participated as a member of Professor Small's Williamsburg circle; he now foresaw his own home as the center of a new intellectual circle, physically represented by a spring that would serve as a place for enlightened postprandial conversation.

Jefferson was devoting considerable thought to what that spring would be like. Onto spare blank pages of his interleaved copy of that year's *Virginia Almanack*, he outlined his plans. Located on the north side of Monticello, the spring would cascade over a terrace. The water would be conducted across the bottom of the terrace to its west side, where it would fall into a cistern beneath a handsomely constructed temple. The temple would be elevated two feet above ground level. Its walls would be made of stone. The first story would be constructed with arches on three sides and a solid wall against the hillside on the fourth, the second with a door on one side and spacious windows on the other three. The floor of each room would measure eight-by-eight with eight-foot ceilings, making the interior space of each a perfect cube. The second floor would contain a small table and a few chairs. Jefferson imagined several possible designs for the roof of the temple: "Chinese, Grecian, or in the taste of the Lanthern of Demosthenes at Athens."[30]

The grounds surrounding the temple would be meticulously landscaped. The area above the spring would be leveled and covered with grass. Nearby a statue of a sleeping figure would recline on a marble slab. A stone or metal plate fastened to a tree near the spring would be inscribed with verses from Horace celebrating the happiness of the man who could have such a peaceful retreat. Beech and aspen trees would be planted partway around the spring, leaving open a vista of the mill pond, the river, the road, or, in time, a neighboring village. The spring would not only gratify the visual sensibilities of Jefferson and his guests, but also gratify their senses of smell and hearing. Interspersed around the area would be planted an abundance of jasmine, honeysuckle, and sweet briar. Beneath the temple would be placed an Aeolian harp.

Though Monticello's intellectual circle had yet to cross from Jefferson's imagination to reality, a new intellectual circle was coming together in Williamsburg with the arrival in 1770 of the Reverend Samuel Henley, who had come to fill the position of Professor of Moral Philosophy at William and Mary. Henley became friends with the Reverend James Madison, president of the college; James McClurg, the Edinburgh-trained physician; and John Clayton, the venerable botanist, as well as George Wythe, John Page, and Thomas Jefferson. The intellectual gatherings of these men took place both informally and formally. In 1772, they founded Virginia's Philosophical Society for the Advancement of Useful Knowledge, and Henley became secretary of this new scientific organization.[31]

A year younger than Jefferson, Henley shared a similar passion for books and learning. Born in Devonshire in 1744, he had been educated at Caleb Ashworth's Dissenting Academy, completing his four years of academic studies in 1766. Two years later he was received into the ministry and obtained a position with a congregation of Protestant Dissenters near Cambridge. He eventually became affiliated with the Church of England, being admitted to Queen's College, Cambridge, in 1770. Here, he ingratiated himself with Cambridge's intelligentsia. He became friends with John Lettice, the poet and divine of Sidney Sussex College; Thomas Martyn, botanist and fellow of Sidney Sussex College; and the poet Thomas Gray, then Regius Professor of History.[32]

Once the professorship at William and Mary became vacant, Governor Botetourt appealed to Edward Montagu, Master of Chancery and Virginia's agent in London, for a man of ability and integrity for the college. After consulting with the Bishop of London, Montagu recommended Henley. He received the King's bounty on January 8, 1770, and reached Virginia that April to take the position at William and Mary.

Coming to Virginia, Henley brought with him an excellent library. His collection of books reveals a wide range of intellectual interests. Henley himself described the library as a "collection of books, consisting of scarce and valuable editions (many on large paper, and in the best bindings) of the Greek and Roman classics, and the principal writers in the Italian, French, and English languages. Together with a large collection of engravings, etchings, and mezzotints, by the greatest masters; many of which were proofs, and the rest choice impressions."[33]

The titles he is known to have had confirm the description. His works of English literature show he was both a scholar and a collector. He had a copy of the rare ten-book first edition of *Paradise Lost* and a sixteenth-century edition of William Langland's *Vision of Pierce Plowman*. Other works in his library show his interest in modern literary trends. He owned several books treating such subjects as aesthetics, antiquities, botany, and literary criticism. Henley's knowledge of botany nicely complemented his study of literature. He would later annotate multiple editions of Shakespeare, and a number of his annotations gloss arcane references to botanical lore.[34]

Before American independence, Henley returned to England, where he established a fine reputation not only as an annotator of literary texts but also as an antiquarian and teacher. During the 1780s, he and Jefferson exchanged several letters, which testify to the friendship they developed in Williamsburg. One time Henley stated, "Different as our situations are from what they once were, I shall ever look back with sincere pleasure on the friendship with which you honoured me." Another time he articulated his pleasure with Jefferson's friendship and stated that "neither length of time, change of situation, nor the convulsions which have torn asunder the bands that once held our united countries" had in the least altered his feelings of friendship.[35]

Jefferson left no details of their personal interactions, but statements made by British friends attest to Henley's pleasant company and affirm his bookishness. As a young man, the botanist and antiquarian Dawson Turner had breakfast with Henley and long remembered his agreeable conversation: "It was impossible for any man to be more amusing and instructive in conversation, or of greater amenity of manner, than Dr. Henley." Seeing Turner was fond of books, Henley gave him some useful book-buying advice.[36]

"Let me offer you, as a young man, a piece of advice," Henley suggested. "Never buy a bad book; never buy a bad edition of a good book; and never buy a bad copy of a good edition." This advice, which modern readers and book collectors might take to heart, affirms the care Henley took assembling his own library.

Jefferson, too, talked books with Henley, as his accounts indicate. He became familiar with the professor's fine collection and, on a few occasions, talked him into selling a few items from it.[37] Henley's writings reveal the literary interests they shared and thus indicate what else they may have discussed. Henley published works discussing Virgil's *Aeneid* and the elegies of Tibullus, but he is best known as the editor and annotator of William Beckford's *Vathek*. In his annotations to *Vathek*, Henley cited Milton more than a dozen times, making separate references to *Comus*, *Paradise Lost*, *Paradise Regain'd*, and *Samson Agonistes*.[38] Henley also glossed Beckford's obscure Oriental allusions. His notes to *Vathek* indicate his familiarity with Arabic, a language Jefferson had been interested in at least since he purchased his copy of the Qur'an as a law student. Henley fueled Jefferson's interest in Orientalism.

Henley's presence in Virginia and his burgeoning friendship with Jefferson may also help explain why Jefferson recommended the works of Thomas Percy to Skipwith. Overall, Jefferson included four titles by Percy on the list. Besides *Reliques of Ancient English Poetry*, he also recommended *Five Pieces of Runic Poetry*, Percy's prose translation of samples from Icelandic and Old Norse verse; *Miscellaneous Pieces Relating to the Chinese*, the first volume of which contains "A Dissertation on the Language and Characters of the Chinese"; and *Hau Kiou Choaan; or, The Pleasing History*, an anonymous Chinese novel written between the Ming and Ching dynasties that is considered a masterpiece of Chinese literature. Percy's English version, in turn, is a landmark of European scholarship: it represents the first long work of Chinese narrative fiction translated into any European language.[39]

The presence of Percy's *Miscellaneous Pieces Relating to the Chinese* on the Skipwith list also suggests why Jefferson was thinking about a Chinese roof for his garden temple. In its second volume, Percy described the art of laying out gardens among the Chinese and provided a description of the Emperor's garden and pleasure houses near Peking. Of the four Percy titles he recommended to Skipwith, Jefferson had yet to acquire for himself at least three of them. The presence of Percy on the list of recommended authors suggests Henley's influence on Jefferson.

In his Williamsburg library Henley had multiple works by Percy. While in Virginia he wrote a lengthy critique of Percy's *Key to the New Testament* and also initiated a correspondence with him. Besides sending Percy a copy of his critique, Henley sent him some specimens of Indian oratory, including the speech of Chief Logan. Whereas Henley encouraged Jefferson's interest in Oriental languages, Jefferson introduced him to Indian oratory. Upon encountering Logan's speech for the first time in late 1774, Jefferson became its champion and began sharing it with others, including Henley, who recognized its literary value. Henley also saw social value in Logan's speech: it gave him a perfect excuse to initiate a correspondence with Percy, who was interested in literature from many different parts of the world.

Henley's letter allowed Percy to expand the breadth of his literary knowledge from the banks of the Yangtze to the banks of the Ohio. Thanking him, Percy called Logan's speech "a masterpiece of its kind." Percy shared the speech with others and reported to Henley that it was "exceedingly admired by all who have seen it. It is the eloquence of *sentiment*, and penetrates through the soul,—infinitely more forcible than the eloquence of language." Percy welcomed other specimens of Native American literature Henley had to share: "Should any other pieces of Indian composition, whether of rhetoric or song, fall in your way, you would confer a very great obligation upon me, by favoring me with translations of them."[40]

Outside his intellectual circle, Henley made a reputation for himself in Virginia as a troublemaker. He and fellow professor Thomas Gwatkin vehemently protested against a proposed American episcopate. Though Henley was more affable privately, he could still be something of an instigator even in literary conversation. After one particular discussion with Henley, William Beckford playfully accused him, "You are answerable for having set me to work upon a Story so horrid that I tremble whilst relating it, and have not a nerve in my frame but vibrates like an Aspen." Henley, in turn, took great pleasure in Beckford's tongue-in-cheek accusation. He responded, "My soul rejoices to know that your imagination hath been wrapped in the thickest gloom: never is the lightening so glorious as when it flashes from the darkest clouds."[41]

Henley's presence enhanced Jefferson's periodic trips to Williamsburg at a time when he was becoming increasingly reluctant to leave Monticello. There is no evidence to show whether Henley visited Monticello, but he did come to know and like Mrs. Jefferson. Much as William Small had done before, Henley exemplified the intimate relationship between science and literature that persisted during the Enlightenment. Whereas Small was a scientist who knew about literature, Henley was a litterateur who knew about science. Henley made less of an impact on Jefferson mainly because the two became friends at a time when Jefferson's intellectual abilities were already well developed. Henley reached Virginia at a time when Jefferson sought peers, not mentors, a time when Jefferson himself was becoming a mentor, when he was starting to imagine his home as the new center of Virginia's intellectual community.

CHAPTER 10

Rude Bard of the North

Among the literary works Jefferson read for pleasure, few pleased him more than those James Macpherson assembled as the poems of Ossian, the legendary third-century Gaelic warrior-poet. Writing before the authenticity of these works came under close scrutiny, Jefferson praised Macpherson "for the collection, arrangement and elegant translation, of Ossian's poems."[1] *Fragments of Ancient Poetry, Collected in the Highlands of Scotland, and Translated from the Galic or Erse Language*, Macpherson's first Ossianic publication, appeared in 1760. The enthusiasm that greeted this work prompted Macpherson to research the traditional poetry of the Scottish Highlands further and to publish two additional titles, both ostensibly ancient Gaelic verse rendered into English prose. *Fingal, An Ancient Epic, in Six Books*, which also contained a number of shorter works attributed to Ossian, appeared in 1762. *Temora*, another Ossianic epic, appeared the following year.

The general trajectory of these three volumes stretches from the genuine to the artificial. *Fragments* approaches traditional Gaelic lays in terms of form and content, whereas *Temora* is more heavily indebted to the Greek and Roman epic tradition for its themes, diction, and imagery. Regardless of their authenticity, these prose-poems achieved tremendous popularity in their day. Collected editions began appearing by the mid-1760s and continued being republished for decades.

Jefferson's enthusiasm was not unique. Around the same time he began reading Ossian, many other Virginians were developing their appreciation of the legendary bard. Colonel William Fleming, for one, owned a copy of Ossian's *Poems*. Additional copies were available for purchase at the *Virginia Gazette* office in the 1770s. Still, Jefferson's fondness for Ossian outstripped that of his friends and neighbors. He became so enthralled that by the early months of 1773 he was reading Ossian on a daily basis, a habit he intended to continue into the foreseeable future. The last week of February 1773, he wrote that Ossian's poems "have been, and will I think during my life continue to be to me, the source of daily and exalted pleasure. The tender, and the sublime emotions of the mind were never before so finely wrought up by human hand. I am not ashamed to own that I think this rude bard of the North the greatest Poet that has ever existed."[2]

His commonplace book provides the best indication of how he read Ossian. From the first book of *Fingal*, Jefferson transcribed the following:

> As two dark streams from high rocks meet, and mix and roar on the plain; loud, rough, and dark in battle meet Lochlin and Innis-fail: chief mixed his strokes with chief, and man with man; steel clanging sounded on steel, helmets are cleft on high; blood bursts and smokes around. Strings murmur on the polished yews. Darts rush along the sky. Spears fall like the circles of light that gild the stormy face of the night. As the troubled noise of the ocean when roll the waves on high; as the last peal of the thunder of heaven, such is the noise of the battle. Tho' Cormac's hundred bards were there to give the war to song; feeble were the voices of a hundred bards to send the deaths to future times. For many were the falls of the heroes; and wide poured the blood of the valiant.[3]

Throughout Ossian's poetry, Macpherson incorporated much figurative language—metaphor, simile, epic simile. This and other passages Jefferson transcribed show his appreciation of these figures of speech. The similes Macpherson put in Ossian's mouth often compare the actions of warriors on the battlefield with natural phenomena. The initial simile in this passage, for example, compares the clash of two chieftains with the confluence of two rivers. The passage also reflects Macpherson's characteristic yet paradoxical use of noise. While describing the clash and clang of shield and sword, Ossian's voice maintains a profound sense of quiet. Time and again, *Fingal* emphasizes the bard's importance on the battlefield. Fallen heroes need someone to sing their song, and Macpherson made the poet as essential to war as the warrior. This particular passage closes on an elegiac note, a sentiment that pervades the Ossianic works and helped them to capture the popular imagination during the eighteenth century.

Melancholy was a component of much verse written and published during the final third of the eighteenth century. Macpherson had a keen ability to recognize literary trends and capitalize on them. Shaping his materials for publication, he combined traditional Gaelic motifs with elements from popular English prose and verse. This, the era of the graveyard school of English verse, was a time when poets made a point of cultivating sadness for purposes of pleasure. Before encountering the poems of Ossian, Jefferson had already developed a fondness for the graveyard school. He had been reading the verse of Edward Young, the author of *Night Thoughts*, at least since he had acquired a four-volume edition of Young's *Works* in the mid-1760s.[4] In addition to their debt to contemporary English verse, the poems of Ossian embody the sentimentalism characteristic of British novels that were being written and widely read around this time. The sentimental, melancholy tone of Jefferson's excerpts from Ossian affirms his enjoyment of these literary trends.

After transcribing lines from the last book of *Fingal* into his commonplace book, he excerpted a passage from "Conlath and Cuthona," a work in which Ossian relates a story of tragic lovers.[5] Closing the poem, Ossian conveys how the people he has lost continue to haunt his memory. Jefferson recorded the work's concluding lines: "Oh that I could forget my friends till my footsteps cease to be seen! till I come among them with joy! and lay my aged limbs in the narrow house!" The narrow house: Macpherson's circumlocution for the grave frequently recurs in the poems of Ossian. It recurs multiple times in Jefferson's works, too: in his literary commonplace book, his correspondence, and other belletristic writings.

Within his commonplace book Jefferson added Greek footnotes to his transcriptions from Ossian. These notes may have been inspired by Hugh Blair's lengthy essay, "A Critical Dissertation on the Poems of Ossian." Published with collected editions of Ossian, Blair's essay devotes some forty pages comparing this legendary Gaelic poet with Homer. Jefferson need not have been influenced by Blair. For years he had been inscribing the margins of his books with excerpts from Herodotus as a means of comparing similar ideas from different times, cultures, and languages. With the notes to Ossian he made in his commonplace book, Jefferson went his source one better. Whereas Macpherson added notes to his text from Alexander Pope's English translation of the *Iliad*, Jefferson quoted the original Greek. Furthermore, he located Latin passages in Virgil and Statius to parallel his excerpts from Ossian.

Editions of *Temora* included some "original specimens" of traditional Gaelic verses from which the works of Ossian were supposedly derived. These samples whetted Jefferson's linguistic appetite. He longed to learn Scottish Gaelic in order to read Ossian in the original and hoped to obtain samples of Ossianic verse from the editor. The critical essays accompanying the various editions mentioned other Ossianic verse in manuscript; Jefferson grew anxious to supplement his collection.

He decided to take advantage of an influential Scottish contact. James Macpherson's brother Charles had visited North America earlier.

During his time in Virginia, he had stayed with Jefferson briefly. In 1773, Jefferson renewed their acquaintance, hoping that Charles could put him in contact with his better known brother in order to obtain copies of Ossian's texts in the original Gaelic.

His carefully worded letter to Charles Macpherson spells out his request in specific terms. Unaware of any printed Gaelic editions of Ossian's works, Jefferson asked that if an edition were in print he would appreciate a copy. If not, then he wanted his brother James to arrange for a manuscript copy of the Gaelic originals. Jefferson even stipulated handwriting style, quality of paper, and exterior decoration: "I would chuse it in a fair, round, hand, on fine paper, with a good margin, bound in parchment as elegantly as possible, lettered on the back and marbled or gilt on the edges of the leaves. I should not regard expence in doing this."[6] Jefferson's desire for such an elegant volume affirms his fondness for Ossian. Never one to judge a book by its cover, he nevertheless understood that a handsome cover enhanced the quality of its contents and contributed to the reading experience. He wanted a volume that was textually accurate but one that was a handsome keepsake as well.

He also asked Charles to supply him with the necessary materials to learn Gaelic, including a grammar, a dictionary, and a catalogue of books written in the language. Closing his letter, Jefferson expressed hope that more of Ossian's works would be published but asserted that even if new editions were planned for the near future, he could not wait for them and wished to have manuscript copies of any and all available texts as soon as possible. Cost was no object: "The glow of one warm thought is to me worth more than money."[7]

Jefferson was hoping for a speedy response, but his letter was delayed and did not reach Edinburgh for several months. The touching personal events he experienced during the intervening time affirmed the ongoing relevance of Ossian. The sentiments expressed in the poems soon became all too real: sadness darkened the halls of Monticello this year.

The week after writing Charles Macpherson, Jefferson left Monticello for Williamsburg, where he attended the Assembly in March and the General Court in April. Other important meetings would be taking place outside the judicial and legislative chambers that spring. The movement toward American independence was gaining momentum, and Jefferson and his fellow burgesses were doing what they could to advance the cause of liberty. When he and Patrick Henry met privately with others at the Raleigh Tavern, they decided to propose the establishment of intercolonial committees of correspondence.

Dabney Carr had just begun serving in the House of Burgesses as a representative from Louisa County. Through Jefferson's influence, Carr was chosen to move the resolutions, which he did in a forceful and eloquent speech. The plan was adopted, and Carr was appointed a member of the first committee. Sadly, he did not live to witness the stirring events that would occur over the next few years. On May 16, 1773, two months after making his remarkable speech, Dabney Carr died suddenly. He was twenty-nine.

Jefferson coped with the loss, it would seem, by reading Ossian, whose works could function therapeutically in much the same way as Drelincourt's *Consolations* or Sherlock's *Practical Discourse Concerning Death*. A tone of contemplative sadness pervades the works of Ossian, who often voices his grief as he remembers absent friends. Ossian's verse embodies the sympathetic pleasure a sorrowful tale can evoke.

Jefferson's reading also shaped his ideas for Carr's tombstone. One inscription he drafted conflates two different passages from *Temora*:

> This stone shall rise with all its moss and speak to other years 'here lies gentle Carr within the dark and narrow house where no morning comes with her half opening pages.' When thou, O stone, shalt fail and the mountain stream roll quite away! Then shall the traveller come, and bend here perhaps in rest. When the darkened moon is rolled over his head, the shadowy form may come, and, mixing with his dreams, remind him who is here.

On second thought, Jefferson decided against this inscription, but he did have Carr buried at Monticello beneath an old tree where, legend has it, the two used to study together. The inscription he eventually chose, less ornate in its language, is nonetheless heartfelt:

> To his virtue, good sense, learning and friendship
> this stone is dedicated by
> Thomas Jefferson
> who, of all men loved him most.[8]

Beyond its emotional impact, Carr's death greatly altered the day-to-day life of the Jeffersons. Jefferson's sister, Martha Carr, came to Monticello in late May and brought her children with her—all five of them. The children ranged in age from the oldest, six-year-old Jane, to Dabney Junior—born just three weeks before his father's death. Jefferson became their guardian and personally supervised the boys' education.

As they grew from children into adults, Jefferson continued recommending books to them. His letters to Peter Carr contain some of his most valuable comments on literature. When Peter was fifteen, his uncle recommended reading Ossian, not only for personal enjoyment but also as a literary model he could use to develop his writing style. Dutifully obeying his uncle, Peter read Ossian but was unimpressed. He responded, "You also advise me to read the works of Ossian, which I have done and should be more pleased with them if there were more variety."[9]

Peter's criticism is understandable to anyone who has attempted to read the Ossianic prose-poems since they have passed from popularity. Though disheartened by Peter's lack of enthusiasm, Jefferson could not have been too disappointed because, after all, he had encouraged his nephews to read critically and think deeply about what they read. Though Peter recognized a repetitive quality in the poems of Ossian, he failed to understand what his uncle had, that carefully crafted literary repetition can have great rhetorical and emotional impact. Jefferson knew that patterns of recurrence can intensify ideas and emotions, and he would use such rhetorical repetition in some of his most persuasive and impassioned political writings.[10]

Before the month of May was out, the family endured another death when John Wayles passed away. With this death, Jefferson came into possession of thousands of acres of land and a large number of slaves. He also inherited Wayles's debts. Consequently, he had to sell more than half the land in order to meet the obligation. Poplar Forest, the only property of those he inherited from Wayles that he kept, would become Jefferson's vacation retreat. Before long, those who purchased land from Jefferson would pay off their notes in depreciated Revolutionary currency. For years to come he would struggle to liquidate his debt to Wayles's creditors.

Less complicated and more gratifying were the books he inherited or otherwise acquired from the estate of his father-in-law. The month after Wayles died, Jefferson traveled to Poplar Forest, where he inventoried his father-in-law's substantial library. By Jefferson's count, the Wayles library contained 669 volumes. Making a record of it on one of the blank leaves bound within the center of his almanac, Jefferson subdivided the books into format from large to small—folio, quarto, octavo, duodecimo. He did not list titles individually. Few other documents survive to record the contents of Wayles's estate, so it is impossible to say how many of these volumes came into Jefferson's possession. Titles that have turned up since the detailed catalogue of Jefferson's great library was prepared suggest that he owned many more volumes from the Wayles collection than the catalogue indicates. The most up-to-date evidence shows that his father-in-law's books significantly augmented Jefferson's personal library.[11]

Law books dominated Wayles's library. Given Jefferson's interest in the laws of Virginia, the most important law book he received from the Wayles estate was John Purvis's *Complete Collection of All the Laws of Virginia*. This statute collection, formerly in the possession of William Byrd II of West-over, contains a long and unique manuscript appendix. Other law books Jefferson received from the estate included works treating such subjects as equity pleading, fraud and conspiracy, and parliamentary jurisdiction. He also received reports of cases, collections of important trials, and some individual ones such as Elizabeth Canning's sensational trial. Canning was a young London woman who had gone missing for weeks only to reappear, claim she had been abducted, and then be accused, tried, convicted, sentenced, and transported to America for perjury.

Jefferson acquired books from Wayles's library treating a number of other subjects. Wayles had an idiosyncratic collection of controversial religious literature, as well as a fairly standard collection of books pertaining to business matters, ranging from such practical works as ready-reckoners and currency converters to more theoretical treatises. One such book was Henry Pollexfen's *Of Trade*, which defined and explained how to determine the balance of trade, discussed the price of gold and its relationship to paper credit, and examined the trade among England, Europe, the East Indies, and Africa. Wayles's library also contained several volumes of music. For example, *Lyric Harmony*, a musical score Jefferson acquired from Wayles's estate that survives at the University of Virginia, contains eighteen ballads, including one titled "To a Lady, Who, Being Ask'd by Her Lover for a Token of Her Constancy, Gave Him a Knife."

In terms of Jefferson's literary interests, Wayles's copy of René Rapin's *Critical Works* may be the most relevant book he received from the estate. Rapin was one of the best-loved literary critics of seventeenth-century France. He advocated a traditional aesthetic that emphasized the value of literature for teaching proper moral conduct, an idea Jefferson shared. Rapin also contributed to the Ancients versus Moderns debate, coming out firmly on the side of the Ancients. His critical works consisted of a series of comparative essays contrasting multiple pairs of ancient orators, poets, historians, and philosophers: Demosthenes and Cicero, Homer and Virgil, Thucydides and Livy, Plato and Aristotle. As the notes on Ossian in his commonplace book show, Jefferson was deeply engaged in the practice of comparing ancient literature from different cultures, an approach this newly acquired volume reinforced.

The books from the library of Reuben Skelton that Jefferson acquired also came through the estate of John Wayles. Skelton had owned an excellent collection of biographical literature, which greatly enhanced Jefferson's library, including Archibald Bower's *History of the Popes*; Edward Harwood's *Biographia Classica*, a collection of biographical sketches of Greek and Roman historians, orators, and poets; *Plutarch's Lives*; and Thomas Stanley's *The History of Philosophy*, which presented biographical and critical sketches of philosophers throughout Western history. These works reinforced Jefferson's recognition of the importance of biography as a literary genre. He also acquired Reuben Skelton's copy of the twenty-volume *Universal History*. As far as general reference books went, the *Universal History* was, in Jefferson's words, "the most learned, and most faithful perhaps that ever was written. Its style is very plain, but perspicuous."[12]

He did not come into possession of Wayles's books until the following year, as one surviving volume verifies. The flyleaf of Wayles's copy of Voltaire's *History of Charles XII* contains a rare dated autograph: "Thos. Jefferson 1774."[13] Though Wayles's books greatly augmented his collection, Jefferson remained dissatisfied with the rate his library was growing. It seemed as if he could hardly accumulate books fast enough. His accounts for 1773 indicate that he was buying and selling books not only for himself but also for his friends and neighbors. In Williamsburg the week after Wayles's death, for example, he picked up a copy of a Latin–English dictionary for a neighbor.[14]

At the same time, he acquired another book for himself, a copy of James McClurg's *Experiments upon the Human Bile*, which included a lengthy but self-effacing introduction advocating medical and scientific experimentation. Though Jefferson's scientific interests prompted him to assemble a good collection of European medical treatises, his acquisition of this homegrown medical book was personally motivated. After studying medicine at Edinburgh, its author, a native Virginian, had returned home to practice medicine. McClurg, like Jefferson, had become active in Virginia's Philosophical Society for the Advancement of Useful Knowledge. Jefferson's purchase of McClurg's book gave him a way to support his friend and patronize the study of science in America. Another personal factor motivated Jefferson's acquisition of McClurg's study of human bile: Dabney Carr's death had been attributed to bilious fever.

Despite these new acquisitions, Jefferson longed to expand his library on a much grander scale. To that end, he visited Westover, the stately manor of William Byrd III, whose library had the reputation of being the finest in Virginia. Byrd III, whose personal tastes ran more toward such works as John Cleland's *Memoirs of a Woman of Pleasure*, had little to do with amassing this impressive collection of books. The Byrd library was started by his grandfather and made great by his father. William Byrd II willed the library to his son, who, sadly, turned out to be a drunk, a profligate, and a gambler. It was mainly through the efforts of his mother, Maria Taylor Byrd, that the library remained intact after her husband's death: she prevented her son from selling the books for ready cash. After her death in 1771, William Byrd III, chronically in debt, began considering the sale of the library.[15]

Jefferson, who was Byrd's attorney, had been familiar with the collection for years, but he began looking at it differently once his client started contemplating its sale. One day, he carefully scrutinized Byrd's library and estimated its value, which he noted in his almanac. As he had with Wayles's library, he listed the number of volumes by format and their estimated value. Even though he greatly underestimated the value of the collection, he still could not afford it.

Another memorandum Jefferson made in that year's almanac indicates the size of his own collection:

Aug. 4. 1773. My library.

vols.

In the Mahogany book case with glass doors   510
Walnut bookcase in N.W. corner of room   180
Walnut bookcase in N.E. corner of room   224
Shelves in N.W. corner of room   151
Shelves in N.E. corner of room   131
Lent out   42
Lying about   18
in all 1256 vols.

Note this does not include vols. of Music; nor my books in Williamsburgh.[16]

The total is amazing, especially considering that it had only been three years since the fire at Shadwell. The number of books lent out and lying about show that Jefferson was encouraging others to read and reading much himself that summer. The books lent out were mainly law books: Jefferson was currently overseeing the legal education of several young men. Those lying about suggest that there were eighteen books that he and his wife were reading, all in various stages of completion. The books they were reading were compelling enough that they refused to return them to the shelves before finishing them, not even for purposes of taking inventory.

For the moment, Jefferson did not make a detailed list of the titles his library contained, but his friend Edmund Randolph drafted a good description of the library as it was constituted around this time, using it to help assess Jefferson's personal character:

> He had been ambitious to collect a library, not merely amassing *number* of books, but distinguishing authors of merit and assembling them in subordination to every art and science; and notwithstanding losses by fire, this library was at this time more happily calculated than any other private one to direct to objects of utility and taste, to present to genius the scaffolding upon which its future eminence might be built, and to reprove the restless appetite, which is too apt to seize the mere gatherer of books.[17]

In other words, despite the large number of volumes Jefferson was amassing, he was not buying books indiscriminately. Rather, he was assembling a fine collection that reflected his practical interests, his tastes, and his quest for knowledge.

Though his collection swelled to more than a thousand volumes that summer, he still felt the need for many more—especially those manuscript compilations of Ossianic verse. When he took this inventory, he had yet to hear from Charles Macpherson. Jefferson's letter had been delayed for several months, finally reaching its intended correspondent in Edinburgh the last week of July. Charles acted as quickly as he could and relayed his request to his brother. James Macpherson wrote back and, not surprisingly, refused. In justifying his refusal, James gave his brother several reasons why he could not comply with the request, all of which seem a little evasive when read in retrospect.

Writing Jefferson to give him the disappointing news, Charles apologized and enclosed the letter from his brother. Though unable to send Jefferson Gaelic texts of Ossian, Charles did supply him with a copy of the Gaelic New Testament translated from the Greek by a Scottish Episcopalian minister, James Stuart. *Tiomnadh nuadh*, as this translation of the New Testament was titled, contains a nine-page appendix called "Rules for Reading the Galic Language." Charles also sent Jefferson a copy of Alexander MacDonald's *Galick and English Vocabulary*, a work sponsored by the Society in Scotland for Propagating Christian Knowledge and prepared for the use of charity schools in the Scottish Highlands. The work was intended to help local Scots learn English, but it could also be used in the reverse. Jefferson later acquired another work by Alexander MacDonald, a compilation of Gaelic songs and poems with a useful glossary to facilitate the study of the language. His acquisition of this last volume suggests that even though he had been unable to obtain copies of Ossian's poems in Gaelic, he still pursued the study of the language, which continued to fascinate him for decades.[18]

Charles ended his letter with a promise to send Jefferson any other Gaelic works that might appear in the future, but he conveyed the unlikelihood of such publications. Charles related this information with sadness. Alas, there were few people left who could properly record the language. The best way for a person to experience poems similar to those of Ossian, he suggested, would be to visit the Highlands and immerse himself within the vestiges of ancient Scottish culture that survived: "In the remote Highlands there are still to be found a number of Ossians Poems, abounding equally in the tender and sublime, with those with which Mr. Macpherson has favored the public, and these are chanted away, with a wildness a sweetness of enthusiasm, in the true spirit of Song."[19]

James Macpherson's refusal did not dampen Jefferson's enthusiasm for the poems of Ossian. Even after their authenticity came into question, he continued to read Ossian with fondness. He even named horses after Ossianic characters. He had one horse named Fingal, another named Ryno after Fingal's son, and a mare named Cuthona after the legendary lover in "Conlath and Cuthona." Imagine its owner astride Fingal on an unexpectedly cool summer morning. The valley of the Rivanna would be filled with fog, and Jefferson could descend from Monticello into the mist below and picture himself in the Scottish Highlands of Ossian's day.

Independent testimony confirms Jefferson's devotion to Ossianic verse. The well-known anecdote the Marquis de Chastellux recorded after his visit to Monticello in 1782 bears repeating. In his *Travels in North America*, Chastellux wrote:

> I recall with pleasure that as we were conversing one evening over a "bowl of punch," after Mrs. Jefferson had retired, we happened to speak of the poetry of Ossian. It was a spark of electricity which passed rapidly from one to the other; we recited them for the benefit of my traveling companions, who fortunately knew English well and could appreciate them, even though they had never read the poems. Soon the book was called for, to share in our "toasts": it was brought forth and placed beside the bowl of punch. And, before we realized it, book and bowl had carried us far into the night.[20]

Jefferson's surviving copy of Edward Gibbon's *History of the Decline and Fall of the Roman Empire* contains a transcription from "Carthon," one of the most popular and influential of the Ossianic prose-poems. The inscription, made in or after 1789 (the year the volume was published), confirms Jefferson's ongoing devotion to the legendary poet but clashes with Gibbon's skepticism on the subject of Ossian. Even though Gibbon questioned the authenticity of Ossianic verse, he found Macpherson's depiction of the ancient Caledonians so alluring that he incorporated it in his history. Favorably comparing the ancient Caledonians to the Romans, Gibbon wrote: "Something of a doubtful mist still hangs over these Highland traditions; nor can it be entirely dispelled by the most ingenious researches of modern criticisms: but if he could, with safety, indulge the pleasing supposition, that Fingal lived, and that Ossian sung, the striking contrast of the situation and manners of the contending nations might amuse a philosophic mind."[21]

The inscription in Jefferson's copy of *The History of the Decline and Fall of the Roman Empire* occurs nowhere near Gibbon's skeptical reference to Ossian. Instead, it occurs late in the *History*, adjacent to a passage describing when Mahomet II visited St. Sophia during the fifteenth century and transformed the church into a mosque. Gibbon wrote:

> By his command, the metropolis of the Eastern church was transformed into a mosch: the rich and portable instruments of superstition had been removed; the crosses were thrown down; and the walls, which were covered with images and mosaics, were washed and purified, and restored to a state of naked simplicity. On the same day, or on the ensuing Friday, the *muezin* or crier ascended the most lofty turret, and proclaimed the ezan, or public invitation in the name of God and his prophet, the imam preached; and Mahomet the second performed the *namez* of prayer and thanksgiving on the great altar, where the Christian mysteries had so lately been celebrated before the last of the Caesars. From St. Sophia he proceeded to the august, but desolate, mansion of an hundred successors of the great Constantine; but which in a few hours had been stripped of their pomp of royalty.

Upon reading this passage, Jefferson recalled the following lines from "Carthon," which he inscribed onto this page: "I have seen the walls of Balclutha, but they were desolate. The stream of Clutha was removed from its place by the fall of the walls. The thistle shook there its lonely head. The moss whistled to the wind. The fox looked out from the windows: the rank grass of the wall waved round his head." Reading about this Muslim takeover of a Christian cathedral, Jefferson compared it to watching an ancient edifice being reversed to a state of nature. For Jefferson, Mahomet II and his followers are like the fox and thistle in Ossian: symbols of decay, not progress.[22]

He continued to read, recommend, and refer to the works of Ossian throughout his life. Entertaining John Adams and his family in Paris one evening, Jefferson devoted a part of their conversation to literature; a teenage John Quincy Adams wrote in his diary that Jefferson was "a great admirer of Ossian's poems." Ossian remained on Jefferson's mind after the Adamses had left Paris for London. He wrote John Adams, "The departure of your family has left me in the dumps. My afternoons hang heavily on me." In another of his deliberate exaggerations, he told Adams that he was almost "ready for the dark and narrow house of Ossian."[23]

To members of his own family Jefferson recommended Ossian multiple times. Responding to his daughter Mary many years later, he used an Ossianic simile to characterize the letter she had sent him: "It was, as Ossian says, or would say, like the bright beams of the moon on the desolate heath." Later, he sent his granddaughters a versification from Ossian by Royall Tyler, "Versification of Ossian's Description of the Palace and Power of Fingal, after Death."[24] He presented a copy of a two-volume Paris edition of *The Works of Ossian* to his oldest granddaughter, Anne Cary Randolph. Anne's sister Ellen—his favorite granddaughter—learned the work well enough to quote appropriate lines from memory.[25]

Jefferson never lost his enthusiasm for the works of Ossian even after he acknowledged their dubious authenticity. When the Marquis de Lafayette presented him with a copy of Frances Wright's *A Few Days in Athens*—a fictitious defense of Epicureanism supposedly translated from a Greek original discovered at Herculaneum—Jefferson wrote the Marquis to convey his fondness for that work and, in so doing, made an appreciative comment about the poems of Ossian that recognized their circumspect origins. He called Wright's book a work "of the highest order. The matter and manner of the dialogue is strictly ancient; and the principles of the sects are beautifully and candidly explained and contrasted; and the scenery and portraiture of the interlocutors are of higher finish than anything in that line left us by the ancients; and like Ossian, if not ancient, it is equal to the best morsels of antiquity."[26]

Judith Lomax, a local poet, visited Monticello during the early nineteenth century after developing a fondness for Ossian herself. "I love to read of Fingal's time," she admitted in one of the poems in her collection of personal verse, *The Notes of an American Lyre*, which she dedicated to Jefferson. She found his home reminiscent of the mist-filled Highlands in Ossian, an idea she expressed in another poem in the collection, "Written at Monticello, Albermarle County, and Composed While Viewing the Clouds Gathering and Rolling about the Mountain." It begins:

A cloud rests on the Mountain's brow,
  And thro' it "dim seen forms" appear
Floating in air, or stationed now
  In gloomy grandeur near.
These forms fantastic, bring along,
  To Fancy's mental eye,
Those times when Ossian, "Son of Song,"
  Awaked the tender sigh.
And still the vision'd scene untrue,
  My mind with transport fills;
For still methinks I seem to view
  The "Spirit of the hills."
And Fancy too, in Selma's hall,
  Awakes the Hero's name;
Methinks I hear the Bard recall
  The deeds of Fingal's fame.

Judith Lomax recognized that one reason Ossian appealed to Jefferson was because his often fog-bound home was reminiscent of the scenery Ossian describes.

Overall, Jefferson's lifelong fascination for the poems of Ossian emerged from a number of intertwining influences: biographical, literary, and anthropological. A similarity between the imaginative Scottish landscapes of Ossian's day and the Virginia Piedmont predisposed Jefferson to appreciation. The deaths in the family, which occurred as his enthusiasm for Ossian was reaching its peak, affirmed the value of the sentiments Ossian expressed. The utility of the Ossianic collections as mourning books gave them additional value. The supposedly ancient origins of Ossianic poetry let Jefferson indulge in the literary trends of melancholy and sentimentality while avoiding forms of literature that he disdained, such as sentimental novels.

Finally, the figure of Ossian let him indulge his fascination with primitive cultures. Though Charles Macpherson suggested that he travel to the Scottish Highlands to hear Ossianic lays still being sung, such a journey was not really possible given Jefferson's personal predilections and political responsibilities. His fascination with Indian oratory, on the other hand, partly arises from his fondness for Ossian. Instead of looking to the north, as Charles Macpherson recommended, Jefferson would look to the west to find in Chief Logan a rude bard of his own.

CHAPTER II

A Summary View of the Rights of British America

In 1773, Virginia welcomed one of the most colorful characters yet to reach its shores, the Florentine viticulturist Philip Mazzei, whose personal memoirs provide a unique glimpse into Jefferson's world, despite their occasional errors.[1] With an eye for detail and an ear for dialogue, Mazzei brought his Virginia experience alive as he wrote his life story. Having left Tuscany the previous decade, he had been living in London, where he befriended many Americans, including Thomas Adams and Benjamin Franklin. Adams came to know Mazzei well and spoke with him at length about Virginia and its leading citizens. Conversing with Mazzei—a great talker—people sometimes found it difficult to get a word in edgewise, but Adams managed to tell him about Thomas Jefferson, whose presence in the colony confirmed that Virginia was not without men of refinement and intellect. Before long, Mazzei—a great dreamer as well as a great talker—made up his mind to immigrate to Virginia, where he hoped to establish vineyards and olive orchards and start producing wine and olive oil on a grand scale. From England, he returned to Tuscany to prepare for his voyage to the New World. After recruiting several men to accompany him, he set sail in September and reached Virginia in late November.

Almost immediately Mazzei established contact with the Jefferson family: upon his arrival he stayed with Jefferson's brother-in-law Francis Eppes. Thomas Adams, having reached Virginia before him, greeted Mazzei and arranged to escort him beyond the Blue Ridge to Augusta County, where he could find land suitable for his ambitious agricultural projects adjacent to Adams's own holdings. On the way there, Adams stopped at Monticello, spent a few days with Jefferson, and introduced him to Mazzei.

The evening they arrived, Mazzei informed his host of his ambitious agricultural plans. Always willing to encourage local agricultural development, Jefferson was impressed and intrigued with what Mazzei planned. Jefferson's interest in viticulture is well known.[2] He also approved Mazzei's scheme for planting olive orchards in Virginia. Mazzei did not record what his host said this evening, but it might have resembled something he said the following decade. In what may be the finest paean to the olive ever written, Jefferson stated: "The Olive is a tree the least known in America, and yet the most worthy of being known. Of all the gifts of heaven to man, it is next to the most precious, if it be not the most precious. Perhaps it may claim a preference even to bread; because there is such an infinitude of vegetables which it renders a proper and comfortable nourishment."[3]

The next morning Jefferson and Mazzei arose before the rest of the household and took the opportunity for a quiet walk while the others slept. Jefferson showed his guest the adjoining property and suggested that if Mazzei purchased it, he would supplement the tract with a parcel of his own land as a way of assisting his project. Mazzei needed no more convincing and agreed to purchase the land right then and there. The following year Mazzei formed an agricultural company to underwrite the cost of his vineyards and orchards, and Jefferson put his name on the list of the company's original subscribers. By the time these two returned to Monticello from their walk, the rest of the household had risen. Adams looked at Jefferson, who could not mask his delight.

"I see by your expression that you've taken him away from me," Adams observed. "I knew you would do that."

"Let's have breakfast first and then we'll see what we can do," Jefferson replied nonchalantly.

His knowledge of Italian was one aspect of Jefferson's learning that his new neighbor appreciated. Mazzei explained, "Jefferson understood the Tuscan language very well, but he had never heard it spoken. Nevertheless, he could converse with my men in Italian, and they were so pleased by the fact that he could understand them that I was touched." Jefferson's graciousness and hospitality also impressed Mazzei. He invited his new neighbor to live at Monticello until he could build a home at Colle, as Mazzei decided to call his new plantation. The widow Martin (the future Mrs. Mazzei) and her daughter, who had accompanied him from Europe, joined Mazzei at Monticello. These additional guests brought Jefferson's hospitality and graciousness near their breaking point, but he endured the presence of these unexpected visitors until the house at Colle became habitable.

Mazzei was also responsible for bringing Carlo Bellini and his wife to Virginia. The Bellinis lived at Monticello for a time, too. A kind-hearted man and a keen linguist, Bellini had much in common with Jefferson, and the two became good friends. Later, Bellini was appointed the first professor of modern languages at William and Mary. When he and Jefferson were apart, they exchanged a lively, if sporadic, correspondence.

Mazzei's activities in Virginia went beyond the realm of agriculture. He became intrigued with all things American and watched with fascination the Revolution unfold. Jefferson informed him of many new developments, including the creation of an intercolonial network of committees of correspondence. He also told Mazzei how Dabney Carr contributed to this development. Caught up in the revolutionary fervor, Mazzei planned to establish a new periodical as a forum to express his ideas. He wrote some essays in Italian, which Jefferson translated into English. Dissatisfied with his translations, and presumably irked by the amount of time these translations were taking, Jefferson asked Mazzei to write his essays in English, which he would then correct.

"You have a way of expressing yourself in your own tongue," Jefferson told him, "which I cannot translate without losing the effect."

So, Mazzei drafted his essays in English, and Jefferson corrected them. "By the time he got through making the corrections on the first sheet," Mazzei recalled, "it looked as if a plague of flies had settled on it." A half dozen times later, Jefferson finally returned Mazzei's work to him without having to blot a line.

"That phraseology," Jefferson told him, "is not pure English, but everyone will understand you, and the effect will be more forceful. That is what matters."

Jefferson's words convey a literary idea he would express many times over: a forceful voice is more important than grammatical correctness. Though not a stickler for the finer points of English grammar, Jefferson was a perfectionist who critiqued his own writings as roughly as he treated Mazzei's first English essay, if not more so. Surviving drafts of letters and legislation in Jefferson's hand also look like they have been settled by plagues of flies. The year after Mazzei arrived, Jefferson entered a period of his life during which he would draft some of his greatest political documents.

Through much of 1773, relations between colonial America and Great Britain had been fairly quiet, but one Act Parliament passed that year, which became known as the Tea Act, led to an event destined to become a classic episode in American history. This piece of legislation reduced the tax on imported British tea, giving British merchants an unfair advantage. Many colonists condemned the Act and boycotted the tea. As all American schoolchildren know, the Boston patriots were especially strenuous in their protests. When British tea ships arrived in the harbor that December, many Bostonians insisted the tea be sent back to Great Britain without payment of taxes. In a meticulously planned and carefully orchestrated effort, a group of patriots disguised as Indians boarded the ships and dumped the tea into the harbor. Parliament reacted swiftly to punish the colony of Massachusetts, passing a series of retaliatory Acts, including the Boston Port Bill, which banned the loading or unloading of any ships in the harbor. It was scheduled to take effect June 1.

News of these punitive Acts spread rapidly through the colonies in the spring of 1774, reaching Williamsburg when the House of Burgesses was in session, finally in session, that is. Partway through the Assembly the previous spring, the one during which Dabney Carr had delivered his memorable speech proposing colonial committees of correspondence, Governor Dunmore had prorogued the Assembly. The governor continued proroguing the Assembly for over a year but now permitted the House of Burgesses to meet. For the most part, Dunmore had simply been ignoring the colonial challenges to the crown's authority. He was managing the colony largely by refusing to entangle himself in local political issues. In so doing, he was avoiding the inevitable. Ultimately, Dunmore had no choice but to confront the colonists.

Dunmore or, properly, John Murray, fourth Earl of Dunmore, had first come to America to fight in the French and Indian War, during which he distinguished himself as a soldier. He subsequently became governor of New York, but after Governor Botetourt's sudden and unexpected death in 1770, Lord Dunmore was transferred to Virginia to assume the governorship of the wealthiest and most populous colony in North America. He reached Williamsburg in September 1771.

Around forty years of age, he was a short, muscular man with ruddy cheeks and a massive chin whose head of prematurely gray hair contrasted with his generally athletic appearance. Unlike his immediate predecessor, Dunmore did not possess the aura of a cultivated gentleman. However, his fine library and collection of musical instruments did give him the trappings of sophistication and suggested that he might be able to fit into Virginia society. His activities during his first few years in the colony primarily involved finagling as much land for himself and his heirs as he could. Though a good soldier, he was in no way qualified to engage in the ensuing political battles.

Reacting to the Boston Port Bill, the House of Burgesses split between older and younger members. Since the older ones lacked the wherewithal to tackle the revolutionary events that were unfolding, it fell to the younger members to assume leadership. Jefferson, Patrick Henry, Richard Henry Lee, and a handful of others agreed that Virginia had to stand up for Massachusetts. To decide a proper course of action, these young men met in the Council chamber, where they took advantage of its library.

The relative uneventfulness of the preceding year had lulled many people into a state of political lethargy from which they needed to be aroused. Patriotism was waning. The best way to reinvigorate the Virginians, remind them of the seriousness of their situation, and assert colonial solidarity, the committee decided, would be to set aside June 1, 1774, the day the Boston Port Bill was scheduled to take effect, as a day of "fasting and prayer to the supreme being, imploring him to avert the calamities then threatening us, and to give us one heart and one mind to oppose every invasion of our liberties."[4] Virginia had not experienced such imposed solemnity since the start of the French and Indian War nearly twenty years earlier, a time outside the memory of many young men and women. Unaware precisely how to word a resolution proclaiming a day of fasting and prayer, the committee consulted the Council's copy of John Rushworth's *Historical Collections*.[5]

This classic of English historical literature represents the first great collected edition of English state papers. Beginning to assemble his huge set of documents during the time of Oliver Cromwell, Rushworth had a pragmatic purpose in mind. He designed the work to counteract the misinformation that was being propagated by contemporary pamphleteers. Rushworth intended the *Historical Collections* to preserve many state papers from being destroyed and thus to prevent subsequent lies from being taken as truth. His work, which ultimately amounted to eight folio volumes, would not be completed until after his death. Jefferson, who had a copy of it in his personal library, would consult it numerous times in the coming years as he searched for seventeenth-century documents pertinent to the history of Virginia. Rushworth set an example for Jefferson's own aggressive efforts to collect and preserve important historical documents.

Explaining how he and his committee drafted the resolution, Jefferson recalled, "We thought Oliver Cromwell would be a good guide in such a case. So we looked into Rushworth, and drew up our Resolutions after the most pious and praiseworthy examples."[6] Using some appropriate "revolutionary precedents and forms of the Puritans" as a basis, they drafted a resolution of their own.[7] Shrewdly, they chose Robert Carter Nicholas, an especially devout House member, to move the resolution. Jefferson's personal reluctance to present a bill calling for a day of prayer suggests that his religious skepticism was already well developed—and well known. Had he moved the resolution, others might have recognized it for what it was, a political ploy rather than a sincere expression of religious devotion.

With Nicholas's help, the bill passed unanimously—to Jefferson's great relief. Had there been any debate, he believed, it would not have passed. Upon its passage, the House ordered the following proclamation to be printed:

> This House being deeply impressed with Apprehension of the great Dangers to be derived to *British America*, from the hostile Invasion of the City of *Boston*, in our Sister Colony of *Massachusetts Bay*, whose Commerce and Harbour are on the 1st Day of *June* next to be stopped by an armed Force, deem it highly necessary that the said first Day of *June* be set apart by the Members of this House as a Day of Fasting, Humiliation, and Prayer, devoutly to implore the divine Interposition for averting the heavy Calamity, which threatens Destruction to our civil Rights, and the Evils of civil War; to give us one Heart and one Mind firmly to oppose, by all just and proper Means, every Injury to *American* Rights, and that the Minds of his Majesty and his Parliament may be inspired from above with Wisdom, Moderation, and Justice, to remove from the loyal People of *America* all Cause of Danger from a continued Pursuit of Measures pregnant with their Ruin.[8]

It did not take long for a copy of this proclamation to reach Governor Dunmore's hands. Shortly after it appeared in print, he called the burgesses to the Council chamber. As he wafted a paper before them, there was little doubt what he had in his hand or on his mind.

"I have in my hand a Paper," he told them, "published by order of your House, conceived in such Terms as reflect highly upon his Majesty and the Parliament of *Great Britain*; which makes it necessary for me to dissolve you, and you are dissolved accordingly."

Undaunted, the burgesses left the capitol, made their way down the Duke of Gloucester Street, and unofficially reconvened at the Apollo, where they agreed to another association. They instructed the Virginia Committee of Correspondence to write to the correspondence committees from the other colonies to propose that each choose representatives to meet in a general congress to discuss matters pertinent to the interests of all, the gathering that would become the First Continental Congress. Subscribers to this Virginia association reinforced their colony's solidarity with the others by declaring that an attack on any one colony should be considered an attack on the whole. The association further recommended that each county in Virginia elect representatives to convene in Williamsburg that August to consider the state of the colony and to choose delegates to the Continental Congress, assuming the other American colonies agreed to it.

On Wednesday, June 1, the day of prayer and fasting was observed throughout Virginia. Local clergymen delivered sermons on the occasion, and citizens were quite moved. Jefferson spent the day in and around The Forest. It did not really matter where in Virginia he was; he could have felt this fast day's effects anywhere in the colony. He long remembered how his fellow Virginians interpreted the event: "The people met generally, with anxiety and alarm in their countenances, and the effect of the day thro' the whole colony was like a shock of electricity, arousing every man and placing him erect and solidly on his centre."[9] The event profoundly affected Jefferson and reinforced his devotion to the cause of liberty. The behavior of his fellow Virginians this day bolstered his decision to pen the harshest denunciation of the crown that he or, for that matter, any colonist had yet written, a work that appeared in pamphlet form as *A Summary View of the Rights of British America*.

Recalling *A Summary View* in *Notes on the State of Virginia*, Jefferson situated it within a list of revolutionary polemics beginning with Richard Bland's 1766 work, *An Inquiry into the Rights of the British Colonies*, which had impressed many Virginia readers by both its erudition and its ideas. Philip Mazzei, for one, read Bland's *Inquiry* with great interest and found it "very well thought out." Jefferson called Bland's work "the first pamphlet on the nature of the connection with Gr. Britain, which had any pretension to accuracy of view on that subject."[10]

Though appreciative, Jefferson was not uncritical of Bland, who "would set out on sound principles, pursue them logically till he found them leading to the precipice which we had to leap, start back alarmed, then resume his ground, go over it in another direction, be led again by the correctness of his reasoning to the same place, and again back about, and try other processes to reconcile right and wrong, but finally left his reader and himself bewildered between the steady index of the compass in their hand, and the phantasm to which it seemed to point."[11]

In *A Summary View*, to continue the metaphor, Jefferson led his readers to the precipice and then took them over the edge. He later described the pamphlet as "the first publication which carried the claim of our rights their whole length."[12] *A Summary View* did not contain any startling new ideas, nor did it contain anything that was not already in the minds or on the lips of his fellow patriots.[13] Its literary qualities gave *A Summary View* its impact. Its daring form, its clarity, its vivid figurative language—these aspects made *A Summary View* a powerful statement of colonial rights.

Proud of *A Summary View* after it appeared in print, Jefferson had not necessarily intended it for publication. Rather, he designed it as a set of instructions for those delegates chosen to represent colonial Virginia at the Continental Congress. He later asserted that he wrote it hastily, but its meticulous construction, moving rhetoric, and clever use of imagery and example belie this assertion. Jefferson was neither the first nor the last author to feign nonchalance as he recalled a published work. In terms of its use of imagery, *A Summary View* contains a series of linked motifs that reinforce the argument and make the British injustice palpable. Jefferson's imagery has a cumulative effect. One image builds on another as readers gradually feel the weight of his argument.

In terms of form, the work begins like any legislative resolution. Resolving that Congress prepare an address to King George III, *A Summary View* loses the feel of a resolution as it assumes the quality of an address. During his first term in the House of Burgesses, Jefferson was criticized because an address to the governor he had written followed too closely the wording of the resolution on which it was based. With *A Summary View*, he embedded an address within the resolution. In its published form, *A Summary View* sounds as if it is directly addressed to the king, and it was read as such. One contemporary British reader characterized it as "an expostulation with his majesty." Emphasizing its similarity to a spoken performance, one modern American reader has characterized it as a dramatic monologue.[14]

While appearing to speak with King George III directly, *A Summary View* drops the submissive language traditionally used to address the crown. Jefferson forthrightly justified his choice of words in the opening paragraph. He explained that the address to the king would be "penned in the language of truth, and divested of those expressions of servility which would persuade his majesty that we are asking favors and not rights."[15] This emphasis on plain speech had been a part of colonial American discourse since the early seventeenth century, when such diverse figures as Captain John Smith and William Bradford stressed the importance of speaking plainly in their writings. Never before had any colonist deigned to address the king so bluntly.

The idea of natural rights provides the theoretical basis for *A Summary View*. All men, Jefferson asserted, have the natural right to emigrate where they will. Furthermore, emigrants are not obliged to remain under the sovereign laws of those places they leave. *A Summary View* became the most renowned articulation of this idea, but the point Jefferson was making had been made before by others. In *An Inquiry into the Rights of the British Colonies*, Bland had also asserted the natural right of emigration. For precedent, Jefferson cited the ancient Saxons who left Europe for England. Settling in the British Isles, they felt no compunction to retain the laws of the lands they left behind and instead established a fundamental system of laws unique to Britain. Similarly, those who left England for America were under no compunction to follow English law in the New World. Earlier American colonists had accepted English law merely as a matter of convenience.

Warming up to his argument, Jefferson denied the crown any responsibility for helping to establish the colonies. Instead, he emphasized that the American settlers alone were responsible for successfully planting the British colonies in North America: "Their own blood was spilt in acquiring lands for their settlement, their own fortunes expended in making that settlement effectual. For themselves they fought, for themselves they conquered, and for themselves alone they have right to hold." Self-sufficiency has long been recognized as an important aspect of the American national character. As Jefferson's words clarify, self-sufficiency had become a part of the American character well before nationhood. The American colonists invested their bodies and blood in their struggle. They had earned their rights "at the hazard of their lives and loss of their fortunes."[16]

Jefferson's words echo the promotion literature that had been encouraging people to immigrate to America throughout the colonial period. They are especially reminiscent of words Captain John Smith wrote in *A Description of New England* and reiterated in *The Generall Historie of Virginia*. Encouraging Englishmen to immigrate to the New World, Smith had asked the rhetorical question: "Who can desire more content that hath small meanes, or but onely his merit to advance his fortunes, then to tread and plant that ground he hath purchased by the hazard of his life?"[17] Whereas Smith was writing in anticipation, beckoning people to immigrate, Jefferson was writing in retrospect, showing how the early colonists had answered Smith's call and risen to the challenge.

The early settlers established the American colonies by and for themselves, but it was not long before the crown claimed the colonies for its own and began apportioning America as a means of currying political favor. The land that was originally designated by the name Virginia was "parted out and distributed among the favorites and followers of their fortunes." *A Summary View* uses the image of the body or, more precisely, the mutilated body to make the point: "No exercise of such a power of dividing and dismembering a country has ever occurred in his majesty's realm of England."[18]

This imagery of dismemberment also had precedents in early American literature. William Byrd II prefaced his *History of the Dividing Line Betwixt Virginia and North Carolina* with a brief history of Virginia, which depicts the history of North America as a series of dismemberments. Byrd personified Virginia and conveyed the pain it experienced as it had one limb after another lopped off. Emphasizing how the early colonists put themselves in physical danger and then using a figurative comparison linking the land with the body, Jefferson gave colonial America an organic quality and inextricably linked the land with the people who live on it.

Addressing specific issues, Jefferson chose examples that reinforced the association between colony and colonist, land and body. Barred by Parliament from shipping goods anywhere save Great Britain, the colonists had been led into some absurd restrictions. To illustrate their absurdity, he cited an Act effectively forbidding an American subject from making "a hat for himself of the fur which he has taken perhaps on his own soil."[19] The example of the hat distinguishes the colonists from the king: to the American colonists, the crown had come to symbolize Great Britain's tyrannical power over them; Jefferson represented the colonists themselves by more humble garb, a homemade hat.

The example also reinforces the link between land and body. A product of the land, the hat covers the body and protects it from the elements. In other words, the British legislation effectively deprived colonists of the protection the land offered them. It also denied them their characteristic self-sufficiency. Influencing matters as personal as articles of clothing, the legislation represented a serious incursion of government into the realm of personal freedom.

A further example gives weight to Jefferson's argument, both literally and figuratively. Though colonial America produced significant quantities of iron, British law prevented Americans from manufacturing anything from the iron they produced. In *A Summary View*, Jefferson observed that "the iron which we make we are forbidden to manufacture; and, heavy as that article is, and necessary in every branch of husbandry, besides commission and insurance, we are to pay freight for it to Great Britain, and freight for it back again, for the purpose of supporting, not men, but machines, in the island of Great Britain."[20]

By using iron as a metaphor, Jefferson was able to use a representation of weightiness to give thrust to his argument. Juxtaposing Britain and America, his words establish other binary oppositions: agrarian and industrial, man and machine. From the viewpoint Jefferson espoused, iron is useful for husbandry in America. Iron ore is taken from the land but only to be turned into implements that contribute to the land's improvement. In Britain, on the other hand, American iron simply becomes a part of the industrial machinery. Were they to acquiesce to British demands, Americans would become nothing more than cogs in the imperial British machine.

Figurative uses of the machine were common to eighteenth-century sociopolitical discourse, but metaphors of the time typically compared the workings of an efficient government to those of a well-oiled machine. Elsewhere in *A Summary View* Jefferson used the machine in this sense as he mentioned how the crown should "assist in working the great machine of government."[21] Here he associated Great Britain with industrial machinery and thus contrasted agrarian America with industrial Britain, American men with British machines. Establishing a dichotomy between man and machine, Jefferson anticipated a figurative opposition that would not become prevalent in the literary discourse until the rise of Romanticism during the early nineteenth century.

Closing his discussion of trade restrictions, he distanced himself from the examples he had been using to support his argument. After all, the problem with Britain was not a matter of specific complaints about individual statutes. Rather, it was a matter of rights: "The true ground on which we declare these acts void is that the British parliament has no right to exercise authority over us."[22] Regardless of the practicality or impracticality of the statutes they passed, British lawmakers simply had no right to impose jurisdiction on the American colonists.

The systematic nature of these acts of tyranny on the part of the British had effectively reduced the colonists to a state of slavery. Supporting the point, Jefferson enumerated four Acts passed in consecutive years of the reign of King George III. Listed in series, these Acts verify the systematic nature of British repression and establish a pattern of repetition anticipating Jefferson's next metaphor. After naming the Acts, he characterized them as part of "the connected chain of parliamentary usurpation."[23]

The slavery and chain metaphors connect this series of oppressive Acts with Jefferson's earlier examples and consequently reinforce the motifs of body and iron by associating the two. The crown's efforts to control the physical actions of the colonists and to control the iron and other materials they produce come together in the image of a slave manacled in iron bands. Though the American colonists had complained about the repressive legislation on multiple occasions, neither the crown nor parliament had answered the colonial complaints. Taking a superior stance, Jefferson refused to repeat their numerous, analogous complaints, a refusal that takes on the aura of a slave casting off his chains.

Slavery metaphors had already entered the Revolutionary discourse. The association to which Jefferson and the other Virginia burgesses had affixed their names the previous month, for instance, had accused the British government of "reducing the inhabitants of British America to slavery, by subjecting them to the payment of taxes, imposed without the consent of the people or their representatives."[24] Though a commonplace of current political writing, the slave metaphor still put Jefferson on shaky rhetorical ground. A slaveowner himself who spoke for a land of slaveowners, he knew that he could not cast the American colonists in the role of slaves to a British master without some qualification. He pre-empted possible criticism in this regard by arguing that the crown was responsible for perpetuating slavery, not the colonists. The Americans had been trying to abolish the practice of slavery for years, he asserted, but the crown continued to condone and perpetuate the slave trade. Though not entirely convincing, the assertion is necessary to sustain the argument.

Mentioning the Boston Tea Party, Jefferson did not justify the actions of the rebellious Bostonians, but he did attempt to explain it. He suggested that an "exasperated people, who feel that they possess power, are not easily restrained within limits strictly regular."[25] This forward-thinking explanation identifies the psychological basis motivating the Bostonians' behavior. The British administrators, however, could not or would not understand the subtle psychological reasons underlying the Boston protest. Instead, they meted out punishment quickly and force-fully. After describing the British retribution, Jefferson concluded, "This is administering justice with a heavy hand indeed!"

A heavy hand: choosing this proverbial metaphor. Jefferson again conflated his motifs of weightiness and the body and thus used forceful imagery to reiterate his argument. Images of the hand had occurred frequently in earlier American literature. Think of Captain John Smith's Map of Virginia, which opens with a dedication "To the Hand." Or recall a saying of Poor Richard's from The Way to Wealth: "Help hands, for I have no Lands."[26] In early American discourse, the hand had become an important symbol of American self-sufficiency. Here, Jefferson ironically reversed the traditional American imagery to make the hand a symbol of oppression. Shifting the image of the hand to the British, Jefferson indicated the powerlessness of the colonial legislatures to effect change, an idea he reinforced with an image of dismemberment. The dissolution of one or more colonial legislatures by the crown he called "the lopping off

[of] one or more of their branches."[27] When the British engage in this kind of figurative dismemberment, the colonial citizenry has no choice but, so to speak, to take matters into their own hands.

In his conclusion, Jefferson returned to images of the heavy hand and of dismemberment but only to reject them: "The god who gave us life, gave us liberty at the same time: the hand of force may destroy, but cannot disjoin them."[28] Life and liberty are of one body. One cannot be separated from the other without destruction to the whole.

Jefferson intended to present *A Summary View* before the Virginia Convention. Accompanied by Jupiter, he left Monticello on his way to Williamsburg only to be struck down by a case of dysentery severe enough to turn him back. Though forced to return home, he sent his slave ahead to Williamsburg. So Jupiter, it seems, was responsible for carrying Jefferson's message of natural rights to Williamsburg and giving copies to two of the most prominent delegates at the Virginia convention, Patrick Henry and Peyton Randolph.[29] Presenting copies to these two men in particular, Jefferson displayed his political savvy. Patrick Henry would be able to articulate Jefferson's ideas at the convention, and Randolph, as Jefferson correctly predicted, would be elected chair. What happened to Henry's copy of Jefferson's work is a mystery. Jefferson conjectured, "Mr. Henry probably thought it too bold, as a first measure."[30] Randolph's copy caused quite a stir when it reached Williamsburg.

Once delivered to Peyton Randolph, Jefferson's manuscript was read privately to a large gathering of people at Randolph's Williamsburg home. For those present that evening, its reading was an event to remember. Edmund Randolph, Peyton's nephew, recalled the applause that accompanied the work when it was read aloud at his uncle's home. Everyone gathered there recognized that Jefferson had gone much further than anyone before him had dared to go. "The young ascended with Mr. Jefferson to the source of those rights," Edmund Randolph recalled, but "the old required time for consideration before they could tread this lofty ground, which, if it had not been abandoned, at least had not been fully occupied throughout America."[31] Despite the enthusiasm with which it was received by those gathered at Peyton Randolph's home, the Virginia Convention did not approve the resolution. Reflecting on *A Summary View* many years later, Jefferson understood why the Convention acted as it did: "Tamer sentiments were preferred, and I believe, wisely preferred; the leap I proposed being too long as yet for the mass of our citizens."[32]

Though the Virginia Convention had not approved this resolution, Jefferson's greatest supporters realized that, in a way, they could circumvent the decision of the Convention by putting his words in print and thus giving them a wider currency. Several Virginia patriots subscribed to the publication of *A Summary View*. Jefferson's supporters gave the work its title and supplied a Latin motto from Cicero's *De Officiis*, which can be translated, "It is the indispensable duty of the supreme magistrate to consider himself as acting for the whole community, and obliged to support its dignity, and assign to the people, with justice, their various rights, as he would be faithful to the great trust reposed in him."

In addition, one of the subscribers drafted a short preface to the work, which emphasized its political and philosophical value. In *A Summary View*, the preface explains, "The sources of our present unhappy differences are traced with such faithful accuracy, and the opinions entertained by every free American expressed with such manly firmness, that it must be pleasing to the present, and may be useful to future ages." The subscribers shrewdly preserved Jefferson's anonymity, but the preface did assert that it had been written by one of the "best and wisest" members of the House of Burgesses. Jefferson's authorship of *A Summary View* became widely known.

With the title, motto, and preface added, the subscribers gave Jefferson's manuscript to Clementina Rind, who had taken over the family printing business after her husband's death the previous year. She had continued to publish the newspaper her husband founded, and she had issued a number of other works, too. Now she undertook the task of publishing the first edition of *A Summary View of the Rights of British America*. It would be her most distinguished imprint.

Once *A Summary View* was published, it largely ceased to matter whether the Virginia Convention had approved the work. In printed form, Jefferson's words transcended matters of legislative decision. Virginia delegates to the First Continental Congress brought copies of the pamphlet with them to Philadelphia, where *A Summary View* was reprinted. Though no contemporary American reprintings survive beyond the Williamsburg and Philadelphia editions, external evidence indicates that *A Summary View* was reprinted in Boston, New York, and Norfolk. Copies of one or more of the American editions reached England before year's end. Sending a copy of the Philadelphia edition to Benjamin Franklin, then in London, a sympathetic correspondent wrote, "If you have not seen it, I believe it will please you."[33] The pamphlet was reprinted in London multiple times. *A Summary View* fully established Jefferson's reputation as both an author and a patriot.

CHAPTER 12

The Pen and the Tomahawk

As the mild winter came to a close in March 1775—"the most favorable winter ever known in the memory of man," Jefferson called it—men from all parts of Virginia began wending their way toward Richmond, where they would gather at St. John's Church for the second Virginia Convention, rather than at Williamsburg. As the colonial capital, Williamsburg was becoming increasingly uncomfortable for local citizens who were challenging the British administration. Delegates to the Virginia Convention had been elected by voters across the colony from the counties or corporations where they made their homes. This group of over a hundred men included nearly all of Virginia's foremost leaders. Some, like Peyton Randolph, were old hands at Virginia governance, while others were fairly green. Their youth fueled their enthusiasm and their ardor.

The convention began on Monday, March 20, when the delegates began discussing the dire situation the American colonies faced. By Thursday, the debate had reached a fevered pitch. When it came to a resolution stipulating that the Virginia colonists arm themselves in their own defense, one voice rose above the rest, that of Patrick Henry. When it came to logically justifying such a bold resolution, another voice took its turn, that of Thomas Jefferson. And, when it came to the matter of making this resolution practical, Jefferson was ready, pen in hand, to draft a report.

Furor resulted when Patrick Henry moved a resolution to establish a militia to defend Virginia. Since William Wirt first published his reconstruction of the famous speech in his *Life of Patrick Henry*, Henry's speech has become a part of the popular culture. Many know his famous words by heart. Few can resist repeating them:

Gentlemen may cry, peace, peace—but there is no peace! The war is actually begun! The next gale that sweeps from the north will bring to our ears the clash of resounding arms! Our brethren are already in the field! Why stand we here idle? What is it that gentlemen wish? What would they have? Is life so dear, or peace so sweet, as to be purchased at the price of chains and slavery? Forbid it, Almighty God!—I know not what course others may take; but as for me, give me liberty, or give me death!

All were impressed with Henry's speech, but not all were persuaded. Jefferson, firmly convinced of the justness of their cause before Henry took the floor, rose to speak. The fact that Jefferson addressed this large gathering indicates both his seriousness and his dedication to the cause of liberty: natural shyness generally dissuaded him from addressing large crowds save for matters of extreme gravity. On this occasion, he spoke his mind, arguing "closely, profoundly, and warmly."[1] A well-regulated militia, he explained, would provide the only way to secure a free government. A local militia would obviate the need for a standing army to defend the colony and therefore would eliminate the need for taxes to support one. The combination of Henry's eloquence and Jefferson's logic prompted a majority of the delegates to consent to the resolution. Through their actions, they put Virginia on the defensive.

To make these resolutions a reality, a committee was formed to work out the details. The committee, which included Henry, Jefferson, and the greatest military mind in the colonies, George Washington, prepared a report and presented it before the convention on Saturday. Having demonstrated his literary skill the year before with *A Summary View of the Rights of British America*, Jefferson took primary responsibility for drafting this document. What resulted, the "Report of Committee to Prepare a Plan for a Militia," offers a vivid picture of the colonial militia at the start of the Revolutionary War.

This report stipulates that each company of infantry should consist of sixty-eight soldiers commanded by one captain, two lieutenants, one ensign, four sergeants, and four corporals. The drummer for each company would be furnished with a drum and colors. The committee's report urges all soldiers to "endeavor as soon as possible to become acquainted with the military exercise for infantry appointed to be used by his majesty in the year 1764."[2] Prepared by British Adjutant-General Edward Harvey, *The Manual Exercise as Ordered by His Majesty in 1764* set forth the proper methods of infantry drill and tactics. This same work was already in use by local militia companies throughout Revolutionary

America. During the mid-1770s, new editions of *Manual Exercise* were reprinted up and down the East Coast as militia companies in each colony mobilized themselves for war.

The committee report also stipulates how militiamen should be clothed and armed. Every man would be "provided with a good Rifle if to be had, or otherwise with a common firelock, bayonet and cartouch box; and also with a tomahawk, one pound of gunpowder, and four pounds of ball at least fitted to the bore of his gun." In addition, he should be clothed in "a hunting shirt by way of uniform."[3] A homemade garment, the hunting shirt was a loose frock that reached halfway down the thighs. Instead of being buttoned or fastened in any other way, the shirt was open in front, but the front flaps overlapped by about a foot and were held together with a belt.

This choice of weaponry and uniform was largely based on what was available locally. The preceding year the First Continental Congress had agreed to an association similar to the Virginia associations of earlier years. Like the others, this new association forbade colonists from importing most goods of British manufacture. Consequently, Virginia militiamen would be outfitted in uniquely American fashion. The hunting shirt had long been an article of clothing identified with backwoodsmen, those unsavory and uncivilized characters who inhabited the fringes of colonial society, somewhere in that middle ground between the westernmost plantations and the wilderness. It now became the uniform of a patriot. In the story of the transformation of the backwoodsman into the frontiersman—lout into hero—the Revolutionary soldier plays a conspicuous part. The tomahawk became a useful sidearm for American troops in close combat. Carrying one into battle, the American soldier took on a Native American characteristic. What began as an indigenous weapon became an emblem and implement of American freedom.

An important order of business on Saturday involved electing delegates to represent Virginia in the Second Continental Congress, which was scheduled to convene in Philadelphia the second week of May. The Virginia Convention chose seven Congressional delegates. In descending order of votes received, those elected were Peyton Randolph, George Washington, Patrick Henry, Richard Henry Lee, Edmund Pendleton, Benjamin Harrison, and Richard Bland. The consensus was clear: the first received 107 votes, and the seventh received ninety. The man in eighth place received only eighteen votes: Thomas Jefferson. On the last day of the second Virginia Convention, Jefferson was designated as an alternate to the Second Continental Congress in case Peyton Randolph would be unable to fulfill his responsibilities as a delegate.[4]

Once the second Virginia Convention drew to a close the last days of March, it was not long before the colonists' decision to arm themselves proved to be the right one. Massachusetts had made a similar decision, and members of their militia—the Minutemen—were called into action the following month. Early Wednesday morning, April 19, under orders from General Thomas Gage, about eight hundred British soldiers marched on Concord, where the colonists had a large cache of guns and ammunition. Having been warned by Paul Revere and others, the Minutemen were ready. They assembled at Lexington to try to stop the British advance. Ordered to disperse by the British commander, the Americans refused. The British fired upon them, killing eight and forcing the remainder to retreat toward Concord. The Minutemen, altogether about one-quarter the size of the British force, established a new position on the farther side of the Old North Bridge over the Concord River. This time they successfully resisted the advancing troops and humiliated the British, forcing them to retreat to Boston and harassing them as they went.

The figurative gale from the north Patrick Henry had predicted in his famous speech was not long in coming. News of the Battle of Lexington and Concord reached Virginia quickly, before the month was out. Jefferson later referred to the mood of the country after Lexington and Concord as both a "state of excitement" and a "state of exasperation." Upon learning of the battle, he told a British correspondent: "Within this week we have received the unhappy news of an action of considerable magnitude between the king's troops and our brethren of Boston.... This accident has cut off our last hopes of reconciliation, and a phrenzy of revenge seems to have seized all ranks of people."[5]

Attacked on their own soil, Americans have little patience for diplomacy. The time it took for intelligence to cross the ocean meant that news of an important effort toward reconciliation made by the British prior to the Battle of Lexington and Concord did not reach the American strand until after the battle. In February, Lord North had proposed that any colony agreeing to support the costs of the administration and defense of the colonies would not be burdened with any additional taxes. The House of Commons approved it, and copies of Lord North's conciliatory proposal, as it came to be known, were sent to the colonial governors to present to their respective assemblies.

To present Lord North's proposal, Governor Dunmore called an Assembly. The Virginia delegates to the Continental Congress had already left for Philadelphia, but Peyton Randolph, as Speaker of the House of Burgesses, hurried back to Williamsburg to preside over the Assembly. With Randolph in Williamsburg, Jefferson, as alternate Congressional delegate, had the responsibility to go to Philadelphia instead. Recognizing the importance of Lord North's proposal, he delayed his departure to hear Governor Dunmore present it to the Assembly.

Appointed to the committee formed to respond to North's proposal, Jefferson took primary responsibility for drafting an answer. Upon completing his draft, he met with opposition from one committee member, Robert Carter Nicholas. In Jefferson's words, Carter "combated the answer from *alpha* to *omega*, and succeeded in diluting it in one or two small instances."[6] Despite Carter's critiques, the committee largely accepted what Jefferson had written.

"Virginia Resolutions on Lord North's Conciliatory Proposal" masterfully refutes this misguided attempt at reconciliation on the part of the British. Jefferson's resolutions bristle with memorable phrases. The document begins by expressing gratitude toward the British for their willingness to solve the colonial crisis but otherwise minces few words. Before the first paragraph is out, this set of resolutions explains that Virginia refused the proposal: "With pain and disappointment we must ultimately declare it only changes the form of oppression, without lightening its burthen." Eight similarly structured paragraphs delineate the inadequacy of North's proposal. Parliament had no right to meddle with the support of civil government in colonial America. Or, as Jefferson put it, "For us, not for them, has government been instituted here."[7]

North's proposal provided a colonial tax exemption only by burdening the colonies with a perpetual tax. Furthermore, North solely addressed the matter of taxes; he did not reconcile other grievances the colonies had against Great Britain such as the standing army and violations of free trade. Also, the proposal was directed toward each colony individually. Either North was deliberately seeking to divide the American colonies or he failed to understand how unified they were becoming. Speaking for all Virginians, Jefferson wrote, "We consider ourselves as bound in Honor as well as Interest to share one general Fate with our Sister Colonies, and should hold ourselves base Deserters of that Union, to which we have acceded, were we to agree on any Measures distinct and apart from them."[8]

Anxious to join the Continental Congress, Jefferson did not linger in Virginia after completing the resolutions rejecting North's proposal. On Sunday, June 11, he left Williamsburg for Philadelphia. This trip likely evoked feelings of melancholy on his part. It had been nine years since his first and only previous trip to Philadelphia. His world had since changed much. Then, he had recently passed his bar exam and was looking forward to the start of his career as a lawyer before the General Court of Virginia. Now, he had retired from the practice of law and turned his entire practice over to Edmund Randolph. Then, the rent in the colonial fabric caused by the Stamp Act was being mended with that Act's repeal. Now, the only way for the American colonists to solve their differences with Great Britain was to tear away from it completely. Doing that meant war.

Regardless how eager Jefferson was to reach Philadelphia, he proceeded at a leisurely pace, partly by chance and partly by choice. Between Williamsburg and Annapolis, he stopped to buy a new horse. He subsequently made additional stops for a new harness and some veterinary attention. In Annapolis, he did some sightseeing and shopping. As he noted in his interleaved copy of that year's *Virginia Almanack*, he also toured the new State House. The old one, which had so disappointed him nine years earlier, had since been razed to make way for this handsome new edifice. Construction on the new State House had been completed in 1774. The new building was a distinct improvement over the old one, though some found its modest cupola to lack an appropriate sense of grandeur. The cupola would eventually be replaced with an imposing dome.

He also visited the Annapolis bookshop of William Aikman, who had settled here two years earlier. Bringing with him a wide assortment of books, Aikman had taken over a shop across from the Court House on West Street, where he established a combination circulating library and bookstore. Shortly after its opening, Aikman's Circulating Library contained more than twelve hundred volumes on a variety of subjects. His advertising copy declared that the library contained books covering "the most useful sciences, history, poetry, agriculture, voyages, travels, miscellanies, plays, with all the most approved novels, magazines and other books of entertainment."[9] Jefferson clearly recognized the intellectual, social, and political value of circulating libraries. Many years later, he would say, "Nothing would do more extensive good at small expense than the establishment of a small circulating library in every county."[10]

Since settling in Annapolis, Aikman continued importing books and expanding the collection. He ambitiously hoped to make his library equal to or greater than any other circulating library in America. His bookshop developed a reputation as a congenial gathering place for local men of letters, and as his advertisements indicate, he sold much else beyond books. He also had on hand a supply of "wet goods" that included such items as old Port, London porter, and Cheshire cheese. Before Jefferson left Aikman's shop, he had purchased thirty-one shillings' worth of books.[11]

After spending Saturday night in Annapolis at Middleton's Tavern, he resumed his journey the following day, the second Sunday of his trip. Continuing northward, he reached Philadelphia on Tuesday, June 20, ten days after he had begun. Here he found lodgings with Benjamin Randolph, a cabinetmaker located on Chestnut Street between Third and Fourth. Jefferson's note-filled *Virginia Almanack* reveals how his insatiable curiosity manifested itself during his stay with Randolph, whose parlor contained a large, handsome fireplace. The careful measurements of the fireplace that Jefferson recorded on one of the almanac's blank leaves suggest that he must have climbed halfway into it to obtain such details.[12]

The day following his arrival, Jefferson appeared before Congress to present his credentials. He aroused much curiosity on the part of the other delegates. Save for Elbridge Gerry and Charles Thomson, no one outside the Virginia contingent knew him personally. But all knew him as the author of *A Summary View of the Rights of British America*. Good writing commands respect. The writing skills Jefferson demonstrated in this work had earned him the respect of the other Congressional delegates even before his arrival.

His fellow Congressional delegates attested to the literary quality of *Summary View*. Samuel Ward of Rhode Island, for one, had many good things to say about it. Describing Jefferson's arrival in a letter to his brother the next day, Ward wrote, "Yesterday the famous Mr. Jefferson a Delegate from Virginia in the Room of Mr. Randolph arrived. I have not been in Company with him yet, he looks like a very sensible spirited fine Fellow and by the Pamphlet which he wrote last Summer he certainly is one."[13] *Summary View* had given other delegates a good impression of Jefferson and favorably disposed them to accept him at first sight.

Jefferson brought with him a manuscript copy of "Virginia Resolutions on Lord North's Conciliatory Proposal," which further enhanced his reputation as a writer among the Congressional delegates. By his own account, the document had an important effect on them in terms of "fortifying their minds, and in deciding their measures." Describing the overall impression made on his fellow delegates, John Adams said that Jefferson brought to the Continental Congress "a reputation for literature, science, and a happy talent of composition. Writings of his were handed about, remarkable for the peculiar felicity of expression."[14] Making this statement, Adams did not specify which of Jefferson's writings were handed about, but presumably he meant either his resolutions on North's proposal or copies of *Summary View*, or both.

In the coming days, Jefferson got to know many of the delegates personally. He was impressed with Samuel Adams, whom he found "rigorously logical," "clear in his views," and "abundant in good sense." He later referred to Samuel Adams as the "Palinurus to the Revolution," a reference to the helmsman in the *Aeneid*.[15] He also befriended Silas Deane, with whom he enjoyed much intellectual conversation. As Jefferson interacted with other delegates, he impressed them not only with his capacity for hard work but also with the range and depth of his linguistic knowledge. Speaking with John Adams, James Duane of New York characterized Jefferson by his erudition, calling him "the greatest Rubber off of Dust" he had ever met. "He has learned French, Italian, Spanish and wants to learn German."[16]

True to what he told Duane, Jefferson made an effort to teach himself German. The next year, in fact, he visited Robert Aitken's Philadelphia bookshop, where he purchased a copy of John James Bachmair's *Complete German Grammar*.[17] Bachmair's introductory textbook gave Jefferson the basic rules of German grammar, syntax, and conjugation. Bachmair also provided lists of familiar phrases, dialogue in parallel German/English texts, examples of idioms and proverbs, practical vocabulary lists organized by various trades and professions, and sample letters in German. Overall, Bachmair gave his readers the basic skills to learn and apply the language.

Jefferson progressed far enough in his study of German to translate some verse.[18] "Falle doch auf Doris Augenlieder," a song by Johann Wilhelm Ludwig Gleim, was one item he translated. Another was Christian Felix Weisse's song "Ohn Lieb und ohne Wein." Both works were best known in their musical settings—the likeliest way Jefferson encountered them. Though he learned enough German to translate these songs with the help of a German dictionary, he never mastered the language well enough to read it with ease or speak it with fluency.

Soon after reaching Philadelphia, Jefferson spoke with fellow Virginia delegates and apprised them of what had been happening in Williamsburg. His first day in Congress he met with Edmund Pendleton. He confided in Richard Henry Lee around this same time. In his correspondence, Lee mentioned their conversation: "We had the news of Williamsburg by Mr Jefferson. It seems indeed as if Lord Dunmore was taking true pains to incur the censure of the whole reasonable world."[19] Lee's paraphrase of their conversation suggests that Jefferson was more caustic in his private remarks concerning Governor Dunmore than he had been in his writings.

Congress soon appointed a committee responsible for drafting a declaration to be made public by General Washington before the troops at Boston. John Rutledge and Benjamin Franklin were among the committee members. Known as the *Declaration of the Causes and Necessity for Taking up Arms*, this document went through considerable revision before it reached its final form. Rutledge drafted the initial declaration the committee presented. Congress debated the draft but remanded it to committee, whose membership expanded to include Thomas Jefferson and John Dickinson.

Jefferson composed a draft and then prepared a fair copy for the committee. The surviving manuscripts of both testify to his meticulous literary craftsmanship. Despite such careful composition, Dickinson vehemently disagreed with Jefferson's version and wrote a draft of his own. As the author of the popular and influential *Letters from a Farmer in Pennsylvania to the Inhabitants of the British Colonies*, Dickinson had helped to shape the political opinions of many Americans since the late 1760s, when that book appeared. Recognizing his literary skill and the ongoing influence of his writings, Congress let Dickinson prepare the final version Congress adopted.

In the opinion of Jefferson and other Congressional delegates, including and especially fellow Virginian Benjamin Harrison, Congress overindulged Dickinson. The deference many Congressional delegates paid him seemed both humiliating and disgusting to Jefferson, but when he related this episode in later years, he told it with humor and aplomb. Like Franklin, Jefferson greatly enjoyed telling anecdotes. As a frequent dinner guest observed, "When conveying his view of human nature through their most attractive medium—anecdote—he displayed the grace and brilliance of a courtier."[20] Jefferson's anecdote about the *Declaration of the Causes and Necessity for Taking up Arms* offers a good example.

Retelling the story, he explained what happened after Congress approved Dickinson's final draft of the *Declaration of Causes*.[21] According to proper parliamentary procedure, further discussion on the matter was prohibited, but Dickinson blurted out one final remark.

"There is but one word, Mr. President, in the paper which I disapprove, and that is the word *Congress*," Dickinson said.

To his chagrin, Dickinson did not get in the last word this time: Benjamin Harrison quickly rose from his seat to interject a final comment. "There is but one word in the paper, Mr. President, of which I approve," Harrison stated, "and that is the word *Congress*."

Despite the differences between the final version of the *Declaration of Causes* as approved by the Continental Congress and Jefferson's original, Dickinson did incorporate large chunks of text from Jefferson's fair copy, which form some of the most moving passages in the completed work. In his draft, Jefferson wrote that the colonists had attempted every possible course of peaceful action to reconcile their differences with Great Britain but that liberty ultimately transcended sovereignty. He eloquently observed, "We have pursued every temperate, every respectful measure. We have supplicated our king at various times, in terms almost disgraceful to freedom; we have reasoned, we have remonstrated with parliament in the most mild and decent language; we have even proceeded to break off our commercial intercourse with our fellow subjects, as the last peaceable admonition that our attachment to no nation on earth should supplant our attachment to liberty."[22] Dickinson liked what Jefferson had written and used this passage in the final version of the *Declaration of Causes*, but he softened it considerably by removing the part about disgracing freedom by supplicating the king.

Toward the conclusion of the *Declaration of Causes*, Dickinson paraphrased statements of Jefferson's articulating the American reaction to unprovoked attack. Though both Jefferson and Dickinson had the conflict at Lexington and Concord in mind, their words do not mention the battle. Rather, they speak in general terms regarding any unprovoked attack, and their resulting statements apply to any and all attacks, those past as well as those to come. Their words bear repeating:

> We fight not for Glory or for Conquest. We exhibit to Mankind the remarkable Spectacle of a People attacked by unprovoked Enemies, without any imputation or even suspicion of Offence. They boast of their Privileges and Civilization, and yet proffer no milder Conditions than Servitude or Death.
>
> In our own native Land, in defence of the Freedom that is our Birthright, and which we ever enjoyed till the late Violation of it—for the protection of our Property, acquired by the honest Industry of our fore-fathers and ourselves, against Violence actually offered, we have taken up Arms. We shall lay them down when Hostilities shall cease on the part of the Aggressors, and all danger of their being renewed shall be removed, and not before.[23]

Though intended only for General Washington to read before the troops, the *Declaration of Causes* appeared in print shortly after Congress approved it. The Philadelphia papers published it the second week of

July, and publishers in Massachusetts, New Hampshire, New York, and Rhode Island issued it in pamphlet form. Copies of the pamphlet made their way across the Atlantic, where they found favor with European intellectuals. Christoph M. Wieland, a contemporary German poet, published an appreciation of the *Declarations of Causes* in the newspaper he edited, *Der Teutsche Merkur*: "In every line of this declaration breathes patriotism and the love of freedom, and these lines really deserve to be placed beside the most noble words of Demosthenes and Cicero. It is proof that the fine arts and eloquence bloom no less in the English colonies than among us, and that the Americans can wield the pen as well as the sword."[24]

In the *Declaration of Causes*, Jefferson and Dickinson articulated ideas that remain pertinent for understanding the causes and necessity of taking up arms, especially in the face of unprovoked attack, but neither Jefferson nor his fellow delegates had time to dwell on the matter. They had much else to consider and to write. On Saturday, July 22, with Lee, Adams, and Franklin, Jefferson was appointed to a committee whose task it was to take into consideration Lord North's conciliatory proposal. Having already prepared Virginia's answer to the proposal, Jefferson was a natural for the committee. So far, he had greatly impressed other delegates. Though he almost never spoke aloud in Congress, his work on committees and behind the scenes proved invaluable. John Adams recalled, "Though a silent member in Congress, he was so prompt, frank, explicit, and decisive upon committees and in conversation—*not even Samuel Adams was more so*—that he soon seized upon my heart."[25]

His fellow committee members requested him to write the report. Imagine his thrill at receiving such a vote of confidence from the likes of Benjamin Franklin, the best-known and most-respected mind in colonial America. Jefferson's completed work, "Resolutions of Congress on Lord North's Conciliatory Proposal," contains many of the same arguments as his Virginia report on the same subject, but in places Jefferson sharpened his attack and coined some more memorable phrases. He wondered how the nation of Great Britain would react if faced with a situation similar to what the colonies faced: "With what patience would Britons have received articles of treaty from any power on earth when borne on the point of a bayonet by military plenipotentiaries?" And he claimed that the American colonies deserved to be treated on the same footing as other nations throughout the world: "If we are to contribute equally with the other parts of the empire, let us equally with them enjoy free commerce with the whole world."[26] Jefferson's response impressed Franklin and the other delegates. Congress passed the resolutions.

Jefferson left Philadelphia the first of August to return home for the next Virginia Convention. By now, there was no denying that the American colonies and Great Britain were headed for war. Those who had retained hope that relations between them would be resolved amicably could do so no more. Those who had avoided taking sides could do so no longer. Those supporting the cause of American freedom would stay and, if need be, fight it out. Those remaining loyal to the crown would return to England or relocate to Canada or the sugar colonies of the Caribbean. The summer of 1775 was a time of decision: stay or go.

Though his Annapolis bookshop and circulating library were thriving, William Aikman recognized that his loyalty to the crown would make doing business in Maryland increasingly difficult. Before the year's end, he boxed up his books, closed his doors, and relocated to Jamaica. Samuel Henley left Virginia to return to England, but he hoped to return soon: he left his fine library in Williamsburg. Jefferson's friend John Randolph—Peyton's brother—decided that he could not support the American cause, so he left for England that year, too. With Aikman's departure, Maryland lost a figure who was instrumental in promoting intellectual life in Annapolis. With Henley's departure, colonial Virginia lost its greatest literary scholar. With Randolph's departure, Virginia lost one of its finest bookmen. The looming war was taking its toll on the literary culture of early America.

The letter Jefferson wrote John Randolph on the occasion of his departure indicates the conflicting emotions he was feeling. Having agreed to purchase Randolph's violin, Jefferson provided instructions for its care and handling before conveying his regret at Randolph's departure: "I am sorry the situation of our country should render it not eligible to you to remain longer in it. I hope the returning wisdom of Great Britain will, e'er long, put an end to this unnatural contest. There may be people to whose tempers and dispositions Contention may be pleasing, and who therefore wish a continuance of confusion. But to me it is of all states, but one, the most horrid."[27]

This letter provides keen insight into Jefferson's attitude toward his personal and political responsibilities. "My first wish," he stated, "is a restoration of our just rights; my second a return of the happy period when, consistently with duty, I may withdraw myself totally from the public stage and pass the rest of my days in domestic ease and tranquillity, banishing every desire of ever afterwards hearing what passes in the world."

Jefferson encouraged Randolph to do what he could to inform the English of the justness of the American cause and the steadfastness of the

Americans to fight for their rights. He claimed that he would rather not have to fight for independence: "I am sincerely one of those, and would rather be in dependance on Great Britain, properly limited, than on any nation upon earth, or than on no nation. But I am one of those too who rather than submit to the right of legislating for us, assumed by the British parliament, and which late experience has shewn they will so cruelly exercise, would lend my hand to sink the whole island in the ocean."

He had one more thing to say to Randolph, but it did not fit in this impassioned letter. He put it in a postscript:

> P. S. My collection of classics and of books of parliamentary learning particularly is not so complete as I could wish. As you are going to the land of literature and of books you may be willing to dispose of some of yours here and replace them there in better editions. I should be willing to treat on this head with any body you may think proper to empower for that purpose.

This postscript shows Jefferson taking advantage of his friend's departure in order to augment his own library, but his motives were not entirely selfish. His comments reveal what Jefferson really regretted about the split between America and Great Britain. Wanting more "books of parliamentary learning," Jefferson recognized America's ultimate debt to English law. Regardless of their current differences, there was no denying that the laws and government of the colonies were based on English law and government and would remain so, even after independence.

Jefferson sincerely regretted that by splitting with England he would be parting with a place whose literary heritage meant so much to America. The violation of their rights at the hands of King and Parliament required the colonists to stand and fight, but in so doing they were taking sides against a place that, in terms of cultural influence, had meant the world to them. Sadly, Jefferson realized that he was making war against the Land of Literature and of Books.

CHAPTER 13

The Declaration of Independence

The third week of September 1775, Samuel Ward wrote George Washington an anxious letter from Philadelphia, asking him if he knew where Jefferson was. The Continental Congress had reconvened the preceding week, but Jefferson, who was emerging as one of its hardest working and distinguished delegates, had yet to show. Though Ward did not realize it, personal reasons were keeping Jefferson home beyond the date Congress was scheduled to reconvene: he had to bury his second daughter, Jane Randolph Jefferson. Born the first week of April the year before, the baby had received her name from both her grandmother and her aunt. Jane, Thomas's favorite sister, had died as a young woman; her namesake had not lived to see her second birthday. The child's bereaved father lingered at Monticello until the last week of September. Once he left home, he made excellent time and reached Philadelphia before the month's end.

Whatever grief he brought with him dissipated amidst the rigorous Congressional committee work he undertook upon his arrival. But the specter of death followed Jefferson to Philadelphia: before another month was out, Peyton Randolph died in an apoplectic fit, as a stroke was called back then. Randolph's sudden illness occurred during a dinner party at the country house of Philadelphia wine merchant Henry Hill. Within five hours yet "without a groan," Randolph passed away.[1]

His obesity made Randolph prone to such illness, yet his death still came as a shock. He was only in his mid-fifties. Francis Lightfoot Lee, the Virginia delegate elected to replace Richard Bland, became quite disturbed upon learning of Randolph's death the next morning. "I am so concern'd," he wrote, "that I cant think of politicks." Richard Henry Lee reported the news to General Washington, concluding, "Thus has American liberty lost a powerful Advocate, and human nature a sincere friend."[2] Jefferson took his death hard, too. Randolph had been a friend and mentor since the death of his father. Still, Jefferson would not let his grief impede the weighty tasks Congress faced that year.

Writing to England to inform John Randolph of his brother's death, Jefferson situated the sad news within an impassioned defense of American liberty. He spoke bluntly:

> Believe me Dear Sir there is not in the British empire a man who more cordially loves a Union with Gr. Britain than I do. But by the god that made me I will cease to exist before I yeild to a connection on such terms as the British parliament propose and in this I think I speak the sentiments of America. We want neither inducement nor power to declare and assert a separation. It is will alone which is wanting and that is growing apace under the fostering hand of our king. One bloody campaign will probably decide everlastingly our future course; I am sorry to find a bloody campaign is decided on.[3]

Perhaps Peyton Randolph's death that year was inevitable, but other American and British deaths could be prevented if the king would only acknowledge the inequity of his American policy. The chance of such an acknowledgment, Jefferson realized, was now almost impossibly remote.

The Continental Congress remained in session until mid-December, but Jefferson, who faced many administrative responsibilities, lingered in Philadelphia until the year's end before returning to Monticello. Here, a few months into the new year, death would claim the oldest but last surviving Jane Jefferson. Thomas's mother was only in her mid-fifties, too. The cause of her death is uncertain, but, like Randolph, she apparently died of apoplexy, passing away less than an hour after its onset.

It is difficult to say how much the unexpected deaths of these loved ones affected Jefferson or influenced the composition of the *Declaration of Independence*. People faced death frequently in the eighteenth century. At a time of high infant mortality and low life expectancy, few could go long without having to cope with the death of a loved one. If Jefferson's experience differed from that of his contemporaries, it was because his belief system differed: though most of his friends and neighbors could take comfort in their belief in an afterlife, Jefferson's religious skepticism deprived him of the solace such beliefs offered. Whatever paradise the future might hold would come through man's doing. Suffice it to say that the presence of death in Jefferson's life during the mid-1770s lent a personal sense of urgency to the cause of freedom.

In times of grief, Jefferson's books gave him great comfort. Those who have studied the intellectual background of the *Declaration of Independence* have catalogued in great detail the influence of important legal and political thinkers on the development of the thought processes that led to Jefferson's composition of the *Declaration*.[4] It is important to understand that grief prompted him to turn to works beyond legal theory and political philosophy. When Jefferson was in mourning, Locke, Kames, and Burlamaqui gave way to Sherlock, Young, and Ossian. The influence of poets, devotional writers, and other belletrists on the *Declaration* cannot be ignored.

Jefferson's surviving correspondence offers little insight regarding these personal tragedies, so it is difficult to discern precisely how this series of deaths affected him. His reticence in personal matters suggests a capacity to compartmentalize the private and public aspects of his life. Other documentary evidence confirms Jefferson's capacity to separate his intellect from his emotions, but he could never completely disassociate the two. Anyone who applies profound learning to speak with passionate intensity in the cause of freedom and country must let emotion and intellect run together, at least part of the time.

While Jefferson was spending the rest of the winter at Monticello, a new pamphlet appeared in Philadelphia, Thomas Paine's *Common Sense*. Thomas Nelson, Jr., who remained in Philadelphia after Jefferson had left, sent him a copy of Paine's rousing manifesto as soon as it was published. Many thousands of copies circulated throughout colonial America in the late winter and early spring of 1776. Contemporary testimony verifies the work's wide-ranging influence. John Penn, a delegate from North Carolina on his way to Philadelphia for the spring session of the Continental Congress, wrote that throughout his journey he heard nothing praised "but Common Sense and Independence. That was the cry throughout Virginia."[5]

Jefferson recognized Paine's influence and appreciated his literary style, but he downplayed the impact of *Common Sense* on Virginia readers. Recalling the work in *Notes on the State of Virginia*, he contradicted what John Penn said. Jefferson observed that though "copies of the pamphlet itself had got into a few hands" in the early months of 1776, the idea of American independence "had not been opened to the mass of the people in April, much less can it be said that they had made up their minds in its favor."[6] The account of *Common Sense* in *Notes on the State of Virginia* reflects less the reality of the situation and more Jefferson's rhetorical purpose. He wanted to depict Virginians as people who made up their minds independently. Despite what Jefferson may have said in

Notes on the State of Virginia, *Common Sense* shaped people's minds throughout Virginia and the other colonies. In a way no one before him had done, Paine took the current American political ideas and put them in a form colonists could read, appreciate, and understand.

Though he deliberately minimized the influence of Paine's work on the thinking of Virginians when he retold the events of 1776 in *Notes on the State of Virginia*, Jefferson did have a keen understanding of local sentiment around the time *Common Sense* appeared. That spring he devoted much effort surveying the opinions of his countrymen to get their thoughts on American independence. He told one correspondent that he "took great pains to enquire into the sentiments of the people on that head. In the upper counties I think I may safely say nine out of ten are for it."[7] In terms of American political history, Jefferson was among the first to survey public opinion and generate data from it.

Late that spring Jefferson, now thirty-three, returned to Philadelphia to resume his role as delegate to Congress. Soon after arriving, he wrote John Page, "I have been so long out of the political world that I am almost a new man in it." A new man: the phrase anticipates the famous definition of an American that Jefferson's friend and correspondent, J. Hector St. John de Crèvecoeur, would make in *Letters from an American Farmer*: "The American is a new man, who acts upon new principles; he must therefore entertain new ideas and form new opinions."[8] Jefferson's use of the phrase to describe himself on the eve of independence shows how in tune he was with the popular sentiments. Approaching the birth of a new nation, he, too, had become a new man and, therefore, was a fit representative to speak for it.

Upon his return to Philadelphia, Jefferson decided to take new lodgings. He vacated the home of cabinetmaker Benjamin Randolph and found a home several blocks outside the city center. Anticipating another hot summer in Philadelphia, he wanted to escape the city congestion. Explaining his decision, he wrote, "I think, as the excessive heats of the city are coming on fast, to endeavor to get lodgings in the skirts of the town where I may have the benefit of a freely circulating air."[9] His new lodgings, the middle floor of a three-story brick house at the corner of Seventh and Market Streets, consisted of a furnished parlor and bedroom.

Using a portable, custom-made writing desk of his own design, Jefferson habitually wrote in the parlor. Benjamin Randolph had built the writing desk according to Jefferson's specifications. "Plain, neat, convenient, and, taking no more room on the writing table than a moderate 4to. volume," as Jefferson described it, the desk was good for any kind of writing.[10] This house and this desk would become famous for the

Revolutionary document Jefferson would draft here this hot Philadelphia summer.

The *Declaration of Independence* is Jefferson's best known piece of writing, but he wrote much else in the summer of 1776. Clearly recognizing the significance of the Congressional debates leading to the *Declaration*, he kept meticulous notes of the events that transpired. In fact, his "Notes of Proceedings in the Continental Congress" forms the most thorough account of the proceedings known. Jefferson's notes are even more detailed than John Adams's diary.

The first Friday in June, Richard Henry Lee, voicing instructions from the Virginia Convention, moved to declare that "these United Colonies are, and of right ought to be, free and independent States."[11] The motion absolved Americans from allegiance to the British crown, severed any and all political connections between the American states and Great Britain, provided measures for obtaining assistance from foreign powers, and proposed a confederation uniting the states.

When debate on this motion began the following Monday, those against it argued that it was too rash. Delegates from the middle colonies hesitated to break with Great Britain completely. Foreseeing a time when they might be willing to do so, they argued that unless and until all the American colonies could come together as a whole, the fight for independence would be doomed.

Led by John Adams and the Virginians, those in favor of independence attempted to persuade the reluctant delegates from the other colonies by arguing that officially declaring independence would confirm a preexisting fact. The outbreak of hostilities on the part of the British the previous year had effectively cut the last remaining ties with the colonies. The American people deserved independence, and they looked to the Continental Congress to lead the way. Adams and others effectively refuted the arguments of reluctant Congressional delegates but did not completely convince everyone.

The decision was forestalled until the beginning of July. Should Congress declare independence at that time, it would want to proceed as quickly as possible. To that end, it would be convenient to have a written instrument in place. Congress appointed a committee to draft this document. Besides Adams, Franklin, and Jefferson, the Committee of Five, as it has become known, also included Robert Livingston and Roger Sherman. The committee assigned Jefferson to draft the formal document declaring independence from Great Britain. He proudly accepted the task.

As Jefferson understood it, his purpose in drafting the *Declaration* was not to advance new ideas but to codify the main ideas toward liberty and freedom his fellow Americans had already accepted. The *Declaration* was intended as a purposeful political document, not as an original philosophical or legal treatise on the ideas of natural law and natural rights. Recalling his composition of the *Declaration* after the lapse of several decades, Jefferson wrote, "Neither aiming at originality of principle or sentiment, nor yet copied from any particular and previous writing, it was intended to be an expression of the American mind, and to give to that expression the proper tone and spirit called for by the occasion. All its authority rests then on the harmonizing sentiments of the day, whether expressed in conversation, in letters, printed essays, or in the elementary books of public right, as Aristotle, Cicero, Locke, Sidney, etc."[12]

In another late reminiscence, Jefferson elaborated the relationship between his extensive reading and the composition of the *Declaration*: "Whether I had gathered my ideas from reading or reflection I do not know. I know only that I turned to neither book or pamphlet while writing it. I did not consider it as any part of my charge to invent new ideas altogether, and to offer no sentiment which had ever been expressed before."[13] The comment rings true. Though parts of the *Declaration* echo passages in such works as John Locke's *Two Treatises of Government* and Algernon Sidney's *Discourses Concerning Government*, Jefferson had already read and synthesized these and many similar works before he sat down in the second-floor parlor of his Philadelphia apartment to write the *Declaration*.

Many know the opening paragraph of the *Declaration of Independence* by heart:

> When in the Course of human events, it becomes necessary for one people to dissolve the political bands which have connected them with another, and to assume among the powers of the earth, the separate and equal station to which the Laws of Nature and of Nature's God entitle them, a decent respect to the opinions of mankind requires that they should declare the causes which impel them to the separation.[14]

This paragraph makes no mention of either North America or Great Britain. Rather, it speaks in general terms and situates its purpose within the history of mankind. The phrase "political bands," though somewhat unusual, was not unheard of. Evidence indicates that the phrase was part of the contemporary American parlance. Dr. James MacClurg, one of Jefferson's Virginia friends, for example, used the phrase to refer to the artificial ties that joined men together by "prospect of advantage, or compelled by force."[15]

Jefferson's words posit a cyclical view of history. Laws established for the common good become meaningless when common law diverges from natural law, at which time legal ties must be severed in order to reassert natural law. The process of breaking these political bands is so natural and necessary that their severing need not even be announced. What makes an announcement necessary is the idea of civility. As Jefferson had learned reading such works as Adam Ferguson's *Essay on the History of Civil Society*, the principles of civility required that the dissolution of political ties be properly communicated to the world.

Following this opening paragraph comes the most memorable sentence Jefferson ever wrote and, arguably, the finest articulation of the idea of natural rights ever written. It took much hard work to get the paragraph just right.[16] In his rough draft, he wrote:

> We hold these truths to be sacred and undeniable; that all men are created equal and independent, that from that equal creation they derive rights inherent and inalienable, among which are the preservation of life, and liberty, and the pursuit of happiness....

Though he had minimized the use of conjoined pairs of words when commonplacing legal theory, Jefferson now made use of the structure for rhetorical effect. The conjoined pairs slow the pace of the sentence and let him build his argument gradually. When he returned to revise the passage, he realized he had overdone the word pairs. He subsequently eliminated the first two pairs. He changed the phrase, "equal and independent" to "equal." That revision was simple enough. Revising the first pair was more difficult.

His original phrase, "sacred and undeniable," accomplished much. Besides contributing to the document's deliberate pace, the phrase suggested that the truths he was about to enumerate were sanctioned by God. Out of character for Jefferson, the use of the word "sacred" may have been intended to placate more religious members of the Continental Congress. Actually, the word adds ambiguity to the sentence: "sacred" also had a secular connotation, as his use of it elsewhere reveals. Refuting Benjamin Rush's suggestion that some American place names ought to be changed, Jefferson said that "a name when given should be deemed a sacred property."[17] His use of the word "sacred" here simply means unalterable; it has no religious connotation. Jefferson use of the word this early in his draft of the *Declaration of Independence* anticipates his reuse of it in the last sentence of the *Declaration*, in which the delegates to the Continental Congress, representing the United States as a whole, pledge their "sacred honour." Here again the word "sacred" means unalterable, yet it also implies a religious connotation. Its repetition in the final sentence effectively ties together the introduction and conclusion.

Ultimately, Jefferson canceled "sacred and undeniable" in favor of "self-evident." The change may have been suggested by Benjamin Franklin, who found the word "sacred" inappropriate.[18] Franklin did recognize the secular connotation of the word. He had used it with this meaning himself. Reading a British pamphleteer's suggestion that colonial charters did not matter very much, Franklin wrote, "The Charters are sacred. Violate them, and then the present Bond of Union (the Kingly Power over us) will be broken."[19] If the revision was Franklin's, then perhaps he disliked Jefferson's deliberate ambiguity. Regardless, "sacred and undeniable" was out and "self-evident" was in.

In the document submitted to Congress, "inherent and inalienable" remained the only conjoined word pair left in this phrase, yet Congress would not allow it to remain. It changed the phrase "inherent and un-alienable rights" to "certain inalienable rights." Jefferson disliked the change. The two words he used had long been linked together in the political discourse as a way of characterizing the most basic natural rights. During the previous decade, for example, the phrase "inherent and un-alienable" frequently recurred in the protests against the Stamp Act to reassert the rights of the colonists. A popular belletristic work may have given these words their greatest currency: Lord Lyttelton's *Dialogues of the Dead*.

In one of Lyttleton's series of imaginative conversations between important historical figures, Marcus Aurelius explains to Servius Tullius that Augustus had no legal authority to change the government the way he had, but once it was changed, the government had succeeded to Marcus Aurelius "by a *lawful* and *established* Rule of Succession."

"Can a Length of *Establishment* make Despotism *lawful*?" asks Servius Tullius. "Is not Liberty an inherent, inalienable Right of Mankind?"

"They have an inherent Right to be governed by Laws, not by arbitrary Will," Marcus Aurelius responds. "But Forms of Government may, and must, be occasionally changed, with the consent of the People."[20]

Lord Lyttelton's *Dialogues of the Dead* not only helped popularize the "inherent/inalienable" word pair, but also stressed the validity of over-throwing arbitrary governments in favor of democracy.

Beyond its resonance in both the political and literary discourse, Jefferson's use of this pair of words propels his ideas forward. Situating the phrase precisely where he does, Jefferson gave his sentence additional force. It builds strength as it continues and, in so doing, verbally reinforces the fundamental nature of the truths it delineates. As Jefferson revised the sentence, the concepts articulated seem as sure as one, two, three: "equal," "inherent and unalienable," "Life, Liberty and the pursuit of Happiness."

His original text may be stylistically more effective than the one that appears in the final version of the *Declaration of Independence*. Either way, the sentence offers a moving encapsulation of the idea of natural rights. As adopted by Congress, the passage reads:

> We hold these truths to be self-evident, that all men are created equal, that they are endowed by their Creator with certain unalienable Rights, that among these are Life, Liberty and the pursuit of Happiness.

All of the hundreds of pages and countless hours Jefferson spent reading about natural law and natural rights came down to this one statement. Its simplicity belies the extraordinary amount of intellectual work it took to achieve, but in terms of its straightforwardness and verbal economy, the statement is absolutely appropriate to the ideas it conveys.

This sentence also establishes a grammatical pattern for the remainder of the *Declaration of Independence*. Each beginning with the word "that," the three clauses elaborating the self-evident truths are similarly constructed and anticipate a pattern of repetition that recurs with variation throughout the document. Consider the following set of clauses:

> that to secure these rights, Governments are instituted among Men, deriving their just powers from the consent of the governed, That whenever any Form of Government becomes destructive of these ends, it is the Right of the People to alter or to abolish it, and to institute new Government, laying its foundation on such principles and organizing its powers in such form, as to them shall seem most likely to effect their Safety and Happiness.

As a rhetorical technique, such patterns of repetition are indebted to a number of sources from Cicero's orations to Ossian's prose poems to Christ's "Sermon on the Mount." As an aesthetic device, repetition helps unify the work and offers a way of building intensity.

Political bands between colony and nation, Jefferson explained, should not be broken without just cause, but with just cause they must be broken. Given their treatment at the hands of the British government, the American colonists had sufficient reason to declare themselves independent: "The history of the present King of Great Britain is a history of repeated injuries and usurpations, all having in direct object the establishment of an absolute Tyranny over these States. To prove this, let Facts be submitted to a candid world."

Though Jefferson hinted that he would recount the history to which he alludes, what follows is not a history at all but rather a series of statements using the subject pronoun "he" to refer to King George III and written in the present perfect, a verb tense suggesting that the injuries of the past are continuing into the present. The king himself becomes the primary target of Jefferson's verbal attack in this part of the *Declaration*, which Samuel Adams called the "Catalogue of Crimes."[21] Directing his argument toward King George III, Jefferson established a pattern that would recur in the history of American conflict: he personalized the enemy and directed his vituperation toward an individual leader rather than an entire nation.

Many of these charges contain distinct rhetorical strategies designed to accomplish a variety of effects. The fifth, for example, reads: "He has dissolved Representative Houses repeatedly, for opposing with manly firmness his invasions on the rights of the people." Emphasizing the manliness of the colonial legislators and opposing their actions to the British crown, Jefferson figuratively emasculates the King, implying that his behavior had left Americans "exposed to all the dangers of invasion from without and convulsions within."

Jefferson's phrase "manly firmness" is a literary allusion and, as such, functions as a kind of shorthand for the ideas expressed in the work he was alluding to. The phrase echoes the well-respected eighteenth-century British poet James Thomson, whose verse had garnered a huge popular following in Great Britain and America, especially his long contemplative poem *The Seasons*. Upon first reading this poem, Benjamin Franklin, for one, was moved to tears. Describing the effect Thomson's great poem had upon him, Franklin wrote, "I had read no Poetry for several years, and almost lost the Relish for it, till I met with his *Seasons*. That charming Poet has brought more Tears of Pleasure into my Eyes than all I ever read before. I wish it were in my Power to return him any Part of the Joy he has given me."[22] Jefferson, too, was taken by *The Seasons*. While a young man, he commonplaced several lines from the poem. In fact, his extracts from Thomson include the single lengthiest verse quotation in his entire commonplace book.[23]

As he matured, Jefferson came to prefer Thomson's tragedies, which he ranked above *The Seasons*. In his great library at Monticello, he had the four-volume *Works of James Thomson*. Though this edition begins with *The Seasons* and ends with the poet's dramatic works, Jefferson shelved it among other tragedies, not among the poetry. Specifically, the phrase "manly firmness" derives from Thomson's most successful tragedy, *Tancred and Sigismunda*. Jefferson encountered an excerpt from this play in *The Beauties of the English Stage*, a work from which he excerpted many other passages in his commonplace book. Like the other quotations from *The Beauties of the English Stage*, the passage from *Tancred and Sigismunda* appears under a specific subject heading: it is used to illustrate prudence.

Tancred and Sigismunda tells the story of the young king of Sicily who is thwarted in his love for Sigismunda by her father, Siffredi. Acting in the interests of peace, Siffredi wishes his daughter to marry Osmond, the lord high constable, instead of Tancred. The phrase "manly firmness" occurs in a speech Siffredi makes to Osmond, a speech that emphasizes the importance of avoiding war as long as liberty can be maintained:

> Let us be stedfast in the Right; but let us
> Act with cool Prudence, and with manly Temper,
> As well as manly Firmness. True, I own,
> Th' Indignities you suffer are so high,
> As might even justify what now you threaten.
> But if, my Lord, we can prevent the Woes
> The cruel Horrors of intestine War,
> Yet hold untouch'd our Liberties and Laws;
> O let us, rais'd above the turbid Sphere
> Of little selfish Passions, nobly do it!
> Nor to our hot intemperate Pride pour out
> A dire Libation of *Sicilian* Blood.
> 'Tis Godlike Magnanimity, to keep,
> When most provok'd, our Reason calm and clear,
> And execute her Will, from a strong Sense
> Of what is right, without the vulgar Aid
> Of Heat and Passion, which, tho' honest, bear us
> Often too far.

Applying the phrase "manly firmness" to describe the behavior and attitude of the American colonists in the face of the king's injustice, Jefferson implies all of the positive qualities Thomson associated with it: prudence, good judgment, a belief in the importance of liberty, resistance to war unless absolutely necessary, the value of controlling the passions and maintaining reason, and the importance of upholding what is right.

Jefferson was not the only one to recognize the relevance of Thomson's words to the colonial cause. The phrase had already entered the Revolutionary discourse. One of Jefferson's Virginia supporters had used it two years earlier in the preface he wrote to *A Summary View of the Rights of British America* in order to characterize the rhetorical stance Jefferson took in this work. Furthermore, John Trumbull, one of a group of Revolutionary poets known as the Connecticut Wits, used the phrase in *An Elegy for the Times*, a poem chronicling the plight of Boston in the face of the Port Bill. Abandoning any hope of remedying the injustice through official recourse, the colonists, Trumbull stressed, had to rely on their own strength:

> Ours be the manly firmness of the sage,
>   From shameless foes ungrateful wrongs to bear;
> Alike removed from baseness and from rage,
>   The flames of faction and the chills of fear.

Trumbull emphasized the rational and philosophical aspects of manly firmness, the ability to maintain a sense of reason in the face of injustice. Jefferson's use of the phrase in the *Declaration of Independence* embodies similar concepts.

With the thirteenth and lengthiest indictment of the king, Jefferson varied his structure. He introduced a list of Acts approved by Parliament that contradicted laws passed by the colonial legislators. Again, he used repetition as a rhetorical strategy. Each of the nine Acts is structured as a prepositional phrase beginning with the word "for." The emphasis Jefferson placed on these tends to disappear in modern editions of the *Declaration*, but in the first printing, which Jefferson supervised, each instance of the word appears with an initial capital letter. The remaining two letters of the word appear in small capitals. Furthermore, each "FOR" begins a new line of the printed document and thus leaves considerable white space to the right of the page, further emphasizing and distinguishing each Act named. Take the third and fourth Acts, for example. They appear as follows:

FOR cutting off our Trade with all parts of the world:
FOR imposing Taxes on us without our Consent.

The amount of information these charges provide is remarkably spare given the amount of ink Jefferson and other American political writers had already used to elaborate these complaints. No more justification was necessary. Speaking for the new nation, Jefferson was no longer making an argument but stating facts, the facts that had led to a momentous decision.

The next set of paragraphs shows how British actions had escalated from hurtful legislation to actual violence:

> He has abdicated Government here, by declaring us out of his Protection and waging War against us.
> He has plundered our seas, ravaged our Coasts, burnt our towns, and destroyed the Lives of our people.

Parallels within parallels: Jefferson incorporates within the second sentence of this passage a series of four phrases that emphasize and reinforce the violence of the British. Besides trepanning colonial American sailors and impressing them into the Royal Navy, the King was also attempting to turn sympathetic souls against the American colonists: "He has excited domestic insurrections amongst us, and has endeavoured to bring on the inhabitants of our frontiers, the merciless Indian Savages, whose known rule of warfare, is an undistinguished destruction of all ages, sexes and conditions." Read out of context, Jefferson's depiction of the Native Americans makes them out to be ruthless and bloody savages. Read in light of how he elevated Chief Logan to the level of noble savage in the blank leaves of his *Virginia Almanack*, Jefferson's denigration of the Indian in the *Declaration* becomes an obvious rhetorical strategy. Depicting the Native American in the *Declaration of Independence*, Jefferson was well aware of his use of hyperbole and stereotype but found both useful rhetorical strategies nonetheless.

Retaining the present perfect tense, Jefferson switched from making the king his subject to making himself and his fellow colonists his subject: "In every stage of these Oppressions We have Petitioned for Redress in the most humble terms: Our repeated Petitions have been answered only by repeated injury." British violence, in turn, has been answered with humble colonial perseverance.

In conclusion, Jefferson wrote:

> We therefore the representatives of the United States of America in General Congress assembled do, in the name and by authority of the good people of these states reject and renounce all allegiance and subjection to the kings of Great Britain and all others who may hereafter claim by, through, or under them; we utterly dissolve and break off all political connection which may have heretofore subsisted between us

and the people or parliament of Great Britain; and finally we do assert and declare these colonies to be free and independant states, and that as free and independant states they shall hereafter have power to levy war, conclude peace, contract alliances, establish commerce, and to do all other acts and things which independent states may of right do. And for the support of this declaration we mutually pledge to each other our lives, our fortunes, and our sacred honor.[24]

After composing the *Declaration of Independence*, Jefferson submitted the document to the committee, which made several minor revisions, none affecting its overall impact. On Friday, June 28, the Committee of Five presented the draft to Congress. Debate on it was delayed until Monday, July 1, which many delegates anticipated as a great day. John Penn wrote, "The first day of July will be made remarkable; then the question relative to Independence will be ajitated and there is no doubt but a total separation from Britain will take place."[25]

Benjamin Franklin was not the only Congressional delegate who was early to rise the morning of July 1. John Adams spent the first part of the day trying to catch up his correspondence, but he could scarcely contain his excitement. He wrote Archibald Bulloch: "This morning is assigned for the greatest Debate of all. A Declaration that these Colonies are free and independent states, has been reported by a Committee appointed some weeks ago for that Purpose, and this day or Tomorrow is to determine its Fate. May Heaven prosper the new born Republic—and make it more glorious than any former Republics have been!"

Jefferson, too, was out and about the morning of July 1: he had chosen this day to begin the daily weather log he would maintain the rest of his life. In none of his surviving notebooks does Jefferson say why he chose to start recording weather data when he did. Governor Fauquier had shown him the value and method of keeping accurate weather records more than a decade earlier, but so far Jefferson had refrained from regularly keeping his own. Seen in retrospect, Jefferson's weather log expresses in a different way the same kind of enthusiasm Adams conveyed in his letter to Bulloch: it implicitly acknowledges the birth of a new republic by initiating a detailed written record of its existence literally from Day One. The United States of America would be a nation based on the principles of rational thought, and its history could and would be recorded scientifically.

As Jefferson observed, the temperature at nine o'clock in the morning was already 81 1/2 degrees Fahrenheit.[26] July 1 promised to be a hot day. Congress endured the oppressive heat over its course as the debates continued nonstop for nine grueling hours. But the day ended before a final decision regarding independence was made.

The next day Congress debated Jefferson's draft of the *Declaration of Independence*. New Hampshire delegate Josiah Bartlett wrote a correspondent that "the Declaration before Congress is, I think, a pretty good one. I hope it will not be spoiled by canvassing in Congress."[27] By no means did Congress spoil Jefferson's original draft, but they did not accept it outright. Almost every sentence came under discussion. Jefferson found the process of listening to his finely crafted words being debated, revised, or deleted to be excruciating. Sitting next to him during these proceedings was Benjamin Franklin, who shrewdly recognized the younger man's discomfort and offered a story to make him feel more at ease:

> I have made it a rule, [said Franklin to Jefferson,] whenever in my power, to avoid becoming the draughtsman of papers to be reviewed by a public body. I took my lesson from an incident which I will relate to you. When I was a journeyman printer, one of my companions, an apprentice Hatter, having served out his time, was about to open shop for himself, his first concern was to have a handsome signboard, with a proper inscription. He composed it in these words: *John Thompson, Hatter, makes and sells hats for ready money*, with a figure of a hat subjoined. But he thought he would submit it to his friends for their amendments. The first he shewed it to thought the word *Hatter* tautologous, because followed by the words, *makes hats*, which shew he was a *Hatter*. It was struck out. The next observed that the word *makes* might as well be omitted, because his customers would not care who made the hats. If good and to their mind, they would buy by whomsoever made. He struck it out. A third said he thought the words *for ready money*, were useless as it was not the custom of the place to sell on credit. Every one who purchased expected to pay. They were parted with, and the inscription now stood, *John Thompson sells hats*. *Sells hats!* says his next friend? "Why nobody will expect you to give them away. What then is the use of that word?" It was stricken out, and *hats* followed it,—the rather as there was one painted on the board. So his inscription was reduced ultimately to *John Thompson* with the figure of a hat subjoined.[28]

Franklin's anecdote must have had its intended effect. Jefferson remembered it well and continued to repeat it for many years afterward.

Jefferson regretted the changes Congress made to his version of the *Declaration of Independence* and maintained the superiority of his original text. Sending a copy of the *Declaration* to Richard Henry Lee shortly after Congress approved it, Jefferson also included a copy of his original version, telling him, "You will judge whether it is the better or worse for the Critics."[29]

Writing his autobiography in the last decade of his life, Jefferson used the work as a vehicle to reassert his original text of the *Declaration*. He also included the final text of the document as approved by Congress and devised a way to present both simultaneously. In the autobiography, he introduced the text with the following explanation: "As the sentiments of men are known not only by what they receive, but what they reject also, I will state the form of the declaration as originally reported. The parts struck out by Congress shall be distinguished by a black line drawn under them; and those inserted by them shall be placed in the margin or in a concurrent column."[30]

Coming to the last two paragraphs of the document, Jefferson found it impossible to maintain his stated method. The differences between the documents were too great. Consequently, he supplied the last two paragraphs of both versions in parallel columns. One addition made by Congress is obvious. Jefferson's original did not mention "a firm reliance of the protection of divine providence." This insertion may have upset him the most. Founding the United States of America on principles of reason, he saw no need to conclude the *Declaration of Independence* with reference to religion.

Congress tentatively approved the *Declaration of Independence* on Tuesday, July 2. On Thursday, July 4, it approved the work with its final changes and ordered the document printed. It would not actually be signed until August 2. By this time, Pennsylvania had elected a new slate of delegates to the Continental Congress, which included Benjamin Rush. Yet another man of science to join the ranks of Revolutionary patriots, Rush, an Edinburgh-trained physician, was currently serving as Professor of Chemistry at the College of Philadelphia and had already established himself as a leader in the field with *A Syllabus of a Course of Lectures in Chemistry*, the first American textbook on the subject.[31] He and Jefferson became lifelong friends.

Rush's reminiscence of the event brings alive the experience within the Continental Congress as he and his fellow delegates affixed their names to the *Declaration of Independence*. He recalled the "pensive and awful silence which pervaded the house" as one after another was called to the table of the President of Congress to sign what many believed to be "our own death warrants."[32] The gloom was broken by a remark Benjamin Harrison made to Elbridge Gerry: "I shall have a great advantage over you, Mr. Gerry," the tall, corpulent Harrison said to the slender delegate from Massachusetts, "when we are all hung for what we are now doing. From the size and weight of my body I shall die in a few minutes, but from the lightness of your body you will dance in the air an hour or two before you are dead."

"This speech procured a transient smile," Rush recalled, "but it was soon succeeded by the solemnity with which the whole business was conducted." Several versions of this anecdote survive, and all closely coincide, including the story told by Jefferson himself. Harrison's remark captured a feeling of the moment, the knowledge among the signers that by affixing their names to the *Declaration of Independence* they were putting their lives on the line. Should American independence fail, all would be convicted of treason. Dark humor had been a part of early American culture since the days of Captain John Smith. Among the early colonists, it offered a way to cope with the dangers and privations of the American wilderness. Now, dark humor offered a way to cope with the life-threatening danger that comes when people stand up for what they believe.

Though Jefferson downplayed the originality of the ideas expressed in the *Declaration of Independence*, no other document written before, or since, has synthesized and articulated so well or so succinctly the ideas of natural law and natural right. In addition, the *Declaration of Independence* is one of the greatest statements of defiance ever written. Speaking for the American people, Jefferson let the world know that no longer could they withstand the abuses they were suffering at the hands of the British government. They could not and they would not.

On a stage erected outside the State House at noon on Monday, July 8, the *Declaration of Independence* was proclaimed before a huge crowd. John Nixon read the document to the people, who "declared their approbation by three repeated Huzzas." Despite the scarcity of gunpowder, the soldiers raised their muskets to sound the "Feu de Joy."[33] Church bells rang throughout the day and into the night. The King's arms were pulled down from both the State House and the Court House and burned in one of the many bonfires set throughout the city that evening. The skies were clear as darkness fell. The stars shone and the church bells rang. A new nation was born.

CHAPTER 14

The Book Culture of Philadelphia and Williamsburg, Contrasted

Living in Philadelphia while serving as a delegate to the Continental Congress, Jefferson immersed himself in the city's literary culture. His Congressional colleagues included many of the finest readers and writers in America. Jefferson expanded his circle of acquaintances to include local booksellers and publishers, too. Seldom did he let a week go by without visiting one Philadelphia bookshop or another and making substantial purchases. His July 1776 accounts, combined with other surviving evidence, show him buying some pamphlets on the sixth and some more on the twelfth. He purchased a book on the fifteenth, a pamphlet on the twenty-sixth, more pamphlets on the twenty-ninth, and yet another pamphlet on the thirtieth.[1] His accounts remain silent as to the titles of the books and pamphlets he purchased and the names of the booksellers he patronized, but other evidence can help identify some of the works Jefferson acquired and some of the shops he visited during his time in Philadelphia. He appears to have been best acquainted with three particular booksellers: Robert Bell, Robert Aitken, and John Dunlap. All exerted an influence on him that summer and would remain important contacts in the years to come.

The three booksellers had established themselves in Philadelphia since Jefferson first visited the city ten years earlier. Born in Scotland and apprenticed in England, Robert Bell rose to prominence in Ireland, where he developed a reputation as both bookseller and auctioneer and where he began to reprint works other publishers had already popularized. In the world of books, Dublin had long been known as the place where London imprints were pirated and cheaply reprinted. Bell perpetuated and reinforced the city's reputation as a center for cheap pirated editions, but he had even more audacity than his peers: he claimed the right to reprint whatever books he wished regardless of their place of origin. To that end, he reissued inexpensive reprints of works his Dublin competitors had issued, an endeavor that ultimately caused them to run him out of town.[2]

Finding himself *persona non grata* in Dublin, Bell came to the New World in the late 1760s to get a fresh start. Upon settling in Philadelphia, he opened a bookshop adjacent to St. Paul's Church on Third Street, where the old Union Library used to be. The place had been vacated recently after the Library Company of Philadelphia had absorbed the Union Library. Before long, Bell developed a fine reputation among Philadelphians as bookseller, publisher, and auctioneer. Innovative and aggressive in his marketing, he displayed his flamboyant character both in person and in his advertising copy. He sometimes styled himself "Provedore to the Sentimentalists," and other times used even more outrageous epithets to characterize himself in his role as bookseller. For example, prefaced to a list of sale books appended to his edition of Josiah Tucker's *True Interest of Britain, Set Forth in Regard to the Colonies*—one of the pamphlets Jefferson added to his personal bookshelf in 1776—Bell included a brief note in which he claimed to be "Provedore to the Voluntiers of that Respectable Society, who practically know, that food for the mind, is equivalent to money." Like Jefferson, Bell understood that true bibliophiles prefer books over money.

Bell became best known as an auctioneer, and many contemporary book-buyers came under the sway of what he called his "magic mallet." Printer William McCulloch left the most amusing account of his technique as an auctioneer. Standing before a crowd of anxious book-buyers, Bell "was full of drollery, and many, going to his auction for the merriment, would buy a book from good humour. It was as good as a play to attend his sales at auction. There were few authors of whom he could not tell some anecdote, which would get the audience in a roar. He sometimes had a can of beer aside him, and would drink comical healths. His buffoonery was diversified and without limit."[3]

His auctioneering eventually got him into trouble. Before long, unlicensed book auctions were outlawed in Philadelphia, and the licensing authorities repeatedly denied Bell's application. Publishing a pamphlet in his own defense, he included some tongue-in-cheek admonitory lines of verse he attributed to "Momus":

> PRAY stop, Master Bell, with your selling of Books,
> Your smart witty Sayings, and cunning arch Looks:
> By Auction I mean—'tis a shocking Offence

To sell Wit, or Humour, or e'en common Sense,
Unsanction'd by Law, on any Pretence:
Read the Act of Assembly by Mood, and by Tense,
There's none can vend Knowledge without A Lie-cence.[4]

These lines, of course, refer to Thomas Paine's *Common Sense*, which Bell had published in Philadelphia in early 1776, the imprint that established his renown throughout North America and, incidentally, secured his fortune.

Jefferson had patronized Bell as early as the previous summer, when he subscribed to his three-volume reprint of James Burgh's *Political Disquisitions*, a critical study of English politics and society that significantly influenced the development of American thought. Burgh's solid moral foundation, rationalism, good sense, practicality, and refined literary style found many welcome readers in the New World. Intermittently, Burgh was capable of succinct nuggets of wisdom. Contemporary American readers saw much relevance in his poignant comments on liberty and freedom.

Political Disquisitions was the latest of several major reprints Bell had undertaken in Philadelphia. These ambitious publishing endeavors had begun with a three-volume edition of William Robertson's *History of the Reign of Charles V* and continued with a four-volume edition of William Blackstone's *Commentaries on the Laws of England*. With these reprints, Bell followed the usual practice of the Dublin reprinters: by reducing the size of a book's format as well as its type, he enabled himself to retail the same titles at lower prices than the imported London editions could be had.

"The more Books are sold, the more will be sold," Bell believed. For proof, he invoked the experience of his customers and competitors, calling this idea "an established Truth well known to every liberal Reader, and to every Bookseller of Experience; For the Sale of one BOOK propagateth the Sale of another, with as much certainty as the Possession of one Guinea helpeth to the Possession of another."[5] Jefferson's experience verifies Bell's theory. His accounts show that he patronized Bell's shop frequently when he was in Philadelphia. Though his surviving correspondence makes little mention of Bell, the attitude Jefferson held regarding inexpensive reprint editions shows that the two were in complete accord and suggests Bell's influence. When a book Jefferson wanted was published in London, he was often content to wait until the Dublin edition appeared. His choice of imprints was partly a matter of economy, but it was also a matter of personal taste. He nearly always preferred smaller format books; since the Dublin publishers cut costs by reducing format size, he liked the Dublin editions for their convenience as well as their price.

In Paris some years later, Jefferson helped Laurent Noel Pissot, a publisher who may be considered the French equivalent of Robert Bell, find an American market for his English reprints. Recommending Pissot to Francis Hopkinson, Jefferson explained, "A printer here has begun to print the most remarkable of the English authors, as that can be done here much cheaper than in England or even Ireland. He supposes America could take off a considerable number of copies, and has therefore applied to me to find a sure correspondent for him."[6] By the time Jefferson went to Paris, he clearly understood the value of inexpensive reprints, knowledge his contact with Robert Bell had fostered.

While in Philadelphia, Jefferson also frequented the bookshop of Robert Aitken, located on the east side of Front Street nearly opposite the London Coffee House. Having emigrated from Scotland, Aitken established his Philadelphia shop in 1771, and it soon developed a reputation as the city's "largest and most valuable bookstore." Aitken's approach to the book business varied significantly from Bell's and thus offered customers a much different shopping experience. Whereas Bell concentrated on his own publications, Aitken stocked a wide range of imported books. Aitken also emphasized the elegance of books as material objects. Among the printers in Philadelphia, Aitken reputedly had the finest taste. He was an expert bookbinder, too. Both documentary evidence and surviving examples of Aitken's craftsmanship attest to his taste and his skill. The ever-observant William McCulloch stated, "There was no better finished binding ever done than some of the books executed in his shop."[7] Jefferson purchased a number of books from Aitken in 1776, and Aitken, as he did with so many of his customers, earned his respect and his continued patronage.

Printer and publisher John Dunlap had established his own printing house on the south side of Jersey Market. In practical terms, the location of Dunlap's shop meant that Jefferson could stop there as he walked between Bell's shop and Aitken's. Five years earlier, Dunlap had begun publishing the weekly *Pennsylvania Packet, or General Advertiser*. He came to know Jefferson as a writer before meeting him in person: the previous year Dunlap had issued the Philadelphia edition of *A Summary View of the Rights of British America*. He thus helped give that work greater currency outside Virginia and establish Jefferson's reputation as both writer and thinker. The care with which Dunlap treated this pamphlet suggests that he recognized the importance of the ideas it contained.

Dunlap's edition of *Summary View*, which surpassed the Williamsburg edition in terms of elegance, offers an example of early American printing at its finest. The epigraph from Cicero was printed in all Roman capitals, which Dunlap followed with an English translation printed in italics. The preface, too, appears in italics, with sufficiently generous spacing to make its text fill an entire page. The stately appearance of the preface reinforces the gravity of the ideas it introduces.

Other Congressional delegates recognized Dunlap's keen eye for the visual appearance of the printed page, and in the summer of 1776, Congress chose him to print the *Declaration of Independence*. Presumably, Jefferson spent much time in Dunlap's shop proofreading the *Declaration* before it was issued. A few years later, Jefferson would take advantage of their friendship to their mutual benefit by helping Dunlap establish a partner of his in a Richmond printing venture.[8]

Though Jefferson's accounts for 1776 show him buying several items from Dunlap, not all were for himself. He enjoyed procuring books for friends and neighbors whenever he could. Richard Henry Lee, who had returned to Virginia after presenting his famous motion for American independence, missed the opportunities for book-buying Philadelphia had to offer and wrote Jefferson to ask for a copy of Richard Price's *Observations of the Nature of Civil Liberty*, the work in which Price applied his moral philosophy to the political problems the American colonies faced. Price's pamphlet lent moral support to the colonial cause and earned the respect and friendship of many American leaders.[9] Jefferson acquired a copy of the work for himself, but, always happy for an excuse to return to the bookshop, he went back to Dunlap's, bought another copy of Price's pamphlet, and dispatched it to Lee. Jefferson's book-buying efforts helped fill his friends' bookshelves as well as his own.

In addition to the retail bookshops he patronized, Jefferson also had access to the Library Company of Philadelphia. Established by Franklin and his friends four decades earlier, the Library Company was the first of its kind, and it set an example for many similar subscription libraries throughout colonial America. The "Mother of all the North American Subscription Libraries," Franklin called it.[10] These libraries worked by selling shares and then allowing shareholders to borrow books from the collection. Shareholders also had a say in which titles the library purchased. By the early 1770s, the Library Company contained more than two thousand titles. Its holdings included more history than anything else, but it also had many political works containing ideas that greatly influenced the foundations of American government.

Since the Library Company had numerous titles in common with Jefferson's personal library, it could have served him as a home library away from home. The Library Company granted borrowing privileges to all delegates to the Continental Congress while it was in session. No specific evidence documents Jefferson's use of the Library Company holdings, but more than likely he took advantage of the facility. Many other members of Congress used the collection during their time in the city. Altogether, nine signers of the *Declaration of Independence* held shares in the Library Company of Philadelphia.

The story of Jefferson's literary life in Philadelphia involves not only what he read, but also what he wrote. In addition to the writings required in his role as a delegate to the Continental Congress and active Congressional committee member, he also maintained a lively personal correspondence. While he remained in Philadelphia, Mrs. Jefferson and their three-year-old daughter, Martha, stayed with her brother-in-law, Francis Eppes. Keeping in contact with the family required much letter-writing on Jefferson's part, and he addressed separate letters to his wife and to Eppes. Like all good letter writers, Jefferson shaped his letters to suit his correspondents. Though the letters he and his wife exchanged are lost, the surviving correspondence with Eppes offers clues about what Jefferson wrote his wife.

To Eppes he explained, "I wrote to Patty on my arrival here, and there being then nothing new in the political way I inclosed her letter under a blank cover to you."[11] This remark suggests a division of subject matter appropriate to his correspondents: with his brother-in-law, he discussed politics; with his wife, he discussed people, places, and the details of daily life.

Relating Peyton Randolph's death to Eppes, Jefferson presented the matter as fact. For details, he referred Eppes to his wife: "Our good old Speaker died the night before last. For the particulars of that melancholy event I must refer you to Patty."[12] Jefferson realized that a sad story about the death of an old friend was more suitable in a letter to his wife than in a letter to his brother-in-law. He wrote a detailed account of the episode for her. For Eppes, he found the latest intelligence about the war more pertinent. Stories of personal tragedy were for women, stories of national crisis for men.

Since he could supply information about the war more accurately and expeditiously than the newspapers could, Jefferson assumed responsibility for conveying the latest developments to his family and friends. Though he recognized the newspaper as an essential medium of communication in any democracy, he also understood that the press could propagate much misinformation, especially in times of war, when people are eager for news and, consequently, when rumors run thick and fast. Relating some Congressional news in a letter to another correspondent that summer, Jefferson assured him of its reliability by asserting that the information was "not newspaper, but Official."[13]

Assuming the role of war correspondent in his letters to Eppes from Philadelphia that summer, Jefferson had little good news to report. Read in chronological order, his letters seem darkly foreboding. Anticipating Admiral Howe's next move, George Washington had marched his forces south from Boston to fortify New York against the British. Jefferson did not know how many troops Washington had in New York, but in a mid-July letter to Eppes, he estimated troop strength at around thirty or thirty-five thousand. As Washington had predicted, Howe soon reached New York, established camp at Staten Island, built up his troop strength, and started menacing the city.

In this same letter to Eppes, Jefferson related a threatening incident that had occurred in New York: "The enemy the other day ordered two of their men-of-war to hoist anchor and push our batteries up the Hudson River. Both wind and tide were very fair. They passed all the batteries with ease, and, as far as is known, without receiving material damage." American forces continued firing on the British vessels throughout their progress but with little effect. Jefferson conjectured that the British ploy revealed their intentions of landing above New York. Closing this episode in his letter, he wrote, "I imagine General Washington, finding he cannot prevent their going up the river, will prepare to amuse them wherever they shall go."[14] The light-hearted tone of this sentence rests uneasily atop the episode it concludes. Jefferson's cavalier attitude seems forced, and his deep-seated concern for the troops and their leader shows through the veneer of levity.

A week later Jefferson dropped the light-hearted tone altogether to inform Eppes of the humiliating defeat of the American forces in Canada: "The ill successes in Canada had depressed the minds of many; when we shall hear the last of them I know not; everybody had supposed Crown Point would be a certain stand for them, but they have retreated from that to Ticonderoga, against everything which in my eye wears the shape of reason." Jefferson also had to correct his statistics regarding troop strength from the earlier letter. "When I wrote you last, we were deceived in General Washington's numbers," he explained. "By a return which came to hand a day or two after, he then had but 15,000 effective men."[15] The second week of August Jefferson predicted to Eppes that an attack on New York would occur within three or four days. He expressed a modest amount of confidence in an American victory, but such was not to be. Instead, the British took New York and forced Washington south and west through New Jersey.

With the *Declaration of Independence* adopted, signed, and published, Jefferson grew anxious to leave Philadelphia for Monticello. He disliked the political wranglings that had been going on in Congress since July 4 and thought that his fellow Congressional delegates were devoting entirely too much time to trivialities and ignoring the most important issues facing the new nation. He wrote Richard Henry Lee, "The minutiae of the Confederation have hitherto engaged us; the great points of representation, boundaries, taxation etc. being left open."[16]

His current Congressional term was scheduled to expire the second Sunday in August, but at the Virginia Convention in June, his countrymen had reelected him to another term. He wrote Edmund Pendleton, then serving as Convention president, and asked him to find a substitute. Ultimately, Richard Henry Lee would return to Philadelphia to relieve him. As the end of Jefferson's term approached, he wrote Lee an anxious letter urging him to come as soon as possible. Contributing to his anxiety, news that Martha was quite ill had reached Philadelphia that summer. In his letter to Lee, Jefferson pleaded, "For god's sake, for your country's sake, and for my sake, come. I receive by every post such accounts of the state of Mrs. Jefferson's health, that it will be impossible for me to disappoint her expectation of seeing me at the time I have promised."[17]

Lee was anxious to return to Philadelphia to fulfill his responsibilities, but mechanical problems slowed him down. His old carriage wheels shattered, and he was having trouble finding competent workmen to make new ones. Once he got his wheels repaired, Lee hurried to Philadelphia.[18]

Jefferson had promised Martha that he would leave the city by mid-August, but as August gave way to September he had yet to depart. Finally, on September 3, after completing some last-minute tasks—settling accounts with his barber and his booksellers, getting his horse shod, hiring a peddler to haul some boxes to Virginia—he left Philadelphia to return to Monticello.

The peddler reached Monticello a few days after Jefferson. The boxes from Philadelphia contained items Jefferson had brought to the city that spring and summer. His accounts suggest that he had been buying presents for his wife and daughter: toys, a doll, several pair of women's gloves, butter prints, a thimble. The accounts also show that he had been buying items for himself that would allow him to continue his pursuit of literature and science at home: in addition to numerous books and pamphlets, he purchased a new thermometer and a barometer.

When it came to opportunities for book-buying, the time he spent in Philadelphia had spoiled him. The nearest bookstore to Monticello was in Williamsburg; only during his twice-yearly visits there to serve in the Assembly could he pop into a bookshop and make purchases on impulse. After growing accustomed to Philadelphia's fine bookshops, the *Virginia Gazette* office was disappointing, but he continued buying books there occasionally. Williamsburg did offer some unusual book-buying opportunities, but these depended upon pure chance—people leaving or dying. Over the next two years, however, Jefferson did obtain books formerly in the possession of several others who had spent at least part of their lives in Virginia.

One of the most distinguished collections of books to come up for sale in the mid-1770s was that of Lord Dunmore. After he fled the Governor's Palace in Williamsburg, the Virginia Convention decided to raise funds by auctioning his personal estate, including his books. The auction apparently took place in late June 1776. Though Jefferson was in Philadelphia, several books from Lord Dunmore's library became a part of Jefferson's. Either he had a friend bid for him, or he acquired unsold volumes upon his return to Williamsburg.

Despite their political differences, Jefferson and Dunmore shared similarly eclectic literary tastes. Jefferson obtained Dunmore's copy of Charles Rollin's *Histoire Ancienne*; the *Oeuvres* of Vincent Voiture, the seventeenth-century academician who made a literary reputation for himself as the author of sophisticated yet playfully witty social verse and finely crafted letters; François Pétis's *Histoire du Grand Genghizcan*, the work that initiated the modern study of the Mongol empire and significantly influenced subsequent treatments of the subject; the two-volume *General Collection of Treatys, Declarations of War, Manifestos, and Other Publick Papers, Relating to Peace and War*; and other works pertaining to common law.[19]

Like the colonial governors, the Anglican clergymen and the faculty members of William and Mary generally brought fine personal libraries when they came to Virginia. The Reverend James Horrocks, for one, brought a very good collection of books with him when he came to Virginia to serve as president of William and Mary. Sadly, Horrocks passed away during a trip to England in the 1770s. Remembered as "a Gentleman well versed in several Branches of sound Learning, particularly the Mathematicks," Horrocks left his library in Virginia, which was catalogued and put up for sale. No catalogue survives, so its precise contents remain a mystery, but the books the College of William and Mary acquired from his estate affirm Horrocks's knowledge of mathematics and suggest that his scholarly interests extended to other sciences, as well.[20] Jefferson took advantage of the opportunity to purchase a selection of books formerly in Horrocks's possession. The precise titles he acquired from the Horrocks estate in late 1776 are unknown, but Jefferson likely augmented his own scientific holdings at this time.

Much more is known about the books he acquired from Samuel Henley's library. Prior to his departure for England, Henley had boxed his books in two huge containers and left them in care of the current college president, Jefferson's longtime friend the Reverend James Madison. The fact that Henley left his valuable collection behind when he fled Virginia suggests that he planned to return. A few years after his departure, Madison decided to transport the boxes to the college library for safekeeping but found them so cumbersome that he ordered some men to bring them to the president's house instead. As they were moving them, one of the heavy boxes accidentally burst open, revealing the sorry condition of its contents. Reporting what had happened to Henley, Jefferson told a story to break any bookman's heart: "This accident discovered them to be in a state of ruin. They had contracted a dampness and stuck together in large blocks, insomuch that they could not sometimes be separated without tearing the cover."[21] The notorious heat and humidity of Tidewater Virginia had taken their toll on Henley's prized collection.

Trying to decide what to do with the books, Madison consulted Jefferson, who suggested that they should be overhauled and aired out. As the two discussed the matter, they agreed that it would be in Henley's best interest "to have them sold, as books are now in considerable demand here."[22] Besides, as property of a British subject, Henley's library was subject to confiscation by the Americans, who could seize his books, sell them, and refuse to pay him anything. Madison wrote Henley, who authorized him to sell the books. Even before receiving Henley's approval, Madison set a price for each title, and Jefferson chose which ones he wanted for himself.

The books Jefferson obtained from Henley's library are consistent with the study of science and literature he was cultivating at Monticello. He acquired numerous works to fuel his interest in different languages, both ancient and modern: Anglo-Saxon, Arabic, old French, Greek, Italian, and Latin. Acquiring a book entitled *Poeseos Asiaticae Commentariorum*, a Latin work by Sir William Jones containing a historical and critical survey of Arabic, Persian, and Turkish poetry, Jefferson revealed his interests in the languages of the Near East, an interest initiated by his attention to the Qur'an many years earlier and perpetuated through his contact with Henley. Jefferson would remain intrigued with the subject for years to come. During his presidency, he clipped from the newspapers multiple translations of Persian poetry, including "A Persian Song," which Jones had translated from the original of Hafiz.[23]

Jefferson acquired a number of literary classics from the Henley collection, including John Hoole's English translation of Torquato Tasso's *Jerusalem Delivered*, one of three editions of Tasso's great epic of the First Crusade in his library, the other two being in the original Italian. Some of the books Jefferson obtained from Henley's library were quite rare, including his prized copies of *Paradise Lost* and *Pierce Plowman*. To use Henley's words, these were good books in good editions. Jefferson also acquired from Henley's library a variety of works on art, music, and poetry, including some in-depth critical studies. Elizabeth Montagu's *Essay on the Writings and Genius of Shakespeare*, for example, favorably compared Shakespeare with ancient Greek dramatists and modern French ones, refuted Voltaire's attacks on Shakespeare, and critiqued Samuel Johnson's neglect of Shakespeare's dramatic genius.[24]

In addition, Jefferson purchased many botanical works from Henley's library including a ten-volume set of Linnaeus and John Clayton's *Flora Virginica*. Jefferson knew much about botany from firsthand observation; his acquisition of these authoritative works suggests an attempt to systematize his knowledge. He became a great advocate of the Linnaean system of classification. He especially appreciated the Linnaean system for its capacity to expand and incorporate new information.[25] He also came to know Clayton's work well. Paying homage in *Notes on the State of Virginia*, Jefferson said of Clayton, "This accurate observer was a native and resident of this state, passed a long life in exploring and describing its plants, and is supposed to have enlarged the botanical catalogue as much as almost any man who has lived."[26]

The rest of Henley's books remained unsold and were later destroyed with Madison's personal library when the college president's house burned to the ground. The only volumes from his fine collection that survived were those Jefferson acquired. When he wrote Henley after the fire to tell him what had happened to his unsold books, Henley responded, "I am sorry to learn the fate of my books, prints, etc., and exceedingly regret that no more of them fell into your hands. The pleasure I once took in them, made me feel the more pain for their loss, which however is in some measure alleviated by the consideration that some of them escaped the flames and are in the possession of a friend I so much respect."[27]

The Reverend William Willie of Sussex County, another clergyman with a passion for collecting, passed away in 1776. Upon learning from his executor what Willie had in his library, Jefferson became eager to obtain the prize of his collection, a complete or near-complete set of the *Virginia Gazette*. Currently, Jefferson did not have enough ready cash to pay for the entire set, but he recognized its importance and wanted very much to secure the collection. He put a down payment on the lot and made arrangements to pay off the balance some months later.[28]

His purchase of this multivolume collection represents the first of many sets of newspapers he would add to his library over the course of his life. Jefferson's interest in collecting newspapers shows that he recognized how the quotidian could contribute to history. Some years later, he would assert, "It is the duty of every good citizen to use all the opportunities which occur to him, for preserving documents relating to the history of our country."[29] Jefferson single-handedly rescued much early Virginiana from the waste bin. In many cases, the newspaper issues he preserved now survive in unique copies—if he had not saved them, they would be lost forever.

The most substantial collection of books and manuscripts Jefferson acquired in 1776 came from the Peyton Randolph estate, which included many books from the library of his kinsman Sir John Randolph. The library contained many more books than Jefferson could currently afford, so he signed two bonds to finance his purchase, a smaller one for almost forty pounds, which would come due in February and a huge one, nearly two hundred pounds, which would be due nine months later. Jefferson purchased not only Peyton Randolph's books, but also the bookcases in which they stood.

Volumes he acquired from the Randolph estate affirm his dedication to preserving documents pertinent to the history of Virginia: several contain unique manuscript collections of Virginia laws. If he did not acquire these manuscripts, Jefferson feared that they, too, would be lost forever. Recalling his acquisition of Randolph's legal library many years later, he wrote, "Very early in the course of my researches into the laws of Virginia, I observed that many of them were already lost, and many more on the point of being lost, as existing only in single copies in the hands of careful or curious individuals, on whose deaths they would probably be used for waste paper. I set myself therefore to work to collect all which were then existing."[30] Jefferson understood an important truth: preserving the documents of the past broadens the possibilities for the future.

Given the complex project Jefferson had undertaken shortly before acquiring Randolph's books, these manuscript statute collections gather importance not only as archival material but also as practical works. During the legislative session just ending, Jefferson was appointed chairman of the committee to oversee the revision of the laws of Virginia. Now more than ever, he needed as full a collection of laws as he could assemble.

Proud to come away from the autumn legislative session with this responsibility, Jefferson was quietly relieved that the current Assembly was coming to a close. It had been an especially trying session, the most difficult one he had endured so far. In his autobiography, he described the debates in the House of Delegates that fall as "the severest contests in which I have ever been engaged."[31] The contests Jefferson referred to pitted church against state. It is no coincidence that this head-to-head battle happened when it did: political freedom typically prompts a resurgence of religious freedom. With the declaration of American independence, those Virginians who dissented from the Church of England now clamored for their religious independence.

By 1776, dissenters had come to form a significant percentage of Virginia's population. Though free to practice their beliefs, the law required them to support the Anglican clergy, who remained responsible for the education of Virginia's youth and who were compensated for their efforts through public funds. Reluctant to support the Anglican Church, the dissenters petitioned the Virginia legislature to repeal these legally mandated contributions. Though Jefferson took his catechism in an Anglican church, received his education from Anglican priests, worshiped in an Anglican church, served on the vestry of an Anglican church, and understood how much the Anglican clergy had contributed to the book culture and intellectual life of colonial Virginia, he recognized that in a democracy, no government should dictate religion to its people. Church and state should and must be separate. Though Jefferson knew he would be battling fellow members of the Anglican Church, who were also good friends and shrewd debaters, he felt compelled to try his hardest to achieve the complete separation of church and state. He made the dissenters' cause his own.

Having declared freedom from political tyranny, Jefferson now sought to declare freedom from what he termed "spiritual tyranny." His goal was nothing short of total religious freedom, the freedom for everyone to believe what they want to believe. By the end of this difficult legislative session, he had managed to exempt the dissenters from having to contribute to the Anglican Church, but he knew there would be more battles to come before he achieved his goal.

Acquired at a time when Jefferson was engaged in what amounted to a pitched battle between church and state, the books he purchased from

Peyton Randolph's library take on further significance. Randolph's copy of Gilbert Burnet's *History of the Reformation of the Church of England*—formerly in the possession of Arthur Blackamore, a master of the William and Mary grammar school who had left Virginia ignominiously decades earlier—provided an authoritative and compelling story of what could happen when church and state clash.[32]

Randolph's copy of William Fulbecke's *Parallel of Conference of the Civil Law, the Canon Law, and the Common Law* gave Jefferson a useful methodology to deepen his studies. Fulbecke offered a critical approach to the study of law that Jefferson had applied to other fields of study, namely, the comparative method. In this, one of the earliest English texts of comparative jurisprudence, Fulbecke sought to reconcile how different legal issues were interpreted according to different legal systems.[33] In Fulbecke's *Parallel*, which is grounded in the study of natural law, Jefferson found an amenable approach to understanding the relationship between church and state.

Jefferson's efforts would culminate in his "Bill for Establishing Religious Freedom," which he would draft the following year. Preparing this bill required much intellectual work. His personal library supplied him with the resources he needed. Some idiosyncratic notes survive to show him working out his concept of religious freedom, which his editors have grouped together under the general title "Notes and Proceedings on Discontinuing the Establishment of the Church of England." These miscellaneous papers show Jefferson making use of books from many different parts of his library. He delved into his collections of statutes to compile a list of Acts passed in both Parliament and the Virginia Assembly pertaining to religion.

Jefferson took the philosophical basis of his concept of religious freedom from John Milton's *Reason of Church-Government* and *Of Reformation in England*, John Locke's "Letter Concerning Toleration," and the Earl of Shaftesbury's "Letter Concerning Enthusiasm." He consulted his collection of religious books for much additional information regarding the various faiths around the world. The works of Daniel Waterland and Conyers Middleton, which helped to form the basis of Jefferson's own faith, offered ideas that entered his notes at several points.[34]

The "Bill for Establishing Religious Freedom" came before the Virginia House of Delegates in 1779. It was not adopted then, but when James Madison reintroduced the bill to the House in 1785, it underwent much debate and amendment but was ultimately approved. In early 1786, it passed both the House of Delegates and the Virginia Senate and became law.

Living in France when the bill became law, Jefferson, needless to say, received the news with elation. He ultimately ranked this bill with the *Declaration of Independence* among his proudest accomplishments. Considered as a single Act passed in the legislature of the State of Virginia, the bill seems fairly modest, but in terms of philosophical, social, and political significance, its implications were vast.

News of the bill spread throughout Europe, and it was widely reprinted as an example of American enlightenment. Jefferson explained to Madison:

> The Virginia act for religious freedom has been received with infinite approbation in Europe and propagated with enthusiasm. I do not mean by the governments, but by the individuals which compose them. It has been translated into French and Italian, has been sent to most of the courts of Europe, and has been the best evidence of the falshood of those reports which stated us to be in anarchy. It is inserted in the new Encyclopedie, and is appearing in most of the publications respecting America. In fact it is comfortable to see the standard of reason at length erected, after so many ages during which the human mind has been held in vassalage by kings, priests and nobles; and it is honorable for us to have produced the first legislature who has had the courage to declare that the reason of man may be trusted with the formation of his own opinions.[35]

This excerpt shows how much the bill meant to Jefferson. Not only does it represent the triumph of reason over tyranny, prejudice, and superstition, it also represents the United States and, specifically, Virginia. It represents something else, too: it personally represents Thomas Jefferson. It demonstrates his will, his perseverance, and his desire to work toward the freedom of all men.

Expanding his fine personal library in both Philadelphia and Williamsburg, Jefferson gathered what he needed to broaden his legal and philosophical knowledge in the service of his nation. An ocean may have separated the New World from the Old, but Jefferson saw no reason why he could not recreate at Monticello the intellectual world of Europe, past and present, and surround himself with what the greatest writers and thinkers had to offer.

His aggressive efforts to expand his library during the mid- to late 1770s provide a good context for understanding his comments in this letter to Madison, which identify the "Bill for Establishing Religious Freedom" as a landmark in the history of Western thought: Jefferson

James Madison, engraved by H. B. Hall's Sons, New York. From Lyon Gardiner Tyler, *Encyclopedia of Virginia Biography* (1915). (Collection of Kevin J. Hayes)

had steeped himself in the history of ideas to write the bill, and now, having written it, and having seen it enacted, he was situating his own words and ideas within the intellectual world his books represented. As part of both the *Encyclopedie* and other contemporary publications, the "Bill for Establishing Religious Freedom" showed European readers that America was a place where new thinking was made real.

CHAPTER 15

Of Law and Learning

On Christmas night, 1776, a powerful winter storm covered Virginia with more than twenty inches of snow. During the next few weeks, the weather remained crisp and cold, the temperature seldom creeping above the twenties, the Christmas snow continuing to blanket the land. Though this was the severest winter he could remember, Jefferson had no intention of letting either the snow or the cold hinder his plans. The second week of January 1777, he ventured to Fredericksburg to meet other members of the committee named by the Virginia legislature to revise its laws: Thomas Ludwell Lee, George Mason, Edmund Pendleton, and George Wythe. Since the creation of the United States, all laws present and in force needed to be scrutinized and, in many cases, reworked.

After leaving Philadelphia in September, Jefferson had been thinking much about revising the laws of Virginia. With "no negatives of Councils, Governors and Kings to restrain us from doing right," he observed, the laws could be thoroughly revised "with a single eye to reason, and the good of those for whose government it was framed." Other Virginia legislators agreed, and that autumn the House of Delegates had adopted the "Bill for the Revision of the Laws," elected a committee to undertake the revision, and named Jefferson to chair the committee. This wintertime gathering in Fredericksburg was planned as an organizational meeting. In Jefferson's words, its object was "to settle the plan of operation and to distribute the work."[1]

Regularly laid out in parallel streets and commanding a handsome view, Fredericksburg was an ideal place to begin work on such an important project. Here, the committee had to decide whether to "abolish the whole existing system of laws, and prepare a new and complete Institute" or to "preserve the general system, and only modify it to the present state of things."[2] They decided to keep the parts of the existing system that remained valid, drafted new legislation to replace some of the laws, and added new laws as needed. Less work than drafting an entirely new system, the task they faced was a daunting one nonetheless. Before the committee was through, it would draft a set of more than one hundred bills proposing new laws for Virginia.

Upon determining the scope of the project, these men had to decide who would do what. Some committee members were reluctant to assume the weighty and time-consuming responsibilities involved. "When we proceeded to the distribution of the work," Jefferson recalled, "Mr. Mason excused himself as, being no lawyer, he felt himself unqualified for the work, and he resigned soon after. Mr. Lee excused himself on the same ground, and died indeed in a short time. The other two gentlemen therefore and myself divided the work among us."[3] So, Jefferson, Wythe, and Pendleton assumed the responsibility for revising the laws. And Jefferson himself ultimately did the lion's share of the work.

Rewriting the laws of Virginia was a task for which he was well prepared. From his training under George Wythe through his years before the bar of the General Court of Virginia and within the legislative chambers of the House of Burgesses and the Continental Congress, Jefferson had plenty of practical experience making, interpreting, and upholding the law. What might have served him best, however, was his experience within his library at Monticello. At this time, he had the fullest collection of law books in the nation, and he may have been better read in the law than anyone else in the United States, surpassing even his former teacher and fellow committee member, George Wythe.

The month Jefferson and his committee began their task of rewriting the laws of Virginia, their countryman George Washington was busy to the north retaking ground he had given up to British forces the previous year. That January he routed the British at the Battle of Princeton, established winter quarters at Morristown, and began sending out raiding parties to torment nearby British forces and push them back farther. Though Washington's efforts with his sword were more urgent that Jefferson's efforts with his pen, both endeavors were essential for defining and legitimizing the new nation. Battling the British, Washington was fighting for the principles the United States represented; drafting new laws, Jefferson was taking those general principles and applying them in specific contexts and situations. Jefferson saw rewriting the laws of Virginia not only as a legal task, but also as a literary endeavor. He believed that recent British statutes, not to mention many of the Acts of the Virginia Assembly, were hindered by "their verbosity, their endless tautologies, their involutions of case within case, and parenthesis within parenthesis, and their multiplied efforts at certainty by *saids* and *aforesaids*, by *ors* and by *ands*."[4] Such awkward diction and syntax made them quite difficult to read, not only by the general public but also by the lawyers and judges whose responsibility it was to interpret them. Jefferson began his revision of the laws with the ambitious design of reforming the legalistic prose style.

Once he finished drafting the "Bill for Proportioning Crimes and Punishments," he sent a copy of it to Wythe. In a cover letter, he described the bill and explained the general literary and stylistic approach he was taking. Accuracy, brevity, and simplicity were his watchwords. Though he preserved the wording of laws that had been established and sanctioned by judicial decision, he otherwise avoided "modern statutory language" in the new laws he drafted. As he told Wythe, he was seeking to rescue the statutory language from "the barbarous style into which modern statutes have degenerated from their antient simplicity."[5] Indeed, much of early American literature had a similar impulse. With this particular bill, Jefferson reinforced the value of ancient languages and indulged his linguistic curiosity by adding numerous explanatory notes, citing precedent and quoting them in Anglo-Saxon, Latin, or Law French.

He devoted nearly two years to the task of rewriting the laws, but other activities also kept him busy during this time. His wife, Martha, gave birth to two more children: on May 28, 1777, she gave birth to their only son, who did not live long enough to receive a name, and on August 1, 1778, their daughter Mary was born. Jefferson also had much work to do in the state legislature, which took him away from Monticello for long periods of time. The voters of Albemarle County kept reelecting him to the House of Delegates, so he spent some months in Williamsburg each year attending the increasingly lengthy legislative sessions.

Home at Monticello, Jefferson enjoyed being with his family, keeping up his correspondence, and gathering scientific data. He collected much information about the natural phenomena surrounding him, from the flora that broke through the rich crust of Virginia earth every spring to the rain that poured from the heavens. The war remained far enough away that he could enjoy his home life without feeling threatened and devote his few leisure hours to pursuing personal interests in literature and science.

His time in the Continental Congress had put him in touch with some of the brightest minds in America, and he was eager to maintain these connections. His correspondence was a way not only to continue the business of the new nation but also to enjoy lively intellectual and literary discourse. Benjamin Franklin was the most prominent of his new correspondents. Writing to Franklin, Jefferson made full use of his literary skills. For example, he applied an apt simile to express how easily Virginians had accepted American independence: "With respect to the state of Virginia in particular, the people seem to have deposited the monarchical and taken up the republican government with as much ease as would have attended their throwing off an old and putting on a new suit of clothes."[6] Writing to Silas Deane—after Congress had sent Deane to Paris yet before he compromised his position there by selling his diplomatic correspondence for ready cash—Jefferson told him, "I feel within myself the same kind of desire of an hour's conversation with yourself or Dr. Franklyn which I have often had for a confabulation with those who have passed the irremeable bourne."[7] As he often did, Jefferson became nostalgic when he imagined intellectual conversations from his past and longed to recapture such experiences. Though no substitute for face-to-face encounters, a correspondence did have its own pleasures.

In the spring of 1777, Jefferson established the most important correspondence of his literary life. The third Friday that May he took time from the busy legislative session, put pen to paper, and initiated a correspondence with John Adams, who was still serving in the Continental Congress. In this first letter, Jefferson discussed many different topics— the Continental army, in which Virginia soldiers, he was proud to boast, were serving in great numbers; the Articles of Confederation, which Congress had yet to adopt; the postal system, which was in dire need of reorganization—but he saved his most impassioned comments for a discussion of the importance of the printed word to democracy.

Jefferson voiced concern that the Congressional journals had yet to be published. Without their publication, state legislators were forced to make local policy decisions unaware of what national legislators had resolved. Expressing his dismay, Jefferson summarized what many of his fellow delegates in the Virginia House were feeling: "The journals of congress not being printed earlier gives more uneasiness than I would ever wish to see produced by any act of that body, from whom alone I know our salvation can proceed. In our assembly even the best affected think it an indignity to freemen to be voted away life and fortune in the dark."[8] The printed word not only offers a way to disseminate information, but also helps to ensure freedom.

The following year Jefferson began an important scientific correspondence. Five years earlier, he had learned about a promising young

Florentine named Giovanni Fabbroni from their mutual friend, Philip Mazzei, and had tried to persuade Fabbroni to relocate to Monticello to become music master and tutor to his children. Mazzei had written Fabbroni, telling him that Jefferson was waiting for him with open arms. Mazzei encouraged Fabbroni to come to Virginia by emphasizing the wisdom and friendship Jefferson and his neighbors possessed.[9]

After receiving Mazzei's letter, Fabbroni wrote Jefferson directly, telling him that he wanted very much to come. Influenced by Mazzei's encouraging words, he imagined Virginia as a fine, fertile country populated with warm-hearted inhabitants. But before he could accept the offer, he came under the patronage of the Grand Duke of Tuscany, who magnanimously assigned him the task of traveling to France and England to observe scientific progress in each nation. Though deprived of an amply qualified tutor for his children, Jefferson was pleased to have such an intelligent and well-connected correspondent.

The letter he wrote Fabbroni in mid-1778 offers a glimpse into his mindset as work on the revision of the Virginia laws was entering its late stages. Since Fabbroni had heard all sorts of horrific stories about the war, Jefferson allayed his concerns, assuring him that the danger of war had largely passed: "From the kind anxiety expressed in your letters as well as from other sources of information we discover that our enemies have filled Europe with Thrasonic accounts of victories they had never won and conquests they were fated never to make." Calming Fabbroni, Jefferson indulged in some Thrasonic fervor himself as he boasted that Americans, especially those from Virginia, possessed a "superiority in taking aim when we fire; every soldier in our army having been intimate with his gun from his infancy."[10] Though written to encourage Fabbroni to immigrate to Virginia, Jefferson's words reveal how much he was distancing himself from current events. To him, Monticello was becoming an idyllic retreat completely separated from the dangers of war.

Thoughts of Italy brought music to Jefferson's ears, and he spent much of this letter voicing his musical inclinations. Writing to an accomplished Italian, he expressed his love of music in terms of passion, jealousy, and fantasy: "If there is a gratification which I envy any people in this world it is to your country its music. This is the favorite passion of my soul, and fortune has cast my lot in a country where it is in a state of deplorable barbarism." Ingratiating himself to his new correspondent, Jefferson confessed to Fabbroni one of his domestic fantasies: to have a workforce of skilled craftsmen at Monticello who were also fine musicians. Each would play a different instrument: a tutor who could sing and play the harpsichord, a gardener who could play the French horn, a cabinetmaker on clarinet, a weaver on bassoon, and a stonecutter on hautboy or oboe. Dreaming of an oboe-playing stonecutter, Jefferson was further distancing himself from the war as he imagined himself in a music-lover's paradise.

Jefferson offered Fabbroni the opportunity to correspond on any and all scientific matters, including meteorology. He explained how he was keeping track of local weather conditions. In June 1778, he expanded the scope of his weather data significantly. To the morning and afternoon temperature readings he had been keeping, he now added barometer readings. In his records, he placed the temperature and barometer readings in an initial set of columns and devised a second set of columns to record other pertinent data twice daily, early morning—the same time he took the temperature—and sunset. Jefferson planned to measure wind velocity and rainfall, too. He made space in his weather record for additional columns to list the appearance of buds, leaves, fruit, birds, and insects—the kinds of information he had been including in his *Garden Book*. He also made room for a miscellaneous column to note unusual aspects of the climate.

Less than a week after beginning the expanded weather records, Jefferson recorded a near total eclipse of the sun. His brief entry obscures the amount of effort that went into the observation of this eclipse within Virginia's scientific community. Beforehand, Jefferson had arranged with John Page and the Reverend James Madison to observe the phenomenon from different locations and to compare their notes after the event. The day turned out to be cloudy and his equipment inadequate, so Jefferson was disappointed with his results: he did not see the eclipse until the moon had already covered a third of the sun's disk. Thereafter, clouds interfered with the eclipse off and on throughout its duration.

Observing it in Williamsburg, Madison and Page also experienced a cloudy morning that hindered their initial findings. Happily for them, the clouds broke before the eclipse became total, and the two had a very good view of it. Describing the totality of the eclipse, Madison wrote, "There was really something awful in the Appearance which all Nature assumed. You could not determine your most intimate Acquaintance at 20 yds. distance. Lightening Buggs were seen as at Night."[11]

Frustrated by his efforts to observe the eclipse, Jefferson renewed contact with David Rittenhouse, who had promised to make him an accurate clock for taking astronomical observations. He had met Rittenhouse in Philadelphia and had been impressed with his scientific genius. In *Notes on the State of Virginia*, Jefferson applauded Rittenhouse and the orrery he had created: "We have supposed Mr. Rittenhouse second to no astronomer living: that in genius he must be the first, because he is self-taught. As an artist he has exhibited as great a proof of mechanical genius as the world has ever produced. He has not indeed made a world; but he has by imitation approached nearer its Maker than any man who has lived from the creation to this day."[12]

The letter to Rittenhouse may start as a discussion of astronomical instruments, but by the time it ends, it turns into a treatise on the relationship between genius and governance. People who have a capacity to govern have the responsibility to govern. This rule was not hard and fast: Jefferson acknowledged an important exception. Those who possess true genius should be exempt from governmental responsibility regardless of their administrative abilities. Explaining his ideas to Rittenhouse, Jefferson took Sir Isaac Newton for example: "No body can conceive that nature ever intended to throw away a Newton upon the occupations of a crown. It would have been a prodigality for which even the conduct of providence might have been arraigned, had he been by birth annexed to what was so far below him." Rittenhouse himself, Jefferson continued, offered another good example. Surely, anyone with the capacity to design and construct precise astronomical instruments capable of mapping the heavens should be exempt from governmental administration. Natural genius is "intended for the erudition of the world, like air and light" and should not be "taken from their proper pursuit to do the commonplace drudgery of governing a single state, a work which may be executed by men of an ordinary stature, such as are always and every where to be found."[13] Genius deserves recognition.

Though Jefferson said little about his efforts to revise the laws of Virginia in the letter to Rittenhouse, the ideas concerning natural genius he articulated significantly shaped his composition of the laws, specifically those concerning public education. In addition to the bills regarding religious freedom and crime and punishment, Jefferson's bills concerning education are the most important ones he drafted as part of the revision of the laws of Virginia.

Clustered together in the *Report of the Committee of Revisors*, three bills specifically concern the matter of education: "A Bill for the More General Diffusion of Knowledge," "A Bill for Amending the Constitutions of the College of William and Mary, and Substituting More Certain Revenues for Its Support," and "A Bill for Establishing a Public Library." Though all three encountered opposition from the legislature, each exerted an influence on the development of public education in Virginia and across the United States.

On December 15, 1778, the House of Delegates gave leave for the presentation of the first of these three bills. Richard Parker and George Mason were ordered to prepare "A Bill for the More General Diffusion of Knowledge" for presentation. After Parker presented the bill the following day, many of the delegates were impressed with its purpose, scope, and design. To make Virginians throughout the state aware of these new ideas regarding public education, the House ordered that the public printer issue the bill and distribute four copies of it to each county. Despite the order, the bill was not printed at that time. Nevertheless, word of it got around and sparked much talk about education.

Two days after Parker presented the bill before the House, Jefferson wrote Edmund Pendleton to inform him of its general purpose. Jefferson's letter does not survive, but Pendleton's response indicates what Jefferson had written. Catching his friend's enthusiasm, Pendleton re-used Jefferson's words, telling him, "I have been impatient to see what you call your Quixotism for the diffusion of knowledge, a passion raised by its title and its being yours."[14] Jefferson as an educational Don Quixote: the image fits. He had great dreams for his country and the improvement of its people. Trying to get these bills through the Virginia legislature, he may have been chasing windmills, but he was going to try anyway.

Jefferson recognized that an educated citizenry was the best way to guarantee and perpetuate democracy. The preamble to this bill his editors have called "one of the classic statements of the responsibility of the state in matters of education."[15] Jefferson himself called the bill the most important of all those they drafted: "No other sure foundation can be devised for the preservation of freedom, and happiness."[16] Though some forms of government are better than others when it comes to protecting individual freedoms, those people entrusted with power, even in the best of governments, can pervert it into tyranny. The surest way to prevent such tyrannical usurpation of democracy, Jefferson understood, would be to enlighten the minds of the people and give them a knowledge of history, making them aware of the experiences of others from different times and places and thus enabling them to recognize and overcome dangerous ambition regardless what form it takes.

To guarantee just laws, a nation needs wise and honest people to carry them out. A well-designed educational scheme would allow those citizens "whom nature hath endowed with genius and virtue" to emerge as natural leaders and be trained for leadership or, in Jefferson's words, to be "rendered by liberal education worthy to receive, and able to guard the sacred deposit of the rights and liberties of their fellow citizens." A proper educational scheme would make sure future leaders are "called to that charge without regard to wealth, birth or other accidental condition or circumstance."[17] In short, all citizens deserved an education at public expense, and the new nation deserved a well-educated citizenry.

Jefferson projected two levels of schooling: an elementary school and a grammar school. Each elementary school would teach reading, writing, and basic arithmetic. In the course of learning how to read, children could be taught other subjects simultaneously. Traditionally, American children had learned to read by reading the Bible. In a system of public education, children should learn to read by reading history. Clarifying his scheme for primary education in the *Notes on the State of Virginia*, Jefferson observed that since "the principle foundations for future order" would be laid in these primary schools, what students read is crucial: "Instead therefore of putting the Bible and Testament into the hands of the children, at an age when their judgments are not sufficiently matured for religious enquiries, their memories may here be stored with the most useful facts from Grecian, Roman, European and American history."[18] The books we read as children stick with us all our lives. Jefferson sought to establish a habit of history reading among all children, a habit that would shape their thought and encourage them to continue reading throughout their lives.

The bill stipulated that all free children, male and female, within a school district were "intitled to receive tuition gratis, for the term of three years, and as much longer, at their private expence, as their parents, guardians or friends, shall think proper."[19] Aware that mandating a completely public system of education throughout all grades was much too giant a step for contemporary legislators to take, Jefferson projected a modified form that combined public and private education: the state would support the education of all students for the first three years, and parents would take the responsibility afterward. Jefferson did provide a mechanism whereby bright students from poor families could further their education and proceed to the grammar school: each September, elementary school students would be examined, and the top student whose parents were too poor to afford further education would proceed to the local grammar school to be educated and boarded at public expense.

After this bill was presented to the House of Delegates, news of Jefferson's plan for public education circulated around Virginia and generated enthusiasm among educators. Samuel Stanhope Smith, then rector of Hampden-Sydney Academy and later president of the College of New Jersey (Princeton), applauded the scheme. Though not person-ally acquainted with Jefferson, Smith initiated a correspondence with him to encourage his educational plans. Smith wrote, "The nature of the design must recommend it to every lover of learning and of his country; the idea was greatly imagined; and the whole plan bears an impression of the wisdom of antiquity, when legislation and philosophy were always connected, and but different parts of the same sage characters."[20] Smith did have some reservations about specific aspects of Jefferson's proposed educational scheme, but in general he was quite supportive.

With "A Bill for Amending the Constitutions of the College of William and Mary, and Substituting More Certain Revenues for Its Support," Jefferson proposed to take the college away from the Anglican Church and make it a state institution. As he summarized the present situation of the college, it "was an establishment purely of the Church of England, the Visitors were required to be all of that Church; the Professors to subscribe its 39 Articles, its Students to learn its Catechism, and one of its fundamental objects was declared to be to raise up Ministers for that church."[21]

Of the four different schools within William and Mary, Jefferson wanted to eliminate three. His scheme for a statewide system of grammar schools obviated the need for a grammar school at the college. Making the college a public institution rendered the divinity school inappropriate given the separation of church and state essential to any successful democracy. The Indian school, which had never been very effective in its purpose of educating and christianizing Native Americans, should also be eliminated.

The main reason Jefferson gave in the bill for improving the quality of higher education was much the same as the reason for mandating public education: to guarantee good governance.

> The late change in the form of our government, as well as the contest of arms in which we are at present engaged, calling for extraordinary abilities both in council and field, it becomes the peculiar duty of the Legislature, at this time, to aid and improve that seminary, in which those who are to be the future guardians of the rights and liberties of their country may be endowed with science and virtue, to watch and preserve the sacred deposit.[22]

The bill stipulated that the college curricula be greatly expanded. Altogether Jefferson imagined eight professorships:

Moral Philosophy, the Laws of Nature and of Nations, and of the Fine
    Arts

Law and Police
History, Civil and Ecclesiastical
Mathematics
Anatomy and Medicine
Natural Philosophy and Natural History
Ancient Languages, Oriental and Northern
Modern Languages

Providing for two professorships concerning the law, Jefferson imagined one devoted to law enforcement and the other to legal theory. Putting the professor of natural law also in charge of moral philosophy and art, Jefferson confirmed ideas he articulated elsewhere: law, like art, must follow nature, and the study of law should be tempered by a knowledge of art and literature. Jefferson greatly expanded the linguistic curriculum to include the study of Anglo-Saxon as well as Oriental languages, by which he meant Arabic and Hebrew.

What Jefferson imagined in place of the Indian school might be termed in modern parlance a Native American language research institute. Specifically, "A Bill for Amending the Constitutions of the College of William and Mary" provided for

> a missionary, of approved veracity, to the several tribes of Indians, whose business shall be to investigate their laws, customs, religions, traditions, and more particularly their languages, constructing grammars thereof, as well as may be, and copious vocabularies, and, on oath, to communicate, from time to time to the said president and professors the materials he collects to be by them laid up and preserved in their library, for which trouble the said missionary shall be allowed a salary at the discretion of the visitors out of the revenues of the college.[23]

In the role Jefferson envisioned, the missionary could make a significant contribution to the study of linguistics. As he would explain in *Notes on the State of Virginia*: "Were vocabularies formed of all the languages spoken in North and South America, preserving their appellations of the most common objects in nature, of those which must be present to every nation barbarous or civilised, with the inflections of their nouns and verbs, their principles of regimen and concord, and these deposited in all the public libraries, it would furnish opportunities to those skilled in the languages of the old world to compare them with these, now, or at a future time, and hence to construct the best evidence of the derivation of this part of the human race."[24]

The bill was not enacted, but when Jefferson became governor of Virginia, he also became a member of the college's board of visitors and was able to institute some of his proposed changes, including the abolition of the grammar school and the establishment of several new professorships.

The third bill pertaining to education provided for a public library. It stipulated that the legislature appoint a board of visitors for the library, whose responsibilities would include procuring books and maps and, if necessary, a librarian to administer the collection. The collection would not be a circulating library. In other words, people would not be able to borrow books, but "the learned and the curious" would be welcome to do research in the collection without fees, provided they handled the books carefully and safely.[25]

Jefferson envisioned a pubic library much different from the libraries he knew. Few had the wealth to assemble large collections or sufficient personal contacts among the wealthy to take advantage of Virginia's finest private libraries. Jefferson himself was happy to loan books to young men studying the law or others doing serious research, but such personal patronage was no way to ensure the proper dissemination of books and ideas in a democracy.

He had different models on which he might have based his public library. Though subscription libraries like the Library Company of Philadelphia offered shareholders greater collections of books than they could afford to assemble personally, the library companies were by no means egalitarian. Shares in most were fairly expensive, and membership was generally limited to the well-to-do. Not until the development of mechanics' libraries and their ilk in the early nineteenth century did the subscription library idea embrace the working classes.

Circulating libraries, like the one William Aitken operated in Annapolis, were more democratic than the subscription libraries: books could be borrowed by anyone for a few pence each. As purely commercial ventures, these circulating libraries were subject to the laws of supply and demand, and they became known as places where sentimental readers could borrow the latest novels. Such libraries offered only modest opportunities for intellectual improvement.

Jefferson's concept of a library differed significantly from these models. Like Aitken's circulating library, the public library Jefferson imagined would be available to everyone. Like the Library Company of Philadelphia, it would contain a fine collection of books useful for promoting both democracy and intellectual inquiry. Unlike either, he foresaw a collection of books that would welcome everyone yet cost its patrons nothing. Jefferson's idea of a public library created by and supported from public funds was well ahead of its time. True public libraries like the one he envisioned would not emerge until the mid-nineteenth century.

With all three of these bills, Jefferson conceived an educational system that was supported and perpetuated by the state. He recognized an inextricable relation between democracy and education. Each was essential to the other; together they were self-sustaining. Only a well-educated and informed citizenry could preserve and perpetuate democracy. Conversely, it was the responsibility of a democratic government to make sure that its citizens were well educated. The educational ideas Jefferson included as part of his revision of the laws of Virginia were too forward-thinking for their time. Though none were enacted, they contain the kernel of the modern American educational system.

CHAPTER 16

Lines of Communication

Among the legislation Jefferson drafted as part of his revision of the laws of Virginia is "A Bill for Establishing Cross Posts." Its preamble clearly establishes the bill's purpose. Intended to promote "the more general diffusion of public intelligence among the citizens of this commonwealth," it would help Virginians keep in touch with friends, merchants, and legislators.[1] Jefferson's choice of words echoes the diction of "A Bill for the More General Diffusion of Knowledge." Read in juxtaposition, similar phrases from the two prompt a question: how does the general diffusion of knowledge resemble the general diffusion of public intelligence?

Both require infrastructure: Knowledge can be diffused through the construction of schools and the establishment of a public school system; public intelligence, on the other hand, can be diffused through the establishment of an efficient postal system. By "cross posts" Jefferson specifically meant additional post roads branching off the main north–south route that ran through Virginia and connected it with the other American states. The network of post roads he had in mind was both local and continental in scope: it connected the western parts of Virginia with its eastern part and all of Virginia with the rest of the United States. A network of quality post roads represented state-of-the-art communication technology in Jefferson's day, and he wanted to give Virginia the best system of communication possible.

In February 1779, Jefferson arranged to meet with his committee in Williamsburg to complete the revision of the laws. Since Pendleton was unable to reach Williamsburg, the committee came down to its last two members: George Wythe and Thomas Jefferson. Graciously, Jefferson gave Pendleton more credit than he deserved for his work on the revision. Pendleton's absence may have facilitated what work was left: the fact that only Jefferson and Wythe remained to complete the task of revising the Virginia laws made the effort less contentious and more productive. Once teacher and pupil, now peers and friends, the two met daily to scrutinize the complete set of bills, 126 in all. They examined each bill sentence by sentence and further revised their text until both agreed on the entire manuscript.

The complete revision would not be presented to the Virginia legislature until June, but some of the bills would come before the House of Delegates earlier, including the bill for establishing cross posts. Convinced of their importance and anxious for their construction, Jefferson presented the bill to the House the third week of May. Many legislators found that the plan for establishing cross posts made good sense, and the bill passed the House the following week. It subsequently went before the Virginia Senate, which continued debating the bill into June, when the senators ultimately rejected it.

Returning to Monticello once he and Wythe had completed their lengthy revision of Virginia law, Jefferson discovered that the neighborhood had changed significantly during his absence. In January, the English and Hessian troops who surrendered at Saratoga had been relocated to Albemarle County. The rank-and-file, around four thousand strong, were housed in newly constructed barracks two hours away by horseback. Their leaders were allowed to take up residence locally. Major General William Phillips moved into Blenheim, Edward Carter's estate. The Baron, that is, Major General Friederich von Riedesel, who commanded the Brunswick troops serving the British, moved into Colle, the estate of Jefferson's next-door neighbor, Phillip Mazzei, whom Congress had sent to Tuscany to secure loans to aid the American war effort. Baron von Riedesel even arranged to have the Baroness and their three daughters join him at Colle.

War was much different then, and a clash between nations did not necessarily mean a clash between individuals. Once General Phillips and the Riedesels were settled, they invited the Jeffersons to a dinner party. Jefferson responded cordially: "The great cause which divides our countries is not to be decided by individual animosities. The harmony of private societies cannot weaken national efforts. To contribute by neighborly intercourse and attentions to make others happy is the shortest and surest way of being happy ourselves."[2] Soon, a pleasant social circle formed, which also included some of the officers living in the barracks: Baron de Geismar, Lieutenant Johann Ludwig de Unger, Lieutenant August Wilhelm du Roi, and Chaplain Kohle.

In terms of Jefferson's literary life, perhaps none of the surviving papers documenting his interaction with the Hessian troops are more revealing than the list of books these men borrowed from Monticello.[3] Father Kohle borrowed Origen's *Against Celsus*. After Augustine, Origen was the most important of the early Christian theologians. His *Hexapla*, which presents different versions of the Old Testament in parallel columns, is considered the first attempt to create a polyglot Bible. *Against Celsus*, the most important defense of Christianity written in the early centuries of the church, demonstrates the spirit and power of Christianity. Jefferson remembered the work for its discussion of the controversy over the corporeality of God.[4]

The English stage occupied an important place in their literary discussions, too, gauging by the books listed. Unger borrowed the plays of Sir John Vanbrugh. Being both playwright and architect, Vanbrugh doubly earned Jefferson's admiration. Vanbrugh's buildings were better constructed than his plays, which he largely derived from popular French comedies. Jefferson's opinion of the playwright has gone unrecorded. Lieutenant du Roi borrowed Jefferson's copy of the dramatic works of one of the most popular comic Restoration playwrights, George Farquhar, whose high-spirited yet good-natured plays put his work well above that of most other contemporary playwrights. His works were well known among colonial Virginia readers and theatergoers.

French works Unger borrowed reveal both his wide-ranging belletristic interests and his shrewd, practical bent: the three-volume edition of Jean-François Marmontel's *Contes Moreaux*; the collected works of the influential French literary theorist Nicolas Boileau-Despréaux; and Étienne Bezout's *Cours de Mathématiques*, which Jefferson called "the best for a student ever published."[5] A detailed textbook of mathematics and mechanics, Bezout's *Cours de Mathématiques* was specifically directed toward those serving in the artillery. Unger's interest in this work reveals his curiosity about both science and military service.

Writing to say goodbye to Unger, Jefferson confirmed the younger man's personal and professional interests, encouraging his "fondness for philosophy" and recommending that he place his quest for scientific knowledge above his pursuit of military glory. As if puzzling over this very dilemma, Unger also borrowed Jefferson's copy of Voltaire's *Candide*. Jefferson's library catalogue lists two partial editions of Voltaire's collected works but does not name the specific titles they contained. This list of borrowed books confirms that he did indeed have a copy of *Candide* at Monticello. Voltaire's masterpiece was a popular work in the neighborhood. Philip Mazzei also had a copy of *Candide* in his library at Colle, which the Baroness von Riedesel borrowed.[6]

All too soon, Jefferson's seemingly endless legislative responsibilities took him away from the conviviality and cosmopolitanism his wartime neighbors provided. Reelected to the House of Delegates by the voters of Albemarle County in April, he returned to Williamsburg the first week of May 1779. The Virginia legislature had much urgent work to do that spring. Though Jefferson did not realize it, this legislative session would change his life drastically.

When the state constitution had been adopted three years earlier, it had reformed Virginia's governmental system. Two houses of legislature were created, the House of Delegates and the Senate. Given the far-reaching powers that colonial governors had enjoyed and often abused, the new constitution placed significant restrictions on the executive branch of government, making the governor subject to a council of advisers. Jefferson, in Philadelphia working on the *Declaration of Independence* when the state constitution was passed, was unable to exert as much influence on it as he had wished. He believed that the adopted constitution made the governor far too dependent on both the legislature and his council of advisers. In addition, the new Virginia constitution stipulated that the governor could not serve more than three one-year terms consecutively. Partway through 1779, Patrick Henry, the first state governor, was reaching the end of his third term. It was time for the legislature to choose a new governor. In a joint session, the House of Delegates and the Senate gathered the first of June to cast their ballots.

The results of the election show the level of respect Jefferson commanded among his fellow legislators: he received the most votes on the first ballot, more than either of two old friends who were also on the ballot, John Page and Thomas Nelson, Jr. The results of the first ballot also show the limitations to the respect Jefferson commanded. Though he received more votes than the other two, he did not receive a majority. A runoff between him and second-place finisher John Page was held, and Jefferson bested his old college chum by six votes.

Page apparently felt no animosity after the election. The next day he went to his friend's lodgings in Williamsburg to congratulate him on the victory, but Jefferson was not home. Since Page had to attend court at Gloucester the following day, he would be unable to congratulate the governor-elect properly. Thinking Jefferson might take offense at this unintentional slight, Page wrote a heartfelt letter to tell him that he should not "suspect that I am influenced by some low dirty feelings and avoid seeing you to conceal that Embarasment which might be the Result of them. I can assure you," Page continued, "that I have such Confidence in your good Opinion of my Heart that were it not for the World who may put a wrong Construction on my Conduct I should scarcely trouble you with this Apology. I sincerely wish you all Happiness and will do every thing in my Power to make your Administration easy and agreeable to you."[7]

Their friendship was too strong to let the vagaries of politics interfere with it, and Jefferson wrote Page the following day to reassure him: "It had given me much pain that the zeal of our respective friends should ever have placed you and me in the situation of competitors. I was comforted however with the reflection that it was their competition, not ours, and that the difference of the numbers which decided between us, was too insignificant to give you a pain or me a pleasure had our dispositions towards each other been such as to have admitted those sensations."[8]

Jefferson had not campaigned for the governorship, and he accepted it with reluctance. When Richard Henry Lee congratulated him upon becoming governor, Jefferson responded without enthusiasm: "In a virtuous government, and more especially in times like these, public offices are, what they should be, burthens to those appointed to them which it would be wrong to decline, though foreseen to bring them intense labor and great private loss." Responding to Baron von Riedesel, who had also written to congratulate him upon his election, Jefferson wrote, "Condolances would be better suited to the occasion."[9]

Once again, his public sense of duty was drawing him away from a pleasant social and intellectual circle. Chosen by a group of democratically elected representatives and knowing full well that he had the leadership skills and administrative abilities to govern Virginia, he could scarcely refuse the position, though he understood what the governorship would mean in terms of the time it would take from his domestic pursuits and literary endeavors.

As governor, Jefferson was wary of using his new office to push through reforms without the sanction of the legislature. Though he remained convinced of the validity of his plan for an expanded system of post roads, for example, he made no effort to coerce the legislature into reconsidering the bill. Representative government meant too much to undermine decisions made by those elected by the people, even to introduce what he knew was good for the state and for the nation. Unlike Jefferson, a majority of Virginia senators in 1779 saw no urgency in establishing such a vast, and expensive, network of post roads. The proposed legislation was tabled indefinitely.

War changed the dynamic. In early 1780, the city of Charleston, South Carolina, was under siege, and the American forces there found themselves desperately in need of reinforcements from their French allies. By the middle of May that year, American military leaders were anxiously awaiting the arrival of the French fleet. Writing from military headquarters at Morristown, New Jersey, George Washington sent Jefferson a confidential letter informing him that he expected the French to arrive in a matter of weeks. Since Washington was unsure precisely when or where they would land, he wanted to make sure he would know whenever the French arrived wherever they arrived. Consequently, Washington suggested that men be posted at key positions along the coast and made arrangements to communicate the news of the French arrival as expeditiously as possible. He appointed Major William Galvan, a French volunteer, to take his message to Jefferson first and then to proceed to Cape Henry, where he would establish a lookout for the French fleet.

In his letter to Jefferson, Washington stressed the importance of maintaining the secrecy of Galvan's mission and asked the governor to introduce the major to a confidant near Cape Henry with whom he could live. Washington emphasized the necessity of keeping Galvan "constantly informed of the operations in South Carolina ... as he will be out of the common track of intelligence."[10] Washington's words reminded Jefferson how inadequate the current tracks of intelligence were, especially during wartime.

While stressing the importance of efficient lines of communication, General Washington gave Governor Jefferson no specific directions how to establish them. Washington's letter emphasized the value of an efficient system of communication, not for the general diffusion of public knowledge but rather for the secret communication of military intelligence. Drafting a letter to introduce Major Galvan to a trustworthy person at Cape Henry, Jefferson grew even more convinced of the inadequacy of the current system of communication. In a letter to Galvan dated May 28, 1780, he informed him of the situation at Charleston but admitted that the latest intelligence from there was over a month old. Some of his information was even older than that. In fact, Charleston had fallen to the British two weeks earlier, but Jefferson had yet to learn of the defeat.

He did not wait to learn Charleston's fate before instituting a new system for communicating military intelligence. He closed the letter to Galvan by telling him that whatever urgent news he had to communicate could travel from Cape Henry to Richmond within twenty-four hours.

Jefferson's "Instructions to Express Riders between Richmond and Cape Henry" elaborates the system he put in place for the rapid communication of military intelligence. This document tells each express rider to proceed immediately to his station and "be there in constant readiness, never absenting yourself a moment from your quarters, nor suffering your horse to be out of your instantaneous command." Jefferson also provided detailed instructions concerning how each express rider should handle a communiqué:

> Whenever you shall receive from the express who will be placed next to you any letter or paper from me to Majr. Galvan you will proceed without a moment's delay by night and by day and without regard to weather to carry it down to the next express station. . . . And when you receive a letter or paper from Majr. Galvan to me you are to proceed in like manner with it to this place; always returning to your station, after the delivery, moderately but without delay. You are to give a receipt specifying the hour and minute at which you receive any such paper, and to take a like receipt from the express to whom you shall deliver it.[11]

Having established the express post between Richmond and Cape Henry, Jefferson informed Washington that he would be able to send or receive intelligence between Richmond and Cape Henry in twenty-three hours.[12] That's what he said: not one day or within a day but in twenty-three hours. The figure reveals Jefferson's careful planning and precision, yet such precision would doom him to disappointment. His mathematical calculation of twenty-three hours takes the loyalty and efficiency of the post riders as constants, not variables.

Events during the next week reinforced his decision to establish a system of express riders. The first Monday in June, twenty-four days after the fact, he learned of the fall of Charleston. That same day—though it is unclear how much time passed before Jefferson heard about it—Congress resolved that the governors of Maryland and Virginia engage trusty persons to forward intelligence to Congress as expeditiously as possible. Congress was unaware that the governor of Virginia had already put a system of forwarding intelligence to Congress into place.

This Congressional resolution contains a key component that determines whether this system of communicating military intelligence would work: trusty persons. If only one rider along the line is unreliable or duplicitous, then the whole system fails. Aware of the inherent dangers of such a system yet convinced of its potential value and confident that he could find such persons, Jefferson, with characteristic thoroughness, went well beyond what Congress mandated and sought to establish as many lines of rapid communication as possible and necessary.

Most important, he needed to establish communication between Richmond and the general vicinity of Charleston in order to track the position of the enemy. To head up the operation, he required someone with military knowledge as well as keen powers of judgment. As he told James Wood, "I think the most essential measure is to procure a judicious, sensible officer, not likely to listen to idle tales nor to take alarm at specious dangers." This officer should be dispatched to the vicinity of the British camp

> with a sufficient number of horsemen to leave one at every 40 miles distance, reserving one to be always with himself at the other end of the line for the purpose of conveying his letters from himself to the horse man at the first post. Let him remain as near the enemy as he can safely and shift his position as they shift theirs, always sending proper instructions to the horsemen to make the necessary changes in their stations in order to streighten the line of communication. Let him through these communicate to you from time to time every important movement of the enemy.... If your horsemen are sent on immediately to gain intelligence it should seem that they might obtain and communicate it to you very early, if the enemy should really approach your post.[13]

In this letter to Wood, Jefferson did not mention that he knew someone who could fill the role of "judicious, sensible officer." But he did. The following day he offered the position to an ambitious young man with an eye toward military glory, a twenty-two-year-old Virginian named James Monroe.

A student at William and Mary when the war broke out, Monroe had left college to become a soldier, participating in the campaigns of 1777 and 1778 and rising from lieutenant to major in the process. After serving the governor as a scout, Monroe would begin studying law with Jefferson. The two developed a friendship that would last a lifetime. Speaking of Monroe many years later, Jefferson characterized him as a man with the capacity "to embrace great views of action" and applauded "his character, his enterprise, firmness, industry, and unceasing vigilance."[14] Clearly, Jefferson had already recognized such qualities in him by 1780.

James Monroe, engraved by H. B. Hall's Sons, New York. From Lyon Gardiner Tyler, *Encyclopedia of Virginia Biography* (1915). (Collection of Kevin J. Hayes)

Informing Washington of the express lines between Cape Henry and Richmond and also between Richmond and Cross Creek, Jefferson conveyed his plan to establish another line of rapid communication from Richmond to Washington's headquarters at Morristown, New Jersey. "Perfect and speedy information of what is passing in the South," Jefferson hoped, would aid Washington's military decision-making process.[15] Jefferson's words emphasize the value of gathering detailed, up-to-date information for planning and finely adjusting an overall military strategy. Furthermore, he shrewdly foresaw that the course the war took in the South would determine its eventual outcome. Writing to the governors of Maryland and North Carolina the following month, he explained his plans for additional lines of communication. He also informed Congress of his communication schemes. Before the end of June, Congress approved the lines of communication Jefferson had formed and stipulated that they remain open until further notice.

Had Jefferson been able to find more trusty persons like Monroe, he need not have worried about communication breakdowns, but the typical express riders were scarcely so diligent. Many important messages never made it to the governor or, at least, did not make it there expressly. Even when messages made it through, they could be misinterpreted. Such was the case in Major Galvan's situation.

With the arrival of the French fleet, Washington wrote Jefferson to inform him of the fact, but in so doing apparently made no mention of a second French division yet to arrive. Jefferson dispatched an extract of Washington's letter to Galvan, who interpreted it to mean that his mission at Cape Henry was over. Galvan left for Philadelphia, where his unrequited love for a beautiful widow led him to suicide. Upon leaving Virginia, Galvan disbanded the line of expresses between Richmond and Cape Henry. Consequently, when the second French division arrived, there was no one to herald their arrival and no one there to greet them.

Belatedly, Jefferson wrote the Chevalier d'Anmours, whom the French appointed Vice-Consul to the State of Virginia, to welcome him and apologize for the unintended neglect. He informed the chevalier that the expresses were being reestablished, starting with this very letter. Jefferson also let him know about the checks he had built into the express system, specifically, his requirement that each rider who receives and delivers a communiqué should inscribe the time on it so that sources of delay can be pinpointed and eliminated. "In this way," Jefferson assured d'Anmours, "if they do their duty intelligence should pass between us in 24 hours."[16] Compared with his earlier twenty-three-hour pronouncement to Washington, this one is much less certain and incorporates a big "if." In this letter, Jefferson also let d'Anmours know that along the express line he had established between Richmond and Philadelphia, messages could pass in three days.

Jefferson's comments reflect his wishful thinking more than the reality of the situation. The elaborate communication network he put in place was breaking down, and at the worst possible time—just as British forces were beginning to invade Virginia. In the fall of 1780, about halfway through his second term as governor, Jefferson wrote one correspondent, "I begin to apprehend Treachery in some part of our Chain of Expresses." Thomas Nelson, Jr., now head of the Virginia militia, informed Governor Jefferson the third week of October that British forces had landed. Nelson closed this letter on an ominous note: "I never was in so bad a part of the Country for Intelligence. The Enemy might have secured every pass before I had any Account of their landing. Their numbers I cannot learn, but from their Ships and bringing light Horse with them, I suppose they mean to make their Winter Quarters in this State."[17]

The British arrival, and the failure of intelligence to inform the governor of that fact, reinforced the importance of reestablishing the lines of communication. Jefferson contacted those men responsible for maintaining the lines of express riders and urged them to do their utmost to keep the lines up and running.

Led by the traitor Benedict Arnold, British forces returned to Virginia at the end of December. Once again, communication failed the governor, who did not learn of their arrival for several days. Summing up the situation, Jefferson concluded, "To want of intelligence may be ascribed a great part, if not the whole of the Enemy's late successful incursions to this place." Writing to Governor Jefferson again, Nelson spoke bluntly, "Our Expresses behave most infamously and in what manner to act with them I know not. Unless some rigorous measures are taken with them we shall have no regularity."[18]

References to the system of express riders in Jefferson's official correspondence as governor over the next several months, while the British invasion escalated and intensified, form a chronicle of disappointment. One man Jefferson called upon to establish an express route complained that he had no horses, no money to buy horses, and nowhere to get horses. The man to whom Jefferson gave the responsibility for correcting abuses informed him that the evils inherent in the express system had taken such deep root that it was virtually impossible to destroy them. Another of Jefferson's wartime correspondents reported that one express line was being maintained for about half its length but after that it just petered out, leaving no evidence where either its riders or its horses had gone.

Jefferson's efforts to establish efficient express routes were by no means the only official activities occupying him during his tenure as Virginia governor. In terms of his literary life, the story of the express routes may be the most pertinent aspect of Jefferson's governorship, but his endeavor to establish lines of communication parallel his other endeavors as wartime governor, virtually all of which involved similar frustrations. His strenuous efforts to fill the ranks of the depleted militia, for instance, encountered similar disappointments in terms of manpower, horsepower, and monetary resources.

The encroachment of British troops forced the governor and the Virginia legislators to flee Richmond for Charlottesville around mid-May. After nearly two terms, Jefferson had had enough of being governor. He was overtired and anxious for another to assume leadership of the state. Given the uncertain state of Virginia and its government, he feared that he might end up serving a third term should the Assembly be unable to meet and choose a replacement. Admittedly unprepared for military command by either education or experience, Jefferson believed a military man, specifically, his old friend Thomas Nelson, Jr., would make a better wartime governor. "The union of the civil and military power in the same hands," Jefferson asserted, "would greatly facilitate military measures."[19] When the few state legislators who could make it gathered in Charlottesville late that May, Jefferson placed Nelson's gubernatorial nomination before the Assembly.

Given the chaotic state of affairs in Virginia, Jefferson's departure from the office of governor was not a smooth one. As his second term expired the first of June, he considered himself out of office. Since his successor had yet to assume the governorship, Virginia was effectively without an executive. The British did not know that, however. On Saturday, the second, Lord Cornwallis dispatched Colonel Banastre Tarleton and his mounted regiment to surprise Jefferson and the legislators at Charlottesville.

Captain John Jouett, Jr., a Virginia militiaman, happened to be at the Cuckoo Tavern in Louisa when Tarleton and his men passed by on the main road. Louis Hue Girardin, who heard Jouett's story from Jefferson himself, related, "It was natural enough for him to suspect the enemy's destination. Acquainted with every path and bye road in that part of the country, and mounted on a very fleet horse, he hastened to Charlottesville by a disused and shorter route, and made known the approach, of the British several hours before their arrival."[20] Jouett reached Monticello in time to warn Jefferson of the approaching enemy. If Jefferson had had such dedicated men as Captain Jouett for express riders, the British troops might never have come this far.

To protect his family, Jefferson had already sent them away, remaining at Monticello himself until the last moment. Upon hearing what Jouett had to report, he left Monticello as quickly as possible. Afterward, his political enemies in Virginia decided that he had left his home too hastily and virtually accused Governor Jefferson of both desertion and cowardice—he should have stayed to fight it out with the British cavalry, they claimed. Aware that these accusations were politically motivated and not based on fact, Jefferson found them absurd. He refuted these charges with recourse to literature: the only individual he could think of who would be so foolhardy as to take on British troops single-handedly was not a real person but a fictional character, that renowned knight of La Mancha, Don Quixote. Describing the British forces' approach to Monticello, Isaac Jefferson keenly observed, "It was an awful sight— seemed like the Day of Judgment was come."[21] Did Jefferson's political enemies really expect him to stand and fight such a menace when he was equipped with neither "the enchanted arms of the knight, nor even with his helmet of Mambrino"?

He escaped on Caractacus, a favorite riding horse. The name of the horse reflects its rider's veneration of ancient British history and his attention to Tacitus, whose *Annals* remains virtually the only source for information about Caractacus, a preeminent British chieftain. Besides reflecting Jefferson's literary and historical interests, the horse's name also reflects the political situation around the time it was foaled six years earlier. Sired by Fearnought and foaled just a few days after news of the Battle of Lexington and Concord had reached Virginia, Jefferson named it for the first-century chieftain of western Britain who actively resisted the Roman invasion. What Caractacus lacked in strength he made up for in cunning and topographical knowledge. Ultimately taken prisoner by the Romans, he demonstrated his noble spirit in a speech before Claudius that so impressed the emperor that he released him.

In a memoir of events concerning his last days as governor and the British invasion of Virginia, Jefferson explained that as he departed atop Caractacus, he took a route through the woods and along the mountains. His political enemies accused him of avoiding the public road like a coward, but Jefferson well knew that had he taken the public road, both he and his family might have been detected and taken prisoner. At Enniscorthy, John Cole's plantation, Jefferson overtook his family and dined with them. The next day they traveled together as far as Geddes, the home of Hugh Rose. Learning that the British forces had left Monticello after a short stay, Jefferson returned home briefly but soon rejoined his family at Geddes and escorted them to Poplar Forest, where they would be relatively safe from further depredations on the part of the British.

CHAPTER 17

Notes on the State of Virginia

Jefferson stayed with his family at Poplar Forest through June of 1781. It was during this time that he was thrown from his horse, suffered a bad fall, and broke his arm—not during his retreat from Monticello, as his detractors charged. The injury debilitated him for months but also provided some unexpected leisure, time enough to resume a major writing project he had begun while in the governor's office. This literary effort ultimately took shape as *Notes on the State of Virginia*. In his writings, Jefferson usually refers to this work in the plural, suggesting that he considered it a collection of notes rather than a unified whole. In his preface to the first London edition, he hesitated to mention "the circumstances of the time and place of their composition," which, he asserted, would "open wounds which have already bled enough." Privately, he was more blunt: he told Giovanni Fabbroni the work was written "while our country was wasting under the ravages of a cruel enemy, and whilst the writer was confined to his room by an accidental decrepitude."[1] Unable to leave Poplar Forest, Jefferson was not only physically handicapped, but also handicapped by his separation from most of his books and papers, which he had sent away to distant parts of Virginia for safekeeping in the face of invading British forces. Still, he had enough ideas in mind and enough research materials on hand to get a good start on the manuscript.

For many years, he had accumulated materials pertinent to the history of Virginia. Besides gathering books and manuscripts devoted to its legal and political history, he had collected much additional Virginiana in the form of miscellaneous handwritten notes. Years later he explained, "I had always made it a practice whenever an opportunity occurred of obtaining any information of our country, which might be of use to me in any station public or private, to commit it to writing. These memoranda were on loose papers, bundled up without order, and difficult of re-currence when I had occasion for a particular one."[2]

There's no telling when Jefferson might have given these random notes coherence, but the curiosity of the French regarding their new ally motivated him to assemble his notes and broaden his research. François Marbois, Secretary of the French Legation at Philadelphia, had circu-lated questionnaires regarding all thirteen states among delegates to the Continental Congress the previous year. Joseph Jones, then serving with Virginia's Congressional delegation, recognized the importance of an-swering Marbois's queries and realized that, in terms of both knowledge and passion for the subject, no one was more qualified to respond than Governor Jefferson. Consequently, Jones recopied Marbois's question-naire and sent his transcription to Jefferson. Upon receiving these queries, Jefferson realized that answering them would provide an ex-cellent opportunity for him to assemble his voluminous notes and give them coherence.

Major obstacles prevented him from answering Marbois upon re-ceiving the questionnaire. His gubernatorial responsibilities had left him little time for literary pursuits. During much of his second term, Virginia was besieged by enemy forces. Remarkably, he did manage to find time between invasions to begin drafting his response to Marbois. In late November 1780, after invading British forces had withdrawn yet before Benedict Arnold's invasion the following month, Jefferson was filling in his few spare moments by drafting his notes on Virginia. "I am at present busily employed for Monsr. Marbois without his knowing it," he in-formed the Chevalier d'Anmours and, in so doing, acknowledged his debt to Marbois "for making me much better acquainted with my own country than I ever was before."[3]

The siege of Virginia that occurred in January and the ongoing threat to the state over the next several months prevented Jefferson from completing the questionnaire to his personal satisfaction. There were some queries—those pertaining to commerce, for example—he delib-erately avoided in hopes that Joseph Jones could find someone else to answer them, but there was no one more qualified than Jefferson to undertake the task as a whole. Writing Marbois the first week of March to apologize for the delay, he explained that he would soon have the leisure to complete his notes on Virginia. He did not elaborate what he meant, but he was obviously anticipating the end of his second term as governor and his return home to his family and his books. Looking forward to his retirement from office, Jefferson foresaw his notes on Virginia as an ideal project to complete from the comfort of Monticello.

He had not counted on the war removing him from Monticello or the riding accident that would confine him to Poplar Forest for several weeks. Still, he devoted much energy to *Notes on the State of Virginia* that summer. He could not give his full attention to the project because a more pressing task required his attention. Since his political enemies in the state legislature had accused him of misconduct during his tenure as governor, he had to spend part of that summer preparing a response to the charges, which he would deliver at the next legislative session in December. He expertly answered the charges and ably exonerated himself from wrongdoing, but the accusations wounded him deeply. After the incident, he told James Monroe how he felt about the matter. Jefferson's frankness shows how close the two were becoming: "I had been suspected and suspended in the eyes of the world without the least hint then or afterwards made public which might restrain them from supposing I stood arraigned for treasons of the heart and not mere weaknesses of the head. And I felt that these injuries, for such they have been since acknowledged, had inflicted a wound on my spirit which will only be cured by the all-healing grave."[4]

In early August, he finally returned to Monticello, where he continued working on his notes for Marbois and used his voluminous source materials to double check what he had written so far. Save for a handful of additional details he had yet to find, the manuscript for Marbois was nearing completion. Some pertinent documents he needed were located among the state holdings in Richmond; George Wythe had much additional information in his library. By the third week of December, Jefferson completed a satisfactory draft, had the manuscript copied, and sent one copy to Marbois with a letter apologizing for the delay.

He need not have been apologetic. Though Marbois had distributed his queries to representatives from every state, only a few answered them at all, and none answered them as fully as Jefferson. Marbois graciously thanked him for all his work: "I cannot express to you how grateful I am for the trouble you have taken to draft detailed responses to the questions I had taken the liberty of addressing to you. The Philosophy which has inspired them, the understanding they give me of one of the most important states of the union and the circumstances in which you have taken the trouble to write about them, created the most valuable work that I could take from this country."[5]

No copies of Jefferson's initial set of answers to the queries survive. Almost as soon as he put Marbois's copy in the mail, he began tinkering with his own, revising and expanding its contents, which he would continue over the next few years. Seeking to make the work as authoritative as possible, he elicited the help of others, including family friend Thomas Walker. To encourage Walker's input, Jefferson had made a partial manuscript of the work, mainly the section pertaining to natural history, and sent it to him, asking Walker to read the manuscript and note what facts or observations needed to be corrected, expanded, or deleted.

Before he left Virginia in October 1783, Jefferson made a fair copy of the manuscript of *Notes on the State of Virginia*, which he took with him to Philadelphia that month. When he went to Annapolis in November to serve in Congress, he still had the heavily revised manuscript with him. G. K. Van Hogendorp, a young traveler Jefferson befriended, had a good look at it there. In a subsequent letter to Van Hogendorp, Jefferson reminded him of "the numerous insertions I had made in them from time to time, when I could find a moment for turning to them from other occupations."[6] This description provides a good indication of what the manuscript looked like after nearly two years of revision.

The surviving manuscript of *Notes on the State of Virginia* confirms Jefferson's description. He made many changes to it by inscribing brief passages between the lines. Lengthier revisions he wrote on slips of paper, which he pasted atop canceled passages they replaced. He further expanded his text by composing additional passages on separate slips of paper, which he pasted tab-like to the edges of individual pages. These manuscript tabs must be unfolded to read the manuscript properly.[7]

After significantly expanding his text, Jefferson realized his work had become more than merely answers to a set of queries. It was emerging as a work of considerable importance. He had given the Marquis de Chastellux a copy of the same version he sent Marbois, but after spending two years elaborating his text, he felt like disowning the earlier version. He wrote Chastellux, warning him away from what he had originally given him: "I must caution you to distrust information from my answers to Monsr. de Marbois' queries. I have lately had a little leisure to revise them. I found some things should be omitted many corrected, and more supplied and enlarged. They are swelled nearly to treble bulk."[8] These comments reveal the extent of Jefferson's revisions. He had expanded the manuscript to such an extent that it had grown to three times the size of the version he had originally completed for Marbois.

Despite the length of the expanded version, *Notes on the State of Virginia* is structured much as the original version was structured: as a set of responses to a set of queries. Each chapter addresses a specific query, though Jefferson's answers often extend far beyond the scope of each query. The structure effectively masks the amount of thought Jefferson put into its organization. In the preface to the London edition, he assumed a nonchalant pose by characterizing the work as merely a set of answers to a list of questions: "The following Notes were written in Virginia in the year 1781, and somewhat corrected and enlarged in the winter of 1782, in answer to Queries proposed to the Author, by a Foreigner of Distinction, then residing among us."[9]

Jefferson's statement reinforces what the book's structure implies, that the queries being answered are the same ones Marbois had asked, but that is not the case. The organization of Marbois's original questionnaire differs significantly from the organization of *Notes on the State of Virginia*. As he composed his work, Jefferson greatly revised Marbois's original questionnaire, collapsing multiple queries into single ones in some cases and expanding single ones into multiple queries in others.

The first query in Marbois's list asks about colonial charters, the second about the current state constitution, and the third about state boundaries. Recognizing that the object of the third query made for a better opening, Jefferson combined Marbois's first two queries into one, and shifted them to the middle of his book. Removing these two from the top of the list, he let himself start his work with what had been the subject of Marbois's third query: boundaries.

"Virginia is bounded on the East by the Atlantic" begins Jefferson's answer to the first query in *Notes on the State of Virginia*. Though not one of the most auspicious openings in the history of American literature, this sentence assumes importance by establishing both the physical boundaries that circumscribe the state of Virginia and the parameters that define the book. Jefferson thus created a parallel between the geographical space of Virginia and the textual space of his book. Making the issue of boundaries his first subject, he revealed his personality as well. His desire to establish boundaries before proceeding any further reflects his personal need to exert control over his subject.

By making the Atlantic Ocean his first boundary, Jefferson distinguishes the New World from the Old and, in so doing, emphasizes its uniqueness. After precisely delineating the remaining boundaries, he computes the total area of Virginia. To illustrate its size, he indulges in a little jingoistic breast-beating. By his calculations, Virginia is one-third larger than Great Britain and Ireland put together. Completing his answer to this query, he briefly lists the charters, grants, and other agreements that had created the present boundaries of the state.

Marbois's sixth query asks about Virginia geography. He expected a "notice of the Counties Cities Townships Villages Rivers Rivulets and how far they are navigable. Cascades Caverns Mountains Productions

Trees Plants Fruits and other natural Riches."[10] Jefferson recognized that this single query demanded far more information than could be manageably contained within a single answer, so he split it into five separate queries. Virginia's rivers, for instance, deserved a chapter of their own. Jefferson made it his second.

The names of the first five rivers discussed in this chapter sound familiar to anyone familiar with Virginia geography: James, Chickahominy, Rivanna, York, Potomac. The chapter also mentions the Ohio River. Though Virginia had ceded all territory north of the Ohio to the United States, the land that now forms West Virginia and Kentucky still belonged to Virginia, so the inclusion of the Ohio among Virginia's rivers is perfectly justifiable. Besides, few can quibble with Jefferson's description of the Ohio River. Though he had never seen it himself, he synthesized the accounts of those who had into one grand pronouncement: "The *Ohio* is the most beautiful river on earth." Developing the chapter, Jefferson named other rivers farther west. He included a long discussion of the Mississippi, the western boundary of Virginia, which he called "one of the principal channels of future commerce for the country." But Jefferson did not stop there. Next, he mentioned the Missouri, a river that could open "channels of extensive communication with the western and north-western country." Before concluding the next paragraph, he was considering waterways that could reach as far as Sante Fe and Mexico City.[11]

Over its course, Jefferson's second chapter becomes the antithesis of his first. After establishing his boundaries in the initial chapter, he breaks them in the following one to expand the reach of Virginia across North America to the Gulf of Mexico and the Pacific Ocean. Describing Virginia, Jefferson not only recalled its past; he also anticipated its future. In the beginning, all of North America was Virginia. Such had been the gist of Virginia histories from Captain John Smith to William Stith. Lamenting territory lost to other colonies was already a commonplace of Virginia historiography. In the historical account that prefaced the *History of the Dividing Line*, William Byrd showed how New York had once been part of Virginia and lamented the loss: "Another Limb lopt off from Virginia was New York, which the Dutch seized very unfairly, on pretence of having Purchased it from Captain Hudson, the first Discoverer."[12]

Notes on the State of Virginia perpetuates this discursive tradition. But Jefferson went further than previous Virginia historians. Instead of lamenting the loss, he sought to remedy it. His second chapter looks to the future as it foresees the exploration and expansion of the American West. Indeed, this chapter anticipates an important aspect of Jefferson's presidential policy. Richard Price, for one, read *Notes on the State of Virginia* as proof of Jefferson's qualifications to lead the country.[13] Thanking him for the copy Jefferson gave him, Price mused, "How happy would the united States be were all of them under the direction of Such wisdom and liberality as yours?"

Chapter 3 in *Notes on the States of Virginia* consists of a single sentence in answer to what had been the thirteenth query in Marbois's list. Supplying a "notice of the best sea-ports of the state, and how big are the vessels they can receive," Jefferson observed, "Having no ports but our rivers and creeks, this Query has been answered under the preceding one."[14] Why did Jefferson bother to include this one-sentence chapter at all? Since he had combined some of Marbois's other queries together, he could have easily subsumed this tiny one with the previous query and omitted this chapter altogether.

The chapter represents a literary experiment on Jefferson's part. It may have been inspired by Montesquieu's *Spirit of Laws*, which contained many one-sentence chapters.[15] Alternatively, he may have had a more belletristic source. Laurence Sterne's *Tristram Shandy*, which he alluded to elsewhere in *Notes on the State of Virginia*, set a precedent for the short chapter. The thirteenth chapter of the second book of *Tristram Shandy*, for example, is only three lines long, and it continues a dialogue that had been taking place in the preceding chapter. Jefferson's chapter functions similarly: taking the prefatory query and its one-sentence answer together, this chapter presents a dialogue that continues topics discussed in the previous chapter.

This one-sentence chapter contributes another literary quality to *Notes on the State of Virginia*: it enhances the work's verisimilitude by suggesting that its author is dutifully answering each of the questions he has been asked, one by one, even when he has virtually nothing new to say. The nonchalance Jefferson assumes with this third query is a literary pose that masks the deliberate artistry underlying the structure and content of this work.

Given the time and effort Jefferson spent revising *Notes on the State of Virginia*, he could have restructured the work, removing the queries and revising its contents into distinct sections and chapters, but he did not. He retained the query-and-answer organization to let the work resemble a private manuscript communication. Even as he revised and expanded his text, he did not necessarily envision it as a published work. Rather, he planned to have manuscript copies made for a handful of friends who would appreciate it. When its length became too great to keep having manuscript copies made, he still hesitated to publish it. Instead, he bankrolled the printing costs himself and gave copies to friends with explicit instructions to keep the work from anyone else who might try to reproduce it.

Jefferson's reluctance to publish *Notes on the State of Virginia* helps explain why he retained its structure as a set of answers to a questionnaire. Throughout its composition, he refused to reorganize his work into a more conventional form. He did not want it to seem like something written for public consumption. This impulse also helps explain Jefferson's title. Charles Thomson, who read *Notes on the State of Virginia* after Jefferson had expanded it significantly yet before he had completed his revisions, encouraged him to change the title: "I submit it to your consideration whether you do not owe it to your reputation to publish your work under a more dignified title. In the state in which I saw it I consider it a most excellent Natural history not merely of Virginia but of No. America and possibly equal if not superior to that of any Country yet published."[16] In other words, the finest natural history of North America deserved to be called something else besides *Notes*. Jefferson continued tinkering with his manuscript after receiving Thomson's suggestion, but he refused to change the title.

Even in the printed form of the first edition, *Notes on the State of Virginia* retains the aura of a privately circulated manuscript. In terms of its physical appearance, the highly unusual title page distinguishes Jefferson's book from a published work. The title appears at the tip top. The table of contents appears beneath it, complete with chapter and page numbers. A horizontal rule follows the last item in the table of contents. Unlike a typical eighteenth-century book, neither the publisher nor the place of publication is mentioned on the title page. All that appears below the horizontal rule is a date in Roman numerals.

The date Jefferson chose for his work may be the oddest aspect. The printing of this edition began in 1784 and was completed in 1785. Instead of mentioning either of these years on the title page, Jefferson dated the work earlier. The manuscript of the title page, which Jefferson wrote *after* the printer, Philippe-Denys Pierres, had set the rest of the book in type, contains the date of 1782–1783.[17] In other words, Jefferson dated it from the time he expanded *Notes on the State of Virginia* into something close to its final version. To Jefferson, a date of composition was more pertinent than a date of publication. As far as he was concerned, a date of publication was irrelevant because he did not conceive this private printing a published work at all. He ultimately struck out the year 1783. The first edition of *Notes on the State of Virginia* is dated 1782. This revision reinforces the nonchalant pose Jefferson assumed as he described

Charles Thomson, from Life, 1781–1782, by Charles Willson Peale. (Independence National Historical Park)

the book. Admitting that its composition spanned multiple years would reveal that it was a carefully wrought literary work, an aspect of the work he hesitated to admit.

Comments Jefferson made to recipients of presentation copies reinforce his commitment to keep the work private. Shipping a copy of *Notes* to James Madison, he said that he was intending to "send over a very few copies to particular friends in confidence and burn the rest." He continued, "Do not view me as an author, and attached to what he has written. I am neither. They were at first intended only for Marbois. When I had enlarged them, I thought first of giving copies to three or four friends." Jefferson went so far as to deny that *Notes* made any contribution to literature whatsoever. Mentioning the work to Charles Thomson shortly after it had been printed, Jefferson told him, "In literature nothing new: for I do not consider as having added any thing to that feild my own Notes of which I have had a few copies printed."[18]

Those men privileged enough to receive copies of the privately printed edition respected its author's wishes about keeping the work from the public eye, but some of them found it odd that Jefferson wished to deny the reading public the pleasure and edification the work offered. Louis Guillaume Otto, for one, thanked him for his presentation copy of *Notes on the State of Virginia* but observed, "According to your desire I shall be very careful not to trust your work to any person, who might make an improper use of it, and tho' I conceive that the public would be very much gratified with the interesting particulars contained in it, Your Excellency's determination on this point is a Law, which I shall never attempt to infringe."[19]

Jefferson's efforts to keep his private edition private represent a throwback to an earlier time, a time when it was indecorous or unseemly for respectable people to put their words into print. Through much of the seventeenth century, the colonial South had done without printing presses. Maryland did not get its first press until the last decade of the century, and Virginia did not get its first press until the 1730s. Those who wished to publish their writings sent their manuscripts to London. For many, doing so smacked of Grub Street, that dark region of eighteenth-century London where too many writers working for too little money issued a steady stream of books for the sole purpose of turning a profit. More respectable authors circulated their works in manuscript. If one friend wanted to read something another had written, the author simply had a manuscript copy made for the friend. In this way, writers could control who read their works and ensure that only the most sensitive, convivial souls cast their eyes on them.

Traditionally, the presentation of a manuscript copy of a work functioned as a sign of friendship. The privately printed edition of *Notes* worked in a similar manner. Jefferson explained to Chastellux that the copy he was sending him would serve as a "testimony of the sincere esteem and affection" he felt. Hoping to receive a copy of *Notes on the State of Virginia*, Francis Hopkinson wrote Jefferson: "If you should have any Copies of your Account of Virginia struck off, I shall be much mortified if you do not consider me as one of those friends whom you would wish to gratify."[20] Rest assured, Jefferson earmarked a copy of the first edition for Hopkinson and chose no less a messenger to deliver it than Benjamin Franklin.

Because of its unique circumstances of composition and publication, *Notes on the State of Virginia* occupies a transitional place in literary history. It stands at the crossroads of manuscript culture and print culture. With the early version he completed for Marbois, Jefferson had a few manuscript copies made for friends, including Chastellux. Once the work tripled in bulk, Jefferson realized it had become too long to keep having manuscript copies made, so he reluctantly decided to have the work printed. But even with the first edition, he still treated it like a manuscript work. Instead of publishing it, that is, having a publisher undertake the cost of printing the work and assume the tasks of marketing and distribution, Jefferson assumed the cost of printing and distributed the work himself. The first edition of *Notes on the State of Virginia* was printed, but it was not published in the sense that it was made available to the reading public at large. Jefferson carefully tried to control his readership.

Keeping the work private, he had more freedom to speak his mind. Within his text, Jefferson critiqued both the Virginia constitution and the practice of slavery. The passages against slavery, John Adams said, "are worth Diamonds. They will have more effect than Volumes written by mere Philosophers."[21] Jefferson feared that his critiques would offend Virginia readers, but he hoped that his book would eventually influence political and social behavior in the South. Discussing his reluctance to publish *Notes on the State of Virginia*, he explained to Monroe, "I have taken measures to prevent its publication. My reason is that I fear the terms in which I speak of slavery and of our constitution may produce an irritation which will revolt the minds of our countrymen against reformation in these two articles, and thus do more harm than good."[22] With the first Paris edition, he sent only a few copies to his closest friends in Virginia. Optimistically, he had enough copies printed so that he could send one to every underclassman at William and Mary and thus influence the rising generation of Virginia gentlemen.

Jefferson's actions were well intended, but he was naïve to think that he could control the dissemination of two hundred printed copies the same way an author controlled a few manuscript copies. Once a copy got into the hands of a man who saw profit in the thing, Jefferson realized that the only way he could stop others from publishing surreptitious editions of *Notes on the State of Virginia* would be for him to oversee publication himself. He arranged with the Abbé Morellet to translate the work into French, and eventually found a London publisher to issue an English edition.

Much as the circumstances of its composition and publication mark the *Notes on the State of Virginia* as a transitional work in terms of its relationship to its readers, its contents brand it as a transitional work connecting the Augustan Age to the Romantic Era. A masterpiece of the Enlightenment, it presents an articulate and rational delineation of its subject spoken by the Man of Reason. Occasionally, however, the Man of Feeling takes over from the Man of Reason and imbues the narrative with passion.

Take, for example, Jefferson's description of the Natural Bridge, one of the most famous parts of the book. The subject of the Natural Bridge is not really even pertinent to the fifth query, which asks about Virginia's cascades and caverns, but Jefferson included a detailed description of his favorite geographical landmark in his answer. After carefully delineating its size, providing precise measurements of height, width, and thickness, and describing the Natural Bridge in geometrical terms, Jefferson expressed what it felt like to crawl atop it and gaze downward: "Though the sides of this bridge are provided in some parts with a parapet of fixed rocks, yet few men have resolution to walk to them and look over into the abyss. You involuntarily fall on your hands and feet, creep to the parapet and peep over it. Looking down from this height about a minute, gave me a violent head ach."[23] Over the course of these three sentences, Jefferson switches from the third person ("few men") to the second ("You") to the first ("me"). He thus creates a sense of immediacy, making it seem as if the reader has gone from reading about the Natural Bridge to experiencing it in Jefferson's shoes.

He balanced the description from atop with a view from beneath:

If the view from the top be painful and intolerable, that from below is delightful in an equal extreme. It is impossible for the emotions arising from the sublime, to be felt beyond what they are here: so beautiful an arch, so light, and springing as it were up to heaven, the rapture of the spectator is really indescribable! The fissure continuing narrow, deep, and streight for a considerable distance above and below the bridge, opens a short but very pleasing view of the North mountain on one side, and Blue ridge on the other, at the distance each of them of about five miles.[24]

An unusual geological formation, the Natural Bridge derived its beauty not only from itself but also from its surroundings. As Jefferson's de-

The Natural Bridge, Virginia (1852), by Frederick Edwin Church. (University of Virginia Art Museum, Thomas H. Bayly Building, Charlottesville)

scription suggests, the Natural Bridge was beautiful partly because it framed the beauty of the Virginia wilderness.

To compose this description, Jefferson referred to his memorandum books, in which he had described the Natural Bridge upon seeing it for the first time. This early description contains plenty of measurements and observations but little emotion. Going from the memorandum books to *Notes on the State of Virginia*, Jefferson abbreviated the physical description but enhanced the aesthetic appeal of the Natural Bridge. The delight, the rapture, the sublime terror were all added as Jefferson rewrote his description.

The combination of neoclassical and Romantic elements in *Notes on the State of Virginia* helps explain the diverse reactions to the book. Whereas Charles Thomson had called it an excellent natural history, the English traveler John Davis suggested that the work went well beyond the bounds of natural history. He called *Notes on the State of Virginia* "the book that taught me to think."[25] These two interpretations are not irreconcilable. As a neoclassical work, the book seeks to describe in an encyclopedic way the various features of Virginia: natural, political, and social. Simultaneously, it anticipates the Romantic return to nature. *Notes on the State of Virginia* taught John Davis and others to think because it gave them license to see the world afresh and make their own conclusions about what they observed without regard to what others had said before them.

These classical and Romantic elements of the book also help explain the paradoxical nature of the two queries that begin the work. Whereas Jefferson methodically established the boundaries that contain his subject in his first query, he let his imagination run wild in the second, not only seeing the rivers as geographical features but also foreseeing what they could become in terms of the development of North America. It is the man of Enlightenment in Jefferson that made *Notes on the State of Virginia* into a fine work of natural history and geography, but it is the Romantic dreamer in him that made it one of the classics of early American literature.

CHAPTER 18

The Narrow House

For the Chevalier de Chastellux, the second Saturday in April 1782 "commenced, like every other day in America, by a large breakfast": "ham, butter, fresh eggs, and coffee with milk."[1] Having left Williamsburg five days earlier, Chastellux was headed toward the home of Thomas Jefferson this morning. He had first come to America as a major general in the French Expeditionary Forces, third in command under General Rochambeau. A professional soldier, polished author, and brilliant conversationalist, Chastellux was equally at home on the battlefield, at his desk, or in the salons of Paris. As an author, he had already written a number of works including, most important, *De la Félicité Publique*, a groundbreaking study of social history and the history of social institutions.

During the American Revolution, Chastellux occasionally obtained leave from the service to travel through the United States and witness democracy in its genesis. A year and a half earlier he had ventured from Newport, Rhode Island, to Philadelphia. Since the French navy sailed with a printing press, Chastellux had a small edition of his travel journal printed in quarto to distribute to friends. *Voyage de Newport à Philadelphie*, as he titled this volume of travels, shows that he had already developed a good understanding of the American way of life before he began his tour of Virginia. Later, he combined the text of the Newport edition with his Virginia journal and published them together as *Voyages...dans l'Amérique Septentrionale* or, as the English translation was titled, *Travels in North America*. A delightfully picaresque account of his American experiences, Chastellux's *Voyages* is the finest travel narrative to emerge from the era of the Revolutionary War.

Throughout Virginia, Chastellux traveled with a good-sized entourage: his aide-de-camp, his second aide-de-camp, the Chevalier d'Oyré,

François Jean de Beauvoir, Marquis de Chastellux, from Life, 1782, by Charles Willson Peale. (Independence National Historical Park)

and a half dozen servants, all on horseback. Unsure of the precise route to take this morning, they luckily encountered an Irish immigrant and horse trader, who led them to the foot of the Southwest Mountains. Before the day's end, they parted company with the Irishman and came within view of Monticello. Seeing Jefferson's home for the first time, Chastellux could sense the manner of the man who had built it. Its name, Monticello or "Little Mountain," he thought "a very modest name in-deed, for it is situated upon a very high mountain, but a name which bespeaks the owner's attachment to the language of Italy; and above all to the Fine Arts, of which Italy was the cradle and is still the resort."[2]

What Chastellux wrote in his *Travels* about Jefferson's home constitutes the most detailed account of Monticello as it stood in the early 1780s. His description indicates what Jefferson had completed up to this point as well as what he had yet to complete. Furthermore, Chastellux's account verifies that Jefferson not only designed the building, but also helped to build it:

> This house, of which Mr. Jefferson was the architect, and often the builder, is constructed in an Italian style, and is quite tasteful, although not however without some faults; it consists of a large square pavilion, into which one enters through two porticoes ornamented with columns. The ground floor consists chiefly of a large and lofty *salon*, or drawing room, which is to be decorated entirely in the antique style; above the *salon* is a library of the same form; two small wings, with only a ground floor, and attic, are joined to this pavilion, and are intended to communicate with the kitchen, offices, etc. which will form on either side a kind of basement topped by a terrace.

Including such lengthy detail within his narrative, Chastellux found it necessary to justify the inclusion: "My object in giving these details," he continued, "is not to describe the house, but to prove that it resembles none of the others seen in this country: so that it may be said that Mr. Jefferson is the first American who has consulted the Fine Arts to know how he should shelter himself from the weather."[3] Chastellux's description provides a good indication of how Monticello looked before Jefferson remodeled it during the 1790s.

When the two had met earlier, Jefferson had invited Chastellux to Monticello, so this visit was not unexpected. Consequently, Chastellux was somewhat surprised by the diffidence Jefferson displayed upon his guest's arrival. Chastellux first found his host's "manner grave and even cold." Jefferson's initial reaction reflects his natural shyness but also shows how special his private, domestic world was to him. He so enjoyed the time he spent in his fine, if unfinished, home amid his family and his books that it took him a little while to adjust himself to a visitor, especially one who arrived with nine men and ten horses. But it did not take long for Jefferson to warm to his companionable guest. "But I had no sooner spent two hours with him," Chastellux explained, "than I felt as if we had spent our whole lives together. Walking, the library—above all, conversation which was always varied, always interesting, always sustained by that sweet satisfaction experienced by two persons who in communicating their feelings and opinions invariably find themselves in agreement and who understand each other at the first hint.[4]

Reconstructing the intimate conversations that took place between these two is impossible, but comments made by others who enjoyed the pleasure of Chastellux's company, together with the contents of his *Travels* and the subsequent correspondence he and Jefferson exchanged, partly reveal what they discussed within Jefferson's comfortable home and during their pleasant walks through its environs. Testament to Chastellux's conversational ability survives by no less an authority than Jean-François Marmontel, who said of him: "Never has a man made better use of his own understanding to enjoy that of others. A witticism, a clever remark, a good story opportunely told, delighted him; you might see him leap for joy upon hearing them; and as conversation became more brilliant, the eyes and countenance of Chastellux would become more animated: all success flattered him as if it had been his own."[5] In other words, Chastellux was a good conversationalist not only because he was a good talker but also because he was a good listener.

In *Travels*, Chastellux explains in a general way what he and Jefferson discussed: "Sometimes natural philosophy, at others politics or the arts, were the topics of our conversation, for no object had escaped Mr. Jefferson." After including a lengthy digression in his travel narrative, Chastellux recalled the time he spent at Monticello: "But I perceive that my journal is something like the conversation I had with Mr. Jefferson. I pass from one object to another, and forget myself as I write, as it happened not unfrequently in his society."[6]

The two discussed literature at length, and the depth and breadth of Jefferson's literary knowledge greatly enhanced their conversation. "A man having read a book through," Chastellux observed, has a great advantage in conversation "over him who is only at the beginning."[7] Since Jefferson was so well read, he had something to say about nearly any topic. Though the prose poems of Ossian provided their most notable topic of conversation, the two men also discussed various theories of poetry. Their disagreement over the way poetic meter functioned in English verse sparked a lively discussion. An expert at languages and a great enthusiast of English literature, Chastellux had already authored a book titled *Essai sur l'Union de la Poésie et de la Musique*. Still, Chastellux was unable to sway Jefferson. Their discussion ended unresolved, but their friendship endured. They would take up the topic again at a later time.

Other American conversations Chastellux recorded confirm his literary bent and suggest what else he and Jefferson discussed at Monticello. Staying with a Connecticut family during his New England travels, Chastellux noticed their fine collection of classics and conversed with the eldest son "on various points of literature, and particularly on the manner in which the dead languages should be pronounced." The correct pronunciation of ancient Greek was something Jefferson discussed with others, so it is not hard to imagine him and Chastellux mulling over the subject at Monticello. Traveling through Upstate New York, Chastellux had visited a family whose capacious parlor table held many books and authors worth discussing: Addison, Milton, Richardson, and several other books by important English authors. "The cellar was not nearly so well supplied as the library," he said of this New York home, "for there was neither wine, cider, nor rum, but only some bad cider-brandy, with which I had to make grog."[8] He could not make the same complaint about Monticello, where the wine cellar was stocked nearly as well as the library. In Jefferson's company, Chastellux liberally partook of both.

Not all the time the two spent together at Monticello was filled with conversation. They also played chess, as their subsequent correspondence confirms. Whether talking about literature, playing games of skill, or walking through the woods, Chastellux came to know Jefferson well enough during his time at Monticello to write a flattering character sketch, which Jefferson, as he told its author, "read with a continued blush from beginning to end, as it presented me a lively picture of what I wish to be, but am not. No, my dear Sir," he continued, "the thousand millionth part of what you there say, is more than I deserve."[9]

Given Chastellux's effusive praise, Jefferson's reaction is understandable. Addressing his readers, Chastellux wrote:

> Let me describe to you a man, not yet forty, tall, and with a mild and pleasing countenance, but whose mind and attainments could serve in lieu of all outward graces; an American, who, without ever having quitted his own country, is Musician, Draftsman, Surveyor, Astronomer, Natural Philosopher, Jurist, and Statesman; a Senator of America, who sat for two years in that famous Congress which brought about the Revolution and which is never spoken of here without respect—though with a respect unfortunately mingled with too many misgivings; a Governor of Virginia, who filled this difficult station during the invasions of Arnold, Philips, and Cornwallis; and finally a Philosopher, retired from the world and public business, because the temper of his

fellow citizens is not as yet prepared either to face the truth or to suffer contradictions. A gentle and amiable wife, charming children whose education is his special care, a house to embellish, extensive estates to improve, the arts and sciences to cultivate—these are what remain to Mr. Jefferson, after having played a distinguished role on the stage of the New World, and what he has preferred to the honorable commission of Minister Plenipotentiary in Europe.[10]

As these words suggest, Chastellux was visiting Monticello at a felicitous time in Jefferson's life. Having served as a major figure in American independence, Jefferson now concluded that he had both met his responsibilities to his nation and fulfilled his personal ambitions. As he explained to Monroe the following month: "Before I ventured to declare to my countrymen my determination to retire from public employment I examined well my heart whether it were thoroughly cured of every principle of political ambition, whether no lurking particle remained which might leave me uneasy when reduced within the limits of mere private life. I became satisfied that every fibre of that passion was thoroughly eradicated."[11]

Upon concluding that he had exhausted his political ambitions, Jefferson decided to spend the remainder of his life within the realm of home, family, and intellect. When it came to the matter of education, his responsibilities to his family and his devotion to the life of the mind coincided. Not only was he educating his daughters at Monticello, he was also taking responsibility for the education of his sister's sons and daughters, the Carr children. By this time, the Carrs had moved to Monticello on a more-or-less permanent basis. As far as Jefferson was concerned, the scheme of his life was determined, and he now placed "all prospects of future happiness on domestic and literary objects."[12]

Before they parted company, Jefferson recommended that his new friend take in the Natural Bridge during his tour through Virginia. Chastellux wrote, "Mr. Jefferson would most willingly have taken me there, although this wonder with which he is perfectly acquainted is more than eighty miles from his home; but his wife was expecting her confinement at any moment, and he is as good a husband as he is a philosopher and citizen. He therefore only acted as my guide for about sixteen miles, as far as the crossing of the little Mechum River. Here we parted, and I presume to believe that it was with mutual regret."[13] As Chastellux crossed the river and continued toward the Natural Bridge, Jefferson returned to Monticello to be with Martha as she prepared for the birth of their next child.

By the end of April, Chastellux had completed his tour of Virginia and found himself back in Williamsburg, which, before long, he would leave for Philadelphia on his way back to France. Through the first week of May, Jefferson remained at Monticello during Martha's lying in. So far, they had experienced much bad luck in the matter of children. Though their oldest daughter Patsy was a bright, hearty, athletic nine-year-old, they had lost both their second daughter and their only son in their infancy. Lucy Elizabeth, their fourth daughter, passed away before she turned six months. Mary, their third daughter, was doing well so far. She had celebrated her third birthday the preceding summer.

That spring, Mrs. Jefferson was experiencing a difficult pregnancy, and there was no telling what would happen to either her or the baby she was carrying. Amidst such uncertainty, the aurora borealis appeared around nine o'clock one evening in early May. Jefferson duly recorded the unusual sight in his *Garden Book*. Though beautiful, the appearance of the northern lights did not bode well. Traditionally, they were considered bad omens: signs of illness or death. Two days after the northern lights appeared, again according to Jefferson's *Garden Book*, the buttercups began to bloom. That same day, Martha gave birth to a daughter, whom they named Lucy Elizabeth after the child they had lost the year before. They hoped this Lucy would fair better than her namesake.

The infant seemed to be doing fine in the weeks following the birth. The same cannot be said about her mother. The last months of the pregnancy had been difficult, but the following months were worse. Announcing Lucy's birth to Monroe, Jefferson expressed profound uncertainty about his wife's health: "Mrs. Jefferson has added another daughter to our family. She has ever since and still continues very dangerously ill."[14]

To nine-year-old Patsy, the birth of her youngest sister and the ensuing events became a life-shaping experience. Decades later, she recalled what happened that spring and summer with a clarity transcending the passage of time. She especially remembered the tender care her father devoted to her mother. "As a nurse," she wrote, "no female ever had more tenderness or anxiety.... For four months that she lingered, he was never out of calling; when not at her bedside, he was writing in a small room which opened immediately at the head of her bed."[15] There's no telling what Jefferson wrote in that small room that summer. Virtually no correspondence survives from the period. Most likely, he was continuing to expand *Notes on the State of Virginia*. Regardless what he was working on, the act of writing offered a form of therapy, a way to cope with the threat of his wife's demise. If he wrote anything of a personal nature during Martha's illness, he destroyed it with the rest of the letters they exchanged during their courtship and marriage.

One, and only one, written exchange survives between Thomas and Martha Jefferson, which apparently dates from that summer. This written exchange survives on a scrap of paper folded around a lock of Martha's hair that her husband saved as a memento.[16] On this paper she had written: "Time wastes too fast: every letter I trace tells me with what rapidity life follows my pen. The days and hours of it are flying over our heads like clouds of windy day never to return—more every thing presses on." Recognizing her words as a quotation from one of their favorite works, her husband had completed it: "and every time I kiss thy hand to bid adieu, every absence which follows it, are preludes to that eternal separation which we are shortly to make!"

These words come from a crucial passage late in *Tristram Shandy*. Jefferson had commonplaced the same passage several years earlier. Articulating his thoughts, Tristram recognizes for the first time the destiny that awaits all mankind. The literary effectiveness of the passage requires a sympathetic response on the reader's part.[17] The written exchange between Thomas and Martha Jefferson shows that in their case Sterne's writing had its intended effect. His words emotionally engaged the couple, and they recognized, sadly, how pertinent Tristram's comments were to their own lives.

Having stayed by Martha's bedside throughout the summer months, Jefferson remained there at dawn Friday morning, September 6. As the sun rose, she declined, and her demise became imminent. Her husband could no longer endure the inevitable. Patsy remembered, "A moment before the closing scene, he was led from the room almost in a state of insensibility by his sister Mrs. Carr, who, with great difficulty, got him into his library, where he fainted, and remained so long insensible that they feared he never would revive."[18] At a quarter to noon Martha Jefferson passed away.

During her husband's fainting fit, the family had a pallet moved into the library, where Jefferson remained for weeks. Much as he had nursed his wife, young Patsy took it on herself to nurse him. During this period, she passed her tenth birthday. Having experienced the death of her mother and now faced with the task of nursing her emotionally distraught father, Patsy Jefferson did a lot of growing up that year. Throughout her life, she vividly remembered how her father nervously paced the library floor in the weeks following her mother's death: "He walked almost incessantly night and day, only lying down occasionally, when nature was completely exhausted."[19]

Though Jefferson ended up there by chance and remained there from a kind of emotional lethargy, the library became the place where his grief slowly started to heal. In the past he had sought solace from his books during times of grief. Now, he appears to have acted similarly. A passage from the *Iliad* seemed especially appropriate to convey how he felt toward his wife's death. In book 22, Achilles delivers an emotional apostrophe to the slain Patroclus that shows how he will remember his absent friend. Erecting Martha's tombstone the following year, Jefferson appropriated two lines from Achilles' speech. The original Greek text engraved on the stone can be translated: "Nay, if even in the house of Hades men forget their dead, yet will I even there remember my dear comrade."[20]

With Jefferson ensconced within its walls after his wife's death, the library became a kind of self-imposed sepulchre. What comfort this seclusion could give him was limited, however. After about three weeks, the library walls seemed as if they were closing in on him, and he sought solace in the open air. Shifting the site of his grief from indoors to out, he still kept Patsy by his side. She recalled, "When at last he left his room, he rode out, and from that time he was incessantly on horseback, rambling about the mountain, in the least frequented roads, and just as often through the woods. In those melancholy rambles I was his constant companion, a solitary witness to many a violent burst of grief, the remembrance of which has consecrated particular scenes of that lost home beyond the power of time to obliterate."[21]

Written long afterward, Patsy's recollection may seem clouded by the passage of time and shaped by a deliberately cultivated melancholy, but contemporary documents confirm both her activities and her father's emotions. For almost a month after his wife's death, Jefferson apparently wrote nothing. Eventually taking pen in hand, he conveyed his feelings in a letter to his sister-in-law, Elizabeth Wayles Eppes. Informing her that Patsy was riding five or six miles a day with him, he articulated his emotional state: "This miserable kind of existence is really too burthensome to be borne, and were it not for the infidelity of deserting the sacred charge left me, I could not wish its continuance a moment. For what could it be wished? All my plans of comfort and happiness reversed by a single event and nothing answering in prospect before me but a gloom unbrightened with one chearful expectation."[22]

A letter from Chastellux he received in mid-October brightened Jefferson's spirits considerably. Responding to his friend, Jefferson revealed the therapeutic effect his letter had had: "It found me a little emerging from that stupor of mind which had rendered me as dead to the world as she was whose loss occasioned it. Your letter recalled to my memory, that there were persons still living of much value to me."[23]

This response to Chastellux is dated November 26, from Ampthill, the family plantation of Archibald Cary, where Jefferson had brought his children to have them inoculated against the smallpox. This effort provides the greatest indication that Jefferson was recovering from his grief. He had been unable to prevent his wife's death, but he could take action to protect his children against at least one fatal disease.

While at Ampthill, he received word from James Madison that Congress had once again appointed him minister plenipotentiary to the Court of France. Though he had turned down the appointment earlier, he now accepted it. Summarizing the reasons for his acceptance many years later, Jefferson explained, "I had two months before that lost the cherished companion of my life, in whose affections, unabated on both sides I had lived the last ten years in unchequered happiness. With the public interests, the state of my mind concurred in recommending the change of scene proposed; and I accepted the appointment."[24]

He realized that if he acted quickly, he could sail for France with Chastellux, an opportunity that would allow them sufficient leisure time to indulge in stimulating conversation for weeks—what better way to fill a long and tiresome ocean voyage than in the company of an intellectual kindred spirit. Jefferson wrote Chastellux, expressing his hope to reach Philadelphia before he sailed. The crossing would give Jefferson "full Leisure to learn the result of your observations on the Natural bridge, to communicate to you my answers to the queries of Monsr. de Marbois, to receive edification from you on these and on other subjects of science, considering chess too as a matter of science."[25]

Jefferson left Monticello the week before Christmas and arrived in Philadelphia two days after the holiday. The current minister of France offered him passage in the *Romulus*. That was the good news. The bad news was that the *Romulus* was blocked in by ice a few miles below Baltimore. Jefferson remained in Philadelphia for about a month, but the time was not entirely wasted. He devoted much effort poring over government documents and studying the state of American foreign relations. Throwing himself into the cause of his nation, he had found a way to put his grief behind him. As he had hoped, Chastellux was still in Philadelphia. His companionship provided much comfort.

Before the end of January, Jefferson left Philadelphia for Baltimore and spent nearly a month there doing little beyond waiting for the ice to melt. Before that happened, he learned that a provisional peace treaty between the United States and Great Britain had been signed. He returned to Philadelphia so Congress could excuse him from his appointment. He did not reach home until mid-May.

Since he first began building Monticello, Jefferson always missed his home when he was away. That year he traveled the road to Monticello with mixed feelings. In November, he had decided that the mission to France would take him away, far away, from home for an extended period of time and thus help him forget the great sadness of his wife's death. Now, with the collapse of his mission, he was returning to Monticello much sooner than he had expected. He was unsure how he would handle his feelings of loss.

The evidence suggests that Jefferson squarely confronted the emotional challenge facing him. The library was where he spent the first sorrowful weeks after Martha's death. To the library he returned, this time not to lose himself in grief but to find order. Rebuilt since the Shadwell fire, his library now contained more than 2,500 volumes. A large part of that summer he spent organizing and cataloging the collection.

Classifying his books according to the hierarchy of knowledge set forth by Francis Bacon in the *Advancement of Learning*, Jefferson devised three general categories—history, philosophy, the fine arts—corresponding to Bacon's faculties of the mind: memory, reason, and imagination. Within these three broad categories, he established separate groupings, which he called chapters in his library catalogue. Each chapter has its own organizational scheme. Despite the care with which he organized his books, Jefferson never fully recorded the principles he used to determine individual chapter organization. What his correspondence makes clear, however, is that he devoted enough time and thought to arranging the contents of the individual chapters to become irritated when others ignored his organization.

Jefferson later referred to the organization of the separate chapters as either "chronological or analytical arrangements."[26] This comment is the only known indication Jefferson provided regarding the individual chapter organization. Basically, he had either organized the books chronologically or used some other logical pattern to arrange them—some easier to discern than others.

He subdivided modern history into three chapters, one for foreign, another for British, and a third for American. The books in each of these chapters are organized differently. For the most part, "Modern History / Foreign" is organized geographically, but Jefferson allowed for other subject categories, as well. The first part of the chapter lists chronologies and historical dictionaries. Universal histories and histories of Europe follow. Next come histories of specific nations from different parts of the world, southern Europe first and then northern Europe. Finally, he listed histories of the Near East, Asia, and Africa. Jefferson's analytical arrangement is specific to general, geographic (south to north), and binary (Europe/not Europe).

"Modern History / British," on the other hand, he organized chronologically, according to the closing date of the period of history covered by each work. Those parts of Great Britain separate from England—Scotland, Ireland—each received their own subsections at the end of the chapter. "Modern History / American" is organized chronologically and geographically. Pre-Revolutionary works come first, followed by works chronicling the war, and ending with works detailing postwar history. In the initial group, Jefferson listed general histories first and then histories specific to individual regions and colonies. Whereas European histories were organized from south to north, American histories were organized from north to south, starting with New England and proceeding through New York, New Jersey, Pennsylvania, Virginia, South Carolina, and the Barbados.

Discerning the organizational schemes of each chapter in Jefferson's library catalogue is akin to identifying his patterns of thought. For example, in chapter 17, "Religion," Jefferson made a subcategory of jurisprudence, revealing his understanding that religious beliefs, like law, offer ways to enforce morality and regulate behavior. The organization within the chapter indicates even more about Jefferson's attitude toward religion. It begins with works explaining religious beliefs from ancient Greek and Roman times. George Sale's English translation of the Qur'an comes next, followed by multiple copies of the Old Testament, editions of the Bible incorporating both Old and New Testaments, and then several copies of the New Testament in a number of different scholarly editions.

At first glance, the organization generally seems chronological. The list starts with reference works useful for understanding the numerous gods and goddesses that constitute Greek and Roman mythology. From these beginnings, the catalogue eventually proceeds through Judaism to Christianity. The placement of the Qur'an, much more recent than the sacred scriptures of Judaism and Christianity, disrupts the chronology. Its text was purportedly revealed to Muhammad during the first third of the seventh century, memorized by his followers, and collected in book form after Muhammad's death. In terms of historical chronology, the Qur'an belongs *after* Jefferson's collection of New Testaments. The Qur'an made use of some of the same exemplary figures as the Hebrew

Bible—Abraham, most important—and its text even contains specific references to Christians and Christianity. Alternatively, the Qur'an itself makes its removal from historical chronology justifiable. The text of the Qur'an supposedly transcends matters of chronology—as the word of God, it exists outside of time.

Jefferson did not remove the Qur'an from its historical place because of its timelessness, however. Rather, his religious books, as organized in the manuscript catalogue, follow an analytical scheme that mirrors a chronological one. The idea of progress underlies Jefferson's organization of his religious books, and the list suggests a general progression from pagan to Christian. In *Notes on the State of Virginia*, Jefferson displayed a nonchalant indifference to monotheism and atheism, stating that it little mattered to him were his neighbor "to say there are twenty gods, or no god."[27] The phrase would come back to haunt him. The organization of the library catalogue, on the other hand, suggests that Islam, as a monotheistic religion, represents an advance over the pantheism of ancient times. The catalogue implies that the Islamic belief system improves upon the pagan religions yet falls short of the belief system Christianity represented.[28]

His library catalogue not only reflects how his mind worked, it also reflects Jefferson's state of mind in the summer of 1783. Within a period of just over one year, his library, in terms of its social and personal functions, had transformed itself multiple times. During Chastellux's visit, it represented a location for literary conviviality. Upon his wife's death, it became a site of mourning. Upon his return in May 1783, it became a place of solitude where he could find order by devising his own personal, idiosyncratic scheme of knowledge. The intricate organizational scheme Jefferson devised gave him a way to structure knowledge. Developed in the aftermath of his wife's death, his organizational scheme also offered a way to erect barriers to guard against the vagaries of life and death.

CHAPTER 19

An American Odyssey

On Thursday, October 16, 1783, Thomas Jefferson, now forty, left Monticello to resume his career as a legislator. Earlier that year he had been reelected to the U.S. Congress, the latest session of which was scheduled to convene at Princeton in November. Leaving home, he chose a circuitous route through the Shenandoah Valley. This detour would let him see some of Virginia's more distant scenic areas, places he wanted to describe within his revised and expanded version of *Notes on the State of Virginia*. Patsy, or Martha, as she will now be called, joined her father in the phaeton as he left Monticello, and James Hemings accompanied them on horseback. Think about the time of year and imagine how beautiful the tree-covered hills must have been. Autumn makes a paradise of Virginia, Jefferson told his daughter.[1]

Saturday they reached Madison's Cave, where Jefferson spent much of the day spelunking. The description of this cave, combined with the illustration he sketched for *Notes on the State of Virginia*, brings his experience alive. Reaching the mouth of the cave was no easy task: the entrance was located about two-thirds of the way up a cliff face so steep that, as Jefferson observed, "you may pitch a biscuit from its summit into the river which washes its base."[2] Perhaps Jefferson really did toss a biscuit off the cliff, but he need not have. The proverbial phrase "a biscuit's toss" was a way of indicating proximity, and Jefferson was using the word "biscuit" in a similar manner.

Upon crossing the threshold, he followed the main cave as far back as it would go—about three hundred feet. Calling his illustration an "eye-draught," he suggested that the drawing, though based on his own observations, was not derived by precise measurement. To make his eye-draught as accurate as possible, he followed each of the subordinate caves branching off the main one until they terminated or, at least, became impassable. The lofty, yet irregular ceiling of Madison's Cave contributed to its value as a scenic destination. Jefferson estimated that the height of the ceiling varied from twenty to fifty feet. He also observed water percolating from the ceiling and appreciated the geologic results from an aesthetic standpoint: "This, trickling down the sides of the cave, has incrusted them over in the form of elegant drapery; and dripping from the top of the vault generates on that, and on the base below, stalactites of a conical form, some of which have met and formed massive columns."[3]

From Madison's Cave, the three traveled to the comfortable home of Isaac Zane, where they lingered the better part of a week. Proprietor of the Marlboro Iron Works, Zane wrought fine products for his customers and a substantial profit for himself. Despite his contemporary reputation as a manufacturer and entrepreneur, Zane is better known to literary history as the man who purchased the magnificent library of William Byrd of Westover. Though Jefferson had considered buying the Byrd library shortly after the Shadwell fire, he no longer needed it. By now he had already amassed a collection of books large enough to rival the Byrd collection at its peak. More entrepreneur than bookman, Zane had purchased the library because he thought he could make a profit by reselling it piecemeal. He had the books carted to Philadelphia, where he had contacts in the mercantile business and which had a population large enough to include many well-to-do bookmen among its citizenry.

Consigning the books to Robert Bell, still the city's foremost auctioneer, Zane hoped for a quick profit, but such was not to be. The Byrd books sold slowly. A few prominent Quaker merchants purchased some volumes, and a few congressmen purchased others. Perhaps no one bought more books from the Byrd-Zane collection than James Madison, who was eager to assemble a great personal library of his own. Despite Bell's skill as an auctioneer, his efforts to sell the books had been disappointing. Recently Zane had hired Philadelphia bookseller William Pritchard to replace him, but Pritchard had little more success than Bell in selling the Byrd books.[4]

No doubt the library of William Byrd of Westover occupied part of the conversation during the time Jefferson stayed with Zane, but books were not the only topic the two discussed. Jefferson also mentioned his recent exploration of Madison's Cave. Zane, in turn, informed him about a large and distinctive cave on his property. Zane scarcely realized what he was getting himself into as he spoke. His information piqued his guest's curiosity, and Jefferson convinced his host to show him the cave.

Whereas the entrance to Madison's Cave was horizontal, the one to Zane's was vertical. Reaching Zane's cave required some climbing since its entrance was located atop a ridge. Furthermore, the descent into the cave was a little tricky, and its low ceiling made it more difficult to negotiate than Madison's Cave. Jefferson explained, "You descend 30 or 40 feet, as into a well, from whence the cave then extends, nearly horizontally, 400 feet into the earth, preserving a breadth of from 20 to 50 feet, and a height of from 5 to 12 feet."[5] In practical terms, Jefferson could stand up straight in some parts of the cave, but in others he had to stoop to avoid hitting his head.

During the descent, he noticed that the ambient temperature changed significantly and regretted not having a thermometer with him to record the changes. But Jefferson was not one to give up easily. He wanted those temperature readings, and he was determined to get them. Since he would be stopping in Philadelphia before continuing to Princeton, he was sure he could obtain a proper thermometer there. He secured Zane's promise to take the temperature readings and sent him a thermometer not long afterward, "the only one to be had in Philadelphia."[6] Along with the thermometer, Jefferson supplied precise instructions regarding how to take the cave's temperature. Attesting to his meticulousness, he also asked Zane to take readings in other nearby locations as experimental controls: his ice house, his well, and a spring. Zane complied with the requests of his friend, who subsequently incorporated the temperature readings in *Notes on the State of Virginia*.

From Zane's home, Jefferson proceeded to Harper's Ferry, where he had some more climbing to do before he could appreciate the scenery fully. Behind the tavern here, a steep hill led to a vantage point overlooking the confluence of the Potomac and Shenandoah Rivers. Once he reached the top, he witnessed one of the most majestic sights he had ever seen. He put his experience into words and placed the description within *Notes on the State of Virginia*.

His words are so effusive that some readers challenged their accuracy. When the author of an early-nineteenth-century geography textbook questioned the description's validity, Jefferson refuted him in a personal letter: "I wrote the description from my own view of the spot, stated no fact but what I saw, and can now affirm that no fact is exaggerated. It is true that the same scene may excite very different sensations in different spectators, according to their different sensibilities. The sensations of some may be much stronger than those of others."[7]

It is easy to understand why readers questioned the veracity of Jefferson's description, which constitutes the most highly crafted literary vignette in *Notes on the State of Virginia*:

The passage of the Patowmac through the Blue ridge is perhaps one of the most stupendous scenes in nature. You stand on a very high point of land. On your right comes up the Shenandoah, having ranged along the foot of the mountain an hundred miles to seek a vent. On your left approaches the Patowmac, in quest of a passage also. In the moment of their junction they rush together against the mountain, rend it asunder, and pass off to the sea. The first glance of this scene hurries our senses into the opinion, that this earth has been created in time, that the mountains were formed first, that the rivers began to flow afterwards, that in this place particularly they have been dammed up by the Blue ridge of mountains, and have formed an ocean which filled the whole valley; that continuing to rise they have at length broken over at this spot, and have torn the mountain down from its summit to its base. The piles of rock on each hand, but particularly on the Shenandoah, the evident marks of their disrupture and avulsion from their beds by the most powerful agents of nature, corroborate the impression. But the distant finishing which nature has given to the picture is of a very different character. It is a true contrast to the fore-ground. It is as placid and delightful, as that is wild and tremendous. For the mountain being cloven asunder, she presents to your eye, through the cleft, a small catch of smooth blue horizon, at an infinite distance in the plain country, inviting you, as it were, from the riot and tumult roaring around, to pass through the breach and participate of the calm below. Here the eye ultimately composes itself; and that way too the road happens actually to lead. You cross the Patowmac above the junction, pass along its side through the base of the mountain for three miles, its terrible precipices hanging in fragments over you, and within about 20 miles reach Frederic town and the fine country around that. This scene is worth a voyage across the Atlantic. Yet here, as in the neighbourhood of the natural bridge, are people who have passed their lives within half a dozen miles, and have never been to survey these monuments of a war between rivers and mountains, which must have shaken the earth itself to its center.[8]

This description would draw many tourists to the passage of the Potomac in search of this beauty. Using the second person, he effectively put the reader within the scene. In a way, his word-picture prefigures the visual techniques of the painters of the Hudson River school, who would characteristically depict an individual standing in the foreground of their landscape paintings. Overlooking a beautiful vista, the figure is both an observer of the scene and a participant in it. Writing in second person and describing the scene from a lofty outlook, Jefferson created much the same effect in words.

He enhanced the literary quality of this passage through the use of allusion. Some years earlier, he had commonplaced an epic simile from Ossian that compared the clash of two chieftains on the battlefield with the confluence of two great rivers. Describing two great rivers in *Notes on the State of Virginia*, he used personification to reverse the comparison. In his rendering, the confluence of the Potomac and the Shenandoah resembles a single combat between two great warriors.[9] Furthermore, his words echo a natural description in Herodotus. Annotating his personal copy of *Notes on the State of Virginia*, he cited the precise section of Herodotus he had in mind and revealed his debt to the ancient Greek historian in terms of both diction and ideas expressed. By echoing Herodotus, Jefferson paralleled Virginia with ancient Greece and thus imbued the local landscape with classical splendor.

Shortly before reaching Philadelphia, he received word that Congress would relocate to Annapolis but still intended to convene at Princeton. He stayed in Philadelphia for a few days, spending part of his time buying books. Though his memorandum books, as usual, do not record the titles of the books he bought, they do show him making multiple purchases from William Pritchard. The conclusion is obvious: he was buying books from the Byrd library. Several volumes formerly in the possession of William Byrd became a part of Jefferson's library at Monticello: manuscript collections of laws and early Virginia documents, important legal treatises, and rare editions of Greek classics with learned commentaries.[10]

For the development of his political thought, the most important book he acquired from the Byrd library was James Harrington's *Commonwealth of Oceana*. Casting his political ideas within the framework of a utopia, Harrington had drafted an ideal constitution and elaborated in great detail how it worked within the ideal commonwealth. Harrington provided for two houses of legislation, a senate and a popular assembly. Furthermore, he placed limits on the powers of the executive branch and the term of offices for those serving in governmental posts. He also imagined a magistrate chosen by ballot and devised an elaborate system of checks and balances for the government. Around the time the *Declaration of Independence* was signed, John Adams had commented that the American government had already surpassed anything dreamt of by Harrington. Jefferson's purchase of Harrington's *Oceana* now, before the U.S. Constitution was drafted, suggests that Americans still had much to learn from Harrington.

In Philadelphia, Jefferson was reunited with his dear friend James Madison. After attending college in Princeton, Madison had returned to his native Virginia, where he was elected to the House of Delegates in 1776. Two years later, he was elected to the Governor's Council. In 1780, he was chosen a delegate to the Continental Congress. Describing Madison's progress in a character sketch of his young friend, Jefferson stated, "Trained in these successive schools, he acquired a habit of self-possession which placed at ready command the rich resources of his luminous and discriminating mind, and of his extensive information, and rendered him the first of every assembly afterwards, of which he became a member."[11] The two had met in 1776, and they worked closely together when Jefferson was governor and Madison was serving on the council. Madison had been serving in the Continental Congress almost constantly since 1780, but as the new session of Congress began, his term ended. He was preparing to return to Virginia.

On November 3, Jefferson left Philadelphia for Princeton, arriving the second day of the new Congressional session. At the day's end, to his great frustration, Congress adjourned and agreed to reconvene in Annapolis on November 26. With little else to do, he returned to Philadelphia, where he used the extra time to get some literary business done. By now he had decided to have a limited edition of *Notes on the State of Virginia* privately printed. He showed the fair copy of his manuscript of *Notes on the State of Virginia* to Robert Aitken, who estimated the cost of printing and the amount of time it would take to print it.

While in Philadelphia, Jefferson also had a good look around. Writing to Francis Eppes, he described what he saw and interjected much humor as he conveyed his disapproval of the latest fashions among Philadelphia women. Their elaborate headgear and hairpieces had given way to more low-profile hats, which seemed to change the whole figure in proportion. He observed, "The high head is made as flat as a flounder. Instead of the burthen of lawn, ribbon, false hair etc. the head is covered with a plain chip hat with only a ribbon round the crown. The shoulders are where the chin used to be, and the hips have succeeded to the place of the shoulders. The circumference of the waste is the span of the lady's own hands in order to preserve due proportion. All the residue of the figure is resigned to the possession of a hoop which at each angle before projects like two bastions of a fort."[12] It is good to hear Jefferson laugh again.

On Saturday, November 22, Jefferson left Philadelphia for Annapolis. Madison, on his way home, accompanied him. Together they reached Annapolis three days later. Madison lingered here a few days longer, but eventually said goodbye to his friend. Though parting with one young

Virginia friend, Jefferson rejoined another, James Monroe, who was also currently serving in Congress. Jefferson and Monroe moved into the same rooming house in town and even shared a privy.

Saying hello to Monroe as he said goodbye to Madison, Jefferson would seem to be exchanging one for the other. The two were not exactly interchangeable, however. Madison was more of a scholar. After receiving a good private classical education, he had attended Princeton, graduated, and even stayed an extra year after graduation to study Hebrew. This course of study led some to think he was preparing for the priesthood, but Madison believed far too strongly in religious freedom to wear the collar of an ecclesiastic. Monroe had had a good education, but he was more a man of action than of letters. With the coming of the Revolutionary War, he had left William and Mary before graduating. Now, after having read law under Jefferson, he was trying his hand at being a legislator. Both young men were devoted to both Virginia and the United States, but they differed when it came to the issue of how much power the federal government should wield. The two would remain Jefferson's lifelong friends.

Before leaving Philadelphia for Annapolis, Jefferson had made arrangements for Martha, finding her a place to live and arranging for tutors. Happily, Mrs. Hopkinson—Francis's mother—invited Martha to lodge with her. Francis Hopkinson was one of the most accomplished litterateurs and musicians in early America. Jefferson had known him since they had served together in the Continental Congress together the previous decade. He called Hopkinson "a man of genius, gentility, and great merit."[13] This new arrangement allowed them to renew their friendship and gained Jefferson an amusing correspondent in the bargain. Once Jefferson had settled in Annapolis, Hopkinson wrote to him, anticipating much pleasure in the possibility of their correspondence: "I shall be happy in corresponding with you if you give me any Encouragement. My Fancy suggests a Thousand whims which die for want of Communication, nor would I communicate them but to one who has Discernment to conceive my Humour and Candour with respect to my Faults and Peculiarities. Such a Friend I believe you to be."[14] The delightful letters Jefferson received from Hopkinson in the coming months alleviated the tedium and frustration he experienced during his time in Annapolis.

Jefferson took additional steps to help Martha learn French. He acquired some entertaining books for her: a French translation of *Don Quixote* and a copy of Alain René Lesage's *Gil Blas*, both of which, he said, "are among the best books of their class as far as I am acquainted with them." He also asked Marbois to find her a French tutor. Shortly after reaching Annapolis, Jefferson outlined a general scheme for his daughter's education. "The plan of reading which I have formed for her is considerably different from what I think would be most proper for her sex in any other country than America," he began. His words recall those of his teacher James Maury, who had suggested that local conditions made an American education fundamentally different from a European one. Jefferson continued: "I am obliged in it to extend my views beyond herself, and consider her as possibly at the head of a little family of her own. The chance that in marriage she will draw a blockhead I calculate at about fourteen to one, and of course that the education of her family will probably rest on her own ideas and directions without assistance. With the best poets and prosewriters I shall therefore combine a certain extent of reading in the graver sciences."[15]

His sardonic comment about Martha possibly marrying a blockhead shows that he was recapturing his sense of humor since the dark days surrounding his wife's death. The remark also suggests that he was finding ways to control what he could control and learning to accept what he could not. If his daughter was destined to marry a blockhead, so be it. At least he could assure her and, therefore, her children a good education.

Jefferson did not say where he had purchased copies of *Gil Blas* and *Don Quixote* for his daughter, but during their time in Philadelphia that fall he made substantial purchases at Boinod and Galliard, a new retail establishment specializing in imported French books. He continued to order more books from this shop during his time in Annapolis. Announcing their plans for the business, Messrs. Boinod and Galliard offered customers the opportunity to special order virtually any book: "We shall distinguish ourselves peculiarly in regard to such Books as at this Time are not to be had in the Book-Stores, and which may require a laborious and difficult Search to procure. This Assertion will not appear rash, when it is considered that we have procured punctual, learned and intelligent Correspondents, who will assiduously second our Endeavours to please the Publick."[16] Jefferson took them up on their offer. His Annapolis library, which is known by an inventory prepared shortly before he left the city, contained mostly French books.

Together with this inventory, two other important documents present a picture of Jefferson's literary life during the five and a half months he spent in Annapolis: a lengthy letter he wrote James Madison and the surviving comments of G. K. Van Hogendorp, the young Dutchman who visited Annapolis while Congress was in session. "The best informed man of his age I have ever seen," Jefferson called Hogendorp.[17]

Engaged in the process of drafting legislation to help the government run smoothly, Jefferson was also continuing to study legal theory. Most important, he was deepening his study of natural law. His Annapolis bookshelf contained several crucial new French works on the subject. He was also encouraging younger colleagues to pursue this study as fully as possible. He loaned his copy of Emer de Vattel's *Questions de Droit Natural* to Richard Dobbs Spaight, a representative from North Carolina, and to David Howell, a representative from Rhode Island, he loaned Vattel as well as Fortuné Barthélemy de Félice's *Leçons de Droit de la Nature et des Gens*.

Serving with the author of the *Declaration of Independence*, the junior members of Congress received a thorough grounding in the study of natural law and natural rights. Explaining to a correspondent how he spent his time, Howell, for one, wrote, "I sometimes read. Gov. Jefferson, who is here a Delegate from Virginia, and one of the best members I have ever seen in Congress, has a good Library of French books, and has been so good as to lend me."[18]

Recommending books to his younger colleagues and seeing them in action in Congress, Jefferson, though occasionally frustrated by the slowness of the legislative proceedings, still developed much hope for the new generation of American leaders. In his letter to Madison, he wrote, "I see the best effects produced by sending our young statesmen here [to Congress]. They see the affairs of the Confederacy from a high ground; they learn the importance of the Union, and befriend federal measures when they return. Those who never come here, see our affairs insulated, pursue a system of jealousy and self interest, and distract the Union as much as they can."[19] A successful government, he realized, requires its lawmakers to get to know one another and sympathize with each others' concerns.

For the most part, Jefferson kept to himself when each day's proceedings came to a close. According to Hogendorp, *belles lettres* was his sole diversion.[20] In addition to revising and expanding *Notes on the State of Virginia*, he was also reading widely. He spent his evenings engaged in literary pursuits, partly from preference and partly because he was not in good health. Or should it be the other way around? Jefferson wondered. Could too much reading and study be affecting his physical health? One particular work he had on his Annapolis bookshelf hints that he was asking himself this question and seeking an answer: S. A. D. Tissot's *De la Santé des Gens de Lettres*, a medical treatise devoted to the physical and mental health of the man of letters.

Tissot closely studied the relationship between personal habits and physical health. His general medical handbook, *Advice to the People*, had achieved a popular following among the American reading public in the eighteenth century. Tissot also wrote a number of specific works devoted to different segments of the population. *De la Santé des Gens de Lettres* identifies several different factors adversely affecting the health of the man of letters: the stuffy atmosphere of his study, the vast amounts of tea and coffee scholars consume, the long periods of physical inactivity brought about by hours of reading and writing, and the willingness among scholars to sacrifice their physical health in favor of intellectual endeavor. Isaac Disraeli, one of the work's bookish readers, found that Tissot hit a little too close to home, saying that *De la Santé des Gens de Lettres* "chills and terrifies more than it does good."[21]

Hogendorp came away from Annapolis thoroughly impressed. Summarizing Jefferson's character, he wrote, "He has the shyness that accompanies true worth, which is at first disturbing and which puts off those who seek to know him. Those who persist in knowing him soon discern the man of letters, the lover of natural history, Law, Statecraft, Philosophy, and the friend of mankind."[22] This personal description is remarkably similar to the one Chastellux penned in his journal. Both men noticed a diffidence that warmed into affectionate friendship.

Jefferson's letter to Madison conveys the profound level of affection he extended to close friends and kindred spirits. Once more he was imagining Monticello as the center of an intimate intellectual circle. This time the circle would include James Madison, James Monroe, and William Short, another bright and ambitious young Virginian Jefferson had befriended. Monroe and Short were planning to buy land near Monticello, and Jefferson was urging Madison to do the same. Jefferson argued that rational society was among life's most valuable gratifications: "It informs the mind, sweetens the temper, chears our spirits, and promotes health." In such company, he told his friend, "I could once more venture home and lay myself up for the residue of life, quitting all its contentions which grow daily more and more insupportable. Think of it. To render it practicable only requires you to think it so."[23] Jefferson's sense of the possible is impressive. His advice to Madison applies to everyone. Those who think about the barriers that stand in their way will never reach their goals; those who concentrate on their goals will surmount the intervening barriers with ease.

Jefferson's Monticello dreams would have to wait. On May 7, 1784, Congress appointed him minister plenipotentiary and commissioned him to negotiate treaties of amity and commerce with foreign powers. The appointment would take him to Paris, where John Adams and Benjamin Franklin would join him in this commission. With little hesitation, Jefferson accepted the appointment.

The commission took Jefferson away from what he saw as the tedium, pettiness, and drudgery of Congress. Complaints about Congressional inefficiency occur throughout the letters Jefferson wrote from Annapolis. The critiques that pepper his correspondence belie the extraordinary accomplishments Jefferson made in this, his last term in Congress: he calculated the best possible location for a permanent home for Congress, formulated a plan for carving out new states from the western territories, and designed a decimal system of coinage for the United States. His study of permanent locations for Congress ultimately helped to establish Washington, D.C., as the national capital. In his plan for the western territories, the future states of Illinois, Indiana, Michigan, and Ohio are clearly discernible in nascent form. And the decimal system of coinage Jefferson designed was soon implemented and remains in use today. Take a nickel from your pocket: it almost winks.

After being appointed minister plenipotentiary, Jefferson grew anxious to leave Annapolis but lingered here a few days longer to settle his accounts and divest himself of the personal belongings he had accumulated during his five months here. He sold his home furnishings and his Annapolis library to James Monroe. Since the library consisted mainly of French books he had accumulated recently, Jefferson realized that instead of shipping the library to Paris, it would be more convenient for him to sell the books in Annapolis and replace whatever ones he wished to replace in France.

Leaving Maryland the second week of May, he returned to Philadelphia to speak with Aitken again about printing *Notes on the State of Virginia*. By this time, Jefferson had expanded his manuscript by more than a third. Consequently, Aitken increased his estimate, in terms of both the expense and amount of time it would take to complete. The new estimate was much higher than Jefferson anticipated, but he still wanted Aitken to proceed. When Aitken informed him that the job would take at least three weeks to complete, Jefferson decided against it. He simply could not wait that long. He hoped John Dunlap might print the work more cheaply and expeditiously, but Dunlap was out of town. With the business of his nation rapidly drawing him toward Paris, Jefferson abandoned his hopes of getting *Notes on the State of Virginia* printed in Philadelphia. Instead, he decided to have it printed in Paris if he could find an affordable, reliable English printer there.

By the time he reached Philadelphia, Jefferson was already imagining what life would be like in Paris. He would be able to rejoin Chastellux, who could put him in touch with the leading litterateurs and philosophes of the day. He especially wished to meet the great naturalist the Comte de Buffon. Having taken Buffon to task in the pages of *Notes on the State of Virginia*, Jefferson now hoped to enlighten him on the natural history of North America in person. Such thoughts were in his mind when he passed a Philadelphia hatter's shop one day. The hatter had on display a large panther's skin. Jefferson bought it on the spot and determined to bring it with him to France and present it to Buffon, tangible proof of Buffon's mistake regarding North American wildcats.

Before the end of May, Jefferson had his bags packed. Martha, who would accompany her father to Paris, had her bags packed, too, as did James Hemings, who would travel to France with them. With Martha at his side, Jefferson took the reins of the phaeton and headed north from Philadelphia. Hemings accompanied them on horseback. They crossed New Jersey and soon entered New York. There was little room to spare in the phaeton, but Jefferson found a few books on the well-stocked shelves of James Rivington's New York bookstore he could not live without.

After spending the first week of June in New York, they crossed into Connecticut, where they visited Ezra Stiles, the president of Yale. Given his professional responsibilities as an educator, Stiles was curious to compare his institution with the College of William and Mary. He and Jefferson discussed this subject and others during their time together. Politics and astronomy formed prominent topics of conversation, as their writings suggest. The year before, Stiles had championed Jefferson as the author of the *Declaration of Independence*, the man who "poured the soul of the continent into the monumental act of independence."[24] The letters the two exchanged after Jefferson reached Paris reveal their shared interest in astronomy and other scientific topics. Overall, Stiles was quite impressed. He found Jefferson "a most ingenuous Naturalist and Philosopher, a truly scientific and learned Man, and every way excellent."[25]

From Connecticut, the three travelers passed through Rhode Island to Massachusetts, reaching Boston the third week of June. Here, they arranged to cross the ocean aboard the *Ceres*, a new vessel owned by Boston merchant Nathaniel Tracy, who would be taking the trip with them. Since the *Ceres* would not leave until the first week of July, Jefferson took the opportunity to extend his American odyssey farther north. Leaving Martha in Boston, he ventured into New Hampshire.

Jefferson left no picaresque travel narrative of his journey from Monticello to New Hampshire. Instead, he wrote "Notes on Commerce of the North States," a detailed set of answers to a list of queries drawn up for each state. Remarks he made to George Washington that year reveal the underlying reasons why Jefferson studied its commerce in such detail during his American odyssey: "All the world is becoming commercial. Were it practicable to keep our new empire separated from them we might indulge ourselves in speculating whether commerce contributes to the happiness of mankind. But we cannot separate ourselves from them. Our citizens have had too full a taste of the comforts furnished by the arts and manufactures to be debarred the use of them. We must then in our own defence endeavor to share as large a portion as we can of this modern source of wealth and power."[26] Undoubtedly useful when he composed them, these copious commercial notes, when considered as a literary account of his journey, leave a lot to be desired.

Though he left nothing like Chastellux's *Travels*, Jefferson did observe much else besides the commercial aspects of the American states he visited. In a subsequent letter to Chastellux, he summarized his general impressions of the people he met along the way, especially compared to those he knew in Virginia. Jefferson gave his French friend a candid assessment of the personality traits of Americans from the South compared to those from the North. In the North, he observed, Americans are cool, sober, laborious, persevering, interested, and chicaning. In the South, alternatively, Americans are fiery, voluptuary, indolent, unsteady, generous, and candid. Jefferson's clever diction and sense of balance reveal the care he took crafting this letter. In the northern states, people are "jealous of their own liberties, and just to those of others." He offered an implicit critique of slavery as he said, in contrast, that Americans in the South are "zealous for their own liberties, but trampling on those of others." In the North, people are "superstitious and hypocritical in their religion." In the South, they are "without attachment or pretensions to any religion but that of the heart."[27] In one particular personality trait, Americans from North and South precisely coincide. Regardless which state they call home, Americans everywhere are independent.

PART III

OUR MAN IN PARIS

CHAPTER 20

Bookman in Paris

Boston harbor was cloaked in darkness as the *Ceres* left its mooring shortly before sunrise in early July 1784. The new minister plenipotentiary, his eleven-year-old daughter, and their coachman were snugly aboard, with their considerable baggage stored in its hold. Having driven his phaeton all the way from Monticello, Jefferson was not about to leave it behind. He had it carefully disassembled, crated, and brought aboard as part of his personal luggage. He planned to uncrate it in Le Havre de Grace and make his way to Paris at its reins. Like so many Americans after him, Jefferson was particular about his mode of travel and preferred having his own set of wheels wherever he went.

By noon the following day, the *Ceres* had covered nearly 150 miles. With the passage of another day, Jefferson found himself sufficiently adjusted to sea travel that he was able to do something he loved: keep records. Into his memorandum book, he noted latitude, longitude, distance traveled, temperature, and wind direction. He would continue to keep such statistics every day for the duration of the voyage. He also maintained a list of what he called "miscellaneous circumstances": remarkable occurrences and interesting sights during the voyage.[1] In their first few days at sea, they saw stormy petrels, a sight Jefferson duly noted. Superstitious sailors considered these birds evil omens. As their name suggests, they were harbingers of bad weather. For the time being, the Jeffersons enjoyed fair conditions. On Sunday, the sailors caught some cod—fresh fish for Sunday dinner—and the Jeffersons saw their first whale.

In his record of miscellaneous circumstances, Jefferson did not say what this whale meant to him, but he was becoming fascinated with what it could mean to the United States. During his journey through New England, he recognized the commercial potential of the whaling industry. "Notes on Commerce of the Northern States" contains numerous references to the state of American whaling. In Paris, Jefferson would take an active interest in the whale fishery, especially when it came to its place in trade relations between the United States and Europe. The sperm whale particularly interested him. "An active, fierce animal," he called it, one that required "vast address and boldness in the fisherman."[2] This extract comes from *Observations on the Whale-Fishery*, the brilliant pamphlet Jefferson would present to the French foreign ministry a few years later. Encouraging the French to patronize the American whaling industry, Jefferson would argue persuasively that the exclusion of American whale oil from the French market worked counter to French interests.[3]

The voyage gave him time for reading, and he spent a good part of that time teaching himself Spanish, a fairly simple task according to the story he later told John Quincy Adams. Upon hearing Jefferson's story, Adams recorded in his diary that Jefferson had taught himself Spanish "with the help of a Don Quixote lent him by Mr. Cabot, and a grammar, in the course of a passage to Europe, on which he was but nineteen days at sea. But," young Adams added, "Mr. Jefferson tells large stories."[4] Jefferson's personal correspondence reveals his fondness for hyperbole; Adams's remark suggests that Jefferson also had a reputation for tall talk, an aspect of his character that history has obscured. If there is anything suspicious about what Jefferson told John Quincy Adams, then it is his assertion that he learned the language at this time. Other evidence suggests a prior familiarity with Spanish. Recall what James Duane had told John Adams the previous decade: Spanish was one of several languages Jefferson already knew.

When it comes to the story of his reading aboard the *Ceres*, much additional evidence supports what Jefferson told John Quincy Adams. Embarking on a diplomatic mission overseas, he understood the importance of knowing Spanish. He told Peter Carr that the diplomatic connection between the United States and Spain was making Spanish "the most necessary of the modern languages after the French."[5] The books he acquired from James Rivington's New York bookstore the week he spent in New York included a Spanish dictionary. Apparently unable to purchase a copy of *Don Quixote* in the original before leaving Boston, Jefferson borrowed a two-volume Spanish edition from a member of Boston's prominent Cabot family and agreed to send it back with the *Ceres* when the ship returned to Boston. In his letter of thanks to Mr. Cabot, which has only recently come to light, Jefferson wrote, "I deliver to Mr. Tracy to be returned to you the copy of Don Quixot which you were so obliging as to lend me: for which I return you many thanks.

The winds have been so propitious as to let me get through one volume only: yet this has so far done away the difficulties of the language as that I shall be able to pursue it on shore with pleasure. I have found it a very advantageous disposal of time which could have been applied to no other use, and would have hung heavily on my hands."[6]

This letter reconciles the varying accounts of Jefferson's knowledge of Spanish. Mentioning that he had some difficulties with Spanish suggests that he had studied it beforehand but had not mastered it completely. In other words, when he met Duane in 1775, Jefferson knew the rudiments of Spanish. During this voyage, he refreshed his knowledge by rereading *Don Quixote* with his new dictionary nearby. Presumably, Martha had her French edition of *Don Quixote* handy during the trip, so her father could have consulted the French text whenever he wished to double-check his Spanish. Picture father and daughter aboard ship leisurely sunning themselves on the deck of the *Ceres*, reading *Don Quixote* side by side.

Jefferson understood that reading a familiar text in an unfamiliar language facilitated the language-learning process. Having read *Don Quixote* in French during his youth, he found the Spanish text relatively easy to read, so much so that he boasted about it to John Quincy Adams. He continued to hone his knowledge of the language in Paris, where he purchased separate French and Spanish editions of Fénelon's *Adventures of Telemachus* and, as he sometimes did with editions of foreign language texts, conflated them, that is, had one edition interleaved and bound together with the other. Reading *Telemachus* in a French/Spanish parallel text in Paris, Jefferson continued to improve his knowledge of Spanish.

After two weeks aboard ship, they began seeing more and more vessels coming from the opposite direction. At ten o'clock Saturday evening, July 24, they passed the lighthouse at Scilly. From here, the possibility of dispatching letters arose; several of Jefferson's letters from this date are headed "On board the Ceres off Scilly." In one, he informed John Adams that he was looking for a vessel to take them directly to France. Such was not to be the case. The weather was thick as they approached the coast of Europe, and they encountered no other vessels that could take them to the French coast.

They proceeded through the English Channel as far as the Isle of Wight, where they landed at Cowes that Monday. Despite the last-minute fog, the crossing had turned out to be what few ocean crossings were in Jefferson's day: pleasant *and* expedient. The rugged weather the stormy petrels had foretold had not come to pass. So much for superstition. Throughout the journey, the winds were favorable and the route direct.

Martha's correspondence shows how pleasant the crossing was. In a letter to her Philadelphia friend Eliza Trist, which forms the fullest account of their voyage, she wrote, "We had a lovely passage in a beautiful new ship that had only made one voyage before. There were only six passengers, all of whom papa knew, and a fine sun shine all the way, with the sea which was as calm as a river. I should have no objection at making an other voyage if I could be sure it would be as agreable as the first. We landed in England where we made a very short stay."[7]

Writing to her friend, Martha did not say why they decided to spend a few days in England, but her father, describing the journey to Monroe, told him that she had come down with a fever shortly before they reached Cowes. Consequently, he decided to remain in England until she recuperated. The day after landing, they took the ferry to Portsmouth. A busy seaport and home to the British navy, Portsmouth made a handsome appearance when approached from the sea, crowded as it was with towers and spires and roofs all jumbled together. Here, they found lodgings at the Crown Inn. Jefferson sought the best medical help for Martha he could, which he found in the person of Dr. Thomas Meik, physician to the military garrison at Portsmouth. He also hired a nurse to care for his daughter.[8]

Having placed Martha in good hands, he lingered nearby until her recovery was certain. Allowing her an additional day to recuperate, he decided to take an excursion into the English countryside. From Dr. Meik he had learned that a mutual friend, Elizabeth Blair Thompson, lived in nearby Titchfield. The opportunity of seeing her gave him an excuse for this side trip. The two had been part of the same social circle during their Williamsburg days, and he "recollected with infinite sensibility" the happy times he had passed in her company.[9] In 1769, she had married Samuel Thompson, a captain in the Royal Navy, and the couple settled at Titchfield, where Captain Thompson could live within easy reach of naval headquarters at Portsmouth.

This brief sojourn represents Jefferson's personal introduction to England. He had no previous firsthand knowledge of local traveling customs. What he knew about traveling the English countryside came through reading such spirited novels as *Tom Jones*. Given what transpired over the course of the day he visited Titchfield, his personal experience could easily form a chapter in a picaresque English novel: "A curious adventure, during which our hero is prevented from seeing an old friend by the absence of her husband and the poor judgment of her thick-headed maid-servant."

From Portsmouth, he took the road that looped around the northern shore of the harbor through Fareham to Titchfield, where he called at the Thompson home. One of Mrs. Thompson's servants answered the door and informed him that her mistress was not at home. Though disappointed, Jefferson accepted what the servant had to say and left the Thompson home without seeing his old friend. But the servant had misled the distinguished American visitor. Mrs. Thompson was home, but she was confined to her bedroom, having just lost her baby. Since Captain Thompson was away, the servant thought it best to tell the stranger that the mistress of the house was not at home, seeing it would be inappropriate to let an unaccompanied gentleman into her private chambers, especially during this time of mourning. Disappointed, Jefferson left Titchfield and proceeded toward Gosport, where he could catch the ferry back to Portsmouth.

After sending him off, the servant proceeded upstairs to tell Mrs. Thompson who had called. The news that her old Virginia friend Tom Jefferson, whom she had not seen for many years, had visited and that the servant had sent him away severely mortified Elizabeth. "My stupid servant," she wrote in an apologetic letter to him, "ought to have told you that I was confined up stairs with a little one, (I had just lost,) instead of saying I was not at home." She continued, "Had I known *you* was in the *house*, I should not have denied my self the pleasure of seeing you, and should certainly have interduced you into my Bed Chamber.... I don't know that I was ever more vexed, for believe me I should have rejoyced much to see you."[10] The next day, she dispatched her husband to meet Jefferson at Portsmouth. Captain Thompson's efforts were in vain. A fair wind beckoned, and Jefferson, his daughter, and his coachman were already on their way across the channel by the time the captain reached Portsmouth.

This overnight channel crossing was much less pleasant than their ocean crossing had been. The windowless cabin Jefferson shared with his daughter was dark and confining. "It rained violently," she recalled, "and the sea was exceedingly rough all the time."[11] Their ship set off from England at six o'clock that evening but did not reach Le Havre de Grace until seven the next morning.

Entering France, Jefferson was in for a rude awakening. Though he prided himself on his ability to read French and had spent much of his spare time in Annapolis doing so, he quickly realized that his knowledge of Montaigne and Montesquieu did him little good when it came to making travel arrangements from Le Havre to Paris. His letters say little about the difficulties in communication they encountered. His daughter was more frank. To Eliza Trist, she wrote, "I fear we should have fared as badly at our arival [as on the cramped and stormy voyage] for papa spoke very little french and me not a word, if an Irish gentleman, an entire stranger to us, who seeing our embarrassment, had not been so good as to conduct us to a house and was of great service to us."[12]

They spent two days at Le Havre arranging the final leg of their journey to Paris. The route took them along the Seine, bringing them through what Martha called "the most beautiful country I ever saw in my life."[13] Riding in their elegant Virginia phaeton, they were using a mode of travel that surprised and amazed French countryfolk wherever they stopped. Most took the phaeton to be the contrivance of a wealthy gentleman: every time they stopped to change horses, they were accosted by beggars, an experience virtually unheard of in Virginia.

From Le Havre, they passed through Rouen, Mantes, and Marly. They paused at each place to view the local architectural wonders. At Rouen they saw what Martha described as "a church built by William the conqueror." At Mantes, they visited the twelfth-century church of Notre Dame, which, as Martha said, "had as many steps to go to the top as there are days in the year." Lingering at this cathedral, they enjoyed the statues, the architecture, and the spectacular stained glass. At Marly, they viewed the intricate ironworks that supplied water to the fountains of the royal pleasure gardens. Marly was one of the great tourist destinations of the age, and Jefferson would make his way back there again.

"Behold me at length on the vaunted scene of Europe!" he exclaimed in a letter to Carlo Bellini once he entered the gates of Paris and settled himself within its walls.[14] His words suggest that he entered the city with a sense of grandeur, but the true story of his arrival casts him as an innocent abroad. Arriving in Paris, they checked into the Hôtel d'Orléans on the Rue de Richelieu—without realizing that there were two hotels of that name within the walls of Paris. Jefferson had checked into the wrong one. A few days later he remedied the error and relocated to the Hôtel d'Orléans on the Left Bank.

The first order of business was to get himself and his daughter properly attired for Paris. He also wanted to see Franklin as soon as possible, and he looked forward to renewing his friendship with the Marquis de Chastellux, who would be instrumental in helping to find a school for Martha. In late August, they placed her at Panthemont, an exclusive convent school. Initially, Jefferson was leery about putting her in a Catholic school, but he was assured that many other Protestant girls attended Panthemont and that the school did not make religion a part of its curriculum.

Calling on Franklin within the first few days of his arrival in Paris, Jefferson renewed a friendship that had been firmly cemented in Philadelphia during the mid-1770s. He remembered the keen intellectual conversations they had then and anticipated their renewal. In this, he was not disappointed. Eager for firsthand news of the United States, Franklin listened with great interest to Jefferson about his American odyssey.

The story of his travels offered a helpful corrective to the libels that were filling the British press. As Franklin told Richard Price, "Your Newspapers are full of fictitious Accounts of Distractions in America. We know nothing of them. Mr. Jefferson, just arrived here, after a Journey thro' all the States from Virginia to Boston, assures me that all is quiet, a general Tranquility reigns, and the People well satisfy'd with their present Forms of Government, a few insignificant Persons only excepted."[15] It is not difficult to imagine what else Franklin and Jefferson discussed during their first meeting in Paris. They talked briefly of their commission and the possibility of signing treaties with other nations, but they could do little in this regard until John Adams, the third member of their commission, reached Paris. They talked of absent friends. And they talked about books.

During his time in Paris, Franklin had expanded his personal library significantly. Besides purchasing many books, he had received numerous others as presents from some of the greatest contemporary thinkers, authors, and scientists in Europe. Jefferson apparently complimented him on his impressive library. Franklin called reading the "greatest of all amusements." Jefferson agreed. At this time or another, Franklin made a comment Jefferson enjoyed repeating: "Doctr. Franklin used to say that when he was young, and had time to read, he had not books; and now when he had become old and had books, he had no time."[16]

Jefferson admired Franklin's library, but such admiration made him anxious to start visiting the Paris bookstalls and begin adding to his own collection. The advice Franklin offered on the subject was of minimal use to Jefferson, whose approach to book-buying was much different from Franklin's. Incapacitated by gout and stones, Franklin usually had the books he wanted brought to him. Jefferson, on the other hand, was a great walker. He looked forward to exploring the streets and the bookstalls of Paris on his own.

Franklin's advice about printers may have been more useful than his advice about booksellers. At his instigation, the Duc de la Rochefoucauld had translated a collection of the constitutions of all thirteen American states, which was published as *Constitutions des Treize États-Unis de l'Amérique*. To print the work, Franklin had enlisted the services of Philippe-Denys Pierres, whom he regarded highly. Pierres had just the qualifications Jefferson required: he could print English text accurately and cheaply. Before year's end, Jefferson would make his way to Pierres's print shop on the Rue Saint-Jacques and arrange with him to print *Notes on the State of Virginia*.

After relocating to the other Hôtel d'Orléans, Jefferson was drawn to its nearby bookshops. Many excellent ones were located on the Left Bank. The first bookseller he patronized was Jean Claude Molini, whose shop was on the Rue Mignon. Specializing in Italian books, Molini imported much of his stock from Italy, but he also published some reprints of classic works of Italian literature, including Tasso's *Aminta* and Guarini's *Il Pastor Fido*.

Jefferson's memorandum book makes no mention of what books he bought from Molini the first time he visited his shop, but that year Molini published an edition of Lorenzo Pignotti's *Favole e Novelle*, a collection of verse fables satirizing the follies of the time, which Jefferson did add to his library. Aboard the *Ceres* he had brushed up his Spanish in an effort to improve his qualifications as a diplomat. Now in Paris, he was honing his knowledge of another important modern language. What better way to do so than by reading some humorous topical verse? He later presented the volume to Martha to help her learn Italian.[17] Throughout his time in Paris, he would frequently return to the Rue Mignon to acquire additional books from Molini, Italian and otherwise.

Within his first few weeks in Paris, Jefferson met several other booksellers and found one he preferred above the rest, an old gentleman named Jacques François Froullé. Located on the Quai des Augustins, Froullé's shop was not far from Molini's. Jefferson sometimes visited both on the same day. During his time in Paris, he developed quite an affection for Froullé. Recommending a Paris bookseller to James Monroe, Jefferson singled out Froullé. After buying many books from him and engaging his help in other literary business, Jefferson concluded that Froullé was "one of the most conscientiously honest men" he had ever encountered.[18]

Much as he had bought books for Albemarle friends when he was in Williamsburg and for Virginia friends when he was in Philadelphia, Jefferson bought books for American friends now that he was in Paris. These purchases were on a much grander scale than any purchases he had made for friends in the past. He bought more books for Madison than anyone else. Consider me your bookseller, he had told Madison upon his departure. Jefferson purchased nearly two hundred books for him in Paris, most if not all of them from Froullé.

The books he acquired for Madison cover a wide variety of topics, none more important than those treating the subjects of law and government. The ideas these books contained let Madison apply them in the profound task on which he was engaged, drafting the U.S. Constitution. If Jefferson had any regrets about being in Paris, they involved his inability to help draft this essential document. But he may have aided Madison more than he realized. By selecting pertinent books and shipping them as expeditiously as possible, Jefferson exerted a significant influence on the thought of his friend at a time when he was putting the final touches on the Constitution.

Describing his own characteristic behavior in France some years after returning home, Jefferson wrote, "While residing in Paris, I devoted every afternoon I was disengaged, for a summer or two, in examining all the principal bookstores, turning over every book with my own hand, and putting by everything which related to America, and indeed whatever was rare and valuable in every science."[19] Not only does this statement show how wide-ranging his bookish tastes were; it also provides an insightful portrait of Jefferson in the process of buying books, a process that involved not only his sense of sight but also his sense of touch. Deciding which books to buy, he liked to examine them with his eyes and feel them with his hands. For Jefferson, a book was not only a repository of ideas, it was also a material object, something that gave him a thrill when he came into physical contact with it. In the hands of a sensitive reader, a book has the power to transcend the text it contains and become something magical.

Besides acquiring books for Madison and others who had asked him, Jefferson remembered additional friends as he came across books he thought they might like. The acquisitions he made for Ezra Stiles bring his book-hunting skills alive. Besides showing his thoughtfulness, the following passage, from a letter accompanying some books he sent Stiles, reveals how thoroughly he was combing the Paris bookstalls: "But why, you will ask, do I send you old almanachs, which are proverbially useless? Because, in these publications have appeared from time to time some of the most precious things in astronomy. I have searched out those particular volumes which might be valuable to you on this account."[20] Jefferson shrewdly recognized intellectual value in books that others considered worthless.

After several months of book-buying, he was able to provide some generalizations about the Paris trade to his correspondents on the other side of the Atlantic. Writing home, he informed friends about the price of books in Paris and also about local reading tastes. He found many bargains on French works, but volumes in ancient and foreign languages were quite pricey. As he informed Edmund Randolph, "French books are to be bought here for two thirds of what they can in England. English and Greek and Latin authors cost from 25. to 50. pr. cent more here than in England." Jefferson could speak with some authority about the price of books in England, too, because he was establishing many new contacts in London's world of books. When Jonathan Jackson—"the Sir Charles Grandison of this age," John Adams called him—came over from London in late 1784, he brought multiple books for Jefferson. Writing to Madison, Jefferson made observations similar to those he made to Randolph but also offered a reason why the Greek and Latin books were more expensive in France. Somewhat overgeneralizing, he wrote, "No body here reads them, wherefore they are not printed."[21]

His experience in the Parisian world of books gave Jefferson a good perspective on the literary climate in the United States. Comparing the two places, he identified a lag time of about six years but found that this interval was sufficient for winnowing what was valuable from the literary chaff. As he told Bellini, the French literati are "half a dozen years before us. Books, really good, acquire just reputation in that time, and so become known to us, and communicate to us all their advances in knowledge. Is not this delay compensated by our being placed out of the reach of that swarm of nonsense which issues daily from a thousand presses and perishes almost in issuing?"[22]

To see Jefferson on his daily walks, consider a comment he made to Peter Carr in an admonitory letter from Paris. He recommended his nephew to take a long walk every afternoon, not only to exercise the body but also to give his mind a rest: "Never think of taking a book with you. The object of walking is to relax the mind. You should therefore not permit yourself even to think while you walk. But divert your attention by the objects surrounding you."[23] Jefferson himself may not have taken books with him as he left his home in Paris on his daily walks, but he often returned with some. To him, the bookstalls lining the Quai des Grands Augustins were a part of the city's urban landscape and thus belonged among the objects available to divert his attention as he walked.

Of course, there was much else for him to see throughout the city. Strolling the rues, quais, and boulevards of Paris, Jefferson was a *flâneur* before that term achieved currency. The sights he particularly enjoyed included the Hôtel de Salm, of which he said, "I was violently smitten with the Hôtel de Salm, and used to go to the Thuileries almost daily to look at it"; the Palais Royal, which gave him possible ideas for developing Richmond; and the Grand Colonnade of the Louvre, which, on Jefferson's recommendation, would influence the public buildings in Washington, D.C. For Jefferson, Paris was a visual feast, which satiated him never.[24]

He also began attending the theater during his first few months in Paris, an activity closely allied with his book-buying. For example, four days from the first week of September, his memorandum book records his expenditures for this period as follows:

Sep. 2. Pd. tickets to Italian comedy 18*f.*
3. Pd. for books 17*f*4.
4. Ticket to Italian comedy 6*f.*
5. Pd. Le Gras for books 40*f.*
—pd. for ditto. 62*f*10.[25]

The nature of the surviving evidence permits more to be said about Jefferson's evenings at the theater than his afternoons at the bookshops. Recording that he purchased tickets for "Italian comedy" reveals that he attended the Théâtre des Italiens. Located along the Boulevards across from the Rue Taitbout, this theater had been completed just the year before. There, on Thursday, September 2, he saw two light operas by the foremost composer of *opéra comique*, André-Ernest-Modeste Grétry: *Aucassin et Nicolette*, with libretto by Michel Jean Sedaine, and *Silvain*, with libretto by Jean-François Marmontel. On Saturday he saw two more operas by Grétry with librettos by Marmontel: *Zemire et Azor*, a retelling of the traditional story of Beauty and the Beast, and *La Fausse Magie*, which may be Grétry's most purely comedic work.[26]

Having studied musical composition in Rome and seen *opéra comique* for the first time in Geneva, Grétry was making his reputation in Paris, where he realized the full potential of the genre. He cared less for musical harmony and more for harmony between music and story. He believed that the music should be faithful to the characters portrayed, the words uttered, and the ideas expressed. Putting these beliefs into practice, Grétry succeeded brilliantly. His music complemented the tales his operas told. Furthermore, he did not pander to the crowd. He assumed his audience had sophisticated tastes, and he based his musical compositions on that assumption.[27]

Attending the theater had been a favorite activity of Jefferson's since his William and Mary days, but never had he been able to indulge his passion for the theater as much as he wished. The seat he took at the Théâtre des Italiens this Thursday could scarcely contain his excitement. The performance he witnessed was unlike anything he had seen in Williamsburg or, for that matter, in Philadelphia. Based on a thirteenth-century fable, *Aucassin et Nicolette* told a familiar story of star-crossed lovers whose families were at war. Grétry richly scored the heroic war scenes for brass instruments. The grandeur of *Aucassin et Nicolette* was impressive, but so was the moral of the accompanying work, Marmontel's *Silvain*, which championed the rights of peasant hunters.

By the brief entries in the memorandum book, there is no telling what books Jefferson bought from Gaspar Théodore Le Gras, a bookseller on the Quai de Conti, but there is a close correlation between what he saw at the theater and the dramatic works he was adding to his library. After seeing *Zemire et Azor* and *La Fausse Magie* at the Théâtre des Italiens that Saturday, he added copies of both works to his library. By reading a work he had seen performed, Jefferson could reexperience it through a different medium, thus enhancing his enjoyment and reinforcing his memory.

Despite the high quality of the works of the composers, librettists, and playwrights who plied their trade at the Théâtre des Italiens, they were upstaged that September by three daredevil-scientists, whose balloon ascension was a great scientific event as well as a great display of showmanship.

Jefferson's interest in hydrogen and hot-air balloons was nearly coeval with their invention. Some balloon experiments had been taking place in Philadelphia when Jefferson was in Annapolis, and Francis Hopkinson kept him informed of the latest exhibitions. More belletrist than scientist, Hopkinson found the hydrogen balloon an apt metaphor for the current political activity. In one letter to Jefferson, he playfully observed, "A high flying Politician is I think not unlike a Balloon—he is full of inflammability, he is driven along by every current of Wind, and those who will suffer themselves to be carried up by them run a great Risk that the Bubble may burst and let them fall from the Height to which a principle of Levity had raised them."[28] Despite Hopkinson's flippancy, Jefferson recognized the scientific importance of balloon research. To further his knowledge, he had added to his library the fullest contemporary work on the subject, Barthélemy Faujas de Saint-Fond's *Description des Experience de la Machine Aérostatiques*.

While in Annapolis, Jefferson had prepared a chart of all of the ascensions that had taken place in France, listing date, location, size of balloon, details of its construction and operation, horizontal and vertical distance traveled, and miscellaneous circumstances. Visiting Philadelphia after leaving Annapolis, he had taken the opportunity to attend Dr. John Foulke's lecture and balloon exhibition.

But the balloons Dr. Foulke sent up were not manned balloons—the French ones were. Eager to witness the ascension, Jefferson bought his ticket a day in advance and on Sunday, the nineteenth, joined thousands of others gathered at the Tuileries to watch the three men, the two Roberts brothers and their brother-in-law Colin Hullin, ascend into the sky. They began their ascent just before noon. Their balloon quickly ascended high enough that the thousands of Parisians who had not paid the entry fee could tilt their faces skyward to witness the event. To be sure, this afternoon the streets of Paris resounded with cries of "Ballon! Ballon!" The three would remain afloat nearly seven hours and would travel about 150 miles, landing near Bethune and establishing a record for the longest flight to date. When the Roberts brothers published their account of the flight, *Mémoires de les Expèriences Aérostatiques*, Jefferson bought multiple copies of the pamphlet, one for his own library and others to send home to friends.

Jefferson attended the ascension at the Tuileries with John Adams and his family, who had arrived in Paris two weeks earlier. When Adams had learned of their commission to negotiate treaties of amity and commerce, he was in The Hague while his wife Abigail and their daughter Abigail or Nabby, as she was known among family and close friends, were in London, having recently arrived from America. Learning of his wife's arrival, John Adams was unable to go to her immediately, but he dispatched his son to join her in London and escort her to The Hague. When Adams learned of Jefferson's arrival in Paris—about a month sooner than expected—he decided to join his family in London and escort them to Paris without delay. Even before reaching London, Adams was already imagining the trip from there to Paris. He wrote his son, instructing him to purchase a copy of Samuel Johnson's *Lives of the Poets*, which they would be able to read aloud to amuse themselves on the way from London.

Upon their arrival in Paris, they checked into the Hôtel d'York, which was near the Hôtel d'Orléans, where Jefferson was staying. A few days later they settled at Auteuil, a village on the Right Bank located about four miles west of Paris. Jefferson became a frequent guest in their home and enjoyed their beautiful gardens. Furthermore, Auteuil was near Passy, where Franklin made his home, so Jefferson could meet Adams and travel together with him to Passy, where the three commissioners would plan their strategy.

They held their first meeting on August 30 and met at Passy almost daily for the next several weeks. Joining them was David Humphreys, who had been appointed secretary to the commission. Former aide-de-camp to George Washington, Humphreys had been appointed in time to meet Jefferson in Philadelphia. The two had planned to travel to Paris together. Unable to reach Boston before the *Ceres* set sail, Humphreys had traveled to Paris on his own. Abigail Adams characterized him as a dark-complexioned, stout, well-made, warlike-looking gentleman. She could see industry, probity, and good sense in his face.[29]

Her description hardly sounds as if she is describing a poet, but Humphreys is best known as one of the Connecticut Wits, a group of American poet-patriots that also included John Trumbull and Joel Barlow. Reaching Paris shortly after Jefferson, Humphreys presented him with a copy of Trumbull's epic, *McFingal*. Humphreys himself would continue to write verse in Paris. *A Poem, on the Happiness of America*, which he would publish two years later, celebrates the greatness of America. Humphreys deeply honored Jefferson in this poem, listing him among the founding fathers of the United States and mentioning both his intellectual accomplishments and his patriotism:

> And Jefferson, whose mind with space extends,
> Each science woos, all knowledge comprehends,
> Whose patriot deeds and elevated views
> Demand the tribute of a loftier muse.[30]

Versifying occupied comparatively little of Humphreys's time from his arrival through the first half of the following year, but his responsibilities for the commission kept his pen busy in other ways. Corresponding with nations that the United States hoped would sign treaties occupied a considerable amount of time. So did keeping records of the proceedings of the commission. After eight months, the minutes of the proceedings "already more than half filled a large folio volume."[31]

The hard work of the three commissioners and their diligent secretary went largely for naught. Generally speaking, the Europeans neither knew nor cared about the United States. Mulling over the difficulties he and his fellow commissioners faced among the European nations, Jefferson observed, "They seemed in fact to know little about us, but as rebels who had been successful in throwing off the yoke of the mother country. They were ignorant of our commerce, which had been always monopolized by England, and of the exchange of articles it might offer advantageously to both parties. They were inclined therefore to stand aloof until they could see better what relations might be usefully instituted with us."[32]

The American commissioners did sign a treaty with Prussia, but otherwise their efforts, though time-consuming, bore little fruit. Confidentially informing George Washington of the situation, Humphreys wrote, "As to the state of our own politicks I can only say (and that for

Abigail Adams, after a painting by C. Schessle. From Rufus Wilmot
Griswold, *The Republican Court* (1854). (Collection of Kevin J. Hayes)

your ear alone) that the Treaties in contemplation which extend to all the commercial powers of Europe, tho' progressive, still they go slowly on; insomuch that I have had occasion to remark that there is no Sovereign in Europe but the King of Prussia who seems to do his business himself or even to know that it is done at all."[33]

Realizing that the commission would keep him in Paris for a lengthy period of time, Jefferson decided to relocate to more permanent quarters. On October 16, 1784, he signed a lease for a home on the Cul de Sac Taitbout. The proximity of his new home to the Théâtre des Italiens may have been one factor motivating his choice. By taking a house in the heart of Paris, Jefferson distinguished himself from his suburb-dwelling fellow commissioners. His new house gave the Adamses a home base whenever they ventured into the city. John Quincy Adams and sister Abigail sometimes came to Jefferson's home, dined with him, and then continued to enjoy his hospitality as he treated them to evenings at the theater. Literature was one topic of conversation among them. Young Adams let Jefferson know about his fondness for poetry, especially amatory verses. Speaking of his son many years later, John Adams told Jefferson, "I call him our John, because when you was at the Cul de sac at Paris, he appeared to me to be almost as much your boy as mine."[34]

Sickness put a crimp in Jefferson's activities in late autumn. Toward the end of October, he was struck with a malady that kept him indoors through much of the winter. It is tempting to view his affliction as a sympathetic illness. Back home in Virginia that year the whooping cough was afflicting many children, including his other daughters, Mary and Lucy. Mary recovered, but Lucy did not. Jefferson learned of her death in January. Grief exacerbated his own illness, and it was not until the end of the winter that he recuperated.

Writing Monroe in March, he explained, "I have had a very bad winter, having been confined the greatest part of it. A seasoning, as they call it is the lot of most strangers: and none, I believe have experienced a more severe one than myself. The air is extremely damp, and the waters very unwholesome. We have had for three weeks past a warm visit from the sun (my almighty physician) and I find myself almost reestablished. I begin now to be able to walk 4. or 5. miles a day, and find myself much the better for it." By April, he reported being able "to walk six or eight miles a day, which I do very regularly."[35]

Big changes were taking place in the diplomatic world that spring. Congress had appointed John Adams minister to the court of England and Jefferson minister to the court of France, taking over Franklin's position upon his retirement. Adams would leave for England in May,

John Adams, by Mather Brown. (Boston Athenaeum)

and Franklin would leave for Philadelphia in July. Even with Franklin's departure, Adams and Jefferson retained their responsibilities to negotiate treaties of amity and commerce with other nations. The commission would not expire until the following year, and the two remaining commissioners would make additional efforts to sign treaties with other nations.

Shortly before Adams and his family left Paris, Pierres, at long last, had finished printing *Notes on the State of Virginia*. Jefferson presented a copy to Adams. Though they had read Johnson's *Lives of the Poets* during their trip from London to Paris the year before, they read *Notes on the State of Virginia* on their way from Paris back to London. On the road, Adams wrote Jefferson a letter to express his gratitude: "I thank you kindly for your Book. It is our Meditation all the Day long. I cannot now say much about it, but I think it will do its Author and his Country great Honour." John Quincy Adams liked the book so well that he read it again the next year. Describing one summer night's activity in his diary, he wrote, "In the evening I read about one half of Mr. Jefferson's Notes upon Virginia, and was very much pleased with them; there is a great deal of learning shown without ostentation, and a spirit of philosophy equally instructive and entertaining."[36]

John Adams paid further tribute to *Notes on the State of Virginia*, not in words but in images. The following year Adams engaged the services of Mather Brown, a young New England portrait painter who, after studying with Gilbert Stuart and Benjamin West, had recently established a London studio of his own. Eighteenth-century portrait painters often depicted their subjects with books and even went so far as to letter in spine titles. It was up to the sitter to decide which title or titles were depicted in the portrait.[37] Adams chose to be depicted with his copy of *Notes on the State of Virginia* or, as the volume appears in the portrait, "Jefferson's Hist: of Virginia." Like Charles Thomson, Adams, too, thought the book deserved a more expansive title than the one Jefferson had given it. Associating himself with Jefferson's book, Adams honored his friend and conveyed his respect for his intellectual accomplishments. Though Jefferson had been reluctant to have his book printed, Adams clearly recognized that the book was not only a vehicle for Jefferson's thought, it was also as an icon of his mind.

CHAPTER 21

Talking about Literature

Jefferson traveled to Versailles in May 1785 to assume his position as American minister to the Court of France. Presenting his credentials to King Louis XVI and the Comte de Vergennes, he underwent what he called the "ceremonies usual on such occasions." His matter-of-fact description of the experience shows how little he cared for such pomp. Neither his contemporary correspondence nor his subsequent reminiscences reveal anything further about this visit to Versailles. However, there was one aspect of becoming ambassador Jefferson frequently recalled. Informing French acquaintances and officials of his new position in the forthcoming weeks, he had to endure the same question time and again.[1]

"C'est vous, Monsieur, qui remplace le Docteur Franklin?" they asked. "It is you, sir, who replaces Doctor Franklin?"

"No one can replace him," Jefferson generally replied, "I am only his successor."

The question became tiresome. "The succession to Dr. Franklin, at the court of France," he remembered, "was an excellent school of humility."

Franklin's shoes were tough ones to fill. Not only had he established a scientific reputation that extended to all corners of Europe, but he also had an international reputation as a diplomat and statesman. In short, he was the most famous American in the world. But his lively wit and convivial personality helped make Franklin the darling of Paris. He had become a literary leader in this, the most cosmopolitan city in the world. His French bagatelles were the finest in the language, and his presence in a Parisian salon lent much prestige to the salonnière. Though Jefferson lacked Franklin's flair, he slowly realized that joining the Parisian social scene was a part of the job, and he eventually took the plunge. To some extent, Franklin helped introduce his successor to the literary salons and scientific circles. For the most part, Jefferson found his own place among the literati of Paris.

Even before he left America, Jefferson had made several friends among France's intellectual elite. Crèvecoeur, whose *Letters from an American Farmer* had earned him a honored place among the philosophes, was serving as French consul to New York, New Jersey, and Connecticut when Jefferson left the United States for France. Crèvecoeur had written letters of introduction for him to his Paris friends, including the Duc de la Rochefoucauld, whose friendship could provide much pleasure and influence. "The pearl of all the Dukes," Crèvecoeur called him in a letter to Jefferson. "His House is the Center of reunion where Men of Genius and abilities often Meet," he continued. "You have therefore a great Right To Share his Friendship."[2]

The Marquis de Lafayette, who was also in America when Jefferson reached Paris, wrote his friends and family urging them to help Jefferson. Philip Mazzei was well connected among the intellectual elite of Paris, too. He wrote several letters of introduction and offered Jefferson much personal advice about whom to meet. He also recommended getting to know Rochefoucauld, whose house "is devoted to Philosophy" and whose "garden to experiments for the improvement of knowledge." Chastellux, Jefferson's best friend in Paris, helped introduce him to many different philosophes and litterateurs. Overall, Paris offered someone with Jefferson's interests and abilities plentiful opportunities for intellectual diversion. As Crèvecoeur told him, "I hope You'll be pleas'd with our Social Scene, which is the Shining Side of our nation."[3]

During his first year in France, Jefferson became acquainted with the distinguished people his friends had recommended, but he hesitated to enter the world of the Paris salons. After a year in Paris, he told a correspondent, "I am savage enough to prefer the woods, the wilds, and the independence of Monticello, to all the brilliant pleasures of this gay capital."[4] Not until the time for Franklin's departure neared did Jefferson accept the necessity of joining a salon.

There were definite personal benefits to entering the social scene, as one of Jefferson's anecdotes about Franklin reveals.[5] As he watched Franklin say goodbye to his French friends, Jefferson noticed the ladies smother him with embraces. When Franklin introduced him as his successor to them, Jefferson, referring to their affectionate embraces, wished that Franklin "would transfer these privileges to me."

"You are too young a man," Franklin told him.

Jefferson did make friends with many influential women during his time in Paris. His position as minister to the Court of France required more social activity than he usually enjoyed. But proper conduct in the finest social circles, he slowly realized, would favorably influence French attitudes toward the United States. By establishing a presence in a prominent salon, he could not only assert his own intellectual and social standing among France's literary elite, but also assert his nation's intellectual and social standing. Nearly a year after he arrived in Paris, Jefferson accepted an invitation to visit the country house of the Comtesse d'Houdetot at Sannois.

Considered one of the great romantic figures of her era, the Comtesse d'Houdetot became so despite the defects in her personal appearance. With crossed eyes and a sallow, pock-marked complexion, she hardly had the physical beauty to sustain her reputation, but the Comtesse nonetheless had a sexual appeal men found irresistible. The author of *Les Liasons Dangereuses* said of her, "She knew that the great affair of life is love."[6] The Comtesse also had a keen mind, which accounts for her particular appeal among the philosophes. For decades she had a steady lover in the Marquis de Saint-Lambert, who was a fixture in her salon. But her devotion to Saint-Lambert did not stop Jean-Jacques Rousseau from falling in love with her. Rousseau's love went unrequited, but the Comtesse inspired the heroine of *La Nouvelle Héloïse*, and Rousseau revealed his love for her in the second part of his *Confessions*.

On Monday, June 20, Jefferson left Paris to make his first visit to Sannois. That morning was fairly cool, 55 degrees Fahrenheit to be precise: Jefferson took time before leaving to check his thermometer and record the temperature in his daily weather log. Reaching Saint Denis, he stopped to have breakfast and to see the Basilica before completing the remaining distance to Sannois, where he spent most of the day with the Comtesse and her other house guests. He did not return to Paris until late: the blank space in his weather log suggests that he was not around to take his usual end-of-the-day temperature reading.

He came away from the Comtesse's country house quite pleased with his visit. The next day he wrote Abigail Adams to tell her about it: "I took a trip yesterday to Sannois and commenced an acquaintance with the old Countess d'Hocquetout. I received much pleasure from it and hope it has opened a door of admission for me to the circle of literati with which she is environed."[7]

As Jefferson predicted, his friendship with the Comtesse helped introduce him to other important literary figures. And he would return to Sannois. The Comtesse had a fine garden there and asked his help in obtaining some American plants for cultivation. He also became a frequent visitor to her townhouse. After returning to America, he wrote a heartfelt letter thanking her for the "manifold kindnesses by which you added so much to the happiness of my stay in Paris."[8]

Beyond a few brief references in his correspondence, the record of Jefferson's friendship with the Comtesse is quite sparse. Some comments he made in conversation with Daniel Webster reveal much about his place in her salon. After visiting Monticello and speaking with him at length, Webster noted that Jefferson's French experience was a favorite topic of conversation. Others who recorded conversations with Jefferson confirm the pleasure he took in talking about his time in France, but Webster's account forms one of the most important documents detailing Jefferson's personal life in France.[9]

"Madame Houdetot's society was one of the most agreeable in Paris, when I was there," Jefferson told Webster. "She inherited the materials of which it was composed, from Mad. de Tencin, and Mad. de Geoffrin. St.-Lambert was always there, and it was generally believed that every evening on his return home, he wrote down the substance of the conversations he had held there, with D'Alembert, Diderot, and the other distinguished persons, who frequented her house. From these conversations, he made his books."[10]

According to Webster's notes, Jefferson, even in conversation, said virtually nothing about his personal presence in the Comtesse's salon. Instead, he offered what amounted to a brief history of the Paris salon as it had developed over the course of the eighteenth century. Marquise de Tencin established the most prestigious salon of the early eighteenth century. Upon meeting Marie-Thérèse Geoffrin, Madame de Tencin began grooming the younger woman as her successor. Madame Geoffrin's salon, in turn, became the most influential one of the midcentury and she one of the most powerful women of her day. The Comtesse d'Houdetot took over from Madame Geoffrin, inheriting both her prestige and the membership of her salon.

This line of succession meant much to those who attended these salons. Madame Geoffrin had attracted the likes of Denis Diderot and Jean le Rond D'Alembert to her salon, and the Comtesse d'Houdetot brought them to hers. Even after inheriting such distinguished philosophes, the salonnière could not rest on her laurels. To sustain her reputation, she had to maintain and enhance the quality of her salon by luring new regulars to it. The Comtesse d'Houdetot's greatest coup may have been luring Benjamin Franklin to her salon. Bringing Jefferson into her fold was less impressive, but as the highest ranking American official in France and the author of the increasingly well-respected *Notes on the State of Virginia*, Jefferson did add prestige to the Comtesse's salon at a crucial moment.

He joined the Comtesse's literary circle during a period of transition: Franklin was leaving France that year; Diderot had died the year before and D'Alembert the year before that. Discussing the place of Diderot and D'Alembert in the Comtesse d'Houdetot's literary circle, Jefferson was describing social activities he knew only secondhand from Saint-Lambert. But he had great respect for Saint-Lambert, who would translate his *Act for Establishing Religious Freedom* into French and publish it in a parallel French/English edition. Asserting that Saint-Lambert wrote his books on the basis of what he heard from Diderot and D'Alembert in the salon of Comtesse d'Houdetot, Jefferson was not critiquing him. Rather, he was emphasizing how important conversation within the salons was to French literary culture. As his remarks to Webster suggest, Jefferson realized that some of the finest literature produced in France during the eighteenth century was inspired by and could be traced to conversations that occurred within its salons.

Jefferson's responsibilities as a diplomat and his foray into the world of the Parisian salons frequently coincided. He came to know the great finance minister Jacques Necker, whose wife also had a well-respected salon—despite her awkwardness in conversation. She was what was known in Virginia as a "budge"—a nervous, fidgety person. Jefferson recalled: "She could rarely remain long in the same place, or converse long on the same subject. I have known her get up from table five or six times in the course of a dinner, and walk up and down her Saloon, to compose herself."[11]

Germaine, the Neckers' precocious daughter, grew up within her mother's salon, where she developed a reputation for brilliant conversation and keen philosophical insight. With her marriage in 1786 to Baron de Staël, the Swedish ambassador to Paris, she established a salon of her own in their home on the Rue du Bac. Jefferson visited Madame de Staël's salon as he had visited her mother's. Sometimes he had diplomatic business to transact with the baron, but often he came to enjoy her conversation.[12]

Jefferson fondly remembered the time he spent with Madame de Staël. One Monticello visitor reported, "He amused us very much with an account of interviews which took place between Madame de Staël and himself when he was in Paris and of the laughable mistakes which she would make in her attempts to speak English."[13] This observation makes it sound like Jefferson was making fun of her, but he had great respect for Madame de Staël. She was in her early twenties when he came to know her in Paris. She had not perfected her English, but she had obviously learned to laugh about her mistakes. Their friendship endured after Jefferson left Paris, and they exchanged several letters in the coming years. His regard for her intellect shows in one letter to her: he called France the only country offering "elements of society analogous to the powers of your mind."[14]

Another compliment Jefferson gave Madame de Staël reveals much about what they discussed in Paris. Writing him in 1807, she promised to send a copy of her novel, *Corinne, ou l'Italie*. Jefferson responded, "I shall read with great pleasure whatever comes from your pen, having known its powers when I was in a situation to judge, nearer at hand, the talents which directed it."[15] Jefferson does not say what writings of hers he had previously read. The only work she had published before he left Paris was *Lettres sur les Ouvrages et le Caractère de J.-J. Rousseau*, her controversial defense of Rousseau's writings, especially *La Nouvelle Héloïse*. Jefferson's friendship with Madame de Staël encouraged his interest in the writings of Rousseau. He acquired Pierre Alexandre Peyrou's edition of Rousseau's *Oeuvres Completes* as well as an edition of Rousseau's correspondence, which together formed a thirty-eight-volume collection.[16]

Having been a part of Professor Small's Williamsburg circle in college and having attempted to make Monticello the center of a small intellectual circle himself, Jefferson's salon experiences reinforced the value of the intellectual circle as both a pleasurable diversion and a catalyst for new ideas. He did form a circle of his own in Paris, but as the American ambassador, his Parisian circle was more national in scope than literary or intellectual. His home became a gathering place for Americans in Paris and Parisians with American interests.

William Short, who arrived at the summer's end, quickly became the most constant and loyal member of Jefferson's Paris circle. A Virginian born and bred, Short had attended the College of William and Mary and afterward read law under George Wythe. Jefferson, who recognized Short's "peculiar talent for prying into facts," had helped oversee his education, going so far as to consider him his "adoptive son."[17] Through Jefferson's influence, Short became a member of the Virginia Executive Council, a position he resigned to travel through Europe. In Paris, Jefferson appointed him his private secretary. Short's friendship for his mentor offers yet another example of the personal devotion Jefferson inspired in the talented, intelligent men he encountered. Short would remain a lifelong friend and steady correspondent. As a young man, Short received much encouragement from Jefferson. Once Jefferson eventually retired from public office, no one would encourage his literary ambitions more than Short.

One of the most unusual characters to enter Jefferson's Paris circle was John Ledyard, who makes his first appearance in the memorandum books in June 1785. More is known about Jefferson's contact with this wayward American than his contact with more distinguished Parisians because, unlike Ledyard, Jefferson's French friends did not visit him begging for money. Ledyard had great ambition yet lacked the means to explore the world as he wished. He is mentioned several times in the memorandum books, as Jefferson accounted for the various sums he gave or loaned this daring countryman of his.

He characterized Ledyard as "a man of genius, of some science, and of fearless courage, and enterprise," who had "distinguished himself on several occasions by an unrivaled intrepidity." Already Ledyard had sailed the South Pacific with Captain Cook. When his plans to establish a fur-trading company failed, Ledyard, being "of a roaming, restless character," decided to explore the American West and thought he might get there the hard way—by entering Russia, crossing Siberia to Kamschatka, and taking passage in a Russian vessel bound for Alaska.[18]

Jefferson did more for Ledyard than merely loan him money. He supported this American explorer's ambitious plan for crossing Russia and sought help from another of his close friends in Paris, Baron de Grimm. Though ugly and deformed, Grimm was "the pleasantest, and most conversible member of the diplomatic corps...a man of good fancy, acuteness, irony, cunning, and egoism: no heart, not much of any science, yet enough of every one to speak its language. His fort[é] was Belles-lettres, painting and sculpture. In these he was the oracle of the society, and as such was the empress Catharine's private correspondent and factor in all things not diplomatic."[19] Despite Grimm's intimate relationship with Russian Court, he could not obtain permission for Ledyard to cross Russia. Undaunted, Ledyard decided to go anyway.

Unofficially, Jefferson supported Ledyard's decision to cross Russia without the proper credentials. The two men spent much time discussing ways Ledyard could gather and record scientific information that would survive even if he should be caught and his baggage seized. Jefferson was concerned that any scientific instruments he carried with him would be stolen. He might even be murdered for the sake of them. On the other hand, if he did not bring with him the means to determine latitude, then he would not be able to describe accurately the rivers, mountains, or fertile tracts of land he encountered. Jefferson devised an ingenious solution.

Before Ledyard left Europe, Jefferson recommended that he have the measure of the English foot tattooed onto his arm. Furthermore, he instructed Ledyard how he could determine latitude with nothing more than this measurement, two sticks, and a circle drawn in the dirt. Jefferson also described to him a detailed method of measuring the breadth of a river. Once he took these or any other measurements, Ledyard could then tattoo the results onto his skin using an indelible ink made from the juices of certain herbs. Jefferson also devised a set of secret characters Ledyard could use to tattoo the measurements onto his skin.[20]

Jefferson's concept of the human body as a writing surface is intriguing. In his day, tattoos were associated with primitive culture or, in the Western tradition, with sailors, whose characteristic tattoos expressed their personal and group identity or functioned as talismans.[21] Though the tattoos Jefferson recommended were practical ones, they also identified the person they adorned. The man who went about with a true-to-scale ruler tattooed on his body identified himself as a member of the Enlightenment, someone so committed to scientific discovery that he was willing to disfigure his body for the sake of science.

Ledyard took Jefferson's advice and entered Russia with his forearm adorned with a ruler, complete with one-inch increments. And he apparently tattooed the measurements he took onto his hands. Writing to Jefferson from Barnaul, Ledyard explained, "I am a curiosity myself in this country. Those who have heard of America flock round me to see me. Unfortunately the marks on my hands procures me and my Countrymen the appelation of wild-men."[22] Traveling across Russia, Ledyard walked thousands of miles, making it deep into Siberia—as far as Irkutsk—before the authorities arrested him, escorted him under guard thousands of miles back to European Russia, deported him to Poland, and warned him never to set foot in Russia again. Ledyard returned to Paris to inform Jefferson of his adventures and discuss his latest plans to go to Africa and trace the Nile to its source.

Franklin had established the tradition of hosting a Fourth of July celebration at his home in Passy, and Jefferson perpetuated the tradition. He hosted his first Independence Day party as ambassador in 1785, when friends and fellow Americans gathered at his home in the Cul de Sac Taitbout. Serving good food accompanied by fine wine and lively music, Jefferson gave his guests much to remember. He would continue the tradition throughout his time in France.

Philip Mazzei reached Paris late this July. Practically the first thing he did upon his arrival was to seek out his good friend and Virginia neighbor. "Our meeting," Mazzei wrote, "was very touching to both of us." Though Mazzei had already written letters of introduction for Jefferson to everyone in Paris he could think of, he had inadvertently neglected to write Jean-François Marmontel. Seeing Jefferson in Paris, Mazzei was anxious to remedy this neglect.

"Mr. de Marmontel is one of our great Friends, and admirers of our Cause," Mazzei told Jefferson. "He is goodness itself. He is about 66. years of age, and his good and young wife thinks herself quite happy with an old man so good and so great."[23]

The two agreed to call on him the morning after Mazzei arrived. Reaching Marmontel's home, they found him on his way out. Marmontel insisted on turning back to welcome them properly. A friendship between Jefferson and Marmontel quickly developed. "That morning Jefferson had to go to various other places," Mazzei recalled. "Nonetheless, our chat lasted about two hours. They had much to tell and more to ask each other." Mazzei even recorded a snippet of their conversation. A question Jefferson asked shows that he was starting to plumb the mysteries of international diplomacy.[24]

Why do the ministers of foreign powers make such a mystery out of entirely trivial matters, Jefferson wondered.

"That's true," Marmontel agreed. "They always padlock their lips, but if you take the padlock off you'll see the trunk is empty."

Jefferson cherished this new friendship. He had been reading Marmontel for years, not just the well-known *Moral Tales*, but other works, too. Furthermore, he had been recommending Marmontel's writings to friends at least since the early 1770s. Before long, the two started dining together regularly each week. An accomplished storyteller, Marmontel made a delightful dinner companion. Jefferson described their friendship to Webster: "Marmontel was a very amusing man. He dined with me, every Thursday, for a long time, and I think told some of the most agreable stories, I ever heard in my life. After his death I found almost all of them in his Memoirs, and I dare say, he told them so well, because he had written them before in this book."[25]

These comments about Marmontel contrast sharply with Jefferson's remarks about Saint-Lambert. Though associating the conversation of both men with their writings, Jefferson has the two acting in opposite ways. Saint-Lambert used what he heard in the salon to create his writings; Marmontel wrote up his personal anecdotes and told them in conversation after committing them to paper. For Saint-Lambert, conversation was a rehearsal for writing; for Marmontel, writing served as a rehearsal for conversation. Regardless how either Saint-Lambert or Marmontel actually wrote their works, Jefferson's words show that he recognized a symbiotic relationship between the spoken word and the written. Good talk makes good books; and good books make good talk.

The day Jefferson met Marmontel turned out to be quite busy. As Mazzei and Jefferson prepared to leave, who should show up at

Marmontel's door but Madame de Marmontel's uncle, the Abbé Morellet, whom Mazzei called "one of the most sensible men in France."[26] The two visitors turned around to speak with him, lingering for another hour or so. Having set the tone with these social activities, Mazzei and Jefferson continued in the same vein. Before the day was out they went to see Antoine-Laurent de Lavoisier, whose experiments in chemistry Jefferson was familiar with; the Marquis de Condorcet, whose genius Jefferson appreciated and whose company he would continue to enjoy; and the Duc de la Rochefoucauld, who was becoming a close friend. The pleasures of Rochefoucauld's company, Jefferson told a friend, contributed "much to render my residence in Paris agreeable."[27]

Before the summer was out, Jefferson decided to find a new home, one more suitable to his position as American minister to France. He finally located one after much searching, and made arrangements to rent it. He wrote Abigail Adams: "I have at length procured a house in a situation much more pleasing to me than my present. It is at the grille des champs Elysees, but within the city. It suits me in every circumstance but the price, being dearer than the one I am now in. It has a clever garden to it."[28] The Hôtel de Langeac, as Jefferson's new home was known, provided a stateliness befitting the American ambassador. Its location on the Champs-Elysées at the corner of the Rue de Berri adjoining the Grille de Chaillot at the edge of town near the Bois de Boulogne was more befitting Jefferson's personality. He took possession of the Hôtel de Langeac the third week of October 1785, and from then on had the opportunity to walk regularly through the large wooded area that formed the Bois de Boulogne, an activity that kept his body fit and, given the close connection between walking and thinking, sharpened his mind, too.

The Marquis de Chastellux had been a frequent visitor at his home in the Cul de Sac Taitbout. After Jefferson moved to the outskirts of Paris, Chastellux became a frequent visitor to the Hôtel de Langeac. Perhaps none of his contacts among the Parisian literati were more helpful to Jefferson—or more enjoyable—than the Marquis.

After having his private edition of *Notes on the State of Virginia* printed, Jefferson asked Chastellux to present a copy to the Comte de Buffon. Though Jefferson was quite critical of Buffon in his book, this presentation copy initiated their personal acquaintance. Soon after making this present, Jefferson sent Buffon the panther-skin he had purchased in Philadelphia: physical proof refuting Buffon's primary argument that creatures deteriorated in the New World. Buffon acknowledged the gift of the panther skin in a letter to Jefferson and expressed hope that he and Chastellux would visit soon. Buffon was then living at the Indendant's House in the Jardin du Roi. In early 1786, Chastellux escorted Jefferson there so the two could meet. Jefferson long remembered their meeting.

"When I was in France," he told Webster, "the Marquis de Chastellux carried me to Buffon's residence in the country, and introduced me to him. It was Buffon's practice to remain in his study till dinner time, and receive no visitors under any pretence, but his house was open, and his grounds; and a servant showed them very civilly, and invited all strangers and friends to remain and dine. We saw Buffon in the garden, but carefully avoided him, but we dined with him and he proved himself then as he always did, a man of extraordinary power in conversation. He did not declaim—he was singularly agreable."[29]

Chastellux introduced Jefferson as the author of *Notes on the State of Virginia* and politely reminded Buffon that Jefferson was the man who had disputed his conclusions regarding the natural history of the New World.

Nonplussed, Buffon removed a copy of his latest book from the shelf, presented it to Jefferson, and, apparently addressing his guest in the third person, stated, "When Mr. Jefferson shall have read this, he will be perfectly satisfied that I am right."[30]

Jefferson knew Buffon's theory about nature in the New World was wrong, and others were starting to recognize Buffon's error, too. As a British reader observed, "The ingenious Mr. Jefferson...in his *Notes on the State of Virginia, etc.* has taken occasion to combat the opinions of Buffon; and seems to have fully refuted them both by argument and facts."[31] Jefferson refused to let their differences of opinion get in the way of their friendship—he frequently returned to the Jardin du Roi to visit Buffon. "I often dined with the Count de Buffon, who talked without ceasing, but with great eloquence, on subjects connected with natural history," Jefferson told another acquaintance.[32]

He spoke with Buffon about many scientific subjects. Jefferson was puzzled by Buffon's belligerence toward other fields of study. After a conversation with him in 1788, Jefferson wrote another scientifically inclined friend, the Reverend James Madison:

Speaking one day with Monsieur de Buffon, on the present ardor of chemical enquiry, he affected to consider chemistry but as cookery, and to place the toils of the laboratory on a footing with those of the kitchen. I think it on the contrary among the most useful of sciences, and big with future discoveries for the utility and safety of the human race. It is yet indeed, a mere embryon. Its principles are contested.

Experiments seem contradictory: their subjects are so minute as to escape our senses; and their result too fallacious to satisfy the mind.[33]

Never did Jefferson stop trying to convince Buffon of the superiority of American fauna. He even commissioned a New England hunter to kill a moose and have it stuffed so that he could present it to Buffon as un-equivocal proof. It was an ambitious idea, but the effort took much more time and expense that Jefferson anticipated. When the moose finally reached Paris, it had a bit of the mange about it. Still, there could be no denying the fact that the beast was big.

Besides facilitating Jefferson's entrance into the scientific world of Paris, Chastellux also stimulated his literary interests by prompting him to think more about poetry and ultimately to write a lengthy essay on the subject. Though not generally known for literary criticism, Jefferson found it useful for practicing his critical and analytical skills. He also encouraged students to write literary criticism. To one he advised:

Criticise the style of any book whatever, committing your criticisms to writing. Translate into the different styles, to wit, the elevated, the middling and the familiar. Orators and poets will furnish subjects of the first, historians of the second, and epistolary and Comic writers of the third—Undertake, at first, short compositions, as themes, letters, etc., paying great attention to correctness and elegance of your language.[34]

"Thoughts on English Prosody," the fullest piece of literary criticism Jefferson wrote, is usually dated 1786, but he must have been contemplating it as early as October 1785, when he purchased a 109-volume small-format edition of the British poets published by John Bell in Edinburgh for his daughter. The first Friday of that month Jefferson recorded in his account books, "Pd. Goldsmith for 87. vols. of Bell's poets for Patsy 156f," and the following Thursday, he further recorded, "Pd. Goldsmith for residue of Bell's poets 22 vols. 39f12."[35] These small volumes, each about six inches tall, were just the kind of little books Jefferson enjoyed most. Though his accounts indicate that he was buying them for his daughter, they remained with his books at the Hôtel de Langeac.

Among the literary treasures at the University of Virginia is one volume of the Comtesse de Genlis's four-volume collection of plays written for schoolchildren, *Théatre à l'Usage de Jeunes Personnes*, with evidence of Martha Jefferson's ownership. The volume contains the following inscription in her hand: "Marthe Jefferson Panthmont Juliet 1785." The inscription clearly shows that this volume was in her possession in July 1785. Her frenchification of her Christian name recalls her father's latinization of his Christian name in the books he acquired when he was her age. All but one of the 109 volumes of Bell's English poets survive at the University of Virginia. Though her father acquired this extensive collection for her just three months after Martha inscribed her copy of Genlis, none are similarly inscribed.

Take Bell's edition of *The Poetical Works of Abraham Cowley*, for example. One volume is inscribed "M. Randolph, Monticello," an indication that Martha did not put her ownership inscription into these volumes until after her marriage. The I and T signatures of this surviving Cowley volume do contain her father's unique marks of ownership, indicators that the book was in his possession, not hers, from the time he acquired it until they returned to Virginia.

This lengthy explanation is meant to explain her father's behavior, not to critique it. To be sure, Jefferson was not the last figure in American literary history to purchase books for family members that he wanted to read himself. His talks with Chastellux had stimulated his curiosity about English prosody, and his acquisition of Bell's collection of English poets let him deepen his study of English verse considerably. Jefferson wrote "Thoughts on English Prosody" specifically for Chastellux. Though there is no evidence that he ever fully completed the work or actually sent it to his friend, he did go so far as to write a cover letter explaining the impetus behind it.

"Among the topics of conversation which stole off like so many minutes the few hours I had the happiness of possessing you at Monticello, the measures of English verse was one," Jefferson wrote. "We have again discussed on this side the Atlantic a subject which had occupied us during some pleasing moments on the other," he continued. "A daily habit of walking in the Bois de Boulogne gave me an opportunity of turning this subject in my mind and I determined to present you my thoughts on it in the form of a letter. I for some time parried the difficulties which assailed me, but at length I found they were not to be opposed, and their triumph was complete."[36]

In other words, Jefferson's conversations with Chastellux brought their differing opinions to the surface. Unable to convince Chastellux in person, Jefferson decided to write out his ideas in the form of an essay on English verse. To prepare his written composition, he rehearsed his ideas during his daily walks through the Bois de Boulogne. After many miles and much thought, he realized that Chastellux was right, and he was wrong.

Read in light of his contemporary literary activities, the cover letter's emphasis on the importance of literary conversation shows clearly.

Jefferson's experience within the Comtesse d'Houdetot's salon and in other social and intellectual circles in Paris let him know the value of conversation for encouraging literary discourse. "Thoughts on English Prosody" itself reveals the value of conversation for developing ideas, preventing error, and inspiring thought.

This essay is classic Jefferson. In some ways, his idiosyncratic literary theory follows the standard dictates of Augustan verse, but he departed from prevailing rules of prosody by introducing new terms that precisely define and identify the individual components of a poem. He observed, "It is the business of the poet so to arrange his words as that, repeated in their accustomed measures they shall strike the ear with that regular rhythm which constitutes verse."[37] His emphasis on the regularity of poetic meter aligns him with the common practice of his day.

He challenged the system of prosody outlined by Samuel Johnson, who had applied the rules of Greek prosody to English verse. In ancient Greek, poetic feet are determined by their combination of long and short syllables. Consequently, Johnson had sought to break down English verse into poetic feet composed of long and short syllables. Finding the system inadequate, Jefferson observed: "I am not satisfied whether this accented syllable be pronounced longer, louder, or harder, and the others shorter, lower, or softer. I have found the nicest ears divided on the question." Instead, Jefferson modified Johnson's system of prosody by substituting accent for quality. Usage has established which syllables of a multisyllabic word are stressed or unstressed. "That the accent shall never be displaced from the syllable whereon usage hath established," he explained, "is the fundamental law of English verse."[38]

So far, so good. Jefferson went awry, however, by trying to introduce new terminology for describing the differently accented poetic feet. He borrowed his terms from Greek and Latin grammar. Trochaic verse, where the accent falls on the odd syllables, he called imparisyllabic verse. Iambic verse, where the accent falls on the even syllables, he called parisyllabic verse. Anapestic verse, which incorporates poetic feet consisting of three syllables with an accent on the last, Jefferson called trisyllabic verse. Though he illustrated each of these types of poetic feet with quotations from the British poets—Thomas Gray, William Collins, William Shenstone, Edward Young—his argument in favor of the new terminology is unconvincing.

Quoting lines from Pope's "Epitaph: On Himself" and Swift's "To Mr. Sheridan, Upon His Verses Written in Circles," Jefferson called these two poems "pieces of sport on which they [their authors] did not mean to rest their poetical merit."[39] Here he implicitly acknowledged that verse can be classified in terms of levels of seriousness and importance. Making this distinction, Jefferson anticipated a literary aesthetic that would not emerge until the nineteenth century, the idea of art for art's sake. For the most part, Jefferson accepted the prevailing critical dictate that literature should both delight and instruct. Acknowledging the possibility of poems written for "sport," he was suggesting that some verse could be written purely for delight without regard to its instructive value.

Another section of "Thoughts on English Prosody" describes rules for accenting English. The rules for accenting syllables are so capricious that it would be easier to learn the accent of every word than the rules that govern the placement of accents. Reading English poetry offers a good way to learn how to accent English words. If the reader knows the accent of one word in a piece of poetry, that knowledge often provides the key to correctly reading the entire piece. Learning how to accent English words is only a part of the process because there are also different shades of emphasis.

Among native English speakers, not everyone masters the degrees of emphasis, which depend not only on judgment but also on physical ability. For support, Jefferson used the example of Samuel Foote, who was "known to have read Milton so exquisitely that he received great sums of money for reading him to audiences who attended him regularly for that purpose." The significance Jefferson placed on individual pronunciation in "Thoughts on English Prosody" anticipates a defining aspect of Romantic literature, specifically, the importance of the personal voice.[40]

To facilitate learning the different shades of emphasis, Jefferson outlined a clever way of recording differences of degree in writing. Instead of single accent marks to denote emphasis, he suggested using multiple accent marks—up to four—to denote the degree of emphasis. Read in isolation, an individual word can be scanned in only one way, but placed within two different lines of verse, its emphasis subtly changes according to where it occurs in the line and what other words surround it. In the history of English literary criticism, Jefferson is the first to describe a system for denoting different levels of emphasis. Modern literary critics have lamented that scansion does not record pitch.[41] Jefferson's method of scansion does. Still, it seems too demanding. Requiring those who scan poetry not only to identify the accented syllables but also to discriminate four different degrees of emphasis may be too complex for practical purposes. Jefferson's theory of prosody manifests an impulse that shows in other aspects of his creative life, especially his architectural drawings: precision regardless of practicality.

Discussing line length, Jefferson concurred with the prevailing belief that pentameter verse made the best poetry. Pentameter is the only metrical form with "dignity enough to support blank verse," which Jefferson considered the most precious part of English verse. His defense echoes Milton's preface to *Paradise Lost*. As an advocate for blank verse, Jefferson argued its value over rhymed verse: "The poet, unfettered by rhyme, is at liberty to prune his diction of those tautologies, those feeble nothings necessary to introtrude the rhyming word. With no other trammel than that of measure he is able to condense his thoughts and images and to leave nothing but what is truly poetical."[42]

To prune the prevailing diction of its tautologies: Jefferson had used this idea to guide his reformation of legal language the decade before. Here is yet another similarity Jefferson saw between law and literature: both should express their ideas with elegant simplicity.

Beyond its value as literary criticism, "Thoughts on English Prosody" also provides a good indication of Jefferson's literary tastes. Like the extracts he recorded in his literary commonplace book, the lines he quoted in "Thoughts on English Prosody" indicate the English authors he enjoyed. The essay quotes William Shenstone more than any other author, but it also includes lines from many popular seventeenth- and eighteenth-century authors. Jefferson obviously found the apostrophe to liberty from Joseph Addison's "Letter from Italy" inspiring. He quoted the passage to illustrate parisyllabic verse, but his quotation goes much further than necessary to illustrate the literary point he was making:

> Oh liberty! thou goddess heav'nly bright
> Profuse of bliss, and pregnant with delight
> Eternal pleasures in thy presence reign,
> And smiling plenty leads thy wanton train;
> Eas'd of her load subjection grows more light,
> And Poverty looks cheerful in thy sight;
> Thou mak'st the gloomy face of nature gay
> Giv'st beauty to the sun, and pleasure to the day.

The fact that Jefferson wrote "Thoughts on English Prosody," his only sustained piece of literary criticism, in Paris confirms the liveliness of the intellectual milieu in which he found himself. The literary and social circles he traveled in offered the opportunity to talk about literature, and such talk prompted him to think and eventually write about literature. "Thoughts on English Prosody" may not occupy a prominent place in the history of literary criticism, but in the story of Jefferson's life, the essay shows how intellectually stimulated he was during his time in Paris.

CHAPTER 22

London Town

One snowy February day in 1786, Jefferson received a visit from William Stephens Smith, secretary of the American legation in London, good friend of John Adams, and fiancé to his daughter Abigail. Smith had come to Paris expressly to deliver an urgent message from Adams to Jefferson. Since their joint commission to negotiate treaties of amity and commerce between the United States and other nations would end in May, the two had the responsibility to do as much as they could before its expiration. Though any further efforts in this regard had seemed fruitless, new and unexpected opportunities for negotiating treaties with Portugal, Tripoli, and possibly other nations of the Barbary Coast arose that winter. In recent weeks, Adams had been meeting with Abdrahaman, the envoy of the Sultan of Tripoli.[1] Adams went so far to endear himself to the Tripoline ambassador that he actually began smoking a hookah in his presence. The incongruous sight of this staid New Englander puffing away at a hookah prompted Abdrahaman's secretary to exclaim, "Monsieur, vous êtes un Turk!"

After three such meetings, Adams remained hopeful that a diplomatic agreement between the United States and Tripoli could be hammered out, provided he and Jefferson acted quickly. From Adams's view, a treaty would prevent a grim alternative, "a universal and horrible War with these Barbary States, which will continue for many Years." He felt quite strongly about the matter and conveyed his feelings in an urgent letter to Jefferson. "I am so impressed and distressed with this affair," Adams wrote, "that I will go to New York or to Algiers or first to one and then to the other, if you think it necessary, rather than it should not be brought to a Conclusion."[2]

Jefferson was more skeptical than his fellow commissioner when it came to negotiating with Tripoli. He suspected, shrewdly, that the nation wanted money before it would sign a treaty, and more money than the United States could or should pay. From Jefferson's perspective, the situation with Portugal was more promising, and this, more than Adams's fervent remarks about Tripoli, motivated him to go to London.

Before leaving Paris, he had certain proprieties to observe. For one, he had to present himself at Versailles and apprise the Comte de Vergennes that he would be out of France for some weeks. In the meantime, Jefferson saw no reason to alter his social calendar. Planning to attend a masquerade ball on the evening Smith arrived, he invited his visitor to accompany him. The two became friends almost immediately. Jefferson penned a character sketch of him for James Madison. "You can judge of Smith's abilities by his letters," he observed. Jefferson's words emphasize the importance of being a good writer in his day, a time when people were often judged by the letters they wrote. He compared Smith to James Monroe—no small praise: "For his honesty he is like our friend Monroe. Turn his soul wrong side outwards and there is not a speck on it. He has one foible, an excessive inflammability of temper, but he feels it when it comes on, and has resolution enough to suppress it, and to remain silent till it passes over."[3]

Considering the events that occurred on the evening in question, Jefferson might have given Smith a touch of Yankee naiveté in his character sketch. Though engaged to Nabby Adams, Smith had insufficient experience in the ways of the world to survive a Paris masquerade ball unscathed. When a Dutch baroness approached the two that evening, Jefferson successfully extricated himself from her clutches. Smith was less adept at dealing with a European noblewoman on the prowl. Describing the episode to a correspondent, Smith admitted, "When Mr. Jefferson had made his escape, she had fastened her talons on me."[4]

Upon taking care of a few more pieces of business—acquiring the latest volume of the *Encyclopedie Methodique* for himself and additional copies for Franklin, Hopkinson, Madison, and Monroe; purchasing some lace and cambric to present to Mrs. Adams; and hiring a cabriolet to take them to Calais—Jefferson was ready to go. They left Paris the first Monday in March. Since the snowstorm of the previous week, the temperature had been hovering around the freezing point. The journey to Calais proved cold and uncomfortable. They nonetheless paused at Chantilly for some sightseeing. The Adamses had passed through there on their way to London the year before and had recommended seeing the chateau. The brisk weather persisted at Calais, and storms delayed their passage to Dover. Happily, the cheery inn where they stayed offered several amenities for its channel-crossing patrons. Jefferson and Smith would wait here a day and a half before the weather settled enough for sailing.

After a passage of nine and a half hours, they touched at Dover, finally reaching London late Saturday night, "as early as the excessive rigour of the weather admitted."[5] They met with Adams briefly that evening and rejoined him on Sunday. All in all, Jefferson would spend many pleasurable evenings in the company of John, Abigail, and Nabby Adams. John Quincy Adams had since returned to the United States to attend college, but not William and Mary, as Jefferson had recommended. No, William and Mary would not do, not for an Adams. None of their clan could imagine traveling south of the Charles River, let alone the Potomac, for their education. John Quincy Adams was attending Harvard College, of course.

For his London sojourn, Jefferson found lodgings in Golden Square in the city's West End. On Sunday, he had a good look around the place. Though he found London generally more handsome than Paris, its architecture was wretched in comparison. David Humphreys, who had visited earlier that year, was also disappointed with its buildings. In a letter to George Washington from London, Humphreys observed, "This City is in extent as well as population considerably larger than Paris, the streets are wider and cleaner, and the appearance of some particular squares perhaps more elegant, tho' in general I cannot say I like the style of building here so well as in France."[6]

Adams arranged for Jefferson to meet the Marquis of Carmarthen, the British Minister of Foreign Affairs, and to attend the levees of King George III and his queen. None of these meetings went well. About the Marquis, Jefferson wrote, "The distance and disinclination which he betrayed in his conversation, the vagueness and evasions of his answers to us, confirmed me in the belief of their aversion to have anything to do with us."[7] Shortly after meeting the king, Jefferson observed that the British monarch was as bitter and obstinate as he had imagined.

Recalling the time he met the king and queen after a lapse of forty years, Jefferson reiterated his first impression: "It was impossible for anything to be more ungracious than their notice of Mr. Adams and myself. I saw at once that the ulcerations in the narrow mind of that mulish being left nothing to be expected on the subject of my attendance."[8] Having written in the *Declaration of Independence* that the "history of the present King of Great Britain is a history of unremitting injuries and usurpations" and having enumerated these injuries as a "Catalogue of Crimes," Jefferson should not have expected too warm a reception from His Royal Majesty. But now that the war was over and a peace treaty signed, he had expected the king to cast off his animosity toward the United States of America, set aside his stubbornness, and behave with the civility and grace befitting the crown. Apparently, the king saw it differently.

A few days later, Jefferson encountered a contemporary English celebrity of a different sort. Shortly after mentioning the king in his memorandum book, Jefferson recorded that he saw the "learned pig."[9] He neither elaborated on this encounter nor made any explicit comparisons between it and his meeting with the king, but given his criticism of the king's obstinate behavior, Jefferson seems to have preferred the oinker's company: better a learned pig than a mulish monarch.

The learned pig was a phenomenon of the time. A contemporary advertisement describing its abilities puffed: "He reads, writes, and casts accounts by means of typographical cards, in the same manner that a printer composes and by the same method." In addition, the pig purportedly could solve complex problems in arithmetic. Like many good shows, the pig and its exhibitors toured the provinces before making their London debut. Samuel Johnson learned of the beast's intellectual prowess and regaled friends with conjectures of its abilities, which James Boswell duly recorded in his *Life of Johnson*, thus capturing the pig for posterity. Johnson passed away before the pig's London debut and never had the opportunity to see the pig in person.[10]

Once it reached London, the learned pig was all the rage. Speaking of this renowned porker, one contemporary Londoner observed, "He now draws the attention of the beau monde—women of the first Fashion waited for hours for their turn to see him." Another observed: "The renown of this prodigy of animals is so established, as I am informed, that the proprietor is rapidly amassing a fortune, thro' the sway of fashion, as it would be quite monstrous and ill-bred not to follow the *ton* and go to see the wonderful Learned Pig; it being the trite question in all polite circles, Pray, my Lord, my Lady, Sir John, Madam, or Miss, have you seen the Learned Pig? If answer is given in the affirmative, it is a confirmation of taste; if in the negative, it is reprobated as an odious singularity!" Nabby Adams, having already seen the dancing dogs, the singing duck, and the little hare that beats a drum, anxiously looked forward to seeing the learned pig, too.[11]

During Jefferson's time in England, the following paean to the pig appeared in the London press:

> Though Johnson, learned Bear, is gone,
> Let us no longer mourn our loss,

> For lo, a learned Hog is come,
>   And wisdom grunts at Charing Cross.
> Happy for Johnson—that he died
>   Before this wonder came to town,
> Else had it blasted all his pride
>   *Another* brute should gain renown.[12]

Ever a man of discriminating tastes, Jefferson usually found such crass verse offensive, but Samuel Johnson was not above his reproach. Jefferson, whose prose has been called superior to Johnson's verse, had room to complain.[13] In addition to critiquing his theory of prosody, Jefferson also found fault with his *Dictionary of the English Language*. "Johnson, besides the want of precision in his definitions, and of accurate distinction in passing from one shade of meaning to another of the same word, is most objectionable in his derivations," Jefferson observed. "From a want probably of intimacy with our own language while in the Anglo-Saxon form and type, and of its kindred languages of the North, he has a constant leaning towards Greek and Latin for English etymon."[14] In Jefferson's view, Johnson should have brushed up his Anglo-Saxon and his Gaelic before drafting his derivations.

Boswell's anecdote of Johnson and the newspaper verse indicate that the very idea of a learned pig regaled the spirit and fired the literary imagination. The day Jefferson saw the pig, he, too, found himself in the mood for versifying. As he, Smith, and Richard Peters—another American lawyer in London—were walking the city streets, they approached a signboard displaying a large joint of beef, which turned out to be the sign of a famous London eatery, Dolly's Chop House. Long a fixture on Paternoster Row, Dolly's dated back to the time of Queen Anne, and its steaks were legendary.

John Wilkes, who had become a symbol of liberty for many Americans the previous decade, was known to have visited Dolly's, according to a widely circulated anecdote: "Mr. Wilkes going to Dolly's chop-house, in Paternoster-row, with a friend, in order to observe the humours of the place, accidentally seated himself near a rich and purse-proud citizen, who almost stunned him with roaring for his *stake*, as he called it. Mr. Wilkes in the mean time, asking him some common question, received a very brutal answer: the steak coming at that instant, Mr. Wilkes turned to his friend, saying, 'See the difference between the *City* and the *Bear-Garden*; in the latter the *bear* is brought to the *stake*, but here the *steak* is brought to the *bear*.'"[15]

Dolly's was also known as a place for literary inspiration. Summoning the nine muses to inspire his composition of *The Lousiad*, Peter Pindar observed that some contemporaries preferred the din of Dolly's over more classical forms of inspiration. "Blest with beef, their ghostly forms to fill," these modern bards "Make Dolly's chop-house their Aonian hill, / More pleas'd to hear knives, forks, in concert join, / Than all the tinkling cymbals of the Nine." James Boswell, among the writers who sought both inspiration and sustenance at Dolly's, had devoured "a large fat beef-steak" here some years earlier and duly recorded the event for posterity.[16]

Spying Dolly's Chop House, Jefferson and his two companions decided to patronize the place. Once inside, it seems that one thing led to another, and the three found themselves lingering within Dolly's doors far longer than they planned. Before they knew it, they were scandalously late for a dinner meeting with some unknown person, likely John Adams. As their tardiness neared the point of unforgivableness, they felt the need to draft an apology to their slighted host. They, too, let the sound of knives and forks be their muse.[17] To make their apology as endearing as possible, they wrote it in the form of rhyming couplets. The resulting poem bears the unmistakable smell of Madeira:

> One among our many follies
> Was calling in for steaks at Dolly's
> Whereby we've lost—and feel like Sinners
> That we have miss'd much better dinners
> Nor do we think that us 'tis hard on
> Most humbly thus to beg your pardon
> And promise that another time
> We'll give our *reason* not our *rhime*
> So we've agreed—our Nem: Con: Vote is
> That we *thus jointly* give you notice
> For as our rule is to be clever
> We hold it better late than never.

Since entering public life, Jefferson seldom dropped his guard in his writings, so this poem comes as a delightful surprise within the pages of his collected works. The rhyme of "pardon" and "hard on" is worthy of *Hudibras*, and the adverb *jointly* in the third to last line offers a fine double entendre as it refers to their communal decision as well as the place where they made it, at the sign of a joint of beef.

None of the three were willing to take individual credit for these lines, so they signed their names in the form of a Round Robin—signatures arranged in a circle so that no name would appear above the others. The great object of a Round Robin is, in the words of a subsequent American author who found himself in need of anonymity on a similar occasion, "to arrange the signatures in such a way, that, although they are all found in a ring, no man can be picked out as the leader of it."[18]

Opportunities for levity came to an abrupt halt as Jefferson and Adams sat down with Abdrahaman to try and reach an agreement between the United States and Tripoli. The Americans wanted assurances that the Muslim pirates from Tripoli would no longer accost American merchant vessels; Tripoli, as Jefferson suspected, wanted money, and lots of it.

The North African nations of Tripoli, Algiers, Morocco, and Tunis constituted the Barbary Coast, a land whose pirates had been terrorizing American merchant vessels: attacking ships, taking sailors hostage, threatening their lives, and holding them for ransom. The Muslim states of the Barbary Coast endorsed the practices of piracy and hostage-taking provided they were carried out against infidels in the name of Islam. In colonial times, American vessels had been protected from the Islamic corsairs because Great Britain paid the Barbary states tribute, or protection money to guard against the piracy. With American independence, the Barbary pirates felt free to attack the new nation's merchant vessels because the American government refused to pay tribute to the nations of the Barbary Coast. Sanctioned by their government, the attacks of the Barbary pirates on American merchant vessels represent an early example of state-sponsored terrorism aimed at civilian American targets.

Adams and Jefferson asked Abdrahaman on what grounds his nation made war upon other nations that had done their people no harm. They let him know that as representatives of the United States, they considered friends everyone who had done them no wrong or had given them no provocation. The response they received was darkly foreboding. The conduct of the Barbary Coast pirates, the ambassador explained,

> was founded on the Laws of their Prophet, that it was written in their Koran, that all nations who should not have acknowledged their authority were sinners, that it was their right and duty to make war upon them wherever they could be found, and to make slaves of all they could take as Prisoners, and that every Musselman who should be slain in battle was sure to go to Paradise.[19]

Even now, especially now, it is difficult to read the response of the Tripoline ambassador without a chill. At the time, his words clashed with Jefferson's most heartfelt beliefs. A man of politics, a man of reason, and a man of conscience, Jefferson knew that justifying armed conflict on the basis of a religious text was wrong. As a scholar, he knew that relying on a single text as a source of information or belief led to poor judgment. Throughout his adult life, he had been living by these ideals. Besides having drafted legislation separating church and state, he had made a personal habit of reading many different texts on any and every subject, including religion, to achieve a broad and deep perspective on it.

The ambassador's words gave Jefferson a reminder of the profound danger that could come from relying on a single text without recourse to supplementary texts and alternative interpretations. Surely, if a religious text seemed to sanction war, its readers ought to research how others interpreted that text as a means of achieving some clarity before rushing into battle. Abdrahaman and the Muslim pirates whose behavior he sanctioned saw no need to consult other texts to justify their behavior. Everything they needed to know was in the Qur'an, and what was not in the Qur'an they did not feel a need to know.[20]

Upon returning to Paris, Jefferson sought Vergennes's advice regarding what possible courses of action could be taken against the Muslim states of the Barbary Coast.

Money and fear are the only things they understand, Vergennes told him.

Vergennes's brief comment summarized the dilemma the United States faced. Jefferson and Adams took opposite sides over the issue: Adams was in favor of paying the Barbary states tribute money to protect American merchant ships; Jefferson, who staunchly refused to bargain with nations that sponsored such terrorism, thought war would be a more effective solution. He and Adams weighed the pros and cons in a series of letters they exchanged throughout that year.

Adams was pragmatic; Jefferson took the moral high ground. In his fullest letter on the subject, Adams sets forth a detailed argument for paying the tribute money. Before finishing the letter, he wavered and began to see value in a military response, which would help him pursue a pet project: the development of the U.S. Navy. Adams realized that the European policy of giving in to the Muslim demands had weakened their military forces significantly. Developing this line of thought, Adams rose to eloquence, all the while damaging his own argument against a military solution: "The Policy of Christendom has made Cowards of all their Sailors before the Standard of Mahomet."[21]

Responding to Adams, Jefferson enumerated all of the reasons justifying a military solution:

1. Justice is in favor of this opinion.
2. Honor favors it.
3. It will procure us respect in Europe, and respect is a safe-guard to interest.
4. It will arm the federal head with the safest of all the instruments of coercion over their delinquent members and prevent them from using what would be less safe.
5. I think it least expensive.
6. Equally effectual.[22]

Developing his argument, Jefferson refuted Adams's claim that paying tribute would be more economical by arguing that the United States would not have to combat the Muslim states of North Africa alone. He proposed a coalition of nations willing to battle the Islamic states of the Barbary Coast. In the short term, Adams's argument won out: the United States negotiated treaties with the Barbary states that stipulated annual payments for protecting American merchant vessels from the Muslim pirates. This was not a lasting solution, however, and the problem with the Barbary states would continue for years.

The efforts of Jefferson and Adams to negotiate a treaty with Portugal also went for naught. The meetings with the Portuguese envoy extraordinary, the Chevalier de Pinto, took much longer than expected, but through effort and perseverance, they hammered out a treaty, only to have it end, ultimately, in an impasse. Not until after they had prepared the treaty did Jefferson and Adams learn that though de Pinto had the power to negotiate a treaty, he did not have the power to sign it once negotiated. The carefully drafted treaty went unsigned.

Jefferson's excursion to London proved a disappointment in terms of official business, but in terms of pleasurable diversion, it was a rich and rewarding personal experience. Roaming the London streets, he took advantage of the numerous book-buying opportunities the city offered. As the German traveler Karl Moritz observed during his visit to London a few years earlier, "The quick sale of the classical authors, is here promoted also, by cheap and convenient editions. They have them all bound in pocket volumes; as well as in a more pompous stile.... At stalls, and in the streets, you every now and then meet with a sort of antiquarians, who sell single or odd volumes; sometimes perhaps of Shakespear, &c. so low as a penny; nay even sometimes for an halfpenny a piece."[23]

While in London, Jefferson frequently visited the bookshops of James Lackington, John Stockdale, and others. He added to his library one of the most popular books of 1786, Richard Jodrell's *Persian Heroine*, a tragedy based on an episode from Herodotus. Jodrell's play is better known for its detailed explanatory notes than for its dramatic value. Jefferson would continue to order books from both Lackington and Stockdale after he returned to Paris and would make arrangements with Stockdale to publish the first London edition of *Notes on the State of Virginia*, which would be issued the following year. One day, Jefferson bought a new reading lamp to facilitate what had long been a favorite habit: reading long into the night. Ever a great shopper, he purchased much else in London. The splendor of its shops, he decided, constituted the city's greatest attribute.[24]

Beyond what pleasures Jefferson found on the streets of London, he and Adams had the opportunity to spend much time together visiting England's most renowned pleasure gardens. For a guidebook during their excursions into the countryside, Jefferson brought his copy of Thomas Whately's *Observations on Modern Gardening*, a work he had obtained earlier from another William and Mary professor who had left Virginia to return to England. Jefferson also drafted a narrative of their sight-seeing tour, "Notes of a Tour of English Gardens," which he structured as a set of one-paragraph discussions of each garden they visited.

The opening paragraph provides a general description of his method of sightseeing. Nearly always he walked through the gardens with Whatley's *Observations* in hand. Seeing the originals, he was further impressed with the book. He found the gardens "so justly characterised by him as to be easily recognised, and saw with wonder, that his fine imagination had never been able to seduce him from the truth." Brief as it is, this comment characterizes Jefferson's attitude toward the literary imagination more generally: it should serve to enhance truth, not mask it.

Closing his first paragraph, Jefferson described the purpose underlying his scrupulous attention to the English gardens: "My enquiries were directed chiefly to such practical things as might enable me to estimate the expence of making and maintaining a garden in that style." He did not stick to this purpose consistently. Despite his practical justification for this garden tour, Jefferson's initial observation of Chiswick, the Duke of Devonshire's estate, is aesthetic: "The Octagonal dome has an ill effect, both within and without; the garden shews still too much of art; an obelisk of very ill effect. Another in the middle of a pond useless."[25]

One estate in Shropshire Jefferson was especially anxious to see was Leasowes, the former property of William Shenstone, whose elegiac verse and landscape designs had significantly influenced Jefferson's elegiac verse and landscape designs. Compared with what he had imagined, Leasowes was disappointing. The cascades were beautiful, and from one lookout point there was a fine prospect, but otherwise Leasowes failed to meet his expectations. The gardens had not been properly maintained, and many of the inscriptions about the place had disappeared. Happily, Shenstone had preserved these inscriptions within the pages of his *Works*. In this case, the printed page had outlasted what was written in stone.

Reflecting on the trip, Jefferson told John Page that, all things considered, England had disappointed him: "Both town and country, fell short of my expectations." But its gardens made up for England's other shortcomings. The English pleasure garden, he observed, "is the article in which it surpasses all the earth."[26]

Adams also recorded their tour of English gardens. The differences between the notes both men took reveal important differences in their personalities. Whereas Jefferson was scrutinizing the gardens with an eye toward making improvements at Monticello, Adams had no plans to improve his property in Massachusetts, at least not in terms of its aesthetics. Adams found that the country estates and pleasure gardens provided "the highest Entertainment" of their trip, but he did little beyond name the gardens they visited in his notes. The only ones that called forth appreciative comments on his part were those with literary associations. For its beauty and its grandeur, he especially enjoyed the estate of Lord Lyttelton. He also appreciated the gardens of Alexander Pope and James Thomson.

Leasowes pleased Adams more than Jefferson. He called it "the simplest and plainest, but the most rural of all. I saw no Spot so small, that exhibited such a Variety of Beauties." Adams had no desire for such pleasure gardens himself, nor did he desire to see them developed in the United States: "It will be long, I hope before Ridings, Parks, Pleasure Grounds, Gardens and ornamented Farms grow so much in fashion in America. But Nature has done greater Things and furnished nobler Materials there. The Oceans, Islands, Rivers, Mountains, Valleys are all laid out upon a larger Scale."[27]

One particular place called forth lengthier comments on Adams's part than any other: Stratford-upon-Avon. Adams's detailed description of Stratford is not unusual. Numerous other Shakespeare-loving travelers made this literary pilgrimage and described their visits at length. Karl Moritz observed, "The River Avon is here pretty broad; and a row of neat, though humble, cottages, only one story high, with shingled roofs, are ranged all along its banks. These houses impressed me strongly with the idea of patriarchal simplicity and content." Moritz noted that Shakespeare's house was the worst one in town. Adams concurred. From the inn where he and Jefferson were staying, they walked three doors down to enter Shakespeare's birthplace, a house, in Adams's words, "as small and mean, as you can conceive."[28]

Typically, the guide within the house showed visitors a dilapidated wooden chair in the chimney corner. Moritz observed, "Shakespeare's chair, in which he used to sit before the door, was so cut to pieces that it hardly looked like a chair; for every one that travels through Stratford, cuts off a chip, as a remembrance which he carefully preserves, and deems a precious relique."[29] Despite the sorry condition of the chair, Moritz could not avoid whittling off a sliver for himself, nor could Jefferson and Adams. They, too, cut chips off the old chair, which to literary devotees were akin to pieces of the true cross.

Outside the house, a mulberry tree Shakespeare supposedly planted had been cut down and put up for sale. The house where Shakespeare died had been taken down, too. The spot where the house once stood was preserved as a small garden. In the nearby graveyard, they saw Shakespeare's gravestone and read the famous curse upon anyone who should disturb the bard's bones:

> Good friend for Jesus sake forbeare
> To digg the dust enclosed heare!
> Blese be the man that spares these stones
> And curst be he that moves my bones

Overall, Adams found unsettling the incongruity between the greatness of Shakespeare's work and the meanness of his home and the meager relics remaining there: "There is nothing preserved of this great Genius which is worth knowing—nothing which might inform Us what Education, what Company, what Accident turned his Mind to Letters and the Drama. His name is not even on his Grave Stone. An ill sculptured Head is sett up by his Wife, by the Side of his Grave in the Church. But paintings and Sculpture would be thrown away upon his Fame. His Wit, and Fancy, his Taste and Judgment, His Knowledge of Nature, of Life and Character, are immortal."[30]

In contrast, Jefferson's "Notes of a Tour of English Gardens" makes no mention of their visit to Stratford, which simply shows that Jefferson wrote what he did with a specific purpose in mind: to observe and analyze the gardens they visited in terms of both practical matters and aesthetics. The purposeful notes he took during his travels through other parts of Europe contain many similar gaps.

Jefferson did have other ways to show his appreciation. He had already begun to acquire a new edition of Shakespeare's works. In 1785, John Bell began publishing a new fine-paper, petite-format edition of Shakespeare with detailed scholarly annotations. Each of the plays was issued separately. The annotations following the text were separately issued, too. Jefferson began acquiring the separate numbers of *Bell's Edition of Shakespeare* when publication began. He continued expanding the set through 1788, when the last number was issued. Jefferson not only acquired the plays, he also purchased their accompanying annotations. To Jefferson's ear, these annotations had a familiar ring to them: many were written by his old friend Samuel Henley.[31]

Shortly after he returned to Paris from London, Jefferson ordered a copy of *The Beauties of Shakespeare*, a selection of memorable lines and speeches from the plays and sonnets. He also purchased the quarto edition of Edward Capell's *Notes and Various Readings to Shakespeare*, which contained explanatory notes, variant readings, and a glossary.[32] While the earlier work suggests a dilettantish interest in Shakespeare, the latter shows Jefferson's scholarly bent.

Two years later he ordered *A Concordance to Shakespeare*. Compiled by Andrew Becket and published in 1787, this work is the first concordance to Shakespeare ever published. In his introduction, Becket quoted Samuel Johnson's comment that Shakespeare's plays "are filled with practical axioms and domestic wisdom; and that a system of civil and economical prudence may be collected from them."[33] The comedian John Bernard, who enjoyed much literary conversation with Jefferson, provided further testament to his fondness for Shakespeare. Bernard observed, "In poetry his taste was thoroughly orthodox; Shakespeare and Pope, he said, gave him the perfection of imagination and judgment, both displaying more knowledge of the human heart—the true province of poetry—than he could elsewhere find."[34] The year he left Paris to return to America, Jefferson was trying to obtain an accurate portrait of Shakespeare to hang at Monticello.

He also took the opportunity to see Shakespeare in performance while in London. One evening he saw a production of *Macbeth* starring Sarah Siddons, Britain's leading actress, in the role of Lady Macbeth. Contemporary theater-goers raved over her. David Humphreys told George Washington, "I have frequented the Theatres very often and have found an exquisite pleasure in seeing the famous Mrs Siddons perform who is far superior to any thing I had ever beheld on the stage."[35] Jefferson also saw Mrs. Siddons in *The Merchant of Venice*. By all accounts, her performance as Portia was inspiring, especially her enactment of the character's most famous speech, which had a rare, natural quality to it. Listen:

> The quality of mercy is not strain'd,
> It droppeth as the gentle rain from heaven
> Upon the place beneath. It is twice blest:
> It blesseth him that gives and him that takes.
> 'Tis mightiest in the mightiest, it becomes
> The throned monarch better than his crown.

As one contemporary observer attending this performance commented, "Mrs Siddons spoke the speech on mercy as it certainly should be spoken—but as in truth we never heard it spoken—as a reply to 'On what compulsion must I?' From every other Portia it has always appeared as a *recitation*, prepared for the occasion."[36]

Jefferson's exposure to the arts in London also involved visiting the studios of several expatriate American artists. Having had his own portrait painted by Mather Brown, Adams convinced Jefferson to sit for him. The copy of Jefferson's *Notes on the State of Virginia* depicted in Adams's portrait offers one indication of his deep affection for Jefferson; Adams's desire to obtain a portrait of his friend to hang in his home offers another.

The original portrait Brown painted has disappeared, but from a copy made before its disappearance, Jefferson, at forty-three, still looks like a young man. He is neatly coiffed, his hair curled at the sides and thickly powdered. His always-ruddy cheeks give him a glow. His eyes constitute the most striking feature of the painting. Paradoxically, they have a dreamy yet penetrating quality. They seem to stare into the distance, looking beyond the horizon and deep into the future.

Brown's portrait forms the surest indication of Jefferson's contact with London's world of art. Jefferson's correspondence hints that he immersed himself deeply enough within the artistic community to speak with all of the leading American painters in London. Lately he had been corresponding with George Washington regarding the statue of the president that Jean-Antoine Houdon would create as the centerpiece for the Virginia State Capitol. There was some question whether Washington should be depicted in modern or classical dress. Upon learning Washington's preference for modern garb, Jefferson was "happy to find that modern dress for your statue would meet your approbation. I found

Thomas Jefferson, by Mather Brown. (National Portrait Gallery, Smithsonian Institution; bequest of Charles Francis Adams)

it strongly the sentiment of West, Copeley, Trumbul, and Brown in London, after which it would be ridiculous to add that it was my own. I think a modern in an antique dress as *just* an object of ridicule as a Hercules or Marius with a periwig and a chapeau bras."[37]

This brief comment reveals that Jefferson had spoken about art not only with Mather Brown, but also with John Singleton Copley, John Trumbull, and Benjamin West. His contact with John Trumbull—the artist, not to be confused with John Trumbull the poet—proved beneficial to them both. By the time they met, Trumbull had embarked on a series of paintings depicting important people and events from the Revolutionary War, including *The Death of General Warren at the Battle of Bunker Hill* and *The Death of General Montgomery in the Attack on Quebec*. Unsure whether he should continue the series, Trumbull sought Jefferson's opinion. Jefferson, as Trumbull recorded in his invaluable autobiography, "encouraged me to persevere in this pursuit, and kindly invited me to come to Paris, to see and study the fine works there, and to make his house my home, during my stay."[38] It would not be long before Trumbull took him up on his offer and joined him at the Hôtel de Langeac.

Before leaving London, Jefferson also visited Sir Ashton Lever's Museum. Having written what Charles Thomson called the finest natural history of America yet, Jefferson wanted to see this, the most extensive collection of curiosities from the natural world England had ever seen. "Natural History...is my passion," Jefferson informed one correspondent a few years later.[39] Though some contemporary critics found fault with Lever's collection because it was not organized according to any established scheme for classifying nature, the sheer breadth and depth of the collection made it impressive. From the rotunda of the museum, Jefferson, among numerous other visitors, could have seen hundreds and hundreds of stuffed birds. Lever's Museum helped inspire Jefferson to cover the walls beneath his rotunda at Monticello with numerous specimens from the natural world.

Lever went so far as to add a touch of whimsy to his collection, specifically, to his display of monkeys. Good for him. The world deserves more whimsy. Despite their humor, the displays that filled Lever's Monkey Room were not without serious implications. Stuffed chimpanzees and orangutans were posed in human attitudes. Tailor Monkey, for one, sat cross-legged threading a needle. Carpenter Monkey was planing a bench. Clerk Monkey sat at a writing desk. The sight of these manlike apes led some to chuckle, others to guffaw, and at least one to reconsider the theories of Lord Monboddo, who first posited the idea of evolution.[40]

Leaving England, Jefferson crossed the channel without incident and soon found himself in Calais. The expenses he recorded in his account book include the following: "gave the successor of Sterne's monk at Calais 1f4."[41] Jefferson, of course, was referring to the Franciscan monk Laurence Sterne described in *A Sentimental Journey through France and Italy*. His passion for Sterne's work was well known among his friends.

Earlier that year Abigail Adams had written to complain about their situation in the American embassy in London, alluding to a caged bird in *A Sentimental Journey* and knowing that Jefferson would get the reference: "At present we are in the situation of Sterne's starling."[42]

Inspired by Sterne's own travels through France, *A Sentimental Journey* is nevertheless a fictionalized account that parodies other contemporary travel narratives. Jefferson himself recognized the work's fictional nature and shelved it among romances and novels. Sterne, more than any other modern English novelist in Jefferson's opinion, had the capacity to combine his powers of imagination with his capacity for expressing truth. As Jefferson observed, "We neither know nor care whether Lawrence Sterne really went to France, whether he was there accosted by the poor Franciscan, at first rebuked him unkindly, and then gave him a peace offering; or whether the whole be not a fiction."[43] If the essence is true, the plot need not be.

Identifying a parallel between his own personal experience and something he read in a novel, Jefferson projected himself into the pages of fiction. Before visiting England, he referred to the nation as the land of literature, and of books. During the four weeks he spent here, England ceased being a place in Jefferson's imagination and became real. Upon leaving, however, his English experience took on the quality of a fable. With a king like a mule, a pig like a scholar, and apes like men, London did seem rather like a fantastic place in retrospect. If Jefferson's attitude toward London softened at all in the coming years, it was because of what he read in his books and in the letters of his British correspondents. This, Jefferson's first trip to London, would also be his last.

CHAPTER 23

Summer of '86

Jefferson's springtime activities in London helped shape his summertime activities in Paris. After returning to France in May, he caught up his correspondence, writing several friends to tell them about his trip and inform them of his return. To one he described the painterly skill of John Trumbull, who was planning to visit Paris soon, though not as soon as Jefferson imagined. Trumbull did not reach Paris until late July. Before then, Jefferson had much that required his attention, including some unfinished literary business. The friendship he and William Stephens Smith had formed, combined with new contacts in London's literary world, had given him an idea for marketing Dr. David Ramsay's *History of the Revolution in South Carolina*, a problem that had been preying on his mind for months.

For almost a year, in fact, Jefferson had been involved with the publication of Ramsay's history. The two men had become acquainted when both were serving in Congress. Upon completing his manuscript, Ramsay had written Jefferson, asking him to find a French translator and publisher. Ramsay asked a lot, but Jefferson was willing to do what he could. The history had been a pet project of Ramsay's ever since he had been taken prisoner after the fall of Charleston and exiled to a British P.O.W. camp in St. Augustine, Florida. Incensed by his treatment at the hands of the British during his incarceration, Ramsay decided to write a history of the war in South Carolina. By the time he was through, he had created a work that went far beyond its original scope. Ramsay's two-volume *History of the Revolution of South Carolina* amounts to a history of the Revolutionary War in the South.

The usual way of issuing such a substantial work was to publish it by subscription, which typically involved having a prospectus printed in order to give potential subscribers an idea of the work. Ramsay found this method of publication distasteful. As he explained to Jefferson, he avoided publishing his book by subscription because of "principles of delicacy perhaps excessive."[1]

Ramsay's reluctance to publish his history by subscription resembles Jefferson's reluctance to publish *Notes on the State of Virginia*. During the late eighteenth century, attitudes toward commercial publishing were in a state of flux, especially among Southern gentlemen. The tradition of circulating a written work in manuscript persisted much longer in the South than it did elsewhere in America. If an author wrote something and a friend expressed interest in it, then the author would have a manuscript copy made to present to the friend. Somehow, the idea of putting a written work in printed form for anyone to read was indecorous.

Venturing the cost of publication himself, Ramsay was getting his work into print yet doing so in a way that resembled the manuscript tradition, in which the author bore the cost of making manuscripts. The expense Ramsay incurred and the disappointment he experienced with his *History* suggest that the delicate principles he was clinging to had lost their validity. In terms of the history of books and printing, it was time for authors to set aside whatever feelings of delicacy they may be having and, for better or worse, plunge into the marketplace.

To print *The History of the Revolution in South Carolina*, Ramsay had engaged Isaac Collins, a careful yet relatively unambitious printer working out of Trenton, New Jersey. When Ramsay approached Jefferson about the possibility of a French edition, the American edition was in press but unfinished. For Jefferson, Ramsay went to the trouble of having a partial manuscript copy of his history prepared. A manuscript copy of an author's work still made a heartfelt gift that could endear the recipient to the author. The one Ramsay presented to Jefferson clearly functioned in this manner. Ramsay sent printed sheets of the history to Paris as its gatherings came through the press. In letters accompanying these printed gatherings, Ramsay reiterated his desire for a French edition, but he did so in an ingratiating manner. Ramsay told him: "If a translation is thought proper you shall not in any event lose by it: if it is not I shall have the pleasure of furnishing you with the reading of the first copy of my work that crossed the Atlantic."[2]

Jefferson wrote from Paris, expressing much satisfaction with Ramsay's work, the first history of the war published from an American perspective. He assured Ramsay that he would do what he could: "I am much pleased to see a commencement of those special histories of the late revolution which must be written first before a good general one can be expected."[3]

Though an offhand remark phrased as a cordial note of appreciation, Jefferson's comment says much about his attitude toward history writing. By "special histories," he meant narrowly focused studies written by experts in different fields of inquiry. Once several individual specialists have published their own focused histories of the Revolutionary War, he implied, then a general historian could synthesize these various studies into one authoritative, comprehensive history. History-writing is a cumulative effort requiring many minds.

As promised, Jefferson began seeking a French publisher for Ramsay's *History*. His untiring efforts in this regard display the profound sense of responsibility he felt toward his nation and his countrymen. Dissatisfied with one offer he received, Jefferson sought others but found few that could top it. French publishers were reluctant to compensate authors adequately for translated works because there was no way one publisher could legally prohibit another from issuing a different translation of the same work.

Confident he could do better, Jefferson continued to seek a more lucrative offer for Ramsay. He could not wait too long: he feared that a lengthy delay would open the door for a competing French translation. Eventually, Froullé offered him slightly better terms. Despite his respect for Froullé, Jefferson hesitated to accept the offer. Only after Chastellux assured him that Froullé's was the best offer he could expect did Jefferson close the deal. Froullé's handling of Ramsay's *History* confirmed the respect Jefferson had already developed for him. He would return to Froullé with similar projects. When John Adams sent Jefferson a copy of the first volume of his *Defence of the Constitutions of the United States*, Jefferson took the initiative and arranged with Froullé to have it translated and printed.

With Jefferson hard at work on the French edition, Ramsay was doing what he could to market his book in England, but his naiveté led him astray. Instead of trying to find a London publisher who would edit and publish an edition specifically for British readers, Ramsay sent a huge quantity of the American edition—sixteen hundred copies—directly to the prominent London publisher and bookseller Charles Dilly.

Considering the partisan nature of Ramsay's work, Dilly hesitated to sell it. Ramsay's harsh treatment of Cornwallis, Tarleton, and other British officers would subject Dilly to accusations of libel were he to sell Ramsay's *History* as its text stood. Before putting the book up for sale, Dilly sought the advice of legal counsel. His lawyers strongly advised against selling it. Since the portion of Ramsay's *History* most offensive to British readers was largely restricted to an eighteen-page section, Dilly devised a way to make the book suitable for his local clientele: he asked Edward Bancroft to rewrite this section, which Dilly could have printed as a substitute for the supposedly offensive pages. His lawyers advised against this course of action, too. Dilly slowly realized that he had on hand sixteen hundred copies of a book he could not sell.[4]

When Bancroft let Jefferson know what Dilly was considering, Jefferson was aghast. How could any self-respecting bookseller deliberately tear the guts from a book before selling it? Gutting a book—the phrase is Jefferson's—would help no one. As he informed William Stephens Smith, "They tell me that they are about altering Dr. Ramsay's book in London in order to accommodate it to the English palate and pride.... The French translation will be out in a short time. There is no gutting in that. All Europe will read the English transactions in America, as they really happened. To what purpose then hoodwink themselves? Like the foolish Ostrich who when it has hid its head, thinks its body cannot be seen."[5]

Jefferson devised an alternate plan: he would have Dilly send copies of Ramsay's *History* to Paris, where he could have Froullé sell them from his shop. Any Englishman who wished to read Ramsay's *History* complete and unaltered could obtain a copy from Paris. He wrote Smith, asking him to visit Dilly's shop and have fifty copies sent to Froullé. Jefferson even drafted an advertisement informing British readers that they could obtain a complete and unexpurgated copy of Ramsay's *History of the Revolution in South Carolina* by writing directly to Froullé. He ended his advertising copy by assuring British readers that though the book would be coming from France it would be delivered promptly. Jefferson's forward-thinking effort to promote inter-European commerce was far ahead of its time, as the fruitless results of this venture proved. British consumers hesitated to take advantage of his offer. Nearly two years later, Froullé had sold only nine of the original fifty copies Smith had sent from London. The French translation fared little better.

Though Jefferson's strenuous efforts on Ramsay's behalf largely went for naught, they do reveal his sense of personal and professional responsibility. His friendship with Ramsay partly motivated his efforts, but his sense of professional responsibility motivated him more. As American minister to the Court of France, he understood that he was responsible for carrying out the business in France his countrymen requested of him. When that business involved publishing books about the United States unprejudiced by British accounts, then it became a matter of utmost importance.

Beyond his personal and national responsibilities, another factor motivated Jefferson to do his best to publish Ramsay's *History*. Unquestionably dedicated to the United States, Jefferson did owe allegiance to another republic, one that transcended national and political boundaries: the Republic of Letters. His efforts to make Ramsay's *History* available to European readers exemplify his belief in books without boundaries. Works written in other languages and published in other nations should be made available and affordable to any and all who wish to read them.

The difficulty and expense Jefferson was currently experiencing as he tried to obtain several Spanish volumes reinforced the importance of making books more easily available between different nations. Having honed his knowledge of Spanish during his passage from Boston to Europe, Jefferson was now cultivating his interest in Spanish literature, which took him in two different directions. His curiosity about early American history prompted him to read the accounts of Spanish exploration, but he was also broadening his knowledge of the Spanish belletristic tradition.

The Spanish works he acquired during his time in Europe include Don Vicente García de la Huerta's *Obras Poéticas*, a collection of drama and verse; *Parnaso Español*, a nine-volume collection of poetry edited by Juan José López de Sedano; *Romances de Germanía*, Juan Hidalgo's collection of gypsy romances by various authors, including the great Spanish satirist Francisco de Quevedo; and *La Eroticas*, a collection of verse by Esteban Manuel de Villegas. Villegas's provocative title makes the work seem more salacious than it is. Villegas included translations of verse from Horace and Anacreon and even appended a Spanish translation of Boethius's *Consolation of Philosophy*—hardly the kind of thing that would seem to belong in a book entitled *La Eroticas*.

In the summer of 1786 Jefferson finally received the books he had ordered some months earlier through William Carmichael, U.S. chargé d'affaires in Spain. "Having been very desirous of collecting the original Spanish writers on American history," he explained to James Madison, "I commissioned Mr. Carmichael to purchase some for me. They came very dear, and moreover he was obliged to take duplicates in two instances."[6] The Spanish books he received that summer included two by "El Inca," the Peruvian mestizo chronicler Garcilaso de la Vega: *La Florida* and *Commentarios Reale*. He also received Jose d'Acosta's *Historia Natural y Moral de las Indias* and Juan de Torquemada's massive *La Monarchia Indiana*.

These books reached the Hôtel de Langeac from Spain around the same time John Trumbull arrived from England. Jefferson shelved them in his library and welcomed Trumbull to stay as long as he wished.

Trumbull became not only a part of Jefferson's circle, but also a part of his household. Jefferson announced his arrival to Francis Hopkinson: "Our countryman Trumbull is here, a young painter of the most promising talents. He brought with him his Battle of Bunker's hill and Death of Montgomery to have them engraved here, and we may add, to have them sold; for like Dr. Ramsay's history, they are too true to suit the English palate."[7]

Jefferson's comparison between Trumbull's paintings of the American Revolution and Ramsay's *History of the Revolution in South Carolina* reflects his prejudice against the English, which his encounter with its king and counselors earlier that year had done nothing to dispel. The English still could not face the truth of the American Revolution, he implied. Identifying a similarity between the works of Ramsay and Trumbull, Jefferson also paralleled literature and painting. Both forms of expression allow their creators to articulate truth and exalt the principles for which their countrymen fought and died. Much as Jefferson devoted an extraordinary amount of effort to help Ramsay, he would also exert himself on Trumbull's behalf, introducing him to people he knew in the local artistic community.

Once Jefferson introduced Trumbull to his contacts in Paris, Trumbull immersed himself in the Parisian art world. The two paintings he brought along quickly earned him much respect. As Jefferson told Ezra Stiles, Trumbull's paintings "are the admiration of the Connoisseurs. His natural talents of this art seem almost unparalleled."[8] Trumbull made many friends among the leading artists in Paris and, in turn, introduced Jefferson to them.

Jacques-Louis David was one of Trumbull's new friends whom Jefferson came to know. After Trumbull introduced them, Jefferson returned to David's studio at the Louvre on his own, where he saw *The Oath of the Horatii*. Once Trumbull had left Paris, Jefferson continued to follow David's work. At the Exposition au Salon du Louvre in 1787, he saw David's moving *Death of Socrates*. Jefferson wrote Trumbull and urged him to return to Paris before the exposition was over in order to see this magnificent work, the best item in the entire show. To his eye, David's work was far superior to other contemporary painters. During his time in Paris, Jefferson reached a point where he cared little for any other artists besides David.[9]

Jefferson did appreciate another artist Trumbull introduced him to— for sentimental reasons. Maria Cosway, a beautiful Anglo-Italian painter, captured his heart and turned the summer of 1786 into a whirl of pleasure, the likes of which Jefferson had not known since he had

The Oath of the Horatii (1786), by Jacques-Louis David. (Toledo Museum of Art, purchased with funds from the Libbey Endowment, gift of Edward Drummond Libbey, 1950.308)

courted his wife a decade and a half earlier. The fullest information about the relationship between Mr. Jefferson and Mrs. Cosway occurs in the long letter he wrote her that autumn, which has become known as "Dialogue between My Head and My Heart." Though this letter is worth analyzing as literature, it also contains much factual detail. The challenge is separating fact from fancy.

Jefferson's letter personifies both his mind and his sentiment. Head and Heart engage in a lively debate regarding which one should control his personal behavior. Few contemporary dialogues surpass Jefferson's in terms of their literary quality. With the possible exception of Benjamin Franklin's "Dialogue between the Gout and Mr. Franklin," Jefferson's letter constitutes the finest dialogue in the history of early American literature. Like Franklin's, Jefferson's dialogue anticipates later developments of the form in American popular culture, in which different parts of the body or aspects of the personality—the devil and the angel—debate possible courses of action.

Discussing how Trumbull introduced Jefferson to Maria and her husband, Richard Cosway, himself a talented and fashionable miniaturist, Head reminds Heart, "You will be pleased to remember that when our friend Trumbull used to be telling us of the merits and talents of these good people, I never ceased whispering to you that we had no occasion for new acquaintance."[10] The comment rings true: the circumference of Jefferson's Parisian circle was continually expanding—to the detriment of his studies. The hours he spent with Trumbull and other artist friends took time away from his books, whose companionship he dearly cherished. While he lingered at the Louvre, all those newly arrived Spanish folios back at the Hôtel de Langeac remained unread.

Jefferson first met the Cosways at the municipal grain market, which may seem an odd place for a meeting, but the Halle aux Bleds, as it was called, was known less for what was sold inside than for what was placed on top: a vast rotunda. Jefferson was thoroughly impressed with this great dome—the largest in France—and hoped to model the U.S. Capitol on it. Constructed of wood and based on new principles of carpentry, the rotunda looked, in the words of one contemporary traveler, "as light as if suspended by the fairies."[11] It was made all the more magnificent by glass panels that let light enter and fill the interior.

The cross-hatched streams of light created a dramatic setting for what occurred the day Trumbull, Jefferson, and the Cosways showed up simultaneously. Imagine it: Entering the Hall aux Bleds with Jefferson, Trumbull spies the Cosways in this distance. They notice him and his lanky companion and begin walking toward them. As the Cosways approach, they pass through beams of light and patches of shadow. The four meet, and Trumbull introduces Jefferson to Mr. and Mrs. Cosway. Maria stands in the light, which enhances her natural beauty, showing off her large, blue eyes and the massive curls piled high atop her head. Next to his beautiful wife, her diminutive husband disappears in the shadows. Jefferson left no derogatory comments regarding Richard Cosway, but more than one contemporary said that Maria's husband had a face like a monkey's.[12]

Jefferson was smitten. Though he had other plans for this evening, he canceled them to be with her, even if it meant being with her chimplike husband, too. Jefferson had planned to dine with the Duchesse de la Rochefoucauld d'Anville, but he sent word to her via a "lying messenger" and canceled their plans. Something had suddenly come up: dispatches requiring his immediate attention had unexpectedly arrived. He dined with the Cosways at St. Cloud and then went to Ruggieri's, a fashionable outdoor resort among the *haut monde*, where they witnessed an extraordinary display of fireworks. From Ruggieri's they went to see a performance of Johann Baptiste Krumpholtz, the renowned Austrian harpist.

After that first meeting in early August, Jefferson met Maria Cosway often during the next two months. Sometimes she came with Chimp-Like, but frequently she came alone. Their meetings typically took the form of sightseeing. Together they saw the Pont de Neuilly, a "perfectly horizontal" bridge "remarkable for its elegant simplicity," according to one contemporary traveler.[13] Jefferson agreed. He called it the handsomest bridge in the world. He and Maria also visited Marly, where the impressive machinery cast a great mist into the air and produced a nearly perpetual series of rainbows. Primarily designed to channel water to the king's pleasure gardens, Marly made a beautiful sight—provided a person did not think too much about the amount of money and manpower that went into this unnecessary extravagance.

Together they also saw the chateau at St. Germain en Laye, which was situated amidst a beautiful wooded park; the Pavilion de Musique at Louecinnes, the villa built by Louis XV the previous decade; the Chateau de Madrid, built by Francis I and modeled on the palace in which he was confined in Spain; and the Desert de Retz, which contained what may have been the most unusual sight of all, a house disguised as a ruined Roman column. Recalling their visit, Jefferson exclaimed, "How grand the idea excited by the remains of such a column! The spiral staircase was too beautiful!"

They attended the theater together on at least one occasion: the second week of September they visited the Théâtre Italien. In addition to *Richard Coeur de Lion*—libretto by Michel-Jean Sedaine, music by André Grétry—they also saw a performance of *Les Deux Billets* by the popular contemporary novelist and playwright Jean-Pierre-Claris de Florian. (Jefferson's daughter Martha was also familiar with the works of Florian: a Paris friend had presented her with a copy of *Galatée*, Florian's pastoral romance.)[14] One of several theatrical works Florian collectively called his *Arlequinades*, *Les Deux Billets* tells the story of a harlequin and an unscrupulous rival who has purloined a love letter from him. Jefferson enjoyed the comedy well enough to add a copy of it to his library.

The following week Jefferson suffered a bad fall and fractured his right wrist. The circumstances surrounding this unfortunate fall are a little fuzzy. Friends and family members remembered its details differently. One day in mid-September Jefferson was out with a companion, who might have been Maria Cosway but could have been a male acquaintance. They were out walking together, or they might have been on horseback. While trying to jump a fence—possibly—Jefferson tumbled to the ground, breaking his fall with his arm, breaking his wrist in the process.

Jefferson summoned Dr. Antoine Louis, who was considered the finest surgeon in Paris. Dr. Louis was not at his best the day he treated Jefferson. He set the wrist improperly, and Jefferson remained in great pain through October. The injury crimped his social activities, preventing him from seeing Maria as much as he wished. On Wednesday, October 4, the day before she and Richard Visage de Chimpanzé planned to leave Paris, Jefferson felt well enough to take a carriage ride with her. His wrist had not healed as well as he had hoped. Driving Maria's carriage down the cobblestones, he "rattled a little too freely over the pavement" and reinjured the wrist.[15]

That evening, the pain was so excruciating he could not sleep at all. Making his pain more acute, Jefferson was saddened because he would not be able to say goodbye to Maria before she left Paris. With his left hand, he wrote an apologetic note to her, explaining, "I have passed the night in so much pain that I have not closed my eyes. It is with infinite regret therefore that I must relinquish your charming company for that of the Surgeon whom I have sent for to examine into the cause of this change."[16] Jefferson was apparently hoping she would linger in Paris for his sake, and he ended his letter asking her to notify him if she would delay her departure. He quickly dispatched the note.

Maria was touched by the left-handed message. She dashed off an affectionate note and sent it to him. Once he received it, Jefferson decided that the pain in his wrist was not so great to prevent him from saying goodbye to her in person. He sent away the surgeon he had summoned, hurried off in his carriage to the Cosways' home, and accompanied them as far as the Pavilion de St. Denis, where he treated them to refreshments before saying his final goodbyes.

After taking their refreshments, Jefferson walked the Cosways to their carriage, helped Maria into it, and watched as its wheels began to turn. Sadly, he realized, the wonderful times they had spent together during the preceding weeks had come to a close.

Pierre d'Hancarville, an antiquarian and ancient art specialist, had also accompanied them to the Pavilion de St. Denis. He had been smitten by Maria Cosway's charms, too, and was also saddened to see her go. As Jefferson tells the story, both men were dumbstruck and almost paralyzed by her departure. In the introductory paragraph to his "Dialogue between My Head and My Heart," he explains that the coachman crammed them into the carriage "like recruits for the Bastille." They scarcely had "soul enough to give orders to the coachman," who assumed that Paris was their destination and headed back into the city.

Inside the carriage both men remained quiet for a time, but one of them eventually broke the silence to express his sadness at Maria's departure. With the silence broken, they talked the rest of the way into the city. The coachman let d'Hancarville off first and then brought Jefferson back to the Hôtel de Langeac, where he took a seat by the fire, the pain in his heart supplanting the pain in his wrist.

It was at this time that he began thinking about what he would write to Maria to express how he felt and devised the idea to present his thoughts and feelings as a dialogue between the Head and the Heart. The dialogue was a prominent literary genre in the eighteenth century, and there are numerous examples of it in English and American literature.[17] But Jefferson had a much older model he could turn to, Boethius's *Consolation of Philosophy*. Boethius structured his work as a dialogue between himself and Philosophy, who descends upon him in his despair and urges him to find solace in philosophy. In Jefferson's dialogue, Head performs much the same function as Philosophy in Boethius—at least at first.

A week later, with the letter carefully planned, Jefferson wrote the whole thing out in his left hand, all twelve pages. The letter situates the dialogue within a narrative frame. It begins in Jefferson's voice and tells her about the carriage ride with d'Hancarville from the Pavilion de St. Denis back into Paris. As his opening frame ends, Jefferson, having returned home, is seated by his fire, "solitary and sad" listening to Head and Heart discuss his melancholy predicament.

"Well, friend, you seem to be in a pretty trim," Head says as he makes an ironic observation regarding Heart's forlorn appearance.

"I am indeed the most wretched of all earthly beings," Heart responds. "Overwhelmed with grief, every fibre of my frame distended beyond its natural powers to bear, I would willingly meet whatever catastrophe should leave me no more to feel or to fear."

The words Heart speaks are reminiscent of the letters Jefferson sent John Page two decades earlier. In those, he often assumed the persona of a distraught lover and conveyed his feelings through the use of hyperbole.

Responding to Heart's expression of emotional distraught and overwhelming grief, Head observes, "These are the eternal consequences of your warmth and precipitation. This is one of the scrapes into which you are ever leading us. You confess your follies indeed; but still you hug and cherish them, and no reformation can be hoped, where there is no re-pentance." Castigating Heart for becoming mired in emotion, Head sounds much like Philosophy, who castigates Boethius for turning his back on philosophy: "You are the man, are you not, who was brought up on the milk of my learning and fed on my food until you reached maturity? I gave you arms to protect you and keep your strength un-impaired, but you threw them away."[18]

Head upbraids Heart for becoming so attached to the Cosways. Un-like Heart, Head eschews friendship and social intercourse, activities that disturb his equanimity. Once Head blames Heart for developing a fond friendship that made saying good-bye painful, Heart responds by blaming Head for initiating the friendship. In defense of Jefferson's behavior, Head explains that the visit to the Halle aux Bleds was mo-tivated by public utility. Since a marketplace would be built in Rich-mond, Jefferson had been seeking architectural examples for inspiration. Similarly, the magnificent design of the Pont de Neuilly could be adapted to span the Schuylkill River, something that would greatly encourage Philadelphia's economic development. While sightseeing, Head had concentrated on projects of public utility while Heart spent all his time cultivating the Cosways' friendship. Recalling how Heart be-came carried away with these new friends, Head accuses him of being unable to control his behavior.

Heart turns the argument around, thanking Head for reminding him of all the wonderful pleasures they enjoyed with the Cosways that day. Head, in response, blasts Heart for his incorrigibility. Instead of re-forming his behavior, Heart seems willing to relive such follies again. Head acknowledges the accomplishments of Maria Cosway, her beauty, modesty, musical abilities, and pleasant disposition. But such charms, he continues, only increased the pain experienced at parting.

Heart expresses hope of seeing the Cosways in America. Head dismisses the possibility of an American visit on their part as unrealistic, but Heart insists upon its likelihood. Given her talent as a painter, Maria could find few better subjects for landscape painting than the natural scenery of America. Making this point, Heart launches a paean to the American landscape: "Where could they find such objects as in America for the exercise of their enchanting art? especially the lady, who paints landscapes so inimitably. She wants only subjects worthy of immortality to render her pencil immortal. The Falling Spring, the Cascade of Niagara, the Passage of the Potowmac thro the Blue mountains, the Natural bridge. It is worth a voiage across the Atlantic to see these objects; much more to paint, and make them, and thereby ourselves, known to all ages."

Heart's words lead both Head and Heart to digress on the beauty and progress of America, a subject upon which they both agree, but eventually Head terminates the digression and refocuses their argument on the matter at hand.

Head goes so far as to devise a calculus of pleasure and pain, which must be balanced properly. Do not pursue an acquaintance that promises pleasure until you weigh it against the pain that could result. "The art of life is the art of avoiding pain," Head continues, and "he is the best pilot who steers clearest of the rocks and shoals with which it is beset." The best way to avoid emotional pain is to seek pleasures within ourselves, which no one else can take away. Intellectual pleasure, for instance, is always in our power. Enjoying the life of the mind, "we ride serene and sublime above the concerns of this mortal world, contemplating truth and nature, matter and motion, the laws which bind up their existence, and that eternal being who made and bound them up by those laws."

Many of the ideas Head suggests Jefferson himself believed, but Head is not content to rest his case here. He continues by recommending against all friendships, voicing an idea that does damage to his argument: "Leave the bustle and tumult of society to those who have not talents to occupy themselves without them. Friendship is but another name for an alliance with the follies and the misfortunes of others. Our own share of miseries is sufficient: why enter then as volunteers into those of another?"

In response, Heart rejects the pleasures of solitude and upholds the value of friendship:

In a life where we are perpetually exposed to want and accident, yours is a wonderful proposition, to insulate ourselves, to retire from all aid, and to wrap ourselves in the mantle of self-sufficiency! For assuredly nobody will care for him who cares for nobody. But friendship is precious not only in the shade but in the sunshine of life: and thanks to a benevolent arrangement of things, the greater part of life is sunshine. I will recur for proof to the days we have lately passed. On these indeed the sun shone brightly! How gay did the face of nature appear! Hills, valleys, chateaux, gardens, rivers, every object wore its liveliest hue! Whence did they borrow it? From the presence of our charming companion. They were pleasing, because she seemed pleased. Alone, the scene would have been dull and insipid: the participation of it with her gave it relish. Let the gloomy Monk, sequestered from the world, seek unsocial pleasures in the bottom of his cell! Let the sublimated philosopher grasp visionary happiness while pursuing phantoms dressed in the garb of truth! Their supreme wisdom is supreme folly:

and they mistake for happiness the mere absence of pain. Had they ever felt the solid pleasure of one generous spasm of the heart, they would exchange for it all the frigid speculations of their lives, which you have been vaunting in such elevated terms. Believe me then, my friend, that that is a miserable arithmetic which would estimate friendship at nothing, or at less than nothing.

Heart is now starting to win the argument. He gains control and puts Head in his place:

When nature assigned us the same habitation, she gave us over it a divided empire. To you she allotted the field of science, to me that of morals. When the circle is to be squared, or the orbit of a comet to be traced; when the arch of greatest strength, or the solid of least resistance is to be investigated, take you the problem: it is yours: nature has given me no cognisance of it. In like manner in denying to you the feelings of sympathy, of benevolence, of gratitude, of justice, of love, of friendship, she has excluded you from their controul. To these she has adapted the mechanism of the heart. Morals were too essential to the happiness of man to be risked on the incertain combinations of the head. She laid their foundation therefore in sentiment, not in science.

From this point on, Heart forbids Head from decisions regarding when to make friendships or whom to befriend. Boethius gave Philosophy the last word. In Jefferson's dialogue, Heart wins the argument and gets in the last word. Upon finishing the dialogue, Jefferson resumed his letter in his own voice to provide a closing frame.

Apologizing for the length of this letter in his final remarks, Jefferson gave Maria license to write letters as long or even longer to him. In so doing, he cleverly reminded her of one evening they spent together: "If your letters are as long as the bible, they will appear short to me. Only let them be brim full of affection. I shall read them with the dispositions with which Arlequin, in les deux billets spelt the words 'je t'aime' and wished that the whole alphabet had entered into their composition."

Bringing his letter to a close, Jefferson informed her, "As to myself my health is good, except my wrist which mends slowly, and my mind which mends not at all, but broods constantly over your departure." Jefferson's wrist would give him pain off and on through the rest of his life. He and Maria would see each other again and would exchange letters for years to come. But never would they recapture the magic of the summer of '86.

CHAPTER 24

An Inquisitive Journey
through France and Italy

Jefferson's broken wrist healed very slowly and he considered more drastic treatment. Friends recommended the waters at Aix-en-Provence for their curative properties. Chances are he had little faith in the waters at Aix, but the promised cure gave him a convenient excuse to visit Provence. He had other ways to justify the trip, which would let him visit Italy, a place he had dreamt of seeing for years. Despite what the South of France and the Italian north offered visitors in terms of art and architecture, Jefferson really wanted to observe the agriculture of these regions and the folkways of their people. The story of this European tour has been told before. What has so far gone untold is the story behind the story. Jefferson wrote different versions of his journey for different purposes. How do these various narratives stack up as travel literature?

Excluding the bare-bones account of expenses in his memorandum books, three different sets of documents detailing the trip survive: "Notes of a Tour into the Southern Parts of France etc.," as his trip journal has been titled; "Hints to Americans Traveling in Europe," a set of recommendations Jefferson made to John Rutledge, Jr., and Thomas Lee Shippen, two young American men who were embarking on an extensive European tour; and his correspondence with friends during the journey.

"Notes of a Tour" offers the most detailed account of the trip. Though Jefferson had no intentions of publishing "Notes of a Tour," it does possess qualities he admired in published travel narratives. Characterizing worthwhile books of travel, he said that they "blend together the geography, natural history, civil history, agriculture, manufactures, commerce, arts, occupations, manners etc. of a country."[1] Omitted from this list of characteristics are personal stories of adventure. For the most part, Jefferson excluded such stories from "Notes of a Tour," too. These deliberate omissions make "Notes of a Tour" more frustrating than either "Hints" or his travel correspondence.

"Hints," more travel advice than travel adventure, resembles Lord Chesterfield's travel advice in *Letters to His Son*. Perhaps it should be considered more as didactic literature than as travel writing, but "Hints" does contain much colorful detail excluded from "Notes of a Tour." Telling Rutledge and Shippen which taverns to patronize and which ones to avoid, Jefferson supplied the kind of local information he omitted from "Notes of a Tour."

The letters he wrote during his journey through France and Italy are uneven. Those to William Short and others in Paris contain good information, but his letters to French lady friends embody a sense of fun absent from those he wrote others. The letters to his daughter Martha belong to the category of didactic literature. Mainly, they admonish her to keep studying; infrequently did he reward his older daughter with a glimpse of his travels. Missing from all of these various accounts are the kind of picaresque anecdotes that fill the most beloved eighteenth-century travel writings.

Though Jefferson wrote "Hints" quickly, he took enough time to detail which cities to visit, whose taverns to patronize, and what things to notice while traveling. His advice goes a long way toward explaining why he wrote up his own journey as he did. "Hints" cautions travelers to avoid generalizations based on the behavior of tavern keepers and their ilk. Though travelers encountered them often, such people scarcely represented their nation. "The people you will naturally see the most of will be tavern keepers, Valets de place, and postillions," he explained. "These are the hackneyed rascals of every country. Of course they must never be considered when we calculate the national character."[2]

Jefferson's words show that he approached travel with great seriousness. He was not traveling merely for pleasure. He was traveling to understand the people he encountered, to know them individually but also in the aggregate. He sought to understand the character of the regions and nations he visited. Jefferson's lofty purpose helps explain why his writings are largely bereft of the specific details of traveling. While looking for the big picture, he neglected the quotidian. The conditions of the roads, the quality of the taverns, the food and drink they served: These commonplace details seldom seemed worth noting to him.

His advice to Rutledge and Shippen also reveals why "Notes of a Tour" is largely bereft of humorous detail. The eccentric behavior of tipplers and tavern keepers can lend much charm to stories of travel, but Jefferson excluded them as he characterized the regions he visited. As he told another traveler, "To pass once along a public road thro' a country, and in one direction only, to put up at its taverns, and get into conversation with the idle, drunken individuals who pass their time lounging in these taverns, is not the way to know a country, its inhabitants or manners."[3]

"Hints" also supplies advice regarding how to see what there is to see. Avoid hiring personal guides. Motivated by monetary gain, they assume a direct correlation between how much they say and how much they earn. They spout numerous trivial details, which overload the memory with trifles, fatigue the attention, and waste time. Instead of hiring personal guides, it is better to purchase good guidebooks. "On arriving at a town," Jefferson suggested, "the first thing is to buy the plan of the town, and the book noting its curiosities."[4]

Jefferson's preference for printed guides over personal ones was quite forward-thinking. Hiring local guides while traveling through Europe was standard practice for most eighteenth-century travelers. Though Jean François Royez had published a good road book titled *L'Itinéraire et Guide des Postes d'Italie*, few other travel guidebooks were available. The guidebook publishing industry would not really develop until the early nineteenth century. Jefferson's advice reinforces the importance of the printed word and anticipates the development of the modern travel guidebook. In terms of their form, his own travel notes looked forward to subsequent developments in guidebook literature. On another journey he would place asterisks designating superior accommodations on a list of place names, a feature that would become an essential aspect of the modern guidebook.

"Hints" recommends more general books, too. Before visiting Italy, for example, travelers should purchase a copy of Joseph Addison's *Remarks on Several Parts of Italy*, a work offering a model journey for the well-read tourist. Having prepared for his Italian excursion by rereading the Latin classics, Addison brought his reading to bear throughout his travels, as *Remarks* makes clear: "A Man who is in Rome can scarce see an Object that does not call to Mind a Piece of a Latin Poet or Historian."[5] Using Addison's *Remarks* as a guidebook, travelers could apply their own classical knowledge on the spot. Recalling classical literature while touring the remnants of the Roman Empire reinforces the memory by letting travelers blend their classical knowledge with their personal experience.

Jefferson provided much other useful advice in "Hints." "Walk round the ramparts when there are any," he advised. "Go to the top of a steeple to have a view of the town and its environs." Sightseeing involves great powers of discrimination: "When you are doubting whether a thing is worth the trouble of going to see, recollect that you will never again be so near it, that you may repent the not having seen it, but can never repent having seen it. But there is an opposite extreme too. That is, the seeing too much. A judicious selection is to be aimed at, taking care that the indolence of the moment have no influence in the decision."[6] Modern travelers might take such advice to heart.

Since the two young men who sought his help were from the United States, "Hints" supplies further advice specific to their nationality. Traveling through Europe, Americans should note the following subjects: agriculture, architecture, courts, gardens, heavy machinery, lighter mechanical arts and manufacture, painting and statuary, and politics. Within each of these topics, Jefferson provided more detailed recommendations. Under politics, for example, he recommended observing people in their daily lives: "Take every possible occasion of entering into the houses of the labourers, and especially at the moments of their repast, see what they eat, how they are clothed, whether they are obliged to labour too hard; whether the government or their landlord takes from them an unjust proportion of their labour; on what footing stands the property they call their own, their personal liberty, etc."[7] To understand politics, travelers must examine its folk roots. Only by seeing how people live on a daily basis can travelers understand how well political systems work.

Wending his way through the South of France, Jefferson took his own advice to heart. Writing Chastellux from Marseilles, he characterized his trip as "a continued feast of new objects and ideas." Explaining what he meant, he said that he was getting to know the people who best represented the land: "To make the most of the little time I have for so long a circuit, I have been obliged to keep myself rather out of the way of good dinners and good company. Had they been my objects, I should not have quitted Paris. I have courted the society of gardeners, vignerons, coopers, farmers etc. and have devoted every moment of every day almost, to the business of enquiry."[8]

Jefferson's words echo a remark of Laurence Sterne's from *A Sentimental Journey through France and Italy*. After receiving some seemingly absurd advice from a barber, Sterne's mouthpiece, the Reverend Mr. Yorick, comments: "I think I can see the precise and distinguishing marks of national characters more in these nonsensical *minutiae*, than in the most important matters of state; where great men of all nations talk and talk so much alike, that I would not give nine-pence to chuse amongst them."[9] Though Jefferson shared a similar perspective, he was a different kind of traveler from his fictional predecessor. Of all the types of travelers Sterne identifies in *A Sentimental Journey*—idle travelers, inquisitive travelers, lying travelers, proud travelers, sentimental travelers, splenetic travelers, vain travelers—Jefferson best fits the category of inquisitive traveler. Though his letters sometimes show elements of sentimentality, his quest for new objects and ideas reveals his inquisitive nature. His desire for knowledge overrode his natural shyness: seldom did he hesitate to ask questions when the answers could broaden his knowledge and expand his mind.

Given his impulse to mingle among farmers and laborers, Jefferson wanted to travel alone and anonymously—much to the disdain of his French friends. Determined to keep his identity secret, he left Paris the last Wednesday in February 1787, traveling alone in his carriage and hiring post horses along the way. Besides keeping him incognito, traveling alone gave him much time for reflection. At Dijon, less than a week into his journey, he hired a manservant named Petit Jean, mainly for the sake of propriety. Petit Jean accompanied him for the remainder of the journey. They reached Sens on Friday, and the journey from there to Vermanton on Saturday, March 3, supplied the subject for the first entry in Jefferson's "Notes of a Tour."

This initial, two-paragraph entry established a pattern for the entries to follow. In his first paragraph, Jefferson described the topography, soil, and agriculture of the region. In the second, he depicted its people. He found it strange that families should congregate in villages instead of living on farms of their own and blamed the Catholic Church for the situation: "Are they thus collected by that dogma of their religion which makes them believe that, to keep the Creator in good humor with his own works, they must mumble a mass every day? Certain it is that they are less happy and less virtuous in villages than they would be insulated with their families on the grounds they cultivate."[10] Both his own rural ideal and his religious skepticism shaped Jefferson's understanding of the French.

Thinking about the local diet a few days later, he noticed that though French country folk generally lived on bread and vegetables, the type of bread differed from one place to the next: some people ate good wheat bread while those in a neighboring region ate coarse rye bread. Curious to learn the reason underlying this difference, he asked a local about it. Generally speaking, the people Jefferson approached were happy to respond. "The farmers were very civil, and answered my questions with great readiness," he remembered.[11]

In the rye-eating region, his informant told him, the stony soil prevents red wine grapes from growing. Consequently, the region produces only white wine. Since the production of white fails more often than that of red wine, people in these white-grape-growing regions are less prosperous than those living in the adjacent red-grape-growing regions. Basically, the quality of the bread is contingent on the stoniness of the soil.[12]

"On such slight circumstances depends the condition of man!" Jefferson exclaimed.

By Thursday, March 15, he had reached Lyons. He was having mixed feelings about the French countryside so far. The long, straight, tree-lined roads, which form such a quaint and characteristic aspect of rural France, induced feelings of ennui in him. On the other hand, he enjoyed watching the native plants begin to push forth the new growth of the season; his remarks in "Notes of a Tour" recall comments he made at home in his *Garden Book*. One day he noted, "The wild gooseberry is in leaf, the wild pear and sweet briar in bud."[13]

The weather was the only thing he really complained about, but this was nothing new. He had been complaining about the dreary weather ever since he arrived in France. From Lyons he wrote William Short: "So far all is well. No complaints; except against the weathermaker, who has pelted me with rain, hail, and snow, almost from the moment of my departure to my arrival here. Now and then a few gleamings of sunshine to chear me by the way. Such is this life: and such too will be the next, if there be another, and we may judge of the future by the past."[14] For most people, discussing the weather is a banal activity, but not for Jefferson, who could start talking about the weather and end up pondering the relationship between historiography and eschatology.

Other letters to Short from this journey are peppered with similar reflections, but Jefferson was at his letter-writing best when addressing female friends. Lately, his circle had expanded to include Madame de Tessé and Madame de Tott.

Jefferson's friendship with Lafayette had brought him in contact with Madame de Tessé. Despite being Lafayette's aunt, she was only two years older than Jefferson, and the two got along famously. Like the Comtesse d'Houdetot, Madame de Tessé's wit, charm, and intelligence more than compensated for the defects in her physical appearance. As a contemporary described her, "Madame de Tessé was in every respect a remarkable person: small, piercing eyes, a pretty face marred at the age of twenty by small pox, which, it is said, was no worry to her thanks to her precocious mind; a fine mouth, but slightly misshapen by nervous tic which made her grimace when talking, and, in spite of all that, an imposing air, grace and dignity in all her movements, and above all, infinitely witty."[15] She shared Jefferson's love of art, literature, and gardening. She had a passion for English novels and maintained a lavish garden decorated with all sorts of exotic flora. She and Jefferson often walked through her garden. He greatly admired it and promised to send her some unique American plants once he returned home.

Through Madame de Tessé Jefferson met Madame de Tott or, properly, Mademoiselle de Tott, who had become a part of the Tessé household through a heady combination of intrigue, sympathy, and chance. Once Jefferson's friendship with these two women blossomed, he began dining with them regularly. His correspondence suggests that he was closer to Madame de Tessé, but he was also quite fond of Madame de Tott.

South of Lyons, he began to see remnants of the Roman Empire, or, as he told Madame de Tessé, he began to be "nourished with the remains of Roman grandeur."[16] Using a food metaphor to describe what ancient Rome meant to him, Jefferson revealed how essential contact with the Ancients was to his very being. This comment occurs in the letter he wrote her from Nimes, possibly the finest letter he wrote throughout this journey. He painted a vivid picture of himself at Nimes, where he enjoyed the Maison Quarrée, the Roman building that inspired his design for the Virginia State Capitol.

Describing the pleasure this building gave him, Jefferson depicts himself as a love-struck melancholic:

> Here I am, Madam, gazing whole hours at the Maison quarrée, like a lover at his mistress. The stocking-weavers and silk spinners around it consider me as an hypochondriac Englishman, about to write with a pistol the last chapter of his history. This is the second time I have been in love since I left Paris. The first was with a Diana at the Chateau de Laye Epinaye in the Beaujolois, a delicious morsel of sculpture, by Michael Angelo Slodtz. This, you will say, was in rule, to fall in love with a fine woman: but, with a house! It is all out of precedent! No, madam, it is not without a precedent in my own history.[17]

Jefferson sounds like he just stepped from the pages of an eighteenth-century English novel. Having given his heart to an object that cannot return his love, he has reached the brink of despair and is ready to end it all. He knew Madame de Tessé and her fondness for novels well enough to know she would enjoy this fanciful self-portrait—and recognize it as a literary pose.

Like any good letter writer, Jefferson made his subject matter suit the person he addressed. To Madame de Tessé, he wrote that he had remembered her while seeing sights she would enjoy and imagined seeing them together. Often thinking about her, he had considered writing several times, but he hesitated. At Nimes, "where Roman taste, genius, and magnificence excite ideas analogous to yours at every step," all hesitation disappeared.[18]

The letter he wrote Madame de Tott is personal without being as intimate or affectionate as the one to Madame de Tessé. He told Madame de Tott that he had been thinking of her, too, but in less emphatic terms. Speaking of himself in the third person, his reflections have the quality of a fable: "A traveller, sais I, retired at night to his chamber in an Inn, all his effects contained in a single trunk, all his cares circumscribed by the walls of his apartment, unknown to all, unheeded, and undisturbed, writes, reads, thinks, sleeps, just in the moments when nature and the movements of his body and mind require. Charmed with the tranquillity of his little cell, he finds how few are our real wants, how cheap a thing is happiness, how expensive a one pride."[19]

He also indulged in some creative prose that starts as humorous, pseudoscientific discourse and ends up as a clever dialogue incorporating a charming play on words. Explaining how he was spending his time on the road, he wrote: "Sometimes I amuse myself with physical researches. Those enormous boots, for instance, in which the postillion is incased like an Egyptian mummy, have cost me more pondering than the laws of planetary motion did to Newton. I have searched their solution in his physical, and in his moral constitution. I fancied myself in conversation with one of Newton's countrymen, and asked him what he thought could be the reason of their wearing those boots?"

"Sir," responds the imaginary English conversationalist, "it is because a Frenchman's heels are so light, that, without this ballast, he would turn keel up."

"If so, Sir," Jefferson puns, "it proves at least that he has more *gravity* in his head than your nation is generally willing to allow him."

Jefferson varied the tone and content of his letters to suit different correspondents. Writing to Short from Aix-en-Provence, he not only dropped the melancholic pose, he completely abjured it: "The man who shoots himself in the climate of Aix must be a bloody minded fellow indeed.—I am now in the land of corn, wine, oil, and sunshine. What more can man ask of heaven? If I should happen to die at Paris I will beg of you to send me here, and have me exposed to the sun. I am sure it will bring me to life again."[20] The near-perpetual cloud cover of Paris depressed Jefferson, but the sunshine of Provence gave reason to cheer. In the letter to Short, he scoffs at the man who took suicide as a way out. With gobs of food, casks of wine, and plentiful sunshine, why would anyone want to write the last chapter of his life with a pistol?

In a follow-up letter, Jefferson offered Short a fine appreciation of Provençale, a language Jefferson enjoyed hearing and one he could understand better than French. He observed:

> Provençale stands nearer to the Tuscan than it does to the French, and it is my Italian which enables me to understand the people here, more than my French. This language, in different shades occupies all the country south of the Loire. Formerly it took precedence of the French under the name of la langue Romans. The ballads of its Troubadours were the delight of the several courts of Europe, and it is from thence that the novels of the English are called Romances. Every letter is pronounced, the articulation is distinct, no nasal sounds disfigure it, and on the whole it stands close to the Italian and Spanish in point of beauty. I think it a general misfortune that historical circumstances gave a final prevalence to the French instead of the Provençale language. It loses its ground slowly, and will ultimately disappear because there are few books written in it, and because it is thought more polite to speak the language of the Capital. Yet those who learn that language here, pronounce it as the Italians do.[21]

Jefferson was offering an impassioned plea for linguistic diversity. This letter also anticipates a comment made by another major figure in American literature, who characterized traditional Provençale verse as "the poetry of a democratic aristocracy, which swept into itself, or drew about it, every man with wit or a voice."[22]

As his journey progressed, Jefferson's sense of purpose became more defined. Reaching Nice the second week of April, he wrote Lafayette a letter encapsulating his philosophy of travel. In its basic thrust, the letter contains similar ideas as those in "Hints," but Jefferson polished his prose to a much higher sheen for Lafayette. On the road, he had developed a routine: "In the great cities, I go to see what travellers think alone worthy of being seen; but I make a job of it, and generally gulp it all down in a day. On the other hand, I am never satiated with rambling through the fields and farms, examining the culture and cultivators, with a degree of curiosity which makes some take me to be a fool, and others to be much wiser than I am."[23] Jefferson realized his method of sightseeing differed greatly from that of contemporary travelers, but he happily endured the stares of wide-eyed gawkers he passed along the road.

As he told Lafayette, "You must ferret the people out of their hovels as I have done, look into their kettles, eat their bread, loll on their beds under pretense of resting yourself, but in fact to find if they are soft. You will feel a sublime pleasure in the course of this investigation, and a sublimer one hereafter when you shall be able to apply your knolege to the softening of their beds, or the throwing a morsel of meat into the kettle of vegetables."[24] Such comments account for the tremendous amount of practical detail in "Notes of a Tour." Jefferson was not only recording how the French lived; he was also creating a document that would help improve the lives of Lafayette's countrymen and his own.

From Nice, he extended his journey to Milan. He was growing uneasy about being away from Paris for so long, but he really wanted to observe the rice-growing regions of northern Italy, which were much deeper in Italy's interior than he realized. It was easy to justify the extra travel time: his observations on rice farming would benefit his countrymen, especially the rice farmers in the Carolina lowlands. The Nice-Milan-Nice round trip would take about three weeks. Writing Short before plunging into Italy, he said goodbye for the time being. There was no point in posting letters from Italy. He would arrive in France before his letters.

The absence of personal letters from Jefferson's time in Italy means that "Notes of a Tour" constitutes the main source of information for his Italian experience. The matter-of-fact nature of "Notes of a Tour," however, detracts from á trip that, by all other indications, involved exciting adventure, culinary delight, aesthetic pleasure, and new information.

Learning that the snowy pass through the Alps was still closed to wheeled traffic, he had to leave his carriage and much of his kit in Nice and hire mules and mule drivers to take him through the Alps. Though space for his gear was limited, he managed to find room in his panniers for some books, not just travel guides but also works on Italian history.

In terms of visual pleasure, the Chateau of Saorge provided the most picturesque experience: "The castle and village seem hanging to a cloud in front. On the right is a mountain cloven through to let pass a gurgling stream; on the left a river over which is thrown a magnificent bridge. The whole forms a bason, the sides of which are shagged with rocks, olive trees, vines, herds etc." Jefferson would characterize his all-too-brief time in Italy as a peep into Elysium.[25]

While enjoying the sights, he also looked at the Alps with the eyes of an antiquarian and an agronomist. Describing his trip to George Wythe, he explained, "I took with me some of the writings in which endeavors have been made to investigate the passage of Annibal over the Alps, and was just able to satisfy myself, from a view of the country, that the descriptions given of his march are not sufficiently particular to enable us at this day even to guess at his tract across the Alps."[26]

He also made careful observations on the cultivation of olive trees and other plants, which he recorded in his trip journal and wrote up for the South-Carolina Society for Promoting and Improving Agriculture. "In passing the Alps at the Col de Tende, where they are mere masses of rock, wherever there happens to be a little soil, there are a number of olive trees, and a village supported by them. Take away these trees, and the same ground in corn would not support a single family." Crossing the Alps, Jefferson carefully observed the plant life and formed a scale of plants arranged according to their different powers of resisting the cold.[27]

From Turin he took a day trip to see the basilica of Superga. Located atop a lofty peak, Superga offered an excellent view of the surrounding countryside. He hired a carriage and horses to take him to the peak. The carriage ride down Superga was hair-raising: when his postillion encountered another, the two engaged in an impromptu downhill race, much to the chagrin of their passengers. When Jefferson could take the reins himself, he enjoyed driving fast. As Isaac Jefferson explained, "Traveling in the phaeton Mr. Jefferson used oftentimes to take the reins himself and drive. Whenever he wanted to travel fast *he'd* drive; would drive powerful hard himself."[28] Descending the treacherous switchbacks of Superga at breakneck speed as a passenger, he was not amused.

"Notes of a Tour" mentions neither the fine view from atop Superga nor the nerve-racking downhill race that ended the day. Since neither experience pertained to agriculture or manufacture, he excluded them from his narrative. Sometimes the factual details in "Notes of a Tour" inadvertently convey the charms of travel. Recording the agricultural products and natural resources of Italy, Jefferson occasionally captured its culinary pleasures.

After a few days in Milan, he turned south toward Genoa. Along the way, he passed through Rozzano, where he observed how to make parmesan cheese and recorded the process for posterity. He also sampled mascarpone, which he found delicious.[29] And he fell in love with pasta. When Short traveled through Italy later, Jefferson asked him to buy a mold for making spaghetti and macaroni. Frustrated with the difficulty and expense of importing pasta to Virginia, he eventually designed his own pasta maker. Beyond his importance as author, leader, and thinker, Thomas Jefferson deserves the gratitude of his fellow Americans for domestic reasons, too: he personally introduced macaroni and cheese to the United States.

In Genoa, he spent time enjoying what sights there were to see and made arrangements to return to Nice, where he could retrieve his carriage and resume his roundabout journey through France. Without a proper road, he faced a tough choice between the alternatives: by sea or by a narrow, rocky mule path. Despite his dread of seasickness, the water route offered the most expeditious way to return—or so he thought: he quickly regretted his decision to travel by sea. Before the vessel left the Gulf of Genoa, the wind from the southwest picked up, and he became quite nauseous. The ship's captain recognized that the sea was too rough to reach Nice, so he sought safe harbor at Noli, a sleepy fishing village where the only place Jefferson could find lodgings was at a broken-down tavern. The menu compensated for the tavern's other shortcomings. This evening, he not only had good fish—sardines, fresh anchovies—he also had ortolans—tiny game birds with little meat but lots of flavor—and fresh strawberries, too.

At Noli, he hired three mules and a mule driver to accompany him the rest of the way to Nice. The trip was quite fatiguing. He rode through some places, but more treacherous spots forced him to dismount and lead his mule along a path that barely clung to the side of a steep cliff. Describing this leg of his trip soon after its completion, he made it seem quite arduous. Upon further consideration, he grew nostalgic for that rocky mule track and recommended the same route to others. He told Rutledge and Shippen: "Do not be persuaded to go by water from Genoa to Nice. You will lose a great deal of pleasure which the journey by land will afford you. Take mules therefore at Genoa. Horses are not to be trusted on the precipices you will have to pass."[30]

On the way to Albenga, he enjoyed walking along the Mediterranean shore and letting his mind wander wherever it wished. The ever-changing Mediterranean was beautiful, but he was not content to view it from a distance. Fascinated by the appearance of the water, he got a drinking glass from somewhere, went to the shore, scooped up a glass of water, and held it to the sunlight. When viewed in a drinking glass, the waters of the Mediterranean were remarkably clear and colorless, but on the whole the sea "assumes *by reflection* the colour of the sky or atmosphere, black, green, blue, according to the state of the weather."[31]

Like others who have visited this coastal region, he imagined lingering here and putting behind him other earthly concerns. "If any person wished to retire from their acquaintance, to live absolutely unknown, and yet in the midst of physical enjoiments," he noted, "it should be in some of the little villages of this coast, where air, earth and water concur to offer what each has most precious. Here are nightingales, beccaficas, ortolans, pheasants, partridges, quails, a superb climate, and the power of changing it from summer to winter at any moment, by ascending the mountains. The earth furnishes wine, oil, figs, oranges, and every production of the garden in every season. The sea yeilds lobsters, crabs, oysters, thunny, sardines, anchovies etc."[32]

Reaching Nice was something like leaving the Middle Ages and re-entering the eighteenth century. He checked into the Hotel de York, "a fine English tavern, very agreeably situated, and the mistress a friendly agreeable woman."[33] He also renewed communications in Nice, but fatigue from the journey made him more inclined to sleep than write.

Arriving in Marseilles later that week, he wrote Martha again. Having been her father's riding companion after her mother's death and having been his traveling companion from Philadelphia to Boston to Paris, she remained at Panthemont while he toured southern France and northern Italy. At the very least, she was hoping for some good letters describing the trip en route. The early ones she received contain little colorful detail. From Aix, her father admonished Martha to pursue her studies diligently regardless how difficult they may seem. She was having trouble with Latin, especially as she tried reading Livy's *History* without her teacher's help.

Her father encouraged her to persevere, transforming her study into a matter of national importance. His words are inspiring: "We are always equal to what we undertake with resolution. A little degree of this will enable you to decypher your Livy," he wrote. "If you always lean on your master, you will never be able to proceed without him. It is a part of the American character to consider nothing as desperate; to surmount every difficulty by resolution and contrivance. In Europe there are shops for every want. Its inhabitants therefore have no idea that their wants can be furnished otherwise. Remote from all other aid, we are obliged to invent and to execute; to find means within ourselves, and not to lean on others."[34]

Having learned that his other daughter would soon reach Paris, Jefferson wrote Martha another admonitory letter urging her to be good to Mary and encourage her studies, too. Along with a young slave named Sally—James Hemings's little sister—Mary would reach London the last week of June. Jefferson planned for her to stay with John and Abigail Adams until he could arrange her passage to Paris.

Once Mary reached London, Abigail Adams wrote Jefferson to let him know. She had never met Mary before, but she quickly became fond of her. Mary's face put Abigail Adams in mind of an old song:

> What she thinks in her Heart
> You may read in her Eyes
> For knowing no art
> She needs no disguise.

Recalling these lines in her letter to Jefferson, Abigail Adams indulged her sentimental streak. These same lines recur in novels of the day.[35] Abigail Adams continued, "Her temper, her disposition, her sensibility are all formed to delight. Yet perhaps at your first interview you may find a little roughness but it all subsides in a very little time, and she is soon attached by kindness."[36]

Writing Martha from Marseilles, Jefferson told her about the arduous mule trip to Nice but did little beyond name the places through which he had passed. In fact, the place names fill almost half the letter. Her father kept his comments brief because he wanted to spark her curiosity, not satiate it. He expected her to use his letter as the basis for a self-taught geography lesson. She should have been able to identify all of the places he visited, locate them on a map, and trace her father's route.

From the Mediterranean coast, he headed inland via the Canal de Langueduc. This lazy journey gave him the chance to write Martha the kind of letter she wanted and deserved. He created a vivid picture of his canal passage, complete with image and sound: "cloudless skies above, limpid waters below, and on each hand a row of nightingales in full chorus." The sound of nightingales gave him the opportunity to recall an earlier moment in his trip when he had visited Petrarch's home and its environs. "This delightful bird had given me a rich treat before at the fountain of Vaucluse," he explained. "After visiting the tomb of Laura at Avignon, I went to see this fountain, a noble one of itself, and rendered for ever famous by the songs of Petrarch who lived near it. I arrived there somewhat fatigued, and sat down by the fountain to repose myself. It gushes, of the size of a river, from a secluded valley of the mountain, the ruins of Petrarch's chateau being perched on a rock 200 feet perpendicular above. To add to the enchantment of the scene, every tree and bush was filled with nightingales in full song."[37]

Jefferson mingled the sound of the nightingale with the music of Petrarch's verse to accompany his idyllic canal journey. Long an aficionado of Italian literature, he knew Petrarch well. Earlier he had acquired a precious copy of *Il Petrarca* with other valuable editions from the library of his friend Samuel Henley. The book does not survive, and the exact edition has escaped identity, but its format belongs to early sixteenth-century Italy. Henley's luxurious binding—red morocco—and the fact that Jefferson made note of the binding confirm its special quality.

Even while capturing the beautiful sound of the nightingales in this letter, Jefferson turned it into a lesson for his daughter. He urged Martha to familiarize herself with the nightingale's song while in Europe, so she could compare it with the song of the mockingbird once she returned home to Virginia. Writing his daughter while traveling down the Canal de Languedoc, Jefferson's heart was in Virginia. Celebrations of the mockingbird's song were already an important literary tradition in the American South. Expressing his preference for the mockingbird over the nightingale, he was perpetuating an American tradition.

Though Jefferson conveyed his ideas in many different ways over the course of his trip, similar patterns run through his various forms of travel writing. In "Hints," he told Rutledge and Shippen to make their observations useful for their countrymen. With "Notes of a Tour," he personally exemplified what he recommended to them. He may have depicted himself as a lovesick melancholic gazing at the Maison Quarrée in his letter to Madame de Tessé, but his gazing had a practical intent: he was using the ancient building to inspire ideas for developing the architecture of a new nation. His travel letters to Martha may seem overly didactic, but he held himself to a similar standard: he, too, was using his travels as a way of learning. He never lost sight of what he saw as the main purpose of traveling: to learn new ideas that could help improve mankind.

CHAPTER 25

A Tour through Holland and the Rhine Valley

During his first year in Paris, one of Jefferson's greatest pleasures was spending time with John Adams and his family. Sometimes he would travel to their fine suburban home at Auteuil for an evening of pleasant conversation; other times they would venture to the heart of the city to dine with him and attend the theater. Once Adams became minister plenipotentiary to Great Britain and relocated the family to London, Jefferson missed them very much. "The departure of your family has left me in the dumps," he wrote Adams.[1] Their presence in London, however, did offer him the opportunity of developing a correspondence with Abigail Adams, which both enjoyed immensely.

Dated June 6, 1785—just two weeks after they left Paris—her first letter to Jefferson gave him great pleasure. He replied: "I have received duly the honor of your letter, and am now to return you thanks for your condescension in having taken the first step for settling a correspondence which I so much desired; for I now consider it as *settled* and proceed accordingly."[2] For Jefferson, a literary correspondence was almost like a living, breathing thing. Once established, a correspondence between two friends took on a life of its own, and his correspondence with Abigail Adams was no exception. Their letters are filled with memorable comments. Toward the end of one, Jefferson apologized for its length: "When writing to you, I fancy myself at Auteuil, and chatter on till the last page of my paper awakes me from my reverie."[3] A good correspondence has the quality of an intimate conversation between close friends.

When several months passed without any letters from her, Jefferson wrote, "It is an age since I have had the honor of a letter from you, and an age and a half since I presumed to address one to you. I think my last was dated in the reign of king Amri, but under which of his successors you wrote, I cannot recollect. Ochosias, Joachar, Manahem or some such hard name."[4] Harking back to biblical times to emphasize how long it had been since hearing from her, Jefferson was indulging in the kind of exaggeration characteristic of both his personal correspondence and his personal conversation.

Reporting table talk, Jefferson uses a similarly breezy tone. In another letter, he related a dinner conversation he had had with their friend Guy Claude, Comte de Sarsfield: "Count Sarsfield sets out for London four days hence. At dinner the other day at M. de Malesherbe's he was sadly abusing an English dish called Gooseberry tart. I asked him if he had ever tasted the cranberry. He said, no. So I invited him to go and eat cranberries with you. He said that on his arrival in London he would send to you and demander á diner."[5]

Learning that Adams had written Congress requesting to resign his position and return to Massachusetts, Jefferson entered the doldrums. Or so he told Abigail Adams: "I have considered you while in London as my neighbor, and look forward to the moment of your departure from thence as to an epoch of much regret and concern for me. Insulated and friendless on this side the globe, with such an ocean between me and every thing to which I am attached the days will seem long which are to be counted over before I too am to rejoin my native country. Young poets complain often that life is fleeting and transient. We find in it seasons and situations however which move heavily enough. It will lighten them to me if you will continue to honour me with your correspondence."[6]

Much as the Adamses were growing homesick for Massachusetts, Jefferson was growing homesick for Virginia, as his recent behavior suggested. He told Abigail that he sometimes stayed at Mont Calvaire, a little mountain nearby where a community of lay brothers known as the Hermites kept a boarding house. The place offered a magnificent view, clean air, and quiet. Here Jefferson could concentrate on pressing paperwork without distraction.[7] Mont Calvaire was as close as he could come to Monticello without leaving Paris.

The last letter Abigail Adams wrote Jefferson from London differed greatly from the chatty ones preceding it. This letter contained urgent information regarding her husband's movements. When John Adams had joined Jefferson and Franklin in the summer of 1784 as one of the commissioners appointed to arrange treaties of amity and commerce between the United States and other nations, he was serving at The Hague as American minister to Holland. Appointed minister plenipotentiary to Great Britain while in Paris, Adams assumed this responsibility without officially relinquishing his post at The Hague. Since Adams had taken the new position in London, no one had been appointed to fill the place he had vacated. Consequently, he remained the American minister to Holland, in name if not in actuality. As a condition of his return to the United States, Adams needed to revisit The Hague to take official leave of his former position.

Jefferson received Abigail Adams's letter with much anxiety. To stay afloat, fiscally speaking, the United States had been relying on loans from Holland, which John Adams had been instrumental in securing. Interest payments on the loans would soon come due. Should the nation default on these payments, its credit would disintegrate and so, too, would the prospect of obtaining additional funds from Amsterdam. On Sunday, March 2, 1788, the day he received the news from Abigail Adams, Jefferson dashed off a letter to her husband explaining how precarious were the financial relations between the United States and Holland and how much the situation was affecting him: "Our affairs at Amsterdam press on my mind like a mountain."[8]

He quickly made plans to meet Adams at The Hague and proceed with him to Amsterdam, where they could see the bankers. After some quick repairs to his cabriolet, he left Paris Tuesday morning accompanied by his servant Espagnol. Together they rode in the carriage and hired a series of postillions and horses to bring them to The Hague. Taking the most direct route, they did not do much sightseeing during this first segment of their journey. "A country of corn and pasture affords little interesting to an American who has seen in his own country so much of that, and who travels to see the country and not its towns," he informed William Short.[9] The two made good time the first two days, so good that they hoped to reach The Hague Thursday evening.

But their hopes were soon dashed. By nightfall Thursday, they had only reached Antwerp. Under normal conditions, just one day's travel separated them from The Hague, but it took them three frustrating days to complete the remaining distance. Jefferson wrote, "This remnant employed me three days and nothing less than the omnipotence of god could have shortened this time of torture. I saw the Saturday passing over, and, in imagination, the packet sailing and Mr. Adams on board." Saturday night they spent at Rotterdam, where compensation came in the form of a visual extravaganza. That evening the citizens of Rotterdam celebrated the birthnight of William V, Prince of Orange, with a grand display of fireworks. "The illuminations were the most splendid I had ever seen," Jefferson told Short, "and the roar of joy the most universal I had ever heard."[10]

Happily, Adams had not left The Hague on Saturday as Jefferson had feared, so the two friends were reunited on Sunday. As planned, they continued to Amsterdam, where they initiated the procedures necessary to secure their nation's credit and obtain an additional loan to tide it over for the next few years. Adams, who had negotiated previous loans from the Dutch bankers, was more experienced in these matters. He introduced Jefferson to his contacts in Amsterdam. Together they accomplished what they had set out to accomplish, but the financial business took much longer than Jefferson had imagined. He had been hoping to leave the city less than ten days after his arrival, but as March neared its end, he found himself in Amsterdam still. Despite the delays, the successful completion of their undertaking pleased him greatly. Recalling the experience many years later, he said, "I had the satisfaction to reflect that by this journey our credit was secured, the new government was placed at ease for two years to come."[11]

His fine accommodations helped make the unexpected delays tolerable. He stayed at the Amsterdam Arms, a hotel he subsequently recommended to others, mainly because of its excellent service. "I liked the Valet de place they furnished me," he told John Rutledge, Jr., and Thomas Lee Shippen. "He spoke French, and was sensible and well informed." Not surprisingly, during his spare time in Amsterdam, Jefferson went shopping for books. He familiarized himself with the bookshops, of course, but he also visited a number of other retailers, too. At one, he bought a set of waffle irons. Waffles became a frequent breakfast treat at Monticello in the coming years.[12]

Part of his time in Amsterdam Jefferson devoted to planning his return trip to Paris. He decided to take a circuitous route allowing him to see parts of Europe he had not seen, but he left his route open-ended to accommodate changes in the weather and uncertain road conditions. John Trumbull had toured the Rhine Valley two years earlier, and his recommendations helped shape Jefferson's itinerary. The day before leaving Amsterdam, Jefferson wrote Short to inform him of his intended route, telling him that he would set out for Utrecht and then "pursue the course of the Rhine as far as the roads will permit me, not exceeding Strasburg. Whenever they become impassable or too difficult, if they do become so, I shall turn off to Paris."[13]

As he had the previous year during his travels through France and Italy, Jefferson kept a record of the journey. Read as travel literature, "Notes of a Tour through Holland and the Rhine Valley" suffers from the same defects as "Notes of a Tour into the Southern Parts of France etc.": it contains much useful information but few colorful episodes.

"Hints to Americans Traveling in Europe" provides additional information regarding where Jefferson stayed and what he saw during his trip through Holland and the Rhine Valley.

Missing from the literary record of this journey are the kinds of delightful travel letters he had written to Paris friends from the South of France the previous year. By his own admission, Jefferson frequently felt too tired to write personal letters during this trip. Upon his return to Paris, he wrote Maria Cosway, "I often determined during my journey to write to you: but sometimes the fatigue of exercise, and sometimes a fatigued attention hindered me."[14] This letter to her, one to Trumbull from Amsterdam, and another to William Short from Frankfort constitute the entirety of what can be called the belletristic travel correspondence resulting from Jefferson's excursions through Holland and the Rhine Valley.

The letter to Short indicates one reason why he wrote so little during this trip. After describing his adventures briefly, he decided to tell Short about the rest of them in person once he returned to Paris, "having already given you a sufficiency of egoismes, for want of other subjects."[15] Though Jefferson enjoyed sharing personal anecdotes in conversation, he always felt uncomfortable writing about himself. Such discomfort shows why "Notes of a Tour through Holland and the Rhine Valley" contains so few personal details. From his perspective, stories of his own exploits were useless, whereas information about agriculture was useful. Though Jefferson accepted the critical commonplace that the best literature should both delight and instruct, the instructive dominates his own travel writing. The delightful surfaces infrequently and momentarily.

Leaving Amsterdam the last Sunday in March, he began this new inquisitive journey with a good mental attitude. His mind would make up for what the journey might lack. "Imagination," he wrote Trumbull, "helps me on cheerily over the dull roads of this world." Jefferson was speaking in reference to his European travels, but in this case his words were figurative because the first stage of this trip did not bring him over a road at all but down a canal. From Amsterdam to Utrecht, he took a type of canal boat known as a track scout, which provided a comfortable, yet scenic passage: "To Utrecht nothing but plain is seen, a rich black mould, wet, lower than the level of the waters which intersect it; almost entirely in grass; few or no farm houses, as the business of grazing requires few labourers. The canal is lined with country houses which bespeak the wealth and cleanliness of the country; but generally in an uncouth state and exhibiting no regular architecture."[16]

Back on land, he passed through Cleves, where a hailstorm overtook him. This storm was a sign of things to come. Intermittent showers would persist for the next several days. On Wednesday, April 2, he reached Dusseldorf, "a small pleasant town, pretty well built, paved and fortified," as Trumbull described it. Jefferson found lodgings at Zimmerman's, the "best tavern I saw in my whole journey." Contemporary travelers were similarly impressed. John Owen, a Cambridge scholar who took the same basic route a few years later, also stopped in Dusseldorf, where he found himself "agreeably accommodated by the good offices of Zimmerman."[17]

On Trumbull's advice, Jefferson visited the most important tourist attraction in Dusseldorf, the gallery of paintings in the palace of the Palatine Elector. "I surely never saw so precious a collection of paintings," he told Maria Cosway. Trumbull, who had spent three days in the gallery, enjoyed the room devoted to Peter Paul Rubens most. He recalled, "The fifth apartment may properly be called the monument of Rubens, and magnificently worthy of him; it contains near fifty of his most extraordinary works, and nothing by any other hand. They are of such variety and style, as would almost inspire a doubt of their being the fruits of one mind, but that we see the hand and the color which are so peculiarly and exclusively his. The subjects vary, from lowest ribaldry and profligacy of human nature, to the most sublime conceptions of religion and poetry."[18]

John Owen, too, visited the gallery, where he also enjoyed Rubens's paintings, especially *The Adoration of the Shepherds*, *The Death of Seneca*, and *The Last Judgment*. Discussing all three, Owen observed, "In the first of these the countenance of the Virgin was wonderfully expressive of solemnity and joy—the looks of the shepherds of surprize and congratulation. The Death of Seneca made me shudder. Of the Last Judgment, I *ought* to speak in raptures, but shall refer you to those, whose optics are better qualified to do justice to this vast and sublime groupe."[19] Unlike Trumbull or Owens, Jefferson was unimpressed by Rubens. Though aware of the painter's prestige, he preferred the work of other artists represented in the gallery over what he dismissed as "the old faded red things of Rubens."[20]

Making this critique in the letter to Maria Cosway, Jefferson seems a little self-conscious. Aware that his own aesthetic judgment was at odds with the accepted canons of criticism, he prefaced his remark by admitting that he was no connoisseur of art. Jefferson's words recall Laurence Sterne's critique of connoisseurs in *Tristram Shandy*, a work he alluded to elsewhere in this same letter. Connoisseurs, Shandy asserts, "are stuck so full of rules and compasses, and have that eternal propensity to apply them upon all occasions, that a work of genius had better go to the devil at once, than stand bepricked and tortured to death by 'em." Unlike Sterne's rule-bound connoisseur, Jefferson let nature be his guide in matters of aesthetics. As he explained to Maria Cosway, "I am but a son of nature, loving what I see and feel, without being able to give a reason, nor caring much whether there be one."[21]

Jefferson maintained this same attitude toward artistic appreciation all his life. Three decades later he wrote, "I have always very much dispised the artificial canons of criticism. When I have read a work in prose or poetry, or seen a painting, a statue, etc., I have only asked myself whether it gives me pleasure, whether it is animating, interesting, attaching? If it is, it is good for these reasons."[22] This personal approach to art explains why Jefferson never really developed an extensive critical vocabulary and partly explains his idiosyncratic tastes.

Among the Dusseldorf collection, Jefferson most enjoyed the work of the late-seventeenth-century Dutch painter Adriaen van der Werff: "Above all things those of Van der Werff affected me the most. His picture of Sarah delivering Agar to Abraham is delicious. I would have agreed to have been Abraham though the consequence would have been that I should have been dead five or six thousand years." Neither Owen nor Trumbull shared Jefferson's appreciation. Speaking of van der Werff, Owen observed, "The paintings of this master, whose polished pencil defies the strictness of criticism, present little that can move the heart." Trumbull's critique is even harsher. "Of all the celebrated pictures I have ever seen," he said, the paintings of van der Werff "appear to me to be the very worst—mere monuments of labor, patience, and want of genius."[23]

Conveying a preference for van der Werff over Rubens, Jefferson revealed much about his tastes in art, which parallel his tastes in literature. Critiquing Rubens, he identified the color red as a defining feature of the artist's work but derogates the paintings as being old and faded. Jefferson's choice of words reveals that the paintings of Rubens looked dated to him. He preferred a classical aesthetic that would not go out of style. The Baroque qualities that Rubens's work exemplifies—the bold use of bright colors juxtaposed with shade, the preference for curves over straight lines and right angles, the dynamic quality suggesting movement—looked passé to this exemplar of the Augustan Age. The paintings of van der Werff, alternatively, exemplified the neoclassical aesthetic Jefferson held dear.

Among the early van der Werff paintings on display in Dusseldorf, *Children Playing before a Statue of Hercules* reveals the artist developing his neoclassical style. In the foreground, figures of children indicate van der Werff's capacity for rendering surface textures and his fascination with clothing and other drapery. The statue of Hercules, contrasted against the blue sky of the background, displays the emerging importance of classical myth and motif in late-seventeenth-century art. The artist figure standing to the left of the statue is busy molding a head of clay. His presence in the painting and his behavior make explicit the message that the artist should pattern his work on the classical, a message van der Werff took to heart over the course of his career.

Sarah Presenting Hagar to Abraham, the one painting of van der Werff's Jefferson mentioned by name in his writings, represents the artist's later, fully developed neoclassical style. Gone is any sense of movement. The figures in the painting have a still, posed quality reminiscent of statuary. Straight lines and right angles predominate. Jefferson's appreciation of this painting is consistent with his appreciation of the neoclassical verse of Alexander Pope. Like Pope's heroic couplets, the composition of this painting is balanced and well proportioned, qualities that lend it a sense of propriety.

The Dusseldorf gallery contained dozens of works by van der Werff, most of which embody this neoclassical aesthetic. Singling out *Sarah Presenting Hagar to Abraham*, Jefferson not only named a work exemplifying his tastes, but also chose a work to titillate his reader, Maria Cosway. The painting illustrates the biblical story of the still-childless and presumably barren Sarah giving her scantily clad Egyptian slave to her husband Abraham so that he could produce an heir with her. Van der Werff made Hagar voluptuous, emphasizing her smooth, white skin and giving her an unmistakable softness, especially compared to Sarah's hard, angular features and long, sinewy neck. Though the painting depicts a moment of stillness, Hagar's sensuality anticipates what will happen next: the productive coupling between her and Abraham.

Though confirming the paucity of Jefferson's critical vocabulary, the word he used to describe the painting—"delicious"—expresses a combination of artistic beauty and sensual allure. In his playful letter to Madame de Tessé from the year before, he used the same word as a critical term to describe Michael Angelo Slodtz's *Diana* at the Chateau de Laye-Epinaye. In this letter to Maria Cosway, he makes his titillation more explicit by personally identifying with Abraham and conveying his desire to change places with him at the moment Sarah presents the voluptuous Hagar.

Jefferson mentioned a third artist in his letter to Maria Cosway, one whose work does not exemplify a neoclassical aesthetic: Carlo Dolci.

Jefferson generally enjoyed Dolci's work, but the time he spent at the Dusseldorf gallery turned Dolci into a "violent favorite."[24] Considered the most important Florentine painter of the seventeenth century, Dolci was an excellent portraitist. Like van der Werff's, Dolci's paintings were carefully wrought and highly polished. Similarly, Dolci had a gift for rendering surface textures.[25] His paintings differ from those of van der Werff in terms of their emotional tone. Dolci's work cultivates feelings of contemplative melancholy. Perhaps Jefferson's literary tastes can also help explain his appreciation of Dolci's paintings, which anticipate another aspect of the Augustan Age. The theme of melancholy fills an important role in much of the eighteenth-century English literature Jefferson admired, from the verse of James Thomson and Thomas Gray to the Ossianic prose poems.

Given Maria Cosway's talent as an artist and her close personal relationship with Jefferson, his comments regarding these paintings in the letter to her are doubly appropriate. The description of the Dusseldorf gallery he made in "Notes of a Tour through Holland and the Rhine Valley" is less personal and more cursory. In fact, he described it in a single sentence: "The gallery of paintings is sublime, particularly the room of Vanderwerff." This sentence begins a paragraph that describes his journey from Dusseldorf to Cologne and also contains a description of the renowned Westphalian ham. Look how much attention the ham gets in comparison:

> I observe the hog of this country (Westphalia), of which the celebrated ham is made, is tall, gaunt, and with heavy lop ears. Fatted at a year old, would weigh 100. or 120. lb. At two years old, two hundred pounds. Their principal food is acorns. The pork fresh sells at 2½ d sterl. the lb. The ham ready made at 5½ d sterl. the lb. 106 lb of this country is equal to 100. lb of Holland. About 4 lb of fine Holland salt is put on 100 lb of pork. It is smoked in a room which has no chimney. Well-informed people here tell me there is no other part of the world where the bacon is smoked. They do not know that we do it. Cologne is the principal market of exportation. They find that the small hog makes the sweetest meat.[26]

The amount of space in his travel journal Jefferson devoted to Westphalian ham compared to the amount of space he devoted to the art gallery should not be interpreted as a personal preference. Instead, these varying descriptions suggest a literary priority. From his perspective, a disquisition on painting was much less useful in a travelogue than a record of the processing and marketing of pork. Such practical information he could put to use himself at Monticello. Furthermore, he could share what he learned of hogs and ham with farmers throughout Virginia. The contrast between the comments on art and those on farming in "Notes of a Tour through Holland and the Rhine Valley" shows the focus and purposefulness with which Jefferson recorded his travel experiences.

Staying at a tavern called the Holy Ghost in Cologne, he remained there long enough to notice several incongruities. The city had much commerce yet many poor people. Though Protestant merchants controlled the markets, Catholics controlled the city government and placed severe limits on the Protestants' commercial enterprises. Recently, the Catholic-dominated Cologne legislature had licensed the Protestants to erect a church, but lawmakers were now threatening to revoke this privilege. Jefferson saw Cologne as a negative example that confirmed the importance of the separation of church and state: there can be neither freedom nor progress while the precepts of the church, any church, continue to influence the policies of a nation.

Despite recent storms, the roads remained in good condition until Bonn, after which clay roads predominated. When these clay roads got wet, they became, in Jefferson's words, "worse than imagination can paint." At Coblenz, he stayed at L'Homme Sauvage or, as it was also known, The Wildman, a very good tavern kept by a very good tavernkeeper who served very good bread. During his stay at Coblenz, this gracious tavernkeeper accompanied Jefferson to a nearby winery, where he introduced him to a Moselle expert. Consequently, Jefferson drafted a lengthy description of Moselle wine, one of many such descriptions that appear in his travelogue. After a fine breakfast roll reminiscent of the French rolls he had enjoyed in Philadelphia, Jefferson left L'Homme Sauvage with a sense of civility. His obliging host had kindly provided him with a road map of Germany to guide him through the next portion of his trip.

On Sunday, April 6, he entered Frankfurt, "a large and beautiful city," the contemporary British traveler Adam Walker called it. Jefferson stayed at the splendid Red House. Walker stayed there, too, and his account supplies the kind of description absent from Jefferson's "Notes." Walker observed: "Our inn is superb; it is called the Maison Rouge, or Red House, and said to be the first Inn in Europe. For my part, I must confess, I never saw such an Inn in all my travels: it is a red house, of three stories, containing thirteen windows long in front, and inclosing behind, a considerable square; one side indeed is a garden, at the head of which is a palace fit for a prince, of beautiful and modern architecture."[27]

Here, Jefferson met Baron de Geismar, whom he had befriended during the Revolutionary War when Geismar was among the Hessian troops staying at the barracks in Albemarle County. A career soldier, Geismar was now garrisoned at nearby Hanau, where Jefferson became reacquainted with several of the other Hessian officers he had met during the war. Renewing these friendships, Jefferson recalled the civility he had experienced in wartime Virginia.

Geismar accompanied him on several day trips this week. On Friday, the eleventh, they sailed from Mainz to Rüdesheim and returned by land, stopping at the vineyards along the way. In this region, Jefferson observed, only the area from Rüdesheim to Hochheim produced "wines of the very first quality." Though the wines do not really become drinkable until they are about five years old, the proprietors, he noted, "sell them old or young, according to the prices offered, and according to their own want of money. There is always a little difference between different casks, and therefore when you chuse and buy a single cask, you pay 3, 4, 5, or 600 florins for it. They are not at all acid, and to my taste much preferable to Hocheim, tho' but of the same price." Jefferson purchased several vines, which he planted in his Paris garden and hoped to transplant to Monticello. Inviting Geismar back to Virginia, he promised him "a glass of Hock or Rudesheim of my own making."[28]

Over its course, "Notes of a Tour through Holland and the Rhine Valley" develops a clear sense of purpose. What had started as a miscellaneous account of useful information essentially becomes what could be called "Observations on German Viticulture." From Frankfurt through the remainder of the journey, Jefferson wrote more about wines and winemaking than any other subject.

Strasbourg conjured up further memories of *Tristram Shandy*, in which Sterne's title character tells the story of one Slawkenbergius, a great chronicler of noses, who included within his compilation of nasal lore a series of stories about prodigious proboscises. One such tale tells of a man named Diego, whose extraordinary nose set all tongues wagging upon his entry into Strasbourg. To Maria Cosway, Jefferson wrote, "At Strasbourg I sat down to write you. But for my soul I could think of nothing at Strasbourg but the promontory of noses, of Diego, of Slawkenburgius his historian, and the procession of the Strasburgers to meet the man with the nose. Had I written to you from thence it would have been a continuation of Sterne upon noses, and I knew that nature had not formed me for a Continuator of Sterne."[29]

Maria Cosway did not appreciate Jefferson's remarks. She replied, "How could you [have] led me by the hand all the way, think of me, have

Many things to say, and not find One word to write, *but on Noses?*"[30] Like the reference to Abraham and Hagar, the suggestive reference to Sterne's long-nosed character is tinged with sexual innuendo. Jefferson made similar literary use of Sterne's *Sentimental Journey* in a flirtatious letter to Angelica Church, a young, beautiful American woman, later that year.[31] Hinting that they share a cabin together on a return voyage to the United States, he recalled the intense negotiations between the Reverend Mr. Yorick and the fulsome Italian woman he shares a room with one evening. Jefferson explained, "I allow myself all the months of April, May, and June, to find a good ship. Embarking in either of these months we shall avoid being out during the equinoxes and be sure of fine weather. Think of it then, my friend, and let us begin a negociation on the subject. You shall find in me all the spirit of accommodation with which Yoric began his with the fair Piedmontese."[32]

Regardless of the sexual innuendo, few passages in Jefferson's writings offer as keen an understanding of his own place in literary history as his reference to *Tristram Shandy* in the letter to Maria Cosway. Though Jefferson loved reading Sterne, he understood that as an author he was cut from a different cloth. As much as he wrote and as much as he enjoyed writing, Jefferson knew he would never write in the manner of Sterne. His admission to Maria Cosway that he was no continuator of Sterne comes with recognition, not regret. Though possessing considerable virtuosity in terms of literary genre—biography, character sketch, flirtatious letter, informative journal, legislative bill, political manifesto, state paper, table talk—Jefferson had neither the capacity nor the desire to write the kind of imaginative prose at which Sterne excelled.

Another memorable passage from *Tristram Shandy* highlights the differences between the way Sterne and Jefferson approached the task of writing. In one of the novel's most famous passages, Tristram Shandy observes, "Digressions, incontestably, are the sunshine;—they are the life, the soul of reading!—take them out of this book, for instance,—you might as well take the book along with them;—one cold eternal winter would reign in every page of it; restore them to the writer;—he steps forth like a bridegroom,—bids All-hail; brings in variety, and forbids the appetite to fail."[33] Though Jefferson appreciated Sterne's digressions as a reader, as a writer he largely abjured the digression as a literary device. The *Declaration of Independence* is a masterpiece of concision. In "Notes of a Tour of English Gardens," Jefferson concentrated so intently on his subject that he made no reference to his visit to Shakespeare's birthplace. "Notes of a Tour through Holland and the Rhine Valley" begins without a clear focus, but once it finds one—the wines of Germany—it scarcely deviates from it.

Throughout this trip, Jefferson hoped to find a really good bookseller, but so far such hopes had been thwarted. In Amsterdam, he visited Van Damme's bookshop and requested several titles, mostly classical texts in small-format editions, including some more than two centuries old. Van Damme filled few of Jefferson's requests. Perhaps the biggest indication of his disappointment with the Amsterdam booksellers comes in a letter he wrote John Trumbull shortly before he left the city, asking him to locate a bookseller in London from whom he could purchase what books he wanted: "Will you consult with some Amateur in classical reading to know who is the bookseller for classical authors in London, the most curious and copious, of whom one may get the particular editions they would wish, and send me his address?" Jefferson spoke too soon. When he reached Strasbourg, he visited Armand Koenig's establishment in the Rue des Grandes-Arcades, which proved to be just the kind of bookshop he wanted. "The best shop of classical books I ever saw," he said after purchasing multiple volumes from Koenig.[34]

Trumbull subsequently recommended a London bookseller named Thomas Payne. While evidence indicates that Jefferson continued to rely on Koenig for editions of classical works, he did write Payne after returning from Holland to request many important works of English literature and several books about Anglo-Saxon. Few surviving documents better illustrate Jefferson's attitude toward book buying than his instructions to Payne:

> When I name a particular edition of a book, send me that edition and no other.
>
> When I do not name the edition, never send a folio or quarto if there exists an 8vo. or smaller edition. I like books of a handy size.
>
> Where a book costs much higher than the common price of books of that size do not send it, tho I write for it, till you shall have advised me of the price.
>
> I disclaim all pompous editions and all typographical luxury; but I like a fine white paper, neat type, and neat binding, gilt and lettered in the modern stile. But while I remain in Europe it will be better to send my books in boards, as I have found that scarcely any method of packing preserves them from rubbing in a land transportation.[35]

Though Jefferson spent much time in Strasbourg lingering in Armand Koenig's shop, he visited the city's other attractions, too. He climbed the 662 steps to the top of the steeple of the Strasbourg Cathedral, an effort he recommended in "Hints." This steeple he called "the highest in the world, and the handsomest. Go to the very top of it; but let it be the last operation of the day, as you will need a long rest after it."[36]

Elevated heights usually sent Jefferson into a state of contemplation. From the top of the steeple, Strasbourg lay at his feet, a sea of triangular rooftops and gable windows intermittently punctuated by picturesque towers and lesser steeples. The plains of Alsace spread out before him. He could see well beyond the city limits and, in his mind's eye, even further. Northeastward he saw the route he had taken from Amsterdam. To the northwest was Paris, a city he had come to love, where he was now returning. To the distant west across the ocean was Monticello, to which both his head and his heart were longing to return.

CHAPTER 26

Last Days in Paris

Returning to Paris from the Rhine Valley, Jefferson made up his mind: he would go back to Virginia—not permanently, just for a few months, time enough to bring his daughters home and straighten out his personal and financial affairs. When he had left Monticello in October 1783 to serve as delegate to the Continental Congress, he had planned to be away for only five months. It had now been five years since he had seen home. The third week of November 1788 he wrote Congress to ask for a leave of absence. He argued persuasively that he could make the trip without detriment to his responsibilities as American minister to France. His ministerial duties, he assured Congress, had reached a pause. His most pressing commitments had been fulfilled or would be in a matter of weeks. Most important, he had reached a new consular convention, which he was arranging to have printed. In addition, he had finished composing *Observations on the Whale-Fishery*, which would also be published soon.

The harsh winter weather reinforced his decision to return home. For most Parisians, the winter of 1788–89 was the coldest in memory. Large bonfires, Jefferson wrote, were kept "at all the cross-streets, around which the people gathered in crowds to avoid perishing with cold." As the bitter weather slowly abated in March, he informed Madame de Bréhan: "We have had such a winter Madam, as makes me shiver yet whenever I think of it. All communications almost were cut off. Dinners and suppers were suppressed, and the money laid out in feeding and warming the poor, whose labours were suspended by the rigour of the season. Loaded carriages past [i.e., crossed] the Seine on the ice, and it was covered with thousands of people from morning to night, skaiting and sliding. Such sights were never seen before, and they continued two months."[1] The skaters and sliders obviously enjoyed themselves that winter, but many

Parisians suffered. The severe cold may have exacerbated the city's social unrest and facilitated the onset of the French Revolution.

Several months would pass before Jefferson heard from Congress and learned that it had approved his request, but he anticipated its approval and prepared for his departure. Unsure when he would experience such fine shopping opportunities as he had been enjoying over the past five years, he stepped up his purchases, acquiring numerous items unavailable in Virginia. His most extravagant purchase was a custom-made crane-neck chariot, which he ordered from England. Upon his return, he intended to make his way through Virginia in style. He acquired numerous paintings to hang at Monticello. He also obtained several useful scientific instruments. And he kept buying more books, lots and lots more books.

His artistic, literary, and scientific interests occasionally coincided. That winter he wrote John Trumbull, asking him to commission a painting. He wanted a single canvas depicting Francis Bacon, John Locke, and Isaac Newton, who, he said, were "the three greatest men that have ever lived, without any exception." These three "laid the foundation of those superstructures which have been raised in the Physical and Moral sciences." He gave Trumbull detailed instructions regarding how the painting should be composed. The portrait of each man should appear in a small oval and, for symmetry's sake, all three should be contained within a larger oval.[2]

The story of Jefferson's last year in Paris can be told partly through the books he purchased. That winter Van Damme, the Amsterdam bookseller, sent him a catalogue of a forthcoming sale and urged him to submit his orders prior to the public auction. Jefferson took Van Damme's advice and sent him a list of requests. Though he already owned a Latin edition of *Annales et Historiae de Rebus Belgicis*, Hugo Grotius's history of the Wars of Independence in the Netherlands, he requested the sixteenth-century polyglot edition Van Damme was advertising. The size of this edition made it especially appealing to Jefferson, given his penchant for small-format volumes. He had always enjoyed little books, which facilitated another great pleasure—reading in bed—but now, with the nagging pain in his right wrist, he found small books essential for bedtime reading.

He also hoped to augment his collection of European Americana. He asked Van Damme for *Voyage d'un François Exile pour la Religion*, a book of travels containing firsthand descriptions of Virginia and Maryland, which has been called "one of the most picturesque and lively descriptions of life in an English colony at the end of the seventeenth century."[3]

He also requested *Voyage de la Louisiane*, the travels of the Jesuit missionary Antoine François Laval. Interwoven in Laval's exciting narrative of his missionary work is a considerable amount of useful scientific data.

Reading Van Damme's sale catalogue, Jefferson recognized the gem of the collection, at least as far as Americana went: Thomas Hariot's *Admiranda Narratio*, a sixteenth-century description of Virginia that formed part of a much larger work, Theodor de Bry's collection of voyages. Jefferson would acquire not only the part by Hariot, but also several other parts of de Bry's work. Gleefully, he recalled the purchase of the work many years later. Describing it to John Adams, he wrote, "This is a work of great curiosity, extremely rare, so as never to be bought in Europe, but on the breaking up, and selling some antient library. On one of these occasions a bookseller procured me a copy, which, unless you have one, is probably the only one in America."[4]

News of Jefferson's growing reputation in America also reached him that winter. He learned from Joseph Willard, the president of Harvard College, that the school had granted him an honorary doctorate of laws. Jefferson was now receiving the same kind of recognition Franklin had received before him. Unlike Dr. Franklin, he never went by the title that this or any of his other honorary degrees conferred upon him. Much as he eschewed the title of Colonel Jefferson when he was the leader of the Albemarle militia, he now eschewed the title of Dr. Jefferson.

Expressing his thanks, he gave Willard a report on the state of letters in Europe, naming and describing the most remarkable French publications that had appeared in the past year or two. Mentioning the *Posthumous Works of Frederic II, King of Prussia*, he explained that the sixteen-volume Berlin edition had been severely "gutted" and that the Paris edition was even "more mangled." These comments reinforce his disgust with any and all forms of censorship. Other books Jefferson mentioned to Willard include *L'Etat des Etoiles Fixes au Second Siecle*, a Greek edition of the seventh book of Ptolemy with an accompanying French translation; Joseph-Louis Lagrange's *Mechanique Analitique*, a work seeking, in Jefferson's words, "to reduce all the principles of Mechanics to the single one of the Equilibrium, and to give a simple formula applicable to them all"; and another important work of European Americana, Francesco Saverio Clavigero's *History of Mexico*, which "merits more respect than any other work on the same subject."[5] In addition, he told Willard about the latest scientific developments in Europe, especially in the field of chemistry.

Jefferson's information-packed letter to Willard goes well beyond the note of thanks the honorary degree necessitated. Knowing that his presence in Europe exposed him to news long before it reached America, Jefferson sought to keep Willard and others informed of the latest advancements in science and literature. He wanted to minimize lag time and foster American intellectual development, as his closing remarks suggest: "It is for such institutions as that over which you preside so worthily, Sir, to do justice to our country, its productions, and its genius. It is the work to which the young men, whom you are forming, should lay their hands. We have spent the prime of our lives in procuring them the precious blessing of liberty. Let them spend theirs in shewing that it is the great parent of science and of virtue; and that a nation will be great in both always in proportion as it is free."[6]

Thus, this letter of thanks evolved into a celebration of American freedom. Jefferson recognized that freedom was the one thing that made everything else possible. As the parent of science and virtue, freedom gave people the ability to think and act in ways they could not before becoming free. The unfettered mind has the potential for limitless development. More than an abstract expression on the value of freedom, Jefferson's words convey the personal pride he felt for contributing to the advancement of freedom and embody his hope that such freedom could span the globe.

The biggest news from the Republic of Letters that year concerned the death of Maffeo Pinelli, the great Venetian collector. Pinelli's death resulted in the sale of his extraordinary library and created a fantastic opportunity for collectors from Rome to London. Pinelli had assembled an unparalleled collection of classical and Italian books: printed volumes dating from the earliest days of printing and manuscript volumes antedating the invention of printing. Before the sale, bibliographer Jacopo Morelli prepared a detailed catalogue, which was published at Venice in six octavo volumes. Pinelli's heirs sold the entire collection to London book dealer James Edwards and his associates. Intending to resell the library piecemeal, Edwards arranged to have the books shipped to London. According to legend, one of the ships transporting the books from Venice to London was besieged by pirates, but the story is apocryphal: the Pinelli library reached London intact and unscathed.[7]

Once the books arrived, Edwards had them recatalogued for sale. Copies of *Bibliotheca Pinelliana*, a beefy quarto of more than five hundred pages listing nearly 13,000 items, made their way into the hands of interested collectors throughout Europe, Jefferson included. The sale was scheduled to start in March and would continue into May.

To purchase the books he wanted from the Pinelli sale, Jefferson enlisted the help of Lucy Ludwell Paradise, whom he had met three years earlier at a London dinner party that she and her husband, John Paradise, had hosted. From the time they met, Jefferson took a liking to the Paradises. Lucy was from an old Virginia family but had lived in England since girlhood. John was born at Salonika in Macedonia and educated at the University of Padua before settling in London, where he and Lucy were wed. Seldom has there been a more mismatched couple. Lucy, possessing the haughtiness and beauty of the stereotypical Southern belle, had an urge for social affairs and a fiery temper that frequently plunged her into difficulties. John was a quiet, scholarly type who preferred the company of books and intellectual conversation with a few close friends.

With John's interest in the sciences and his skill as a linguist—he could speak Arabic, French, Greek, Italian, Latin, and Turkish—Jefferson found in him a like-minded soul. Given Paradise's linguistic expertise, especially in both modern and classical Greek, Jefferson asked him about how Greek was pronounced in ancient times. The books Jefferson acquired in 1789 reflect Paradise's influence; they include one work devoted to a discussion of how to pronounce ancient Greek.

Despite his scholarly accomplishments, Paradise was totally inept when it came to practical affairs, and he and his wife often found their finances on the brink of ruin. They sought help from Jefferson, who went well beyond the call of duty in his exertions on their behalf. In an early move to sort out their personal and financial difficulties, he arranged to have Lucy leave Paris and return to London as John remained on the Continent.

Before she left, Jefferson gave her a list of titles he wanted from the Pinelli library and a set of instructions detailing how she should execute his bids. Lucy Paradise had become quite fond of Jefferson and, realizing how indebted she and her husband were to him, was happy to act as his agent.

She undertook the responsibility with great seriousness and found someone to execute Jefferson's commission. Contacting James Robson, she could scarcely have found anyone better: Robson was one of Edwards's associates. She and Jefferson engaged in a lively correspondence through the spring of 1789 as she informed him how the sale was going. He kept adding to his list of requested books and answering her queries about the prices books were fetching. Jefferson's marked-up copy of *Bibliotheca Pinelliana* does not survive, nor does a copy of the list he originally gave her. But their surviving correspondence indicates the kinds of books he wanted from the Pinelli collection.

Several titles he put on his initial list of desiderata are clear from their correspondence: *Epistolae Veterum Graecorum*, a collection of letters by such Greek authors as Democritus, Diogenes, Heraclitus, and

Hippocrates edited by Eilhard Lubin and published with the text in Greek and Latin on facing pages; a polyglot edition of *De Amoribus Anthiae et Abrocomae* by Xenophon of Ephesus, with the text in Greek, Latin, Italian, and French in parallel columns; and *Geographiae Veteris Scriptores Graeci Minores*, John Hudson's collection of Greek geographies, which also included works by thirteenth-century Arabic geographers printed in Arabic and Latin.

Amidst all this classical erudition, Jefferson requested another important piece of Americana. Listed in the Pinelli catalogue under the general heading "Biblia Linguis Exoticis" is a quarto printed in 1663 at Cambridge, Massachusetts, titled "Biblia Indica."[8] This short title represents *Mamusse Wunneetupanatamwe Up-Biblum God Naneeswe Nukkone Testament Kah Wonk Wusku Testament*, that is, John Eliot's translation of the Bible into the Massachusett language. The presence of Eliot's Indian Bible in Pinelli's library shows that this book had already become a precious collectible among European bibliophiles.

Jefferson was interested in the book not only as a bibliographical curiosity, but also for what it could contribute to his knowledge of Native American languages. Around this same time, he acquired another linguistic work. Jonathan Edwards, not the great preacher but his son, presented Jefferson with a copy of his *Observations on the Language of the Muhhekaneew Indians*, which Edwards had read at a meeting of the Connecticut Society of Arts and Sciences in 1787. Much as Jefferson was keeping his American correspondents aware of recent scientific and literary developments in Europe, they were keeping him informed of the latest intellectual developments in the United States.

Many of the books at the Pinelli sale fetched prices higher than Jefferson had stipulated in his instructions, as Lucy Paradise informed him. Her letters reveal the sincere disappointment she felt. Overall, she had been able to acquire only four of the books he requested. The others had sold at prices well above the upper limits he had stipulated in his instructions. Pinelli's copy of John Eliot's Indian Bible, for example, fetched a great deal more than Jefferson had expected. A few years earlier, he had missed the opportunity to purchase William Byrd's copy of the work, which had sold for the ridiculously low price of three pounds. Now, he had missed another opportunity to purchase one. He never did add a copy of Eliot's Indian Bible to his personal library.

"I am Sorry you Could not have had them all," Lucy Paradise wrote to him, referring to the books he had asked her to purchase.

"I am much indebted to you for your attention to my commission about the books, and am well pleased that those which went above the prices I noted, were not purchased," he reassured her. "Sensible that I labour grievously under the malady of Bibliomanie, I submit to the rule of buying only at reasonable prices, as to a regimen necessary in that disease."[9]

Bibliomanie, the French term Jefferson used in his response to Lucy Paradise, was current through much of the eighteenth century. Its English equivalent, bibliomania, entered the language late in the century. In either French or English, the term often had pejorative connotations. The British bibliographer Myles Davies defined bibliomanie as "having too many Books" and said that those who suffer from this malady collect books without reading them or without sharing them with others. Isaac Disraeli defined bibliomania as "collecting an enormous heap of books." In his *Letters to His Son*, Lord Chesterfield associated this bibliographic affliction with excessive pedantry and cautioned against it: "Beware of the *Bibliomanie*," he admonished his son. Abel Boyer's *Royal Dictionary* may offer the most charming definition of bibliomanie: "bookishness, an itch after books."[10]

Jefferson's self-diagnosis—"I labour grievously under the malady of Bibliomanie"—presents another example of the humorous exaggeration characteristic of his personal correspondence. Based on Myles Davies's definition, he did not really suffer from bibliomanie because he read his books and shared them with others. Based on Boyer's definition, perhaps he did suffer from bibliomanie. Jefferson never stopped scratching his itch for books.

In April he took his daughters from school and brought them to the Hôtel de Langeac to live with him. His eagerness to leave Paris for Virginia partly explains his actions: he wanted the girls nearby so they could leave Paris with as little as a week's notice. There may also have been another reason why he pulled his daughters from school when he did: according to family legend, he feared that Martha would convert to Catholicism and take the veil. Though he had been assured by a knowing friend of his that the nuns at Panthemont did not attempt to convert the Protestant girls in their charge, they obviously influenced those who spent their nights and days within the walls of the convent.[11]

As summer approached, Jefferson had yet to learn whether Congress had approved his leave of absence. He became less anxious to leave Paris as the events precipitating the French Revolution unfolded. From the time he read law in Williamsburg, he retained fond memories of standing at the door to the Virginia legislature to watch the House of Burgesses. Now, he had the opportunity to observe another legislative body in action. He recorded his observations in his *Autobiography*, which constitutes one of the finest accounts of what transpired in France in 1789 by one who was there to witness the beginning of the end of monarchical rule in Europe and the start of representative European democracy.

The fact that the French Revolution began during his last year in Paris meant that he was present to bear witness to momentous events. The French Revolution gave him something besides himself to discuss in his autobiography. Assuming the narrative pose of a humble observer, he was being overmodest. The presence of the author of the *Declaration of Independence* in Paris inspired the French revolutionaries. Furthermore, Jefferson did participate in the Revolution as a close personal adviser to the Marquis de Lafayette, who was emerging as an instrumental force in the early days of the Revolutionary movement.

The discussion of the French Revolution in Jefferson's autobiography begins with a slight personal reference: "On my return from Holland, I had found Paris still in high fermentation as I had left it." He then disappears from the autobiography for the next four pages or so as he summarizes the events leading to the Revolution. In places his prose attains a high level of artistry. For example, after delineating the numerous atrocities and injustices committed by the French government on its people, he concluded with an extended metaphor: "Surely under such a mass of misrule and oppressions, a people might justly press for a thoro' reformation, and might even dismount their rough-shod riders, and leave them to walk on their own legs." His characterization of Louis XVI incisively identifies his flaws: "His mind was weakness itself, his constitution timid, his judgment null, and without sufficient firmness even to stand by the faith of his word."[12]

Jefferson does not reenter the story until May 5, 1789, the day the Estates-General convened at Versailles. He explained what compelled him to attend the Estates-General: "The objects for which this body was convened being of the first order of importance, I felt it very interesting to understand the views of the parties of which it was composed, and especially the ideas prevalent as to the organization contemplated for their government." The Estates-General, consisting of the Nobles, the Clergy, and the Commoners, had not been assembled since 1614. The Commoners, collectively known as the Third Estate, represented ninety percent of the French population but shared an equal vote with the Nobles and the Clergy. In Jefferson's account, the Nobles seem "impassioned and tempestuous," whereas the Commoners are "temperate, rational and inflexibly firm."[13]

Once the Estates-General convened, Jefferson went to Versailles nearly every day to follow the proceedings. In June, the Third Estate proclaimed itself the National Assembly and invited the Nobles to join in this new legislative body. Some noblemen accepted the invitation. Before the week was out the king closed the hall where it was meeting. Still calling itself the National Assembly, the Third Estate relocated to the Tennis Court of Versailles, where its members swore not to disband until a constitution was approved. Before the end of June, the king capitulated, ordering the Nobles and the Clergy to join the National Assembly.

As he had in the past, Jefferson hosted a Fourth of July celebration that year. Besides being the last Independence Day he would celebrate in Paris, this occasion takes on further importance due to the heartfelt tribute his friends gave him. But Jefferson makes no mention of the event in his autobiography. His neglect of it stems from both his reluctance to write about himself and his extraordinary focus: once the autobiography takes up the subject of the French Revolution, it scarcely deviates from it.

But this Fourth of July celebration deserves a place in the story of Jefferson's life. Many of his closest friends in Paris attended, including the Lafayettes, John Paradise, Philip Mazzei, and Joel Barlow. Another member of the group of poets known as the Connecticut Wits, Barlow had established his literary reputation two years earlier with *The Vision of Columbus*, an epic poem celebrating the greatness of America. Upon its publication, Barlow had presented Jefferson with a copy. The same year this poem appeared, Barlow was selected by a group of investors to travel to Europe and represent them in a scheme to sell land in the Scioto River Valley to Europeans. In Paris, he and Jefferson became friends, and Barlow became a frequent visitor to the Hôtel de Langeac.

During the festivities, several of those in attendance presented a tribute to Jefferson. Composed by Barlow, this tribute honored Jefferson's efforts as American minister to France: "During your residence in this kingdom your particular kindness and attention to every American who has fallen in your way have endeared you to their hearts." They also commemorated Jefferson's past efforts in helping to secure American independence: "As this is the anniversary of our Independence our sensations of pleasure are much increased from the idea that we are addressing ourselves to a man who sustained so conspicuous a part in the immortal transactions of that day—whose dignity energy and elegance of thought and expression added a peculiar lustre to that declaratory act which announced to the world the existence of an empire."[14] Barlow's tribute verifies Jefferson's growing reputation as the author of the *Declaration of Independence*.

Ten days after this celebration of American freedom came the day that has come to symbolize French independence from monarchical tyranny. Jefferson's autobiography poignantly captures the events leading to the storming of the Bastille. On July 12, he witnessed a group of people confront troops guarding the king. His depiction of the event is stunning:

> As their numbers increased, their indignation rose. They retired a few steps, and posted themselves on and behind large piles of stones, large and small, collected in that Place for a bridge which was to be built adjacent to it. In this position, happening to be in my carriage on a visit, I passed thro' the lane they had formed, without interruption. But the moment after I had passed, the people attacked the cavalry with stones. They charged, but the advantageous position of the people, and the showers of stones obliged the horse to retire, and quit the field altogether, leaving one of their number on the ground, and the Swiss in their rear not moving to their aid. This was the signal for universal insurrection, and this body of cavalry, to avoid being massacred, retired towards Versailles.[15]

Jefferson's storytelling ability and his pictorial sense are impressive. As he describes the swelling crowd before the armed soldiers, he builds the tension, which he heightens by having the people slowly retreat to the large piles of stone. Once they are stationed there, he freezes the action. The people and the soldiers have reached a pause, each group wondering what the other will do. Then, with the scene set, he personally passes through the opening created between the two groups. Only after freezing the people and the soldiers in their place does he bring his carriage through the scene. Against the still, yet tension-filled background, the carriage seems to pass in slow motion. The soldiers, brandishing their weapons, stand to one side. The people stand to the other, the bravest and most brazen of them poised atop the piles of stone, ready to shower the soldiers with flagstones and brickbats. Once Jefferson's carriage has passed, the scene explodes into action. The people pummel the soldiers with stones, forcing them to retreat.

The rest of his story of the French Revolution consists of similarly poignant vignettes, loosely held together within a framework of facts. The extent of his personal contact with the ensuing events shapes the way he constructed each vignette. He was not present at the Bastille on July 14, for example, so he could not narrate firsthand the story of what happened there. His friend Monsieur de Corny did witness what happened and told Jefferson about it later that same day. Meticulously, Jefferson prefaced his account with details regarding how he heard what had happened. His account of the story of the Bastille lacks the visual complexity of the stone fight but graphically depicts the ensuing bloodshed.

Beyond giving the Marquis de Lafayette much helpful advice that summer, Jefferson tried to maintain his role as a neutral observer. Without Jefferson's knowledge, Lafayette arranged for several leading French patriots to meet at the Hôtel de Langeac the last week in August to discuss the important issues they faced. Though Jefferson was a little disturbed by the fact that his home, the home of the American minister to France, would be used as a meeting place for French patriots, Lafayette gave him no choice in the matter. The author of the *Declaration of Independence* played reluctant host to a group of men seeking to free France from monarchical tyranny.

Presumably, Jefferson served a fine meal that afternoon, but he makes no mention of it in the autobiography. Typically omitting any unnecessary detail from his narrative, he began the episode as the discussions began. As was the custom at his table, he served no wine until after the meal, when the tablecloth was removed and wine set on the table. The removal of the tablecloth at this moment in the autobiography provides a brief dramatic flourish akin to the opening of the curtain in the theater.

Lafayette is the star of this drama. Jefferson deliberately refrained from active participation. He wrote, "The discussions began at the hour of four, and were continued till ten o'clock in the evening; during which time I was a silent witness to a coolness and candor of argument unusual in the conflicts of political opinion; to a logical reasoning, and chaste eloquence, disfigured by no gaudy tinsel of rhetoric or declamation, and truly worthy of being placed in parallel with the finest dialogues of antiquity, as handed to us by Xenophon, by Plato and Cicero."[16] His reference to these major figures in ancient history, philosophy, and rhetoric emphasizes the significance he placed on the scene he was witnessing. He would continue to follow events closely throughout his time in France.

Jefferson finally received Congressional approval for his leave in September, so he began to prepare for what he thought would be a temporary return to Virginia. In the autobiography, he ends the story of the French Revolution where his personal association with it ended. In so doing, he eloquently takes leave of France. Abigail Adams had observed that no one can leave Paris without a feeling of *tristesse*.[17] Jefferson's parting words reflect a similar tone. His goodbye message remains the finest paean to France ever written by an American. Recalling an anecdote from Cornelius Nepos, he offered a fitting way to close the story of his last days in Paris:

And here I cannot leave this great and good country without expressing my sense of its preeminence of character among the nations of
the earth. A more benevolent people, I have never known, nor greater
warmth and devotedness in their select friendships. Their kindness
and accommodation to strangers is unparalleled, and the hospitality of
Paris is beyond anything I had conceived to be practicable in a large
city. Their eminence too in science, the communicative dispositions of
their scientific men, the politeness of the general manners, the ease and
vivacity of their conversation, give a charm to their society to be found
nowhere else. In a comparison of this with other countries we have the
proof of primacy, which was given to Themistocles after the battle of
Salamis. Every general voted to himself the first reward of valor, and
the second to Themistocles. So ask the travelled inhabitant of any
nation, In what country on earth would you rather live?—Certainly in
my own, where are all my friends, my relations, and the earliest and
sweetest affections and recollections of my life. Which would be your
second choice? France.[18]

PART IV

SERVANT OF THE PEOPLE

CHAPTER 27

The Young Idea

L eft Paris": So reads Jefferson's memorandum book for Saturday, September 26, 1789. Two days later his party, which included his two daughters, James Hemings, and James's sister Sally, reached Le Havre, where Jefferson befriended a seafaring man from Massachusetts named Nathaniel Cutting. Better known to posterity as a diarist than a sailor, Captain Cutting tirelessly recorded the incidents of everyday life to create a lasting record of his seafaring adventures. Cutting's diary chronicles his friendship with the Jeffersons in great detail and thus supplements the laconic memorandum book. Few surviving documents better capture Jefferson's personal interactions with his daughters. Since it took several days to find passage from Le Havre to the Isle of Wight, Cutting spent much time in their company, postponing his own journey to be with them.

The night the Jeffersons arrived in Le Havre, they dined with Cutting at their hotel, L'Aigle d'Or. After dinner, he invited them to tea at the Wheatcrofts, a prominent local family. That evening the tea service accidentally broke, spilling hot tea and crockery everywhere, but the accident scarcely spoiled the pleasantries. Their remaining nights in Le Havre followed a similar pattern, without the broken crockery but with musical accompaniment from Miss Wheatcroft on pianoforte.

When the Jeffersons' luggage arrived a few days later, Captain Wright, who ran the service between Le Havre and the Isle of Wight, had already sailed, so they were delayed further. Given the ferocious weather, perhaps they were better off staying at Le Havre for the time being. Cutting could "not recollect to have heard the Wind blow so very violently before, since I have known this Country"—strong words from this seasoned sailor.[1] The storms continued through much of Thursday, October 1. Once the rain lessened that afternoon, Cutting returned to

L'Aigle d'Or, where he found the Jeffersons seated comfortably by the fire.

Taking a seat and ordering more tea, he joined the conversation, which settled on the subject of John Ledyard. Cutting knew Ledyard personally—an eccentric genius, he called him—but had lost track of him in recent years. Having encouraged Ledyard's journey to Siberia and having spoken with him at length upon his return, Jefferson knew more about his exploits than anyone save Ledyard himself. Jefferson described Ledyard's adventures to Cutting, whose record of their conversation supplies important details about Ledyard's Russian adventures unavailable elsewhere.

Once Captain Wright returned from Cowes Friday evening, the Jeffersons could prepare to leave Le Havre. But recurring storms created further delays. The captain intended to sail on Tuesday, October 6, but the weather—the squally, dirty, tempestuous weather—postponed their voyage. Jefferson spent the day searching for a pair of sheepdogs to take to Virginia for breeding purposes. Not a great dog fancier, he did like Normandy sheepdogs, which he called "the most careful intelligent dogs in the world." Besides, such dogs were essential to his plans for raising sheep in Virginia. The search proved exhausting. Jefferson related, "We walked 10. miles, clambering the cliffs in quest of the shepherds, during the most furious tempest of wind and rain I was ever in. The journey was fruitless."[2]

Returning to town, they encountered a gruesome sight, "the body of a man who had that moment shot himself. His pistol had dropped at his feet," Jefferson observed, "and himself fallen backward without ever moving. The shot had completely separated his whole face from the forehead to the chin and so torn it to atoms that it could not be known. The center of the head was entirely laid bare."[3] Jefferson reacted to the sight of this suicide like a modern-day forensic scientist. Besides getting a good look at the destruction the bullet did to the man's face, he also noticed the position of the gun and its relationship to the position of the man's body. His description is neither emotional nor judgmental. Jefferson saw suicide as the result of mental disease and sought to understand it as such.[4]

Apparently, the sight of the dead man did not hurt Jefferson's appetite. That evening he had dinner with a local merchant, complete with a variety of excellent wines. After dinner they viewed their host's collection of valuable prints. Walking in the rain Wednesday, Jefferson encountered a visibly pregnant Normandy sheepdog, which he purchased and named Bergère. Buzzy, as its French name came to be pronounced in Virginia, turned out to be a great favorite at Monticello.[5]

The care with which Cutting treated the Jeffersons before, during, and after the passage to the Isle of Wight is touching. He arranged for coaches to take them from their hotel to the point of embarkation and saw them all safely aboard before midnight. A southerly breeze hurried them along at first, but the wind shifted to the north partway through the voyage and slowed them considerably. Regardless which way the wind was blowing, all the Jeffersons became seasick. Rain and contrary winds persisted though Thursday evening. Finally, around two o'clock Friday morning, they anchored in Cowes harbor. Cutting went ashore, found accommodations at the Fountain Inn, and returned to accompany them to their lodgings.

The Jeffersons did not reach the inn until four that morning. Five hours later, Cutting was amazed to find them seated in the breakfast room enjoying hot buttered rolls and tea. He wrote, "I had the pleasure to see a vivifying smile upon those countenances over which the *nausea marina* yesterday threw the palid Veil of weakness and discouragement."[6]

Aware they would soon part ways, Cutting took advantage of their time together and enjoyed breakfast with them the next three mornings. Coming down about half past eight one morning, he saw Jefferson and his younger daughter seated before an open copy of Don Antonio de Solís's *Historia de la Conquista de México*. Cutting noted how tenderly Jefferson oversaw the education of his daughters. While in Paris, he had purchased other books for Mary, including a copy of Pierre Coste's tiny two-volume edition of Jean de La Fontaine's *Fables Choisies*.[7] Cutting's diary supplements the story of the Jefferson girls. Most of the other evidence concerning Jefferson's relationship with Martha and Mary or, as she now insisted upon being called, Maria comes from his letters. Writing his daughters while separated from them, he typically admonished them to pursue their studies with diligence. In these letters, Jefferson comes off as a stern taskmaster. Cutting's diary, alternatively, shows how tender-hearted he could be as he helped Maria with her Spanish.

The diary also captures how Cutting felt upon seeing father and daughter bent over a book together: "I was prodigiously pleased with his method of instilling into her tender mind an accurate knowledge of Geography at the same time that he inculcated the purest principles of the Language."[8] In his educational writings, Jefferson had advocated the importance of teaching foreign tongues in conjunction with other subjects such as history and geography. In practice, he did just that. Cutting continued, "The lovely Girl was all attention, and discover'd a degree of sagacity and observation beyond her years, in the very pertinent queries she put to her excellent Preceptor. I could not help participating [in] the pleasure this indulgent Parent must experience in the Delightful Task! To rear the tender thought and teach the young idea how to shoot!"

Cutting's words echo lines from James Thomson's *Spring*, which captures the joy of teaching:

> Delightful Task! to rear the tender Thought
> To teach the young idea how to shoot,
> To pour the fresh Instruction o'er the Mind,
> To breathe th' enlivening Spirit, and to fix
> The generous Purpose in the glowing Breast.

These oft-quoted lines embody a view of education that both Jefferson and Thomson shared with John Locke. The organic metaphor in *Spring* nicely conveys Jefferson's personal attitude toward education. Ideas must be planted in the mind and then carefully nurtured to ensure that they take root.

After saying his final goodbyes, Cutting reflected upon the friendship he had formed with the Jeffersons. His reflections, duly recorded in the pages of his diary, constitute the fullest contemporary description of the Jefferson family from their time in Europe. In addition, Cutting's heartfelt words and affectionate tone affirm the devotion Jefferson could inspire in articulate, sensitive men:

> I never remember to have experienced so much regret at parting from a Family with whom I had so short an acquaintance. I have found Mr. Jefferson a man of infinite information and sound Judgement, becoming gravity, and engaging affability mark his deportment. His general abilities are such as would do honor to any age or Country. His eldest Daughter is an amiable girl about 17 years of age, tall and genteel, has been 5 years in France, principally in a convent, for her Education, and though she has been so long resident in a Country remarkable for its Levity and the forward indelicacy of its manners, yet she retains all that winning simplicity, and good humour'd reserve that are evident proofs of innate Virtue and an happy disposition.— Characteristicks which eminently distinguish the Women of America from those of any other Country. The youngest Daughter is a lovely Girl about 11 years of age. The perfect pattern of good temper, an engaging smile ever animates her Countenance, and the chearful attention which she pays to the judisious instructions and advice of her worthy Father, the Pertinent queries which she puts to him, and the evident improvement she makes in her knowledge of Foreign Lan-

guages, History and Geography, afford a pleasing Presage that when her faculties attain their maturity, she will be the delight of her Friends, and a distinguish'd ornament to her sex.[9]

The word "ornament," in this sense, has fallen from usage, but it was not uncommon in the day. Basically, Cutting meant that Maria would mature into a person who adds distinction to her time, place, sex, and station.

The Jeffersons remained in Cowes a few weeks after Cutting's departure. John Trumbull had booked passage for them aboard the *Clermont*, which embarked from London and made a special stop at Cowes to pick up the Jefferson party. Once aboard the *Clermont*, they were plagued by seasickness for the first five days of the journey, but the remainder of the crossing turned out to be quite pleasant. In Jefferson's words, they experienced "the finest autumn weather it was possible to have the wind having never blown harder than we would have desired it."[10]

Buzzy gave birth to puppies either at Cowes or during the journey, but otherwise the crossing was uneventful—until the *Clermont* approached the Virginia capes, where thick fog made it impossible to locate a pilot boat. For three days they searched but to no avail. The captain of the *Clermont* finally decided to brave the capes and enter the Chesapeake on his own. Martha Jefferson remembered the experience well:

After beating about for three days the captain, who was a bold as well as an experienced seaman determined to run in at a venture without having seen the capes. We were near running upon what he conjectured to be the middle ground when we cast anchor at ten o'clock at night. The wind rose, the vessel drifted down dragging her anchors one or more miles, but we had got within the capes whilst a number of vessels less bold were blown off the coast some of them lost and all of them kept out three or four weeks longer. We had to beat up against a strong head wind which carried away our topsails and were very near being run down by a brig coming out of port who having the wind in her favor was almost upon us before we could get out of the way. We escaped however with only a loss only of a part of our rigging.[11]

Mooring safely at Norfolk on Monday afternoon, November 23, the Jeffersons disembarked, thinking their adventures over, but an hour or two later, before their luggage had been unloaded, the *Clermont* caught fire. The fire started in the middle steerage, and the flames burst through the cabin and out the windows. Happily, their luggage escaped the conflagration. Martha's account explains that their trunks had been put in their staterooms and "the doors pulled to *accidentally* as our Captain acknowledged but seeing them open he thought it as well to shut them. They were so close that the flames did not penetrate, but the powder in a musket in our room was silently consumed and the thickness of the travelling trunks alone saved their contents from the excessive heat. I understood at the time that the state rooms alone of all the internal partitions escaped burning."[12]

Accommodations in Norfolk were limited, but a couple of gentlemen staying at Lindsay's Hotel gave up their rooms for the Jeffersons. Once they settled in, Jefferson got himself caught up on the news. He was surprised to read in the papers that President Washington had appointed him secretary of state. "I made light of it," he said later, "supposing I had only to say 'no' and there would be an end of it."[13] Saying no to George Washington would be more difficult than Jefferson imagined.

They took the roundabout way to Monticello, stopping at the homes of many friends. In fact, they did not reach Monticello until a month after they touched at Norfolk. Word of their arrival preceded them—Martha recalled what happened as they neared home:

> The negroes discovered the approach of the carriage as soon as it reached Shadwell and such a scene I never witnessed in my life. They collected in crowds around it and almost drew it up the mountain by hand. The shouting etc had been sufficiently obstreperous before but the moment it arrived at the top it reached the climax. When the door of the carriage was opened they received him in their arms and bore him to the house, crowding round and kissing his hands and feet some blubbering and crying others laughing. It seemed impossible to satisfy their anxiety to touch and kiss the very earth which bore him. These were the first ebulitions of joy for his return after a long absence which they would of course feel.[14]

Written decades after the fact, Martha's recollection embodies the rhetoric of the antebellum plantation novels in its depiction of the gratitude of the slaves and the benevolence of the master. Other evidence confirms her description, however.[15]

Shortly after the Jeffersons returned to Monticello, Thomas Mann Randolph, Jr., came courting. While a student at the University of Edinburgh, he had visited the Jeffersons in Paris, where his romance with Martha may have begun. Now back in Virginia, their courtship progressed rapidly, and soon young Randolph asked for Martha's hand.

Her father, a little disappointed that the marriage would cut short his daughter's studies, was otherwise pleased with the match. By God, she had beaten the odds and escaped marrying a blockhead. Randolph was "a young gentleman of genius, science and honorable mind." To a European correspondent, Jefferson explained that Randolph's "talents, dispositions, connections and fortune were such as he would have made him my own first choice, yet according to the usage of my country, I scrupulously suppressed my wishes, that my daughter might indulge her own sentiments freely. It ended in their marriage."[16]

The wedding took place the last Tuesday of February 1790, the Reverend Matthew Maury performing the ceremony. Once the wedding festivities wound down, Jefferson had no time to spare. Saying no to George Washington had proven more than difficult: it had proven impossible. Accepting the appointment, he came to understand what Washington already knew: Thomas Jefferson was the most qualified man in the nation to serve as secretary of state. Before leaving for New York, the nation's temporary capital, he made arrangements for Maria to live with the Eppes family at Eppington. He insisted she study her Spanish grammar in his absence and read at least ten pages a day in *Don Quixote*.

There were good reasons why the coming generation needed to know Spanish. The commercial and diplomatic relationship between Spain and the United States, Jefferson told young Randolph, "is already important and will become daily more so. Besides this the antient part of American history is written chiefly in Spanish." Jefferson took his own advice to heart. Having expanded his collection of Spanish Americana in Europe, he was now busily reading it. Packing his bags for New York, he included a book by Francisco López de Gómara, the Spanish historian who served as secretary to Hernando Cortés.[17]

Leaving Monticello on Monday, March 1, accompanied by James Hemings, Jefferson stopped in Richmond for a week to take care of some additional business. Much construction had occurred at the state capital in his absence. There was one street that, to Jefferson's eyes, could "be considered as handsomely built in any city of Europe." He especially enjoyed seeing the new state capitol building under construction. Some adjustments were necessary to make it conform to his original plans, but by and large he felt great pride even as he realized that it would take much time to finish. Once completed, the capitol would be "an edifice of first rate dignity," one "worthy of being exhibited along side the most celebrated remains of antiquity."[18]

From Richmond, Jefferson and James Hemings took the stagecoach to Alexandria, where they met Robert Hemings, who had driven the phaeton from Monticello. They reached Alexandria on Wednesday, the tenth, staying over that night and the next on the occasion of a public dinner in Jefferson's honor at the Fountain Tavern. Finding a vessel bound from Alexandria for France, Jefferson took the opportunity to write William Short, asking him to wind up his affairs in France and providing detailed instructions about how to pack all of his books for shipment. The fine library Jefferson had assembled in Paris would be coming to Monticello.

He had planned to drive his phaeton from Alexandria to New York, but an unexpected storm dumped eighteen inches of snow on the city overnight. With no desire to drive through such slop, Jefferson sent the phaeton to New York by water and decided to "bump it" in the stage-coach himself. The overland route turned out to be bumpier than he imagined. As he wrote his new son-in-law upon reaching his destination, "The roads thro the whole were so bad that we could never go more than three miles an hour, sometimes not more than two, and in the night but one."[19] He could have walked all the way to New York faster.

The month after he reached the city, he subscribed to Christopher Colles's *Survey of the Roads of the United States*. The earliest American road guide, Colles's *Survey* was based on maps prepared on George Washington's orders during the Revolutionary War. It contained a series of copperplate engravings illustrating routes from Connecticut to Virginia. The journey from Alexandria had shown Jefferson how much roadwork was needed. Subscribing to Colles's *Survey*, he encouraged the improvement of American travel conditions.

In Philadelphia, he paused long enough to visit Benjamin Franklin. Since returning, Franklin had added a three-story wing to his home, largely to accommodate the fine library *he* had assembled in Paris. Franklin avoided placing a staircase in the new wing of his home: he did not want to take precious space away from his books. Similarly, Jefferson would minimize the staircases at Monticello to maximize interior space. In the past, the two bookmen had discussed their libraries at length. On this occasion, Franklin's physical condition dampened his guest's enthusiasm: Jefferson found his old friend on his deathbed.[20]

Despite his failing health, Franklin had many questions about mutual friends in Paris, which he asked "with a rapidity and animation almost too much for his strength."

Jefferson had heard that Franklin was continuing to write his autobiography and asked him about it.

"I cannot say much of that," Franklin replied, "but I will give you a sample of what I shall leave."

Thomas Jefferson, engraved by H. B. Hall's Sons, New York. From Lyon Gardiner Tyler, *Encyclopedia of Virginia Biography* (1915). (Collection of Kevin J. Hayes)

Saying these words, he directed his grandson Billy Bache to hand him the manuscript from atop a nearby table. Bache did so, and Franklin gave the manuscript to Jefferson, urging him to take it with him and read it as his leisure. The manuscript he presented was a narrative describing the informal discussions that took place in 1774 and 1775 between Franklin and some British representatives, who met secretly to try to restore amicable relations between Great Britain and America.

Jefferson glanced at the manuscript and, realizing what it was, thanked Franklin for letting him read it and assured him he would return it.

"No, keep it," Franklin replied.

Unsure precisely what Franklin meant, Jefferson glanced at the manuscript again, folded it, and reassured him again that he would return it.

"No," Franklin insisted. "Keep it."

Jefferson put the manuscript in his pocket and took leave of his old friend. Franklin would pass away the following month. After his death, Jefferson pronounced him "the greatest man and ornament of the age and country in which he lived." He further observed, "His memory will be preserved and venerated as long as the thunders of heaven shall be heard or feared."[21]

Reaching New York in late March, Jefferson hoped to find a house on Broadway. Unable to locate anything suitable to his tastes there, he took a small house in Maiden Lane. Knowing he would not be returning to France as ambassador, he slowly realized that he would never see France again. The first week of April he undertook the melancholy task of putting pen to paper to say goodbye to his French friends. To one he explained: "Could I have persuaded myself that public offices were made for private convenience, I should undoubtedly have preferred a continuance in that which placed me nearer to you: but believing on the contrary that a good citizen should take his stand where the public authority marshals him, I have acquiesced. Among the circumstances which reconcile me to my new position, the most powerful is the opportunities it will give me of cementing the friendship between our two nations."[22]

The most memorable phrase from this set of goodbye letters occurs in one to Lafayette. Confronting the violence associated with the French Revolution, Jefferson diminished the bloodshed and waxed philosophic: "So far it seemed that your revolution had got along with a steady pace: meeting indeed occasional difficulties and dangers, but we are not to expect to be translated from despotism to liberty in a feather-bed."[23] These oft-quoted words remain applicable as new democracies face brutal violence as they emerge from political and religious tyranny.

Diplomacy was not the only task the first secretary of state faced. Within Washington's administration, there were three executive departments, each headed by a secretary. Alexander Hamilton served as treasury secretary, and Henry Knox served as secretary of war. Attorney General Edmund Randolph rounded out the cabinet. As secretary of state, Jefferson had the most demanding job of all four men. Not only did he oversee foreign affairs, he also oversaw domestic policy. His concern for the new government prompted him to oversee treasury matters in order to keep an eye on Hamilton. Jefferson realized that the course the government took during its first administration would establish the nation's direction for centuries to come. He took the same care and seriousness in nurturing the new government as he did in raising his daughters.

Fresh from the French Revolution, he began his duties as secretary of state with much enthusiasm. His experience in France had revitalized his passion for republicanism. Describing his state of mind at this time, he recalled, "I had left France in the first year of her revolution, in the fervor of natural rights, and zeal for reformation. My conscientious devotion to these rights could not be heightened, but it had been aroused and excited by daily exercise."[24]

Given his passionate devotion to the principles of natural law and natural rights, Jefferson was shocked when he started hearing high-ranking members of Washington's administration questioning the value of a republican form of government and wanting something closer to a monarchy. The ideas John Adams was articulating in print made him seem like a monarchist, too. But Adams's position as vice president, which largely involved presiding over the Senate, isolated him from decisions made by Washington and his cabinet. Hamilton was emerging as a much more dominant force on the national political scene.

In a brief character sketch, Jefferson identified Hamilton's positive traits but also recognized his major shortcoming: "Hamilton was, indeed, a singular character. Of acute understanding, disinterested, honest, and honorable in all private transactions, amiable in society, and duly valuing virtue in private life, yet so bewitched and perverted by the British example, as to be under thorough conviction that corruption was essential to the government of a nation."[25]

To paraphrase Jefferson's last remark more objectively: Hamilton was convinced that the best way to further the public interest would be to encourage private self-interests. Often called the father of American capitalism, Hamilton sought to make money rule America. Jefferson accused Hamilton of being a monarchist, but this accusation is imprecise. While appreciating the British system of government and hoping the United States would emulate it, Hamilton was against making the president into a king. What he really wanted was to make money king.

While disagreeing with Hamilton's policies, Jefferson held little personal animosity toward him when they first began serving together in Washington's cabinet. He tried working with Hamilton as much as possible. Upon his arrival, Jefferson found himself thick in the controversy over the proposal for the federal government to assume the debts incurred by individual states since the beginning of American independence. States like Virginia that had already retired much of their debt independently were reluctant to assume responsibility for states like Massachusetts that had been unable to pay off their debts. James Madison successfully led the fight against the assumption of state debt in Congress.

Convinced of the proposal's importance, Hamilton tried to win over the secretary of state. Jefferson vividly remembered Hamilton catching up with him while on the way to see President Washington shortly after he settled in New York. The two walked back and forth past Washington's house for half an hour as Hamilton argued for the proposal's validity. Unwilling to commit himself so quickly, Jefferson forestalled a decision. Instead, he and Madison invited Hamilton to dinner, when they could discuss the matter at length and devise a workable solution.

Since the assumption of state debts favored New England, Jefferson and Madison realized the South would need an incentive to approve the measure. Or, as Jefferson put it: "But it was observed that this pill would be peculiarly bitter to the southern States, and that some concomitant measure should be adopted, to sweeten it a little to them. There had before been propositions to fix the seat of government either at Philadelphia, or at Georgetown on the Potomac; and it was thought that by giving it to Philadelphia, for ten years, and to Georgetown permanently afterwards, this might, as an anodyne, calm in some degree the ferment which might be excited by the other measure alone."[26] Hamilton agreed. If they would find enough votes in Congress to pass the assumption bill, he would find enough votes to move the seat of the federal government to Philadelphia first and then, ten years later, to the banks of the Potomac.

Jefferson's personal animosity toward Hamilton did not begin until one evening in April 1791, when they dined with Vice President Adams, and the conversation turned to the British constitution.[27]

"Purge that constitution of its corruption, and give to its popular branch equality of representation," Adams observed, "and it would be the most perfect constitution ever devised by wit of man."

"Purge it of its corruption, and give to its popular branch equality of representation," Hamilton responded, "and it would become an *impracticable* government: as it stands at present, with all its supposed defects, it is the most perfect government which ever existed."

These words convinced Jefferson that Hamilton was attempting to reshape the American republic into a mirror image of the British system. Jefferson subsequently scrutinized everything Hamilton did in order to keep his ideas and ambitions in check. Political parties per se had yet to form, but in their opposition to the federal policies of Adams and Hamilton, Jefferson and Madison began laying the foundation of what would be called the Anti-Federalist or Republican Party. Essentially, the clash between the policies of Hamilton and Jefferson initiated the development of the Federalist and Republican parties.

Not all of Jefferson's responsibilities in Washington's administration were so contentious. One of the most agreeable tasks he undertook as secretary of state let him pursue his scientific interests and indulge his penchant for precision. Washington asked him to prepare a report on weights and measures and, basically, to create the standards that would ensure smooth-running systems of commerce and transportation. This responsibility came unexpectedly: Jefferson was caught without his mathematical books. Having somewhat neglected his mathematics in recent years, he wrote David Rittenhouse, asking him to send whatever textbooks he could spare. Jefferson also had the opportunity to consult the holdings of the New York Society Library. Furthermore, he asked people in New York about any recent developments in the field. Count Paolo Andreani, for one, remembered a work on the subject of weights and measures recently published in Milan.[28]

The first of many official reports he would write as secretary of state, Jefferson's completed work was published as *Report of the Secretary of State, on the Subject of Establishing a Uniformity in the Weights, Measures and Coins*. More than merely a government document, Jefferson's *Report* amounts to a learned treatise on standards and measurements. He sent copies to his scholarly friends, a group that included George Wythe and Ezra Stiles. The always gracious Wythe thanked Jefferson for the *Report*, saying the book "is deposited among my treasures." Stiles was "extremely pleased with it as a philosophic Production." He told his students at Yale about the *Report* and had them study it. The letter of thanks he wrote Jefferson includes much additional literary news, the kind of information he enjoyed reading. Stiles ended his letter by expressing hope that one day Jefferson would become President of the United States, an idea he did not necessarily want to hear.[29]

The thank-you letters from Wythe and Stiles were among the few pieces of literary correspondence Jefferson received during his tenure as secretary of state. Others came as cover letters accompanying presentation copies of books he received. Mercy Otis Warren, for instance, presented him with a copy of her *Poems, Dramatic and Miscellaneous*. Thanking her for the book, Jefferson applauded it as proof that Americans could excel at poetry. Though the letter does not mention the Comte de Buffon by name,

Jefferson clearly had Buffon's theories in mind when he suggested that the superiority of her verse refuted the hypothesis that "supposed a degeneracy even of the human race on this side of the Atlantic."[30]

Once Congress adjourned on Saturday, August 14, the U.S. government began the long, slow process of moving its operations to Philadelphia. Correctly surmising that he would never be this far north again, Jefferson took the opportunity to visit Rhode Island with the president. They left New York the day after Congress adjourned, sailing up Long Island Sound and reaching Newport Tuesday. Washington was feted and toasted and honored; Jefferson was happy to remain in the president's shadow. They left Newport Wednesday and reached Providence that afternoon. More festivities ensued. Perhaps Jefferson enjoyed the visit to the library of Rhode Island College best. Like most New England college libraries, the collection was heavy in religious treatises, but it did show some signs of Enlightenment. In addition to its divinity collection, the college library contained works on aesthetics, astronomy, botany, chemistry, commerce, conic sections, electricity, optics, and surgery.

The president and the secretary of state returned to New York on August 21.[31] Jefferson spent the rest of the month arranging to leave New York permanently. He settled several bills, paying for some madeira and some porter. He bought more books and had local bookbinder Thomas Allen bind some volumes for him.[32] On Wednesday, September 1, 1790, he and Madison left New York together in Jefferson's trusty phaeton. They proceeded through New Jersey, Pennsylvania, and Delaware, reaching Rock Hall, Maryland on the tenth, when Thomas Lee Shippen caught up with them.

Shippen was one of the young men for whom Jefferson had written "Hints to Americans Travelling in Europe." He had followed Jefferson's hints during his long sojourn in Europe and had become a seasoned traveler. Shippen also became a fine travel writer, as his account of this current trip indicates. Unlike Jefferson, Shippen recorded many incidental details regarding their experience.[33]

Like Jefferson and Madison, Shippen hoped to cross the Chesapeake Bay from Rock Hall to Annapolis. Forced to wait a long time for a boat to take them across, they did the same things modern-day visitors to the Chesapeake would do. Shippen explained, "We talked and dined, and strolled, and rowed ourselves in boats, and feasted upon delicious crabs."

It took them six hours to cross the bay, but their horses, which crossed on a separate vessel, took eighteen. With more time on their hands, they toured Annapolis. Here Shippen met an old Annapolis friend named Shaaff, who showed them around the city: "We passed 3 hours on the top

George Washington, engraved by H. B. Hall's Sons, New York, after a painting by Gilbert Stuart. From Lyon Gardiner Tyler, *Encyclopedia of Virginia Biography* (1915). (Collection of Kevin J. Hayes)

of the State House steeple from which place you descry the finest prospect in the world, if extent, variety Wood and Water in all their happiest forms can make one so. My good friend Shaaff was not displeased at my comparing him to the Diable Boiteux whose office he seemed to fill in opening the roofs of the houses and telling us the history of each family who lived in them."

Shippen was referring to the popular novel by Alain-René Lesage, Jefferson's favorite French novelist. In fact, Jefferson kept a copy of *Diable Boiteux* in his vacation library at Poplar Forest. This novel tells the story of a student named Cleofas who releases a spirit named Asmodée, a lame, misshapen devil who walks about on crutches. Leading Cleofas on a tour of Madrid, Asmodée shows him what the city is really like by lifting the roofs from the houses and portraying what goes on behind closed doors. Lesage's voyeurism has the potential to be mean-spirited, but his light tone and delicate touch save the narrative from scathing exposé.

Mann's Tavern, where they stayed in Annapolis, Shippen placed "among the most excellent in the world." They feasted on turtle here and enjoyed some mellow old madeira. Their accommodations the next night at Queen Anne's were, in Shippen's words, "a most perfect contrast to Mann's—Musquitos, gnats, flees and bugs contended with each other for preference, and we had nothing decent to eat or drink. You may imagine how much we slept from the company we were in."

Once they reached Georgetown, Jefferson and Madison lingered here to scout locations for the new national capital. Several local men joined the party, which became quite a sizable group. Since Shippen left them at Georgetown, the colorful story of their adventures ends here, too. Jefferson reached Monticello on Sunday, September 19.

He did not stay long. Less than two months later, he left home for Philadelphia. He and Madison first stayed together at a boarding house, but Jefferson eventually rented a four-story brick house on Market Street and Eighth, right across from the offices of the State Department.[34] He threw himself into his work, relying on his correspondence with his daughters to keep him connected to home. The month after he arrived, Jefferson wrote his daughter Martha, scolding her for not writing: "Perhaps you think you have nothing to say to me. It is a great deal to say you are all well, or that one has a cold, another a fever etc., besides that there is not a sprig of grass that shoots uninteresting to me, nor any thing that moves, from yourself down to Bergere."[35]

His letters to Maria admonish her to continue studying Spanish. Hers inform him of her progress in *Don Quixote* and, upon completing that, her intention to read *Lazarillo de Tormes*, which is considered the first Spanish picaresque romance. Maria also mentioned that she had been reading William Robertson's *History of America* and reminded him of his promise to send her copies of Edward Gibbon's *History of the Decline and Fall of the Roman Empire* and Jean-Jacques Barthélmy's *Voyage de Jeune Anacharsis*. Maria would never become as bookish as her big sister, but these letters show that she was trying to obey her father and pursue her studies as diligently as she could.[36]

Actually, Jefferson's letters to and from his daughters constitute the fullest literary correspondence he maintained while secretary of state.

Maria provided other bookish information beyond her studies. She told her father that for Christmas she had presented Martha a copy of Comtesse de Genlis's *Tales of the Castle: or, Stories of Instruction and Delight*, a collection of didactic juvenile fiction—a gift that may reflect Maria's own tastes more than those of her married sister. A contemporary educator recommended *Tales of the Castle* as a book that "young ladies, from the age of six to sixteen years, may read with advantage." Like her father, Maria apparently bought books for Martha she wished to read herself. Martha, in turn, presented her sister a copy of Richard Cumberland's *Observer*, a collection of essays that is part conduct manual and part literary criticism.[37]

Since her marriage, Martha had been neglecting her studies—but she had a good excuse. To her father the third week of January 1791, she wrote, "I can give but a poor account of my reading having had so little time to my self that tho I have the greatest inclination I have not as yet been able to indulge it."[38] This letter does not say so, but Martha was pregnant with her first child. The following week, in fact, she gave birth to Anne Cary Randolph, Thomas Jefferson's first grandchild.

Grandpa Jefferson wrote one letter of congratulations to Martha and another to her sister. The charming letter he wrote Maria on this occasion is notable for the self-effacing humor it contains: "I congratulate you my dear aunt on your new title. I hope you pay a great deal of attention to your niece, and that you have begun to give her lessons on the harpsichord, in Spanish etc."[39] Telling Maria to give the newborn baby harpsichord lessons and teach her Spanish, Jefferson was poking fun at himself and his unflagging insistence that Maria attend to her studies. Still, his comments are not entirely tongue-in-cheek. He felt that the sooner children acquire good study habits, the more quickly they will learn and the longer those habits will last.

With this letter to Maria, Jefferson enclosed a book for her sister, John Gregory's *Comparative View of the State and Faculties of Man with Those of the Animal World*, a pioneering work of comparative psychology and one of the most widely read eighteenth-century manuals on child rearing. Presenting the book, Jefferson said that it contained much useful advice for the young mother. Later that spring, he sent Martha a large package containing more books, some for her, some for her husband, and others for her sister, including the promised copy of Barthélemy's *Voyage de Jeune Anacharsis*, which Jefferson called "a very elegant digest of whatever is known of the Greeks."[40]

The most unusual book he sent Martha in this shipment was *Sacontalá: or, The Fatal Ring, an Indian Drama*, William Jones's English translation from the original Sanskrit play by Kalidasa, who was known as the Indian Shakespeare. *Sacontalá* tells a tale of a maiden and a great raja, who first seduces the maiden and then spurns her. After she gives birth, the raja ultimately accepts the woman and their son.

Sacontalá may have been one of those books Jefferson bought for his daughter because he wanted to read it himself. He had great respect for Jones's linguistic skills and was fascinated by the transmission of languages throughout the world. The process of translation Jones described in his preface was the kind of scholarly information Jefferson appreciated. Noticing considerable similarities between Latin and Sanskrit, Jones translated *Sacontalá* verbatim into Latin, creating an interlinear text, which he then rendered into English. Though Jefferson sent the book to Martha, the catalogue of his library indicates that *Sacontalá* ended up among his books, not hers.

Living in Philadelphia again, he took advantage of the great literary opportunities the city had to offer. He subscribed to Matthew Carey's *American Museum* and other magazines. He bought many books and borrowed more from friends. But one particular book he borrowed from James Madison stirred up no end of trouble. Having borrowed Thomas Paine's *Rights of Man*—one of the first copies to reach America—from John Beckley, clerk of the House of Representatives, Madison loaned it to Jefferson, urging him to read the book quickly and return it. When Beckley called for it, Jefferson had yet to finish the book. Beckley let him keep it for the time being but asked him to send it directly to Jonathan Bayard Smith, whose son, Samuel Harrison Smith, intended to reprint it. Though Jefferson would become good friends with Samuel Harrison Smith in the coming years, at this time he did not personally know either him or his father.

Once he finished reading Paine's *Rights of Man*, Jefferson found it necessary to write a cover letter to Jonathan Bayard Smith explaining why he was sending the book to him. The letter became something more than mere explanation as Jefferson interjected his opinion about the book. Jefferson's reason for supplying his opinion was a literary one: he wanted to "take off a little of the dryness" of this otherwise formulaic letter of thanks. Reading what Jefferson wrote, Samuel Harrison Smith realized that the secretary of state's words made good advertising copy. Without securing Jefferson's permission, he incorporated a passage from the letter in his preface:

> The following Extract from a note accompanying a copy of this Pamphlet for republication, is so respectable a testimony of its value, that the Printer hopes the distinguished writer will excuse its present

appearance. It proceeds from a character equally eminent in the councils of America, and conversant in the affairs of France, from a long and recent residence at the Court of Versailles in the Diplomatic department; and, at the same time that it does justice to the writings of Mr. Paine, it reflects honor on the source from which it flows, by directing the mind to a contemplation of that Republican firmness and Democratic simplicity which endear their possessor to every friend of the "Rights of Man."

After some prefatory remarks, the Secretary of State observes:

"I am extremely pleased to find it will be re-printed here, and that something is at length to be publicly said against the political heresies which have sprung up among us.

"I have no doubt our citizens will *rally* a second time round the *standard* of Common Sense."

Jefferson was shocked when he saw his private words published as part of this book. He had not intended to make his opinion in this matter public. From the surface of the printed page, the word "heresies" glared the brightest. To many readers, there was little doubt that Jefferson had in mind the policies of Vice President Adams, as articulated in his *Defence of the Constitutions of Government of the United States* and in his *Discourses on Davila*, published serially in the *Gazette of the United States*. In June, an essay series signed "Publicola" and secretly written by John Quincy Adams attacked Jefferson's remarks and perpetuated the controversy.

Upon the release of Smith's edition of Paine, Jefferson wrote President Washington to explain how his words happened to appear in this book. Washington accepted the explanation, but others were unconvinced. Hamilton saw the preface to Smith's edition of Paine as a clever ploy on Jefferson's part. He told others that Jefferson's comments marked his opposition to the government. But, as Jefferson told Madison, Hamilton was twisting his words. Hamilton asserted that Jefferson was attacking the federal government, but Jefferson was really critiquing the enemies of the government, those who demonstrated monarchical tendencies. The bitterness expressed over this issue shows how tensions between the two were escalating during Jefferson's time as secretary of state.

In late May 1791, Jefferson escaped the temporary capital for a vacation to upstate New York. From Philadelphia, he traveled to New York, where he joined Madison, and together they continued farther north to visit some of the most scenic areas in the nation. As he had on his travels through Europe, Jefferson kept a journal of the trip and also wrote several letters describing the experience. These documents contribute to the story of Jefferson as a travel writer, but they share the same shortcomings as his European travel writing. The matter-of-fact quality of his journal precludes good writing. Alternatively, the letters he wrote to his daughters offer fine examples of Jefferson's literary craftsmanship, though they illustrate only a small segment of the journey.

The last week of May they sailed the length of Lake George—the highlight of the trip. Jefferson wrote his older daughter. "Lake George is without comparison the most beautiful water I ever saw: formed by a contour of mountains into a bason 35 miles long, and from 2 to 4 miles broad, finely interspersed with islands, its waves limpid as chrystal and the mountain sides covered with rich groves of Thuya, silver fir, white pine, Aspen and paper birch down to the water edge, here and there precipices of rock to checquer the scene and save it from monotony. An abundance of speckled trout, salmon trout, bass and other fish with which it is stored, have added to our other amusements the sport of taking them."[41]

Numerous birch trees offered the opportunity to teach Maria about how their bark was used as paper. Her father wrote, "Such a moment is now offered while passing this lake and its border, on which we have just landed, has furnished the means which the want of paper would otherwise have denied me. I write to you on the bark of the Paper birch, supposed to be the same used by the antients to write on before the art of making paper was invented, and which being called the Papyrus, gave the name of paper to the new invented substitute."[42] Jefferson fibs a little here as he tells her that the lack of paper prompted him to use birch bark for the letter. This letter is only known by a surviving draft written on regular paper. It wasn't Jefferson's want of paper that prompted him to write on birch bark but his wanting to bring natural history alive for his younger daughter. Maria appreciated his thoughtfulness. She thought the birch bark "prettier than paper."[43]

Jefferson and Madison also visited numerous historical sites where battles had been fought during the American Revolution. Jefferson's letters to his daughters say nothing about the war. Instead, he wrote his son-in-law that he and Madison had visited "the principal scenes of Burgoyne's misfortunes, to wit the grounds at Still water where the action of that name was fought and particularly the breastworks which cost so much blood to both parties, the encampments at Saratoga and ground where the British piled their arms, and the field of the battle of Bennington, about 9 miles from this place. We have also visited Forts William Henry and George, Ticonderoga, Crown point etc. which have been scenes of blood from a very early part of our history."[44]

The differences in content among these letters show how Jefferson carefully shaped his experiences to suit his recipients. Though his responsibilities as secretary of state gave him relatively little time to indulge his literary inclinations, the distance separating him from his family turned his daughters into keen literary correspondents. Jefferson's letters to them, read in conjunction with the contemporary comments he made against Hamilton and Adams, make one similarity obvious: Jefferson took the same attitude toward the American government that he took toward educating his daughters. American democracy, too, was a young idea that had to be taught how to shoot.

CHAPTER 28

The Anas

The late eighteenth century was the era of the ana, a time that saw many excellent collections of memorable sayings from remarkable people. It was the time of James Boswell's *Life of Johnson*—"the Ana of all Anas," Robert Southey called it.[1] It was also the time of Thomas Jefferson's *The Anas*, the finest work of its kind in American literature. *The Anas* contains notes on Jefferson's conversations during his time as secretary of state. He did not set out to create a literary work while fulfilling his responsibilities in Washington's cabinet. But as he continued serving as secretary of state, he realized that what Washington and other members of his administration were saying was worth putting down on paper. Jefferson was motivated to create *The Anas* for much the same reason he was motivated to take detailed notes of the proceedings of the Continental Congress a decade and a half earlier: they were useful at the moment—for recording important political business—but they were also useful in the long run, as a record of the beginnings of American democracy.

Once he left the office of secretary of state, Jefferson had his notes—"loose scraps," he called them—bound together. Some years after John Marshall published the final volume of his *Life of Washington* in the early nineteenth century, Jefferson decided to recopy and edit his notes. He wanted to refute the opinionated inaccuracies that plague Marshall's biography. Jefferson combined his notes and related correspondence into three volumes, which he had bound in marbled paper and labeled A, B, and C.

In "Explanations of the 3 Volumes Bound in Marbled Paper," a document typically edited as the introduction to *The Anas*, Jefferson described the genesis of the work. When he began serving as secretary of state, he took no notes of his meetings with the president or members of his cabinet. Slowly he realized the importance of creating a written record of what they said. He recorded his memoranda on whatever odd slips of paper he had on hand and set these rough notes aside with the intention of making a fair copy of them.

During his retirement from the presidency, he went through these various "ragged, rubbed, and scribbled" notes and gave "the whole a calm revisal." Much as *Notes on the State of Virginia* had emerged from the set of miscellaneous handwritten notes about Virginia that Jefferson had gradually assembled, *The Anas* emerged from the notes he kept while serving in Washington's administration. He omitted details that were "incorrect, or doubtful, or merely personal; or private, with which we have nothing to do."[2] Historians might wish he had left these loose scraps alone. The fact that he went through and edited the lot, however, enhances the significance of *The Anas* as a carefully crafted literary work.

The Anas has never been well edited. "Explanations" clearly shows that Jefferson intended the collection to stop at the time he retired as secretary of state and left Washington's administration, but his editors have frequently tacked onto *The Anas* notes of other conversations Jefferson recorded during his time as vice president and president, thus destroying the focus and purposefulness of *The Anas*. Complicating matters further, the materials he had collected together in the three similarly bound volumes were disbound in the early twentieth century and redistributed among his papers in chronological order. Given the state of the documents, the editors of the ongoing edition of Jefferson's papers have concluded that it is impossible to reconstitute what he originally gathered together as a distinct unit. Consequently, they present his notes individually with the rest of his papers in chronological order. Exercising little caution, previous editors have included many documents Jefferson did not intend to be part of the three volumes bound in marbled paper; overly cautious, the editors of the Jefferson papers have eliminated *The Anas* as a distinct work.[3]

They go too far. Though it is impossible to reconstitute the precise contents of those three volumes, to ignore a carefully crafted three-volume work documenting Washington's administration is to ignore an important part of Jefferson's literary life. Despite the editorial vagaries, despite the fact that its title is not even Jefferson's, *The Anas* deserves consideration as a whole.

Jefferson was aware of the literary tradition of anas, which extended back at least as far as Athenaeus's *Dipnosophistarum*, a delightful collection of table talk from ancient times covering a variety of subjects including law, literature, medicine, and philosophy. Before he gave those loose scraps a calm revisal, Jefferson obtained a copy of Natale Conti's sixteenth-century-edition Athenaeus—Benjamin Franklin's old copy, no less. In the seventeenth century, both English and French authors began compiling collections of table talk. Jefferson also had in his library a six-volume folio edition of John Selden's *Opera Omnia*, which included *Table-Talk*, a collection of anas Samuel Johnson found superior to its French rivals.[4] Instead of chronologically organizing his work, Selden arranged *Table-Talk* by subject. Jefferson, on the other hand, understood that a chronological organization would contribute significantly to his own work's historical and literary importance.

Dated August 13, 1791, the first item in *The Anas* is titled "Notes of a Conversation between A. Hamilton and Th:J." According to this item, Jefferson mentioned to Alexander Hamilton a letter from John Adams disavowing authorship of the Publicola essays and denying a desire to make either the presidency or the senate hereditary. As part of this initial entry, he recorded Hamilton's response. Jefferson began writing down the response by paraphrasing what Hamilton said. Partway through the entry, however, Jefferson switched to direct discourse, placing Hamilton's words within quotation marks. Jefferson's use of a direct quotation in this instance is rare in his recordings of firsthand conversations in *The Anas*.

"I own it is my own opinion," Hamilton said, "tho' I do not publish it in Dan and Bersheba, that the present government is not that which will answer the ends of society, by giving stability and protection to its rights, and that it will probably be found expedient to go into the British form. However, since we have undertaken the experiment," he continued, "I am for giving it a fair course, whatever my expectations may be. The success indeed so far is greater than I had expected, and therefore at present success seems more possible than it had done heretofore, and there are still other and other stages of improvement which, if the present does not succeed, may be tried and ought to be tried before we give up the republican form altogether."[5]

Though Jefferson enclosed Hamilton's words in quotation marks, he still qualified them, noting beforehand that the remarks he transcribed were substantially Hamilton's. After the quotation, Jefferson reiterated: "This is the substance of a declaration made in much more lengthy terms, and which seemed to be more formal than usual for a conversation between two, and as if intended to qualify some less guarded expressions which had been dropped on former occasions." Jefferson closed with a statement regarding where and when he made this entry: "Th:J has committed it to writing in the moment of A. H.'s leaving the room."[6]

This final comment reflects Jefferson's penchant for precision. Realizing the inherent possibilities for error when recording speech, he made sure to acknowledge the fact. By emphasizing the quotation's immediacy, he stressed its accuracy. Of all remembered quotations, those transcribed directly after they occurred are more likely to be accurate than those transcribed after the passage of time.

The diction Jefferson used within the quotation is unusual enough to suggest that he was trying to capture Hamilton's phraseology. Unlike the paraphrases Jefferson made in his legal commonplace book, his entries in *The Anas* include many colorful expressions and figures of speech. In this first entry, he has Hamilton applying the proverbial phrase, "from Dan to Beersheba." Making reference to the northernmost and southernmost places in Judea, this traditional saying is typically used to indicate something that is done to the farthest extent possible.

If he were simply trying to capture the gist of Hamilton's remarks, Jefferson need not have included this colorful saying. Clearly, he was doing something more than merely recording the substance of Hamilton's remarks. He was also attempting to capture the flavor of what Hamilton said. His inclusion of this particular phrase also enhances the literary quality of *The Anas*. Not only does it give *The Anas* a greater geographical resonance, but it also echoes important works of English literature. "From Dan to Beersheba" was a favorite saying of Laurence Sterne, who used it in both *A Sentimental Journey through France and Italy* and *Tristram Shandy*.[7]

Jefferson had had numerous conversations with Hamilton and other members of Washington's administration prior to August 13. Why hadn't he recorded any of these earlier discussions? For example, why hadn't he noted the after-dinner conversation he had with Adams and Hamilton in April, the conversation that initiated his split with Hamilton? What was it about this August conversation that compelled Jefferson to get it down on paper and to initiate the series of notes that would become *The Anas*?

Based on internal evidence within *The Anas*, Hamilton's remarks on this occasion were noteworthy because of their contradictory nature and their strange tone. Speaking formally in support of the current government, Hamilton seemed to be refuting earlier informal comments he had made against the government. Jefferson had long since retired from the practice of law, but he retained his lawyer's mind. Getting Hamilton's words down on paper, he created a written record he could compare with less guarded remarks Hamilton might make in the future.

Much as he began taking notes about wildflowers before he turned them into his *Garden Book*, Jefferson began taking conversation notes before he conceived them as a unified collection. Four months separate this first entry from the next in *The Anas*. When he recorded the August 13 conversation with Hamilton, he apparently had not considered it as the first entry in a series of anas. Instead, it was simply an isolated conversation recorded on a scrap of paper. After the second one, dated December 25, 1791, the entries grow more frequent. Though quite different from the first, this second entry gave Jefferson a better idea of the work as a whole.

This entry records another contemporary conversation, not one he personally had but one he had heard about secondhand, a conversation between Alexander Hamilton and Senator James Gunn of Georgia. They had been talking about Rufus King of New York. King's erratic voting record provided Gunn with numerous instances to illustrate his legislative vagaries. For example, Gunn mentioned to Hamilton the recent bill to reapportion congressional representation in accordance with the 1790 census. Though Jefferson heard about this conversation secondhand, he recorded it using direct discourse.

The use of direct discourse often lends a narrative a greater sense of immediacy. But in this instance and elsewhere in *The Anas*, Jefferson used direct discourse when reporting conversations mediated by others. In this case, he heard about the conversation between Gunn and Hamilton from an acquaintance of Gunn's, not from Gunn himself. Following his source, who was ostensibly repeating what Gunn and Hamilton had said, Jefferson placed their words in quotation marks and included tag clauses to clarify who said what. Like the first episode in *The Anas*, Jefferson also recorded how he learned of this conversation.[8]

"I wish Sir you would advise your friend King, to observe some kind of consistency in his votes," Gunn told Hamilton. "There has been scarcely a question before Senate on which he has not voted both ways. On the Representation bill, for instance, he first voted for the proposition of the Representatives, and ultimately voted against it."

"Why," Hamilton replied, "I'll tell you as to that Colo. Gunn, that it never was intended that bill should pass."

Juxtaposing the account of his August conversation with Hamilton and the December conversation between Gunn and Hamilton, Jefferson applied an innovative method of editing, which he would continue to use throughout *The Anas*. The way he presents his material anticipates montage, a discursive practice that would not be defined or codified into theory for another century. As it has since been practiced, montage occurs when two texts are placed together, and their juxtaposition creates a new concept.[9] The first two episodes in *The Anas* function in this manner. The initial episode records a private comment Hamilton made that nevertheless has the quality of a formal declaration, a comment supporting the kind of representative government the United States exemplified. The second episode records what Hamilton said to someone else on a separate occasion. This comment undermines the notions of representative government and thus contradicts what Hamilton had said earlier.

Together, the two episodes create a picture of Hamilton more complex than that presented by either individual episode. Hamilton emerges from *The Anas* as a duplicitous figure, one who says one thing to Jefferson and something else to Senator Gunn. Using montage to create this image of Hamilton, Jefferson avoided partisan editorializing and simply allowed the concept of Hamilton to emerge within the minds of his readers through his juxtaposition of the two episodes.

The third episode in *The Anas* is a lengthy one that records conversations that occurred between Jefferson and President Washington on the last two days of February 1792, a leap year. These conversations concerned Jefferson's plan for doubling the velocity of post riders and his general ideas for putting the American government on a solid footing before the end of Washington's first term, at which time Jefferson planned to retire.

On the afternoon of the twenty-eighth, Washington did not have time to discuss these issues at length, so he invited Jefferson back the next morning. Jefferson returned after breakfast, and the two engaged in a lengthy discussion. Washington coaxed him into remaining secretary of state a little longer. For this lengthy anecdote, Jefferson used indirect discourse instead of quoting either himself or Washington. He ended the entry by commenting that the conversation "is here stated nearly as much at length as it really was, the expressions preserved where I could recollect them, and their substance always faithfully stated."[10]

In *The Anas*, this entry is dated March 1, 1792, the day after the conversation at Washington's home concluded. The next three entries are dated from January, but the one after the last of these three is dated March 7, which begins, "The subject resumed" and refers to the same subject the three January entries discuss. Though Jefferson organized *The Anas* chronologically, he was not so committed to his organization that he never deviated from it. In this case, he understood that it would be better to group these four entries together instead of placing the three brief January entries before his February conversations with Washington

and the March 7 entry afterward.[11] The deviation from strict chronological order further reinforces the care Jefferson took in effectively
organizing his materials.

Wherever he could, Jefferson tried to capture the tenor of each conversation he recorded, as two separate entries from March 11, 1792,
clarify. The first records a conversation between Jefferson and Washington concerning a possible treaty with Algiers. A senate committee
consisting of Ralph Izard, Rufus King, and Robert Morris wished to
consult with President Washington regarding the necessity of applying
to the House of Representatives for funds to negotiate the treaty. Washington sought Jefferson's opinion before speaking with the committee.

Jefferson recorded what Washington asked and how he responded.
The most intriguing aspect of their conversation concerns how Washington learned of the committee's concerns: Izard rudely informed him
at a dinner party. Washington described Izard's indecorous behavior to
Jefferson, who made sure to get the episode down:

> Mr. Izard made the communication to him setting next to him at table
> on one hand, while a lady (Mrs. Mclane) was on his other hand and the
> Fr. minister next to her, and as Mr. Izard got on with his communi-
> cation, his voice kept rising, and his stutter bolting the words out
> loudly at intervals, so that the minister might hear if he would. He
> [Washington] said he had a great mind at one time to have got up in
> order to put a stop to Mr. Izard.[12]

Directly after this entry but separated from it with a horizontal rule,
Jefferson recorded a second entry of the same date: "Mr. Sterret tells me
that sitting round a fire the other day with 4 or 5. others of Mr. Smith (of
S. C.) was one, some body mentioned that the murderers of Hogeboom,
sheriff of Columbia county, N. York, were acquitted. 'Aye,' says Smith,
'This is what comes of your damned *trial by jury*.'"[13]

Jefferson's record of this exchange is fascinating. He phrased the
words of his immediate source—Samuel Sterett—as indirect discourse,
but he presented the words of William Loughton Smith, a congressman
from South Carolina, as direct discourse. In this instance, Jefferson found
it crucial to get Smith's words down precisely, expletive and all. The
phrase "trial by jury" was one of the most revered phrases in Jefferson's
vocabulary. Two years earlier he told Thomas Paine that he considered
trial by jury as "the only anchor ever yet imagined by man, by which a
government can be held to the principles of its constitution." He maintained this belief throughout his life. Three decades later, he informed a

correspondent, "Trial by jury is the best of all safeguards for the person, the property, and the fame of every individual."[14]

This entry in *The Anas* refers to the brutal slaying of Sheriff Cornelius Hogeboom. While serving a writ, Hogeboom was shot to death in October 1791. Those tried for his murder were acquitted of all charges. The acquittal disturbed many people, but Smith's startling response to the verdict disturbed Jefferson even more so. He refrained from editorializing in *The Anas*, letting the quotation from Smith speak for itself. Jefferson's straightforward record of the incident nonetheless registers his shock.

He also noted the setting of this conversation, which not only enhances the drama, but also provides an interpretive frame through which to understand the context of Smith's remark. Occurring within a small group of men seated around a fire, the conversation took place at a casual time, a time when men were less guarded than they were during more formal occasions. With a bottle going round, perhaps, tongues loosened and true feelings emerged.

This entry also reflects Jefferson's growing sense of purpose as he compiled *The Anas*. Upon its completion, *The Anas* not only would be a lively record of Washington's administration, but also would form a set of comments reflecting the varying beliefs of many people involved with the establishment of the U.S. government and, more generally, involved in the experiment of American democracy.

Restricted as it is to conversations that occurred among those in government, *The Anas* reveals little about Jefferson's daily life. For example, it does not mention that in April 1793—the month he turned fifty—his domestic arrangements in Philadelphia changed significantly. He moved from the townhouse he had been renting on Market Street to a three-room cottage on the east bank of the Schuylkill River near Gray's Ferry. Considerably smaller than his townhouse, the cottage had no room for his excess furniture and books, which he sent back to Monticello. The cottage was a kind of halfway house between the center of Philadelphia and the top of Monticello. Though Jefferson wanted to retire from public life, the keen responsibility he felt toward his nation and its president prevented him from retiring as soon as he wished. The Schuylkill cottage let him enjoy the countryside while fulfilling his duties as secretary of state.

Jefferson's description of the cottage and its grounds in letters to his daughter Martha make it seem idyllic. Her sister Maria, who was attending a Philadelphia boarding school, visited often. "She passes two or three days in the week with me, under the trees, for I never go into the house but at the hour of bed," Jefferson told Martha. "I never before knew the full value of trees," he continued. "My house is entirely embosomed in high plane trees, with good grass below, and under them I breakfast, dine, write, read and receive my company. What would I not give that the trees planted nearest round the house at Monticello were full grown."[15]

When the weather was sunny, Maria enjoyed sauntering along the banks of the Schuylkill. Across the river, she and her father could see Bartram's Gardens and Gray's Gardens, too. On rainy days, the two stayed indoors catching up their correspondence.[16]

Within the family, Maria's difficulty writing letters was notorious. Describing one particular day at the cottage in a letter to Martha, Jefferson captured a delightful moment as Maria tried writing a letter to her brother-in-law: "Maria's brain is hard at work to squeeze out a letter for Mr. Randolph. She has been scribbling and rubbing out these three hours, and this moment exclaimed 'I do not think I shall get a letter made out to-day.'"[17] With great charm, Jefferson used direct discourse to capture his daughter's mood. Why didn't he use direct discourse more often in *The Anas*? Recording the conversations of his nation's leaders, it seems, he held himself to a higher standard. He hesitated to put words in the mouths of others when he could indirectly convey what they said.

One of the most unusual entries in *The Anas* reports a conversation about Philip Freneau between Washington and Jefferson that occurred on May 23, 1793. Two years earlier, poet and essayist Freneau had turned to journalism and briefly edited the *New York Daily Advertiser*. When Jefferson became secretary of state, he offered Freneau the post of translating clerk for the state department. Freneau accepted the position and relocated to Philadelphia, where he established the *National Gazette* with Jefferson's approval. Freneau's purpose was to counter the Federalist tendencies of John Fenno's *Gazette of the United States*. Like Jefferson, Freneau saw the federal government backsliding to aristocratic English ways and filled his paper with harsh invective against the prevailing governmental policies.[18]

In the May 23 conversation Jefferson recorded, Washington expressed his displeasure with an article that had appeared in the *National Gazette* the previous day. Furthermore, Washington made some general comments about the negative tenor of all of Freneau's articles and implied that Jefferson should do something to censure Freneau. Jefferson wrote:

He was evidently sore and warm, and I took his intention to be that I should interpose in some way with Freneau, perhaps withdraw his appointment of translating clerk to my office, but I will not do it: his paper has saved our constitution which was galloping fast into monarchy, and has been checked by no one means so powerfully as by that paper. It is well and universally known that it has been that paper which has checked the career of the Monocrats, and the President, not sensible of the designs of the party, has not with his usual good sense, and sang froid, looked on the efforts and effects of this free press, and seen that tho some bad things had passed thro' it to the public, yet the good had preponderated immensely.[19]

The Anas does not mention which article in Freneau's paper provoked Washington's ire this May, but Jefferson's editors conjecture that it was an article applauding Philadelphians for their enthusiastic reception of Edmund Charles Genet, the new French minister to the United States.

At war with other European nations, including Great Britain and Spain, France wanted the support of its longtime ally, the United States. Genet was appointed to secure American support by renegotiating the 1778 treaty between the two nations. Genet was further instructed to outfit privateers to attack British and Spanish vessels and also to plan expeditions against Florida and Louisiana, both Spanish possessions.

Hamilton strongly opposed Genet's reception. Washington cordially received him but issued a proclamation of neutrality, refusing to take sides in the European conflict. Jefferson welcomed him initially, but Genet quickly wore out his welcome. Starting from Charleston, South Carolina, he stirred up support for the French cause at the grassroots level, convincing many Americans that the cause of France was theirs, too—the cause of freedom.

The enthusiasm Genet expressed for André Michaux's planned expedition across the continent pleased Jefferson at first. Since coming to America in 1785, Michaux had traveled the East Coast extensively. In 1792, he approached the American Philosophical Society with a plan to cross the continent. Long an advocate for Western exploration, Jefferson took the responsibility for raising funds to support Michaux's scientific excursion. To that end he actively solicited subscribers among Society members and other interested parties. Once Jefferson had enough subscribers to support the expedition, he gave Michaux a set of instructions prepared by himself on behalf of the American Philosophical Society.

These instructions anticipate subsequent ones he would write for the Lewis and Clark expedition. Jefferson told Michaux to find the shortest and most convenient route to the Pacific, to concentrate on following the Missouri River and its tributaries, to note "the country you pass through, its general face, soil, rivers, mountains, its productions animal, vegetable, and mineral so far as they may be new to us and may also be useful or very curious," and to record the culture of the native inhabitants.[20]

Echoing advice he had given John Ledyard earlier, Jefferson recommended that Michaux tattoo the most important observations on his skin. Other information could be recorded on birch bark for safekeeping. "When you shall have reached the Pacific ocean," Jefferson continued, "if you find yourself within convenient distance of any settlement of Europeans, go to them, commit to writing a narrative of your journey and observations and take the best measures you can for conveying it by duplicates or triplicates thence to the society by sea." The preservation of new information should be the utmost goal: "It is strongly rec.mmended to you to expose yourself in no case to unnecessary dangers, whether such as might affect your health or your personal safety: and to consider this not merely as your personal concern, but as the injunction of Science in general which expects its enlargement from your enquiries, and of the inhabitants of the US. in particular, to whom your Report will open new feilds and subjects of Commerce, Intercourse, and Observation."[21]

Doing what he could to encourage Michaux's expedition, Genet approached Jefferson in June and asked him to write a letter of recommendation to Isaac Shelby, the governor of Kentucky. Jefferson complied, informing Governor Shelby of Michaux's expedition and applauding him as "a man of science and merit" who "goes to Kentuckey in pursuit of objects of Natural history and botany, to augment the literary acquirements of the two republicks."[22]

Within *The Anas*, Genet makes his first appearance on July 5, 1793, when he called on Jefferson to inform him of the alternate instructions he had prepared for Michaux. Genet's instructions were all written out, and he read them to Jefferson very quickly. What Jefferson heard came as a shock: Genet had singlehandedly transmogrified the scientific expedition sponsored by the American Philosophical Society into a military expedition. Genet's instructions to Michaux included addresses to be delivered to the inhabitants of Louisiana and Canada encouraging them to rise up against their Spanish and British governors. Furthermore, Genet had arranged with American military leaders in Kentucky to capture New Orleans on behalf of the French government.

According to Genet's plan, two particular generals would form battalions of men recruited from Kentucky and Louisiana and bolster their ranks with whatever Indians they could recruit. Once they captured New Orleans, they would establish Louisiana as an independent state connected in commerce with France and the United States. Closing his remarks, Genet told Jefferson that he was communicating his message to him as a private citizen, not as secretary of state.

Seldom in *The Anas* did Jefferson record what he himself said in conversation, but in this instance he recorded his disapproval. Jefferson phrased his own response as indirect discourse, but reading *The Anas*, you can almost hear him talking: "I told him that his enticing officers and souldiers from Kentuckey to go against Spain, was really putting a halter about their necks, for that they would assuredly be hung, if they commenced hostilities against a nation at peace with the US."[23]

When Genet had approached him the previous month to write a letter of recommendation Michaux could present to Governor Shelby, it apparently had not occurred to Jefferson to record the incident. To him, Michaux's expedition was a purely scientific venture. It was a matter for the American Philosophical Society, not the American government. Now recognizing Genet's ulterior motives, he realized that Michaux's expedition was indeed pertinent to American diplomacy. He hastily filled in his previous encounter with Genet concerning Michaux's expedition.

Having informed Jefferson of Michaux's extrascientific mission, Genet asked him if he would revise his letter of recommendation to Governor Shelby in order to identify Michaux as something more than "a person of botanical and natural pursuits." Instead, Genet wished Jefferson's letters to depict Michaux as a French citizen "possessing his confidence." Without agreeing to the mission Genet planned for Michaux, Jefferson agreed to rewrite the letter.

Against Washington's policy of neutrality, Genet also began outfitting privateers to harass British vessels. When he outfitted a captured British ship as a privateer to sail against the British in July, Genet went too far. Washington asked Jefferson to draft a letter to Gouverneur Morris, the current American minister to France, asking for Genet's recall. Washington then called a meeting of his cabinet to discuss the letter Jefferson drafted.

They met on Tuesday, August 20, 1793, and Jefferson detailed the meeting in *The Anas*. The level of consensus among them was extraordinary. The president and all the members of the cabinet agreed with the reasons for Genet's recall that Jefferson outlined in the letter, which is considered one of his most accomplished diplomatic papers.[24] Hamilton did take issue with one particular phrase, which happened to be Jefferson's favorite phrase in the whole letter. In his draft, Jefferson suggested that Genet's actions were leading to a rift between France and the United States. A conflict between these two republics, Jefferson wrote, would present the spectacle of *"liberty warring on herself."*[25]

Hamilton moved to strike out the phrase. He argued that Great Britain and its allies would take offense with the statement and questioned whether the cause of France was really the cause of liberty. Regardless, it was not up to the United States to declare what the cause of France really was. Despite their difference of opinion, Jefferson gave Hamilton's argument a fair amount of space in *The Anas*. The same cannot be said for his depiction of Henry Knox's reaction to Hamilton's position: "Knox according to custom jumped plump into all his opinions."[26]

Washington sided with Jefferson. "With a good deal of positiveness," Washington "declared in favor of the expression, that he considered the pursuit of France to be that of liberty, however they might sometimes fail of the best means of obtaining it, that he had never at any time entertained a doubt of their ultimate success, if they hung well together, and that as to their dissensions there were such contradictory accounts given that no one could tell what to believe."[27]

Suspecting the phrase might generate dissension within the cabinet, Jefferson had an elaborate counterargument planned. One of Jefferson's reasons for including this particular phrase was literary. So far, his role as secretary of state had severely limited his writing abilities. In his official correspondence, he had "avoided the insertion of a single term of friendship to the French nation." As a result, the official letters "were as dry and husky as if written between the generals of two enemy nations." Furthermore, the phrase about liberty warring on herself would clarify that the U.S. complaint was against Genet, not against France. As he argued during this meeting and recorded in *The Anas*, Jefferson "thought it essential to satisfy the French and our own citizens of the light in which we viewed their cause, and of our fellow feeling for the general cause of liberty." Furthermore, this brief phrase was the only mention of liberty in the entire letter. Surely, the subject of the letter demanded at least one reference to liberty.[28]

Washington spoke again, declaring "his strong attachment to the expression" but leaving the matter to his cabinet to decide. Jefferson found himself on the short end of the stick. The sentence, he recorded, "was struck out, of course, and the expressions of affection in the context were a good deal taken down."[29]

The Anas concludes with the entry for December 1, 1793, thirty days before Jefferson's resignation as secretary of state took effect. In his final entry, Jefferson recorded something he had heard from his friend and supporter John Beckley, who was repeating what Tobias Lear had told him:

Langdon, Cabot, and some others of the Senate, standing in a knot before the fire after the Senate had adjourned, and growling together about some measure which they had just lost, "ah!" said Cabot, "things will never go right till you have a President for life and an hereditary Senate." Langdon told this to Lear, who mentioned it to the President. The President seemed struck with it, and declared he had not supposed there was a man in the US. who could have entertained such an idea.[30]

Washington's appearance in this closing episode is consistent with his character throughout *The Anas*. Whereas Jefferson is an advocate for the democratic principles embodied in the U.S. Constitution and Hamilton is an advocate of the British form of government, President Washington is the stabilizing force whose good nature prevents him from thinking ill of others. In *The Anas*, Washington's positive attitude and his level-headedness allow him to effectively mediate between Jefferson and Hamilton. Written to record what went on during Washington's administration and edited to refute Marshall's *Life of Washington*, *The Anas*, in terms of form, is a documentary record of the conversations that occurred during Jefferson's time as secretary of state. Like no other document before the emergence of modern recording equipment, it dramatizes what went on behind the scenes of an American presidency.

CHAPTER 29

Letters from a Virginia Farmer

Writing to Mann Page in the summer of 1795 to apologize for not joining him in Fredericksburg as they had planned, Jefferson began by listing excuses—"the heat of the weather, the business of the farm"—but he stopped short. Instead of providing any more specific reasons for his absence, he decided to supply a general excuse or, as he put it, "one round reason for all." He said, "I have laid up my Rosinante in his stall, before his unfitness for the road shall expose him faultering to the world."[1] Jefferson's "round reason" is both figurative and literary. The name Rosinante refers to Don Quixote's superannuated steed. Once again, Jefferson was casting himself in the role of Cervantes' hero. But no longer was he tilting at windmills: Thomas Jefferson was now Don Quixote in retirement.

The sentiments he expressed in this letter pervade his correspondence from his return to Monticello in early 1794 through the next three years. Four predominant themes recur in the personal letters he wrote during this period. They extol the pleasures of retirement, describe his enjoyment of the farmer's life, reinforce his dedication to reading and study, and celebrate his ignorance of current political intrigue. To an extent, each of these aspects is a literary pose, and sometimes these different poses contradict one another. But all the personae Jefferson assumed in his letters of the mid-1790s—retired gentleman, farmer, scholar, political naif—reflect the profound satisfaction he felt upon returning to Monticello, where he hoped to remain the rest of his days.

The Retired Gentleman

In many of the letters from this period, Jefferson told correspondents how happy he was to have retired from public life. To one, he asserted

Thomas Jefferson, from Life, 1796–1797, by James Sharples, Senior.
(Independence National Historical Park)

that nothing—neither politics nor private business—could lure him
from home again: "The length of my tether is now fixed for life from
Monticello to Richmond." In a letter to Edmund Rutledge, whose son
had recently visited Monticello, he recreated the son's experience for his
father: "He found me in a retirement I doat on, living like an Ante-
diluvian patriarch among my children and grand children, and tilling

my soil."[2] Jefferson's figurative comparison is not unusual for the eighteenth-century Virginia planter. A generation earlier, William Byrd II had made much the same comment to characterize his situation at Westover.

Using the plural "grandchildren," Jefferson revealed another recent development: the year after giving her father a granddaughter, Martha gave him a grandson and namesake. Thomas Jefferson Randolph had been born September 12, 1792. She ultimately delivered twelve children, with eleven surviving into adulthood. The Christian names of Thomas Jefferson Randolph's younger brothers read like a roster of his grandfather's best friends: Benjamin Franklin Randolph, George Wythe Randolph, James Madison Randolph, and Meriwether Lewis Randolph. Martha's daughters—Anne, Cornelia, Ellen, Mary, Septimia, and Virginia—would all become special objects of Thomas Jefferson's love. Some of his most delightful letters are those he wrote his granddaughters.

The oldest boy was known in the family as Jefferson, but his sisters often called him Jeff. He became his grandfather's pride and joy. When Martha was away from Monticello during the mid-1790s, she sometimes left Anne and Jeff with their grandfather, who frequently wrote to inform her of their well-being. His letters reflect his love for the children. Writing to Martha the winter following his grandson's third birthday, he explained, "They are both well, and have never had even a finger-ach since you left us. Jefferson is very robust"—"robust as a beef," according to a follow-up letter. "His hands are constantly like lumps of ice, yet he will not warm them. He has not worn his shoes an hour this winter. If put on him, he takes them off immediately and uses one to carry his nuts etc." As a solution to this dilemma, Grandpa decided to put both children in moccasins, "which being made of soft leather, fitting well and lacing up, they have never been able to take them off."[3] Thomas Jefferson was well known for his cool temper; he was pleased to see Anne's temper develop similarly. Jeff, on the other hand, had a fiery temper. Anne's grandfather hoped that her example would eventually mellow her brother's temper. It did.

Numerous letters reflect Thomas Jefferson's pleasure at retiring from public life. The one he wrote Pierre Auguste Adet is among the best. Adet became French minister to the United States in 1795, but his background was in the sciences. A virtuoso in chemistry, he had devised and published a new system of chemical nomenclature. Adet was like many of the French philosophes Jefferson befriended in Paris: while serving his country, he did what he could to make advances in the cause of science.

After assuming his ministerial post, Adet wrote Jefferson to initiate a scientific correspondence with him. In response, Jefferson regretted that Adet had not come to Philadelphia when he was still serving as secretary of state: "It would have been a circumstance of still higher satisfaction and advantage to me if fortune had timed the periods of our service together, so that the drudgery of public business, which I always hated, might have been relieved by conversations with you on subjects which I always loved, and particularly in learning from you the new advances of science on the other side the Atlantic." These comments reflect a slight twinge of regret at not being in Philadelphia, a great city for scientific and literary conversation. Still, Jefferson closed the letter by reinforcing the pleasures of Monticello: "My books, my family, my friends, and my farm, furnish more than enough to occupy me the remainder of my life."[4] Placing his books on the same level as family, friends, and farm, Jefferson showed how integral his library was to the idyllic life he planned to lead into the foreseeable future.

The Farmer

In many personal letters of the mid-1790s, Jefferson depicted his life at Monticello as that of a simple farmer. He celebrated the virtues of the soil. He detailed his agricultural schemes and experiments. And he proudly described the pleasures of overseeing his fields.

During his last year as secretary of state, he had prepared for his return to farming. He consulted Senator George Logan, whom Jefferson called the best farmer in Pennsylvania in terms of both theory and practice. Logan offered much good advice about what books belong in a proper agricultural library. Jefferson also spent time talking agriculture with George Washington. Since these conversations were outside the purpose of *The Anas*, Jefferson did not record what Washington said on the subject of farming, and these valuable discussions have been lost to history.

He also spoke with John Spurrier, an English farmer who had settled in Delaware. Upon his retirement, Jefferson took Spurrier's advice about growing horse beans, but they would not take to the soil at Monticello. Jefferson nonetheless appreciated Spurrier's advice on this and many other agricultural matters. Spurrier, in turn, appreciated Jefferson's attention. When he collected his lifetime of agricultural experience in a book titled *The Practical Farmer*, Spurrier dedicated it to Jefferson, whom he called "a promoter of every degree of useful knowledge" who set "an example worthy of imitation."[5]

Before retiring from the State Department and returning to Monticello, Jefferson tried to learn as much as he could about crop rotation. Senator Logan gave him more information on this subject than everyone else combined. The summer preceding his retirement, Jefferson devised an elaborate plan for rotating crops at Monticello and submitted it to Logan for his approval. Jefferson initiated his scheme in 1794, but he never stopped tinkering to improve it. Learning about John Beale Bordley's pamphlet, *Sketches on Rotations of Crops*, the following winter, he asked James Madison to find a copy for him. Madison located the book and sent it to Monticello. Jefferson's new agricultural collection was growing quickly. By the time he was through, he would possess the greatest agricultural library in the nation.

Eighteenth-century agricultural writers clashed when it came to the matter of experience. Those like Spurrier, who incorporated the word "practical" into the titles of their works, emphasized the importance of agricultural experience and differentiated themselves from authors who treated agriculture solely on theoretical principles. Applauding Logan for his agricultural theory *and* practice, Jefferson suggested that both were necessary to the farmer, an idea his own behavior confirms. He formulated agricultural theories, put them into practice, sought additional information through conversation and reading, and modified his practice according to his experience in the field and the ideas of others.

The Duc de La Rochefoucauld Liancourt, an old friend from his Paris days who visited Monticello in 1796, highly approved Jefferson's dual approach to agriculture: "Much good may be expected, if a contemplative mind, like that of Mr. Jefferson, which takes the theory for its guide, watches its application with discernment, and rectifies it according to the peculiar circumstances and natures of the country, climate and soil, and conformably to the experience which he daily acquires."[6] In his letters, Jefferson depicted himself as an amateur when it came to agricultural endeavors, but his meticulousness belies the amateurish pose he struck.

Perhaps the most delightful letters that take farming as their subject are those that speak in more general terms instead of those that discuss specific agricultural practices. In 1795, William Branch Giles, a Virginia congressman who tirelessly battled the Federalist policies of Alexander Hamilton and John Adams, received a delightful invitation from the former secretary of state. Inviting Giles to Monticello, Jefferson cautioned him against talking politics. He wrote: "If you visit me as a farmer, it must be as a condisciple: for I am but a learner; an eager one indeed, but yet desperate, being too old now to learn a new art. However, I am as much delighted and occupied with it, as if I was the greatest adept. I shall talk with you about it from morning till night, and put you on very short allowance as to political aliment. Now and then a pious speculation for the French and Dutch republicans, returning with due dispatch to clover, potatoes, wheat, etc."[7]

Stressing the joys of the farmer's life, Jefferson painted an idyllic picture designed to make his correspondents in the political world wince with jealousy. In a letter to Madison one April, he engaged his friend's senses of taste, smell, sight, and sound: "Asparagus is just come to table. The Lilac in blossom, and the first Whip-poor-will heard last night."[8] This passage presents a beautiful picture of rural harmony. It does contain a fib, however. According to Jefferson's *Garden Book*, the asparagus had come up the week before; it would not come to the table until the following week. In his imagination, he hurried the asparagus along to create for Madison a more alluring picture of the natural fecundity of Monticello.

Jefferson's love of books was well known to his correspondents, but in his letters from the mid-1790s he sometimes downplayed his scholarly activities and literary pursuits in favor of his agricultural activities. He wrote John Adams, "I return to farming with an ardour which I scarcely knew in my youth, and which has got the better entirely of my love of study. Instead of writing 10. or 12. letters a day, which I have been in the habit of doing as a thing of course, I put off answering my letters now, farmer-like, till a rainy day, and then find it sometimes postponed by other necessary occupations."[9] Few of his correspondents understood Jefferson's love of study more than Adams, who naturally recognized his friend's farmerlike pose and knew full well that few activities could distract him from the pen and the book. Telling Adams that he was neglecting his literary work, Jefferson was writing to someone who knew that he would never neglect his studies given half a chance to pursue them.

The Scholar

When he was not in the field tending his crops, Jefferson could be found indoors setting his library to rights. It had been years since he had had time to organize his books, and the library was in rough shape. Much as his fields had suffered from years of neglect, so, too, had his library. A large box of books he had ordered from Froullé two years earlier had only just arrived in February 1794 after bouncing around "from port to port in America by various mistakes."[10] Upon opening the crate, Jefferson was shocked by what he saw. Most of the books were damp and mildewed, and some were already rotten.

He realized what had gone wrong and wrote Froullé to explain the situation: "It happened unfortunately that being shipped from Havre in the winter, the books, as always happens in a winter passage, had been much wetted, and lying wet in America for a twelvemonth before they were opened, were some of them completely rotted. In this way the volumes of plates to the Encyclopedie suffered more than any others, because being larger than the rest, they were laid in the top of the box, and received the first and greatest effect of the salt water."[11] To prevent subsequent shipments from similar damage, Jefferson insisted that all books be packed in a good solid trunk and covered with sealskin.

During his tenure as secretary of state, he had brought a good portion of his library to Philadelphia. When he relocated to his small Schuylkill cottage, he returned many books to Monticello. Upon vacating the cottage, he sent home the remaining books. Still, some of his books stayed in Philadelphia, those he had loaned to friends who had not returned them. Jefferson's experience was not dissimilar to that of Benjamin Franklin, who joked "that a man lost 10 per cent. on the *value*, by lending his books."[12] Anxious to get his entire library back together, Jefferson asked a friend and neighbor who was going to Philadelphia to retrieve what books he had lent to others.

Jefferson solicited Madison's help in this matter, too, asking him to collect some of the books that had gone astray. Edmund Randolph, who had taken over as secretary of state upon Jefferson's retirement, had borrowed books in such diverse fields as agriculture, geology, history, law, and philosophy. The books Randolph had borrowed included a standard agricultural treatise Jefferson sorely needed in his role as farmer: Jethro Tull's *Horse-Hoeing Husbandry*. Randolph was embarrassed upon receiving Jefferson's request for the return of this volume: he could not find the book anywhere. He ended up buying Jefferson a replacement copy of Jethro Tull.

Few contemporary comments survive to show what Jefferson was doing in the mid-1790s to organize his library, but a remark he made two decades later suggests that he was thoroughly working his way through the entire collection, systematically putting his books in order.[13] Generally speaking, each case contained three shelves, and he stacked three cases atop one another to make standing cases nine feet tall. He carefully arranged his books according to the system of organization he had established in 1783, pasting labels listing the shelf number of each volume onto the spine.

Once he had a handle on his collection and restored a degree of order to his books, Jefferson realized that his law library contained several unnecessary duplicates. Most came from the libraries of John Wayles and Peyton Randolph and mainly consisted of reports of cases in equity and common pleas. He also had a duplicate of that great classic of English law, *Coke upon Littleton*. With shelf space at a premium, he decided to hold a sale. He compiled a list of law books he wished to sell, cross-checked this list with John Worrall's *Bibliotheca Legum*, and composed a newspaper advertisement. Neither the list nor the advertising copy survives, but his correspondence shows that he was selling his extra copy of *Coke upon Littleton*. With the 1639 fourth edition of *Coke upon Littleton* in his library, he found Francis Hargrave's modern edition unnecessary.

Jefferson never did publish his advertisement or hold a public sale of these books, but he wrote friends to let them know what he had to sell. Archibald Stuart, who had read law with Jefferson, was one person who needed books and would put them to good use. Jefferson sent Stuart a copy of the advertisement he had drafted and let him know that he could have whatever books he desired from the list and pay for them whenever he wished. Stuart accepted the offer and acquired several law books from his mentor, mostly reports of cases.[14]

Jefferson was paring down his library, but this did not mean that he planned to stop buying books. Still suffering from bibliomanie, he sent a long list of desired titles to Froullé with special instructions. His requests indicate his wide-ranging interests and depth of learning. Having acquired the first two volumes of Christian Gottfried Shütz's edition of Aeschylus at Strassbourg, he asked Froullé for the third in order to complete the set.

He also requested from Froullé a copy of the *Geoponica*, which shows how deep his interest in agricultural books went. Known in a Greek and Latin text dating from the tenth century, the roots of this early treatise on farming went back several centuries further. As Jefferson explained, the *Geoponica* "gives the state of Agriculture in Greece in the time of Constantine Porphyrogeneta to whom it has been ascribed. The age and country make it curious."[15] Froullé came through, locating a good edition of the work. Jefferson later acquired other editions of the *Geoponica*.

Though he wished to limit himself to Monticello and the surrounding region the rest of his days, Jefferson did not plan to limit his mind or his imagination. Content to stay in the Virginia Piedmont, he remained ever curious about the world at large. Books gave him a way to gratify his curiosity. His correspondence of the mid-1790s indicates that he was broadening his knowledge of the Orient. He asked Froullé for a copy of *The Fables of Pilpay*, a collection of ancient Hindu fables derived from the Sanskrit *Pantchatantra*. But he did not want just any edition. He asked Froullé specifically for the Greek edition published in Berlin. The request he sent Froullé lists other works pertaining to the Orient: Sharaf al-Din 'Ali's four-volume *Histoire de Timur-Bec*; *Instituts Politiques et Militaire de Tamerlan*, the French translation of Abu Talib al-Husayni's Persian edition of the *Tuzukat*; and François Pétis's *Histoire du Grand Genghizcan*. Apparently, Jefferson had not finished organizing his library when he placed this order. He already had a copy of the same edition of Pétis's life of Genghis Khan. He later gave his extra copy to his granddaughter Cornelia to help her learn French.[16]

In his instructions, Jefferson told Froullé that James Monroe would collect the books from him and pay for them. When he was serving as minister to France, Jefferson had purchased books for numerous friends, including Monroe. Now that Monroe had taken over Jefferson's former position as minister plenipotentiary to France, he took the responsibility of carrying out Jefferson's requests. Books were not the only items Jefferson wanted from Europe. He asked Monroe to send him twenty or thirty pounds of macaroni, too.[17]

During the mid-1790s, Jefferson received several books as gifts. From Paris, William Short sent him a copy of the octavo edition of *Don Quixote* published in Madrid and sponsored by the Real Academia Española. Short's gift was a sensitive one showing how well he knew his friend: the Academia edition of *Don Quixote* was better known in a lavish quarto format, but Short chose the handier octavo. Though smaller in size, the octavo *Don Quixote*, Short assured Jefferson, contained the identical text as the quarto.

Through John Adams, Jean Jacques Cart presented Jefferson a copy of his *Lettres...sur le Droit Public de ce Pays et sur les Événemens Actuels*, a work that told a poignant tale of political oppression. Since the canton of Vaud had come under the control of the City of Berne in the sixteenth century, Berne had gradually oppressed the inhabitants of Vaud, effectively turning them into second-class citizens. They were deprived of the basic civil and political rights that citizens of Berne retained. Furthermore, Berne persecuted any inhabitants of Vaud who sympathized with the French Revolution.[18] Cart's moving series of letters impressed many of the day's foremost thinkers. Hegel translated them into German to inform his countrymen of Berne's misrule. Cart's *Lettres* convinced Adams of Berne's tyrannical rule, too. On Adams's recommendation, Jefferson read the book, which also convinced him of the injustice the inhabitants of Vaud suffered. Ever the American patriot, Jefferson told Adams that Cart and the inhabitants of Vaud should follow the example of the United States.[19]

In 1795, George Wythe presented his former student with a copy of the reports of Virginia legal cases he had compiled, *Decisions of Cases in Virginia, by the High Court of Chancery*. Thanking Wythe for the volume, Jefferson wrote, "I shall read it with great pleasure and profit, and I needed something the reading of which would refresh my law-memory."[20] This exchange initiated a series of letters about books that culminated in their collaboration on a major scholarly, yet public-minded project.

Both Jefferson and Wythe encouraged one another to continue pursuing the study of ancient languages. In October 1794, Jefferson sent his former teacher a copy of a linguistic work by Ludolf Kuster, *De Vero Usu Verborum Mediorum apud Grecos*. In the cover letter accompanying this book, Jefferson wrote, "I inclose for your perusal a little treatise by Kuster on the use of the Middle voice in Greek. I never saw a copy of it till I met with this, nor had ever heard of it. I presume therefore it may be new to you; and if it gives you half the pleasure it did me, mine will be doubled still. His position is that the middle voice is always intransitive, and is never confounded with either the active or passive in its signification. According to my own observation, since his work suggested the idea, I have found it almost always true, but I think not absolutely always." Though the two had been peers for what seemed like ages now, Jefferson still liked to show off his linguistic knowledge for his former teacher. He closed the letter by inviting Wythe to Monticello, where he hoped to gratify his taste for books by introducing him to "a collection now certainly the best in America."[21] Jefferson had room to boast. His library was the finest private library in the nation by now, superior even to the one left by Benjamin Franklin.

Busy with legal work, Wythe, nearing seventy, had little time to spare for classical Greek linguistics. Neither did he have the time to visit Monticello. Regrettably, he returned the book unread: "You send Kuster for my perusal. I can peruse nothing but court papers. This employment by habit is become delectable. In it I regret only that I cannot participate [in] the elegant entertainment to which Monticello invites. I return the book, supposing you to possess but one copy, lest by detaining it I should deprive you of a pleasure I am forbidden to enjoy; which, with Aesops leave, would be more than brutish."[22] Ending his letter with a moral reminiscent of Aesop's *Fables*, Wythe couched his refusal with reference to one of Jefferson favorite works.

Wythe did approach Jefferson to ask his help to compile a complete set of Virginia laws and statutes. He knew no one more qualified. Jefferson now possessed the fullest collection of Virginia law books in print and manuscript ever assembled, and he was happy to help, but he apologized because his collection of laws and statutes was in a chaotic state. Much work was necessary to get then into a usable order. He did not have time to copy law himself, but he was hoping to hire a young man from Charlottesville for the task. The excuse he offered is characteristic of his letters from the mid-1790s: "I am become too lazy, with the pen, and too much attached to the plough to do it myself. I live on my horse from an early breakfast to a late dinner, and very often after that till dark. This occasions me to be in great arrears in my pen-work."[23]

After the Virginia Assembly passed a bill calling for a printed collection of state laws, Wythe informed Jefferson that the legislators desperately needed his help. He personally guaranteed Jefferson that if he loaned his collection of Virginia laws to the state that they would be returned in good condition. Unable to refuse his old teacher or, for that matter, unable to resist Virginia when it needed him, Jefferson agreed. He boxed up his law books and sent them to the binder, who bound the collection and then forwarded it to Wythe. Jefferson's personal collection would eventually form the basis for William Hening's *Statutes at Large*, the standard edition of Virginia laws.

The Political Naif

Throughout his correspondence of the mid-1790s, Jefferson celebrated his ignorance of national politics. Sometimes he pretended to know nothing about current political events. After Madison sent him some newspapers from Philadelphia, he responded with a letter of thanks, explaining, "I have never seen a Philadelphia paper since I left it, till those you inclosed me; and I feel myself so thoroughly weened from the interest I took in the proceedings there, while there, that I have never had a wish to see one, and believe that I never shall take another newspaper of any sort. I find my mind totally absorbed in my rural occupations."[24] It's easy to recognize Jefferson striking a deliberate pose in this passage. In fact, the catalogue of his library listed dozens of volumes of newspapers.

In a letter to George Washington, he observed, "I cherish tranquility too much to suffer political things to enter my mind at all." Writing Edmund Randolph, he applied his reading to his current situation: "I think it is Montaigne who has said that ignorance is the softest pillow on which a man can rest his head. I am sure it is true as to every thing political, and shall endeavour to estrange myself to every thing of that character."[25] He later reused Montaigne's metaphor to refer to metaphysical speculations: "I have for very many years ceased to read or to think concerning them, and have reposed my head on that pillow of ignorance which a benevolent creator has made so soft for us knowing how much we should be forced to use it."[26] Jefferson already had one edition of Montaigne's *Essais*, but he acquired another when he was in France. His metaphor echoes a passage from the essay, "Of Experience": "Oh, what a soft, easy, and healthy pillow is ignorance and incuriosity to rest a well-made head!"

Despite Jefferson's attempt to play the political naif, some of his letters from this period betray his ongoing interest in politics. In the letter to Edmund Rutledge discussing his son's recent visit to Monticello, Jefferson explained that when young Rutledge came down from Philadelphia, "I pestered him with questions pretty much as our friends Lynch, Nelson, etc. will us when we step across the Styx, for they will wish to know what has been passing above ground since they left us."[27] This clever sentence compares Jefferson's personal situation with that of someone who has crossed into the next life. His figure of speech gives this letter an aura of nonchalance, but it also reveals that Jefferson remained curious about political events in Philadelphia, despite what he may have claimed in letters to others.

After describing his ignorance of politics in the letter to Edmund Randolph, he admitted there was one political topic that interested him. He wanted to help disclose the "shameless corruption" of some members of Congress and to expose their "implicit devotion to the treasury." Even from the distance of Monticello, he was keeping a watchful eye on Hamilton and his schemes and hoped that Randolph, as secretary of state, would follow the example Jefferson had set. Staying abreast of such issues, he hoped "to reform the evil on the success of which the form of the government is to depend."[28] Despite his professions to the contrary, Jefferson remained passionately devoted to his nation. He wanted to see it established on a firm footing that would let it endure for centuries.

One of the greatest freedoms he enjoyed upon his retirement was the freedom to speak his mind without worrying about how his political enemies might twist his words. As a private American citizen, he had the right to say whatever he wished. As he informed Pierre Adet, "I am now a private man, free to express my feelings, and their expression will be estimated at neither more nor less than they weigh, to wit the expressions of a private man."[29]

The letter from the mid-1790s that best exemplifies Jefferson's newfound freedom of speech is the one he wrote on April 24, 1796, to his old friend and neighbor Philip Mazzei, who had returned to Italy and was now living in Pisa. As a part of this letter—the "Mazzei letter," as it would become known—Jefferson critiqued the present state of American government:

> The aspect of our politics has wonderfully changed since you left us. In place of that noble love of liberty and republican government which carried us triumphantly thro' the war, an Anglican, monarchical and aristocratical party has sprung up, whose avowed object is to draw over us the substance, as they have already done the forms, of the British government. The main body of our citizens, however remain true to their republican principles, the whole landed interest is with them, and so is a great mass of talents. Against us are the Executive, the Judiciary, two out of three branches of the legislature, all the officers of the government, all who want to be officers, all timid men who prefer the calm of despotism to the boisterous sea of liberty, British merchants and Americans trading on British capitals, speculators and holders in the banks and public funds a contrivance invented for the purposes of corruption and for assimilating us in all things to the rotten as well as the sound parts of the British model. It would give you a fever were I to name to you the apostates who have gone over to these heresies, men who were lions in the field and councils when you were here.

Jefferson liked the idea this last sentence expressed but realized he could make it much stronger, so he completely rewrote the second half of it. As revised, the sentence reads, "It would give you a fever were I to name to you the apostates who have gone over to these heresies, men who were Samsons in the field and Solomons in the council, but who have had their heads shorn by the harlot England."[30]

Jefferson's revision is much stronger than his original. Samson made for a more powerful figure than a lion. Continuing this paragraph, he enhanced its literary quality with an allusion to an early-eighteenth-century work of English literature that was now an established classic, *Gulliver's Travels*. Jonathan Swift's masterpiece had become standard fare for young readers throughout early America. George Washington, for one, read it as a boy.[31] Alluding to *Gulliver's Travels*, Jefferson wrote: "In short we are likely to preserve the liberty we have obtained only by unremitting labors and perils. But we shall preserve them, and our mass of weight and wealth on the good side is so great as to leave no danger that force will ever be attempted against us. We have only to awake and snap the Lilliputian cords with which they have been entangling us during the first sleep which succeeded our labors."[32]

Jefferson's allusion reveals his familiarity with *Gulliver's Travels*, though no copy of the work is listed among his books. This and other references in his writings confirm his appreciation of Jonathan Swift. John Bernard, whose reminiscences are so important for understanding Jefferson's literary tastes, recorded, "His prose favorites were Swift and Bolingbroke."[33] In a way, the image of Lemuel Gulliver both echoes and supersedes the image of Samson. In their respective stories, the two characters find themselves tied up by those who wish to restrain their movements. Whereas Samson can only break his bonds and destroy the Philistines through his own destruction, Gulliver needs only to wake up and move about to snap the cords that bind him.

The freedom of speech Jefferson exercised in the Mazzei letter reveals the strength of his decision to retire from public life. Anyone considering a return to politics would hardly speak so freely. While enjoying the life of a Virginia farmer, he neglected one crucial aspect of American presidential politics as it was constituted at the time: a person did not necessarily have to run for office in order to be elected to office. Just as John Adams was emerging as the de facto leader of the Federalists, Jefferson emerged as the de facto leader of the Republicans. Without campaigning, without running, without even expressing an interest in the American presidency, Jefferson came in second in the presidential balloting. Since president and vice president did not run on the same ticket back then, the man who came in second in presidential balloting served as vice president.

Despite the ideal life Jefferson had created for himself, he could not ignore the voice of the people. He accepted the vice presidency, exchanging the idyllic world of Monticello for the turbulent political world of Philadelphia. Suddenly, he could no longer speak freely as a private citizen. As second in command, he had to watch what he said and what he wrote. But during his vice presidency, one of the letters from this Virginia farmer—the Mazzei letter—would come back to haunt him.

CHAPTER 30

The Vice President
and the Printed Word

After being elected vice president of the United States, Thomas Jefferson was elected president of the American Philosophical Society, an office aligning him with some of the greatest scientific minds in early America. Benjamin Franklin had served as president of the Society until his death in 1790. David Rittenhouse had succeeded him and served until his death in 1796. Accepting the office and the honor, Jefferson expressed hope not only for what the Society could contribute toward the advancement of science, but also for what science could contribute toward the advancement of mankind: "I feel no qualification for this distinguished post but a sincere zeal for all the objects of our institution, and an ardent desire to see knowledge so disseminated through the mass of mankind that it may at length reach even the extremes of society, beggars and kings."[1] As he had many times before, Jefferson emphasized the direct relation between science and liberty. Freedom from tyranny brings opportunities for scientific inquiry; scientific advances reinforce and extend freedom. Given his ideas about how science could contribute to the advancement of mankind, Thomas Jefferson made an ideal choice to lead the American Philosophical Society into the next century.

His association with the Society extended back almost two decades. In 1779, the Reverend James Madison contributed a paper to the Society containing a series of meteorological observations he and Jefferson had recorded. The year after he was elected to the Society, Jefferson was chosen as one of its councilors. Unaware precisely what his responsibilities as councilor entailed, he consulted his old friend Charles Thomson, who was also serving as councilor. Thomson gave him a general overview of the organization's basic purpose. In his words, the American Philosophical Society "has for its object the improvement of useful knowledge more particularly what relates to this new world. It comprehends the whole circle of arts, science and discoveries especially in the natural world."[2]

Averse to "being counted as a drone in any society," Jefferson wanted to contribute whatever he could. Since he was elected councilor shortly after completing his set of answers to Marbois's queries about Virginia, he asked Thomson if a manuscript copy of the work might make a worthwhile contribution.[3] Not surprisingly, Thomson told him that the American Philosophical Society would gladly welcome a copy of his manuscript. Jefferson, who kept tinkering with the work, revising and expanding it into what would become *Notes on the State of Virginia*, never quite got the manuscript into a form suitable for presentation, but he did contribute to the American Philosophical Society in other ways. While serving as secretary of state and living in Philadelphia, he became quite active in the organization. In 1791, he was elected a vice president of the Society for the first time. He continued being reelected to the position through 1794.

Once he returned to Monticello after resigning his position as secretary of state, Jefferson kept an eye out for scientific discoveries that he could report. When some fossilized remains from a previously unknown prehistoric creature were discovered in a cave beyond the Blue Ridge, he drafted a letter to David Rittenhouse informing him of the discovery. Jefferson characterized the bones as being of the lion family but "preeminent over the lion in size as the Mammoth is over the elephant."[4] He promised to deposit the fossils with the Society and coined a named for this new discovery, calling it the Great Claw or megalonyx. When he wrote his letter, Jefferson was unaware of Rittenhouse's death. The letter ultimately reached Benjamin Smith Barton, the nation's foremost naturalist, who read it before the Society in August 1796.

Even before learning of his election as president of the American Philosophical Society, Jefferson was planning to attend its meetings regularly as he had done while secretary of state. The opportunity to pursue his scientific interests while serving as vice president of the United States was just one of several reasons why he was happy he had been elected to second highest office in the nation instead of the first. Expressing his relief upon becoming the nation's vice president, he told Elbridge Gerry, "The second office of this government is honorable and easy. The first is but a splendid misery."[5]

He said much the same to Count de Volney but with more literary flair. In an earlier letter, Volney had quoted a speech made by Clorinda, a leader of the pagan forces in Tasso's *Jerusalem Delivered*. Pledging to defend her land and hoping for mighty conquests, she says, "L'altè Non temo, è l'humile Non Sdegno": Great tasks I dread not, nor do I scorn the humble. Jefferson altered the expression to suit his acceptance of the vice presidency instead of the presidency. He told Volney, "I change the sentiment of Clorinda to 'L'altè temo, l'humile non sdegno' ": Great tasks I dread, but I do not scorn the humble.[6]

Comparing it with the American presidency in a letter to Benjamin Rush, Jefferson called the vice presidency "a more tranquil and un-offending station.... It will give me philosophical evenings in the winter, and rural days in summer."[7] In other words, his time in Philadelphia would let him see his scientist friends formally at the meetings of the American Philosophical Society and informally at dinner gatherings. He would also have the opportunity to escape Philadelphia and return to Monticello during the summer when the Senate was not in session.

Shortly before John Adams's inauguration, Jefferson told Rush that he would be in Philadelphia briefly for the event. He also alluded to "Memoir on the Megalonyx," hoping that "the publications of the society may admit the addition, to our new volume, of this interesting article, which it would be best to have first announced under the sanction of their authority."[8] When it came to the megalonyx essay, Jefferson's at-titude toward publication differed significantly from his earlier attitude toward the publication of *Notes on the State of Virginia*. The change reflects the difference in purpose between the two works. *Notes on the State of Virginia* was a contribution to science, but it was also a social document, a work challenging the practice of slavery and the constitu-tion of Virginia. The paper on the megalonyx was purely a contribution to science, and Jefferson was anxious to see it into print.

"Memoir on the Megalonyx" is just one of many works he published during his vice presidency. During this four-year period, his relationship with the printed word would become increasingly complex. Though severely attacked in the newspapers throughout his vice presidency, Jefferson held firm in his belief that a free press was essential to de-mocracy. He staunchly refused to respond directly to newspaper attacks but did find ways to respond indirectly. Throughout his time as vice president, the printed word, paradoxically, was Jefferson best friend and worst enemy.

Prior to his departure for Philadelphia in early 1797, he spent much time composing "Memoir on the Megalonyx." He related the discovery and then explained which bones had been discovered. Since the bones resembled those of a lion, he double-checked his copy of Buffon for comparison. Estimating the size of the megalonyx, he conjectured that it was more than three times the size of a lion. His comparison puts the beast in perspective: what the mammoth was to the elephant the megalonyx was to the lion. The megalonyx made a formidable antagonist for the mammoth in prehistoric America. While engaged in writing a scientific paper, Jefferson was obviously having fun imagining the prehistoric—he visualized the epic battles that occurred in Virginia between some of nature's greatest creatures.

He was not necessarily willing to consign the megalonyx to prehistoric times, however: he had read printed accounts from the early American explorers attesting to the presence of huge, lionlike creatures. Captain John Smith, for one, found evidence of large wildcats in early-seventeenth-century Virginia. Furthermore, Jefferson had heard legends and firsthand accounts from trappers and backwoodsmen suggesting that the megalonyx still lived. Read in retrospect, his ideas seem naive, but he deserves credit for keeping an open mind about what lurked west of the Appalachians. He refused to make conclusions based on insufficient evidence.

He hypothesized that the westward migration of the American people had driven the largest creatures even farther west: "In the present interior of our continent there is surely space and range enough for elephants and lions, if in that climate they could subsist; and for mammoths and megalonyxes who may subsist there. Our entire ignorance of the immense country to the West and North West, and of its contents, does not authorize us to say what it does not contain."[9] Jefferson's "Memoir on the Megalonyx" can be read as an impassioned plea for the scientific exploration of the American West. As such, it anticipates his presidential policy.

Until the continent was thoroughly explored, scientists had to use what evidence was available, including traditional stories. Arguing for the possibility of the megalonyx's survival, Jefferson drew upon on local legend for support. The settlers of Greenbriar County told how they became alarmed the first night there when they heard the "terrible roarings of some animal unknown to them."[10] This ferocious beast circled their camp, coming close enough for them to see its eyes, which looked like balls of fire. Their frightened horses laid down on the earth, and their dogs were too scared to bark.

Some may accuse Jefferson of letting his imagination get the better of him, but his use of local legends in a scientific paper should not be critiqued too harshly. In the absence of supporting evidence, he was unwilling to discount the information legends could provide. Though he incorporated such fantastic detail, he did not accept traditional stories without question. "Memoir on the Megalonyx" shows that he tested the authenticity of local legends by cross-checking their details with information he found in natural histories and books of travel. To test an oral account, he would scan his library for books describing other parts of the world where similar phenomena occurred and then compare that information with what he gleaned from local legends to reconcile folk history with printed accounts.

It turns out that Jefferson's megalonyx was actually a giant sloth of the Pleistocene epoch. Still, science has given him credit for the discovery: this prehistoric beast is now known as *Megalonyx jeffersonii*. While outdated as science, "Memoir of the Megalonyx" remains important to the history of both science and literature. Jefferson's paper is considered the first American essay on vertebrate paleontology. The open-mindedness it embodies and the imagination it shows are qualities all important scientific papers should exemplify.

Having completed this paper, Jefferson left Monticello for Philadelphia. He wanted to enter the city unobtrusively. He told Madison, "I hope I shall be made a part of no ceremony whatever. I shall escape into the city as covertly as possible."[11] Such was not to be the case. Upon his arrival on Thursday, March 2, 1797, he was greeted by sixteen rounds of fire from an artillery company. He was installed as president of the American Philosophical Society Friday evening. The presidential and vice presidential inaugurations were scheduled for the following day.

On Saturday morning, William Bingham, president pro tempore of the Senate, administered the oath of office. Jefferson's initial act as president of the Senate was to swear in eight new senators. Afterward, he delivered his first address as vice president.

"Gentlemen of the Senate," he began. "Entering on the duties of the office to which I am called, I feel it incumbent on me to apologize to this honourable house for the insufficient manner in which I fear they may be discharged. At an earlier period of my life, and through some considerable portion of it, I have been a member of legislative bodies, and not altogether inattentive to the forms of their proceedings; but much time has elapsed since that, other duties have occupied my mind, and in a great degree it has lost its familiarity with this subject." Continuing his speech, he affirmed his dedication to fairness and impartiality: "The rules which are to govern the proceedings of this house, so far as they shall depend on me for their application, shall be applied with the most rigorous and inflexible impartiality, regarding neither persons, their views or principles, and seeing only the abstract proposition subject to my decision."[12] After his speech, he and the senators left their chamber to go downstairs to the chamber of the House of Representatives, where a joint session of Congress would witness John Adams take the oath of office.

Jefferson lingered in Philadelphia through the following week. On Friday, March 10, he presented his "Memoir on the Megalonyx" to the American Philosophical Society. That same day, he went to see a Bengal elephant, which was being displayed on Market Street. With his mind filled with epic battles between mammoth and megalonyx, the sight of the elephant fired his imagination all the more. As large as that elephant was, there were similar yet larger creatures that once roamed the wilds of prehistoric America. Having seen the elephant, Jefferson left Philadelphia for Monticello the second week of March.

Another Philadelphia entertainment that year sparked a controversy that raged throughout Jefferson's vice presidency. On the Philadelphia stage, James Fennel performed a one-man show during which he recited several famous orations, including Chief Logan's great speech, which Jefferson had been instrumental in popularizing. His inclusion of it in *Notes on the State of Virginia* had reinforced its importance and prompted numerous reprintings. Logan's speech names one Colonel Cresap as the man responsible for the slaughter of his family. Putting the speech into context in *Notes on the State of Virginia*, Jefferson supplied some additional explanation but unintentionally confused Colonel Thomas Cresap with his son, Captain Michael Cresap, calling him "a man infamous for the many murders he had committed on these much injured people [the Shawnee]." Jefferson explained how Cresap satisfied his thirst for revenge by attacking a canoe full of women and children: "Cresap and his party concealed themselves on the bank of the river, and the moment the canoe reached the shore, singled out their objects, and, at one fire, killed every person in it. That happened to be the family of Logan, who had long been distinguished as a friend of the whites."[13]

When Luther Martin, the attorney general of Maryland, learned of Fennel's performance, he was reminded of what Jefferson had said against Michael Cresap, who happened to be the father of Martin's recently deceased wife. The crafty Martin saw he could launch a brutal attack on Jefferson but disguise it as an altruistic attempt to clear the family name of his dead wife. Martin wrote an open letter to Fennel and published it in *Porcupine's Gazette*, the paper edited by William Cobbett, one of Jefferson's most virulent critics. Cobbett, who had established his reputation by attacking Jefferson and the Republicans under the pen name Peter Porcupine, was happy to publish Martin's letter. Martin questioned the veracity of Logan's speech, asserting that it was a deliberate fiction created by Jefferson to slur Cresap.

Martin subsequently wrote a series of open letters addressed to Jefferson but published in the newspapers. There was something underhanded about Martin's approach: writing his attack in the form of a private letter and then publishing it, he was deliberately obscuring the boundaries between public and private. His open letters baited Jefferson to respond. Jefferson refused to take the bait—publishing a response to Martin in the newspapers would only result in an endless stream of attacks and counterattacks.

Jefferson did take Martin's argument seriously and began preparing a defense. He wrote everyone he knew who had had some experience with either Logan or Cresap. Eventually, he gathered the pertinent documents together and published them in 1800 as a pamphlet, *An Appendix to the Notes on Virginia Relative to the Murder of Logan's Family*.

The form Jefferson chose for his response says much about his intentions. The pamphlet implicitly let Martin know that though Jefferson refused to involve himself in newspaper controversy, he was responding to Martin's charges in his own way. The pamphlet form let him develop his argument more fully than he could have in a newspaper article. With the pamphlet, Jefferson could determine the structure and scope of his response. He had room enough to present all of the various letters and testimonials he had solicited. Being a separate publication instead of a periodical contribution, Jefferson's pamphlet essentially closed the book on Martin's argument. The pamphlet form also gave Jefferson's response a much greater sense of permanence. Today's newspaper usually gets tossed by the time tomorrow's arrives. But a pamphlet gets bound up with others and placed on a library shelf, where it endures.

Martin's critique of Logan's speech was one of many newspaper attacks Vice President Jefferson suffered. Another concerned the 1796 letter he had sent Philip Mazzei. Upon receiving the letter, Mazzei had excerpted a paragraph that seemed to critique George Washington and sent copies of the excerpt to others. Jacob Van Staphorst, a correspondent of both Mazzei and Jefferson, upbraided Mazzei for circulating a personal letter without his correspondent's permission. Van Staphorst understood what Mazzei apparently did not: what is written in a personal letter should remain personal. Mazzei went even further, however: he sent the excerpt to a French correspondent, who translated and published it in the French press with a detailed commentary. Noah Webster obtained a copy of the article from the *Moniteur*, the French paper in which it appeared in early 1797, had it translated from French back into English, and published it in the New York *Minerva* on May 2, 1797. Several other Federalist papers reprinted the "Mazzei letter," as it became known, including *Porcupine's Gazette*.

Jefferson's keen literary abilities had come back to haunt him. The most memorable sentence of the Mazzei letter, the one about "Samsons in the field and Solomons in the council," whose heads were "shorn by the harlot England," proved so memorable that it was repeated over and over again. In its retranslation into English from the French, Jefferson's words got twisted. In the *Minerva*, the passage read, "Solomons in council, and Sampsons in combat, but whose hair has been cut off by the whore England."[14] In the retranslation, the fine literary qualities of Jefferson's original disappear. It sounds vulgar and mean-spirited.

It was not long before Jefferson learned about the publication of his letter to Mazzei. The first week of May 1797, he left Monticello to attend a special session of Congress. One morning he stopped for breakfast at Bladensburg, Maryland, where he learned the letter's fate. The attacks on his character and his policy were swift in coming, as Jefferson knew they would be, but he again refused to enter into a newspaper controversy.

Jefferson's fullest expression of his general position toward newspaper controversy occurs in a letter he wrote Maryland congressman Samuel Smith the following year. After explaining his position concerning war with France, he cautioned Smith against publishing what he wrote in this letter and offered him a lengthy discussion of why he avoided newspaper publication:

> At a very early period of my life, I determined never to put a sentence into any newspaper. I have religiously adhered to the resolution through my life, and have great reason to be contented with it. Were I to undertake to answer the calumnies of the newspapers, it would be more than all my own time, and that of 20. aids could effect. For while I should be answering one, twenty new ones would be invented. I have thought it better to trust to the justice of my countrymen, that they would judge me by what they *see* of my conduct on the stage where they have placed me, and what they know of me *before* the epoch since which a particular party has supposed it might answer some view of theirs to vilify me in the public eye.... Though I have made up my mind not to suffer calumny to disturb my tranquillity, yet I retain all my sensibilities for the approbation of the good and just. That is indeed the chief consolation for the hatred of so many who, without the least personal knowledge, and on the sacred evidence of Porcupine and Fenno alone, cover me with their implacable hatred. The only return I will ever make them, will be to do them all the good I can, in spite of their teeth.[15]

Jefferson deserves credit for taking the moral high ground, but his words mask an important aspect of his relationship with the press: though he refused to contribute to the newspapers himself, he was not averse to encouraging friends and supporters to write newspaper articles critiquing his enemies. As secretary of state, he had hired Philip Freneau as his translating clerk, thus putting him in a position to edit a paper friendly to his side and against the Federalists. With a few minor exceptions, Jefferson never contributed to Freneau's *National Gazette*, but he continually sanctioned Freneau's attacks on the Federalists.[16]

When Jefferson told Smith that he never authored any newspaper articles, he was taking a narrow view of authorship. To him, the author was the one who put pen to paper and strung words together to form the sentences and paragraphs that comprise a newspaper article. But this is not the only possible definition of an author. Seen from a broader perspective of authorship, Jefferson can be considered the author of many articles that appeared in Freneau's and other papers friendly to his views, especially the Philadelphia *Aurora*. Owned and edited by Benjamin Franklin Bache until his death by yellow fever in 1798, the *Aurora* was one of Jefferson's staunchest supporters. When William Duane took over editorial responsibilities upon Bache's death, he maintained support for Jefferson's policies. The articles Bache and Duane wrote for the *Aurora* were often written with Jefferson's advice and approval. He discussed his ideas with Freneau, Bache, Duane, and others, encouraged them to articulate these ideas in the press, and applauded them for their efforts.

James Thomson Callender was another journalist who received Vice President Jefferson's encouragement and support. Callender first emerged as a controversial author in Great Britain, which he fled to avoid being prosecuted for sedition for his highly critical work *Political Progress of Britain*. He reached Philadelphia in 1793, where he joined the circle of Republican propagandists led by Bache. Callender contributed to the *Aurora* and published controversial books and pamphlets on his own. *The History of the United States for 1796*, which originally appeared in a series of eight pamphlets, exposed Alexander Hamilton's affair with Maria Reynolds, a married woman. Callender's exposé effectively destroyed Hamilton's political career.[17]

Later explaining their relationship, Jefferson downplayed his support of Callender. He told James Monroe that on the strength of *Political Progress of Britain* he considered its author "a man of science fled from persecution." Similarly, he told Abigail Adams that he considered Callender "a fugitive from persecution for having written that book, and in distress."[18] Consequently, Jefferson sought to do whatever he could to help him. His support of Callender alienated Abigail Adams, who broke off their friendship in the face of Callender's mean-spirited attacks on her husband, the president. Jefferson and Abigail Adams subsequently exchanged a series of letters regarding the matter, accusatory on her side, explanatory on his. Jefferson's letters left her unconvinced. Indeed, his explanations to both her and Monroe obscure the extent of his support.

His memorandum books tell a different story: On June 20, 1797, Jefferson paid Callender $15.14 for his *History of the United States for 1796*. On October 8, he gave him twenty dollars "for his pamphlets." On December 12, sixteen dollars. Two days later $4.33 "for pamphlets." Three days after that $1.25 for a copy of *The History of the United State for 1796* for a friend. On December 23, five dollars "for books and pamphlets." On February 9, 1798, $97.50 for five copies of Callender's latest book, *Sketches of the History of America*. March 23: sixteen dollars. May 23: three dollars "for books." June 25: five dollars "for his next book."[19] To Jefferson's mind, his payments to Callender were instances of literary patronage, but the sums he paid were all out of proportion for what he got, especially that one on February 9: $97.50 for five books!

Shortly after receiving the June 25 payment, Callender left Philadelphia in fear of the Sedition Act, which President Adams would soon sign into law. Severely critical of the president's policies, Callender knew he would be one of the first to face prosecution. He fled to Virginia, where he continued his campaign in the newspapers and in pamphlets— and where Jefferson continued to support him. But Callender's days were numbered. *The Prospect before Us*, a severe critique of the Adams administration he published in 1800, led to his prosecution and conviction under the Sedition Act.

But even from jail, Callender kept up his attacks. He expected great changes soon. As the 1800 presidential election approached, he foresaw Jefferson's victory and imagined being pardoned, vindicated, and rewarded for his unwavering support of the Republican cause. Starting his presidency with a spirit of reconciliation, Jefferson had no place in his administration for Callender or, for that matter, any other contentious, mean-spirited journalist and pamphleteer. Callender felt betrayed. Scoundrel to the core, he switched sides and began launching attacks on Jefferson.

It did not take long for his attacks to become personal. Callender was the one who first published the salacious rumor about a romantic liaison between Thomas Jefferson and Sally Hemings. The story gave Jefferson's enemies the chance to attack him on personal grounds. It quickly entered the political discourse and captured the popular imagination.

Though its publication was motivated by personal vindictiveness, the story of Thomas Jefferson and Sally Hemings has long outlived the person who gave it currency. Callender drowned himself in the James River in 1803, yet the story he published remains a part of the historical discourse and continues to fascinate the popular imagination.

In the face of newspaper attacks on his personal and professional conduct, Vice President Jefferson did more than merely uphold the freedom of the press. He vigorously sought to reestablish the freedom of the press in the face of its biggest threat since the Bill of Rights had been passed. Hard on the heels of the Alien Act, which authorized the expulsion of any alien deemed dangerous to the United States without a hearing, the Sedition Act proved to be the last straw. No longer could Jefferson stand by and witness the erosion of basic American freedoms. With the Federalists in control of the executive, legislative, and judicial branches of the federal government, he had no recourse at the national level. He decided to make a stand at the state level and drafted what would become known as the "Kentucky Resolutions," which declared the Alien and Sedition Acts unconstitutional.

He wrote the "Kentucky Resolutions" in secrecy and kept his authorship secret for decades, so little information survives to explain their genesis. His editors persuasively suggest that Jefferson began writing them to present before the Virginia legislature, but since the Kentucky legislature was scheduled to meet before the Virginians, Jefferson took the opportunity to have John Breckinridge, his contact in Kentucky, present them. The Kentucky General Assembly convened the first week of November 1798. Breckinridge introduced the "Kentucky Resolutions" early the second week of the month. By the end of that week, both the General Assembly and the Kentucky Senate had passed the resolutions. The third week of November, the governor approved them.[20] The Kentuckians had made a few minor changes in the wording, but by and large, the resolutions passed as Jefferson had written them. They lack the pithy, aphoristic quality of earlier legislative resolutions he had written, but they gain power in the aggregate. The "Kentucky Resolutions" stand as a stern warning to the federal government: the states will not tolerate the federal abuse of power.

Late in 1798, Jefferson received a letter from William G. Munford, reputedly one of the brightest young Virginians of his generation. This was the kind of letter Jefferson liked best—Munford wrote asking advice about books. Jefferson responded with a detailed list of reading. Munford's initial letter to him does not survive, but he apparently expressed an interest in studying law. Jefferson's reading list emphasizes law and history but also includes sections on politics, moral philosophy, mathematics, and fine arts.[21]

Munford appreciated Jefferson's list of recommended reading and wrote back to ask him if he would acquire some of the books for him. Requesting the vice president to run errands for him, Munford asked a lot, but Jefferson did not seem to mind. He was always happy to encourage learning, especially among bright and ambitious young men. On Munford's behalf, he visited nearly every bookshop in Philadelphia to find the requested books. By late February 1799, he had located four of them. On his search, Jefferson came across two other books he thought Munford would appreciate, which he also included: Nathaniel Chipman's *Sketches of the Principles of Government* and the Marquis de Condorcet's *Outlines of an Historical View of the Progress of the Human Mind*, the English translation Benjamin Franklin Bache had recently published.[22]

Recommending this last work, Jefferson emphasized Condorcet's established reputation. He had become friends with Condorcet in Paris and had several of his works in his Monticello library, including the French first edition of this particular work. Jefferson's annotated copy, which survives at the Library of Congress, shows how carefully he read the work.

Condorcet's celebration of the printed word makes for memorable reading:

> To the press we owe those continued discussions which alone can enlighten doubtful questions, and fix upon an immoveable basis, truths too abstract, too subtile, too remote from the prejudices of the people or the common opinion of the learned, not to be soon forgotten and lost. To the press we owe those books purely elementary, dictionaries, works in which are collected, with all their details, a multitude of facts, observations, and experiments, in which all their proofs are developed, all their difficulties investigated. To the press we owe those valuable compilations, containing sometimes all that has been discovered, written, thought, upon a particular branch of science, and sometimes the result of the annual labours of all the literati of a country. To the press we owe those tables, those catalogues, those pictures of every kind, of which some exhibit a view of inductions which the mind could only have acquired by the most tedious operations; others present at will the fact, the discovery, the number, the method, the object which we are desirous of ascertaining; while others again furnish, in a more commodious form and a more arranged order, the materials from which genius may fashion and derive new truths.[23]

The general purpose of Condorcet's book is to tell the story of mankind's progress, and the printing press is an essential player in the drama.

Munford never really followed the educational scheme Jefferson outlined for him. In fact, he never lived up to his potential as a scholar or, for that matter, as a gentleman. After visiting Europe, he returned to Virginia a changed man. He now called himself W. G. Montfort. From Bishop James Madison's perspective, he had assumed the character of a scoundrel. Rumors circulated that he was now an agent for the French government. Before the results of the 1800 presidential election were finalized, the ungrateful Munford came out against Jefferson and attacked him in the newspapers. The remainder of his history is brief but mysterious. In 1804, he was in Bordeaux, France, where he died of smallpox. William Lee, U.S. consul at Bordeaux, found three of Jefferson's letters among Munford's effects, which he sent back to him.[24]

One of these letters, which Jefferson had written Munford on June 18, 1799, is among the finest letters he ever wrote. The only reason Munford has not completely disappeared from the pages of history is because he was the recipient of this letter. For a brief moment in his otherwise short life, William G. Munford was able to solicit Thomas Jefferson's most heartfelt thoughts on the importance of scientific progress and the value of the printing press. Echoing Condorcet, perhaps recalling ideas he and Condorcet had discussed in Paris, Jefferson observed, "While the art of printing is left to us science can never be retrograde; what is once acquired of real knowledge can never be lost. To preserve the freedom of the human mind then and freedom of the press, every spirit should be ready to devote itself to martyrdom; for as long as we may think as we will, and speak as we think, the condition of man will proceed in improvement."[25]

Even when read out of context, Jefferson's words are stirring. Read in light of the almost constant barrage of newspaper attacks he suffered as vice president, his enduring faith in a free press is awe-inspiring. The onslaught of insensitive and mean-spirited political attacks was a small price to pay for a free press, which offered the best way to ensure mankind's progress.

Throughout his vice presidency, Jefferson had been working on a new book, and it began to coalesce during his last year in the office. Before he began presiding over the Senate, he had commonplaced the British treatises on parliamentary procedure. This formed his "Parliamentary Pocket-Book," which he used throughout his vice presidency. Nearing the end of his term, he wanted to put the rules of parliamentary procedure into a more permanent form for others to use once he retired. The result would be *A Manual of Parliamentary Practice*.

The first known reference to the project occurs in a letter to George Wythe on February 28, 1800. Recognizing Wythe as the nation's foremost expert on the subject, Jefferson asked his help in clarifying several minor points. Jefferson explained to Wythe the difficulties he was having in codifying the rules of order: "In the course of this business I find perplexities, having for 20. years been out of deliberative bodies and become rusty as to many points of proceedings: and so little has the Parliamentary branch of the law been attended to, that I not only find no person here, but not even a book to aid me.... Some of them are so minute indeed and belong so much to every day's practice that they have never been thought worthy of being written down."[26] Jefferson was caught between oral tradition and the printed word. Many of the rules of order had evolved as representative government had evolved but had never been recorded. Jefferson was hoping Wythe could remember the unwritten rules.

Without knowing the unwritten rules, Jefferson hesitated to publish his *Manual of Parliamentary Practice*. Initially, he decided to make the book as thorough as he could and then deposit a manuscript copy with the Senate. In the coming years, future senators and vice presidents could revise and refine the manual. There was a danger with this solution: someone else might publish it without his approval, errors and all. If he published it himself, at least he would be able to oversee its publication.

Another problem: existing as a single manuscript in the Senate, the work would not be able to influence any other legislative bodies. Speaking of printed books in general, Condorcet had said, "These multiplied copies, spreading themselves with greater rapidity, facts and discoveries not only acquire a more extensive publicity, but acquire it also in a shorter space of time."[27] As Jefferson realized, the state legislatures needed much help in the area of parliamentary procedure, too. By printing his manual, Jefferson would contribute greatly to the advance of the democratic process. Yet still he hesitated.

Wythe could not understand Jefferson's hesitation. He wrote on multiple occasions to encourage his former student to publish the work. He told Jefferson, "I am persuaded the manual of your parliamentary praxis will be more chaste than any extant, and, if you can be persuaded to let it go forth, that it will be canonized in all the legislatures of America."[28]

After working on the *Manual* through the summer of 1800 and into the fall, Jefferson left Monticello in late November to resume his responsibilities in the Senate. This time he would not have to go all the way to Philadelphia: the U.S. capital had finally relocated to its permanent home at Washington, D.C. Though some impressive government buildings were under construction—the Capitol, the President's House—Washington still had a primitive look. But it was improving slowly as businessmen and entrepreneurs were flowing into the new city to meet the needs of the federal government, which had grown significantly during the Adams administration. Jefferson had convinced Samuel Harrison Smith to relocate from Philadelphia and establish a newspaper here. For Smith, the decision to relocate was a gamble: a staunch supporter of Republican policy, he was depending on Jefferson's election to the presidency for his paper's survival.

Jefferson first knew Smith as the publisher of the Philadelphia edition of Thomas Paine's *Rights of Man*. Though Jefferson disliked Smith's publication of his private letter in the preface to this work, he found Smith himself quite likeable. Jefferson subscribed to the *Universal Gazette*, the Philadelphia newspaper Smith began in 1797. He earned Jefferson's enduring respect late that year as an advocate of free public schools: Smith wrote an essay on the subject and submitted it to a contest sponsored by the American Philosophical Society. His essay tied for first place and was published as *Remarks on Education*. After relocating to Washington, Smith established the *National Intelligencer and Washington Advertiser*. It quickly earned a reputation as the finest newspaper in the capital and is now recognized as the most important political newspaper in nineteenth-century America.[29] Jefferson chose Smith to publish his *Manual of Parliamentary Practice*.

Though Smith and his new bride, Margaret Bayard Smith, would become best friends with Jefferson, he did not really start socializing with them until after they moved to Washington in 1800. Jefferson did not meet Mrs. Smith until December, when he visited their Washington home to deliver his manuscript. Mrs. Smith, whose letters, journals, and reminiscences form an important record of early-nineteenth-century social life in Washington, D.C., tells the story best:

> In December, 1800, a few days after Congress had for the first time met in our new Metropolis, I was one morning sitting alone in the parlour, when the servant opened the door and showed in a gentleman who wished to see my husband. The usual frankness and care with which I met strangers, were somewhat checked by the dignified and reserved air of the present visitor; but the chilled feeling was only momentary, for after taking the chair I offered him in a free and easy manner, and carelessly throwing his arm on the table near which he sat, he turned towards me a countenance beaming with an expression

of benevolence and with a manner and voice almost femininely soft and gentle, entered into conversation on the commonplace topics of the day, from which, before I was conscious of it, he had drawn me into observations of a more personal and interesting nature. I know not how it was, but there was something in his manner, his countenance and voice that at once unlocked my heart, and in answer to his casual enquiries concerning our situation in our *new home*, as he called it, I found myself frankly telling him what I liked or disliked in our present circumstances and abode. I knew not who he was, but the interest with which he listened to my artless details, induced the idea he was some intimate acquaintance or friend of Mr. Smith's and put me perfectly at my ease; in truth so kind and conciliating were his looks and manners that I forgot he was not a friend of my own, until on the opening of the door, Mr. Smith entered and introduced the stranger to me as *Mr. Jefferson*.

I felt my cheeks burn and my heart throb, and not a word more could I speak while he remained. Nay, such was my embarrassment I could scarcely listen to the conversation carried on between him and my husband.[30]

She may not have contributed any further to the conversation, but she remained attentive. The manuscript of Jefferson's *Manual of Parliamentary Practice* made a strong impression on her. She recalled, "The original was in his own neat, plain, but elegant hand writing. The manuscript was as legible as printing and its unadorned simplicity was emblematical of his character." Though Mrs. Smith never recaptured her equanimity this day, Jefferson remained cordial throughout his visit and expressed friendship for them upon his departure.

"And is this," Mrs. Smith reflected once he left, "the violent democrat, the vulgar demagogue, the bold atheist and profligate man I have so often heard denounced by the Federalists? Can this man so meek and mild, yet dignified in his manners, with a voice so soft and low, with a countenance so benignant and intelligent, can he be that daring leader of a faction, that disturber of the peace, that enemy of all rank and order?" Previously, Mr. Smith had tried to convince his wife that Jefferson was nothing like the way the newspapers portrayed him, but even he could not change her mind. Mrs. Smith's attitude reflects the power of the press in shaping public opinion. Not until she met Jefferson personally did she change her mind about him.

Jefferson retrieved his manuscript from Smith in January to make a few last-minute corrections but soon put it back in his hands. Smith finished printing the work just before Jefferson resigned as president of the Senate. As Wythe had predicted, *A Manual of Parliamentary Practice* began being used in the Senate, in the House of Representatives, and in state legislatures across the nation.

In a way, Jefferson's task in writing the *Manual of Parliamentary Practice* was not dissimilar to the situation he faced writing "Memoir on the Megalonyx." Explaining the bones of this unknown creature, he brought in local legend for support. Instead of accepting these traditional tales at face value, he compared them with printed accounts from books of travel and natural history in his library. Elaborating the rules of parliamentary procedure, he compared traditional rules with what the books in his library had to say on the subject. Both works combine oral tradition and the printed word to form original contributions to science. "Memoir on the Megalonyx" sought to advance man's understanding of how the world works. *A Manual of Parliamentary Procedure* sought to advance democracy by streamlining the way the legislative process works. Both compositions demonstrate how freedom of expression can contribute to the progress of mankind.

CHAPTER 31

The First Inaugural Address

At daybreak on Wednesday, March 4, 1801, cannon fire sounded from Capitol Hill as an artillery company discharged its weapons to welcome the day. Those within earshot were reminded that this was no ordinary Wednesday morning. Today was the day Thomas Jefferson would be inaugurated third president of the United States, the first to be inaugurated in Washington, D.C.

Later that morning, around ten o'clock, the Alexandria company of riflemen reached the corner of New Jersey Avenue and C Street and paraded before Conrad and McMunn's boarding house, where Jefferson lived. A boarding house, even a handsome and commodious one such as Conrad and McMunn's, may seem an odd place for the president-elect to be staying on the eve of his inauguration. But the place suited Jefferson: located on the south side of Capitol Hill, this house "commanded an extensive and beautiful view" overlooking a vista of "grass, shrubs and trees in their wild uncultivated state." Here Jefferson had a separate drawing-room to receive visitors, but otherwise "he lived on a perfect equality with his fellow boarders, and ate at a common table."[1]

As noon approached, he left the boarding house for the Capitol. Unlike Washington and Adams before him, Jefferson avoided a fancy carriage—he simply walked. Jefferson was accompanied by several of his fellow citizens, including military officers from Alexandria, marshals of the District of Columbia, and a number of congressmen. Though taller than most of the others, Jefferson blended in with the crowd. One observer who saw him this day recorded, "His dress was, as usual, that of a plain citizen, without any distinctive badge of office."[2]

In the past, Jefferson had abjured all forms of ceremony. Now that he was about to be inaugurated president, he saw no reason to change his ways. The military salutes, arranged without his knowledge, were the only aspects of the day that gave it a ceremonial quality. As the president-elect entered the Capitol, the artillery company fired another round to mark the occasion.

Inside the Senate chamber, many people were gathering to witness the inauguration. The senators were already here, having convened this morning to swear in Vice President Aaron Burr as president of the Senate. Since then, members of the House of Representatives had been streaming into the Senate chamber. Many other government officials were admitted, too. What space remained was filled by the general public. People came from throughout the United States. There were some international visitors here, too. The English traveler John Davis, for one, arrived early enough to get a good spot. He observed, "The Senate-Chamber was filled with citizens from the remotest places of the Union. The planter, the farmer, the mechanic and merchant, all seemed to catch one common transport of enthusiasm, and welcome the approach of the Man to the chair of Sovereign Authority."[3]

By one estimate, about a thousand people were assembled there that morning, not counting the legislators but including more than 150 women. Margaret Bayard Smith, one of the women present, noted, "The Senate chamber was so crowded that I believe not another creature could enter." Another observer called it "the largest concourse of citizens ever assembled here."[4] By noon, the crowd noise grew deafening. When Jefferson entered shortly after noon, the people rose from their seats to welcome him. Burr vacated the chair of the Senate for Jefferson. Once he was seated, the crowd grew quiet. After a few moments of silence, he rose to deliver his inaugural address.

"Friends and Fellow Citizens," he began. "Called upon to undertake the duties of the first executive office of our country, I avail myself of the presence of that portion of my fellow-citizens which is here assembled to express my grateful thanks for the favor with which they have been pleased to look toward me, to declare a sincere consciousness that the task is above my talents." The humble pose Jefferson assumed is typical of his public utterances. Continuing this first long sentence, he explained how he felt as he began his presidency: "I approach it with those anxious and awful presentiments which the greatness of the charge and the weakness of my powers so justly inspire."[5]

Since Jefferson's victory in the presidential election had been delayed until February 17—when the House of Representatives finally decided the contest after Jefferson and Aaron Burr tied with the same number of electoral votes—he had had only a few weeks to write his inaugural address. But he really did not need much time. The speech incorporated ideas he had been thinking about for a lifetime. As his opening sentence reveals, he had polished the address until it glistened. The last part of this sentence reveals his ongoing fondness for conjoined word pairs. He used other literary devices to enhance his message, too. Assonance links the pair of adjectives modifying "presentiments": "anxious and awful." The finely balanced parallelism between "the greatness of the charge" and "the weakness of my powers" brings together two seeming opposites.

Jefferson next spoke of the nation's rapidly growing power and prosperity, characterizing the United States as a "rising nation, spread over a wide and fruitful land, traversing all the seas with the rich productions of their industry, engaged in commerce with nations who feel power and forget right, advancing rapidly to destinies beyond the reach of mortal eye." This beautifully constructed phrase has a vast sweep in terms of both time and space. Jefferson's words begin in the recent past, characterize the present state of the nation, and anticipate the future, when the United States would extend its commercial reach around the globe. From Jefferson's optimistic perspective, the nation's future seemed boundless.

His choice of words unified the different forms of discourse he used. The phrase "rising nation" uses the rhetoric of the Revolutionary era, embodied, for example, in the poem Philip Freneau and Hugh Henry Brackenridge wrote for their 1771 commencement from the College of New Jersey, *The Rising Glory of America*. Jefferson's diction also incorporates utopian discourse: asserting that the United States is "spread over a wide and fruitful land," he echoed Samuel Johnson's *Rasselas*, which depicts an idyllic valley, "wide and fruitful."[6]

At this point in his speech, Jefferson interjected his personal reaction to American prosperity: "When I contemplate these transcendent objects, and see the honor, the happiness, and the hopes of this beloved country committed to the issue and the auspices of this day, I shrink from the contemplation, and humble myself before the magnitude of the undertaking." Though phrased as a personal observation, this sentence reiterates the past-present-future pattern in "the honor, the happiness, and the hopes," with alliteration reinforcing the links between the three. Having so far limited his rhetorical flourishes to conjoined word pairs, Jefferson now provided a list of three parallel words, in part for variation but also as a mirror for the concepts he was developing. He had used the list of three as a rhetorical device with great effectiveness in the *Declaration of Independence*. His use of it here is no less effective: honor represents the past, what the United States has accomplished; happiness reflects the present state of the nation; and hope symbolizes its future. As

Jefferson remarked elsewhere, "Hope is so much pleasanter than despair, that I always prefer looking into futurity through her glass."[7]

Drafting his inaugural address, he had imagined delivering it before the combined legislature and included the congressmen and senators in his speech. His responsibilities as president humbled him, but he took strength from the help that those he now faced would provide. The faces in the crowd reminded him that he would not confront such daunting tasks alone.

Applying another list of three—three prepositional phrases this time—Jefferson said that he knew he could rely on Congress's "resources of wisdom, of virtue, and of zeal." He reminded the legislators of the importance of their responsibilities as lawmakers and expressed his desire for their help. To emphasize his point, he used one of his favorite metaphors for talking about government, the ship of state: "I look with encouragement for that guidance and support which may enable us to steer with safety the vessel in which we are all embarked amidst the conflicting elements of a troubled world."

With variation, Jefferson used this metaphor in his private writings, too. In a letter to John Dickinson a few weeks after the inauguration, he wrote, "The storm through which we have passed, has been tremendous indeed. The tough sides of our Argosie have been thoroughly tried. Her strength has stood the waves into which she was steered, with a view to sink her."[8] The differences between the ways Jefferson formulated this metaphor affirm the care he took composing the inaugural address. The word "Argosie" gave his ship-of-state comparison a poetic quality. Considering such poetic diction inappropriate when speaking to the entire nation, Jefferson used more straightforward language in his address.

Next he mentioned the divisiveness that had polarized the United States during the previous administration. Despite the vicious attacks he had suffered at the hands of the press during his vice presidency, Jefferson reasserted the freedom of speech and validated the election process. Now that the people had made their choice, it was time for all citizens to accept the decision of the majority and work toward advancing the cause of the United States. Though the majority should and must rule in a democracy, the rights of the minority should and must be protected.

After outlining these ideas, Jefferson offered a general call for unity: "Let us, then, fellow-citizens, unite with one heart and one mind. Let us restore to social intercourse that harmony and affection without which liberty and even life itself are but dreary things. And let us reflect that, having banished from our land that religious intolerance under which mankind so long bled and suffered, we have yet gained little if we countenance a political intolerance as despotic, as wicked, and capable of as bitter and bloody persecutions."

This call for national unity has much personal resonance. Imploring the nation to "unite with one heart and one mind," Jefferson echoed his "Dialogue between My Head and My Heart." Jefferson knew from personal experience how difficult it could be to reconcile the two, but he also knew how essential the effort was both for the individual body and for the body politic. As president, he effectively unified head and heart—according to his most enthusiastic supporters. Shortly after his inauguration, William Thornton, the director of the U.S. Patent Office, observed, "We have now a philosopher also at our head, whose heart appears in every action."[9]

Pairing life and liberty, Jefferson echoed the most famous usage of these two words in the English language, which occur in the *Declaration of Independence*: "life, liberty, and the pursuit of happiness." Jefferson's reference to banishing religious intolerance in the inaugural address recalls another important document he wrote, "A Bill for Establishing Religious Freedom." Throughout his life, Jefferson closely linked religious and political tyranny, seeing their elimination as the cornerstone of democracy and the capstone of the Enlightenment.

In his effort to reconcile opposing political views, he made a commonsense observation: "But every difference of opinion is not a difference of principle." Over the next several sentences, Jefferson gradually developed this notion, building to what would be the most quoted line from this address: "We are all Republicans, we are all Federalists."

This call for reconciliation and consensus won over many of those who heard his words this Wednesday afternoon and many more who read them during the next week or two. Continuing his speech, he encouraged all Americans to speak their minds. In the United States, contradictory opinions can and will be tolerated because they are subject to debate and reason. Considering the freedom citizens have to express themselves, Jefferson offered a paean to the greatness of American democracy, celebrating its superiority to all other types of government and calling the American form of government "the world's best hope."

Anticipating his policy of Western exploration and expansion, he characterized America as a place "with room enough for our descendants to the thousandth and thousandth generation." Jefferson saw no end to what the nation could and would accomplish. He was already foreseeing a United States that would endure for thousands of generations. And why not? With "a wise and frugal Government, which shall restrain men from injuring one another, shall leave them otherwise free to regulate their own pursuits of industry and improvement, and shall not take from the mouth of labor the bread it has earned," the American people could accomplish much.

Next, Jefferson outlined his duties and responsibilities as president. To this end, he sketched out the essential principles of American government, which he formulated as one long, breathtaking list:

> Equal and exact justice to all men, of whatever state or persuasion, religious or political; peace, commerce, and honest friendship with all nations, entangling alliances with none; the support of the State governments in all their rights, as the most competent administrations for our domestic concerns and the surest bulwarks against antirepublican tendencies; the preservation of the General Government in its whole constitutional vigor, as the sheet anchor of our peace at home and safety abroad; a jealous care of the right of election by the people—a mild and safe corrective of abuses which are lopped by the sword of revolution where peaceable remedies are unprovided; absolute acquiescence in the decisions of the majority, the vital principle of republics, from which is no appeal but to force, the vital principle and immediate parent of despotism; a well-disciplined militia, our best reliance in peace and for the first moments of war till regulars may relieve them; the supremacy of the civil over the military authority; economy in the public expense, that labor may be lightly burthened; the honest payment of our debts and sacred preservation of the public faith; encouragement of agriculture, and of commerce as its handmaid; the diffusion of information and arraignment of all abuses at the bar of the public reason; freedom of religion; freedom of the press, and freedom of person under the protection of the habeas corpus, and trial by juries impartially selected.

In this list of principles, Jefferson used some of the same rhetorical devices he had used so effectively earlier in the speech. This long sentence also incorporates much figurative language. He applied three different metaphors as he developed the list. Calling the general government a "sheet anchor," he reiterated his ship-of-state metaphor. The phrase "the sword of revolution" introduces the threat of violence, which the American government must guard against by peacefully correcting any abuses that may arise. Making commerce handmaid to agriculture, Jefferson used dramatic imagery to acknowledge the importance of trade to the American economy, while reinforcing his agricultural ideal.

He supplied another metaphor that effectively unifies the entire list: "These principles form the bright constellation which has gone before us and guided our steps through an age of revolution and reformation." This evocative sentence is the first of three that summarize his list of principles. The next two share a similarly high level of literary craftsmanship.

Describing how the United States had acquired such principles, Jefferson observed, "The wisdom of our sages and blood of our heroes have been devoted to their attainment." In terms of both imagery and structure, this sentence recalls the Samsons-in-the-field, Solomons-in-the-council sentence that had been turned against him during his vice presidency. He still liked the complementary images the sentence embodied, but he had learned his lesson: instead of applying a clever metaphor this time, he spoke in realistic terms. He referred to the real sages and real heroes who had helped to establish the United States.

The final sentence characterizing the set of American principles twice makes use of the list of three as a rhetorical device and hooks it to another metaphor: "They should be the creed of our political faith, the text of civic instruction, the touchstone by which to try the services of those we trust; and should we wander from them in moments of error or of alarm, let us hasten to retrace our steps and to regain the road which alone leads to peace, liberty, and safety." The road—another favorite metaphor of Jefferson's—provides a land-based equivalent to the ship-of-state metaphor and effectively grounds his principles.

"I repair, then fellow-citizens, to the post you have assigned me," he continued. Getting down to the business of being president, Jefferson asserted his qualifications for the position and asked for patience and tolerance in order "to retain the good opinion of those who have bestowed it in advance, to conciliate that of others by doing them all the good in my power, and to be instrumental to the happiness and freedom of all." Reusing the list of three as a rhetorical device again but varying it by using three infinitive phrases, Jefferson reinforced the actions he intended to take as president.

At the conclusion of his speech, applause resounded through the Senate chamber. Jefferson had clearly touched the hearts of those in attendance. A sentimental observer noticed that tears "bedewed many manly cheeks." When the applause abated, Chief Justice John Marshall proceeded to administer the oath of office. Regardless of their divergent political views, even Marshall recognized the effectiveness of Jefferson's inaugural address. In his opinion, this speech was both judicious and conciliatory.[10]

Margaret Bayard Smith came away from Jefferson's inauguration awe-inspired. She wrote her sister-in-law that she left the Senate chamber with a glow of enthusiasm that lingered for hours. "The changes of administration, which in every government and in every age have most generally been epochs of confusion, villainy and bloodshed, in this our happy country take place without any species of distraction, or disorder," she observed. "This day, has one of the most amiable and worthy men taken that seat to which he was called by the voice of his country." Generally speaking, she said that the inaugural address contained "principles the most correct, sentiments the most liberal, and wishes the most benevolent, conveyed in the most appropriate and elegant language and in a manner mild as it was firm. If doubts of the integrity and talents of Mr. Jefferson ever existed in the minds of any one, methinks this address must forever eradicate them."[11]

Jefferson had given Samuel Harrison Smith an advance copy of his inaugural address that morning so that he could print it in the *National Intelligencer* and have copies available directly after the inauguration. As the crowd left the Senate chamber, multiple rounds of artillery fire sounded in celebration. The cries of newsboys, eager to distribute copies of the *National Intelligencer* containing Jefferson's speech, sounded almost as loud. Throughout the afternoon, people crowded around the *Intelligencer* office clamoring for copies of the inaugural address. Demand was so great that Smith could hardly print copies fast enough to meet it. Catching up her correspondence later that day, Mrs. Smith related what had happened as she left the Capitol: "On coming out of the house, the paper was distributed immediately. Since then there has been a constant succession of persons coming for the papers."[12]

Newspapers throughout the nation reprinted Jefferson's inaugural address. The speech was available in other formats, too. It was issued as a pamphlet in Baltimore, New York, Philadelphia, and Washington. One pamphlet issued in Washington presented the text in English, French, German, and Italian. The speech was also available as a broadside. Publishers in Albany, Baltimore, Boston, Hagerstown, Hartford, New York, Newport, and Philadelphia all issued broadside reprints.

Some of these broadsides were quite special. The Boston firm of Adams and Rhoades issued a copy of the speech printed on silk. Philadelphia publisher Matthew Carey offered copies printed on superfine wove paper with a miniature likeness of Jefferson, and more expensive versions printed on satin. Carey sent President Jefferson a paper copy; Jefferson wrote back to request a satin print. His appreciation of fine printing partly accounts for the request, which also shows how proud Jefferson was of what he had written.

People were buying copies of his speech not only to read but also to possess. These silk and satin printings were handsome keepsakes intended to be framed and hung on the wall as constant reminders of the principles Jefferson represented. Advertising one of these fancy copies, the *Independent Chronicle* made clever use of the speech's most memorable words: "The work will be executed with neatness, and in a form calculated to adorn the Parlours of all the *Federal Republicans.* A few copies will be struck on white satin—at different prices."[13] Multiple copies of silk broadsides survive handsomely mounted and framed.

Several magazines reprinted Jefferson's speech later that month: the *Connecticut Magazine*, the New York *Weekly Museum*, and the *Philadelphia Repository and Weekly Register*. On the special request of its readers, the *Baltimore Weekly Magazine* reprinted it in May. And almanac-maker Joshua Sharp issued the address as part of his *Citizen's and Farmer's Almanac, for the Year 1802.*

John Davis incorporated the entire address in his *Travels of Four Years and a Half in the United States of America*, which he dedicated to Jefferson. Davis's popular book of travels brought Jefferson's words to many English readers, including some of the era's most distinguished men of letters. Reading Jefferson's inaugural address in Davis's *Travels*, Percy Bysshe Shelley was inspired to add a paean to America in his long poem *Revolt of Islam*:[14]

> There is a People mighty in its youth,
> A land beyond the Oceans of the West...
> That land is like an eagle, whose young gaze
> Feeds on the noontide beam, whose golden plume
> Floats moveless on the storm, and in the blaze
> Of sunrise gleams when Earth is wrapped in gloom...
> Yes, in the desert, then, is built a home
> For Freedom!

Other English readers were also impressed with the stirring words Jefferson spoke this day. Alexander Baring, a young but prominent British financier living in the United States, said that the inaugural address confirmed his high opinion of Jefferson, whom Baring called "a visionary theorist." Subsequent events would confirm this opinion. Two years later Baring would take charge of financing the Louisiana Purchase.[15]

In June, Philadelphia publisher R. T. Rawle reprinted Jefferson's inaugural address as an appendix to a new edition of *Notes on the State of Virginia*, one of several editions issued that year. The controversial outcome of the presidential election had created much interest in Jefferson's book. New editions had begun to appear even before the election had been decided. In February, the New York firm of Furman and Loudon issued a new edition of *Notes on the State of Virginia*.[16] Another New York firm issued its own edition of the work later that year. Two Boston editions appeared, as did an edition by a publisher in Newark, New Jersey.

While the election made readers curious about what Jefferson had to say in *Notes on the State of Virginia*, the fine writing he demonstrated in the inaugural address made them anxious to enjoy what else he had written. Rapine, Conrad, and Company, a bookseller located at the corner of South B Street and New Jersey Avenue near the Capitol, began advertising a new edition of *Notes on the State of Virginia* shortly after the inauguration. In a newspaper advertisement that ran for months, the title appeared on a list advertising several current works, including Charles Brockden Brown's *Edgar Huntley* and *Arthur Mervyn*.[17] Now fifteen years old, Jefferson's book was being read as avidly as the latest popular novels.

One contemporary commentator saw similarities between the inaugural address and *Notes on the State of Virginia*, at least in terms of their literary quality. Discussing the address, he mentioned the principles of American government Jefferson delineated, observing, "They are compressed within such precise limits, as to enforce them on the memory, and expressed with such classical elegance, as to charm the scholar with their rhetorical brilliancy." Directly after this statement, this reviewer mentioned "the peculiar happiness attached to Mr. Jefferson's literary performance" and used *Notes on the State of Virginia* to support his point: "His Notes on Virginia are strewed with flowers selected from the parterre of the Belles Lettres."[18]

Benjamin Rush wrote from Philadelphia to congratulate Jefferson on his brilliant speech. Rush's letter, which incorporates phrases from the inaugural address, shows how infectious Jefferson's words could be: "You have opened a new era by your speech on the 4th of March in the history of the United States. Never have I seen the public mind more generally or more agreeably affected by any publication. Old friends who had been separated by party names and a *supposed* difference of *principle* in politics for many years shook hands with each other immediately after reading it, and discovered, for the first time, that they had differed in *opinion* only, about the best means of promoting the interests of their common country."[19]

Rush mentioned several men who had enjoyed the speech, including his friend Joseph Wharton, who had read it "*seven* times, and with increasing pleasure."[20] Wharton's experience shows the value of the printed word over the spoken. Those who attended Jefferson inauguration could only hear it once—and some not even that much. Margaret Bayard Smith reported, "The speech was delivered in so low a tone that few heard it."[21] Buying reprints, especially fancy silk reprints designed as wall hangings, people could reread the speech as often as they wished. Advertising a broadside of the inaugural address, Baltimore publisher William Pechin puffed, "It is handsomely printed on a large size type, and in a form which will not only be convenient for perusal, but will give it a chance of durability beyond what its insertion in a daily paper can ensure."

A moving composition as a whole, the inaugural address contained many memorable phrases that could be easily extracted from it. Congratulating Jefferson on the speech, Pierre Samuel Du Pont de Nemours observed, "With these maxims you will enchant one half of the human race, and finally the other half."[22] Du Pont de Nemours clearly recognized the ease with which phrases and sentences could be detached from Jefferson's inaugural address for purposes of quotation. Benjamin Rush greatly appreciated the aphoristic quality of Jefferson's address, too, as he said in his letter of congratulations: "You have concentrated whole chapters into a few aphorisms in defense of the principles and *form* of our government." Rush also echoed what was becoming the speech's most famous passage: "In the third month of the year 1801," Rush observed, "we have become 'all Republicans, all Federalists.' "[23] Already Jefferson's literary abilities were serving him well as president.

After his inauguration, President Jefferson left the Senate chamber on his way back to Conrad and McMunn's. Upon his exit from the Capitol, more rounds of artillery sounded. Accompanied by Vice President Burr, Chief Justice Marshall, and several other dignitaries, he walked back to his boarding house. Two more weeks would pass before he would relocate to the President's House on Pennsylvania Avenue.

Jefferson had made no plans for the evening of his inauguration. Throughout Washington, the rest of the day was devoted to festivities, but there is no indication that the new president took part. Once darkness fell, the city looked quite different than it had the night before. After dark, there was "a pretty general illumination."[24] People throughout Washington placed candles in their windows to celebrate the start of Jefferson's presidency.

When he went down to dinner at Conrad and McMunn's, according to a story Margaret Smith heard, Jefferson took the same seat he had always taken at the table, the lowest seat at the end of the long dinner table, which was also the coldest, being the farthest from the fire. Mrs. Smith was indignant that more was not done to give the new president a place of honor at the table, but her story ably captures Jefferson's character.

Though he may have done nothing special to celebrate his inauguration that evening, Jefferson realized how much the nation had changed with his election. The general illumination confirmed the public support for the democratic ideals he had articulated in his inaugural address—each light in every window was a vote of support. A new era in American democracy had begun.

CHAPTER 32

The Wall of Separation

W riting to Benjamin Rush a few months before the 1800 presidential election, Thomas Jefferson made one of his most famous pronouncements: "I have sworn upon the altar of god eternal hostility against every form of tyranny over the mind of man."[1] Save for the fact that these words occur in a private letter to a trusted friend, they have the aura of a campaign slogan. But Jefferson was not solely inveighing against political tyranny. He was also speaking against religious tyranny. Read within the context of this letter, his words are tinged with irony: they occur in a paragraph recalling ideas about Christianity he and Rush had discussed in Philadelphia during the winter of 1798–99. Their energetic conversations had encouraged Jefferson to think about religion further, and he had promised to write up his thoughts on Christianity for Rush. This letter reiterates that promise.

After his inauguration, Jefferson wrote his friend again, thanking him for the kind things he had said about the inaugural address. Jefferson also told Rush about the responsibilities he now faced as president. His most onerous task concerned the midnight appointments made by his predecessor. In the waning days of the Adams administration, the Federalist-controlled Congress had passed the Judiciary Act of 1801, which created a new tier of courts and judgeships. Almost until the last hour of the last day of his presidency, John Adams had continued making appointments to fill these new positions. The Federalists had entered panic mode in the closing days of the Adams administration. Not only were they losing the presidency; they were also losing their majority in the Senate and the House. Adams loaded the judiciary with Federalists to let his party retain a modicum of control over the remaining branch of the national government. Federalists were hoping that Adams's appointees could exert control by legislating from the bench.

Nothing Adams did during his presidency irked Jefferson more than the matter of the midnight appointments. Jefferson admitted to Rush that he was determined to remove many of Adams's appointees—"to expunge the effects of Mr. A's indecent conduct"—in order to achieve something close to judicial parity between Federalists and Republicans. While optimistic about his chances of accomplishing this goal, Jefferson correctly surmised that his political enemies would interpret his behavior as partisan.[2] Nowhere in this letter does Jefferson reiterate his promise to record his thoughts on Christianity for Rush. That task would seem to involve more time than the new president could spare.

Letters he wrote Moses Robinson, Elbridge Gerry, and Joseph Priestley in the weeks following the inauguration, however, show that he had not stopped thinking about religion. Early in his presidency, Jefferson was devoting much thought to the relationship between church and state. Writing Moses Robinson, the former senator from Vermont who had been one of his staunchest supporters during his tenure as secretary of state, Jefferson reiterated his hope of reconciling Federalists and Republicans and emphasized the need for patience. Understanding that it would take New England longer to accept the new government than it would the rest of the nation, he placed the blame squarely on the shoulders of the clergy, who, he said, "had got a smell of union between church and state, and began to indulge reveries which can never be realized in the present state of science."[3]

To Jefferson, the Enlightenment had progressed far enough in America that it was impossible to revert to the darkness of the religious past. No longer could people see "advances in science as dangerous innovations," he told Robinson. Only by accepting such advances and reconciling them with their faith could clergymen hope to practice their religious beliefs in the enlightened era. To summarize the situation, Jefferson applied a proverb, slyly associating Christianity and Islam along the way: "Since the mountain will not come to them, they had better go to the mountain." Only by accepting "the liberty and science of their country" and divesting Christianity from "the rags in which they have enveloped it" can the New England clergymen restore the "original purity and simplicity of its benevolent institutor." Of all the religions, Jefferson continued, Christianity is the "most friendly to liberty, science, and the freest expansions of the human mind."[4]

Jefferson's contemporary remarks to Elbridge Gerry, his first friend in New England, echo what he told Robinson. More than anything, New England's religious heritage was holding it back: "Your part of the Union tho' as absolutely republican as ours, had drunk deeper of the delusion, and is therefore slower in recovering from it. The aegis of government, and the temples of religion and of justice, have all been prostituted there to toll us back to the times when we burnt witches." Jefferson advised Gerry to stick to his principles and lead the people of New England away from religious superstition. His vivid imagery shows how much Jefferson disliked the attempts of the narrow-minded, overzealous clergy to restrain progress: "The people will support you, notwithstanding the howlings of the ravenous crew from whose jaws they are escaping."[5]

Few men shaped Jefferson's religious views more significantly than Joseph Priestley. Theologian *and* man of science, Priestley established a reputation for his advanced thinking in both realms. His experiments on the principles of gases made him England's most respected scientist in that field. His denial of the Holy Trinity made him a leader of the Unitarian movement but antagonized the Anglican hegemony. Together with his outspoken views on governmental reform, his religious opinions made him unwelcome in his native land, so he left England for the United States. Considering Priestley's situation, Jefferson observed, "His antagonists think they have quenched his opinions by sending him to America, just as the pope imagined when he shut up Galileo in prison that he had compelled the world to stand still."[6]

Leaving England in 1794, Priestley settled in Northumberland, Pennsylvania. Though befriended by many prominent Americans, including Washington and Jefferson, Priestley still did not escape censure here. Peter Porcupine attacked him in the press; angry preachers attacked him from the pulpit. During the Adams administration, Secretary of State Timothy Pickering wanted to prosecute him under the Alien and Sedition Acts. Not until Jefferson was elected could Priestley feel safe from persecution.[7]

Jefferson had been corresponding with Priestley for years, but he took special pleasure in writing him after his inauguration. The new president could now assure his friend that the kind of trouble he had encountered during the Adams administration was at an end. To illustrate his point, Jefferson used a favorite literary analogy, comparing Priestley to Gulliver and his small-minded enemies to the Lilliputians. Then he continued: "It is with heartfelt satisfaction that, in the first moments of my public action, I can hail you with welcome to our land, tender to you the homage of its respect and esteem, cover you under the protection of those laws which were made for the wise and good like you, and disdain the legitimacy of that libel on legislation, which under the form of a law, was for some time placed among them."[8] Jefferson would maintain a lively correspondence with Priestley during his first term as president.

The growing conflict with the Barbary Coast gave Jefferson an object lesson in what could happen when nations let religion dictate policy. For years, the Muslim states along the north coast of Africa had followed a policy of extorting money from other nations wishing to sail the Mediterranean. The vessels of any nation refusing to pay tribute would be at the mercy of Muslim pirates, whose governments gave them free rein to launch attacks in the name of Islam, capturing merchant ships, kidnapping their sailors, and holding them hostage. During the Adams administration, the United States had paid protection money to Tripoli and the other Barbary states to safeguard American merchant vessels from attack. Jefferson had long opposed this policy. As president, he refused to cave in to such extortion. In May 1801, the Pasha of Tripoli declared war on the United States.

President Jefferson realized there was little hope in reasoning with the Pasha. He never fully articulated his thoughts on the subject, but the contemporary remarks of an American in Tunis are similar in tone and diction to comments Jefferson made elsewhere concerning the detrimental effects religion could have on policy: "The ignorance, superstitious tradition, and civil and religious tyranny, which depress the human mind here, exclude improvement of every kind; consequently the same habits, customs and manners, which were observed in the East three thousand years ago, are still prevalent here: Everything is done to the greatest possible disadvantage."[9] Jefferson dispatched a naval squadron to Tripoli. Though the squadron experienced some early successes, the Tripoline War would drag on for years.

In the early weeks of his administration, Jefferson assembled an excellent cabinet to advise him in matters both foreign and domestic. His choice of Albert Gallatin for treasury secretary surprised no one. Since emigrating from Switzerland as a young man, Gallatin had established himself as the foremost authority on public finance in the nation. While serving in the House of Representatives, he had harshly critiqued the policies of Alexander Hamilton. To facilitate a smooth-running economic policy, Gallatin established the House Committee on Ways and Means.[10]

James Madison, whom Jefferson selected as his secretary of state, would be his closest confidant throughout his administration. Since Madison would not reach Washington until May, Levi Lincoln, whom Jefferson tapped for attorney general, served as provisional secretary of state until Madison's arrival. Being from Massachusetts, Lincoln helped balance the cabinet geographically. Despite his New England origins, Lincoln was a Jeffersonian through and through. The son of a farmer, he was apprenticed to a blacksmith until his precociousness led him to enroll at Harvard. During the Revolutionary War, he joined the Minutemen. He also wrote a patriotic essay series titled "Farmer's Letters." The persona Lincoln assumed for these letters confirms his affinity with Jefferson. As attorney general, Lincoln would resume this persona in his polemical *Letters to the People, by a Farmer*, which attacked the Federalists for politicizing the clergy.[11]

President Jefferson chose Henry Dearborn as secretary of war, and General Samuel Smith served as acting secretary of the navy, a cabinet-level post John Adams had established during his administration. Samuel Smith used his influence to get his brother Robert officially appointed to the position. Robert Smith, though without naval experience, was an expert organizer. Through his efforts, the U.S. Navy established a sophisticated logistical network to maintain naval supply lines, which allowed American vessels to exert continual pressure on Tripoli.[12]

Jefferson moved to the President's House before the end of March. Meriwether Lewis moved in the following month. Lewis served as Jefferson's personal secretary, an office Jefferson described as "more in the nature of that of an aid de camp, than a mere Secretary."[13] John Adams had been the first president to live in what would eventually be called the White House when the seat of government was relocated to Washington in 1800. Abigail Adams disliked the unfinished, cavernous residence. She called it a "great castle," in part because of its function as the president's house but also because of its size, dampness, and darkness. Jefferson also found it quite roomy. As he wrote his daughter Martha that spring, "Capt. Lewis and myself are like two mice in a church."[14]

Unlike Abigail Adams, Jefferson did not mind the unfinished state of the President's House. Monticello had been a work-in-progress ever since he first moved in three decades earlier. A home was a canvas on which Jefferson painted. He saw the condition of the President's House as an opportunity, not a disadvantage. It gave him the chance to contribute significantly to its design. Indeed, some of the White House's most distinctive features were designed by the nation's third president during his residence there. In early May, James and Dolley Madison stayed at the President's House for a few weeks until their home was ready. Dolley Madison's conviviality helped make it the center of Washington society.

Once the Madisons settled in their own home, Jefferson perpetuated the convivial atmosphere Dolley Madison had helped to establish. During the Jefferson administration, the president's dinner table became

Dolley Madison, after a painting by Gilbert Stuart. From Rufus Wilmot Griswold, *The Republican Court* (1854). (Collection of Kevin J. Hayes)

the place where many complex political issues were resolved. While serving as minister plenipotentiary in Paris, Jefferson had discovered his flair for entertaining. Throughout his two terms as president, he typically invited ten or twelve people to dine. Playing host, he encouraged intellectual conversation and helped iron out political disagreements.

Samuel Harrison Smith and his wife, Margaret Bayard Smith, were frequent guests at the President's House. Mrs. Smith's letters and reminiscences bring their experience alive. By limiting his company to twelve or less, Jefferson kept his dinners informal and his dinner conversation "general and unreserved." Sitting next to him during her first dinner at the President's House, Mrs. Smith found his manners "easy, candid and gentle."[15] In her reminiscences, she recorded one particular dinner conversation. Though written many years after the fact, the words she recorded are consistent with other accounts of Jefferson's dinnertime conversation and confirm his fondness for tall talk—Jefferson took great pleasure whenever he could pull someone's leg.[16]

"How I wish that I possessed the power of a despot," he said one evening, shocking his dinner guests in the process. Strange words for a man who had sworn an oath against tyranny! If I were a despot, he continued, "I might save the noble, the beautiful trees that are daily falling sacrifices to the cupidity of their owners, or the necessity of the poor," speaking of the beautiful magnolias, poplars, and tulip trees in the District of Columbia that were being destroyed for firewood.

"And have you not authority to save those on the public grounds?" one guest asked.

"No," Jefferson replied wistfully, "only an armed guard could save them. The unnecessary felling of a tree, perhaps the growth of centuries seems to me a crime little short of murder, it pains me to an unspeakable degree." Expressing a desire for despotism, Jefferson was talking tall, but the sadness he conveyed toward the loss of these great old trees was genuine. Jefferson was a conservationist before that term became current. While president, he advised his overseer at Monticello, "Use great economy in timber, never cutting down a tree for fire-wood or any other purpose as long as one can be found ready cut down, and tolerably convenient."[17]

Other dinner guests recorded additional instances of Jefferson's tall talk, but at least one of them, Dr. Samuel Mitchill, did not realize when Jefferson was pulling his leg. Having read *Notes on the State of Virginia*, Dr. Mitchill—physician, professor, and congressman—asked the president about one particular description.[18] Mitchill reported their conversation in a letter to a friend:

I asked Mr. Jefferson some questions about the sublime prospect he has described in that work of the passage of the Potomac through the mountains. My chief object was to be directed to the proper place for observation—the place where he himself stood when there. He told me the place no longer existed, for during the reign of Federalism under

Adams's administration, the spot, which was a projecting point of rock on the brow of the mountain, had been industriously blown up and destroyed by gunpowder! A company of Federal troops quartered there were several days employed in boring and blasting the rock to pieces, doubtless with the intention of falsifying his account, and rendering it incredible by putting it out of the power of any subsequent traveller to behold the like from the same point of view. What shameful, what vandalic revenge is this!

Like Dr. Mitchill, others were drawn to the Blue Ridge from Jefferson's glowing depiction of them. John Bernard observed, "Mr. Jefferson, in his *Notes on Virginia*, had given such a vivid description of these hills that I could not resist the temptation during the previous summer to visit the 'passage of the Potomac,' though then residing at a hundred miles' distance." Bernard was rewarded for his effort. The view, he concluded, was "unquestionably the sublimest scene in America, after the Falls of Niagara."[19]

Bernard, who occasionally visited the President's House during the Jefferson administration, also testified to the conviviality of his dinner gatherings. The two had met in Philadelphia when Jefferson was vice president. After establishing a reputation as a stage comedian in England, Bernard had been offered a lucrative salary by the Chestnut Street Theater. He accepted the offer, reached Philadelphia in 1797, and quickly emerged as one of the finest comedians on the American stage. He also became a fixture on Philadelphia's social scene. Bernard established a Beefsteak Club in Philadelphia, which Jefferson visited while vice president.[20]

Besides contributing his own witticisms to the dinner conversation, Bernard enjoyed the president's lively sense of humor. Recalling Jefferson's conversation, he wrote, "With specimens of his humor I could fill pages." In his memoirs, Bernard provided a general overview of Jefferson's manner of speaking and recorded many snippets of conversation that occurred at the president's table: "In all the chief requisites of the social character Mr. Jefferson appeared to me to possess few equals. His heart was warmed with a love for the whole human race; a *bonhommie* which fixed your attention the instant he spoke. His information was equally polite and profound, and his conversational powers capable of discussing moral questions of deepest seriousness, or the lightest themes of humor fancy. Nothing could be more simple than his reasonings, nothing more picturesque and pointed than his description."[21]

Bernard's memoirs are the source for several quips and anecdotes unrecorded elsewhere. In his presence, Jefferson retold his favorite stories. To illustrate the president's capacity for humor, Bernard recorded what Jefferson said to Benjamin Rush upon learning that Rush and H——, "a well-known wit of Philadelphia," had nearly lost their lives on a packet boat from New York to Baltimore.

"Well, doctor, such a fate would have suited your genius precisely," Jefferson told Rush. "You, you know, are always for going to the bottom of things; though it would have been inappropriate for our friend H——, who prefers skimming the surface."

Summers in Washington can be unpleasant, and many of the city's residents, then as now, clear out before the heat and humidity reach their peak. By late June his first year in office, President Jefferson was already planning to return to Monticello. He wrote his daughter Martha, "I begin with pleasure to make memorandums, lay by what is to be carried there etc. etc. for the pleasure of thinking of it, of looking forward to the moment when we shall be all there together."[22]

He did want to stay in Washington long enough to host his first Fourth of July celebration as president. Mrs. Smith usually spent the summer at their house in the country, so she was not around to enjoy the celebration. Her husband, who remained in town to run his newspaper, did attend the festivities. On July 4, 1801, Smith and a guest entered the President's House about noon, when they were astonished to find Jefferson surrounded by five Cherokee chiefs. Throughout his presidency, Jefferson welcomed Native Americans to the White House. Furthermore, he wrote several addresses to them that effectively utilize Native American rhetoric.

On this occasion, shortly after Smith had arrived, the president invited his company into the dining room, where four large sideboards were covered with refreshments—"cakes of various kinds, wine, punch, etc." The company eventually swelled to more than a hundred guests. To accompany this pleasant holiday afternoon, the U.S. Marine Band played patriotic airs.[23]

It was Jefferson who titled this band "The President's Own" and thus defined the mission of the Marine Band, which continues to provide music for the president. Jefferson greatly improved the band as he sanctioned the recruit of several Italian musicians to its ranks. He recognized the importance of music to the nation as a whole and to the military in particular. As president, he did what he could to encourage the development of music in the United States.

He left Washington for Monticello that year on July 30 and stayed away for the next two months, taking full advantage of the time by enjoying the company of his grandchildren. Anne, the oldest, had turned ten earlier that year. At four, Ellen was learning to read, but she did not let on how much she knew during her grandfather's visit. A little shy or a little coy or maybe a little of both, Ellen feigned ignorance in order to surprise and amaze her grandfather at a later time. While he was home that summer, two more grandchildren were born. On August 22, Martha gave birth to Virginia Jefferson Randolph, and on September 20, Maria gave birth to Francis Eppes.

Jefferson returned to Washington the last day of September. The most important literary task he faced was drafting his first annual message to Congress. Much official correspondence demanded his attention, but he still managed to find time to write his grandchildren. One particular letter gave him more satisfaction than just about any other, the first letter he ever wrote his granddaughter Ellen, which responds to her first letter to him. As short as it is, four-year-old Ellen's letter contains multiple comments about books. In the body of the letter, she wrote, "I hope you will bring me some books my dear grand papa." In a postscript, she added, "Make hast to come home to see us and all our books in the press."[24] Here was a little girl after her grandfather's heart. Not only did she express a desire for more books, but she was also already helping arrange her books and those of her siblings.

Ellen's grandfather was amazed by her precociousness. He responded, "When I left Monticello you could not read, and now I find you can not only read, but write also. I inclose you two little books as a mark of my satisfaction and if you continue to learn as fast, you will become a learned lady and publish books yourself." He would continue to send Ellen and his other grandchildren books throughout his presidency.[25]

It is impossible to identify all the books Jefferson acquired for Ellen and the others, but sporadic evidence provides some indication. Maria Edgeworth was one of the girls' favorites: *The Modern Griselda*, *Moral Tales for Young People*, *The Parent's Assistant; or, Stories for Children*, and *Rosamond* all became a part of his granddaughters' bookshelf. While purchasing Edgeworth's works for them, Jefferson sometimes questioned their value. Presenting a copy of *Moral Tales* to one granddaughter, he said that it seemed "better suited to your years than to mine." Though his daughter Martha enjoyed *The Modern Griselda* and shared it with her children, Jefferson expressed uncertainty about the book. Describing it to Anne, he explained, "The heroine presents herself certainly as a perfect model of ingenious perverseness, and of the art of making herself and others unhappy. If it can be made of use in inculcating the virtues and felicities of life, it must be by the rule of contraries."[26]

The Modern Griselda was one of Edgeworth's most daring efforts. *The Parent's Assistant*, a more conservative work, makes its instructive value apparent from its title page. *The Parent's Assistant* presented a collection of stories and plays, all designed for the purposes of moral inculcation. For example, the virtuous title character of "Simple Susan," one of Edgeworth's best-known tales, experiences many personal tribulations but is ultimately rewarded in the end.[27] Jefferson was happy to present this work to his granddaughters. One of them remembered when he gave it to them. They drew lots to determine who would get to read the book first: "She who drew the longest straw had the first reading of the book—the next longest straw entitled the drawer to the second reading—the shortest, to the last reading and ownership of the book."[28]

During his presidency, Jefferson subscribed to *Captain John Smith and Princess Pocahontas*, John Davis's romantic retelling of the story of Virginia's early years. The work does not appear in his library catalogue. More than likely, he gave it to his grandchildren. In 1802, the Reverend Thomas Davis sought subscriptions for *Miscellaneous Poetry*, an anthology of British verse, and the president subscribed to the book. The work is also not listed in his library catalogue; this, too, seems intended as a present for his grandchildren. He also subscribed to Richard Dinmore's 1802 anthology, *Select and Fugitive Poetry*—the first volume of poetry printed in Washington, D.C. Jefferson initialed this volume with his characteristic identifying marks, but he subsequently presented it to his daughter Martha.[29]

Hard-to-get books Jefferson had to order from elsewhere. Philadelphia book dealer Nicolas Gouin Dufief was an important source for books. During his presidency, Jefferson also developed a good relationship with Baltimore book dealer J. P. Reibelt. Altogether, they exchanged dozens of letters. Reibelt would write to inform Jefferson of the latest titles he had imported, and Jefferson would write back to purchase some books and special order others. Sometimes, Reibelt would pack up entire boxes of books and send them to the President's House on approval. Jefferson would then pick and choose the ones he wanted and return the ones he did not.[30]

The book culture of Washington, D.C., continued to develop throughout Jefferson's presidency. Dinmore ran a bookstore and circulating library at "the first door west of the President's Square." Jefferson subscribed to Dinmore's circulating library and purchased other books from him, too.[31] Late in 1801, William Duane opened the Apollo Press and Aurora Bookstore at the corner of Pennsylvania Avenue and Sixth Street N.W., and Jefferson bought several books there.[32] He also continued to shop at Rapin, Conrad, and Company and began to patronize John March's Store, a stationery shop and book bindery on High Street in Georgetown.

John March's reputation as a bookbinder rivaled that of Robert Aitken. March was especially skilled with tree calf bindings, that is, calf bindings decorated with elaborate wood-grain patterns. Surviving examples of March's bindings testify to his craftsmanship and his aesthetic sensibilities. The first week of November Jefferson paid him to have dozens of volumes bound. He would bring dozens more volumes there in the coming years.

After March's death the first week of June 1804, Joseph Milligan took over the business. Capitalizing on the excellent reputation March had established, Milligan kept the name John March's Store. Milligan also perpetuated the shop's reputation. He stocked an excellent selection of books, and could turn out handsome tree calf bindings himself. Jefferson observed, "For elegant bindings to choice books, there is no one in America comparable to him. His bindings are so tasty, so solid, and as heavy as blocks of metal."[33]

By the second week of November, Jefferson had finished a draft of his "First Annual Message." (The president's annual message would not be known as the "State of the Union" until the twentieth century.) He sent a copy of it to James Madison, asking him to give it a "serious revisal, not only as to matter, but diction." Jefferson's instructions did not stop here. "Where strictness of grammar does not weaken expression, it should be attended to in complaisance to the purists of New England. But where by small grammatical negligences the energy of an idea is condensed, or a word stands for a sentence, I hold grammatical rigor in contempt."[34]

Elsewhere Jefferson similarly criticized those who advocated grammatical rigor. To one like-minded author, he wrote, "I concur entirely with you in opposition to Purists, who would destroy all strength and beauty of style, by subjecting it to a rigorous compliance with their rules. Fill up all the ellipses of Tacitus, Sallust, Livy, etc., and the elegance and force of their sententious brevity are extinguished."[35] Jefferson's comments react to the criticism his inaugural address had received. Finding it difficult to critique the substance of his inaugural address, some of his bitterest critics had attacked his grammar. He was happy to clean up his grammar to minimize criticism in this regard, but he shunned grammatical correctness if it detracted from the power of his words.

On Tuesday, December 8, 1801, Jefferson sent Meriwether Lewis to the Capitol with his first annual message and a cover letter explaining it. The explanation was necessary because Jefferson was breaking with a tradition established by George Washington and perpetuated by John Adams. Both had delivered their annual messages to Congress orally, but Jefferson preferred communicating through the written word. Early in the first year of his presidency, he had decided against delivering the address orally. He felt that a written message would be more convenient, saving time and freeing Congress from having to answer it without having the time to consider it properly.

In his message, Jefferson celebrated the fact that the United States had remained at peace during his first year in office. The general peace allowed Americans "quietly to cultivate the earth and to practice and improve those arts which tend to increase our comforts."[36] The word "increase" introduces a leitmotif that recurs throughout the message. Jefferson would repeat and elaborate the connotations of the word, which comes to mean "increase and multiply."

Continuing his message, he admitted that there was one exception to the general peace: the war with Tripoli. He explained that he had sent a small squadron there and reported what had happened. The schooner *Enterprise* had engaged a Tripolitan cruiser and defeated it without loss of life on the American side. "The bravery exhibited by our citizens," Jefferson stated, will be "testimony to the world that it is not the want of that virtue which makes us seek their peace, but a conscientious desire to direct the energies of our nation to the multiplication of the human race, and not to its destruction." Though brave and devoted to defending their nation, American sailors were still anxious to return home to their families and farms.

The subject of the 1800 census gave Jefferson the opportunity to reiterate his central theme. The results of the census promised "a duplication in little more than twenty-two years. We contemplate this rapid growth, and the prospect it holds up to us, not with a view to the injuries it may enable us to do to others in some future day, but to the settlement of the extensive country still remaining vacant within our limits, to the multiplications of men susceptible of happiness, educated in the love of order, habituated to self-government, and value its blessings above all price." With keen foresight, Jefferson created an idyllic picture of North America gradually filling up with the burgeoning American population.

Hearkening back to an idea he had been advocating publicly at least since his revision of Virginia law, he offered another way to help disseminate news and ideas throughout the nation. He recommended eliminating postage on newspapers "to facilitate the progress of information." Newspaper postage was just one of many internal taxes Jefferson thought could be eliminated. In fact, he advocated eliminating all internal taxes in his message to Congress.

Bringing the message to a close, he provided its most memorable sentence: "Agriculture, manufactures, commerce, and navigation, the four pillars of our prosperity, are the most thriving when left most free to individual enterprise." Jefferson's careful word choice unites this part of the message with its earlier part. Much as the schooner *Enterprise* defeated its Tripolitan rival, American enterprise will overcome all obstacles and ensure a prosperous and mighty nation.

On New Year's Day, 1802, an extraordinary gift arrived at the President's House, an enormous Cheshire cheese, which had already become known as the Mammoth Cheese. The cheese had been made to celebrate Jefferson's election by the Republican citizens of Cheshire, a small community in western Massachusetts. It had been transported partly by sea and partly by land from Massachusetts to Washington, and it met great fanfare wherever it went. The last leg of the journey took it down Pennsylvania Avenue to the President's House, where it arrived the first morning of the new year. John Leland, the Baptist preacher who came up with the idea for this great cheese, personally presented it to President Jefferson. In his presentation speech, Leland called it "the greatest cheese in America, for the greatest man in America."[37]

The huge cheese was four feet in diameter, thirteen feet in circumference, and seventeen inches tall. Its crust was stained red and adorned with the motto "Rebellion to tyrants is obedience to God."[38] It deserves a place in early American literary history because it inspired numerous verses, whose tone and content divided sharply according to party lines. The Republican *Ode to the Mammoth Cheese*, for example, ends with the following lines:

> All that we want or wish for in life's hour,
> Heaven still will grant us—they are only these,
> Poetry—Health—Peace—Virtue—Bread and *Cheese*.

A Federalist poem that appeared in the *Courier of New Hampshire* the first week of January 1802 included a stanza about the Mammoth Cheese:

> But, Muse, you'll not forget to squeeze
> A word out 'bout the "Mammoth Cheese";
> Such Cheese no man before set face on;
> 'Tis bigger than Don Quixot's bason—
> Such Cheese, my stars! 'twould make one swoon
> To view—'tis bigger than a moon!
> This Cheese is surely honour'd more,
> Than ever any Cheese before;

To feel the weight and force, forsooth,
And crash, of Presidential tooth.
Ye maggots, that dwell in the Cheese,
With horror how your limbs will freeze,
How will you kick, and squirm, and claw,
Beneath the Jeffersonian jaw!

The Mammoth Cheese symbolized the support Jefferson received from religious groups who benefited from his policy of religious freedom. Early in his presidency, he received many other messages of support, none so extravagant but many as heartfelt. Recently, he had received a letter from Connecticut written by members of the Danbury Baptist Association congratulating him upon his election. On this busy New Year's Day, Jefferson drafted a response to the association, thanking them for their support and outlining his basic principles toward the relationship between church and state. His words are inspiring:

> Believing with you that religion is a matter which lies solely between man and his God, that he owes account to none other for his faith or his worship, that the legislative powers of government reach actions only, and not opinions, I contemplate with sovereign reverence that act of the whole American people which declared that their legislature should "make no law respecting an establishment of religion, or pro-hibiting the free exercise thereof," thus building a wall of separation between church and State. Adhering to this expression of the supreme will of the nation in behalf of the rights of conscience, I shall see with sincere satisfaction the progress of those sentiments which tend to restore to man all his natural rights, convinced he has no natural right in opposition to his social duties.[39]

Though written as a letter to the Danbury Baptist Association, Jef-ferson knew his words would be published throughout the United States. With his response to the Danbury Baptists, he took the opportunity to influence public attitudes toward the separation of church and state. Sending a copy of his letter to Levi Lincoln, Jefferson explained his reaction to this and similar addresses he had received: "I have generally endeavored to turn them to some account, by making them the occasion, by way of answer, of sowing useful truths and principles among the people, which might germinate and become rooted among their politi-cal tenets. The Baptist address now inclosed admits of a condemnation of the alliance between church and state, under the authority of the

Constitution."[40] Jefferson intended his statement as a gloss on the First Amendment, and such it has become. His wall-of-separation metaphor brilliantly encapsulates the proper relationship between church and state.

Jefferson's metaphor is so well known that some think he coined it, but the phrase "wall of separation" occurs repeatedly in earlier literature. It was used often enough to become proverbial. The Boston preacher Samuel Willard said, "Man, by the instigation of *Satan* was allured and invited, and by the abuse of his own free will led away to fall from his obedience, and became a Covenant-breaker; whereby a wall of separation was set up between him and God." In her *Moral Tales*, Madame Le Prince de Beaumont told the story of two star-crossed lovers divided by a wall of separation. And, to cite one further example, Frederick Schiller spoke of a wall of separation between good and evil in *Don Carlos: A Tragedy*.[41] In these various works, the wall of separation connotes a barrier that is impenetrable, impermeable, unbreakable. Jefferson played upon these traditional associations to build his wall of separation between church and state.

In terms of Jefferson's personal life, the most important event of his first term as president was his daughters' visit to Washington. They arrived on November 21, 1802. Not surprisingly, Margaret Bayard Smith's correspondence provides the best information about their stay. She characterized Maria as "beautiful, simplicity and timidity personified when in company, but when alone with you of communicative and winning manners." Martha she described as "rather homely, a delicate likeness of her father." Still, Mrs. Smith found Martha more interesting than her sister. Speaking more in terms of personality than appearance, she called Martha, "one of the most lovely women I have ever met with, her countenance beaming with intelligence, benevolence and sensibility, and her conversation fulfils all her countenance promises. Her manners, so frank and affectionate, that you know her at once, and feel perfectly at your ease with her."[42]

Mrs. Smith also fell prey to the charms of Martha's daughter Ellen, whom she called "without exception one of the finest and most intelligent children I have ever met with." Finding Ellen "singularly and extravagantly fond of poetry," Mrs. Smith recited for her *The Hermit*, by Oliver Goldsmith. Ellen listened "with the most expressive countenance," looking Mrs. Smith in the eye and clasping her arms around her.

Martha and Maria left Washington the first week in January 1803. The President's House seemed empty again after their departure, but Jefferson would see his family again when he returned to Monticello for a brief visit in March. Shortly before he returned to Washington from that quick trip home, he received a copy of Joseph Priestley's *Socrates and Jesus Compared* in the mail. Priestley's work gave him much to think about on the road to Washington. He explained, "It became a subject of reflection, while on the road, and unoccupied otherwise. The result was, to arrange in my mind a Syllabus, or Outline of such an Estimate of the comparative merits of Christianity, as wished to see executed, by some one of more leisure and information for the task than myself."[43]

He briefly outlined his thoughts for a book comparing the development of moral philosophy from the ancients to the time of Christ. He sketched out his ideas in a letter to Priestley and developed them further for Benjamin Rush. Here was the long promised outline of his ideas on Christianity. He titled it "Syllabus of an Estimate of the Merit of the Doctrines of Jesus, Compared with Those of Others."

Start with the ethics of the ancients, he suggested. Next, discuss the ethics of the Jews. After that, present the life, character, and doctrines of Jesus. Avoid altogether the issue of Christ's divinity. Discuss the problematic nature of the evidence of Christ's life and teaching, recorded "by the most unlettered of men, by memory, long after they had heard them from him; when much was forgotten, much misunderstood, and presented in very paradoxical shapes." Despite the fragmentary nature of Christ's system of morality, enough evidence survives to show that it was "the most benevolent and sublime probably that has been ever taught, and eminently more perfect than those of any of the antient philosophers."[44] In his "Syllabus," Jefferson characterized Jesus: "His parentage was obscure, his condition poor, his education null, his natural endowments great, his life correct and innocent; he was meek, benevolent, patient, firm, disinterested, and of the sublimest eloquence." Jesus' system of morals "if filled up in the true style and spirit of the rich fragments he left us, would be the most perfect and sublime that has ever been taught by man."[45]

Jefferson's use of the wall-of-separation metaphor in his letter to the Danbury Baptist Association elegantly describes the proper relationship between church and state in an enlightened world. To understand Jefferson's general attitude toward Christianity, Samuel Willard's application of the metaphor may be more useful. Willard placed God on one side of the wall and man on the other. For Jefferson, there was no doubt where Jesus stood: Christ is on our side.

CHAPTER 33

"Life of Captain Lewis"

History of the Expedition under the Command of Captains Lewis and Clark, the most substantial work of American literature to appear in the first two decades of the nineteenth century, was based on journals Meriwether Lewis and William Clark kept during their transcontinental expedition. Eight years would pass between their return in 1806 and the publication of *History of the Expedition*. During that time Nicholas Biddle began preparing their unwieldy journals for publication but wearied of the task before its completion. Paul Allen took over as editor and saw the work through the press.[1]

Initially, Allen asked Jefferson to write a biographical sketch of both Lewis and Clark. Jefferson knew little of Clark's life but said he would write a biography of Lewis for *History of the Expedition*. Since Lewis and Clark's return from their journey, Jefferson had been anxious for the publication of their story. Allen was hurrying the work along as fast as he could, but he agreed to forestall publication briefly to accommodate Jefferson's biography of Lewis. Though Jefferson knew Lewis well, he wanted to learn more about him before completing the biographical sketch. Consequently, he dispatched a messenger to Lewis's family to retrieve additional information about the explorer's early life.[2]

Allen saw the biography of Lewis as a valuable addition to the completed book. Explaining what he hoped Jefferson's contribution would add to *History of the Expedition*, Allen provided a perceptive, if cynical, comment on reading tastes in early-nineteenth-century America: "I wish very much to enliven the dulness of the Narrative by something more popular splendid and attractive. The publick taste has from a variety of adventitious causes been gorged to repletion on fanciful viands and the most nutritive and invigorating aliments will not be relished unless seasoned with Something of that character. Biography partakes to a certain extent of this quality, and is essentially connected with subjects dear to every heart."[3] Allen's words emphasize the importance of biography as a popular literary genre, but his negativity toward the narrative of Lewis and Clark makes it sound like his heart was not entirely devoted to his editorial task. Jefferson, on the other hand, understood the book's inherent interest and was happy to participate in its publication.

Upon completing his biography of Lewis, Jefferson turned it into a letter by adding an introductory paragraph in the margin of the manuscript's first page.[4] Before submitting the letter to Allen, he ran it past Allen's editorial predecessor, offering Biddle the opportunity to revise the biography as he saw fit. Biddle found Jefferson's biographical sketch of Lewis "very interesting" and saw no need for revision. He forwarded it to Allen unchanged.[5]

Details within the biography, combined with remarks in an earlier letter to Allen, show that Jefferson expected him to print the entire biographical sketch. Allen greatly appreciated Jefferson's life of Lewis. He printed not only the biography in its entirety, but also the introductory paragraph Jefferson had added at the last minute. Jefferson's letter forms the book's introduction, which Allen titled "Life of Captain Lewis."

Though written five years after he left office, "Life of Captain Lewis" provides a convenient way to retell the story of President Jefferson's involvement in the Lewis and Clark expedition while simultaneously examining one of the fullest biographical works he wrote.

In his opening paragraph, Jefferson sketched out his theory of biography writing: "The ordinary occurrences of a private life, and those also while acting in a subordinate sphere in the army, in a time of peace, are not deemed sufficiently interesting to occupy the public attention."[6] Jefferson's approach to biography resembles his approach to autobiography. Much as he excluded personal details—"egotisms"—when writing about himself, much as he omitted personal and private information from *The Anas*, he saw no need for private details of personal life in a published biography. Lengthy accounts of ancestry are also unnecessary to biography. A brief account of minor incidents from a person's youth is permissible—provided the incidents help reveal important aspects of character.

Jefferson's Lewis is a prodigy of the backwoods. Stories of the boy's hunting excursions prove it. Jefferson wrote: "When only eight years of age he habitually went out, in the dead of night alone with his dogs, into the forest to hunt the raccoon and opossum, which, seeking their food in the night, can then only be taken. In this exercise, no season or

Meriwether Lewis, from Life, 1807, by Charles Willson Peale. (Independence National Historical Park)

circumstance could obstruct his purpose—plunging through the winter's snows and frozen streams in pursuit of his object."[7] Jefferson's "Life of Captain Lewis" presents a vivid picture of a hardy and determined boy American readers could appreciate. From colonial times through the nineteenth century, the coon hunt was practically a rite of passage for boys growing up in the South.

No document better reveals how carefully Jefferson crafted the story of young Lewis than a manuscript fragment in an unknown hand that survives among his papers. This fragment lists several of the same details as Jefferson's "Life of Captain Lewis," but the two accounts differ in places. The fragment begins:

> M. Lewis, born August 18, 1774 in Albemarle. At first went to common day schools, learning to read, to write and Arithmetic with ordinary facility, he was early remarkable for intrepidity, liberality and hardihood, at eight years of age going alone with his dogs at midnight in the depth of winter, hunting wading creeks when the banks were covered with ice and snow. He might be tracked through the snow to his traps by the blood which trickled from his bare feet.[8]

In its details, this fragment is close enough to the "Life of Captain Lewis" to confirm it as Jefferson's source. Apparently, this manuscript fragment is what Jefferson's messenger brought back from his quest to learn more information about Lewis's early life. While incorporating information from this source, Jefferson made three crucial changes.

His source text uses a favorite rhetorical device of Jefferson's—the list of three—but the three qualities it ascribes to young Lewis—intrepidity, liberality, hardihood—did not jibe with Jefferson's understanding of him. In Jefferson's version, young Lewis is remarkable "for enterprise, boldness, and discretion." This phrase echoes advice Jefferson had given Peter Carr many years earlier. He recommended hunting to Carr as a good form of exercise because it could give "boldness, enterprize, and independance to the mind."[9] Revising his source, Jefferson remained true to its structure but substituted personal characteristics he generally admired and personally recognized in Lewis.

Jefferson also eliminated the gory detail. The image of a barefoot boy traipsing through the snow with so little regard for personal safety that he leaves bloody footprints wherever he walks was not an image Jefferson wanted for the hero of "Life of Captain Lewis." He wanted to depict the man he chose to lead a great expedition across the continent as someone with more cognizance of personal danger.

The third way Jefferson's "Life of Captain Lewis" diverges from his source concerns its factual organization. To give the story more impact, Jefferson changed the order of its details. The source text describes Lewis's early education before the coon hunting episode and then returns to the subject of his education. Jefferson withheld the story of Lewis's formal education until after he related the coon hunt. In Jefferson's version, Lewis perfected his woodcraft as a boy, studied Latin as a teen, and left school at eighteen to become a farmer. Describing the early life of Meriwether

Lewis, Jefferson created a hero who exemplified a personal ideal. As Lewis matures from adolescence to adulthood in Jefferson's version, he moves from the wilderness to the world of books to a farm of his own. But Lewis was too restless to stay farmer for long. He joined the army, participated in the Whiskey Rebellion, and rose to a captaincy.

Once he set Lewis on the path to military glory in "Life of Captain Lewis," Jefferson paused his biographical sketch to recount the history of the exploration of the American West. Seemingly a digression, this section greatly contributes to the story as a whole. Nicholas Biddle, for one, found it quite valuable. After reading "Life of Captain Lewis" in manuscript, Biddle observed, "The account of the previous projects for exploring the country west of the Mississipi contains new and curious information."[10] This section performs an important role in the story of Lewis's life, too. Jefferson recognized the Lewis and Clark expedition as *the* defining event in Lewis's life. The biography of Meriwether Lewis and the history of the expedition were inextricably linked. A section on the prehistory of the expedition suited his "Life of Captain Lewis."

Jefferson's prehistory begins in Paris, where he and John Ledyard discussed the possibility of exploring the American West. Calling Ledyard to mind, Jefferson inserted a brief biography of him into "Life of Captain Lewis." This life of Ledyard also seems like a digression, but it offers an important parallel. Using the biographical parallel as a rhetorical technique, Jefferson borrowed a leaf from Puritan historiography. In *Magnalia Christi Americana*—to name one of several Puritan histories he had in his library at Monticello—Cotton Mather frequently used biographical parallels to illuminate the lives of his subjects. This literary device derives from a form of biblical exegesis known as typology.[11] The practice of typology involved identifying parallels between types (characters from the Old Testament) and antitypes (characters from the New Testament). The Old Testament types foreshadow the New Testament antitypes. Including a brief biography of Ledyard within his life of Lewis, Jefferson nationalized and secularized this traditional form of exegesis. John Ledyard, the type, prefigures Meriwether Lewis, the antitype.

The specific details of Ledyard's life reinforce the scriptural resonance. The last letter Jefferson received from him came from Egypt, where the ever ambitious, ever adventurous Ledyard was planning to trace the Nile to its source. Shortly after writing this letter, Ledyard died in Cairo under mysterious circumstances. In other words, Ledyard had died seeking the headwaters of the great river of the Old Testament. Similarly, Lewis would explore the headwaters of the Missouri, the great east–west river of the American continent—the New Canaan, according to Puritan historiography. Where the type had failed, the antitype would succeed.

Placing the prehistory of the Lewis and Clark expedition where he did, Jefferson allowed himself to skip a big chunk of Lewis's life, specifically, the time from the Whiskey Rebellion through Lewis's appointment as his presidential secretary in 1801. Jefferson resumed the story on January 18, 1803, the day he submitted his confidential message to Congress that proposed an expedition across the American continent. Although Jefferson breezed past this message in the "Life of Captain Lewis," it is worth lingering over here.

He pitched the expedition to Congress as a commercial venture but suggested that in terms of international diplomacy, it would be better if other nations considered it undertaken for "literary purposes." This phrase indicates how closely Jefferson associated literature and science. An expedition undertaken for literary purposes was one that would be written up and offered to the world as a contribution to science. He explained:

> While other civilized nations have encountered great expense to enlarge the boundaries of knowledge, by undertaking voyages of discovery, and for other literary purposes, in various parts and directions, our nation seems to owe to the same object, as well as to its own interest, to explore this, the only line of easy communication across the continent, and so directly traversing our own part of it. The interests of commerce place the principal object within the constitutional powers and care of Congress, and that it should incidentally advance the geographical knowledge of our own continent can not but be an additional gratification. The nation claiming the territory, regarding this as a literary pursuit which it is in the habit of permitting within its dominions, would not be disposed to view it with jealousy, even if the expiring state of its interest there did not render it a matter of indifference.[12]

Jefferson greatly admired the voyages of discovery that had been sponsored by the philosophical societies of France and Great Britain and underwritten by their governments. These journeys were landmark events in the history of the Enlightenment, events that contributed to man's greater understanding of the world. Similarly, the Lewis and Clark expedition would be America's contribution to the mapping of the globe. Jefferson may have persuaded Congress to fund the expedition by emphasizing its commercial nature, but by the end of his confidential message, the literary purposes he mentioned reflect his personal impulses more closely.

After recalling the message to Congress and Lewis's subsequent scientific training in "Life of Captain Lewis," Jefferson got down to his instructions for the expedition. At this point in the manuscript that would become "Life of Captain Lewis," Jefferson inscribed a brief note to Paul Allen: "Here insert the instructions verbatim."[13] Though Jefferson had told Allen to include whatever details he wished, this note clearly indicates that Jefferson expected Allen to print the entire biographical essay *and* the complete set of instructions.

Jefferson's desire to include the instructions within the biography of Lewis affirms an impulse he had articulated and exemplified in other writings from *The Anas* to his autobiography. He found the inclusion of important historical documents essential to history writing. Contemporary readers appreciated the inclusion. A headnote to a contemporary reprint of "Life of Captain Lewis" called the instructions "the most valuable part of this paper" and suggested that subsequent American explorers could use these instructions as a pattern to follow.[14]

Besides contributing to the historical accuracy of the "Life of Captain Lewis," "Instructions to Lewis" enhances the literary complexity of the entire work. Where the biography meets the instructions, Jefferson's narrative voice splits in two. The casual, easygoing voice of biographer Jefferson gives way to the authoritative, official voice of President Jefferson.

"Instructions" meticulously outlines the preparations and procedures Lewis should follow. It describes the ammunition, provisions, and scientific instruments he should bring; tells him how to maintain communications; and explains what to do after crossing the Mississippi, that is, after leaving the United States and entering Louisiana, which the French had recently obtained from Spain. Establishing these details, Jefferson carefully articulated the expedition's purpose: "The object of your mission is to explore the Missouri river, and such principal streams of it, as, by its course and communication with the waters of the Pacific ocean, whether the Columbia, Oregan, Colorado, or any other river, may offer the most direct and practicable water communication across the continent, for the purposes of commerce."[15]

Specific instructions explain how to record latitude and longitude and how to make other useful measurements. These instructions recall earlier ones Jefferson had given John Ledyard and André Michaux. Jefferson not only emphasized accuracy but also stressed the importance of making multiple copies of the records for safekeeping. Lewis should record such "objects worthy of notice" as animals, climate, fossils, minerals, and soil. Jefferson could have retitled "Instructions to Lewis" as "Hints to Americans Traveling in North America."

Jefferson wanted Lewis to gather ethnological data, too, so he consulted Benjamin Rush, who gave him a detailed set of guidelines. Jefferson simplified Rush's guidelines considerably. Whereas Rush was more a man of pure science, Jefferson was a scientist who kept an eye toward practical matters. Rush—"always for going to the bottom of things"—requested information that would be difficult to obtain. He wanted to know at what age Indian women begin and cease to menstruate. He also wanted Lewis to take the pulse of children, adults, and elders morning, noon, and night.[16] In "Instructions," Jefferson alternately emphasized gathering information on disease prevention and cures. He wanted Lewis to gather as much information as possible about Indian languages and asked him to compile basic vocabulary lists.

He mentioned the native inhabitants again as he emphasized the peaceful nature of the expedition:

> In all your intercourse with the natives, treat them in the most friendly and conciliatory manner which their own conduct will admit; allay all jealousies as to the object of your journey; satisfy them of its innocence; make them acquainted with the position, extent, character, peaceable and commercial dispositions of the United States; of our wish to be neighbourly, friendly, and useful to them, and of our dispositions to a commercial intercourse with them; confer with them on points most convenient as mutual emporiums, and the articles of most desirable interchange for them and us.[17]

Stressing the importance of avoiding unnecessary risk, Jefferson explained, "We value too much the lives of citizens to offer them to probable destruction." If confronted by superior forces, Lewis and his men should return to safety instead of engaging them in combat. Their safety and the preservation of their new information should be paramount: "In the loss of yourselves we should lose also the information you will have acquired. By returning safely with that, you may enable us to renew the essay with better calculated means. To your own discretion, therefore, must be left the degree of danger you may risk, and the point at which you should decline, only saying, we wish you to err on the side of your safety, and to bring back your party safe, even if it be with less information."[18]

"Instructions" also suggests what Lewis should do upon reaching the Pacific. Ideally, the expedition should return overland. If possible, a few men should take a copy of a complete set of records and return by water. If an overland return journey proves impossible, then Lewis should get a passing ship to take him and his party wherever it happens to be going. Jefferson wrote:

> As you will be without money, clothes, or provisions, you must endeavour to use the credit of the United States to obtain them; for which purposes open letters of credit shall be furnished you, authorizing you to draw on the executive of the United States, or any of its officers, in any part of the world, on which draughts can be disposed of, and to apply with our recommendations to the consuls, agents, merchants, or citizens of any nation with which we have intercourse, assuring them, in our name, that any aids they may furnish you shall be honourably repaid, and on demand. Our consuls, Thomas Hewes, at Batavia, in Java, William Buchanan, in the Isles of France and Bourbon, and John Elmslie, at the Cape of Good Hope, will be able to supply your necessities, by draughts on us.[19]

"Instructions to Lewis" is Jefferson's "Passage to India." His meticulous preparations are impressive, but his imaginative vision is stunning. He not only saw Lewis and his party crossing the continent, but also foresaw the possibility of them sailing around the world, turning their continental journey into a round-the-world excursion. The United States already had men stationed at key points around the circumference of the globe. Crossing North America and sailing from the Pacific Coast, the intrepid American could connect the world together.

Jefferson addressed "Instructions" solely to Lewis because Clark had yet to join the expedition. Not until after Jefferson wrote these instructions did Lewis invite William Clark to join as co-leader. Lewis knew Clark well and recognized his leadership skills. The two had served together under Anthony Wayne in the Battle of Fallen Timbers. Some years older than Lewis, Clark had more wilderness experience. The two men complemented one another and, needless to say, proved a successful team.[20]

When Jefferson presented the set of instructions to Lewis, he was unaware that the United States had officially acquired Louisiana. He received the news the first week of July. The purchase of Louisiana from France, as he explained in "Life of Captain Lewis," "increased infinitely the interest we felt in the expedition, and lessened the apprehensions of interruption from other powers."[21]

Jefferson officially announced the cession of Louisiana on July 4, 1803. Samuel Harrison Smith, who attended the Independence Day festivities at the White House, reported the celebration to his wife, who was out of town. Concerning the Louisiana Purchase, Smith wrote, "This mighty event forms an era in our history, and of itself must render the administration of Jefferson immortal." The military welcomed the dawn with an eighteen-gun salute. At noon, company gathered at the President's House. Smith, who had attended Jefferson's previous Independence Day celebrations, found this one the best yet: "It was more numerous than I have before marked it, enlivened too by the presence of between 40 and 50 ladies clothed in their best attire, cakes, punch, wine &c in profusion."[22]

"Life of Captain Lewis" says nothing about the holiday celebrations. Jefferson did mention that Lewis did not leave the city until July 5, implying that Lewis intentionally stayed to celebrate Independence Day. The implication reinforces Lewis's patriotism and underscores the Lewis and Clark Expedition as a nationalistic venture.

Writing his biography of Lewis as a preface to *History of the Expedition*, Jefferson was deprived of retelling the story of the expedition itself. Once he set Lewis and Clark on their journey across the continent, he could do no more at this point in his story than introduce the narrative that follows.

"Life of Captain Lewis" does not mention the communications Jefferson received from Lewis and Clark during their expedition, but they exchanged multiple letters through the summer and into the fall of 1803, as Lewis and Clark made their way to St. Louis. During this period, Jefferson was busy gathering information about the huge new territory the United States had acquired. He assembled the various accounts of Louisiana into a form suitable for both Congress and the increasingly curious reading public. His distillation of these various accounts appeared as a pamphlet titled *An Account of Louisiana, being an Abstract of Documents, in the Office of the Department of State, and of the Treasury*. A largely unadorned set of facts, Jefferson's *Account of Louisiana* is punctuated by colorful details. Some indicate his gullibility; others, his prescience. All serve to bring the land of Louisiana alive for his readers. His admiration of the explorers is obvious, his understanding of the potential of Louisiana's resources boundless, and his recognition of its natural wonders both beautiful and awesome. Consider what he had to say about the following topics:

On communication in Louisiana:

Many of the present establishments are separated from each other by immense and trackless deserts, having no communication with each other by land, except now and then a solitary instance of its being attempted by hunters, who have to swim rivers, expose themselves to the inclemency of the weather, and carry their provisions on their backs for a time, proportioned to the length of their journey. This is particularly the case on the west of the Mississippi, where the communication is kept up only by water between the capital and the distant settlements; three months being required to convey intelligence from the one to the other by the Mississippi.

On the west side of the Mississippi in upper Louisiana:

It is elevated and healthy, and well watered with a variety of large, rapid streams, calculated for mills and other water-works.... Some of the heights exhibit a scene truly picturesque. They rise to a height of at least three hundred feet, faced with perpendicular *lime and free-stone*, carved into various shapes and figures by the hand of nature, and afford the appearance of a multitude of antique towers.

On Louisiana as a source of salt:

There exists, about one thousand miles up the Missouri, and not far from that river, *a salt mountain*.... This mountain is said to be one hundred and eighty miles long, and forty-five in width, composed of solid rock salt, without any trees, or even shrubs on it.

On the effects of hurricanes in lower Louisiana:

The whole lower part of the country ... is subject to overflowing in hurricanes, either by the recoiling of the river, or reflux from the sea on each side; and, on more than one occasion, it has been covered from the depth of two to ten feet, according to the descent of the river, whereby many lives were lost, horses and cattle swept away, and a scene of destruction laid.... These hurricanes have generally been felt in the month of August. Their greatest fury lasts about twelve hours. They commence in the southeast, veer about to all points of the compass, are felt most severely below, and seldom extend more than a few leagues above New Orleans. In their whole course they are marked with ruin and desolation.[23]

Jefferson presented this information to Congress on November 14, 1803. Two days later, he sent a copy of *An Account of Louisiana* to Lewis. In the cover letter accompanying this pamphlet, Jefferson expressed concern about how far Lewis and Clark intended to go before winter. He received no response. In January 1804, he wrote two follow-up letters, asking their whereabouts and informing Lewis that he had been elected to the American Philosophical Society, a prestigious honor designed to secure for the Society some of the curiosities the explorers were accumulating.

Lewis and Clark welcomed the Indians they encountered to travel east to Washington to meet President Jefferson. Several accepted the offer. On Wednesday, July 11, 1804, White Hairs, a principal chief of the Great Osages, arrived at the head of a delegation of twelve men and two boys. Jefferson was thoroughly impressed by their stature and their demeanor. He conveyed his impressions to members of his cabinet. He told Treasury Secretary Albert Gallatin they were "certainly the most gigantic men we have ever seen." To Navy Secretary Robert Smith he called them "the finest men we have ever seen." Jefferson informally welcomed them the next day and presented a formal welcome speech a few days later.[24]

His formal welcome reveals his mastery of the rhetoric of Indian diplomacy. Instead of using the typical, and increasingly clichéd, language of the Indian treaty—burying the hatchet, brightening the chain—Jefferson structured his address using the metaphor of fatherhood. President Jefferson presents himself as the Great Father to his children the Osage. He begins his address with the words "My children," which he repeats at the start of his next three paragraphs. He expresses hope for friendship and commiserates with the Osages' recent tragedy, a massacre at the hands of the Sauk:

> My children. I sincerely weep with you over the graves of your chiefs and friends, who fell by the hands of their enemies lately descending the Osage river. Had they been prisoners, and living, we would have recovered them: but no voice can awake the dead; no power undo what is done. On this side the Missisipi where our government has been long established, and our authority organised our friends visiting us are safe. We hope it will not be long before our voice will be heard and our

arm respected, by those who mediate to injure our friends, on the other side of that river.[25]

Jefferson's use of the first person plural reinforces the fact that he is speaking for the entire nation. His message depicts the United States as the Indians' protector and avenger. Recognizing the importance of Indian oral tradition, Jefferson made the voice a prominent motif in this address. The act of enforcing the law of the land is a matter of making others hear the voice of the United States.

While maintaining the fatherhood metaphor, Jefferson also introduced the notion of brotherhood. Explaining what the Louisiana Purchase means to them, he stated:

My children. By late arrangements with France and Spain, we now take their place as your neighbors, friends and fathers: and we hope you will have no cause to regret the change. It is so long since our forefathers came from beyond the great water, that we have lost the memory of it, and seem to have grown out of this land, as you have done. Never more will you have occasion to change your fathers. We are all now of one family, born in the same land, and bound to live as brothers; and the strangers from beyond the great water are gone from among us.[26]

Despite the metaphors, despite the hierarchical relationship Jefferson establishes, this address has a frankness that is refreshing. Two centuries had passed since the first permanent English settlement was established. Several generations of Americans now knew no other home. Born in America, they were as much a part of the land as were the Indians.

The day Chief White Hairs arrived in Washington, July 11, another momentous event was taking place at Weehawken, New Jersey, where Aaron Burr and Alexander Hamilton met to fight a duel. This conflict had been brewing for a long time. The two had been political rivals since the late 1780s, and Burr had frequently been the object of Hamilton's wrath, both in public and in private. As vice president, Burr had antagonized the Republican Party, which replaced him with George Clinton as vice presidential candidate in the 1804 national election. Burr ran for governor of New York but was roundly defeated. Meanwhile, Hamilton's incessant attacks on Burr showed no sign of surcease. When Hamilton refused to take back the derogatory comments he made during the New York governor's race, Burr demanded satisfaction. Hamilton accepted the challenge.

Burr fired first, sending a ball through Hamilton's torso. As Hamilton fell to the ground, he fired wildly. Once the smoke cleared, Burr remained standing, but Hamilton was on the ground with the ball lodged in his spine. He died the next day. Many Americans considered Burr a cold-blooded murderer.[27] His adventures in the West would menace Jefferson during his second term as president.[28]

In his address to Chief White Hairs, Jefferson depicted the United States as a land of harmony, where truth and justice reigned. The reality was somewhat different. A place where the nation's second highest officer used physical violence to avenge a personal wrong hardly seems like an exemplar of modern civilization. Generally speaking, Jefferson considered the duel a barbarous way to settle a dispute. But in the story of his second term in office, violence or the threat of violence forms a prominent leitmotif.

The fall of 1804 Jefferson was elected to his second term—the first landslide victory in presidential history. George Clinton was chosen vice president. The winter he spent preparing for his second term as president, Lewis and Clark spent at Fort Mandan. Once the Missouri melted the following spring, they sent their barge back. Accompanying the numerous specimens they had gathered, Lewis sent a detailed letter describing their progress and a copy of Clark's journal.

Jefferson took the information from Lewis and Clark, combined it with information from explorers he had sent to other parts of North America, and compiled *Message from the President of the United States Communicating Discoveries Made in Exploring the Missouri, Red River, and Washita, by Captains Lewis and Clark, Doctor Sibley, and Mr. Dunbar,* which he presented to Congress on February 19, 1806. He heard nothing more from the expedition for several months.

In June 1806, Jefferson received some sad news about George Wythe. The previous year his grandnephew George Wythe Sweeney, a notorious gambler, had stolen several books from Wythe's library and tried to sell them at public auction. After that scheme failed, he forged his granduncle's name on a half dozen checks drawn on the Bank of Virginia. Desperate for money, Sweeney devised an even more nefarious scheme: to murder his granduncle to receive his inheritance. On May 25, 1806, he put a huge quantity of arsenic in Wythe's morning coffee. Michael, a house servant, also drank some of the coffee. Both became violently ill, experiencing bouts of uncontrollable vomiting and diarrhea. Michael died first. The autopsy determined that he had been poisoned. There was only one suspect.

Wythe lived long enough to add a codicil to his will, disinheriting his grandnephew.

"Let me die righteous," he said on Friday, June 6. Wythe died two days later on Sunday, the eighth.[29]

He bequeathed his scientific instruments and his library to Jefferson. As might be surmised by Wythe's professional and scholarly interests, his library was filled with law books and annotated editions of Greek and Latin classics. There were a number of titles Jefferson already had in his library, especially among his law books. He sold or gave away some of these duplicates. For example, he received from Wythe's estate a copy of the 1738 English edition of Grotius's *Rights of War and Peace*, with annotations by the French jurist Jean Barbeyrac. He already had the 1724 French edition of Grotius's work with Barbeyrac's notes. Being a two-volume quarto, the French edition was more convenient, so Jefferson held onto it, letting someone else have Wythe's copy of Grotius.[30]

Jefferson also received Wythe's copy of the two-volume folio edition of Lord Raymond's *Reports of Cases of King's Bench and Common Pleas*. Since he already had the three-volume octavo edition published in Dublin in 1792, he gave Wythe's copy of Raymond's *Reports* to his nephew Dabney Carr, Jr., who had passed the bar ten years earlier and was currently serving as the commonwealth's attorney for Albemarle County. The gift shows that Jefferson was continuing to further the education of his nephews, even after they had become established.[31]

Perhaps Jacob Tullius's parallel text edition of Longinus's *De Sublimitate* was the first book from Wythe's bequest Jefferson read. Longinus's concept of the sublime had already influenced Jefferson's aesthetic sensibilities. As his appreciation of Ossian suggests, Jefferson closely associated the sublime and the melancholy. His copy of Wythe's Longinus reinforces the association. Opening the book's cover, Jefferson inscribed the following: "The gift of a friend a few days before he died."[32]

Death threatened another member of Jefferson's intimate circle of family and friends that summer. His son-in-law Thomas Mann Randolph, who was currently serving his second term in the House of Representatives, had allegedly insulted a congressional colleague, the fiery John Randolph of Roanoke. Their dispute threatened to end in a duel. Jefferson wrote Randolph's friends, encouraging them to talk him out of the duel. He also wrote his son-in-law directly, reminding him of the wife and children who were depending upon him. Thankfully, cooler heads prevailed, and threats of a duel dissipated.[33]

The day Meriwether Lewis returned to St. Louis, September 23, 1806, he wrote a letter informing the president of their success. Jefferson received the letter in late October, time enough to include their story in his annual message to Congress. In an early draft of the message, Jefferson told a longer version of the Lewis and Clark Expedition, which he abbreviated in revision. He officially announced their success and applauded their accomplishments: "They have traced the Missouri nearly to its source, descended the Columbia to the Pacific ocean, ascertained with accuracy the geography of that interesting communication across our continent, learned the character of the country, of its commerce, and inhabitants, and it is but justice to say that Messrs. Lewis and Clarke, and their brave companions, have, by this arduous service, deserved well of their country."[34]

Meriwether Lewis returned to Washington in December. In "Life of Captain Lewis," Jefferson resumed the biography from the time of Lewis's successful return: "Never did a similar event excite more joy through the United States. The humblest of its citizens had taken a lively interest in the issue of this journey, and looked forward with impatience for the information it would furnish."[35]

Partly as a reward for his successful journey, Jefferson appointed Lewis governor of upper Louisiana Territory. Lewis did not assume his gubernatorial responsibilities until he returned to St. Louis in March 1808. He was at his best in the rough-and-tumble life of a wilderness explorer, and the tedious duties of an administrator depressed him greatly. Exacerbating his increasingly precarious mental state, he engaged in much land speculation and lost considerable sums. He decided to leave St. Louis in September 1809.

At Fort Pickering (what is now Memphis), Lewis encountered his old friend Captain Gilbert Russell, who found him in "a state of mental derangement." Russell took it upon himself to assume what would now be called a suicide watch. Already, Lewis "had made several attempts to put an end to his own existence."[36] After six days, Lewis seemed to recover his presence of mind enough to travel. Major James Neely, who accompanied him on the road to Nashville, disagreed. Lewis seemed deranged to him.

Partway across Tennessee, two of their horses escaped. Lewis asked Neely to remain behind to locate the horses, promising to stop for the night at the first house he encountered. He stopped at the house of one Mrs. Grindle. She gave him a room but became quite concerned when she heard him pacing the floor incessantly and talking to himself. Unbeknownst to Mrs. Grindle, one of her servants had supplied him with some gunpowder. Late that night, Meriwether Lewis shot himself, first in the chest, then in the head. He died around sunrise.

Explaining his suicide in "Life of Captain Lewis," Jefferson offered a forward-thinking psychological interpretation that took both his experience and his natural predilections into account:

Governor Lewis had, from early life, been subject to hypochondriac affections. It was a constitutional disposition in all the nearer branches of the family of his name, and was more immediately inherited by him from his father. They had not, however, been so strong as to give uneasiness to his family. While he lived with me in Washington I observed at times sensible depressions of mind: but knowing their constitutional source, I estimated their course by what I had seen in the family. During his western expedition, the constant exertion which that required of all the faculties of body and mind, suspended these distressing affections; but after his establishment at St. Louis in sedentary occupations, they returned upon him with redoubled vigour, and began seriously to alarm his friends. He was in a paroxysm of one of these, when his affairs rendered it necessary for him to go to Washington.... About three o'clock in the night he did the deed which plunged his friends into affliction, and deprived his country of one of her most valued citizens, whose valour and intelligence would have been now employed in avenging the wrongs of his country, and in emulating by land the splendid deeds which have honoured her arms on the ocean. It lost to the nation the benefit of receiving from his own hand the narrative now offered them of his sufferings and successes, in endeavouring to extend for them the boundaries of science, and to present to their knowledge that vast and fertile country, which their sons are destined to fill with arts, with science, with freedom and happiness.[37]

These closing remarks to "Life of Captain Lewis" reveal Jefferson's literary craftsmanship as well as his unshakable optimism. Lewis's suicide makes it tempting to end his story in melancholy thoughts, but Jefferson avoided the temptation. He kept his eye on the rhetorical purpose of his "Life of Captain Lewis": an introduction to *History of the Expedition*. Jefferson ends on a hopeful note, explaining that the explorations of Lewis and Clark will allow Americans to fulfill their destiny.

CHAPTER 34

The President as Patron
of Literature

In September 1807, Thomas Jefferson was at Monticello enjoying the end of his summer vacation before returning to Washington. The successful return of Lewis and Clark the previous year had marked the high point of his second term as president. Since then, he had experienced several difficulties, punctuated by an event that threatened an international crisis. On June 22, the *H.M.S. Leopard*, aggressively searching for deserters from the British navy, had fired on the *Chesapeake*, an American frigate, killing three sailors and wounding several others. Tensions between Great Britain and the United States had escalated through the summer. Many Americans clamored for war, and the situation remained unresolved. Jefferson would face some tough decisions upon his return to Washington.

Amidst the political turmoil, he was happy for any diversion that could take his mind off the weighty responsibilities he faced as president. Late this September, one diversion came in the form of an odd little Englishman in a dark blue coat and an old, white woolen hat. The man turned out to be an itinerant printer and traveling bookseller in his late forties named Jonathan Brunt.[1] The appearance of a traveling bookseller at Monticello was nothing new: Jefferson had been greeting chapmen at his door since boyhood. But even among that strange breed of fellows who traveled the nation selling books, Jonathan Brunt was out of the ordinary.

Jefferson grew weary of the numerous gawkers who came by Monticello to catch a glimpse of him and his house, but he usually welcomed fellow bookmen. Samuel Whitcomb, a bookseller who visited Monticello many years after Jefferson retired from public life, left a detailed record of his visit. Jefferson answered the door himself, shook Whitcomb's hand, and invited him inside. Though Whitcomb had no letter of introduction, Jefferson seemed genuinely pleased with him. When Whitcomb asked if he would be willing to subscribe to a new book, however, Jefferson fibbed: he told Whitcomb that he never subscribed to anything.[2]

Of course, Jefferson had been subscribing to books through much of his life. As president, he realized that subscribing to new publications gave him a way of patronizing American literature and encouraging its development. Subscribing to books was just one of several ways Jefferson patronized literature during his administration. He continued to subscribe to numerous publications even after he left the presidency, but he had to draw the line somewhere. His blanket response to Whitcomb let him politely refuse this door-to-door salesman's request. Jonathan Brunt left no comparable record of his visit to Monticello; presumably Jefferson's reaction to him was similar to his reaction to Whitcomb: cordial, yet reluctant to make his guest too comfortable.

Since the mid-1790s Brunt had been crisscrossing the United States, haplessly seeking a livelihood. He had been traveling long enough to develop a routine: he would visit a print shop, work briefly for the local printer, print some pamphlets of his own composition, and get back on the road, walking from one place to the next selling books along the way. Once he had exhausted his stock, he would locate a printer wherever he ended up and repeat the process. The pamphlets he printed include extracts from various sources, snippets on patriotism and politics combined with autobiographical rants. Brunt's competence as a printer offered him the opportunity to express himself and to record his aberrant thoughts for posterity. Using the printed word as his medium, he could record his ideas in a way denied to others in a similarly precarious psychological state.

Erratic as they are, Brunt's writings offer an insider's look into mental illness in early America. His paranoia is obvious early in his writings. He lashed out against the "speculators," a vague term encompassing everyone who wished to do him harm and anyone who tried to restrict his personal freedom. It is impossible to know what Brunt said to Jefferson this September day, but his writings indicate the tone and tenor of his discourse. There may be no better way to introduce Jonathan Brunt than to let him do the talking.[3]

The History of Jonathan Brunt

I was born in a small village, in the county of Derby, near the county of York, in Old England, on the eight of May 1760.... When near fifteen years old I went 'prentice to a Stationer, Printer, and Bookseller, at Sheffield in Yorkshire, about six miles from the place where I was born. As my natural and acquired abilities are not very great, they were not suitable employments, because I could not excel a majority of my fellow-workmen in quickness and judgment. As I am of a very private turn of mind, Agriculture (the natural and most useful employment of man) would have suited me better. During my servitude I was religiously inclined, tho' frequently overcome with my private besetting sin, which made me very unhappy.

After working two years at Sheffield, and one year at London, in different Printing-Offices, I saved, by industry and frugality, upwards of fifty pounds. With this sum, and one hundred pounds I was entrusted with by my parents, through the improper influence of an indulgent mother, I kept a Bookseller's shop, and engaged in the Printing Business, at Sheffield, on a contracted plan, but did not succeed very well, thro' want of more spirit and property to carry it on. . . .

Before I had been two years in business, I unfortunately made too free with the second woman-servant who lived with me, and, though of very short duration, I made some foolish and wicked promises, (only conditional, that she was free from every other man) but they were soon after set entirely aside by the young woman taking a false oath before a Magistrate. If I was wrong and unfit at that time, (through the foul sin of self-pollution) for intercourse with a woman, she was equally as unfit for an intercourse with the other sex, from causes unknown to me at this time. How severely such a conduct is censured by the commands of God. Through this indiscretion I paid more than the law of the land required: and was accused of many things of which I was quite innocent.

In a few years after I committed a worse fault with a young woman who lived with me. I obeyed the Law: but the fruit of this bad proceeding (a girl) died at the age of about seven months. In about half a year after the child's death, this young woman was married to another man. . . .

Above ten years ago I arrived in America, with an intention to procure an honest living, by following the printing business in different parts, which conduct I have mostly observed to the present day. . . .

Travelling on the Green Mountain in Vermont, the beginning of January 1795, or six, when there was a large fall of snow, I unfortunately missed the main road, and got entangled in the woods, about nine o'clock one Saturday morning, where I walked about six or seven hours on the hills and in the vallies, in the latter of which the snow was more than knee deep, when I began to feel great pain in my feet and ankles, caused by the intense frost, when I fortunately heard the sound of an axe, towards which I immediately directed my course, at which house I arrived one or two hours before sun-set, which happened to be on the main road I had left, by mistake—the said house had been empty some time before, but two young men had come there one or two days before my misfortune, to repair that house. The said young men had prepared a bucket of cold water on my arrival, but I did not make the experiment of plunging my feet and legs into the water, because of the great pain I felt therein—I stayed at the said house a few days where poultices were applied to my sore feet, and then they removed me to several farm-houses for the space of three months, during which time a gradual cure was nearly compleated by salving and nursing—except a small piece of bone coming out of one of my great toes, the bad effects of which I sensibly feel to the present day....

When I was in New York the beginning of December 1797,... John Moulson enquired for me, pretending that he had seen my own father at Sheffield, the 10th of July, 1797, and that my father had paid £21. 12s to him, for my use and service, that is, to procure return passage to England for me.... When on or about the 15th of December 1797, the said J. M. came to me, and said he would take me to a Doctor, without any expence; but instead thereof, he treacherously decoyed me into the City Hospital, pretending to the Doctors, (for there were more than one) and Steward (who was a villainous Englishman) that I was crazy, or insane. These persons seemed to favor his views, as their intention was to increase their patients, and I was taken down into No. 2, when and where I discovered too late their tyrannical designs, and solicited to go out of the Hospital immediately; on which the understrappers in waiting, (a Scotchman and an Irishman) by order of the Steward, thrust me into a cold cell; on using violence, or taking hold of me, *I called out murder, and said I was betrayed.* During this illegal and cruel persecution, the said J. M. was either in the Doctor's or Governess' room.—They locked me up in the said cell a few days, they afterwards permitted me to be a prisoner at large.... They detained and confined me 18 weeks in the said Hospital, with the perfect use of my reason, or the rational powers of my mind—the pretended allegation of *insanity* being entirely false and groundless, if not malicious. If I had not behaved peaceably and orderly during the said confinement, the miscreants about me would have put me in the strait jacket....

It is worthy of remark, that during my confinement, a speculator came to me, and said, that I might go out of the Hospital with *somebody....* I was determined not to surrender my personal liberty to any one, or put myself at the disposition of another, either man or woman; but that I would act according to the good Laws of the United States, if they would permit me.

At last they thought on another plan to cause me to forfeit the ways of honor; they obliged me to sign a palpable lie, to regain my personal liberty, viz. "*Cured of mania.*" I scarcely knew whether to sign the lie, or attempt to get over the part-picked fence; for fear of being used ill, if I failed to get out of the city, I thought it best to sign the lie. . . .

In the eastern states, in the midst of plenty, from the years 1796 to 1800, some depraved miscreants, preparing some unfortunate bodies, and then castrating them, gave me the unlawful contents to eat secretly— but I express my abhorrence of such bad cannibal practices and principles. Before I came to America I could not have supposed that one such depraved wretch had existed therein. About the year 1798, some evil disposed persons in Virginia and New-York state, joining in a secret combination, attempted to carry me off, by putting dreadful poison into some good milk or hasty-pudding. . . .

It is difficult to say how much personal information Brunt offered as he introduced himself to Jefferson. Brunt himself admitted, "I sometimes talk too much, at other times too little."[4] Perhaps he stopped short of confessing his private besetting sin of self-pollution or expressing his paranoia about people feeding him human body parts or poisoning his hasty pudding. Chances are he revealed enough to make Jefferson recognize what John Moulson had recognized the previous decade: Jonathan Brunt was quite insane.

Actually, Jefferson did know something about this strange little man before meeting him in person. Brunt had written the president from Schenectady six years earlier, sending him a pamphlet he had edited and partly composed.[5] Brunt was hoping to curry Jefferson's favor in order to obtain a post with his administration. The pamphlet he sent was titled *Rush's Extracts*. It excerpted passages from a charge that Judge Jacob Rush had given a grand jury in Northampton County, Pennsylvania. Rush's comments amount to an impassioned treatise on patriotism. This pamphlet also contains a series of essays composed by Brunt, one accusing some people of cannibalism, another attacking those who thought he was insane, and another retelling the story of his hospitalization in New York.

Nearly a year after sending him a copy of *Rush's Extracts*, Brunt wrote President Jefferson again, explaining his circumstances and asking for a position: "As I have followed the Printing-Business in America without much success, thro' the minds of the people being somewhat contaminated with *corrupt* speculations; (which is not actuated by a principle of laudable enterprize in *honest Industry;*) I hoped you would not be displeased if I enquired of you, if it would be practicable to get a place as a writer or copyist under your Government."[6] Needless to say, Jefferson had no place in his administration for him.

With few other options, Brunt continued to roam the country, working as an itinerant printer and bookseller. In 1804, he was in Frankfort, Kentucky, where he printed *Extracts from Locke's Essay on the Human Understanding*. He sent a copy of this pamphlet to Jefferson, too. Jefferson kept it and had it bound with numerous other contemporary political pamphlets. Reprinting Locke for a popular audience was a worthy endeavor, but Brunt was not content to stop there. He appended his own writings to Locke's. Brunt again lashed out against the speculators and viciously attacked his other great enemy, scheming women.

Leaving Monticello after his brief visit in September 1807, Brunt made his way to Lynchburg, where he worked in the local printing office for a day and a half before going to Raleigh, North Carolina, where he could not find regular work but managed to print another pamphlet to keep him going. He reached Augusta, Georgia, by the end of November, when he wrote President Jefferson again, urging him to have Congress "obtain restitution for the personal injuries I have received in America from evil-disposed persons." But Jefferson could do nothing to remedy Brunt's phantom grievances. In January 1808, the forlorn Jonathan Brunt was back in North Carolina, where he was robbed of what little money he had on him.[7]

Brunt was one of many office seekers who approached Jefferson during his administration. Jefferson could do little for those seeking personal favors, but he took a passionate interest in literary men with ideas that could contribute to scholarship and to the public good. He gave Brunt a few dollars in charity, but he did much more to help serious writers who approached him during his presidency.

John Daly Burk, another colorful character who sought President Jefferson's help, had considerably more presence of mind than Jonathan Brunt. Born in County Cork, Ireland, Burk attended Trinity College until he began aggressively advocating Irish independence. Expelled from college, Burk became embroiled in further controversy that obliged him to leave Ireland. He immigrated to Boston, where he began the city's first daily newspaper and wrote political plays exemplifying Republican values. He continued as newspaperman and playwright after removing to New York, where he took over the *Time Piece*, Philip Freneau's staunchly Republican paper. Attacks on President Adams led to Burk's indictment for sedition and libel. He fled to Virginia to avoid prosecution.

Aware of Burk's literary talents and Republican values, Jefferson encouraged him to write the history of Virginia. With Jefferson's election to the presidency, Burk, like so many others, no longer needed to worry about being prosecuted for libel. He settled in Petersburg, became an

American citizen, and began writing his most substantial work, *The History of Virginia*.[8]

In early 1803, Burk asked Jefferson if he could borrow books relating to Virginia history from his personal library. Jefferson responded cordially, describing his collection of Virginia laws and statutes and the near-complete file of the original *Virginia Gazette* he had obtained from Parson Willie three decades earlier. Jefferson gave Burk free use of his books, offered to help in any other way he could, and asked to subscribe to the *History of Virginia*.[9]

Burk did not take advantage of Jefferson's offer right away, but when he began drafting the second volume of his history, he reached the point where Jefferson's materials would be most useful. In 1805, he wrote again to reiterate his request. Jefferson agreed to send his priceless collection of Virginia newspapers to his old friend John Page, who was now serving as governor of Virginia. Burk would be able to access them at the Governor's House in Richmond. Writing to Burk, Jefferson emphasized the rarity of his collection: "These also being the only collection probably in existence, I purchased and cherish it with a view to public utility. It is answering one of its principal objects when I put it into your hands."[10]

Since Burk had sent him a copy of the first volume of the *History of Virginia*, Jefferson acknowledged its receipt but apologized for not reading it and for not being able to help him even more:

> Altho' I have not yet had time to peruse the volume you have published (for indeed my occupations permit me to read almost nothing) yet occasional recurrence to parts of it, and the opinions of others who have read it, occasion me to regret that I am not in a situation to give you the benefit of all my materials. Were I residing at home I could do it, and would with pleasure: and should a 2d edition be called for after my return to live at Monticello, I am persuaded it will be in my power, as it is certainly in my wish, to furnish you with some useful matter, not perhaps to be found elsewhere.[11]

Burk greatly appreciated Jefferson's help and dedicated the volume to him. In his dedication, Burk observed, "The History of Virginia, by a sort of national right, claims you as its guardian and patron and I inscribe it to you because I conceive you to be the first and most useful citizen of the republic."[12]

The third volume of Burk's history, which took the story of Virginia to 1775, appeared in 1805. He planned a fourth volume but never finished it. Attending a dinner in 1808, Burk denounced the French government and called the French people a "pack of rascals." Incensed with Burk's remarks, Felix Coquebert, a Frenchman living in Virginia, challenged him to a duel. On April 11, 1808, Coquebert shot and killed the historian of Virginia.

Though Burk died before he could complete the fourth volume of his history, it was continued by Skelton Jones and finally completed by Louis Hue Girardin. Much as Jefferson invited Burk to his home, he also invited Girardin, who took full advantage of the invitation. When he published the final volume of Burk's history, Girardin also dedicated it to Jefferson. Expressing his gratitude, Girardin explained, "During my residence in the vicinity of Monticello, I enjoyed the incalculable benefit of free access to Mr. Jefferson's Library; and, as his historical collection was no less valuable than extensive, that happy circumstance proved of infinite service to my undertaking."[13]

Abiel Holmes, a New England historian, similarly took advantage of President Jefferson's aid when compiling his *American Annals; or, A Chronological History of America*. Initially Holmes did not ask for his help. Instead, he wrote the president to inform him of the work. Jefferson responded with a lengthy discussion on the value of chronology as a genre of history writing and complimented Holmes on his ambitious project. A thorough chronological history of America, Jefferson said, would be "precious to the man of business."[14] While Jefferson believed that people should grow up reading history, he realized that history-reading could be difficult for modern men whose fast-paced lifestyle left little time for pleasure reading. As a genre of history-writing, the chronology provided an ideal solution.

Jefferson specifically recommended three titles to Holmes for his research. *Memoires de l'Amerique*, a four-volume work containing much information about the exploration and settling of North America, was, in Jefferson's view, the fullest available compilation of French materials pertaining to American history. He also recommended Bishop White Kennett's *Bibliothecae Americanae Primordia*—the first systematic attempt to create a bibliography of American literature—and *The American and British Chronicle of War and Politics*, which detailed events in British–American relations from 1773 to 1783. Jefferson offered to loan Holmes his copies of any or all of these works.[15]

Holmes appreciated Jefferson's offer. He had a copy of Bishop Kennett's bibliography but lacked the other two. He wrote back to Jefferson, explaining his own research in more detail and asking to borrow both. Jefferson realized that the *Memoires de l'Amerique* would be more useful to him and promised to send it along. Jefferson also agreed to loan

Holmes his copy of *The American and British Chronicle of War and Politics*, but he hesitated to send it until Holmes really needed it. Jefferson explained, "I do not propose [to send] it now because it is a manual to which I am constantly turning."[16]

Upon the publication of his *American Annals*, Holmes wrote President Jefferson an affectionate letter of thanks: "Your early approbation of the plan of my work, and your valuable contribution of materials towards its execution, were a great encouragement to me during the labours of it. In the favourable reception which it has met abroad, as well as at home, I cherish a grateful sense of the patronage afforded it by the literati of our own country, and particularly by the President of the United States."[17]

Jefferson's old friend Charles Thomson was another man of letters who benefited from the president's literary advice. After serving as secretary to the Continental Congress for fifteen years, Thomson had left public life and retired to Harriton, his wife's family estate, where he devoted much time and effort to scholarly pursuits. He translated the Greek Old Testament (the Septuagint) and the New Testament, too.

Jefferson had lost touch with Thomson, but he was greatly pleased to see an advertisement for his translation of the Bible in the newspapers. The advertisement detailed plans to publish the book in quarto and asked for subscribers. Eager to subscribe, Jefferson hoped Thomson would reconsider the format: "Folios and Quartos are now laid aside because of their inconvenience. Every thing is now printed in 8vo 12mo or petit format. The English booksellers print their first editions indeed in 4to because they can assess a larger price on account of the novelty, but the bulk of readers generally wait for the 2d edition which is for the most part in 8vo. This is what I have long practised myself. Johnson of Philadelphia set the example of printing a handsome edition of the bible in 4 v. 8vo I wish yours were in the same form."[18] Here, Jefferson refers to the edition of *The Holy Bible* published in 1804 by the prolific Philadelphia printer Benjamin Johnson, who deserves recognition for reprinting much English belletristic literature and literary biography in the United States.

Thomson respected Jefferson's advice and agreed to alter the format. The first two octavo volumes reached the President's House in December 1808, the month after Madison was elected president and just a few months before Jefferson would leave office. Jefferson thanked Thomson for the book and looked forward to reading it upon his retirement: "I thank you, my dear and antient friend, for the two volumes of your translation which you have been so kind as to send me. I have dipped into it at the few moments of leisure which my vocations permit, and I perceive that I shall use it with great satisfaction on my return home. I propose there, among my first emploiments, to give to the Septuagint an attentive perusal, and shall feel the aid you have now given me."[19]

Thomson's advertisement was just one of many literary items in the newspapers that President Jefferson noticed. Throughout his time in office, he regularly scanned papers from across the nation and enjoyed reading the original American poetry and reprints of English verse. Not only did he read the papers from all the major cities on the eastern seaboard; he also read papers from Kentucky, Louisiana, and Ohio. Furthermore, he read several British papers and periodicals, including the *London Sporting Magazine*. He frequently clipped verse from the newspapers, pasted them onto loose scraps of paper, and sent them home for his grandchildren, who turned them into scrapbooks.[20]

Anne, his oldest granddaughter, was the recipient of the earliest poems he sent from Washington. As her younger sisters grew, their grandfather sent them poems for scrapbooks of their own. Sending Ellen some verse, Jefferson wrote, "As I expect Anne's volume is now large enough, I will begin to furnish you with materials for one. I know you have been collecting some yourself; but as I expect there is some tag, rag, and bobtail verse among it you must begin a new volume for my materials."[21]

Jefferson's words sound nonchalant: he supposes that Anne's volume has grown large enough to warrant a new volume. But the date of this letter to Ellen belies her grandfather's nonchalance. He wrote her on March 4, 1805, the day he was inaugurated for his second term as president. Insisting she exclude whatever miscellaneous materials she had collected to that point, Jefferson was ensuring that Ellen's scrapbook would be a record of his second term as president just as Anne's was a record of his first. Later, he decided to divide his second term as president in half to give their younger sister Cornelia a chance to start a scrapbook of her own. The first week of March 1807—two years after directing Ellen to start a scrapbook—Jefferson sent some newspaper verse to Cornelia.[22] As they survive, the poems are arranged somewhat differently. Jefferson himself may have reorganized the scrapbook material once he retired from the presidency. The existing state of the scrapbooks suggests that Jefferson, just as he did with *The Anas*, recognized that juxtaposing two different texts could give rise to new ideas not present in either of the texts individually.

Many of the selected poems take current events for their subject. Some concern the much-dreaded embargo. Jefferson's dismay with the depredations of British ships had reached the breaking point after the

Leopard–Chesapeake affair. He decided to punish the foreign powers through the use of an embargo. In other words, he would deprive other nations of American goods by keeping American vessels at home. Though well intended, the embargo significantly damaged the business of American merchants who made their livelihood in the shipping trade. Given the animosity toward the policy among many Americans, especially Jefferson's natural enemies in New England, who relied heavily on the merchant trade, enforcing the embargo proved difficult. Jefferson and Secretary of State James Madison devoted extraordinary efforts toward its enforcement. So did Treasury Secretary Albert Gallatin, even though he was privately opposed to it. Although the embargo had little effect on the foreign powers, Jefferson's forward-thinking policy anticipated modern approaches toward solving international disputes through economic coercion.

Not surprisingly, newspaper commentary on the embargo split along party lines: the Republican papers supported the embargo while the Federalist papers criticized it. Contemporary criticism often took the form of verse. Jefferson clipped poems supporting the embargo, and to his credit, he even clipped some of the negative ones. One of the negative poems Jefferson clipped ends with the following lines:

> Our ships all in motion,
> Once whiten'd the ocean,
> They sail'd and return'd with a cargo;
> Now doom'd to decay,
> They have fallen a prey
> To Jefferson, worms and Embargo.

Corresponding with her grandfather the president, eleven-year-old Ellen broached the subject of the embargo. The last week of January 1808, she reported to him a comment her Aunt Virginia had made: "She says that the embargo has thrown the dissipated inhabitants of Williamsburg in great confusion. The Ladies say they cannot give up tea and coffee and the gentlemen wine." In his response to Ellen, Jefferson wrote, "You give a bad account of the patriotism of the ladies of Williamsburg who are not disposed to submit to the small privations to which the embargo will subject them. I hope this will not be general and that principle and prudence will induce us all to return to the good old plan of manufacturing within our own families most of the articles we need."[23]

Several of the poems he clipped from the papers possess a personal dimension. Jefferson himself was the subject of many laudatory poems.

Sometimes he encountered poems that encapsulated ideas he used to guide his life, including one titled "No Place Commends the Man Unworthy Praise." Now attributed to John Lyly, the sixteenth-century English author who popularized an ornate and convoluted style of writing known as Euphuism, this poem elevates personal qualities above the privilege of birth:

> What doth avail to have a princely place,
> A name of honour, and a high degree;
> To come by kindred of a noble race,
> Except we princely, worthy, noble be!
> The fruit declares the goodness of the tree.
> Do brag no more of birth, or lineage then;
> For virtue, grace and manners make the man.

Rarely did Jefferson annotate the poems he clipped, but this poem contains a brief pencil note in his hand: "As good now as when it was written."[24] The titles of several poems in the surviving scrapbooks show how much Jefferson looked forward to retiring from office and returning to Monticello once and for all: "The Happy Fireside," "Home," "The Pleasures of Retirement," and "To My Armchair."

One of the most important and touching pieces he added to his personal collection of verse was a poem by Robert Burns, "To Mary in Heaven." Jefferson enjoyed the poet's Scottish dialect and generally characterized his work as "the beautiful poetry of Burns."[25] This particular poem had personal ramifications: Jefferson's beloved daughter Mary had died in childbirth on April 17, 1804. In some of his lines, Burns almost seemed to be speaking for Jefferson as he lamented the death of his Mary:

> Thou ling'ring star with lessening ray,
>   That lov'st to greet the early morn,
> Again thou usher'st in the day
>   My Mary from my soul was torn.
> O Mary! dear, departed shade!
>   Where is thy place of blissful rest?[26]

The best account of the death of Mary Jefferson Eppes comes from her niece Ellen. Though only eight years old at the time of her aunt's death, Ellen remembered the experience well:

One morning I heard that my aunt was dying; I crept softly from my nursery to her chamber door, and being alarmed by her short, hard breathing, ran away again. I have a distinct recollection of confusion and dismay in the household. I did not see my mother. By and by one of the female servants came running in where I was with other persons, to say that Mrs. Eppes was dead. The day passed I do not know how. Late in the afternoon I was taken to the death-chamber. The body was covered with a white cloth, over which had been strewed a profusion of flowers. A day or two after, I followed the coffin to the burying-ground on the mountain side, and saw it consigned to the earth.[27]

Back at Monticello in September 1808, Jefferson was home to attend Anne's wedding on the nineteenth. Still in her teens, she married a young man named Charles Lewis Bankhead. Anne was the gardener in the family, and she had been instrumental in helping her grandfather plant his gardens and in overseeing them while he was in Washington. In her first known letter to her grandfather after her marriage, Anne still sounds like a schoolgirl. She assures him that she was spending her mornings reading French, studying history, and "doing sums."[28]

Alas, the schoolgirl had to grow up all too quickly. Abandoning his plans to read law under Jefferson, Charles Bankhead turned profligate and became a drunken, abusive husband. Edmund Bacon related a story of Anne having to hide in the potato bin to escape her husband's drink-induced violence. Her mother hoped for someone to live with the couple in order to protect Anne from her husband.

The same month that Anne was married, her brother Jeff turned sixteen. His grandfather was doing all he could to advance his education. That month Jefferson presented him with several scholarly editions of classic authors—Homer, Virgil, Ovid, Boethius. Later that fall, Jeff moved to Philadelphia to live and study natural history with Charles Willson Peale. While in Philadelphia, he would also study anatomy, surgery, and botany. As a present for the family, Peale painted a portrait of Thomas Jefferson Randolph, which his grandfather greatly enjoyed.[29]

Jeff took a break in his studies to be with his grandfather in Washington at the end of his administration. Jefferson continued to entertain nightly throughout his presidency. His grandson provides a good indication of Jefferson's dinnertime conversation: "cheerful, often sportive, and illustrated by anecdotes."[30] Frances Few, a young woman who had the good fortune to dine at President Jefferson's table late in his second term, recorded the episode in her diary. Her account shows that

Thomas Jefferson Randolph, by Charles Willson Peale. (Monticello, Thomas Jefferson Foundation, Inc.)

Jefferson's time in office, though trying, had not dulled his sense of humor or mellowed his disgust with formality. Rather, his time as president had given him many new experiences that he turned into anecdotes. An anecdote about the Danish minister he related to Miss Few has another anecdote embedded within it.

One evening, President Jefferson invited the Danish minister to dinner. His guest was happy for the opportunity to visit because he had been wanting to tell Jefferson that the Danish government disapproved of the way the president was being treated. As chief magistrate, he deserved more respect.

"Great men," the Danish minister said, "ought to be surrounded by an atmosphere of ceremony."

Jefferson responded with an anecdote about one of the present kings of Europe who was fond of hunting.

"The day was uncommonly fine and the king was all ready for the chase when one of his courtiers announced a number of strangers," Jefferson explained. "Before the ceremony of introducing them was over the king's patience was quite exhausted and turning to a courtier he said in a foreign language 'Oh how I hate ceremony.' The courtier bowed and said, 'Sire you do not remember that you are yourself ceremony.' "[31]

On Saturday, March 4, 1809, James Madison was inaugurated as president. After the inauguration at the Capitol, a large group of people gathered at the Madisons' home. Mr. and Mrs. Samuel Harrison Smith were among the guests, and, not surprisingly, Mrs. Smith's letters and reminiscences form the fullest account of the event. When the Smiths arrived, the house was "completely filled, parlours, entry, drawing room and bed room. Near the door of the drawing room," Mrs. Smith observed, "Mr. and Mrs. Madison stood to receive their company. She looked extremely beautiful, was drest in a plain cambrick dress with a very long train, plain round the neck without any handerkerchief, and beautiful bonnet of purple velvet, and white satin with white plumes. She was all dignity, grace and affability."[32]

Though Mrs. Smith enjoyed greeting the fourth president of the United States, she really wanted to see the third. After shaking hands with President Madison, she spied Jefferson across the room. Their eyes met, and she quickly approached him. He warmly greeted Mrs. Smith, took her hand, and held it as they talked.

"Remember the promise you have made me, to come to see us next summer, do not forget it," Jefferson said.

She assured him that she and her husband would visit soon. Reflecting on his presidency, she told him, "You have now resigned a heavy burden."

"Yes indeed," Jefferson replied, "and am much happier at this moment than my friend."

That evening the Madisons hosted the very first inaugural ball. As the ex-president entered, the Marine Band played Jefferson's March. Mrs. Smith observed, "He spoke to all whom he knew, and was quite the plain, unassuming citizen."[33] Mrs. Smith was not the only one who recorded conversations with Jefferson this evening. John Quincy Adams noted what he and Jefferson talked about, too.

Remembering the impression Adams had made upon him in Paris, Jefferson asked if he was as fond of poetry as he had been in his youth.

"Yes," Adams responded, explaining that he had not lost his relish for good poetry, though his "taste for the minor poets, and particular for *amatory verses*, was not so keen as it had been."

Jefferson replied that he was "still fond of reading Homer, but did not take much delight in Virgil."[34]

Mrs. Smith summarized Jefferson's general conduct at this inaugural ball: "Mr. Jefferson did not stay above two hours; he seemed in high spirits and his countenance beamed with a benevolent joy. I do believe father never loved son more than he loves Mr. Madison, and I believe too that every demonstration of respect to Mr. M. gave Mr. J. more pleasure than if paid to himself."[35]

Jefferson's behavior after leaving office, at least in terms of his literary patronage, differed little from his behavior as president. He continued to encourage others to write. He loaned books to many who were writing books of their own. He wrote voluminous letters to would-be biographers and historians describing men he had known and important historical events in which he had played a part. And he continued subscribing to the works of many American authors. When Philip Freneau wrote seeking subscribers for a new edition of his *Poems*, for example, Jefferson was happy to oblige.

Freneau also asked Jefferson to circulate the subscription list among his Virginia neighbors. This Jefferson hesitated to do, partly because of his reluctance to leave Monticello and partly because of his awareness that his country neighbors generally disliked subscribing for books sight unseen. He explained to Freneau: "The inhabitants of the country are mostly industrious farmers employed in active life and reading little. They rarely buy a book of whose merit they can not judge by having it in their hand, and are less disposed to engage for those yet unknown to them. I am becoming like them myself in a preference of the healthy and chearful emploiments without doors, to the being immured within four brick walls. But under the shade of a tree one of your volumes will be a pleasant pocket companion."[36]

While Jefferson continued to patronize American men and women of letters after leaving the presidency, there was one man he was powerless to help, the forlorn Jonathan Brunt. Since visiting Monticello in September 1807, Brunt continued to roam the nation looking for printers who would give him employment or, at least, let him use their printing plants long enough to print pamphlets to keep him going until the next town with a print shop. In 1809, Brunt trekked across Tennessee in search of work. While in Knoxville, he printed an autobiographical pamphlet titled *The Little Medley*. He traveled as far west as Nashville and considered going from there to New Orleans.

From Nashville, Brunt wrote Jefferson again. This time he asked a special favor: "The principal intention of this letter is to request your Excellency to let me come to Monticello, to have a private room there, for I must die ere long, except Deity work another miracle for me,—The sooner I get out of this knavish world the better.—I hope sir, your religious principles are the same you had in your youth.—Tho' I have wrote to a printer at New Orleans, about the printing business there, yet I do not want to go there:—The warmness of the climate is not the only reason."[37]

Without waiting for a response from Jefferson, Brunt abandoned his plans to go to New Orleans and trudged back across Tennessee and Virginia. He reached Monticello three days before Christmas. Finally, Jefferson had the life he had been longing for throughout his presidency. The laughter of his grandchildren filled the halls of Monticello. He had no room for a crazy printer who wanted to come here to die. On this December day, he gave Brunt two dollars in charity and sent him on his way. Brunt continued wandering the country. He showed up at Monticello at least twice more, once in November 1811 and again in January 1815. Jefferson gave him a dollar or two in charity on both occasions. Though Jefferson had no place for Brunt in either his administration or his home, he always had a soft spot in his heart for this weird little man in a blue jacket and an old white woolen hat.

PART V

MONTICELLO

CHAPTER 35

Return to Monticello

During his presidency, Thomas Jefferson had accumulated a considerable number of personal possessions, including, of course, lots and lots of books. Anticipating his retirement by more than a year, he had sent much of his presidential library back to Monticello, enough books to fill eight trunks. Together with four other packages, these book-filled trunks weighed two and a half tons.[1] As his retirement approached in February 1809, enough other stuff remained—books too essential to pack, papers, furniture, lamps—that he summoned overseer Edmund Bacon to come up from Monticello to help. Together they filled about thirty packages to be sent home by water. The rest they loaded onto wagons driven to Washington. Bacon recalled, "I had three wagons from Monticello—two six-mule teams loaded with boxes, and the other four sorrel Chickasaw horses, and the wagon pretty much loaded with shrubbery from Maine's nursery. The servants rode on these wagons. I had the carriage horses and carriage, and rode behind them."[2] Bacon left Washington on March ninth or tenth. Jefferson followed on Saturday, the eleventh.

For contemplative souls, moving is a time for reflection. As Jefferson prepared to leave Washington for good, he apparently thought less about what he had accomplished as president and more about what he intended to accomplish once he returned to Monticello. The books and papers that partly filled those trunks gave him much to do once he returned home. He wanted to catch up on his reading, which his presidential responsibilities had prevented him from doing. And he had many different writing projects planned. Some works he would write himself, others he would encourage friends to write. Jefferson contributed to literary history not only as an author but also as a facilitator, someone who recognizes literary talent in others and encourages them to pursue the writing projects that suit them best. Jefferson's literary patronage continued throughout his retirement.

According to Bacon, shrubbery from Thomas Main's nursery formed a significant part of Jefferson's baggage, but there was one plant Jefferson was leaving behind, a potted geranium. Correctly assuming that he would not be taking this potted plant home, Margaret Bayard Smith asked if she could have it: "I have seen in your cabinet a *Geranium*, which I understood you cultivated with your own hands. If you do not take it home with you, I entreat you to leave it with me. I cannot tell you how inexpressively precious it will be to my heart. It shall be attended with the assiduity of affection and watered with tears of regret each day as I attend it, will I invoke the best blessings of Heaven, on the most venerated of human beings!" With a request like that, Jefferson was happy to put the geranium into her nurturing hands.[3]

He left the President's House in his phaeton with two servants accompanying him on horseback. At Georgetown he took the ferry across the Potomac for the last time. The weather was tolerable this Saturday, and they made it as far as Barnett's Tavern by nightfall. The weather grew worse on Sunday. The roads got so bad Jefferson found that traveling by horseback was more efficient than in the phaeton, though riding a horse through an incessant snowstorm was quite fatiguing, too. On one day of this trip he traveled eight hours through "as disagreeable snow storm as I was ever in."[4]

Ahead of him, Bacon was having an even more difficult time. On Monday, March 13, the snow came down fast and hard. By the time he reached Shackelford's Tavern at Culpeper Courthouse, it was already "half-leg deep." The deep snow did not put off the locals. Looking forward to Jefferson's arrival, many had braved the weather and gathered at Shackelford's. Bacon remembered:

A large crowd of people had collected there, expecting that the President would be along. When I rode up, they thought I was the President and shouted and hurrahed tremendously. When I got out of the carriage, they laughed very heartily at their mistake. There was a platform along the whole front of the tavern, and it was full of people. Some of them had been waiting a good while and drinking a good deal, and they made so much noise that they scared the horses, and Diomede backed, and tread upon my foot, and lamed me so that I could hardly get into the carriage the next morning.[5]

The noisiest of the bunch, a tall, boisterous geyser, expressed his determination to see "Old Tom." Others anxiously asked when he would arrive. Bacon guessed that Jefferson was making good time in the phaeton, comparatively speaking, and predicted that he would reach Shackelford's that evening. He went inside and told the proprietor to build a large fire in a private room for the former president.

Actually, Jefferson was making better time than his overseer realized. While Bacon was indoors speaking with tavernkeeper, Benjamin Shackelford, the crowd outside saw Jefferson in the distance making his way through the snow. They shouted for joy. Hearing their shouts, Bacon went back outside to see the phaeton slowly approaching.

"When he came up," Bacon remembered, "there was a great cheering again. I motioned to him to follow me; took him straight to his room and locked the door. The tall old fellow came and knocked very often, but I would not let him in. I told Mr. Jefferson not to mind him, he was drunk. Finally the door was opened, and they rushed in and filled the room. It was as full as I ever saw a barroom. He stood up and made a short address to them."[6]

Tuesday night, the fourteenth, Jefferson reached Gordon's Tavern. He had enjoyed Nathaniel Gordon's hospitality many times during his back-and-forth trips between Monticello and Washington and recommended the place to others. He was now only twenty miles from home. Barring another hellacious snowstorm, he would be home the next day. Finally, he would be among his family, his friends, and his books: "moored in the midst of my affections, and free to follow the pursuits of my choice."[7]

These last words come from a letter he wrote Martha two weeks before he left Washington. Each time he had returned to Monticello from Washington, she and her husband would bring their children to come stay at Monticello. Now that he was retired, he wanted Martha, his only surviving child, to move to Monticello permanently. But he was concerned that managing such a large household would overburden her. In his letter, he suggested that Anna Marks, his sister and her aunt, should also move to Monticello in order to manage the household.

Martha was shocked and dismayed at his suggestion. Devoted to her father, she, too, was looking forward to his retirement when they could be together. Her response contains what may be the strongest words she ever wrote him: "As to Aunt Marks it would not be desirable to have her if it was proper. I had full proof of her being totally incompetent to the business the last summer. The servants have no sort of respect for her and take just what they please before her face. She is an excellent creature and a neat manager in a little way, but she has neither head nor a sufficient weight of character to manage so large an establishment as yours will be. I shall devote my self to it and with feelings which I never could have in my own affairs."[8] Martha's devotion to her father and her willingness to leave Edgehill, her nearby estate, to live at Monticello strained her relationship with her husband, who devoted more time to his own political career.

The unseasonably cold weather that year was slowing the onset of spring. Upon his arrival at Monticello, Jefferson observed, "No oats sown, not much tobacco seed, and little done in the gardens. Wheat has suffered considerably. No vegetation visible yet but the red maple, weeping willow and Lilac."[9] He had much work to do to get the place in shape but looked forward to spending his days on horseback overseeing the farm. The freedom to do whatever he wanted to do whenever he wanted to do it was a delicious pleasure. As he informed Charles Willson Peale the first week of May, "I am totally occupied without doors, and enjoying a species of happiness I never before knew, that of doing whatever hits the humor of the moment without responsibility or injury to any one."[10]

Jefferson's adverb "totally" is typical of his personal correspondence, which is filled with absolute statements. Despite what he said to Peale, he was not spending all his time outdoors. He had plenty of indoor occupations to keep him busy. He devoted several hours each day to reading and writing. But one of the most extensive writing projects he had planned for his retirement came to naught: his plans to assemble a polyglot Indian vocabulary was ruined while his books and papers were being transported. Of the thirty packages he sent by water from Washington to Monticello, only twenty-nine made it. He related the sad story to Benjamin Smith Barton:

I have now been thirty years availing myself of every possible opportunity of procuring Indian vocabularies to the same set of words: my opportunities were probably better than will ever occur again to any person having the same desire. I had collected about 50. and had digested most of them in collateral columns, and meant to have printed them the last year of my stay in Washington. But not having yet digested Capt Lewis's collection, nor having leisure then to do it, I put it off till should return home. The whole, as well digest as originals were packed in a trunk of stationary and sent round by water with about 30. other packages of my effects from Washington, and while ascending James river, this package, on account of its weight and presumed precious contents, was singled out and stolen. The thief being disappointed on opening it, threw into the river all its contents of which he thought he could make no use. Among these were the whole of the vocabularies. Some leaves floated ashore [and] were found in the mud; but these were very few, and so defaced by the mud and water that no general use can ever be made of them.[11]

Though Jefferson enjoyed reading melancholy literature, he was too much of an optimist to indulge his melancholy sensibilities in his own writings. But in this letter to Barton, he temporarily gave way to such feelings. The destruction of his manuscripts was a grave disappointment, but the image of the individual leaves of his irreplaceable manuscript floating atop the surface of the James River and washing ashore is beautiful.

For the most part, it was great to be home. The only negative aspect of living at Monticello was the steady stream of visitors who came to see him. Jefferson's visitors were both a blessing and a curse—depending on who they were and how many of them there were. Edmund Bacon's reminiscences provide a good indication of the traffic that streamed through Monticello:

After Mr. Jefferson returned from Washington, he was for years crowded with visitors, and they almost ate him out of house and home. They were there all times of the year; but about the middle of June the travel would commence from the lower part of the state to the Springs, and then there was a perfect throng of visitors. They traveled in their own carriages and came in gangs—the whole family, with carriage and riding horses and servants; sometimes three or four such gangs at a time. We had thirty-six stalls for horses, and only used about ten of them for the stock we kept there. Very often all of the rest were full, and I had to send horses off to another place. I have often sent a wagonload of hay up to the stable, and the next morning there would not be enough left to make a hen's nest. I have killed a fine beef, and it would all be eaten in a day or two. There was no tavern in all that country that had so much company. Mrs. Randolph, who always lived with Mr. Jefferson after his return from Washington and kept house for him, was very often greatly perplexed to entertain them. I have known her many and many a time to have every bed in the house full, and she would send to my wife and borrow all her beds—she had six spare beds—to accommodate her visitors.[12]

As Bacon's remarks suggest, Jefferson's hospitality knew no bounds. Some guests were welcomed with open arms. Mr. and Mrs. Samuel Harrison Smith, for example, had promised to visit Monticello that summer, and Jefferson was overjoyed on their arrival. On Friday, August 4, the Smiths ascended the road to Monticello. Before they reached the house, they met Jefferson on horseback. Returning home from his morning ride, he had recognized them from the distance and hurried to their coach to greet them. Mrs. Smith recorded in her diary, "He received us with one of those benignant smiles, and cordial tones of voice that convey an undoubted welcome to the heart."[13]

Combined with a handful of accounts by other visitors, Mrs. Smith's diary makes it possible to reconstruct a typical day in the life of Thomas Jefferson in retirement. On her first night at Monticello she had difficulty sleeping, so she rose in time to see the sun rise. As early as she arose, Jefferson was up before her. Toward the end of his life, he boasted that the sun had not caught him in bed for fifty years.[14] Upon rising, he would read or catch up his correspondence. Mrs. Smith's sleeping difficulties allowed her to watch the sunrise on successive mornings, a beautiful sight from atop Monticello. She mentioned in her diary "the various appearances the landscape assumed as the fog was rising. But the blue and misty mountains, now lighted up with sunshine, now thrown into deep shadow, presented objects on which I gaze each morning with new pleasure."

Breakfast was more modest than she had imagined. With tea or coffee, they enjoyed "excellent muffins, hot wheat and corn bread, cold ham and butter." After breakfast, as Mrs. Smith learned her first morning at Monticello, "it was the habit of the family each separately to pursue their occupations. Mr. J. went to his apartments, the door of which is never opened but by himself and his retirement seems so sacred that I told him it was his sanctum sanctorum."

This daily routine worked well for a family whose patriarch had continually impressed upon his children and grandchildren the value of reading and the importance of staying busy. Some houseguests found the interval between mealtimes too long, however. As Mrs. Smith observed, "Visitors generally retire to their own rooms, or walk about the place; those who are fond of reading can never be at a loss, those who are not will some times feel wearied in the long interval between breakfast and dinner."

For about two hours after breakfast one morning, Jefferson welcomed the Smiths into his library. Mrs. Smith had heard so much about his library beforehand that she eagerly looked forward to seeing it. Her

Monticello, West Front. (Monticello, Thomas Jefferson Foundation, Inc.)

reaction was ambivalent. Jefferson's library was distributed throughout a suite of three rooms. She observed that the collection would be much more impressive if it were contained within one large room, but even as she made this observation, she greatly overestimated the size of the library at 20,000 volumes—about three times more than it actually contained.

Jefferson relished the opportunity to show off some of his most prized volumes to his visitors. He showed the Smiths examples from his early Americana collection, his architectural collection, his collection of Middle English literature, and his collection of Greek romances. *Historia de Nueva España* contained Archbishop Francisco Antonio Lorenzana's collection of Hernán Cortés's letters from Mexico. Robert Castell's *Villas of the Ancients Illustrated* Mrs. Smith called a volume of fine views of ancient villas around Rome, with maps of the grounds, and minute descriptions of the buildings and grounds. Engraved architectural works made ideal conversation pieces. Another visitor to Monticello recorded that Jefferson showed him his copy of Robert Wood's *Ruins of Balbec*.[15] Wood included dozens of engravings illustrating what was left of the

Library and Book Room. (Robert C. Lautman, Thomas Jefferson Foundation, Inc.)

renowned City of the Sun, a set of melancholy images that allowed readers to imagine the grandeur of the ancient past.

To demonstrate his collection of Middle English literature, Jefferson chose to show the Smiths his copy of William Langland's *Vision of Pierce Plowman*. There's no telling precisely why he chose *Pierce Plowman* to display on this occasion. He had other sixteenth-century black letter editions of classic English literature, including Chaucer's *Workes* and

John Lydgate's *History of Troy*. Perhaps the personal association made Langland's *Vision of Pierce Plowman* more special than the others: Jefferson had acquired the volume from the library of his old friend Samuel Henley. The Henley-Jefferson copy of *Pierce Plowman* does not survive, and there has been some question about the precise date of the edition. Mrs. Smith's description of the work—"an old poem written by Piers Plowman and printed 250 years ago"—confirms that the copy Jefferson owned must have been the 1550 London edition.[16]

A handsome volume printed in black letter, *Pierce Plowman* was more than just a bibliographical curiosity. It was also important to both literary history and the history of the English language. Jefferson did not just show this book to the Smiths—he also read from it. Perhaps he began at the beginning. *Pierce Plowman* is structured as a dream vision. As it starts, the speaker of the poem, dressed as a hermit, is wandering through the Malvern Hills on a summer morning. Growing weary, he stops to rest on the bank of a river, falls asleep, and starts to dream. Listen:

> In a somer season, when set was the sunne
> I shope me into shroubs, as I a shepe were
> In habyte as an hermet, unholy of werkes
> Went wyde in thys world wōders to here
> And on a May morning, on Malverne hilles
> Me befell a ferly, of a fayry me thought.
> I was wery of wandering, and went me to rest
> Under a brode banke, by a bourne side
> And as I lay and lened, and loked on the water
> I slombred into a sleping...

Jefferson continued reading for about a page. When reading Langland's *Pierce Plowman* or Chaucer's *Canterbury Tales* aloud, he tried to assimilate its pronunciation to modern-day English. Still, he could only go so far. Mrs. Smith, though proud of her knowledge of English literature, found *Pierce Plowman* "almost as unintelligible as if it was Hebrew."

Perhaps sensing Mrs. Smith's dislike of *Pierce Plowman*, Jefferson tried to find something more to her tastes: a Greek romance. She explained, "He took pains to find one that was translated into French, as most of them were translated in Latin and Italian." Previous readers have hesitated to credit Mrs. Smith's powers of observation, but her description precisely coincides with the catalogue of Jefferson's great library.[17]

Mrs. Smith's diary does not say for sure that Jefferson read from Xenophon of Ephesus, but he must have. It was the only Greek romance in French he had. Xenophon told the story of a young married couple from Ephesus who are separated during a voyage. They endure attacks by pirates and robbers, shipwreck, enslavement, and seduction. Throughout their trials and tribulations, the two remain faithful to each other. Eventually, they are reunited. They return to Ephesus and live happily ever after.[18]

Her diary also indicates Jefferson's playfulness. One day during their visit he offered to take her on a carriage ride around the grounds of Monticello. She thought it was a good idea at first, but the longer the ride lasted, the more she questioned her decision. Jefferson led her down some pathways that scarcely seemed as if they were wide enough to accommodate the carriage. In places, she was terrified that they would not make it through safely. Once they passed the most treacherous spots, Jefferson spoke to reassure his passenger.

"My dear madam," he said, "you are not to be afraid, or if you are you are not to show it; trust yourself implicitly to me, I will answer for your safety; I came every foot of this road yesterday, on purpose to see if a carriage could come safely; I know every step I take, so banish all fear."

Mrs. Smith also enjoyed seeing Ellen, her favorite among Jefferson's granddaughters. But perhaps no one enjoyed the grandchildren more than Jefferson himself. For their summer games, he took on the role of chief referee. His granddaughter Virginia recalled:

One of our earliest amusements was in running races on the terrace, or around the lawn. He placed us according to our ages, giving the youngest and smallest the start of all the others by some yards, and so on, and then he raised his arm high with his white handkerchief in his hand, on which our eager eyes were fixed, and slowly counted three, at which number he dropt the handkerchief and we started off to finish the race by returning to the starting-place and receiving our reward of dried fruit—three figs, prunes or dates to the victor, two to the second, and one to the lagger who came in last. These were our summer sports with him.[19]

The Jeffersons typically had dinner in the late afternoon. Reporting his daily habits to a correspondent, Jefferson said, "I have lived temperately, eating little animal food, and that not as an aliment, so much as a condiment for the vegetables, which constitute my principal diet." Enough recipes survive from the Monticello kitchen to fill a good-sized cookbook. They enjoyed such dishes as Mexican black bean soup. They got the recipe from the grocer who sold them the beans. Pumpkin soup was another favorite, and Martha had a good recipe for okra soup, with lima beans and tomatoes.[20]

As had been his habit throughout his adult life, Jefferson served no wine until after dinner. Dr. Benjamin Rush enjoyed a glass and a half of wine each day. Jefferson told a correspondent that he would usually double "the Doctor's glass and a half of wine, and even treble it with a friend; but halve its effects by drinking the weak wines only. The ardent wines I cannot drink, nor do I use ardent spirits in any form."[21]

The time after dinner Jefferson devoted to conversation or reading. Warm summer evenings often drew friends and family outdoors. Francis Walker Gilmer, who became a frequent visitor during Jefferson's retirement, left the most poetical description of evenings at Monticello. His night thoughts provide a companion to Mrs. Smith's description of mornings at Monticello. Gilmer observed:

> The prospect from Monticello is most interesting on a summer's night. The elevation prevents or at least very much diminishes the descent of dews, and you walk with impunity at all hours on the lawn or terrace. The distant summits reflecting the silvery light, the moon beams floating on the mists below, the pale clouds hanging lightly on the declivities of the mountains, the motionless leaf, the softly murmuring wave, the glittering tapers in the surrounding vale, altogether remind one of that beautiful description of night in the Iliad.

> As when the moon, refulgent lamp of night:
> O'er heaven's clear azure spreads her sacred light,
> When not a breath disturbs the deep serene
> And not a cloud o'ercasts the solemn scene;
> Around her throne the vivid planets roll
> And stars unnumbered gild the glowing pole.
> O'er the dark trees a yellower verdure shed
> And tipped with silver every mountain head
> Then, shine the vales, the rocks in prospect rise
> A flood of glory bursts from all the skies.[22]

Jefferson went to bed fairly early, around nine or ten, but he often spent hours reading before he fell asleep. He slept between five and eight hours a night, depending upon how "the book I am reading interests me."[23]

That summer Jefferson received the kind of request that any great writer longs to receive—any great writer besides Jefferson, that is. John W. Campbell, a publisher from Petersburg, Virginia, wrote to ask if he could publish a collected edition of Jefferson's works. Though flattered, Jefferson was unsure whether Campbell's editorial project would be a worthwhile commercial venture. However, Jefferson did take the request as an opportunity to reflect on his life as a writer.

Outside of official writings, he told Campbell, he had really only published two works: *Notes on the State of Virginia* and *A Summary View of the Rights of British America*. He downplayed the significance of *A Manual of Parliamentary Practice*, which he called "a mere compilation, into which nothing entered of my own but the arrangement, and a few observations necessary to explain that and some of the cases."[24]

His official papers had historical value, but he questioned their commercial prospects: "Many of these would be like old news papers, materials for future historians, but no longer interesting to the readers of the day. They would consist of Reports, correspondencies, messages, answers to addresses." As he thought about his writings as secretary of state, he saw some potential interest in them for contemporary readers. Though his official reports for the State Department were written for practical purposes, they could be read now as "Essays on abstract subjects." He was thinking specifically about the following works: "Report on Commerce," "Report on Copper Coinage," "Report on Desalination of Sea Water," "Report on Fisheries," and *Report . . . on the Subject of Establishing a Uniformity in the Weights, Measures and Coins.*

The numerous reports, resolutions, and declarations he drafted in the Virginia legislature and the Continental Congress, including the "Act for Establishing Religious Freedom" and the *Declaration of Independence*, do not belong in a collection of his writings, he told Campbell. Since they were public writings, Jefferson denied any personal claims to them. "So that on a review of these various materials," he concluded, "I see nothing encouraging a printer to a re-publication of them. They would probably be bought by those only who are in the habit of preserving state-papers, and who are not many."[25]

Reviewing his literary output, Jefferson was again reminded that he was no continuator of Sterne, but he also realized the profound influence of his writings on the formation and perpetuation of American democracy. His writings helped bring the Enlightenment into the realm of politics and government.

Campbell was not discouraged by Jefferson's response, but he did reconceive the project in light of it. He wrote back proposing an octavo volume that included *A Summary View*, his reports as secretary of state, and his presidential messages to Congress. Campbell also made arrangements to co-publish the work with the experienced Philadelphia firm, Hopkins and Earle. Jefferson approved the plan and sent Campbell his personal copy of *A Summary View* and also a bound volume containing his reports as secretary of state. Campbell held onto them for two years before deciding that, after all, the proposed volume "would at this day not be interesting to the mass of readers."[26]

Though Jefferson downplayed the significance of *A Manual of Parliamentary Practice* in his letter to Campbell, there had been considerable demand for it. The first edition, too small to meet the demand, was quickly exhausted. William Dickson, a publisher in Lancaster, Pennsylvania, reprinted the *Manual* in 1810. The following year, Joseph Milligan wrote Jefferson, asking if he could publish a new edition of the work.

"I am perfectly willing that you should print another edition of the *Parliamentary Manual*," he told Milligan. "I have no right to refuse it, because no copy right was retained, or would have answered any view I had in publishing it. If it can be made to promote order and decorum in debate it will do great good." Jefferson did take the chance to revise and update the *Manual* for Milligan's edition. When he originally compiled the work, John Hatsell's three-volume *Precedents of Proceedings in the House of Commons* had been one of his most important reference works. Hatsell had added a fourth volume to his collection, which Jefferson had not seen before completing the first edition. Revising the *Manual* became another writing project for Jefferson's retirement. For the Milligan edition, he made many changes and additions, some inspired by Hatsell, and others made to sharpen the rules of order he had originally written.[27]

Jefferson did find fault with Milligan's plan to publish the *Manual* in octavo: "I wonder you should think of printing them in 8vo. It is essentially a book for the pocket, and which members will carry to their house in their pocket occasionally, and some habitually."[28] Milligan took Jefferson's advice to heart and chose a smaller format for the book. Sending some preliminary proof sheets to Jefferson for his approval, Milligan explained, "As you will see by the Enclosed proof of the first 12 pages of the Manual I have had it printed to meet your Idea as to size and think that it is certainly a great improvement as it may be bound like the Volume of the British Spy herewith sent so as to make an Elegant pocket Volume." This other book Milligan sent was the fourth edition of William Wirt's *Letters of the British Spy*, handsomely bound in calf and gilt. Its small format made it ideal for Jefferson's vacation library.[29]

Milligan's edition of the *Manual* appeared in 1812. Other American publishers issued reprints in 1820, 1822, and 1823. Jefferson's *Manual* influenced not only legislatures in the United States, but also foreign legislatures. In his lifetime, it was translated into French (1814), German (1819), and Spanish (1826). Think back to the time when Jefferson chuckled at the proceedings of the colonial Maryland legislature. *A Manual of Parliamentary Procedure* established methods that allowed any legislature to proceed with fairness and decorum. A half a century later, Jefferson's chuckle became a grin of satisfaction.

Late in the summer of 1809, Jefferson learned of a French writer and politician who needed his help. In August he received a letter from Lafayette, introducing Destutt de Tracy and letting him know that Tracy would be sending him a manuscript he was hoping to publish in America, a redaction of Montesquieu's *Spirit of Laws*.[30] Jefferson had appreciated Montesquieu's work for decades, even as he disliked its incongruities. He called the work "a book of paradoxes; having, indeed, much of truth and sound principle, but abounding also in inconsistencies, apocryphal facts, and false inferences."[31] Upon receiving the manuscript, Jefferson recognized how well Tracy had methodized Montesquieu. He saw great value in the work and agreed to help him get it into print.

Jefferson took no action immediately, but after about a year, he translated one chapter into English and sent it to William Duane to see if he would be interested in publishing Tracy's entire work. Duane agreed. He lined up a translator and, when the translation was finished, sent it to Jefferson for his approval. Jefferson made some minor changes to the translation, but there was one aspect of it he could not remedy: overall, it lacked the fluidity to be the work of a native English speaker.

Jefferson devised an ingenious solution. He imagined a fictional author for the work and drafted a "short Proem" in which this author introduces himself. Since Tracy did not want to be identified as the author, Jefferson had to develop a distinct personality for his fictional author. He decided to make him a Frenchman now living in America, and wrote the proem from this point of view. The use of a fictional persona was a commonplace literary device of the period. Some of the finest writers in early America, including Benjamin Franklin, wore the masks of many different personae. Jefferson rarely used the technique. Consequently, this proem marks an unusual departure for Jefferson— but one that is great fun. It begins:

> I am a Frenchman by birth and education. I was an early friend to the revolution of France, and continued to support it, until those entrusted

with its helm, had evidently changed its direction. Flying then from the tyrannies of the monster Robespierre, I found, and still enjoy, safety, freedom, and hospitality, among you. I am grateful for these boons, and anxious to shew that gratitude, by such services as my faculties and habits enable me to render. Reading and contemplation have been the occupations of my life, and mostly on those subjects which concern the condition of man.

At this point, Jefferson's preface seems like a fantasy piece. Often throughout his personal correspondence he had explained that the Revolutionary times in which he lived had taken him from his natural, scholarly pursuits. Writing from a persona, Jefferson became in imagination what he had always wanted to be, a man whose lifetime occupations involved reading and contemplation.

Duane published the work in 1811 as *A Commentary and Review of Montesquieu's Spirit of Laws*. Tracy was thrilled with the result. He also appreciated Jefferson's ongoing efforts to promote the work. A half a dozen years later, Tracy sought Jefferson's help publishing another work, *A Treatise on Political Economy*. Jefferson ended up translating the work himself and arranged for Milligan to publish it.

Nearly a year passed between the time Jefferson first received Tracy's manuscript of *A Commentary and Review of Montesquieu's Spirit of Laws* and the time he approached Duane about publishing it. Another arduous writing project had intervened. During that time, Jefferson wrote another book, one he had not planned to write, and did not want to write, but one that circumstances demanded of him.

The acquisition of Louisiana during Jefferson's presidency had generated a local controversy in New Orleans. Below the levee was a part of the Mississippi riverbed opposite the suburb of Ste. Marie known as the batture, which was dry for about half the year and submerged the other half. Most people in New Orleans treated the batture as public property, but one resident, Monsieur Jean Gravier, who owned the property in the facing suburb, laid claim to the batture. Townsfolk feared that Gravier would reclaim the batture, a project that might alter the course of the Mississippi, hinder navigation, and possibly endanger the levees. Clearly, something had to be done.

Jefferson learned of the controversy in 1807. Attorney General Caesar Rodney recommended that the batture was the property of the U.S. government, which could justifiably eject intruders. Jefferson had concurred: after consulting with the rest of his cabinet, he authorized U.S. marshals to forcibly remove anyone who settled on the batture.

Before President Jefferson's decision was executed, Gravier had secretly conveyed his supposed title to the batture to Edward Livingston. A formidable attorney, Livingston took up the fight. Upon retiring from office, Jefferson put the batture controversy behind him, or so he thought. But in May 1810, he was shocked to learn that Livingston was suing him for $100,000 for trespass and damages: Thomas Jefferson, private citizen, was being sued for decisions he had made while president of the United States.

Shocked at this unprecedented suit, Jefferson sprang into action. He hired three expert attorneys, George Hay, Littleton Waller Tazewell, and William Wirt, and began preparing a brief that is a masterpiece of legal erudition. By midsummer, he had drafted the work, which he shared with his former cabinet members, James Madison, Albert Gallatin, and Caesar Rodney. He revised and polished the brief in light of their feedback.

The result of the case was anticlimactic: *Livingston v. Jefferson* did not come to trial until December 1811, and the case was dismissed for lack of jurisdiction. Jefferson was disappointed with the result. Knowing he held the upper hand, he had been looking forward to the fight. Most of all, he wanted to lay the case before the public. With the case dismissed on a technicality, the only way for him to present his arguments to the public would be for him to publish his brief.

Jefferson arranged with New York publisher Ezra Sargeant to issue the work. To Jefferson's mind, Sargeant's was the only publisher in America who could issue a book so complicated. Filled with quotations from French, Greek, Latin, and Spanish, double columns of parallel texts, numerous marginal glosses, and lengthy footnotes, Jefferson's brief presented a challenge to even the best of printers.

The work appeared in March 1812 as *The Proceedings of the Government of the United States, in Maintaining the Public Right to the Beach of the Missisipi, Adjacent to New-Orleans, against the Intrusion of Edward Livingston*, a closely printed volume of more than eighty pages. Jefferson presented copies to Congress and many other figures in the federal government.

In the preface to the *Proceedings*, Jefferson apologized for the arid quality of the document, originally written solely for the use of his counsel. Remarkably, the *Proceedings* found a handful of enthusiastic readers. William Wirt, one of the attorneys Jefferson had hired and author of *Letters of the British Spy*, one of the most respected contemporary works of American literature, was ecstatic about it: "It is by far the best piece of grecian architecture that I have ever seen, either from ancient or modern times. I did not think it possible that such a subject could be so deeply and at the same time so airily treated—because I never before had seen such a union of lightness and solidity, of beauty and power, in any investigation."[32]

While a legal brief is not usually a place for fine writing, Jefferson's *Proceedings* does contain several charming nuggets of humor and wisdom, starting on the first page with an allusion to one of Shakespeare's history plays, *Henry IV, Part 1*. In a hilarious exchange with Prince Hal, Falstaff boasts about having successfully attacked two rogues clad in buckram. Before he finishes one speech, the two rogues have become four. As Hal questions him, Falstaff's boast continues to grow. The four rogues become seven, and the seven become eleven. Jefferson, in tracing the transfer of title to seven arpents of riverfront property from a Monsieur Pradel to the widow Pradel to Monsieur Renard to the widow Renard to Monsieur Gravier, who married the widow Renard, Jefferson observed, "How these 7 arpents, like Falstaff's men in buckram, became 12 in the sale of the widow Pradel to Renard, 13 in Gravier's inventory, and nearly 17, as is said in the extent of his fauxbourg, the plaintiff is called on to show, and to deduce titles from the crown, regularly down to himself."[33]

The aphorisms Jefferson composed to punctuate the *Proceedings* need no explanation:

> Sound reason ... should constitute the law of every country.
> Common sense [is] the foundation of all authorities, of the laws themselves, and of their construction.
> There is more honour and magnanimity in correcting than preserving an error.
> He who has done his duty honestly, and according to his best skill and judgment, stands acquitted before God and man.[34]

Judge John Tyler was also impressed. He read the *Proceedings* "with great delight."[35] Writing to Jefferson to express his appreciation, the judge told him, "You still retain the power of turning whatever you touch to gold—Your Streams are brought from so many fountains—like the great Missisippi so strong and irresistible that Livingston and his bold, but corrupt Enterprize, are swept together into the Gulf without hope of redemption."

CHAPTER 36

Letters to an Old Friend

As a literary device, the dream vision reached its peak during the time of *Pierce Plowman*. By no means did it disappear from the literary discourse once the medieval period gave way to the Renaissance. John Bunyan's *Pilgrim's Progress*, the best-known dream vision of the seventeenth century, influenced such works as Benjamin Franklin's "Silence Dogood, No. 4," the best-known dream vision in early American literature. But Franklin was not the only early American author and, for that matter, not the only signer of the *Declaration of Independence* who wrote dream visions. Benjamin Rush greatly enjoyed writing them and sometimes built dream visions into his personal letters.

Writing John Adams on October 17, 1809, Rush described a dream that is set several years in the future. As it begins, Rush sees his son Richard reading a history of the United States. Richard offers to let him read the book. His father refuses until Richard informs him that the book mentions his friend John Adams. Rush takes the volume and reads the entry for 1809, which begins: "Among the most extraordinary events of this year was the renewal of the friendship and intercourse between Mr. John Adams and Mr. Jefferson, the two ex-Presidents of the United States." This historical account explains that their initial exchange of letters in 1809 was followed by a correspondence extending for years and containing "many precious aphorisms, the result of observation, experience, and profound reflection." The account ends observing that both Adams and Jefferson "sunk into the grave nearly at the same time, full of years and rich in the gratitude and praises of their country."[1]

Responding to Rush's fanciful letter, Adams exclaimed, "A Dream again! I wish you would dream all day and all Night, for one of your dreams puts me in spirits for a Month. I have no other objection to your Dream, but that it is not History. It may be Prophecy."[2] Rush's dream

Benjamin Rush (1805), by Ellen Sharples, after James Sharples, Senior. (Independence National Historical Park)

vision was prophetic indeed. The reconciliation of Thomas Jefferson and John Adams, who had not communicated since March 1801, the month Jefferson took over the presidency from Adams, would not happen as soon as Rush dreamed, but it would happen within a few more years, largely due to Rush's persistence.

The first week of January 1811 Rush encouraged Jefferson to write Adams. No dream vision this time: Rush's letters to Jefferson are not nearly as playful as his letters to Adams. He understood what would persuade Jefferson to change his mind: he appealed to his humanity and his sense of the future. Rush observed, "Posterity will revere the friendship of two ex-Presidents that were once opposed to each other. Human nature will be a gainer by it. I am sure an advance on your side will be a cordial to the heart of Mr. Adams."[3] Jefferson told Rush he would be happy to write John Adams but suspected that his advances would be rebuffed. To explain why, Jefferson related the story of his disheartening correspondence with Abigail Adams over James Callender. To convince Rush, Jefferson sent her letters and copies of his responses, the first time he had shared them with anyone.

Naturally enough, Jefferson assumed that Abigail Adams had written to him with her husband's approval. She had not. She and Jefferson exchanged letters discussing Callender from May to November 1804, when she finally showed her husband Jefferson's letters and letter book copies of her letters to him. After reading the correspondence, Adams wrote in the letter book: "I have no remarks to make upon it at this time and in this place."[4] For once, John Adams was speechless.

Rush was moved by the confidence Jefferson had in him. After reading the letters Jefferson had written Abigail Adams, Rush found that they reflected his "kindness, benevolence, and even friendship."[5] In light of her letters, Rush did not push Jefferson to pursue the correspondence with John Adams—though he did mention that Adams had made some favorable comments about him in a recent letter.

A chance encounter changed everything. Jefferson's friend and neighbor Edward Coles happened to visit New England in the summer of 1811. Supplied with letters of introduction from President Madison, he visited Quincy, Massachusetts, where he met John Adams. Naturally enough, Jefferson's name came up in conversation. Adams told Coles how icy and awkward their last meeting had been. He interpreted Jefferson's cool demeanor as a sign of insensitivity. Coles disagreed. Having heard Jefferson tell the story of his last meeting with Adams on multiple occasions, Coles told Adams that Jefferson had been sensitive to Adams's feelings and had wanted to part on friendly terms. In light of Coles's information, Adams softened considerably. He expressed kind feelings for Jefferson, admiring his character and appreciating his services to the nation.[6] As he conveyed his friendship for Jefferson, Adams became effusive.

"I always loved Jefferson," he said, "and still love him."

Upon his return to Virginia, Coles visited Jefferson, told him about his visit to Massachusetts, and repeated what Adams had to say. Afterward, Jefferson wrote Rush and told him about Coles's visit to Quincy. Referring to Adams's expression of friendship, Jefferson wrote, "This is enough for me. I only needed this knowledge to revive towards him all the affections of the most cordial moments of our lives." He was ready to resume his correspondence with Adams, but he saw one difficulty: "There is an awkwardness which hangs over the resuming a correspondence so long discontinued, unless something could arise which should call for a letter." Taking advantage of Rush's desire to reunite them, Jefferson hinted how to resolve this difficulty: "In your letters to Mr. Adams, you can, perhaps, suggest my continued cordiality towards him, and knowing this, should an occasion of writing first present itself to him, he will perhaps avail himself of it, as I certainly will should it first occur to me. No ground for jealousy now existing, he will certainly give fair play to the natural warmth of his heart."[7]

Rush took the hint. On December 16, the same day he received Jefferson's letter, he wrote Adams, repeated what Jefferson had told him, and suggested he "receive the olive branch which has thus been offered to you by the hand of a man who still loves you." The next day Rush wrote back to Jefferson, telling him that he had written Adams and expressing hope that the two would resume their correspondence: "Patriotism, liberty, science, and religion would all gain a triumph by it."[8]

On New Year's Day, 1812, Adams drafted a brief letter to Jefferson. The ostensible purpose of the letter was to present a copy of John Quincy Adams's two-volume pedagogical work, *Lectures on Rhetoric and Oratory*. Instead of directly mentioning the book or its author, Adams chose a clever metaphor ideally suited to Jefferson: "As you are a Friend to American Manufactures under proper restrictions, especially Manufactures of the domestic kind, I take the Liberty of sending you by the Post a Packett containing two Pieces of Homespun lately produced in this quarter by One who was honoured in his youth with some of your Attention and much of your kindness."[9]

Adams's letter arrived before either volume of the *Lectures*. Consequently, Jefferson took the metaphor literally and assumed that Adams was indeed sending some homespun fabric. Before receiving this gift, Jefferson wrote a letter of thanks to his old friend, which begins with a celebration of American textile manufacture. The same day he wrote Adams, January 21, Jefferson also wrote Rush, informing him that they had resumed their correspondence and enclosing copies of Adams's letter and his response.

Writing to Rush, Jefferson characterized his letter to Adams. He called it "a rambling, gossiping epistle." With this description, Jefferson was being nonchalant: his letter is carefully crafted. Mentioning that he had made "openings for the expression of sincere feelings," Jefferson provided a better indication of its craftsmanship.[10] Like a well-designed home, this letter contains entryways to welcome the invited guest.

Jefferson's letter is divided into three sections, all roughly equal in length. After the long initial discussion of domestic textile manufacture, he started the second paragraph suggesting that Adams's letter had jogged his memory and prompted him to recall past events in which both men played important parts. Much as he had done in some of his political writings, Jefferson presented a brief historical survey of his subject, encompassing past, present, and future. Imagining the future, he asserted that the United States would thrive, continuing "to multiply and prosper until we exhibit an association, powerful, wise and happy, beyond what has yet been seen by men."[11]

A rhetorical question separates the second section from the third, which is largely personal in nature: "But whither is senile garrulity leading me?" This question serves as an abrupt transition to the next topic, his personal life. He told Adams about what he has been reading in his retirement: "I have given up newspapers in exchange for Tacitus and Thucydides, for Newton and Euclid; and I find myself much the happier."[12] He informed Adams that he remained active, spending three or four hours a day on horseback and periodically making the seventy-mile trek to Poplar Forest. His health was not perfect. He could seldom walk more than a mile. This lack of mobility did not bother him much because there were few activities he enjoyed more than staying at home with his grandchildren and his first great-grandchild.

Unused to writing about himself at such length, Jefferson stopped short, telling Adams that he would rather be reading about him than writing about himself. He asked Adams to respond with a letter "full of egotisms, and of details of your health, your habits, occupations and enjoyments."[13]

Rush was delighted to learn that his two friends and fellow signers had successfully resumed their correspondence. He told Jefferson, "Few of the acts of my life have given me more pleasure than the one you are pleased to acknowledge in your last letter." Rush made Jefferson privy to some information about the health of Adams's daughter Abigail, who had breast cancer and had recently undergone a mastectomy. Rush was not so specific about her affliction, but he did say that she had been "saved from certain death by a painful operation."[14] Rush also wrote

Adams to congratulate him on the resumption of his correspondence with Jefferson.

Adams received Jefferson's letter on February 1. Noticing that it was postmarked January 23 at Milton, Virginia, he was amazed that the letter had traveled so far so fast. He made the speed of the mail the subject of the opening paragraph of his response. Adams knew that the improvement of post roads had been a pet project for Jefferson throughout his public life; his information about the speed of this letter let Jefferson know that his efforts to improve the American transportation infrastructure had not been in vain.

In his response, Adams took advantage of the openings Jefferson had built into his letter. Actually, Adams's response helps explain precisely what Jefferson had meant by his term "openings": startling facts about his life in retirement, direct questions, and unusual diction designed to provoke comment. Jefferson's discussion of his reading prompted Adams to exclaim, "What an Exchange have you made? Of Newspapers for Newton! Rising from the lower deep of the lowest deep of Dulness and Bathos to the Contemplation of the Heavens and the heavens of Heavens."[15] Adams also informed Jefferson about his health. He was walking every sunny day, sometimes three or four miles a day. He rode occasionally but never more than ten or fifteen miles at a stretch. His hands trembled sometimes. That tremble was really the only malady that bothered him.[16]

A great literary stylist in his own right, Adams reacted to the most unusual instance of Jefferson's diction with a synonymous phrase of his own. After writing several pages, Adams explained, "My Senectutal Loquacity has more than retaliated your 'Senile Garrulity.'"[17] Adams's playfulness enhances his affection for Jefferson. Knowing Jefferson's enjoyment of neologisms, Adams invented a word himself, making an adjective from the noun senectute. Adams's new word further ingratiated Jefferson: it takes its inspiration from a favorite work of theirs, Cicero's *De Senectute*.

Jefferson eventually received both volumes of John Quincy Adams's *Lectures* and realized what Adams had meant by the two pieces of homespun. Wanting to make Adams a similar present, he already had something in mind. *The Proceedings of the Government of the United States, in Maintaining the Public Right to the Beach of the Missisipi Adjacent to New-Orleans, against the Intrusion of Edward Livingston* was going through the press that winter. Informing Rush of his plan to send Adams a copy of the book, Jefferson said that the gift "may not be unassuming to one who is himself a profound lawyer."[18]

The cover letter accompanying this presentation copy of *The Pro-ceedings* begins, "I have it now in my power to send you a piece of homespun in return for that I recieved from you. Not of the fine texture, or delicate character of yours, or, to drop our metaphor, not filled as that was with that display of imagination which constitutes excellence in Belles lettres, but a mere sober, dry and formal piece of Logic."[19] Unlike less accomplished politicians, Jefferson recognized the impropriety of carrying a metaphor too far and knew precisely when to drop it.

Adams responded to the gift with gratitude, humor, and shock. Re-ferring to the actions taken by Edward Livingston, he commented, "Neddy is a naughty lad as well as a saucy one." His tone soon grows serious: "Good God! Is a President of U. S. to be Subject to a private Action of every Individual? This will soon introduce the Axiom that a President can do no wrong; or another equally curious that a President can do no right."[20]

As their correspondence developed, certain topics would dominate for a few months and then give way to others. The third week of May 1812, for example, Adams expressed curiosity about Native American tradi-tions and asked Jefferson if he could recommend any books on the subject. He was especially curious about indigenous religious practices and wanted to know if the American Indians had "any order of Priesthood among them, like the Druids, Bards or Minstrells of the Celtic nations."[21]

Jefferson responded swiftly and at considerable length. Early Amer-ican accounts contained much good information on Indian customs, but their information on religious traditions was scanty. He recommended three authors: Theodor de Bry, Joseph-François Lafitau, and James Adair. The works of all three were useful but flawed. Lafitau, for ex-ample, spent several years in Canada among the Iroquois collecting data. He documented his experience in *Moeurs des Sauvages Amériquains Comparées aux Moeurs des Premiers Temps*, which used the comparative method to show how the Native Americans resembled the Ancients. Lafitau actually concluded that the American Indians descended from the Ancients. Furthermore, he asserted that the religion of both could be traced back to a pure, primitive religion.

The problem Jefferson had with Lafitau was not his theory but the way he derived it. While Jefferson greatly appreciated the comparative method, he realized the approach was valid only when it was applied inductively, not deductively. Lafitau began with a preconceived theory about the shared heritage between people of the New World and those of the Old. Consequently, he selected only those empirical facts that supported his theory. The same could be said about James Adair, who theorized that the American Indians were descendants of the Jews. Even with these drawbacks, Lafitau's work contained numerous firsthand observations that made it a valuable sourcebook. Furthermore, his literary style made *Moeurs des Sauvages Amériquains* a pleasure to read. Jefferson observed, "He was a man of much classical and scriptural reading, and has rendered his book not unentertaining."[22]

Recognizing Adams's curiosity about Native American religious practices, Jefferson discussed how Adair, De Bry, and Lafitau depicted the religious leaders among the Indians:

> Lafitau calls them by their proper names, Jongleurs, Devins, Sortileges; De Bry praestigiatores, Adair himself sometimes Magi, Archimagi, cunning men, Seers, rain makers, and the modern Indian interpreters, call them Conjurers and Witches. They are persons pretending to have communications with the devil and other evil spirits, to foretel future events, bring down rain, find stolen goods, raise the dead, destroy some, and heal others by enchantment, lay spells etc. And Adair, without departing from his parallel of the Jews and Indians, might have found their counterpart, much more aptly, among the Soothsayers, sorcerers and wizards of the Jews, their Jannes and Jambres, their Simon Magus, witch of Endor, and the young damsel whose sorceries disturbed Paul so much; instead of placing them in a line with their High-priest, their Chief priests, and their magnificent hierarchy generally.[23]

Though this passage begins as a summary of the texts Jefferson was discussing, it shifts toward a critique of Western religious practices. But Jefferson did not stop here. Speaking of Indian attitudes toward Christian ministers, Jefferson observed: "So little idea have they of a regular order of priests, that they mistake ours for their Conjurers, and call them by that name."[24] Jefferson may have been interpreting the attitude toward priests held by American Indians, but his tone suggests that their opinions, at least when it came to Christian ministers, were right on target.

That fall he and Adams took up the topic of early American literature. Adams introduced the subject. He was motivated by a pamphlet volume John Quincy Adams had found in Berlin containing three early-seventeenth-century works of Americana: Edward Johnson's *Wonder-Working Providence*, Thomas Morton's *New English Canaan*, and William Wood's *New Englands Prospect*. John Adams was especially happy to acquire *New English Canaan*. He had heard about this rare work but had never seen a copy. Though Adams was not a great bookman like Jefferson, he spoke of this pamphlet volume lovingly. Writing to Jefferson, he personified the volume, calling it an adventurer for having made it as far as Berlin. Adams explained, "I have enquired for it, more than half a Century: but have never been able to learn that any Copy of it ever was seen in this Country. The Berlin Adventurer is I believe the only one in America." In truth, it was not quite the only copy in the nation. Abiel Holmes had located a copy earlier while preparing his *American Annals.* Curious to learn more about *New English Canaan*, Adams asked Jefferson if he knew anything about the book. He even named some reference works Jefferson could use as starting points.[25]

Jefferson was happy to help his friend. He did not have a copy of *New English Canaan* at Monticello, but he did have some of the reference books Adams recommended. He checked these and examined other works of Americana. His search was hampered because he had loaned out many relevant books, some to Louis Hue Girardin, who was completing Burk's *History of Virginia*, and others to William Waller Hening, who was compiling the Virginia *Statutes*. Jefferson found Thomas Morton's *New English Canaan* listed in Bishop White Kennett's *Bibliothecae Americanae*. The most useful volume he had at Monticello for Adams's purpose was Nathaniel Morton's *New-England's Memorial*, which detailed Thomas Morton's exploits in New England. Writing Adams in October 1812, Jefferson told him where he looked and took the time to transcribe several pages from Nathaniel Morton's *New-England's Memorial*.

He did not write Adams again until May 1813. By this time, he had received the sad news that Benjamin Rush had died the previous month. Jefferson lamented, "Another of our friends of 76. is gone, my dear Sir, another of the Co-signers of the independence of our country. And a better man, than Rush, could not have left us, more benevolent, more learned, of finer genius, or more honest. We too must go; and that ere long. I believe we are under half a dozen at present; I mean the signers of the Declaration."[26] Jefferson's fondness for Rush shows in this passage, which also recognizes the special bond the signers shared. Thirty-seven years earlier they had put their lives on the line by signing the *Declaration of Independence*. With the resounding success of American democracy, they took great pride in their accomplishment. And they took an ongoing interest in the welfare of one another.

Jefferson tried to remember who else survived. Besides himself and Adams, he thought of Elbridge Gerry and Charles Carroll of Carrollton.

It was impossible to forget Gerry: he had yet to retire from public service. The year before, in fact, he had been elected vice president. The only other signers who might survive were Robert Treat Paine and William Floyd, but Jefferson was unsure whether either one was alive. He asked Adams if he knew.

Responding to Jefferson, Adams honored Benjamin Rush, too: "I know of no Character living or dead, who has done more real good in America."[27] He informed Jefferson that Paine was still alive. At eighty-two, he was alert, droll, and witty, but quite deaf. Adams thought Floyd was still alive, but he was unsure. Actually, Floyd was living in happy obscurity in western New York. Ten years earlier, he had relocated his family to a small town on the Mohawk River.[28]

Charles Thomson, though not a signer, had been instrumental to the cause of American independence as secretary to the Continental Congress. He, too, was alive and would remain so into the next decade, when his longevity became a subject of discussion for Jefferson and Adams. In 1822, Jefferson wrote, "Charles Thomson still lives at about the same age [ninety-three], chearful, slender as a grasshopper, and so much without memory that he scarcely recognizes the members of his household. An intimate friend of his called on him not long since: it was difficult to make him recollect who he was, and, sitting one hour, he told the same story 4. times over." Adams reassured Jefferson that Thomson was not quite as bad as all that.[29]

A potential source of friction between Adams and Jefferson arose in late spring 1813. Adams had been reading Thomas Belsham's *Memoirs of the Late Reverend Theophilus Lindsey*. Essentially a study of the rise of the Unitarian Church in England, Belsham's work includes an appendix containing several related documents. Among these are two letters Jefferson wrote to Joseph Priestley. The earlier letter is the one Jefferson wrote Priestley soon after his inauguration in March 1801 informing him that he no longer had to worry about being persecuted for his ideas and beliefs. The second one was the 1803 letter to Priestley in which Jefferson outlined his ideas for a work tracing the history of moral philosophy from antiquity to the time of Christ.

Adams took offense at what Jefferson had to say in the earlier letter, which hinted that President Adams had held little hope for intellectual or scientific advancement. Adams asked Jefferson to explain what he meant. Jefferson had not seen Belsham's *Memoirs*, but he located copies of the letters in his files. Regarding the first, Jefferson said, "It recalls to our recollection the gloomy transactions of the times, the doctrines they witnessed, and the sensibilities they excited. It was a confidential communication of reflections on these from one friend to another, deposited in his bosom, and never meant to trouble the public mind."[30] Though Adams had asked him to explain what he had written, Jefferson did not really offer an explanation. Instead, he described his impressions upon rereading the letter now after a lapse of a dozen years. He reminded Adams of the circumstances under which the letter was written and emphasized the impropriety of publishing private messages.

Adams could tell by this response that his question had put Jefferson on the defensive. He wrote a follow-up letter with a calming effect. "Be not surprised or alarmed," Adams said. "You have right and reason to feel and to resent the breach of Confidence, I have had enough of the same kind of Treachery and Perfidy practiced upon me, to know how to sympathize with you. I will agree with you, in unquallified censure of such Abuses. They are the worst Species of Tyranny over private Judgment and free Enquiry. They supress the free communication of Soul to Soul."[31] Nevermore would the slightest hint of controversy enter their correspondence.

The second letter from Jefferson to Priestley appended to Belsham's *Memoirs* prompted Adams to ask about Jefferson's religious views. Jefferson responded by supplying the background behind the "Syllabus of an Estimate of the Merit of the Doctrines of Jesus, Compared with Those of Others." He even promised to send a copy of the syllabus with the proviso: "I enclose it *to you* with entire confidence, free to be perused by yourself and Mrs. Adams, but by no one else; and to be returned to me."[32]

The confidence Jefferson expressed in Abigail Adams marks another important development in his correspondence. At the end of the July 15, 1813, letter from Adams to Jefferson, the following postscript appears in a different hand, a hand Jefferson had not seen for eleven years now. Reading this postscript gave him great personal satisfaction:

> I have been looking for some time for a space in my good Husbands Letters to add the regards of an old Friend, which are still cherished and preserved through all the changes and vicissitudes which have taken place since we first became acquainted, and will I trust remains as long as
> A Adams

Once again, Abigail Adams was happy to call Jefferson her friend. He wrote her a chatty letter responding to her postscript and talking about how much he enjoyed reading. He also offered a charming comment about his grandchildren: "I have compared notes with Mr. Adams on the score of progeny, and find I am ahead of him, and think I am in a fair way to keep so. I have 10 1/2 grandchildren, and 2 3/4 great-grand children; and these fractions will ere long become units."[33]

Sadly, Mr. and Mrs. Adams had a death in the family to report. In August, John Adams informed Jefferson that their daughter Abigail had passed away. The mastectomy had not removed all the cancer, which had spread to other parts of her body. At forty-nine, she had lost her long battle with cancer. Burdened with extreme pain during the final months of the affliction, she was, in her father's words, "a monument to Suffering and to Patience."[34]

Abigail Adams wrote Jefferson separately. Her grief reinforced the insignificance of past squabbles and the importance of Jefferson's friendship. She summed up the situation with a literary allusion she knew he would appreciate: "But altho, time has changed the outward form, and political 'Back wounding calumny' for a period interrupted the Friendly intercourse and harmony which subsisted, it is again renewed, purified from the dross."[35] Abigail Adams was alluding to a speech by Duke Vincentio in *Measure for Measure*, which applies equally to the attacks that both John Adams and Thomas Jefferson had suffered throughout their public lives:

> No might nor greatness in mortality
> Can censure scape; back-wounding calumny
> The whitest virtue strikes. What king so strong
> Can tie the gall up in the slanderous tongue?

In the fall of 1813, Jefferson sent Adams a letter destined to be one of his most famous. His subject is what he called the "natural aristocracy." Though this letter is typically cited as the one in which Jefferson defined precisely what he meant by the phrase, the ideas this letter expresses occur in virtually all of his earlier discussions of education. His definition is actually quite simple: the natural aristocracy is not founded on wealth or birth—it is founded on "virtue and talents." The American educational system must be structured to ensure that those with virtue and talents are recognized and given opportunities for education and advancement. In short, the natural aristocracy is "the most precious gift of nature for the instruction, the trusts, and government of society."[36]

Jefferson may have told Adams that he had quit reading the newspapers, but he was still keeping abreast of national affairs. Incidental remarks about the War of 1812 occur throughout their correspondence during this period. Jefferson also remained cognizant of world affairs.

One event prompting his extended comments was the news of Napoleon Bonaparte's exile to Elba in 1814. This event gave Jefferson the opportunity to reflect on Napoleon's rule. "The Attila of the age," he called him in a July 5, 1814, letter to Adams. "The ruthless destroyer of 10. millions of the human race," he continued, "whose thirst for blood appeared unquenchable, the great oppressor of the rights and liberties of the world." Jefferson characterized the pitifulness of Napoleon's exile, in contrast to the greatness of his ambition: "How miserably, how meanly, has he closed his inflated career! What a sample of the Bathos will his history present! He should have perished on the swords of his enemies, under the walls of Paris."[37]

After these reflections, Jefferson quoted some pertinent lines from Pietro Metastasio's libretto *Adriano in Siria*. Jefferson had the London edition of Metastasio's *Opere* in twelve pocket-sized volumes in his library at Poplar Forest, from which he had recently returned. This quotation suggests that he had been reading Metastasio on vacation. Writing to Adams, Jefferson quoted the original Italian, which can be translated:

> The lion stricken to death
> Realizes that he is dying,
> And looks at his wounds from which
> He grows ever weaker and weaker.
> Then with his final wrath
> He roars, threatens, and screams,
> Which makes the hunter
> Tremble at him dying.

Perpetuating the metaphor, Jefferson observed, "But Bonaparte was a lion in the field only. In civil life a cold-blooded, calculating unprincipled Usurper, without a virtue, no statesman, knowing nothing of commerce, political economy, or civil government, and supplying ignorance by bold presumption."[38]

Jefferson's words echo something he had written two decades earlier. In the first draft of the Mazzei letter, he had used the phrase "lions in the field and councils" to describe leadership qualities he admired. It was not enough to be valiant on the battlefield. A good leader needed the skills to negotiate the political labyrinth. Calling Napoleon a "lion in the field only," Jefferson suggested that he was not a good leader because he was incompetent when it came to matters of administration, commerce, and diplomacy.

Jefferson's reuse of this phrase to describe Napoleon provides a fascinating insight into his literary life. He had devised the phrase while drafting the Mazzei letter, which he deleted in favor of "Samsons in the field." Still, he did not forget his original phrase. It remained dormant until Jefferson found the opportunity to use it. That opportunity came while reading *Adriano in Siria* soon after learning about Napoleon's exile. Metastasio's imagery prompted Jefferson to recall his original phrase and apply it to Napoleon. Read in light of the first draft of the Mazzei letter, this letter helps tie together Jefferson's diverse body of writings and highlights a consistent theme that runs throughout his writing: the meaning of leadership.

When some of the first letters from the John Adams–Thomas Jefferson correspondence were published, they touched their readers' hearts—as Benjamin Rush predicted they would. One prominent English reader, Thomas Love Peacock, remarked, "We know nothing more beautiful in the records of the retirement of illustrious men, than the manner in which these veteran statesmen renewed and continued their correspondence."[39] What they resumed in 1812, John Adams and Thomas Jefferson would continue for the rest of their lives. The Adams–Jefferson correspondence offers a penetrating look into the lives of two men who were great leaders and great writers. Theirs is the finest correspondence in the history of American literature.

CHAPTER 37

The Library of Congress

Patrick Magruder, the ailing Librarian of Congress, left Washington in late July 1814 on his physician's advice to visit the Virginia hot springs in order to recover his health. Before leaving, he put J. T. Frost in charge. Frost, the congressional clerk who acted as assistant librarian, was aided by Samuel Burch, another clerk in the House of Representatives. Unaware of the impending crisis, Magruder did not tell Frost what to do in case of attack. He simply instructed him to air out the books according to regulation. For the sake of the Library of Congress, Magruder chose the worst possible time to take sick leave. Had he stayed in Washington to fulfill his official responsibilities, however, chances are he could have done little more to save the library from destruction than Frost and Burch were able to do.[1]

In August, British troops massed in Chesapeake Bay for an assault on Washington. To protect the city, the District of Columbia called out the militia. All of the congressional clerks went with the militia, excluding Frost, who was too old to serve, but including Burch. George Magruder, Patrick's brother and chief clerk, served as a colonel in the militia. Understanding the dire situation Frost faced alone, Colonel Magruder arranged a furlough for Burch so that he could help Frost save the books. Burch returned on Sunday evening, August 21.

On the twenty-second, they received word to pack up the books and papers and remove them from the Capitol for safekeeping. As Frost packed, Burch scoured Washington for wagons or carts or carriages to transport whatever books and papers they could. Wherever he went, he met with the same result: every wagon and nearly every cart belonging to the city had been turned into transport vehicles for the military. The few privately owned conveyances he encountered were loaded with the personal effects of citizens fleeing in the face of approaching enemy forces. Burch tried to impress a few of the vehicles he came across to stop and aid the Library of Congress. With neither legal authority nor military might, his attempts were in vain.

But Burch was not one to give up easily. He sent messengers into the country to see if they could have more luck than he was having in the city. His messengers managed to obtain one cart and a team of oxen. Frost and Burch loaded the cart with the most valuable congressional records and sent it to the safest place they could think of beyond the city limits. Meanwhile, the two continued packing. Once Bladensburg fell, there was no stopping the enemy. Frost and Burch needed to get out of Washington. They fled the city, leaving behind the three thousand volumes that then comprised the Library of Congress.

British troops ran roughshod over the Capitol building, looting what they could and destroying what they could not take away. The west side of the Capitol, where the library was housed, was constructed of timber and covered with shingles. Once the marauders set a torch to some books, the library went up like a tinder box. By the time the smoke cleared, little remained but charred bits of old folios.

News of this bibliographical carnage saddened Jefferson deeply. He predicted that people the world over would react to the news similarly: they would see the library's destruction as an act of barbarism that did not belong to a civilized age. Jefferson's prediction was accurate. Many people were incensed with the wholesale destruction of books on the part of the British troops. At the risk of being prosecuted for libel, some English commentators spoke out against the actions taken by British forces. Using words closely paralleling Jefferson's, a Nottingham editor condemned the destruction of the Library of Congress as "an act without example in modern wars or in any other wars since the inroads of the barbarians who conflagrated Rome and overthrew the Roman Empire."[2]

Jefferson's patriotism for America and his passion for books doubled the anger he felt upon learning what had happened. But he also had personal reasons to lament the library's destruction. Established shortly before he became president, the Library of Congress had developed largely through the encouragement and support Jefferson provided during his presidency.

The shipment of books forming the nucleus of the original Library of Congress had reached Washington two months after Jefferson's inauguration in 1801. Samuel Otis, then secretary of the Senate, informed President Jefferson of the shipment's arrival. Jefferson subsequently called upon Otis to make a statement about the books at the next session of Congress. Congress proved reluctant to appropriate money for additional book purchases, but the legislators who supported the library sought the help of the greatest bookman ever to occupy the White House. After some gentle prodding from the president, Congress passed the appropriations bill.

A law passed in January 1802 established the position of Librarian of Congress and made it a presidential appointment. That same month, Jefferson appointed John Beckley the first Librarian of Congress. Beckley concurrently served as Clerk of the House of Representatives. After Beckley's death in 1807, Patrick Magruder succeeded him as Clerk of the House of Representatives. Jefferson had hoped to separate the two positions, but in the absence of other qualified candidates, he appointed Magruder to the position of Librarian of Congress.

The January 1802 Act also established the Joint Committee on the Library, which consisted of members from both the Senate and the House of Representatives. Throughout his presidency, Jefferson worked closely with this committee. Upon its establishment, Senator Abraham Baldwin of Georgia was chosen as chair. Jefferson prepared a detailed catalogue of suitable books the committee should consider acquiring for the library and sent the list of desiderata to Baldwin. With the catalogue, Jefferson included a lengthy cover letter explaining its underlying rationale. The letter provides a good indication of what he considered the library's purpose.

Agreeing with Baldwin that "books of entertainment" were beyond the scope of the Library of Congress, Jefferson "confined the catalogue to those branches of science which belong to the deliberations of the members as statesmen." He excluded those "classical books, ancient and modern, which gentlemen generally have in their private libraries, but which cannot properly claim a place in a collection made merely for the purpose of reference."[3] This comment assumes that all congressmen and senators were well read in the ancient classics, an assumption that was becoming increasingly difficult to make.

Though history remained the most respected form of literature through the early decades of the nineteenth century, Jefferson saw no reason to include any in the Library of Congress—at least not narrative history. He explained, "In history, I have confined the list to the chronological works, which give facts and dates with a minuteness not to be found in narratives composed for agreeable reading."[4] Jefferson's words emphasize that the Library of Congress should be purely a reference library, and a chronological list of historical events made for a much better reference work than an artfully crafted historical narrative.

Legislative proceedings demanded a significant collection of law books. "Under the law of nature and nations," he told Baldwin, "I have put down every thing I know of worth possessing because this is a branch of science often under the discussion of Congress and the books written in it not to be found in private libraries."[5] Recall the comment Jefferson made to George Washington about books treating the laws of nature: when several reach a consensus on a particular issue, they form a powerful argument. A large collection of books treating the laws of nature and nations allowed for much consensus-making among lawmakers. In addition, the Library of Congress should contain reports of cases and special legal treatises.

The collection of parliamentary treatises should be as full as possible. "The Parliamentary section I have imagined should be compleat," Jefferson continued. "It is only by having a law of proceedings, and by every member having the means of understanding it for himself, and appealing to it, that he can be protected against caprice and despotism in the chair."[6] A good collection of parliamentary books would help congressmen and senators fulfill their responsibilities as lawmakers, all of whom should have a general knowledge of parliamentary procedure and have the opportunity to double-check specific procedures whenever necessary.

In 1803 Jefferson tried to persuade Congress to purchase some books that survived from the library of Benjamin Franklin. N. G. Dufief, who was selling Franklin's library piecemeal in Philadelphia and having little success, had written President Jefferson—one of his best customers—to enlist his help. Dufief catalogued the two thousand or so volumes that remained from Franklin's library and sent the manuscript catalogue to Jefferson, urging him to persuade Congress to allocate funds for the purchase of the collection and thus to honor a Founding Father and one of the greatest minds America had yet produced by preserving his library as a national treasure.

Essentially, Dufief was suggesting a radical shift in the purpose of the Library of Congress. Instead of a working reference library for legislators, it should be a repository for books that contributed to the cultural and intellectual history of the nation. As the frequency of his Franklin anecdotes show, Jefferson retained fond memories of his old friend. Furthermore, he admired Franklin's great personal library, which he came to know in Paris and saw for the last time in Philadelphia weeks before Franklin's death. Already, he had personally acquired several volumes from Dufief formerly in the possession of Benjamin Franklin.

Still, Jefferson hesitated to change what he saw as the fundamental purpose of the Library of Congress.

Instead of recommending to the Joint Committee on the Library that they purchase what remained of Franklin's collection, Jefferson marked up the catalogue Dufief sent him to indicate which books Congress should notice in particular. Dufief's original catalogue does not survive, but the reconstructed catalogue of Franklin's library lists many books that suit the purpose of the Library of Congress that Jefferson outlined in Jefferson's letter to Baldwin: numerous collections of debates in the House of Commons, several volumes of laws and statutes, *The Parliamentary Register*, *A Complete Collection of the Lords' Protests*, a fifteen-volume collection of the *Journal of the House of Commons*, and many other related works.[7]

The time Jefferson spent reading and annotating the manuscript catalogue of Franklin's library went for naught. Upon receiving it, the Joint Committee of the Library informed him that it had already exhausted its annual budget. Jefferson wrote Dufief to return the catalogue and give him the disappointing news that Congress could not afford the Franklin books. He did agree to buy a few more volumes from Franklin's library for his own collection. Dufief eventually put the rest of the library up for auction. Franklin's collection—second only to Jefferson's among private libraries in early America—was so thoroughly dispersed after Franklin's death that it has largely disappeared.

Jefferson's thoughts on the dispersal of Franklin's library have gone unrecorded, but its sorry fate may have prompted him to rethink the purpose of the Library of Congress. Should it remain a working library for legislators or should it assume a purpose similar to the one Dufief suggested? In other words, should it begin collecting books from all fields of study that have cultural or historical significance to the United States?

Franklin's library may have turned Jefferson's thoughts to his own library. Other great personal libraries in early America had met a similar fate as Franklin's. Around the same time that Dufief was selling the Franklin library, he was also selling piecemeal what remained of the great library of William Byrd of Westover. One important early American library that remained intact was James Logan's. His library survived because he had had the foresight to donate it to the city of Philadelphia. The Loganian Library was a monument to a man who spent a lifetime carefully assembling his collection. Logan's library now survives as part of the Library Company of Philadelphia.

Before enemy soldiers destroyed the Library of Congress, Jefferson had not decided what to do with his library. One idea was to present it to the university he wanted to establish, but the creation of this university remained a distant prospect. Coinciding with an acute personal need for ready cash, the destruction of the Library of Congress crystallized Jefferson's thoughts in the matter: he would sell his collection to the government to form the kernel of a new Library of Congress.

Jefferson's decision marks a fundamental shift in his conception of what the Library of Congress should be. His library contained many of the same kinds of books he had recommended to Baldwin a dozen years earlier. It was rich in law books, especially books treating the laws of nature and of nations, and its collection of parliamentary books was unsurpassed in America. But it also contained thousands of books that fell outside his recommendations to Baldwin: books of entertainment, classical books, narratives composed for agreeable reading.

Whereas Jefferson had recommended selected books from Franklin's library for Congress to buy, he insisted that Congress should purchase his entire collection. He wanted to ensure that the collection he had spent five decades assembling would remain intact. When William Short learned of Jefferson's plan to sell his library to Congress, he congratulated him because it would preserve his library from the fate suffered by the library of William Byrd of Westover. Were he to leave his library in private hands, Short conjectured, his books would be dispersed and the integrity of the collection ruined. Occasionally encountering stray books from Byrd's library in Philadelphia, Short had been saddened by the dispersal of that once great collection. He told Jefferson, "The fate of that of Westover was a sufficient warning. It was scattered in the winds, and separate volumes are every now and then to be found in the book-sales here."[8]

But Jefferson was motivated by the desire not only to preserve his own library as a whole, but also to have it form the basis for a great new Library of Congress—a purpose John Adams well understood. When Adams learned of Jefferson's plan to sell his library to Congress, he told him, "I envy you that immortal honour."[9]

Jefferson did not necessarily see the sale of his library to Congress as a personal honor, but he did see it as another opportunity to inscribe himself onto the nation. In this respect, his careful library organization was more important than the individual books it contained. He cleverly devised a way for the Library of Congress to use the meticulous organizational scheme he had invented. More than the opportunity to preserve his personal library, as Short surmised, more than the opportunity for personal glory, as Adams surmised, Jefferson saw the sale of his highly organized library to Congress as an opportunity to determine how the new national library codified information.

On September 21, 1814, he drafted a letter to Samuel Harrison Smith describing his plan to sell his personal collection to the Library of Congress and soliciting Smith's help. Jefferson began, "I learn from the newspapers that the Vandalism of our enemy has triumphed at Washington over science as well as the arts, by the destruction of the public library with the noble edifice in which it was deposited." He reminded Smith of the greatness of his personal library, which he and his wife had seen when they visited Monticello: "You know my collection, its condition and extent. I have been fifty years making it, and have spared no pains, opportunity or expense, to make it what it is."[10]

He also emphasized his efforts to assemble an unsurpassed collection of Americana. His personal library formed a collection that "can never again be effected, because it is hardly probable that the same opportunities, the same time, industry, perseverance and expense, with some knowledge of the bibliography of the subject, would again happen to be in concurrence."[11] Though Jefferson was typically modest when writing about himself, he was not afraid to praise his library. Stressing the significance of his Americana collection in the letter to Smith, he indicated that he had reconceived the purpose of the Library of Congress more along the lines Dufief had suggested.

Jefferson sent Smith the catalogue and asked him to give both it and his letter to the Joint Committee on the Library so that Congress could set the terms of remuneration. Though Jefferson refused to sell his library piecemeal, he hoped to hang onto some of the classical and mathematical books until his death—but he did not insist on this point. The most important thing was to maintain the collection's integrity.

Smith presented Jefferson's offer to the Joint Committee on the Library. The committee liked the idea but could not approve such a substantial purchase without the support of both the Senate and the House of Representatives.

On Friday, October 7, Robert Goldsborough, chairman of the Joint Committee on the Library, submitted the following resolution: "Resolved, by the Senate and House of Representatives of the United States of America in Congress assembled, That the joint library committee of the two Houses of Congress be, and they are hereby, authorized and empowered to contract on their part, for the purchase of the library of Mr. Jefferson, late President of the United States, for the use of both Houses of Congress."[12]

The following Monday, Jefferson's letter to Smith was read before the Senate. Acting as a committee of the whole, the Senate debated the resolution. No amendments were proposed, and the resolution passed.

Before the day was out, the Senate sent a message to the House of Representatives informing it of the resolution and asking for its approval. The resolution was referred to a committee of the whole to be debated the next day, where it faced a more difficult time than it had in the Senate. The debate over the purchase of Jefferson's library in the House of Representatives has been called "one of the most mean-spirited party battles in Congressional annals."[13]

On Tuesday, October 11, Jefferson's letter to Smith was read before the House. Much "desultory conversation" followed. Congressmen questioned the value of the library and wondered about the books it contained. To give members of the House more time to examine the library catalogue, the committee of the whole agreed to postpone debate until a later time.

Debate was resumed the following Monday, the seventeenth. According to the annals of Congress, this time the debate was both desultory *and* considerable. Charles Ingersoll, a representative from Pennsylvania, remembered what happened. Years later he recalled, "The discussion and votes in the House of Representatives on the purchase of Jefferson's library betrayed the English prepossessions of some, the narrow parsimony of others, the party-prejudices of nearly all."[14] Among those against the purchase, some Congressmen objected to the potential cost of the library, others to its size, and still others to the nature of Jefferson's collection, which, they insisted, contained too many foreign works. After seeing the catalogue of Jefferson's library, one contemporary observer commented, "According to the Catalogue of names a great proportion of the books are in foreign languages, and wholly unintelligible to 9/10ths of the members of Congress."[15] Others objected to the large number of scientific works. Some found many of the works listed in the catalogue downright objectionable.

The names of several prominent authors entered the debate. One congressman did not think that the works of Voltaire deserved a place in the Library of Congress. To be sure, Jefferson owned a sizable Voltaire collection. His fifty-eight-volume collection of Voltaire's *Oeuvres* combined some volumes from the 1775 Geneva edition—the same edition John Adams owned—and other volumes from the 1785 Kehl edition, which Jefferson preferred because, as he said, it was "the last edition corrected by the author himself."[16] Jefferson owned a number of separately published Voltaire works, too. When the newspapers got word of these debates, they attacked the small-mindedness, shortsightedness, and anti-intellectualism of the opposing congressmen. The Petersburg *Courier*, for one, observed, "Another great objection is, that Mr. Jefferson's library contains the works of Voltaire—what a pitiful observation!

Will it be said that the works of an author, which hold the first rank on the shelves of all the libraries of Europe, and which may be found in the libraries of Oxford and Cambridge, and in those of the four Scotch universities, for the express purpose to be perused by students, should be prohibited or forbidden a place in the Library of Congress?"[17]

Ingersoll remembered objections to multiple authors in Jefferson's library. One congressman even objected to the presence of John Locke! Learning about the kinds of objections Jefferson's enemies in Congress were making, the Petersburg *Courier* remarked that if the opponents of the resolution had their way, then Locke's works would be committed to the flames and replaced by the *Arabian Nights' Entertainment* or Monk Lewis's *Tales of Wonder*.

Jean-Jacques Rousseau was another author Congress objected to, according to Ingersoll. The only volume by Rousseau listed in the catalogue of Jefferson's great library is *Letters on the Elements of Botany*. Though Rousseau encouraged young women to study botany in this work, its educational program was hardly controversial. Numerous earlier works popular in America had encouraged women to pursue their interests in the sciences.[18] If this was the work congressmen were complaining about, then they were grasping at straws. On the other hand, there may have been other Rousseau works listed in the catalogue Jefferson prepared for Congress. The catalogue of his library at Poplar Forest reveals that he owned Pierre Alexandre Peyrou's edition of Rousseau's *Oeuvres Completes* as well as an edition of Rousseau's correspondence, thirty-eight volumes of Rousseau in total. Perhaps these volumes had originally been in his Monticello library, and Jefferson transferred then to his vacation library to minimize controversy.

Those congressmen who advocated the purchase of Jefferson's library understood its fundamental worth. They argued "that so valuable a library, one so admirably calculated for the substratum of a great national library, was not to be obtained in the United States; and that, although there might be some works to which gentlemen might take exception, there were others of very opposite character; that this, besides, was no reason against the purchase, because in every library of value might be found some books to which exceptions would be taken, according to the feelings or prejudices of those who examined them."[19]

The key phrase in this passage—"the substratum of a great national library"—shows that the library's supporters recognized that the new Library of Congress could be something much greater than the original one. It would not only be a working library for legislators but also a library for the nation.

Congressman Cyrus King of Massachusetts was one of the most vocal opponents. He moved to amend the resolution by letting the committee purchase a portion of Jefferson's library. King's amendment not only went against Jefferson's express desire to prevent his library from being dismembered, but also negated the idea of a great national library in favor of a modest collection of legislative books. The amendment was discussed briefly but voted down.

Before the day was out, John Reed, another representative from Massachusetts, moved to amend the resolution by limiting the price to be given for the library to $25,000. Debate on Reed's proposed amendment "continued with considerable vivacity" the following day.

John Hulbert, a junior representative from Massachusetts, broke ranks with his senior colleagues. He spoke against Reed's amendment and in favor of the purchase of Jefferson's library. The *Annals of Congress* notes that Hulbert's speech—the first he had delivered in the House of Representatives—was "very ingenious and handsome."[20] Regardless of either its ingenuity or its handsomeness, Hulbert's speech did nothing to quash the mounting controversy. The debate raged on, becoming "rather too animated" at times—so animated, in fact, that it had to be checked by the Speaker of the House. A vote was taken, and Reed's amendment was denied.

Other amendments were proposed, debated, and rejected. Debate spilled over to Wednesday, October 19, when the resolution was finally approved by the House with one amendment, that Congress must approve the purchase once the Joint Committee on the Library had reached terms with Jefferson. Basically this amendment gave Congress the opportunity to debate the purchase of Jefferson's collection all over again at a later date. The amended resolution was sent back to the Senate, which approved the measure two days later. Announcing the measure's approval, the *Alexandria Gazette* quipped, "Congress have agreed to purchase Mr. Jefferson's Library, *trumpery and all*."[21]

After much correspondence between Jefferson, Smith, and Joseph Milligan, the exact size of the library was determined—6,487 volumes (nearly 6,700 once many errant volumes were located), and the entire collection was valued at $23,950. This figure derives from the arbitrary values assigned to each volume according to format—folio, quarto, octavo, duodecimo.

Some contemporary observers found this estimate absolutely parsimonious. William Thornton, who had also become familiar with Jefferson's library during a visit to Monticello, understood the amount of learning necessary to assemble such a collection and realized that a similar collection could not be obtained without great trouble, great expense, and great risk. Thornton advised Congress to offer Jefferson $50,000 without hesitation. Another contemporary observer, calling Jefferson's library "a collection that any monarch in Europe would be proud to own," valued it at £50,000 sterling.[22]

One keen bookman found that the arbitrary amounts assigned to each volume undervalued the collection significantly. To make his point, he looked up selected titles from Jefferson's library in European auction catalogues to compare what Congress paid—on average about $3.50 per volume—with what copies of the same titles fetched at auction in Europe. By this method, the three folio volumes of Theodor De Bry's *Voyages* in Jefferson's library were worth £400 sterling; *Purchas His Pilgrimage* was worth £56 sterling; and Captain John Smith's *Generall Historie of Virginia* was worth £42 sterling.[23]

The whole idea of assigning a monetary value to Jefferson's great library was offensive to some. As one enthusiastic supporter commented, "The mere ordinary valuation of such a library, as an article of merchandize, can give no just idea of its intrinsic value. There is a sort of intellectual *advance* stamped on the selected books of great men, which has been always recognized in every country and age."[24]

Before the end of November, Robert Goldsborough introduced to the Senate a bill to authorize the purchase of Jefferson's library. On December 3, the Senate passed the bill, informed the House of Representatives about its passage, and requested their concurrence.

When debate on the issue in the House resumed in January 1815, Jefferson's enemies renewed their attack. One congressman moved to postpone consideration of the bill indefinitely. The motion was denied. Another moved to postpone consideration of the bill until March 4—the day after this session of Congress was scheduled to end. The motion was denied. Cyrus King moved to recommit the bill to a select committee with instructions to authorize the purchase of those "books belonging to said library as might be necessary or useful to Congress in their deliberations and to dispose of the remainder at public sale." The motion was denied—emphatically.

King then moved to recommit the bill to a select committee to remove from the library once it arrived in Washington "all books of an atheistical, irreligious, and immoral tendency, if any such there be, and send the same back to Mr. Jefferson without any expense to him." King withdrew the motion before it could be denied.[25]

The discussion continued. Though the editors of the *Annals of Congress* reported the early debate over Jefferson's library in detail, they misjudged the interest of the later parts of the debate among their readers. Anxious to learn more about the attitudes toward the Library of Congress voiced by early-nineteenth-century legislators, readers of the *Annals* reach a dead end as they confront the following sentence: "This subject, and the various motions relative thereto, gave rise to a debate which lasted till the hour of adjournment; which, though it afford much amusement to the auditors, would not interest the feelings or judgment of any reader." Despite the arguments of the bill's detractors, its supporters maintained the importance of Jefferson's library as "a most admirable substratum for a National Library."[26] The bill authorizing its purchase passed on January 30, 1815.

After the first bill had passed in December, Francis C. Gray and George Ticknor, two young Boston bookmen, became anxious to see Jefferson's library before it was carted off to Washington. They planned a literary pilgrimage to Monticello. For each, John Adams wrote separate letters of introduction to Jefferson. The one Adams wrote for Ticknor is a pure delight. It begins, "The most exalted of our young Genius's in Boston have an Ambition to see Monticello, its Library and its Sage." Adams predicted that Jefferson would get along famously with both young men. As you are all "gluttons for books," he continued, "I think you ought to have a Sympathy for each other."[27]

Hiring a carriage in Charlottesville on Saturday, February 4, Gray and Ticknor left at noon on their way to Monticello. The clouds and rain this afternoon gave the day a gloomy cast. The tall, bare oak trees covering the land leading to the top of Monticello reinforced the somber mood. Describing the trek to Jefferson's mountaintop home, Ticknor observed, "The ascent up this steep, savage hill was as pensive and slow as Satan's ascent to Paradise." Gray's description was less figurative but no less entertaining: "The forest had evidently been abandoned to nature; some of the trees were decaying from age, some were blasted, some uprooted by the wind and some appeared even to have been twisted from their trunks by the violence of a hurricane. They rendered the approach to the house even at this season of the year extremely grand and imposing."[28]

Once inside Monticello, Ticknor was reminded of the home where the Man of the Hill lives in *Tom Jones.* Upon entering, Henry Fielding's great hero is surprised to see the home "furnished in the most neat and elegant Manner. To say the Truth, *Jones* himself was not a little surprized at what he saw: For, besides the extraordinary Neatness of the Room, it was adorned with a great Number of Nick-nacks, and Curiosities, which might have engaged the Attention of a Virtuoso."[29]

Ticknor was more specific in his description of the curiosities that adorned the hall at Monticello: "On one side hang the head and horns of an elk, a deer, and a buffalo; another is covered with curiosities which Lewis and Clarke found in their wild and perilous expedition. On the third, among many other striking matters, was the head of a mammoth, or, as Cuvier calls it, a mastodon, containing the only *os frontis*, Mr. Jefferson tells me, that has yet been found. On the fourth side, in odd union with a fine painting of the Repentance of St. Peter, is an Indian map on leather, of the southern waters of the Missouri, and an Indian representation of a bloody battle, handed down in their traditions."[30]

Gray was struck by his host's physical appearance. His journal contains one of the best personal descriptions of Jefferson in his old age, though it does border on caricature:

> He is quite tall, six feet, one or two inches, face streaked and speckled with red, light gray eyes, white hair, dressed in shoes of very thin soft leather with pointed toes and heels ascending in a peak behind, with very short quarters, grey worsted stockings, corduroy small clothes, blue waistcoat and coat, of stiff thick cloth made of the wool of his own merinoes and badly manufactured, the buttons of his coat and small clothes of horn, and an under waistcoat flannel bound with red velvet. His figure bony, long and with broad shoulders, a true Virginian.[31]

Both Gray and Ticknor were fascinated with his books. The latter's knowledge especially impressed Jefferson, who called Ticknor "the best bibliograph I have met with."[32] A "bibliograph" is an expert in the history of books—Jefferson invented the term. After breakfast the next morning, their host escorted his guests into the suite of rooms that formed his library and passed an hour or so there pointing out his literary treasures. Gray noted many different aspects of the library. He was impressed with Jefferson's collection of English literature, noting the sixteenth-century black letter edition of Chaucer's *Workes* and the ten-book first edition of *Paradise Lost*.

Gray's journal brings alive the conversation that occurred in Jefferson's library this morning. French language and literature was a prominent topic of discussion. Jefferson told them that the *Dictionnaire de Trévoux* was better than the *Dictionnaire de l'Academie Française*. Pierre Charron's *De la Sagesse*, an early-seventeenth-century treatise on the relationship between knowledge and practical wisdom, he called "an excellent work." And he showed them William Duane's edition of Destutt de Tracy's *Commentary and Review of Montesquieu's Spirit of*

Laws, which Jefferson told them was "the best book on politics which had been published for a century."[33]

Whereas Gray mentioned several different books and authors in his account, Ticknor singled out one particular multivolume collection. Describing the six-volume set titled *Book of Kings*, Ticknor called it "the most curious single specimen—or, at least, the most characteristic of the man and expressive of his hatred of royalty."[34]

The story of this curious multivolume collection goes back at least three years. In April 1812, Madame de Tessé had sent Jefferson a copy of the two-volume *Mémoires* of Wilhelmine, consort of the Margrave of Bayreuth and sister of Frederick the Great. Thanking her, Jefferson wrote, "I am much indebted to you for this singular morsel of history which has given us a curtain view of kings, queens and princes disrobed of their formalities. It is a peep into the stable of the Egyptian god Apis. It would not be easy to find grosser manners, coarser vices, or more meanness in the poorest huts of our peasantry. The princess shews herself the legitimate sister of Frederic, cynical, selfish, and without a heart."[35] Mentioning the stable of Apis, Jefferson referred to a superstitious practice in ancient Egypt where an ox was chosen to represent Apis, and women engaged in wanton behavior before the ox.

These *Mémoires* reminded Jefferson of other works he had in his library, such as *Authentic and Interesting Memoirs of Mrs. Clarke from Her Infancy to the Present Time; Likewise, a Faithful Account of Mr. Wardle's Charges Relative to his Royal Highness the Duke of York; Together with a Summary of the Evidence, as Taken in the House of Commons*.[36] Jefferson was also reminded of *The Book*, a work so titled because, in his words, "it is the *Biblia Sacra Deorum et Dearum sub-coelestium*, the Prince Regent, his Princess and the minor deities of his sphere, [which] form a worthy sequel to the memoirs of Bareuth; instead of the vulgarity and penury of the court of Berlin, giving us the vulgarity and profusion of that of London, and the gross stupidity and profligacy of the latter, in lieu of the genius and misanthropism of the former."[37]

Associating these various titles in his letter to Madame de Tessé, Jefferson got the idea of collecting them together as a single work. He continued, "The whole might be published as a Supplement to M. de Buffon, under the title of the 'Natural history of Kings and Princes,' or as a separate work and called 'Medicine for Monarchists.' "[38]

Once he devised this idea, Jefferson did not immediately act upon it— but he did not forget it, either. It was not until October 17, 1814, that he gathered these three works, along with a fourth, Comtesse de La Motte's *Mémoires Justificatifs*, which retold the story of the infamous diamond necklace affair, and sent them to Joseph Milligan to be bound and lettered. Jefferson's instructions were very specific: he wanted to make sure all six volumes had a uniform appearance. And there was a sense of urgency, too: "Pray do it immediately and return it by the stage that they may be replaced on their shelves should Congress take my library."[39]

Jefferson's detailed instructions, combined with the timing of this letter—written after the Senate had approved the purchase of his library—show that he was not going to the trouble and expense (it cost him five dollars) of having these volumes uniformly bound and lettered for his own library; he was doing it specifically for the Library of Congress. Instead of either of the collective titles he suggested to Madame de Tessé, he chose a more neutral title, but one that contributes irony to the collection. Though he did not title the collection "Medicine for Monarchists," there can be no doubt that he intended the *Book of Kings* to function as such. Jefferson obviously imagined the gilt letters glaring from their spines toward any congressman lured by the idea of a monarchy.

Ticknor's description captures the glee Jefferson felt as he showed them the *Book of Kings*: "These documents of regal scandal seemed to be favourites with the philosopher, who pointed them out to me with a satisfaction somewhat inconsistent with the measured gravity he claims in relations to such subjects generally."[40]

Gray and Ticknor left Monticello on Tuesday, February 7. Thoroughly impressed with these two promising Bostonians, Jefferson had hoped they would stay longer. He called Gray a young man "of great information and promise" and Ticknor a man "of great erudition, indefatigable industry, and preparation for a life of distinction in his own country."[41] Jefferson would correspond with Ticknor through the remainder of his life.

Once he learned of Congress's final approval of the sale, Jefferson still had to arrange transportation for his library—a matter easier said than done. He estimated the weight of the books and the number of wagons it would take to transport them. He also devised an ingenious way to pack the books for shipping: since they were shelved in pine bookcases, they could be sent to Washington as they stood. By using the bookcases as shipping crates, Jefferson could make sure the books retained the precise shelf order he had given them. A little waste paper was needed to protect them—individual sheets between each volume and some extra wads of paper stuffed in the empty spaces to prevent them from jostling about on the wagon journey to Washington. Once packed with paper, the bookcases could be enclosed with covers nailed to the front of each case. Finalizing plans for shipping the library, Jefferson explained, "The books should go in their cases, every one in its station, so that the cases on their arrival need only be set up on end, and they will be arranged exactly as they stand in the catalogue."[42]

Jefferson's shipping plans indicate his desire for the Library of Congress to follow his meticulous organizational scheme. His correspondence with the new Librarian of Congress reiterates the importance Jefferson placed on his organization. Accused of dereliction of duty, Patrick Magruder had resigned his position after the original Library of Congress was destroyed, and President Madison appointed George Watterston to succeed him. As Jefferson had wanted to do, Madison separated the position of the Librarian of Congress from the position of Clerk of the House of Representatives, making the librarian a full-time post. Journalist, novelist, poet, travel writer, Watterston was amply qualified for the job. He earned Madison's respect when he dedicated *The Wanderer in Jamaica* to Dolley Madison because of her efforts to "promote the cause of general literature."[43] Watterston's first responsibility was to oversee the installation of the new Library of Congress on the third floor of Blodgett's Hotel, the temporary location of Congress at the corner of 7th and E Streets N.W.

Looking forward to his new responsibilities, Watterston wrote Jefferson asking for his thoughts on the organization of the library. Jefferson responded enthusiastically. The letter he wrote to Watterston has been called "one of the fundamental documents in the development of library science in America."[44] Jefferson offered Watterston a detailed comparison between alphabetical and subject organization:

> Two methods offer themselves the one Alphabetical, the other according to the subject of the work. The former is very unsatisfactory, because of the medley it presents to the mind, the difficulty sometimes of recollecting an author's name, and the greater difficulty, where the name is not given of selecting the word in the title which shall determine its Alphabetical place. The arrangement according to subject is far preferable, altho' sometimes presenting difficulty also, for it is often doubtful to what particular subject a book should be ascribed.... Yet on the whole I have preferred arrangement according to subject, because of the peculiar satisfaction, when we wish to consider a particular one, of seeing at a glance the books which have been written on it, and selecting those from which we expect most readily the information we seek.[45]

Basically, Jefferson informed Watterston that there was little he needed to do in the way of arrangement: "You will receive my library arranged very perfectly in the order observed in the Catalogue, which I have sent with it. . . . On every book is a label, indicating the chapter of the catalogue to which it belongs, and the order it holds among those of the same format, so that altho' the Nos. seem confused on the catalogue, they are consecutive on the volumes as they stand on their shelves and indicate at once the place they occupy there."[46]

Before packing them with paper and nailing on the covers, Jefferson went through his entire library a final time, moving volumes that were misplaced and cross-checking the catalogue with the shelf placement. He spent the last two weeks of March and the first two of April straightening the library and making sure the books were ready for shipping. He enlisted the help of his granddaughters Ellen, Virginia, and Cornelia.[47] Jefferson also prepared a detailed index of authors or key title words for anonymous works. Some books loaned out had yet to return, but the collection was largely in order by the third week of April, when the wagons began arriving to transport the books and their cases to Washington. Joseph Milligan came down from Georgetown to help prepare the books for shipment.

On May 8, 1815, the day the final wagonload of books left Monticello, Jefferson wrote Samuel Harrison Smith: "Our tenth and last waggon load of books goes off today. . . . It is the choicest collection of books in the United States, and I hope it will not be without some general effect on the literature of our country."[48] Understatement was another literary device at which Jefferson excelled.

With Milligan's help, Watterston stood his shelves up in the temporary home of the Library of Congress. Jefferson's plan to make his system of library organization determine the system of organization for the Library of Congress would seem to have worked. But when it came time to publish a catalogue, Watterston could not leave well enough alone. He retained Jefferson's general division into chapters but alphabetized the books within each chapter. Some he alphabetized according to author and others according to key title word. Upon seeing the printed catalogue, Jefferson was flabbergasted. He told a correspondent, "The form of the catalogue has been much injured in the publication; for although they have preserved my division into chapters, they have reduced the books in each chapter to alphabetical order, instead of the chronological or analytical arrangements I had given them."[49]

Jefferson dwelt on his disappointment with the Library of Congress for altering his meticulous organizational scheme. In his personal copy of the printed library catalogue, he rearranged the titles to restore his original order. He eventually had Nicholas P. Trist make a fair copy of the entire catalogue. Born in Virginia and raised in Louisiana, Trist graduated from the College of Orleans and then came to Monticello in 1817 on Jefferson's invitation. There he fell in love with Jefferson's granddaughter Virginia. Her love for him was a stabilizing force in Trist's otherwise restless young life. He attended West Point without graduating, returned to Louisiana after becoming engaged to Virginia in 1821, and after his mother's death a few years later, returned to Monticello, where he became Jefferson's personal secretary.

Having Trist restore the original order of the library he sold to Congress, Jefferson may have overreacted. Though Watterston reorganized the titles in the catalogue, he retained Jefferson's shelf organization, as the shelf numbers in the printed catalogue indicate. In addition, Watterston titled the printed volume *Catalogue of the Library of the United States*, a title showing that he understood that the new Library of Congress was not just a library for legislators: it was a library for the nation. Furthermore, the Library of Congress continued to follow Jefferson's chapter divisions until nearly the end of the nineteenth century. His elaborate organizational scheme and his role in reestablishing the Library of Congress on a new foundation have earned him the title of the "Father of American Librarianship."[50]

Though Watterston's alphabetical rearrangement obscured Jefferson's analytical organization of books within each chapter, that organization did not disappear. The new cataloguing system at the Library of Congress, which has become the cataloguing system of every important university library in the nation, retains vestiges of Jefferson's organizational scheme. Any library patron browsing the stacks in, say, American history who notices that the volumes are generally arranged from North to South can see the books through Jefferson's eyes.

CHAPTER 38

The Retirement Library

O nce the last wagonload of books left Monticello for Washington, the suite of rooms that had contained Jefferson's great library looked desolate. Altogether, about 25,000 pounds of books, which had covered about seven hundred square feet of wall space, were carted from Monticello to Washington. Because Jefferson had sold the bookcases with the books in them, the rooms were now a foot wider on each side. The bare walls, like the walls of Balclutha, had a melancholy look. Standing within this empty suite once the final wagon had left, Jefferson realized an important truth about himself. Well, perhaps he did not realize it at this precise moment. Perhaps he knew it all along. But at this particular moment he could have been reminded of it more poignantly than ever before. As he said in his next letter to John Adams, "I cannot live without books."[1]

Jefferson knew what he needed to do next. He had to start a new library. Actually, he had begun making plans for a new collection even before shipping his books to Washington. Earlier that year he had spoken about rebuilding his library at Monticello with George Ticknor, who graciously offered his help. Since Ticknor was going to Europe for an extended stay, he would be in an ideal position to acquire books Jefferson could not readily obtain in America—scholarly editions of ancient Greek and Roman texts.

He prepared a catalogue of desiderata, confining it "principally to the books of which the edition adds sensibly to the value of the matter," especially in terms of "translations, notes, and other accompaniments." Jefferson also reiterated his desire for small-format editions. He especially liked octavos because of their convenience and versatility. They were small enough to hold in the hand yet large enough to be opened on a table. The typeface was also important to him, but that feature was difficult to discern without seeing the books in person. Since the booksellers' catalogues Jefferson used for reference did not mention typeface, Ticknor would be most helpful in selecting well-printed books. Italics Jefferson found "disagreeable to the eye," and Black Letter tried his patience. He urged Ticknor to compare multiple editions of the same works and evaluate them in terms of format, quality of translation, notes, and typeface and make his judgment by taking all of these factors into consideration. Like his great library, his retirement library would be for reading, not for show. As he told Ticknor, "I like good bindings and handsome, without being over elegant for use."[2]

Ticknor received Jefferson's catalogue but was puzzled by some of the editions listed, which seemed to him inferior to the newer editions available. He wrote back, conveying his preference for recent German editions over those Jefferson specified. Choosing his words carefully, Ticknor said that if Jefferson insisted, then he would obtain whatever editions he stipulated. Ticknor expressed the matter in a way that would charm any bookman: "An old edition or copy in which we have been accustomed to read is like an old friend, who is not to be set aside for a younger one, even though he should be of more promise."[3]

Not nearly as inflexible as Ticknor had feared, Jefferson was happy to trust the young bibliograph's powers of discrimination. He replied, "I must pray you therefore to avail me of your better opportunities of selecting, and to use your own judgment where you find that there is a better edition than that noted by me." He did reiterate his preference for smaller formats: "Be so good as to remember my aversion to folios and 4tos and that it overweighs a good deal of merit in the edition. The nerveless hand of a more than Septuagenaire wields a folio or 4to with fatigue, and a fixed position to read it on a table is equally fatiguing." Jefferson also gave Ticknor his opinion about editorial amenities. He appreciated explanatory notes but did not care for critical interpretations.[4]

When Jefferson received the volumes Ticknor selected, he was delighted with his thoughtful choices. They included Christian Gottlob Heyne's nine-volume octavo edition of Homer's *Iliad*, Heyne's four-volume edition of Virgil, and Georg Alexander Ruperti's four-volume octavo edition of Juvenal. In Jefferson's words, all three were "of the first order." He liked Heyne's *Iliad* best. In his letter of thanks, he told Ticknor that the work "exceeds anything I had ever conceived in editorial merit. How much it makes us wish he had done the same with the Odyssey." Since Jefferson also had a copy of Jean Baptiste d'Angge de Villoison's Venice edition of the *Iliad* at Monticello, he compared the two. He recognized Villoison's influence but still found Heyne's edition superior. The new edition encouraged him to reread Homer's *Iliad* afresh. As he told Ticknor, "This style of editing has all the superiority your former letters have ascribed to it, and urges us to read again the authors we have formerly read to obtain a new and higher under-standing of them."[5]

Comparing Heyne's edition with Villoison's was a fairly easy matter for Jefferson, who could use the ingenious revolving bookstand he had in-vented. Shaped like a cube when not in use, the stand could be unfolded to hold five books simultaneously. Hinged at the top, the four vertical sides could be lifted up and angled out. A lip at the bottom of each let a book rest on the angled surface. Furthermore, the top of the cube could be tilted up to hold a fifth book directly above one of the lower books. Even when fully loaded with books, the stand could be easily revolved to let Jefferson quickly peruse multiple texts in succession.

With Heyne's *Iliad* on top and Villoison's *Iliad* below it, Jefferson could open both books to their corresponding passages and look at them simultaneously, quickly dropping his eyes from the top volume to the bottom one, with no more difficulty than reading footnotes. Jefferson had long enjoyed parallel text editions; his invention let him parallel different translations directly. For further reference, he could place re-lated books—different editions, other translations, pertinent historical works—on the three remaining sides.

When Jefferson first began assembling his retirement library, he saw it predominantly as a collection to amuse himself in his old age. After arranging the sale of his great library to Congress, he informed one correspondent, "I have now to make up again a collection for myself of such as may amuse my hours of reading."[6] Reiterating the idea that his retirement library would be for amusement, not for use, he told Adams that fewer books would suffice. Though Jefferson may have intended to keep his new library small, once his bibliomanie took hold, he began buying books at a furious rate. In the decade following the sale of his great library, he amassed a new collection of impressive proportions. His retirement library would grow to more than fifteen hundred volumes in nearly a thousand titles. Though one-quarter the size of his great library, the retirement collection is remarkable in terms of both size and quality, given the comparatively brief period of time he spent assembling it.

With a few modifications, Jefferson used the same organizational scheme for his retirement library he had used for the great library. Furthermore, he bought some of the same titles that had been part of his former library. But he also added many new and different kinds of books that had not been in his great library. Though it is convenient to refer to this collection as Jefferson's retirement library, many of the books within

Thomas Jefferson's Revolving Bookstand. (Monticello, Thomas Jefferson Foundation, Inc.)

it reflect new attitudes toward literature that were emerging in the early nineteenth century. Indeed, Jefferson's retirement library has much in common with the libraries of a new generation of writers who were making their mark in the early nineteenth century. This old neoclassicist was reading books like a Romantic.

Retaining his memory-reason-imagination scheme, Jefferson organized his collection by placing history first. He began with civil history, followed by natural history. Civil history he subdivided into ancient and modern. Some of the works of ancient history are throwbacks to his youth, such as his copy of the Foulis edition of Cornelius Nepos. He first read Nepos as a boy, and the work had remained a favorite throughout his life. Acquiring a replacement copy, he could reread the book whenever he wished. With this new acquisition, he may have had a different purpose in mind—to share with his grandchildren. To Thomas

Thomas Jefferson's Organizational Scheme for His Retirement Library, from Thomas Jefferson Papers, Series 7, Miscellaneous Bound Volumes. (Library of Congress, Manuscripts Division)

Rogers, the compiler of *A New American Biographical Dictionary*—another work in the retirement library—Jefferson commented that no books interest children more than "such works as Cornelius Nepos."[7]

Other books shelved among ancient history reflect a modern attitude toward the classics. Jefferson acquired a copy of John Lemprière's *Classical Dictionary*, the great repository of classical lore that fired the imagination of John Keats, Percy Bysshe Shelley, and other Romantic poets. While organizing and condensing centuries-old materials known to most every schoolboy, Lemprière let his readers look at the classics afresh. His work remains the finest classical dictionary ever compiled.

The collection of modern history in Jefferson's retirement library combines old standards with new favorites. He owned such works of European history as Jacques Stoer's early-seventeenth-century Geneva edition of Francesco Guicciardini's *Historia d'Italia* and a six-volume edition of Davila's *Historia delle Guerre Civile di Francia*. He also owned the latest works about Egypt, including *Pièces Diverses et Correspondance Relatives aux Opérations de l'Armée d'Orient en Égypte*, a detailed treatment of Napoleon's Egyptian campaign, and Sir Robert Wilson's *History of the British Expedition to Egypt*—famous for charging Napoleon with cruelty against his prisoners at Jaffa and his own soldiers at Cairo.[8]

Napoleon's Egyptian campaign captured the Romantic imagination. Both Samuel Coleridge and Robert Southey closely followed his journey to Egypt and became fascinated with all things Egyptian. Jefferson got caught up in the contemporary fascination with Egyptian art and culture, too. He obtained a model of the pyramid of Cheops and what was supposed to be a statue of Cleopatra reclining with a serpent twisted around her. After careful study, Jefferson concluded that the statue did not depict Cleopatra at all, but Ariadne. This perceptive conclusion also reveals his knowledge of recent European art scholarship.[9]

Southey was represented in Jefferson's retirement library by his *Life of Nelson*, one of the great biographies in the history of English literature. Jefferson's resentment toward the British navy did not stop him from appreciating the personal qualities Southey attributed to Admiral Nelson. As part of his biography, Southey presented a series of anecdotes from Nelson's boyhood showing his innate courage, honor, and determination, exemplary traits that foreshadow his subsequent accomplishments. Jefferson used the same method in his "Life of Captain Lewis." Overall, Southey depicted Nelson as a man who embodied many fine personal characteristics: altruism, bravery, patience, patriotism, and selflessness.

As the presence of Cornelius Nepos under ancient history and Southey's *Life of Nelson* under British history indicate, Jefferson did not make a separate subdivision for biography in his classification scheme. Rather, he subsumed biography within history. Similarly, he shelved American biography with American history—though that's not what he told Daniel Webster. When his copy of William Wirt's *Sketches of the Life and Character of Patrick Henry* reached Monticello, Jefferson joked that he "had been greatly perplexed in deciding where to place the volume, but had finally arranged it under the head of Fiction."[10] Jefferson was pulling

Webster's leg. The catalogue of his retirement library reveals that he shelved Wirt's *Life of Henry* with other works treating the American Revolution. Jefferson made the same joke with Henry Lee's *Memoirs of the War in the Southern Department of the United States*, which he called a "historical novel."[11] He also shelved Lee's *Memoirs* with other books of American history. In fact, he kept it right next to Wirt's *Life of Henry*.

Since the war, many American patriots had biographies written about them, and Jefferson added several of these to his collection. He subscribed for six copies of William Barton's *Memoirs of the Life of David Rittenhouse* without realizing how big the book would be. Presenting one copy of this beefy six-hundred-page octavo to John Adams, Jefferson wryly commented, "Even its episodes and digressions may add to the amusement it will furnish you. But if the history of the world were written on the same scale, the whole world would not hold it."[12]

Jefferson's new books gave him the opportunity to rethink his attitudes toward biography and historiography. The conversations about books and authors that occurred in his library with family, friends, and visitors helped hone his ideas. When the British traveler Francis Hall came to Monticello, for example, he and Jefferson discussed many different topics. Their conversation eventually settled on history writing. Jefferson told Hall an anecdote about Benjamin Franklin that he had heard from the Abbé Raynal:

> The Abbé was in company with Dr. Franklin, and several Americans at Paris, when mention chanced to be made of his anecdote of Polly Baker, related in his sixth volume, upon which one of the company observed, that no such law as that alluded to in the story, existed in New England: the Abbé stoutly maintained the authenticity of his tale, when Dr. Franklin, who had hitherto remained silent, said, "I can account for all this; you took the anecdote from a newspaper, of which I was at that time editor, and, happening to be very short of news, I composed and inserted the whole story." "Ah! Doctor," said the Abbé making a true French retreat, "I had rather have your stories, than other men's truths."[13]

Jefferson related this anecdote to show "how history, even when it calls itself philosophical, is written." Good writing sometimes overrides good reporting. A highly crafted hoax is more seductive than plain truth.

With Hall, Jefferson also discussed a specific book in his collection of American history, Carlo Botta's *Storia della Guerra dell'Indepenza degli Stati Uniti d'America*. Originally, Botta had presented Jefferson a copy of the work. Since this presentation copy had gone to the Library of Congress with the rest of his great library, Jefferson obtained a replacement copy. Hall wrote, "Mr. Jefferson preferred Botta's Italian History of the American Revolution, to any that had yet appeared, remarking, however, the inaccuracy of the speeches."[14]

Hall's brief account confirms more extensive remarks about Botta's history Jefferson made to others. "Botta," he wrote Adams, "has put his own speculations and reasonings into the mouths of persons whom he names, but who, you and I know, never made such speeches. In this he has followed the example of the antients, who made their great men deliver long speeches, all of them in the same style, and in that of the author himself." Jefferson later reemphasized his appreciation of Botta's history of the American Revolution, despite the interpolated speeches: "He has given that history with more detail, precision and candor, than any writer I have yet met with. It is to be sure compiled from those writers; but it is a good secretion of their matter, the pure from the impure, and presented in a just sense of right in opposition to usurpation."[15]

Organizing his books on natural history, Jefferson devised four different levels of substructure. The first level contained a general section on natural history, which is not subdivided further. Other sections at the same level treat, in order, animals, vegetables, minerals, physics, the earth, and the heavens. Jefferson further subdivided all of these categories.

The section on animals he split into "Brutes" and "Man." A copy of *Fauna Americana* presented by its author, Richard Harlan, Jefferson placed in "Brutes." The object Harlan set for this work was the "concise and scientific description and classification of the mammiferous animals of N. America."[16] With Jefferson, Harlan shared an interest in vertebrate paleontology and sought to describe both living and extinct species. Though considered the first systematic presentation of the zoology of North America, *Fauna Americana* is marred by insufficient data and its author's overreliance on A. G. Demarest's *Mammologie*.[17] Jefferson nonetheless admired the work as he admired all contributions to the development of American intellectual life.

The subsection devoted to man is subdivided into three categories: structure, physiology, and occupations. Structure has only one subdivision—anatomy—and only one book within it, Caspar Wistar's *System of Anatomy for the Use of Students of Medicine*, the first American textbook of anatomy. Physiology is further subdivided into surgery and medicine. Surgery, too, has only one book within it, Samuel Cooper's *First Lines of the Practice of Surgery*, an introductory text.

Jefferson's collection of medical books in his retirement library is remarkably tiny, especially compared with other great early American libraries. Fascinated with how the human body worked, William Byrd II recorded the workings of his own body in his secret diary and assembled a personal collection of several hundred medical books. In addition to having one of the finest general collections of medical books in eighteenth-century America, Benjamin Franklin also had a significant collection of books on the two maladies that afflicted him late in life, gout and stones of the urinary tract. Seeking to understand and remedy his afflictions, Franklin kept buying the latest books on these subjects almost to the time of his death.[18] The paucity of medical books in Jefferson's retirement library testifies to the relatively good health he enjoyed in his waning years.

The migraine headaches that had beset him through his public life had lessened considerably during his retirement years. He was occasionally bothered by rheumatism, but his general therapy for it was simply to endure. Jefferson's small collection of medical books also suggests his skepticism toward medical theory. Dr. Robley Dunglison, who attended Jefferson in his final illness, observed, "Mr. Jefferson was considered to have but little faith in physic; and has often told me that he would rather trust to the unaided, or rather uninterfered with, efforts of nature than to physicians in general." Jefferson joked that "whenever he saw three physicians together he looked up to discover whether there was not a turkey buzzard in the neighborhood."[19]

Measured by the books in his retirement library, Jefferson's medical concerns leaned more toward public health than personal health. He had multiple works about yellow fever, including Benjamin Rush's *Observations on the Origin of the Malignant Bilious, or Yellow Fever in Philadelphia* and Nathaniel Potter's *Memoir on Contagion, More Especially as It Respects the Yellow Fever*. Jefferson had lost many friends to yellow fever, including Benjamin Franklin Bache, who died of yellow fever in 1798, just as he was establishing himself as one of the nation's finest newspapermen. Hore Browse Trist—Nicholas's father—had died of yellow fever in Natchez, Louisiana, where President Jefferson had sent him to fill the post of customs collector.

Occupations, the third subdivision within the "Man" subsection, is further divided into agriculture and a section Jefferson labeled "Technics," which included such diverse works as William Roscoe's *On the Origin and Vicissitudes of Literature, Science and Art, and Their Influence on the Present State of Society*, a paper delivered at the opening of the Liverpool Royal Institution. Roscoe, a self-proclaimed literary historian, was a guiding force in establishing this institution, which he saw as central to the purpose of joining "the pursuits of literature with the affairs of the world."[20] Despite his ongoing animosity toward Great Britain, Jefferson remained interested in British developments in science and literature. Political boundaries matter little to those who see themselves as citizens of the Republic of Letters.

"Technics" also included books on inland navigation, such as Robert Fulton's *Treatise on the Improvement of Canal Navigation*, which proposed a system of canals and other innovative forms of transportation to connect all the major cities; Albert Gallatin's *Treatise on Internal Navigation*; and Elkanah Watson's *History of the Rise, Progress, and Existing Condition of the Western Canals in the State of New York, from September, 1788, to 1819.*

Jefferson's shelf of agricultural books shows him still hoping to carry out Mazzei's dream of cultivating olives and wine grapes in Virginia. In addition to Augustus Hillhouse's *Essay on the History and Cultivation of the European Olive-Tree*, he owned a presentation copy of John Adlum's *Memoir on the Cultivation of the Vine in America, and the Best Mode of Making Wine*. James Madison, who had a copy of Adlum's work in his library at Montpelier, encouraged local viticulture, too. Presenting the book to Jefferson, Adlum also gave him some wine; Jefferson appreciated both. In his letter of thanks, he told Adlum that he had no knowledge of viticulture from "either practice or reading."[21] Jefferson was being modest. Besides Adlum's treatise, his retirement library also included two important French works on viticulture.

Minerals, another subcategory within natural history, seems poorly conceived. There are only a few books listed within the category, all devoted to geology. The subcategory "The Earth," which occupies the same level in natural history as minerals, is further subdivided into geography and geology. Apparently, Jefferson created two different categories for geology and never sufficiently distinguished them. The geology books point to another problem with Jefferson's organizational scheme: where to put books that belonged in more than one category. He shelved Amos Eaton's *Geological and Agricultural Survey of the District Adjoining the Erie Canal* with his geology books. Given its purpose, Eaton's work might belong with canal literature. Sometimes Jefferson's rigorous organization cut across more natural subject divisions.

His organization was not so rigid as to prevent him from relocating a book from one section to another, if he deemed it appropriate. In his great library, he shelved his copy of Paul Philippe Gudin's poem *L'Astronomie* with other volumes of didactic verse. After selling his library to

Congress, he bought a replacement copy of Gudin's *L'Astronomie*, which he now shelved within a category titled "The Heavens." A poem would hardly seem to belong with other serious astronomical works, but upon rereading it, Jefferson realized that Gudin's set of explanatory notes was the best part of the book, so he recategorized it. Telling a correspondent about Gudin's *L'Astronomie*, Jefferson explained, "You will find the notes really of value. They embody and ascertain to us all the scraps of new discoveries which we have learnt in detached articles from less authentic publications."[22] In the new edition of *L'Astronomie*, Gudin even speculated about the possibility of life on other planets.

Geography, including books of travel, contained many new works and one old favorite, Joseph Addison's *Remarks on Several Parts of Italy*. Though Jefferson had recommended Addison's work as a guidebook for those traveling to Italy, the copy of Addison in his retirement library shows that it still made good pleasure reading for someone who had no intention of ever traveling to Italy again. Not content solely with this longtime favorite, Jefferson also acquired one of the latest volumes of Italian travel, James Sloan's *Rambles in Italy, in the Years 1816–17*. Furthermore, Jefferson owned American works of exploration and travel that he had been instrumental in bringing to fruition, including Zebulon Pike's *Account of Expeditions to the Sources of the Mississippi and Through the Western Parts of Louisiana to the Sources of the Arkansaw, Kansas, La Platte, and Pierre Jaun Rivers*.

"Philosophy"—what would now be termed "Science"—corresponds to reason in Bacon's tripartite division of knowledge. Jefferson split "Philosophy" into two categories, mathematics and ethics, each of which is further subdivided. He divided his mathematical books into "The Science of Quantity," or mathematics proper, and "The Science of Space," or geometry. He divided ethics into three categories: "Morality," both ancient and modern; "Moral Supplements"; and "Social Organization," which roughly corresponds to politics but encompasses a wide variety of works. What Jefferson meant by "Moral Supplements" is obvious from its subdivisions: religion and law. His unusual category title suggests that he saw man as naturally a moral creature but also perceived the need to bolster man's inherent morality by external means.

Fine arts, Jefferson's third major division, corresponds to the imagination in Bacon's categories of knowledge. Within fine arts, Jefferson made two categories: "Beaux Arts," which included books on architecture, gardening, music, painting, and sculpture, and "Belles Lettres." Two of the most important new works reflecting Jefferson's interests in the latest developments in both art and literature were Stendhal's two-volume *Histoire de la Peinture en Italie* and Moritz Retzsch's illustrated edition of Goethe's *Faust*.

Histoire de la Peinture en Italie, Stendhal's first important book, anticipated the Romantic rediscovery of Michelangelo. While assuming the role of art historian, Stendhal also treated contemporary attitudes toward art. To him, aesthetic appreciation was more a matter of feeling than intellect. The work of Correggio, his favorite artist, Stendhal approached almost as a lover. In short, Stendhal's *Histoire* could be called the bible of the Romantic artist.[23] Jefferson shared Stendhal's attitude toward art. Both saw aesthetics as the province of the heart, not the head.

The presence of Retzsch's *Faust* in Jefferson's retirement library further reinforces his affinity with the Romantics.[24] As an illustrator, Retzsch drew his figures in outline form. Deceptively simple, Retzsch's outlines provoked the imagination of his readers. Shelley, to cite one of his most prominent admirers, found poetic inspiration in his etchings. He admitted that Retzsch's illustrations to *Faust* made his head pulse in much the same way that others' hearts pulsed. He explained, "What etchings those are! I am never satiated with looking at them, and I fear it is the only sort of translation of which Faust is susceptible—I never perfectly understood the Hartz Mountain scene, until I saw the etching.— And then, Margaret in the summer house with Faust!—The artist makes one envy his happiness that he can sketch such things with calmness, which I dared only to look upon once, and which made my brain swim round only to touch the leaf on the opposite side of which I knew that it was figured."[25] Jefferson left no such emotional reaction, but the presence of Retzsch's Goethe in his library shows how open-minded he was to new forms of art and literature.

An 1822 letter to Nicholas Trist, who had temporarily returned to New Orleans, provides a further indication of what the Jeffersons were reading at Monticello. Trist was known in the family as a great Byron enthusiast. His affinity to Byron may partly explain Trist's restlessness. Jefferson knew he would be happy to learn that "the tragedy of Lord Byron was immediately put into the hands of the family and was I believe read by every member of it."[26] The letter does not say which of Byron's poetic tragedies they were reading. The historical drama *Marino Faliero, Doge of Venice* is the likeliest possibility. Philadelphia publisher Matthew Carey had just issued the first American edition of *Marino Faliero* the year before. Lately, Jefferson had been ordering numerous books from Carey.

Jefferson left no reaction to *Marino Faliero* himself, but Byron's tragedy contained much both to delight and dismay him. Rebelling against the aristocratic oligarchy that controls Venice, Faliero voices some stirring words in favor of rebellion:

> We will renew the times of truth and justice,
> Condensing in a fair free commonwealth
> Not rash equality but equal rights,
> Proportion'd like the columns to the temple,
> Giving and taking strength reciprocal,
> And making firm the whole with grace and beauty,
> So that no part could be removed without
> Infringement of the general symmetry.

Faliero's words are stirring, but he makes an unlikely figure to voice the rhetoric of rebellion. While rebelling against his fellow aristocrats, he nonetheless feels antipathy toward his low-born soldier-conspirators. The personal conflict Faliero experiences creates much of the drama's tension.[27]

Another letter to Trist, this one by Jefferson's granddaughter Ellen, also suggests that Byron's poetry was well known at Monticello. Playfully upbraiding Trist for a comment he had made in a letter to her, Ellen quoted Byron's *The Island*, a humorous poem retelling the story of the mutiny on the *H.M.S. Bounty* that appeared in 1823, the year before her letter to Trist. She wrote:

> I must say with old Laddy Grippy "weel! this beats print," though to say the truth I am more tempted to quote from Sir Anthony Absolute "Why Jack, you d——d impudent dog!" only I am afraid you might be shocked at so flagrant an usurpation of the rights of your sex, which reserves as a peculiar privilege, the use of such energetic expressions, and although the words G-d d——m, or as the French write it, godam or godem, are considered by this ingenious people in common with other foreigners, as the very basis and root of the English tongue, or as Lord Byron expresses it
>
> ————those syllables intense.
> Nucleus of England's native eloquence,
>
> yet with the injustice which has uniformly marked your proceedings wherever women were concerned, you forbid us to avail ourselves of what would give so much bone and sinew to our sayings.[28]

Suddenly, Ellen is all grown up. In addition to *The Island*, she also alluded to *The Entail; or, The Lairds of Grippy*, a satirical novel by John

Galt published the same year as *The Island*, and Richard Brinsely Sheridan's stage comedy *The Rivals*, a perennial favorite. Besides giving Ellen the daring to say things that proper young ladies were not supposed to say, these three works, none of which were in Jefferson's retirement library, show that there was a powerful undercurrent of literary activity flowing through Monticello that is not represented by her grandfather's library catalogue.

Jefferson's open-mindedness toward new forms of literary expression did not extend to the novel. While serving as vice president, he received a copy of *Wieland, or The Transformation; An American Tale* presented by its author, an ambitious young novelist named Charles Brockden Brown. The two men were unacquainted personally. Brown gave the book to Vice President Jefferson in the hopes of securing his patronage. With this presentation copy, Brown included a cover letter that amounted to a spirited defense of fiction. After admitting that he did not know whether Jefferson enjoyed "mere works of imagination and invention," Brown argued that fiction could combine an "artful display of incidents," a "powerful delineation of characters," and a "train of eloquent and judicious reasoning" to create an emotional narrative.[29]

Thanking Brown for the gift, Jefferson assured him that his defense of fiction was unnecessary. "Some of the most agreeable moments of my life," he explained, "have been spent in reading works of imagination which have this advantage over history that the incidents of the former may be dressed in the most interesting form, while those of the latter must be confined to fact. They cannot therefore present virtue in the best and vice in the worst forms possible, as the former may."[30] What Jefferson told Brown in this letter closely resembles what he had told Robert Skipwith a quarter century earlier when he recommended several novels to him. Jefferson's theory of fiction had not changed much during the intervening years. He closed his letter of thanks by assuring Brown that he would read the book with great pleasure in the future.

Designed to encourage the young author, Jefferson's letter to Brown does not really reflect his personal tastes. This presentation copy of *Wieland* is not among the books Jefferson sold to the Library of Congress, nor is it listed in the catalogue of his retirement library. The mystery of its whereabouts is not hard to fathom: most likely, he gave *Wieland* to his daughter Martha, who was fond of novels. *The Foundling of Belgrade*, an anonymous novel Jefferson received as a gift during his presidency, likely went the same way. He did not need to read beyond the cliché-ridden opening paragraph of *The Foundling of Belgrade* to see that it was not his kind of book: " 'Villain!' exclaimed a voice from behind, while a rapier passed under the arm of Alfonso. Bleak and stormy was the night, and, the alternate brightness, and total absence of the moon, served but to perplex the way-lost traveller on the heath."[31]

The catalogue of his retirement library provides a much better indication of his personal attitude toward novels than either his letter to Brown or a list of books Jefferson received as presents. The catalogue lists no modern novels whatsoever. The few works of prose fiction his retirement library contained—*Don Quixote*, Bocaccio's *Decameron*—were shelved with poetry, in a subdivision titled "Prosaic Narrative Poetry." *Gargantua and Pantagruel*, the other great narrative of prose fiction he owned, formed part of Rabelais's *Oeuvres*, which he shelved in a miscellaneous category titled "Levities, Pastoral, Anatomy, Lyric, etc."

His daughter and his granddaughters kept trying to interest him in novels. They read passages, sometimes long passages, from Sir Walter Scott's novels to him, but he was not impressed. He did purchase several works by Sir Walter Scott from Washington bookseller R. C. Weightman, all poetry: *Ballads and Lyrical Pieces*, *The Lady of the Lake*, *The Lay of the Last Minstel*, *Marmion*, and *The Vision of Don Roderick*. Regarding *The Lay of the Last Minstrel*, Scott puffed the work as follows: "The poem now offered to the public is intended to illustrate the customs and manners which anciently prevailed on the borders of England and Scotland. The inhabitants, living in a state partly pastoral and partly warlike, and combining habits of constant depredation with the influence of a rude spirit of chivalry, were often engaged in scenes highly susceptible of poetical ornament." Jefferson clipped Scott's comment about this poem from the newspaper. Furthermore, he clipped additional selections from *The Lay of the Last Minstrel*.[32] Scott's verse appealed to Jefferson for much the same reasons Ossian appealed to him, yet Scott's poetry could not sustain his interest the way Ossianic verse could. None of these titles appear in the catalogue of the retirement library. More than likely he presented them to his granddaughters. When *Ivanhoe* appeared in 1819, Martha persuaded her father to read it. Before getting halfway through *Ivanhoe*, he pronounced it "the dullest and dryest reading he had ever experienced."[33]

He tried to dissuade his grandchildren from novel-reading by ridiculing the conventions of the Gothic novel. He told them that when he was a young man, he had trouble with insomnia until he devised an ideal solution. He would mentally compose a love-and-murder novel. On sleepless nights, he would resume the composition of this novel wherever he left off. Before getting three more pages into it, he would find himself sound asleep.[34]

Jefferson's fullest condemnation of the novel occurs in a letter to Nathaniel Burwell:

A great obstacle to good education is the inordinate passion prevalent for novels, and the time lost in that reading which should be instructively employed. When this poison infects the mind, it destroys its tone and revolts it against wholesome reading. Reason and fact, plain and unadorned, are rejected. Nothing can engage attention unless dressed in all the figments of fancy, and nothing so bedecked comes amiss. The result is a bloated imagination, sickly judgment, and disgust towards all the real businesses of life.[35]

Fictional narratives from other cultures, however, did appeal to Jefferson. When Baron Lescallier sent him a copy of *Enchanted Throne: An Indian Story*, his translation of the collection of traditional Persian tales known as *Vikramacarita*, Jefferson enjoyed it very much. Thanking Lescallier for the present, Jefferson told him, "I have read it with satisfaction, and with the more as a piece of natural history, presenting to us, as in a map, the mind of the man of Persia, and the means of measuring it."[36] Fiction from different parts of the world provided important insights into other nations and cultures.

The catalogue of Jefferson's retirement library shows that he also subscribed to many of the day's learned journals. As catalogued, his library is weighted toward American magazines, but he also enjoyed British journals. His favorite was the *Edinburgh Review*. Ellen recalled that he "read new publications as they came out, never missed the new number of a review, especially of the Edinburgh, and kept himself acquainted with what was being done, said, or thought in the world from which he had retired."[37]

Jefferson called the *Edinburgh Review* "unrivalled in merit" and predicted that if it were "continued by the same talents, information, and principles," it "would become a real Encyclopedia, justly taking its station in our libraries with the most valuable depositories of human knowledge."[38] His idea that a set of magazines could evolve into an encyclopedia helps explain why he grouped both together in his library under a category titled "Polygraphical," which basically meant collections of various writings. A periodical that lasts long enough and explores a wide variety of topics could, indeed, became encyclopedic.

The section of the retirement library devoted to philology was impressive. Jefferson's sizable collection of Anglo-Saxon books included nearly all of the important studies of the language. But the collection was weak in Anglo-Saxon poetry: the only major Anglo-Saxon poem Jefferson owned was *Judith*, which forms part of Edward Thwaites's *Heptateuchus*. One of the scholarly works he owned, Joseph Bosworth's *Elements of Anglo-Saxon Grammar*, Jefferson called "a treasure of Anglo-Saxon learning."[39] His copy of Bosworth, which survives at the American Philosophical Society, shows how closely he was studying Anglo-Saxon. Tipped into the volume is a closely written page of notes he took while reading the work. Jefferson's study of Anglo-Saxon would culminate in his *Essay on the Anglo-Saxon Language*, the fullest literary essay he had written since "Thoughts on English Prosody."[40]

Jefferson was also interested in Chinese. During his presidency, he had clipped from the newspaper a Confucian poem titled "A Very Ancient Chinese Ode," which had been translated from the Chinese by Sir William Jones.[41] Keen to learn more, Jefferson added two books treating the Chinese language to his retirement library: Robert Morison's *Dialogues and Detached Sentences in the Chinese Language, with a Free and Verbal Translation in English* and Morison's *View of China for Philological Purposes*. The first Protestant missionary to China, Morison encountered much hostility from the Chinese government. The only way he could hope to accomplish his mission was to lie low and bide his time. He obtained a position as translator of the East India Company in China and studied the language.[42] He designed *Dialogues* as an introductory Chinese textbook. The more advanced *View of China* taught the language by offering an overview of Chinese culture.

Though Jefferson told Adams that his new collection of books would be for amusement, the library catalogue suggests that Jefferson's idea of amusement differed greatly from the average reader's. In the early nineteenth century, novels were offering hordes of readers the opportunity for light-hearted reading that provided much pleasure but required little concentration. Jefferson had no thoughts of whiling away his remaining years reading novels. In his retirement, he found amusement by teaching himself to read Chinese!

CHAPTER 39

The Life and Morals of Jesus of Nazareth

Few authors in Jefferson's retirement library were better represented than Baron d'Holbach, the renowned freethinker who had dared to question the basic tenets of Christianity. Holbach had established his reputation with *Christianisme Dévoilé*, a scathing attack tracing human evil back to religion in general and Christianity in particular. He developed his ideas along these same lines in subsequent treatises. *Système de la Nature*, his most famous work, denied the existence of a deity. Long, ponderous, and often confusing, *Système de la Nature* nonetheless provoked contemporary readers to rethink their understanding of Christianity. To give his ideas greater currency, Holbach digested the work as *Bon Sens*. These two works were part of the great library Jefferson sold to Congress, and he bought replacement copies of both for his retirement library. Neither of these anonymously published works verifies Jefferson's interest in Holbach, however: he attributed both to Diderot. The catalogue of his retirement library shows that Jefferson really became interested in Holbach during the last ten years of his life. Altogether, he had nine works by Holbach in his retirement library.

A brief comment Jefferson made shortly before he sold his great library explains his interest in Holbach. Thanking Thomas Law for a copy of his latest work, *Second Thoughts on Instinctive Impulses*, Jefferson agreed with him that morality was an innate human quality. Refuting those who argued that morality stemmed from the love of God, Jefferson chose several renowned atheists to make his point: "Diderot, Dalembert, D'Holbach, Condorcet, are known to have been among the most virtuous of men. Their virtue then must have had some other foundation than the love of god."[1]

What is the relationship between morality and religion? If we are innately moral creatures, then do we need religion at all? Jefferson asked himself such questions. A succinct answer occurs in the catalogue of his retirement library, which positions religion as a supplement to morality, a man-made invention designed to help people bolster their God-given moral sense. Jefferson realized the answers he sought were more complicated that what his scheme of knowledge in the library catalogue suggested. To pursue his quest, he needed more books. He withheld Law's *Second Thoughts* from the collection he sold to Congress and had it bound up with some other pamphlets on ethics.[2] And he started buying the works of Holbach to see if he could discern his system of morality.

The draft of an essay Jefferson kept in his copy of Holbach's *Système Social* reveals how thoroughly he studied its author's collected works. Jefferson's essay, which has been ignored since its initial publication in an obscure agnostic weekly in 1830, attempts to synthesize Holbach's diverse writings into a unified moral philosophy. "On the Writings of the Baron d'Holbach on the Morality of Nature and That of the Christian Religion," as Jefferson titled his essay, discusses seven Holbach works. Instead of listing them in chronological order, he listed the titles in the order he thought people should read them. With each title, he provided a brief interpretive comment. Talking about *Christianisme Dévoilé*, sixth in the list, Jefferson wrote, "After a preliminary of the substance of what had before been suggested on natural morality, he gives a general view of the insufficiency of the christian substitute, and its actual destructiveness of the real morality accommodated to the social relations of men."[3]

In the last paragraph of "On the Writings of Baron d'Holbach," Jefferson added an extra comment about the fifth work in his list, *Tableau des Saints*. His previous remarks were largely objective, but in this final comment, he critiques Holbach's depiction of Jesus. Holbach "adopted the views of those who consider Jesus as an impostor, and cavilled unworthily at his morals. While, had he examined the character and life of that sage of nature, with candor, making allowances for the circumstances under which he acted, he would have seen in him, the great reformer of the Jewish religion."[4]

Jefferson's study of Holbach confirmed his opinion that morality did not require religion but did not deter his respect for Christ. Before reading Holbach, he had already come to the conclusion that Jesus was the greatest moral philosopher in Western culture. This viewpoint marks a departure from an idea from Bolingbroke he had commonplaced in his youth. Bolingbroke contended that the morals of the Ancients exceeded Christian morality. The epithet Jefferson used to describe Christ in the last paragraph of his essay on Holbach—"sage of nature"—provides the key to understanding his attitude toward Christ and also toward the proper relationship between morality and religion. Much as law, which parallels religion in Jefferson's scheme of knowledge, could be subdivided into natural law and positive law, religion could be divided into the natural and the man-made. Jefferson largely avoided the phrase "natural religion." Man's innate moral sense *was* his natural religion. The system of morality Jesus represented was superior because Christ himself was a "sage of nature." In a way, Jefferson's interpretation of Christ's life resembles his interpretation of Patrick Henry's life. Henry understood natural law because he was a child of nature; Jesus understood morality because he was a sage of nature.

The other epithet Jefferson used to describe Christ in this essay—"the great reformer of the Jewish religion"—suggests that Jefferson was still thinking about ideas from his 1803 "Syllabus of an Estimate of the Merit of the Doctrines of Jesus, Compared with Those of Others," which depicts a similar relationship between Judaism and Christ's teachings. "On the Writings of Baron d'Holbach" also confirms that Jefferson was still thinking deeply about Christianity. His thoughts about religion and moral philosophy form an important part of his literary life from his presidency through his retirement.

A year after writing his "Syllabus," Jefferson assembled "The Philosophy of Jesus," a preliminary compilation of Christ's moral teachings clipped from the Holy Gospel. Describing the work to a correspondent, he explained that he had chosen only those nuggets of moral wisdom that were genuinely Christ's own. It was a simple matter, really. Christ's wisdom was embedded in the writings of the Evangelists like "diamonds in dunghills."[5] Jefferson used this simile time and again to ridicule the Holy Gospel in comparison to Christ's teachings. The twelve apostles were objects of Jefferson's ridicule, as well. A "band of dupes and impostors," he called them. Paul was the "first corrupter of the doctrines of Jesus."[6] Instead of remaining true to Christ's teachings, the apostles twisted what Jesus said to suit their own selfish impulses.

The pressures of being president had stopped Jefferson from taking "The Philosophy of Jesus" any further, but he returned to the project in his retirement, encouraged by his old friend Charles Thomson. After Thomson sent his latest work, *Synopsis of the Four Evangelists*, Jefferson addressed a letter of thanks to him at Harriton House, describing his own attempt to reduce the Evangelists to their essence: "I too have made a wee little book, from the same materials, which I call the Philosophy of Jesus." He mentioned his plans to turn this book into a polyglot text, displaying Greek, Latin, French, and English texts in parallel columns.[7]

Jefferson drafted this letter in January 1816. Somehow it miscarried and did not reach Harriton House until April. The eighty-six-year-old Thomson suffered a debilitating stroke that spring and spent much time in his physician's care. Accidentally, he left Jefferson's letter at his doctor's home, where visitors read it and grossly misinterpreted what Jefferson had to say. Rumors of Jefferson's miraculous religious conversion spread from Philadelphia to Washington. According to the rumors, Jefferson now admitted Christ's divinity, accepted Jesus Christ as his one true personal savior, and had even written a book professing his faith in Christianity.

Friends were surprised to hear these rumors, pleasantly surprised. Several of them wrote Jefferson directly to see if the rumors were true. Margaret Bayard Smith, for one, asked him if he had undergone a change in his attitude toward religion.

"A change from what?" Jefferson replied. "I have ever judged of the religion of others by their lives: and by this test, my dear Madam, I have been satisfied yours must be an excellent one, to have produced a life of such exemplary virtue and correctness. For it is in our lives, and not from our words, that our religion must be read."[8] Jefferson's reply to Mrs. Smith was polite, but essentially he was saying the same thing to her that he had said to others more bluntly: a person did not need religion to live a virtuous life.

Matthew Carey, the prominent Philadelphia bookseller and publisher, also heard the rumors. They made good sense to him. He had recently received a large order of books from Jefferson, several of which pertained specifically to religion: the Venerable Bede's *Historia Ecclesiastica Gentis Anglorum*; James Duport's *Metaphrasis Libri Psalmorum Graecis Versibus Contexta*, a parallel text edition of the psalms in Greek and Latin, which Jefferson had recommended to John Adams; Joseph Priestley's *Harmony of the Evangelists*; and *The Lord's Prayer in above a Hundred Languages*.[9] Eager to capitalize on Jefferson's religious experience, Carey offered to publish the book he told Thomson he had written.

"I write nothing for publication, and last of all things should it be on the subject of religion," Jefferson replied. Continuing his explanation, he offered Carey a keen insight into the futility of religious controversy: "On the dogmas of religion as distinguished from moral principles, all mankind, from the beginning of the world to this day, have been quarrelling, fighting, burning and torturing one another, for abstractions unintelligible to themselves and to all others, and absolutely beyond the comprehension of the human mind."[10]

His refusal to publish anything he had written on the subject of religion is consistent with his refusal to publish other writings of his, but his message to Carey is disingenuous: he had already granted someone else permission to publish his "Syllabus." Furthermore, he was planning to rework "The Philosophy of Jesus" for publication. These strange and uncharacteristic developments resulted from Jefferson's contact with Francis Adrian Van der Kemp, a Dutch clergyman and scholar now living in upstate New York.

Van der Kemp was a good friend of John Adams. In fact, he had visited Adams at Quincy three years earlier. Coincidentally, Van der Kemp had arrived at the Adams home around the same time they had received Jefferson's "Syllabus." Jefferson had told Adams not to show the "Syllabus" to anyone else besides his wife, but Adams did let Van der Kemp read it. Impressed with the document, Van der Kemp asked if he could copy it, but Adams refused. Van der Kemp thought little more about Jefferson's "Syllabus" until 1816, when he happened to read Thomas Belsham's *Memoirs of the Late Reverend Theophilus Lindsey*. Reading Jefferson's letter to Priestley in Belsham's appendix, the letter that sketched out the ideas that would become the "Syllabus," Van der Kemp remembered the "Syllabus" and grew anxious to obtain a copy of it. He wrote Jefferson, not only asking for a copy of the "Syllabus," but also requesting permission to publish it in the British periodical press.[11]

Jefferson's first impulse was to refuse this request, too, but Van der Kemp did not stop there. He continued by telling Jefferson about his plans to write a life of Christ along the same lines as Jefferson had suggested in his letter to Priestley. It was almost as if Van der Kemp had spoken the magic words to unlock Jefferson's heart. Always happy for others to take his ideas and run with them, Jefferson decided to do whatever he could to encourage Van der Kemp—even if that meant going against his rule about publishing his ideas on religion. He still did not want to publish either the "Syllabus" or "The Philosophy of Jesus" under his own name, being "unwilling to draw on myself a swarm of insects, whose buz is more disquieting than their bite," but he did grant Van der Kemp permission to publish the "Syllabus" in a British periodical and to publish both works with his life of Christ.[12]

Thrilled to have another scholar follow through on his ideas, Jefferson made his offer before he checked too carefully into Van der Kemp's background. All Jefferson really knew was that he was a friend and correspondent of John Adams. He decided to write Adams to see what he was getting himself into. Adams gave Van der Kemp a good recommendation: "His head is deeply learned and his heart is pure," Adams said. "A Gentleman here asked my Opinion of him. My Answer was, he is a *Mountain of Salt* of the Earth."[13] What Adams did not tell Jefferson, what Adams perhaps did not know himself, was that Van der Kemp was one of those people who could conceive grandiose projects yet who could not always see them through to completion.

Van der Kemp did manage to get the "Syllabus" published. It appeared in the *Monthly Repository of Theology and General Literature* before the year's end. As promised, he published it anonymously, but he gave the editor of this journal enough information that it was not hard for readers to guess its author. The editor composed a headnote for the "Syllabus" identifying the author as "an eminent American Statesman," one of the "leading men in the American revolution." John Quincy Adams, currently serving as ambassador to the Court of St. James, read the journal and easily recognized Jefferson's authorship.[14]

Though Van der Kemp never did write his life of Christ, Jefferson's correspondence with him was not a total waste of time. Jefferson spoke more frankly to him than to some of his other correspondents, and Van der Kemp had managed to coax from Jefferson several memorable quotations on the subject of religion. On the uselessness of critiquing religious arguments, Jefferson stated, "Ridicule is the only weapon which can be used against unintelligible propositions." The idea of the Holy Trinity Jefferson called "the mere Abracadabra of the mountebanks calling themselves the priests of Jesus."[15] Most important, it was Van der Kemp's failure to write his life of Christ that helped Jefferson realize how to reshape "The Philosophy of Jesus." He would not make this realization right away. The project lay dormant a few more years until a letter from another old friend got Jefferson thinking again.

William Short wrote Jefferson in October 1819. Though Short had learned much from Jefferson, he had never really learned to be concise. His letters always said more than they should have, and this one was no exception. Short boasted that he was now following the principles of Epicurus. The boast sounded jejune to Jefferson, who took the opportunity to give his former protégé a lesson on moral philosophy. Jefferson discussed the teaching of Epicurus and then summarized the moral philosophy of Cicero, Epictetus, Plato, Seneca, and Socrates. After discussing the Ancients, Jefferson reached Jesus of Nazareth, whom he called "the greatest of all the Reformers of the depraved religion of his own country." Extracted from the Gospel, Christ's teachings would form "a system of the most sublime morality which has ever fallen from the lips of man." Like Epictetus and Epicurus, Jesus gave us laws for governing ourselves, but he went much further than the Ancients: he also gave us "the duties and charities we owe to others."[16]

Jefferson mentioned "The Philosophy of Jesus" and told Short that he was considering another literary project pertaining to the subject of moral philosophy, an English translation of Epictetus. By the end of this letter, Jefferson concluded that he would do neither: "With one foot in the grave, these are now idle projects for me. My business is to beguile the wearisomness of declining life, as I endeavour to do, by the delights of classical reading and of Mathematical truths, and by the consolations of a sound philosophy, equally indifferent to hope and fear."[17]

Short was unused to hearing such defeatist language from his mentor. He wrote back to encourage Jefferson to keep working on "The Philosophy of Jesus." Short made a convincing argument: the genuine moral teachings of Jesus may seem evident to Jefferson, but they did not seem so to others. In the history of biblical scholarship, no one had been able to separate Christ's true teachings from the surrounding biblical text. Short argued that Jefferson should take advantage of his personal insight and perform the task for the benefit of mankind.[18]

He needed no more convincing. Jefferson soon assembled all the Bibles he would need for the project—he would destroy eight Bibles to prepare his polyglot text. He took out his scissors and a pot of paste and got to work. He stopped talking about it as an expansion of "The Philosophy of Jesus" and formed a much greater plan for the work. Now that Van der Kemp's plans for writing a life of Christ had fallen through, Jefferson realized if he wanted a life of Christ, he had to compose it himself. With neither the desire nor the inclination to write a narrative biography, he devised an innovative way to write the life of Christ: he would compose his biography from extracts clipped from the Gospel. It was a brilliant stroke—not only would *The Life and Morals of Jesus of Nazareth Extracted Textually from the Gospels, in Greek, Latin, French and English*, as he decided to call the work, contain Christ's moral teachings; it would also tell the story of the man whose life exemplified that philosophy. It would be a biography of Christ devoid of Christian miracles.

The precise date Jefferson began *The Life and Morals of Jesus of Nazareth* is uncertain. So, too, is the date he completed it. The best guess is that he finished the work in the summer of 1820. Jefferson wrote Short two letters on the subject that year, one in April and another in August. Neither letter mentions the work specifically, but both discuss the subject of Jesus' life. The second letter implies that Jefferson had brought the biography to completion.[19]

The biggest cliché about Jefferson's literary life is that he wrote only one book, *Notes on the State of Virginia*. Those who make this assertion ignore *A Manual of Parliamentary Practice*, the *Proceedings* concerning the batture at New Orleans, *The Autobiography*, and the numerous other near book-length official reports he compiled as secretary of state and as president, but they also ignore *The Life and Morals of Jesus of Nazareth*. Though Jefferson used scissors and paste instead of pen and ink to create this work, his composition is as careful as that of any piece of writing.

Jefferson's decision to compose this biography from biblical extracts enhances its complexity as a literary work. His compositional process reflects an approach characteristic of the Romantic era. Like the catalogue of his retirement library, Jefferson's *Life of Jesus* reveals his affinity to the Romantics, who were currently experimenting with fragmenting texts as they rebelled against traditional narrative forms and explored the limits of knowledge. Jefferson's technique of using clippings anticipated experimental literary methods of the twentieth century and let him view the meaning of Christianity in a bold new way.[20]

He gave his work all the trappings of a proper book. He wrote out a title page and drafted a detailed table of contents. He even included some maps, inclusions that help to situate Jesus in a historical time and place and thus demythologize him.[21] And Jefferson had the whole thing handsomely bound in morocco.

A revision he made to his table of contents shows his emerging sense of purpose. He first called it "A Table of the Texts of this Extract from the Evangelists and of the order of their Arrangement." He later deleted the prepositional phrase "of this Extract" and, after the word "Evangelists," added the phrase, "employed in this Narrative." This seemingly minor revision effectively changes the genre of the book. Jefferson clearly realized that the work he was creating was more than "The Philosophy of Jesus," more than a series of extracts. It was a full-fledged narrative, a retelling of the story of Jesus stripped of superstition. *The Life and Morals of Jesus of Nazareth* may be the finest biography of Christ ever written.

"The Gospel According to Luke" provided the first source text Jefferson used for his *Life of Jesus*. He omitted the entire first chapter of Luke. This omission excludes the story of the birth of John the Baptist and thus eliminates an episode Jefferson saw as an unnecessary digression. By omitting the first chapter of Luke, Jefferson also eliminated the story of the Annunciation—Gabriel is not among the *dramatis personae* in this retelling of the life of Christ. Jefferson also avoided any reference to Mary being a virgin. Nothing happens in Jefferson's *Life of Jesus* that cannot happen in nature. Jefferson excluded all supernatural elements from his narrative, regardless how central they had been to the traditional story of Christ's life.

Jefferson's *Life of Jesus* begins as the second chapter of Luke begins, with Joseph and Mary leaving Nazareth and traveling to Bethlehem. Jefferson retained the first seven verses of the chapter, which tell the story of Christ's birth in a manger. He excised verses eight through twenty, which relate the story of an angel announcing the birth of Jesus to the nearby shepherds and their adoration of him. Jefferson found nothing wrong with the shepherds, but the angels had to go. This section of the Gospels contains some of the most quoted and heartfelt passages in the Bible. Jefferson wasted no sentiment here. In the Gospel according to Luke, multitudinous angels appear, praise God and say, "Glory to God in the highest, and on earth peace, good will toward men." In the Gospel according to Jefferson, there are no angels whatsoever.

After quoting a part of the twenty-first verse of the second chapter of Luke, which supplies the name of Jesus, Jefferson excised verses twenty-two through thirty-eight—the story of the presentation of Jesus in the temple. He resumed the story at the thirty-ninth verse, when Joseph and Mary return to Nazareth. With so much of the intervening text removed, Jesus grows into adolescence very quickly.

Even with the verses he retained, Jefferson tinkered with the text. Verse forty of the second chapter of Luke reads: "And the child grew, and waxed strong in spirit, filled with wisdom: and the grace of God was upon him." There was one part of this sentence Jefferson found inappropriate, the closing independent clause. In Jefferson's version, the verse reads: "And the child grew, and waxed strong in spirit, filled with wisdom." To Jefferson's mind, the grace of God had nothing to do with Christ's wisdom.

Jefferson retained the next several verses from the second chapter of Luke, which tell how Joseph and Mary became separated from their son for three days but eventually found him "in the temple, sitting in the midst of the doctors, both hearing them, and asking them questions." Mary, too, has a question for him.

"Son, why hast thou thus dealt with us? behold, thy father and I have sought thee sorrowing," she asks.

"How is it that ye sought me?" Jesus asked in turn. "Wist ye not that I must be about my Father's business?"

That's how Luke told the story. In Jefferson's version, Jesus does not reply to his mother's question at all. He says nothing.

Jefferson ended what can be considered his first chapter with the verse that ends the second chapter of Luke: "And Jesus increased in wisdom and stature, and in favor with God and man." Jefferson liked the beginning of this verse, not its ending, so he eliminated the closing prepositional phrase. In his version, the chapter ends, "And Jesus increased in wisdom and stature."

From this point in his biography, Jefferson's editing process became more complex as the different books of the Gospel tell varying stories of Christ's life. Starting with the third chapter of Luke, Jefferson began to intercut passages from other books of the Gospel. The early verses of the third chapter of Luke establish the setting in terms of both time and place, but Jefferson disliked the syntax of the passage: the opening sentence does not even end until the second verse. The original text of the first four verses of the third chapter of Luke reads:

> Now in the fifteenth year of the reign of Tiberius Caesar, Pontius Pilate being governor of Judea, and Herod being tetrarch of Galilee, and his brother Philip tetrarch of Ituraea and of the region of Trachonitis, and Lysanias the tetrarch of Abilene, Annas and Caiaphas being the high priests, the word of God came unto John the son of Zacharias in the wilderness. And he came into all the country about Jordan, preaching the baptism of repentance for the remission of sins.

Jefferson omitted the phrase "the word of God came unto John the son of Zacharias in the wilderness" and the entire sentence following it. In its place, he substituted the first independent clause of Mark 1:4: "John did baptize in the wilderness." Jefferson's substitution recalls the process of condensation he had used in his writing ever since he began his legal commonplace book. It makes the factual information less wordy and more precise. Furthermore, his revision eliminates references to both God and repentance.

Jefferson intercut a passage from Matthew to describe John's baptism of Jesus (3:4–6, 13). After quoting from Luke (3:23) to record that Jesus was now "about thirty years of age," he related a story from John (2:12–16) showing how Jesus chased the money changers from the temple. He also included the memorable phrase, "Make not my Father's house a house of merchandise."

After this episode, Jefferson flashed forward, intercutting the story of Herodias asking her father for the head of John the Baptist from the sixth chapter of Mark. This biblical episode was one of Jefferson's favorites. Hanging at Monticello was a finely rendered copy of Guido Reni's *Herodias Bearing the Head of St. John*.

Jefferson also included the story of Jesus choosing his apostles and a long excerpt from the fifth chapter of Matthew. This chapter begins Christ's Sermon on the Mount, which extends over the next two chapters

Herodias Bearing the Head of St. John, after the original by Guido Reni. (Monticello, Thomas Jefferson Foundation, Inc.)

of Matthew. Not even the Sermon on the Mount was sacrosanct from Jefferson's scissors. After including the first twelve verses of the fifth chapter of Matthew, he intercut three verses from Luke (6.24–26), which record a different sermon by Jesus. Recognizing that the Sermon on the Mount as recorded in Matthew was incomplete, Jefferson audaciously completed it by adding another text Jesus spoke.

Toward the end of the fifth book of Matthew, he added another excerpt from Luke (6:34–36) to the Sermon on the Mount: "And if ye lend *to them* of whom ye hope to receive, what thank have ye? for sinners also lend to sinners, to receive as much again. But love ye your enemies, and do good, and lend, hoping for nothing again; and your reward shall be great, and ye shall be the children of the Highest: for he is kind unto the unthankful and *to* the evil. Be ye therefore merciful, as your Father also is merciful." This passage is a substitution for a passage from the Sermon on the Mount as recorded in Matthew (5:48), which is similarly worded: "Be ye therefore perfect, even as your Father which is in heaven is perfect." Recognizing that both sentences shared the same syntax, Jefferson logically concluded that the sentence in Matthew was a mistranscription for Christ's words. The sentence in Luke, Jefferson decided, more closely resembled what Christ said.

Separating what Christ said from what others attributed to him seemed a simple process to Jefferson. As he told William Short, "The difference is obvious to the eye and to the understanding, and we may read, as we run, to each his part; and I will venture to affirm that he who, as I have done, will undertake to winnow this grain from its chaff, will find it not to require a moment's consideration. The parts fall asunder of themselves as would those of an image of metal and clay."[22]

Jefferson continued the Sermon on the Mount with the entire sixth chapter of Matthew and the first two verses of the seventh: "Judge not, that ye be not judged. For with what judgment ye judge, ye shall be judged: and with what measure ye mete, it shall be measured to you again." After some further changes, he skipped ahead to a later passage in Matthew (12:35–37), which he used to complete the Sermon on the Mount: "A good man out of the good treasure of the heart, bringeth forth good things: and an evil man out of the evil treasure bringeth forth evil things. But I say unto you, That every idle word that men shall speak, they shall give account thereof in the day of judgment. For by thy words thou shalt be justified, and by thy words thou shalt be condemned." Jefferson considered the Sermon on the Mount to represent Jesus Christ at his best and felt that there was nothing religious about it at all. Rather, it forms a compendium of Christ's moral precepts that everyone interested in living an upright life can follow.

The conclusion of the *Life of Jesus* is simultaneously the most natural and yet the most daring part of the whole biography. It ends with one compound sentence describing Christ's burial. Jefferson formed the sentence from the beginning of a verse from John (19:42) and the ending of a verse from Matthew (27:60): "There they laid Jesus, and rolled a great stone to the door of the sepulchre, and departed."

Of course, neither John nor Matthew ended Christ's story here. Both books of the New Testament tell the story of Christ's resurrection next. To Jefferson, the story of the resurrection had no place in the biography of Jesus of Nazareth. It, too, was another supernatural element that Jefferson eliminated from his life of Christ.

While all these revisions to the Bible may make it seem like Jefferson was an atheist himself, he was not. Few documents provide a better indication of Jefferson's attitude toward a supreme being than Samuel Whitcomb's 1824 interview with him. Whitcomb, who was an atheist, confronted Jefferson on the subject.[23] Jefferson professed his belief in a supreme being. Whitcomb suggested that "if the Being of God was admitted it seemed to go far toward proving the Truth of and preparing the way for the admission of Christianity."

Jefferson disagreed.

"Jesus was one of the best men that ever lived," Jefferson told him.

"But," replied Whitcomb, "how could He make such pretensions to Divinity and..."

"He never did so," replied Jefferson, cutting Whitcomb off in mid-sentence.

"Well," Whitcomb responded, "He professed to have Divine Aid in working miracles."

"No he did not," Jefferson responded. "Paul was the first who had perverted the Doctrines of Christ."

Whitcomb made some additional remarks and "concluded by saying that the Clergy in our Country were investigating these subjects with considerable independence."

Jefferson disagreed once more. Whitcomb did not record his precise response, but his summary captures its essence: "He dissented and expressed himself warmly in a phrase which I suppose was not English but some other language 'The Clergy were all———.'"

He did not tell Whitcomb about his *Life of Jesus*. He did not even tell his family about the book. This was one of those books Jefferson liked to read by himself late at night just before falling asleep. Reading the wisdom of Christ before bed, Jefferson gave himself much to ponder as he drifted off to sleep.

Christians may take offense at Jefferson's decision to omit the resurrection. From a literary perspective, the conclusion to his *Life of Jesus* offers a good example of his use of understatement. The quiet simplicity of Christ's death and burial provide a stirring contrast to his posthumous reputation. The ending of Jefferson's *Life of Jesus* is reminiscent of the ending of *Paradise Lost*. As Milton rewrote the story of Adam and Eve, there is a profound sense of calm as the two leave Paradise and enter the world. The ending of Jefferson's *Life of Jesus* is similarly low key. There's no mourning, no fanfare, no weeping; once the physical burial is complete, the people move on. Jefferson leaves the reader with the image of the sepulchre once everyone has left, an image simple in composition, complex in terms of its symbolic resonance: "There they laid Jesus, And rolled a great stone to the door of the sepulchre, and departed."

CHAPTER 40

The Autobiography

R ereading Benjamin Franklin's autobiography in the spring of 1820, William Short regretted that Jefferson had yet to write his life story. Short had asked him to do so earlier but without result. Tenaciously, he wrote again that year to reiterate the request: "I have lately read over again Dr Franklin's plain and simple narration of the events of his own life. It has renewed my desire to see the same kind of work from yourself; but I will not be importunate in asking it at your hands against your own inclination, notwithstanding the great gratification it would give to your invariable and faithful friend."[1] While aware of Franklin's autobiography and other recent books devoted to the lives of the patriots, Jefferson had so far avoided writing the story of his life. The year following Short's letter, however, he finally relented.

After heading his manuscript with the date January 6, 1821, Jefferson drafted his opening sentence: "At the age of 77, I begin to make some memoranda and state some recollections concerning myself, for my own more ready reference and for the information of my family." The revisions he made to this sentence verify the discomfort he felt writing about himself. After inscribing the phrase "recollections concerning myself," he went back and revised it to read: "recollections of dates and facts concerning myself."[2]

Limiting himself to dates and facts, Jefferson, paradoxically, sought to make his personal story as impersonal as possible. He had few literary models to guide him in his composition. The presidential memoir had yet to emerge as a lucrative, almost obligatory work. In addition to Franklin's, Jefferson knew other famous autobiographies of the era, including Rousseau's *Confessions*. To be sure, he would not be using Rousseau as a model. Jean-François Marmontel's *Memoires*, which Jefferson knew from the four-volume *Oeuvres Posthume de Marmontel*, offered another possible model for his own memoirs.

Having become good friends with Marmontel in Paris, Jefferson knew from personal experience that he was an expert anecdotalist and recognized a quality in Marmontel's *Memoirs* that resembled his conversation. An expert anecdotalist himself, Jefferson, unlike either Franklin or Marmontel, included relatively few of his personal anecdotes in his autobiography. Short was hoping for a work patterned on Franklin's, but Jefferson's autobiography would be something very different.

As far as openings go, Jefferson's first sentence leaves a lot to be desired. It doesn't make for the kind of start that suggests a terrific life story is to follow. But it does offer an indication of the autobiography as a whole. Though not as highly crafted or carefully revised as his most famous writings, Jefferson's autobiography is not without valuable literary qualities. His seemingly modest opening, for example, embodies a deliberate literary pose. While he claims to be writing the story of his life solely for the benefit of himself and his family, Jefferson understood that it would reach a much wider audience after his death. The care with which he preserved his public papers—and destroyed his most intimate private papers—shows his understanding that whatever documents he saved would be read, studied, and published.

The early pages sustain the initial pose, making the book seem like a reference guide for personal use. When George Wythe enters the story, for example, Jefferson avoided saying much about him, despite how important Wythe was to his legal education. Instead, Jefferson referred to a character sketch he had written the previous year: "For a sketch of the life and character of Mr. Wythe see my letter of Aug. 31. 20. to Mr. John Saunderson."[3] The cross-reference to a letter from his files confirms the uneasiness Jefferson felt as he wrote the story of his life. He had recently written a good sketch of Wythe. Why bother writing another?

Though it might seem cumbersome to locate this letter to read his account of George Wythe, it was no problem for Jefferson, who maintained a huge and highly organized file of his correspondence. Always fascinated with the latest technology, he had begun using a polygraph almost as soon as the device was invented. While president, he had acquired one from Charles Willson Peale. Invented by John Isaac Hawkins and developed and produced by Peale, the polygraph, applying the principle of the pantograph, held two pens and allowed its user to write a letter and make a copy of it simultaneously. The early polygraphs were finicky, however, and Jefferson suggested improvements to Peale and purchased new models as they improved in reliability and ease of use. He meticulously made copies of his letters and organized his correspondence so that he could locate any letter effortlessly.

At times, the text of Jefferson's autobiography suggests an uncharacteristic impatience. Describing his relationship with Patrick Henry, Jefferson initially recalled his law student days when he listened to the debates over the Stamp Act from the lobby door of the House of Burgesses and heard Henry present his famous Virginia Resolutions. Jefferson included little other information about the role Henry played in his life. Since he had recorded his impressions in several letters to William Wirt, who had incorporated much of what he wrote in *Sketches of the Life and Character of Patrick Henry*, Jefferson found it unnecessary to write about Henry all over again. Instead of repeating what had been written, he simply referred readers to Wirt's text.

Shifting from his education to his public life, Jefferson corrected some errors that had entered early American history. Discussing the origins of the intercolonial committees of correspondence, for example, he refuted an error John Marshall had perpetuated in his *Life of George Washington*—that Massachusetts was responsible for initiating these committees. In a series of letters two years earlier, Jefferson had argued convincingly that Virginia deserved credit. Instead of repeating his previous arguments, he again referred his readers to the letters. But he did admit an error he had made in one of them.

Jefferson never had a problem admitting when he was wrong. As he said earlier, "Error is the stuff of which the web of life is woven: and he who lives longest and wisest is only able to wear out the more of it."[4] Admitting his error in the autobiography, he exemplified this idea. Some of the minor topics discussed in the autobiography seem introduced primarily for the purpose of correcting errors in his previous writings. Jefferson saw this book as one of his last opportunities to set the record straight.

Once he reached the Revolutionary period, Jefferson's writing style loosened up considerably. The stiffness that characterizes its early pages disappears, and his voice seems clearer and more natural. Recalling Revolutionary days, he was transcribing anecdotes he had been rehearsing for decades. Mentioning some Virginia patriots who were reluctant to advocate independence, for example, he wrote that they had "stopped at the half-way house of John Dickinson who admitted that England had a right to regulate our commerce, and to lay duties on it for the purposes of regulation, but not of raising revenue."[5] Jefferson's metaphor—"the half-way house of John Dickinson"—has the quality of a favorite expression, and his correspondence bears out his fondness for the phrase: in one letter Jefferson called the English constitution a "halfway house," too.[6] Furthermore, his words reflect a larger metaphor that had been an important aspect of his public writings: the metaphor of the journey.

Infrequently, Jefferson included snatches of remembered conversation in the autobiography. Portraying his first time as a delegate to the Continental Congress, he incorporated a conversation with William Livingston, a delegate from New Jersey twenty years his senior. Jefferson greatly admired a work he thought Livingston had written and complimented him on it. Instead of expressing gratitude, Livingston rebuked Jefferson, bluntly telling him he had not written the piece.

While this anecdote effectively illustrates Livingston's contentiousness, its insignificance makes it frustrating. The conversations that occurred behind the scenes of the Continental Congress were some of the most important conversations that ever occurred in American history or, indeed, in the history of democracy. One longs to read more, but the autobiography thwarts that desire. Beyond a couple of Franklin anecdotes, Jefferson recorded few other personal conversations in the pages of his autobiography.

Instead of retelling the story of the congressional proceedings in 1776 that led to the *Declaration of Independence*, Jefferson included the extensive notes he had taken during the proceedings. This inclusion is consistent with his belief that histories should incorporate primary documents. He also included his original version of the *Declaration*. He underlined the passages Congress had omitted and situated the replacement text Congress drafted in an adjoining column. He justified the inclusion of his draft by arguing that the sentiments of men are known by what they receive as well as what they reject.

His inclusion of the *Declaration* in his autobiography marks a departure from something Jefferson told John Campbell a dozen years earlier. Then he had suggested that the *Declaration* should be excluded from his collected writings because he could make no personal claim to it since it belonged to the American public. Including it within his autobiography, Jefferson was now making a personal claim to it—not to the official text as adopted by the Continental Congress, but to his version. By including his original, he was demonstrating the pride he took in it and reasserting his belief that the original was superior to the official text. Furthermore, by placing his original text of the *Declaration* in his autobiography, Jefferson was making sure that it would become a part of history, that it would be reprinted and remembered. The strategy worked: literary anthologies today typically reprint this version of the *Declaration*.

A number of paragraphs in the autobiography begin with dates. Some are the dates that historical events occurred; others are the dates in 1821 when Jefferson was writing the work. On February 6, exactly one month after starting his autobiography, he wrote about thirteen hundred words—a good day's work. But on Wednesday, the seventh, he grew weary of writing. Referring to the "Bill for Amending the Constitution of the College of William and Mary" and discussing his strenuous efforts to reform the college curriculum, he wrote, "I shall recur again to this subject towards the close of my story, if I should have life and resolution enough to reach that term; for I am already tired of talking about myself."[7]

Jefferson's weariness is understandable. The autobiography was not the only literary task occupying his time that year. He was still maintaining a voluminous correspondence, which often became burdensome. Five years earlier, he had complained to Charles Thomson: "My greatest oppression is a correspondence afflictingly laborious, the extent of which I have long been endeavoring to curtail. This keeps me at the drudgery of the writing-table all the prime hours of the day, leaving for the gratification of my appetite for reading only what I can steal from the hours of sleep. Could I reduce this epistolary corvée within the limits of my friends, and affairs, and give the time redeemed from it to reading and reflection, to history, ethics, mathematics, my life would be as happy as the infirmities of age would admit."[8] Shortly before starting the autobiography, he made a similar complaint to his grandson, Francis Eppes.[9] During the intervening years, he had been unable to reduce this "epistolary corvée."

Writing to friends and family gave him much pleasure, but responding to others fatigued him. James Madison had forwarded a long, closely written letter about the Missouri Compromise from one of his correspondents. Jefferson could not bring himself to read the entire letter, let alone respond to it. He told Madison, "Could I have devoted a day to it, by interlining the words as I could pick them out, I might have got at more. The lost books of Livy or Tacitus might be worth this. Our friend would do well to write less and write plainer."[10] Jefferson's words reveal new priorities: sorting out the intricacies of political controversy had become far less important to him than delving into the complexities of classical history.

He wrote several other letters to Francis Eppes, who was attending South Carolina College in Columbia. He sent his grandson books, provided advice about his studies, asked questions about the college's curriculum, and answered questions about his reading. When Francis wrote asking him about the works of Lord Bolingbroke and Thomas Paine, his grandfather responded with a fine comparison between two, analyzing both their opinions and their writings. His response amounts to a lesson on literary style:

> These two persons differed remarkably in the style of their writing, each leaving a model of what is most perfect in both extremes of the simple and the sublime. No writer has exceeded Paine in ease and familiarity of style; in perspicuity of expression, happiness of eluci-dation, and in simple and unassuming language.... Ld. Bolingbroke's, on the other hand, is a style of the highest order: the lofty, r[h]ythmical, full-flowing eloquence of Cicero. Periods of just measure, their members proportioned, their close full and round. His conceptions too are bold and strong, his diction copious, polished and commanding as his subject.[11]

Other correspondence came from unexpected quarters. In February 1821, Jefferson received a letter from Prof. Jared Mansfield of the U.S. Military Academy at West Point. Established during his presidency, the Academy wished to honor Jefferson for playing an instrumental part in its creation. Consequently, Prof. Mansfield asked him to sit for a portrait. Though flattered, Jefferson, at seventy-seven, answered by quoting Voltaire, who, when requested by a female friend to sit for a bust by the sculptor Jean-Baptiste Pigalle at the same age, responded: "I am seventy-seven years old, and M. Pigalle is supposed to be coming to model my face. But, Madame, I must first have a face. You would hardly be able to guess where it ought to be. My eyes have sunk three inches, my cheeks are nothing but old parchment badly glued on to bones which have nothing to hold to. The few teeth I had have departed." Applied to Jefferson, Voltaire's words are hyperbolic. In his old age, Jefferson still had a full set of teeth.[12]

Commissioned by the Academy, the portraitist Thomas Sully came to Monticello in March and stayed for nearly two weeks. Born in England, Sully had immigrated to the United States in his adolescence with his family. His actor-parents traveled around the nation to perform, and they brought Thomas and his many siblings with them; once he turned painter, Sully continued traveling the country executing his commis-sions. These experiences gave him many good stories and much insight into the character of the nation, an essential quality for any good portrait painter. The turning point in Sully's career came in 1807, when he visited Gilbert Stuart's studio in Hartford, Connecticut. Stuart's painting style significantly influenced Sully's, and Sully emerged as the finest American portraitist after Stuart.[13]

During his Monticello sojourn, Sully spent much time talking about art and architecture with Jefferson. He recommended several books, the most notable being Jean Nicolas Louis Durand's *Recueil et Parallèle des Édifices de Tout Genre, Anciens et Modernes*, a large collection of engravings consisting of architectural plans illustrating works from ancient Egypt to eighteenth-century Europe with an accompanying history of architecture by Jacques-Guillaume Legrand. Given Jefferson's appreciation of the comparative method when it came to so many other fields of study—anthropology, biography, law, literature—Durand's comparativist outlook appealed to him. Sully promised to find him a copy of Durand's work. He was unable to make good on this promise, but Jefferson did obtain a copy of Durand's work for the University of Virginia library.[14] The evidence of Sully's visit to Monticello suggests that he developed a deep and abiding respect for Jefferson.

Jefferson was not the only member of the household to engage Sully in artistic discussion. Ever eager to expand her knowledge and test her abilities, Ellen, now twenty-four, talked art with Sully, too. She expressed more interest in landscape painting than in portraiture, though. As Sully knew, good art teachers were hard to come by, so he offered her the next best thing: after returning to Philadelphia, Sully found "a work on Landscape painting," which he sent Ellen as a gift, hoping it would "supply the place of a teacher."[15]

Two paintings resulted from Sully's Monticello visit—or three, if you count the extraordinary portrait of Martha Jefferson Randolph that Sully would paint several years later. The half-length portrait of Jefferson he painted that March served as a study for the elegant full-length portrait he would create for the military academy. Once it was hung, the portrait awed visitors to West Point. James Fenimore Cooper, for one, was thoroughly impressed. Visiting West Point in 1823, he found "a dignity, a repose . . . a loveliness about this painting, that I never have seen in any other portrait." Sully's portrait prompted Cooper to rethink his formerly negative attitude toward Jefferson: "It has really shaken my opinion of Jefferson as a man, if not as a politician; and when his image occurs to me now, it is in the simple robes of Sully."[16] Despite the grandeur of the full-length portrait, the half-length one is often considered the finest Sully ever painted. He left it unfinished for several years, but in 1830, William Short commissioned him to complete the work. Sully added some final touches, and Short presented it to the American Philosophical Society.

Martha Jefferson Randolph, by Thomas Sully. (Monticello, Thomas Jefferson Foundation, Inc.)

The half-length portrait depicts a very different Jefferson from the one Jefferson himself was depicting in his autobiography. In his own verbal portrait, Jefferson subsumed his personal life within his public life. He avoided showing his inner feelings or depicting his private relationships in favor of describing what he had contributed to the development of his nation.[17] Painting Jefferson at Monticello in his retirement, Sully captured the private Jefferson.

Sully's painting confirms Francis Calley Gray's description of Jefferson. Gray had emphasized the fact that even though Jefferson's homemade garments were unfashionable, he was proud of their local manufacture. Wearing a thick coat trimmed with a fur collar in Sully's painting, Jefferson appears warm and comfortable yet hardly stylish. Sully's portrait captures its subject's nonchalance toward personal appearance. While a diplomat in Paris, Jefferson had made a point of dressing in the latest fashions. At home in retirement, he wore what he pleased.

The face above the fur collar is the best part of Sully's painting. Jefferson's sandy red hair had now turned almost completely gray, but he still had plenty of it. In the portrait, his long hair frames his distinctive face. Four decades earlier Mather Brown had depicted the piercing quality of Jefferson's eyes. Like Voltaire's, his eyes had sunk a little over the course of his life, but they had lost none of their penetrating power.

Sully's painting is lit in a distinctive manner, and Jefferson's body is positioned to give light and shadow their full effect. His body faces out, his right shoulder angled slightly forward and his head turned to his right. The light comes from his right, slightly above and behind him. Consequently, the front of his face is brightly lit. His prominent nose casts a dark shadow, and the left side of his head is slightly shaded. There is figurative truth in this likeness: though part of Jefferson remains in shadow, his intentions are clear to those who look him straight in the eye.

His mouth may be the most unusual feature of the portrait. Jefferson's thin lips seem tightly clenched, making his mouth a horizontal line. The position of his lips suggests a touch of vanity. Jefferson seems to be holding his mouth immobile to avoid displaying any unnecessary wrinkles. Alternatively, the tight-lipped manner in which he holds his mouth offers a literal equivalent for the tight-lipped manner he was using to narrate his autobiography. Just as Jefferson hesitated to reveal his personal life in the autobiography, he was also trying to reveal little about himself as he sat for Sully—but to no avail. Sully's keen eye saw through Jefferson's pose: the portrait depicts his natural dignity, his stately being, and his wisdom.

Progress on the autobiography slowed during Sully's visit. Jefferson accelerated the story by skipping big chunks of his life. Reaching 1779, the year he was elected governor of Virginia, he deliberately avoided retelling what happened when he was in office, which he excused with the following statement: "Being now, as it were, identified with the Commonwealth itself, to write my own history during the two years of my administration, would be to write the public history of that portion of the revolution within this state."[18] Seeing the story of his life while Virginia governor as identical to the history of Virginia during his governorship, Jefferson saw no reason to retell it, especially since Louis

Hue Girardin had recently told it so well. Instead, he referred readers to Girardin's *History of Virginia*. Its author, Jefferson explained in his autobiography, "had free access to all my papers while composing it, and has given as faithful an account as I could myself."[19]

Usually, aspects of Jefferson's personal life emerge in the autobiography solely to illuminate his public life. Recalling the offer Congress made in November 1782 to appoint him to negotiate a peace treaty in Europe, he explained why he accepted, when he had previously declined similar appointments: his wife had died in the interim. Instead of making his wife's death a distinct episode in the autobiography, he mentioned it only as it pertained to his diplomatic career. Jefferson often relived his wife's death over in his own mind: the scrap of paper that held a lock of her hair shows much evidence of folding and unfolding.[20] He refused to share his intimate memories with his readers.

One of the finest episodes in the autobiography stems from his last term in the Continental Congress. Recording a conversation with fellow Virginia delegate John Francis Mercer, Jefferson revealed much about himself:

> Our body was little numerous, but very contentious. Day after day was wasted on the most unimportant questions. My colleague Mercer was one of those afflicted with the morbid rage of debate, of an ardent mind, prompt imagination, and copious flow of words. He heard with impatience any logic which was not his own. Sitting near me on some occasion of a trifling but wordy debate, he asked how I could sit in silence hearing so much false reasoning which a word should refute? I observed to him that to refute indeed was easy, but to silence impossible. That in measures brought forward by myself, I took the laboring oar, as was incumbent on me; but that in general I was willing to listen. If every sound argument or objection was used by some one or other of the numerous debaters, it was enough: if not, I thought it sufficient to suggest the omission, without going into a repetition of what had been already said by others. That this was a waste and abuse of the time and patience of the house which could not be justified.[21]

Upon relating this anecdote, Jefferson drew some general conclusions regarding legislative bodies, taking examples from earlier sessions of Continental Congress, European legislative bodies, and the Virginia House of Burgesses—"the most dignified body of men ever assembled to legislate," he said elsewhere.[22] Continuing his autobiography, he observed:

I believe that if the members of deliberative bodies were to observe this course generally, they would do in a day what takes them a week, and it is really more questionable, than may at first be thought, whether Bonaparte's dumb legislature which said nothing and did much, may not be preferable to one which talks much and does nothing. I served with General Washington in the legislature of Virginia before the revolution, and, during it, with Dr. Franklin in Congress. I never heard either of them speak ten minutes at a time, nor to any but the main point which was to decide the question. They laid their shoulders to the great points, knowing that the little ones would follow of themselves. If the present Congress errs in too much talking, how can it be otherwise in a body to which the people send 150. lawyers, whose trade it is to question everything, yield nothing, and talk by the hour? That 150. lawyers should do business together ought not to be expected.[23]

After these incisive remarks, Jefferson wrote, "But to return again to our subject." His words seem almost apologetic. They suggest that he considered this anecdote and the conclusions he drew from it a digression, an indulgence, something not directly pertinent to his narrative. The story of Jefferson's life is a great story, but time and again throughout the autobiography, he backs away from revealing too much of himself. Whenever he catches himself supplying "recollections of myself," he reverts to "recollections of dates and facts."

By the time Jefferson left Monticello for his annual spring visit to Poplar Forest on Saturday, April 21, 1821, he had taken his life story up to his visit to London in 1786. He did not resume the autobiography until after he returned to Monticello. In recent years, his visits to Poplar Forest had become increasingly important to him. Located in Bedford County about seventy miles from Monticello, the Poplar Forest property had belonged to Jefferson ever since the death of his father-in-law John Wayles. Throughout that time, it had remained a working farm. It never really became a vacation retreat until Jefferson began building there during his second term as president.

The house Jefferson built at Poplar Forest was octagonal. Constructed on a slope, it had one story in the front and two in the rear. The center room, twenty feet square, served as the dining room. The drawing room, Jefferson's chambers, three other bedrooms, and the pantry encircled the center room. There was a portico in front, connected to the center room by a vestibule; a terrace on one side; and a verandah in the rear, opening out from the drawing room. Ellen, who often accompanied her grandfather here, found the center room beautiful, the whole house "very pretty and pleasant."[24] Ellen's reminiscence of their visits to Poplar Forest provides the fullest account of their time there. Her sisters, Cornelia and Virginia, often came to Poplar Forest, too, and fondly remembered their experiences.

The seventy-mile trip from Monticello required two overnight stops. Virginia recalled her grandfather's behavior on the road: "His cheerful conversation, so agreeable and instructive, his singing as we journeyed along, made the time pass pleasantly, even travelling through the solitudes of Buckingham and Campbell counties over indifferent roads." Other contemporary accounts verify how much he loved to sing as he traveled. Isaac Jefferson remembered, "Mr. Jefferson [was] always singing when ridin' or walkin'; hardly see him anywhar outdoors but what he was a-singin'. Had a fine clear voice."[25]

Virginia remembered their road food: "Our cold dinner was always put up by his own hands; a pleasant spot by the road-side chosen to eat it, and he was the carver and helped us to our cold fowl and ham, and mixed the wine and water to drink with it." Her reminiscence jibes with her grandfather's advice for traveling through the Virginia countryside: "Cold victuals on the road will be better than any thing which any of the country taverns will give you."[26]

"The roads were not bad for country roads," Ellen recalled. "We always stopped at the same simple country inns, where the country-people were as much pleased to see the 'Squire,' as they always called Mr. Jefferson, as they could have been to meet their own best friends. They set out for him the best they had, gave him the nicest room, and seemed to hail his passage as an event most interesting to themselves." When Jefferson and his granddaughters reached Poplar Forest, the news spread around Bedford County quickly. His neighbors brought him all kinds of fruit, game, poultry, and vegetables. One time a neighbor brought a quarter of a bear cub.[27]

These reminiscences tell a rosy picture of the journey from Monticello to Poplar Forest. With the passage of time, the memories of Jefferson's granddaughters took on a sentimental hue. The letters they wrote at the moment tell a more realistic story. That spring Ellen and Cornelia accompanied their grandfather; Virginia stayed home. Cornelia's first letter to her from the trip captures the difficulties of travel. The day they left Monticello, they reached Warren's Tavern at the peak of a ferocious rainstorm. They were intending to go farther, but the roads were so bad that they were stuck at Warren's all night. The next day they planned to reach Hunter's Tavern but only got as far as Flood's—"horrid Old

Flood's"—where Cornelia and her sister slept "between the sheets that Dr. and Mrs. Flood had been sleeping in for a month." Well, "not *between* them exactly," Cornelia continued, "for finding the counterpane clean we pinn'd the top sheet down close all round and laid upon that."[28]

The hours they spent at these taverns could be quite tedious. They usually brought books along to help them pass the time. On one trip, Ellen brought Catherine Hutton's epistolary novel, *The Miser Married*, which relates the story of a debt-ridden and deceitful widow who marries a miser named Winterdale.[29] Ellen found the first half "insufferably stupid and dull, but," as she wrote to her mother, "the rest amused me a good deal; the character of Lady Winterdale is so well drawn that it redeems the whole book." Ellen was happy she brought some books to read on the road: "We found them a great relief to the ennui of the journey; we got in so early in the evening, and loitered so long at the tiresome taverns, where we stopped to have the horses fed, that reading was a most valuable resource during these weary hours."[30]

That spring they reached Poplar Forest "fatigu'd to death...after the most tedious journey that ever was made," Cornelia said. "I am sure I almost died on the road from impatience."[31]

Since Jefferson had designed Monticello as his personal paradise, a vacation home might seem superfluous. Though life at Monticello often seemed idyllic during his retirement, there was one aspect of it he disliked but was powerless to control: the magnificent home of a well-respected former president proved to be a mecca for gawkers. Poplar Forest offered an escape from the curious and gave him the opportunity to indulge his favorite activities without interruption. As Ellen said, "At Poplar Forest he found in a pleasant home, rest, leisure, power to carry on his favorite pursuits—to think, to study, to read—whilst the presence of part of his family took away all character of solitude from his retreat."[32]

Grandpa Jefferson made sure the children brought much to keep themselves busy throughout their vacation. Ellen typically brought drawing materials and embroidery. Besides the books to read on the road, they also brought other books to read while at Poplar Forest. In one of her letters, Cornelia mentioned bringing a "long row of books."[33] One time Ellen brought the fifth volume of the *British Theatre*, which formed part of the multivolume collection edited by Elizabeth Inchbald.[34] This particular volume contained four works by Shakespeare—*Coriolanus*, *Othello*, *The Tempest*, and *Twelfth Night*—and Ben Jonson's *Every Man in His Humour*.

Jefferson always had plenty of books on vacation. He kept a separate library at Poplar Forest but usually brought some current books with him. Thomas Law's *Second Thoughts on Instinctive Impulses*, for example, he received just before leaving Monticello for Poplar Forest one year. He brought it with him and enjoyed it immensely. The peacefulness of Poplar Forest gave him much time to reflect on Law's ideas and to compose a response to him that amounted to an essay on man's moral sense. As the letter's conclusion explains, "The leisure and solitude of my situation here has led me to the indiscretion of taxing you with a long letter on a subject whereon nothing new can be offered you."[35]

For the most part, the Poplar Forest library was largely a collection of classics. Many of the volumes it contained were small-format books, which Jefferson shelved in handsome mahogany bookcases.[36] The thirty-eight-volume collection of Bell's beautifully illustrated edition of Shakespeare that he had acquired in Europe found its way to Poplar Forest. The 109-volume collection of British poets he had ostensibly purchased for Martha in Paris also became part of Jefferson's vacation library. His granddaughters read their way through this collection of British poets. In one letter, Cornelia quoted lines from William Shenstone's *Poetical Works*, some of the same lines her grandfather had quoted in "Thoughts on English Prosody" three decades earlier.[37]

Jefferson's collection of ancient classics at Poplar Forest was quite full. He had a ninety-eight-volume collection of carefully edited classical works, which he called his petit format library. Other fine editions of classic texts included an edition of Aeschylus with illustrations by the renowned Italian printmaker Domenico Cunego, the rare Aldine edition of Cicero's *De Philosophia* published at Venice in 1541, and a sixteenth-century Greek/Latin parallel text edition of Aesop's *Fables*. That year there were a few empty slots in the Poplar Forest library: Jefferson had recently loaned Francis Eppes his miniature editions of Euripides, Sophocles, and Aeschylus, leaving them at Flood's so that Francis could pick them up there when he passed that way. Sending the tragedies of these three authors to his grandson, Jefferson advised, "The 1st. you will find easy, the 2d. tolerable so; the last incomprehensible in his flights among the clouds."[38]

The Poplar Forest library also included a number of French and Italian authors. Jefferson's collection of French authors included works from many longtime favorites—Corneille, Diderot, Molière, Montesquieu, Voltaire—and some breezier works, such as the scandalous works of the famous seventeenth-century courtesan Ninon de Lenclos. Besides Pietro Metastasio, Jefferson's collection of Italian poetry included works by such authors as Ariosto, Guarini, Petrarch, and Tasso. Ellen remembered him reading Dante, too.[39]

Also included in his library were new editions of old favorites, including an 1817 Edinburgh edition of Lord Kames's *Elements of Criticism*, the 1819 Madrid edition of *Gil Blas*, an edition of Ossian, a six-volume edition of Laurence Sterne's *Works*, and the 1819 edition of F. D. Philidor's *Chess Rendered Familiar by Tabular Demonstrations of the Various Positions and Movements*, which described many different "critical situations and moves" and provided a general introduction to the game by J. G. Pohlman. Playing chess was obviously another frequent activity at Poplar Forest. Jefferson's vacation library also included a new edition of a work by his old friend Madame de Staël, *De la Littérature Considérée dans ses Rapports avec les Institutions Sociales*, which surveyed the literary past in a groundbreaking effort to discern the relationship between literature and society.[40]

Jefferson kept some basic books on mathematics, chemistry, and history at his vacation home, as well, but of all the libraries he assembled in his lifetime, the Poplar Forest collection was the most purely belletristic. The only surviving catalogue of this library is a brief sales catalogue made decades later when it was sold. His granddaughters' letters reveal that Jefferson catalogued the Poplar Forest library himself. This is no surprise. It would have been more astonishing if Jefferson had *not* catalogued the library.

A letter Cornelia wrote from Poplar Forest in 1817 confirms how carefully he organized this library. She had been planning to spend one day copying the illustration of Desdemona from her grandfather's copy of *Othello*. Instead, she and Ellen had to "put numbers" onto all of the books.[41] Numbering the books in his library was the second step in Jefferson's cataloging process, coming after the books were physically arranged on the shelves in the proper order but before the catalogue itself was written.

Jefferson allowed much time for reading at Poplar Forest. His daily vacation schedule was much the same as his Monticello routine. After a long, leisurely breakfast consisting of good food and good conversation, he and his family would go their separate ways until the afternoon, when they would gather for dinner. After dinner, Jefferson would retire for a few hours. He would spend the late afternoon into the evening with his grandchildren. They would go to bed around nine.

Her grandfather's conversation greatly impressed Ellen, who enjoyed not only what he said but also how he listened. She remembered, "He seemed really to take as much pleasure in these conversations with us, as if we had been older and wiser people." Ellen "not only listened with intense interest to all he said, but answered with perfect freedom," conveying her own opinions, asking questions, and making remarks. Spending time with her grandfather at Poplar Forest, she "felt as free and as happy as if I had been with companions of my own age."[42]

Ellen also remembered the subjects her grandfather discussed during their time at Poplar Forest: "He would talk to us about his own youth and early friends, and tell us stories of former days. . . . His conversation was at this time particularly pleasant—easy, flowing and full of anecdote."[43] Ellen's reminiscence offers additional testimony to Jefferson's fondness for anecdotes. Her account of their conversation shows what happened to all those wonderful anecdotes Jefferson omitted from the autobiography: he withheld them to tell his family. The story of his private life Jefferson saved for a private audience.

Once the family came together in the late afternoon, they stayed together until bedtime. They often went outdoors at dusk. Describing a typical evening activity in a letter to his daughter from Poplar Forest, Jefferson wrote, "About twilight of the evening, we sally out with the owls and bats, and take our evening exercise on the terras."[44] There was a new moon on May 1 that year. Imagine how extraordinary the stars looked from the terrace of their remote home at Poplar Forest.

After they came indoors, his granddaughters would bring him his tea, and they would sit together quietly, all reading. Ellen, again: "He would take his book from which he would occasionally look up to make a remark, to question us about what we were reading, or perhaps to read aloud to us from his own book, some passage which had struck him, and of which he wished to give us the benefit." Reading plays was a popular evening activity. Cornelia's interest in *Othello* suggests that reading Shakespeare was a regular activity at Poplar Forest. Ellen admitted that it was her grandfather who exposed her to Shakespeare. He even presented her with the first copy of Shakespeare she ever owned. Ellen's reminiscence does not say which edition of Shakespeare her grandfather bought for her. More than likely, he gave her John Sharpe's tiny nine-volume edition, *The Plays of William Shakespeare in Miniature*, which he had ordered in 1807 but which does not appear in his own library catalogue.[45]

One year at Poplar Forest Cornelia was reading Shakespeare with a purpose: she was planning a home theatrical. She wrote Virginia suggesting possible titles they might perform and offering advice on how to adapt the plays to suit the players. *Macbeth*, she said, had to be trimmed down significantly. But there was a danger in abridging the play. Shrewdly, Cornelia observed that what is tragic in the original could become comic in an abridgment. If they wanted to do a comedy instead,

The Taming of the Shrew was one of her favorites. She also liked *King Lear* very much. In fact, *Lear* might be the best play of Shakespeare's for the family to perform. With Lear's three daughters, there were plenty of good female roles. Some of the minor male roles—such as the husbands of Regan and Goneril—could be eliminated altogether. Their brothers could play the major male roles: Kent, Gloucester, and Lear. Who should play Lear? Well, that part could go to whomever "chose to rave."[46]

That year they returned to Monticello on May 6. Within two weeks, Jefferson was back at work on the autobiography. Reaching the period of the French Revolution, he appears genuinely pleased to have something besides himself to discuss. Though Jefferson's autobiography is one of the finest firsthand accounts of the French Revolution available, as autobiography it is frustrating. Once he introduces this subject, he disappears from the narrative for several pages.

Upon relating the story of the French Revolution, Jefferson admitted that the minuteness of his account was "disproportionate to the general scale of my narrative. But," he continued, "I have thought it justified by the interest which the whole world must take in this revolution."[47] Jefferson shrewdly understood how important the story of the French Revolution was, yet he continually underestimated the importance of his own life story. Though a delegate to the Continental Congress, author of the *Declaration of Independence*, governor of Virginia, author of *Notes on the State of Virginia*, minister plenipotentiary to France, secretary of state, vice president, and president of the United States, Jefferson seems unwilling to admit that the whole world took interest in the story of his life.

The autobiography ends with Jefferson's journey from Virginia to New York after his appointment as secretary of state, during which he saw Benjamin Franklin for the last time. He related their conversation about the autobiography Franklin was writing: "I told him I had learnt with much pleasure that, since his return to America, he had been occupied in preparing for the world the history of his own life."[48] Jefferson then related how Franklin presented him with a fragment of his autobiography and insisted he keep it. After Franklin's death, Jefferson had returned the manuscript to his grandson, William Temple Franklin. Ever since then, Jefferson had wondered what had happened to the manuscript and questioned whether he should have given the manuscript to Temple Franklin, who virtually turned his back on America after his grandfather's death.

Continuing his own autobiography, Jefferson tried to remember as best as he could what had been in the autobiographical fragment Franklin had given him. Filling a gap in Benjamin Franklin's autobiography seems like a strange thing for Thomas Jefferson to do within the pages of his own autobiography, but this section, too, represents an effort to correct what he perceived as an error on his part. Jefferson always re-gretted the loss of historical documents and sought to safeguard them as best he could. Even as he related an episode from Franklin's life, he revealed something of himself: his profound belief in the importance of primary documents to the telling of history.

Jefferson's autobiography ends in anticlimax. After discussing Franklin at length, he added one more sentence—"I arrived at New York on the 21st. of Mar. where Congress was in session"—followed by the statement: "So far, July 29. 21." Having spent nearly seven months on the task, Jefferson was tired of writing about himself. His "So far" hints that he might return to finish the story of his life at a later date. He never did.

The reason Jefferson stopped when he did is not hard to fathom: the next phase of his life, his tenure as secretary of state, he had already written. "Explanations of the 3. Volumes Bound in Marbled Paper" discusses his early experiences as secretary of state, and *The Anas* fills in the remainder of the story. His time as vice president and president could be omitted by much the same excuse he had used to avoid telling the story of his governorship. To write the story of his life as vice president and president of the United States would be to write the public history of the nation.

CHAPTER 41

The University of Virginia from Dream to Reality

The last week of November 1821, Jefferson wrote an eloquent letter to William Short, conveying his hopes for the University of Virginia: "It will be a splendid establishment, would be thought so in Europe, and for the chastity of its architecture and classical taste leaves everything in America far behind it."[1] These words convey the profound satisfaction Jefferson felt at the moment. Finally, his dream of the ideal university was becoming a reality. It had been a long time coming. Construction of the Rotunda had yet to begin, but the rest of the campus was definitely showing signs of progress. Six pavilions, eighty-two dormitories, and two hotels had been completed. Once built, the Rotunda would be the university's centerpiece. It would unify the campus in terms of both its architecture and its function: Jefferson had designed the Rotunda as the library. Just as he had imagined how Monticello would appear before it was finished, he could now imagine how the University of Virginia would appear when it welcomed its first class of students. Maybe not the next year and maybe not even the year after that, but soon it would open, soon it would emerge as a great university.

Jefferson had been dreaming of the ideal university at least since the late 1770s, when he drafted the "Bill for Amending the Constitution of the College of William and Mary," whose twofold purpose had been to turn William and Mary from a school under the auspices of the Church of England into a public institution and to modernize its curriculum to embrace many new fields of study. Though he had established several professorships, he never could implement the full-scale reforms he had envisioned for William and Mary.

Eventually he realized that instead of changing an existing institution, what he really needed to do was to start a new one from scratch. In his last full year as vice president, his plans for a new university developed far enough for him to solicit help from others to design a curriculum. He wrote Joseph Priestley to get his thoughts on the matter, but Jefferson's letter shows that his concept for a state university was already well developed: "We wish to establish in the upper and healthier country, and more centrally for the state, an University on a plan so broad and liberal and *modern*, as to be worth patronising with the public support, and be a temptation to the youth of other states to come, and drink of the cup of knoledge and fraternize with us."[2] He also told Priestley about his desire to recruit professors in Europe and offer them salaries sizable enough to ensure that they would come to Virginia to stay.

Learning of a bill to establish a state university in the General Assembly of Virginia in 1805, Jefferson wrote Littleton Tazewell to offer some thoughts on both the faculty and the administration of the proposed university. When it came to the faculty, Jefferson reiterated ideas he had shared with Priestley and made some further suggestions. He recommended a small board of visitors. The responsibilities of serving as a visitor required intellect, tact, and decisiveness. A university's board of visitors had to analyze all the different fields of study, distribute them into professorships, and superintend the curriculum. Jefferson doubted whether there were enough qualified candidates in Virginia to fill a large board of visitors.[3]

He suggested that the curriculum be as flexible and open-ended as possible. It should be able to change with the times. He was already foreseeing a university that would last for centuries: "What is now deemed useful will in some of its parts become useless in another century." The constitution and statutes of the ideal university should be written to let it keep pace with the progress of knowledge. It should not be like the tradition-bound European universities—Cambridge, Oxford, the Sorbonne—which, he asserted, "are now a century or two behind the science of the age."[4] Actually, Jefferson had great respect for Cambridge and Oxford: this assertion is another hyperbole used for rhetorical purposes.

Jefferson also offered some thoughts on the architecture of the ideal university. The letter to Tazewell represents his earliest known articulation of the idea of a university as a village. This idea would ultimately guide his plans for the University of Virginia. Five years after writing Tazewell on the subject, he expanded his notion of the ideal campus when he offered the following advice to the Trustees for the Lottery of East Tennessee College:

I consider the common plan followed in this country, but not in others, of making one large and expensive building, as unfortunately erroneous. It is infinitely better to erect a small and separate lodge for each separate professorship, with only a hall below for his class, and two chambers above for himself; joining these lodges by barracks for a certain portion of the students, opening into a covered way to give a dry communication between all the schools. The whole of these arranged around an open square of grass and trees, would make it, what it should be in fact, an academical village, instead of a large and common den of noise, of filth and of fetid air. It would afford that quiet retirement so friendly to study, and lessen the dangers of fire, infection and tumult.[5]

Jefferson would follow this advice himself when it came to designing the campus of the University of Virginia.

Taken together, the letters to Priestley, Tazewell, and the Tennesseans show that Jefferson had already formed the basic aspects of his dream university. He imagined its administration, architecture, curriculum, and faculty. There was one thing he needed to make his university a reality, something that no amount of imagination could produce: money, and lots of it. Since he wanted to make the university a public institution, he knew that the capital had to come from the state; therein lay the problem. To build the great university he envisioned would require substantial appropriations from the state legislature. Given the difficulty of obtaining public funds for education, Jefferson slowly realized that it might be better to start his "academical village" on a more modest scale.

In 1814, his nephew Peter Carr was serving as president of the board of trustees for Albemarle Academy, a local institution established years before that had since fallen on hard times. The board wanted to breathe new life into the school. The fact that Carr had assumed leadership as an educator was enough to make his uncle proud: Jefferson had overseen Carr's education, and now Carr was helping to educate a new generation. That year Jefferson was named a trustee to the Albemarle Academy. The original plans for revamping the school were fairly modest. Once Jefferson came on board, the Albemarle Academy began to dream big.

Later that year, he wrote Carr a detailed letter outlining a plan for the academy. This letter forms an important contribution to the history of American educational writing. Jefferson reiterated the statewide system of elementary and secondary education he had been advocating ever since he drafted "A Bill for the More General Diffusion of Knowledge." Though the resources of the Albemarle Academy were modest, he saw no reason to limit the curriculum. If they could only afford to hire four professors, so be it. They should make sure they hired professors who could teach as many subjects as possible.

According to Jefferson's elaborate plan, the first professor would teach ancient and modern languages, ancient and modern history, rhetoric, and oratory; the second professor, anatomy, mathematics, medicine, and physics; the third professor, botany, chemistry, minerals, and zoology; and the fourth would teach philosophy. Jefferson admitted that these fields of study were more "than ought to be imposed on, or can be competently conducted by a single professor permanently." As the school grew, professorships could be subdivided periodically "until each professor shall have no more under his care than he can attend to with advantage to his pupils and ease to himself."[6] In other words, the professorships would become increasingly specialized over time. Jefferson did more than merely project the future of the Albemarle Academy in his letter to Carr; he foresaw the growth of the modern American university.

Capital remained the biggest obstacle preventing the Albemarle Academy from becoming what Jefferson imagined it could be. The board of trustees petitioned the General Assembly of Virginia, asking it to appropriate funds for the school. The board also petitioned to have the name changed to Central College. The state did have some funds available. To its credit, the legislature had created the Literary Fund in 1810 to support education. The Literary Fund stipulated that confiscations, derelict personal property, escheats, fines, forfeitures, and penalties accruing to the state would be appropriated to encourage learning.[7] While a good start, the Literary Fund alone could not provide the kind of capital Jefferson needed to see his educational plans into reality. He realized that he needed help—inside help, someone within the legislature to do his bidding.

The first week of January 1815, Jefferson wrote Senator Joseph C. Cabell to seek his aid in pushing through legislation to benefit Albemarle Academy. He could hardly have made a better choice. A Virginian through and through, Cabell had been born in Amherst County, attended William and Mary, and read law in Richmond. Jefferson met him around 1800, when Cabell, then in his early twenties, had embarked on a program of self-improvement. As he had done for so many other bright, ambitious young men, Jefferson supplied Cabell with a reading list. Actually, he gave him two reading lists, one devoted to English history and another encompassing a wide range of subjects: ancient history, botany, chemistry, ethics, mathematics, medicine, natural history, and politics.[8] Poor health forced Cabell to leave his studies for Europe, where he became the traveling companion of Washington Irving. Back in

Virginia, Cabell entered politics and, in 1810, was elected state senator. He would emerge as one of the most active members of the Virginia Senate.[9]

Jefferson expressed much confidence in Cabell, telling him that the trustees of Albemarle Academy were counting on him as the "main pillar of their support."[10] To fill in the necessary background about the school and its goals, he sent Cabell a detailed letter on July 5, 1815, accompanied by several supporting documents: a copy of his letter to Peter Carr, copies of the petitions to the legislature, and a copy of his letter to John Adams in which he defined the natural aristocracy and explained how his educational system would be able to identify and educate the leaders of tomorrow.

This letter to Cabell shows that Jefferson was thinking about an institution that was much more than a local academy: he was dreaming about his ideal university again.[11] He told Cabell about the possibility of obtaining world-class professors who would make their school superior to any in the United States, possibly superior to any university in Europe. Jefferson's dreams were infectious. Upon reading all the documents he had sent, Cabell needed no more convincing. He took the cause on as his own and fought hard to get the legislation and funds necessary to make the Albemarle school into a great institution, to make Jefferson's dream come alive. Indeed, their correspondence can be read as a chronicle of the early history of the University of Virginia.

A postwar windfall proved a boon for public education in the state. In 1815, Virginia received a surplus from the U.S. government for expenditures made during the War of 1812. It was up to the legislature to decide what to do with this windfall. The day the vote was scheduled, Cabell shrewdly arranged to have the *Richmond Enquirer* publish Jefferson's letter to Peter Carr outlining his system of state education and his plans for the Albemarle Academy. The letter exerted an important influence on the legislators, who voted to add the surplus to the Literary Fund.[12]

Jefferson's plans were being implemented, but he counted progress not in days or weeks, or even months, but in years. In the prehistory of the University of Virginia, one major event is followed by a year of legislative wrangling before another major event occurs. In 1816, the General Assembly passed a bill for establishing a college in Albemarle County. Albemarle Academy would now be Central College. The first meeting of the board of visitors would not take place until May 5, 1817— but what a meeting it would be. No governing board of any American university, before or since, has had a more distinguished membership, which included two former presidents and the current one—Thomas Jefferson, James Madison, and James Monroe, who had been inaugurated earlier that year.

Five more months passed before the cornerstone of the first pavilion was laid on October 6. Central College was finally being built. But Jefferson was not content to stop there. He still wanted to transform the college into a university. Doing that meant going back to the legislature. On February 22, 1818, it passed a bill establishing a state institution of higher learning to be called the University of Virginia.

From Jefferson's perspective, the most natural thing to do would be to turn Central College into the University of Virginia, but the legislature had stipulated three possible locations for the University of Virginia: Charlottesville, Lexington, and Staunton. A conference was scheduled for the first week of August 1818 at Rockfish Gap, about thirty miles west of Monticello. Jefferson presided over the conference. Not surprisingly, the Central College site was chosen as the location for the University of Virginia. The conference also decided upon a general architectural plan and sketched out the curriculum. They decided that the University of Virginia would offer coursework in such disciplines as anatomy and medicine, ancient languages, law, mathematics, modern languages, moral philosophy, natural history, and natural philosophy.

Jefferson took the responsibility of writing a report of the Rockfish Gap conference, which was published as a pamphlet titled *Proceedings and Report of the Commissioners for the University of Virginia, Presented December 8, 1818*. More than merely a set of practical instructions for establishing the University of Virginia, *Proceedings and Report* was recognized as a major treatise on American education. The leading periodicals of the day reviewed the pamphlet and, for the most part, were quite appreciative. The reviewer for the *Analectic Magazine*—to take a periodical Jefferson read, for example—called *Proceedings and Report* "a remarkable instance of practical republicanism" and said that it contained "many novel suggestions worthy the attention of our seminaries of learning already established."[13] *Niles' Weekly Register* reprinted the entire text of *Proceedings and Report*. A headnote explained: "We take a sort of national pride in seeing such papers—from an American pen. It would do honor to any age and any nation.—It is, we believe, with a few variations, from the ever luminous pen of Thomas Jefferson."[14] Beyond their appreciation for his educational scheme, these comments affirm Jefferson's widespread recognition as a great writer.

The fullest notice appeared in that staid and stodgy Boston quarterly, the *North American Review*. While applauding the ambitious educational scheme Jefferson outlined, its reviewer, the Harvard professor Edward Everett did have some misgivings about the design of the campus and the curriculum. Everett was unsure whether it was a good idea to house the professors so close to their students and complained that the plan made no provisions for religious worship. Furthermore, *Proceedings and Report* made inadequate provisions for a university library—"the life and soul of any university."[15]

In terms of the proposed curriculum, Everett approved Jefferson's plan for teaching modern languages and hoped that Yale College and Harvard would follow suit. He also liked the idea of teaching Anglo-Saxon. There was one gap in the modern language curriculum: Portuguese should be taught, as well. Furthermore, Everett wanted to see a professor of divinity. He disliked the idea suggested in *Proceedings and Report* that religion was a subset of ethics and, therefore, important only as a moral supplement. Jefferson's educational scheme institutionalized ideas embodied in his library catalogue, his "Syllabus of an Estimate of the Merit of the Doctrines of Jesus," and *The Life and Morals of Jesus*. But Everett bristled at this approach to religion: "The result of this hazardous experiment it is not for us to anticipate."[16]

Like the British quarterlies on which it was patterned, the *North American Review* assumed a role as guardian and protector of the English language. Even as Everett recommended *Proceedings and Report*, he took issue with Jefferson's neologisms: "We beg leave to commend the whole Report to our readers, as an uncommonly interesting and skilful paper; well assured that they will overlook a little *neologism* in the language, and a few unauthorised words such as *location, centrality, grade*, and *sparse*, for the sake of the liberal zeal for science which it breathes and inculcates."[17]

Jefferson typically enjoyed reading the *North American Review*. He was more tolerant of it than one University of Virginia alumnus, who recommended that a fellow writer throw all his back issues of the journal "out of the window to the pigs."[18] For the most part, Jefferson was pleased with what the *North American Review* said about *Proceedings and Report*. Speaking of its review, Jefferson told John Adams: "I was relieved on finding in it much coincidence of opinion, and even, where criticisms were indulged, I found they would have been obviated had the developments of our plan been fuller. But these were restrained by the character of the paper reviewed, being merely a report of outlines, not a detailed treatise, and addressed to a legislative body, not to a learned academy."[19] Perhaps the reviewer's observation that *Proceedings and Report* lacked a detailed plan for a library hurt Jefferson most. He did have great plans for the university library, but this report was not the place to develop them. He agreed that the library was the life and soul of any university.

The reviewer's critique of Jefferson's neologisms also upset him. It reminded him of the critique of Americanisms that frequently recurred in the British quarterlies. Writing to Adams, Jefferson defended his use of the word "location": "It is a good word, well sounding, obvious, and expresses an idea which would otherwise require circumlocution." Identifying himself as "a friend to *neology*," Jefferson offered Adams a spirited defense of it. Neology was "the only way to give to a language copiousness and euphony." Language must progress with the sciences. As new discoveries are made, new words must be invented to name these discoveries. Jefferson was on a roll. He continued:

And give the word neologism to our language, as a root, and it should give us its fellow substantives, neology, neologist, neologisation; its adjectives neologous, neological, neologistical, its verb neologise, and adverb neologically. Dictionaries are but the depositories of words already legitimated by usage. Society is the work-shop in which new ones are elaborated. When an individual uses a new word, if illformed it is rejected in society, if wellformed, adopted, and, after due time, laid up in the depository of dictionaries. And if, in this process of sound neologisation, our transatlantic brethren shall not choose to accompany us, we may furnish, after the Ionians, a second example of a colonial dialect improving on its primitive.[20]

Though *Proceedings and Report* established the general scheme for the University of Virginia, it still required legislative approval. Finally, on January 25, 1819, the Virginia legislature passed the university bill. Jefferson was officially appointed to the board of visitors the next month, and at the board's first meeting the month after that, he was elected rector of the University of Virginia. He had won the war to establish his ideal university, but many skirmishes remained. While passing the university bill, the legislature still had not appropriated sufficient funds to complete construction, hire the necessary professors, or purchase books for the library. It was not until four years later, in March 1823, that Jefferson could order work on the Rotunda to begin. And not until near the end of 1823 did he receive sufficient financing to hire professors and purchase books.

Jefferson had devoted much time and thought to the makeup of the University of Virginia faculty. He really wanted to hire professors from abroad, but he also knew that doing so would prompt criticism in the United States. Earlier, he had tentatively offered positions to some of the leading intellectuals in America. When Thomas Cooper was teaching chemistry and mineralogy at the University of Pennsylvania, Jefferson invited him to join the Virginia faculty. Cooper was interested in the position, but his radical philosophy and outspoken views against the church made him unwelcome in Virginia. Jefferson offered a professorship to George Ticknor, who turned the position down in favor of a Harvard professorship. He offered the mathematical chair to Nathaniel Bowditch, the Massachusetts astronomer and mathematician whose *New American Practical Navigator* had been recognized for its profound improvement over any similar work. He politely refused the position.[21]

To obtain world-class professors from Great Britain, Jefferson knew he needed to send an agent there personally. He first asked Cabell, who turned down the opportunity. Subsequently, Jefferson asked Francis Walker Gilmer, a young man he had watched mature into a bright and ambitious attorney.

The Gilmers lived in Albemarle County close to Monticello. Francis was born in 1790, but he was orphaned as a boy with the death of his father in 1795 and mother in 1800. He remained in Albemarle after his mother's death, attending James Ogilvie's school and studying French with the finest French teacher in the neighborhood, Martha Jefferson Randolph. Gilmer was an excellent student; his quest for knowledge was nearly insatiable. He attended William and Mary, graduating in 1810. He read law in Richmond under William Wirt and also became a protégé of the Abbé Jose Francisco Corrêa de Serra, the Portuguese philosopher and scientist who was a frequent guest at Monticello. Gilmer began practicing law and pursuing literary projects, as well, including an anthropological essay on the Cherokee, a geological essay on the Natural Bridge, a book titled *Sketches of American Orators*, and a new edition of Captain John Smith's *True Travels* and his *Generall Historie of Virginia*.[22]

On November 25, 1823, Jefferson drafted the formal letter asking Gilmer to undertake the mission to Great Britain on behalf of the University of Virginia. In this letter Jefferson also offered him the chair in law at the University of Virginia.[23] It was not just Gilmer's legal knowledge that qualified him for the position; his wide knowledge in other fields of study enhanced his qualifications. Reiterating the offer in a later letter, Jefferson emphasized that the range of Gilmer's knowledge would help make him an excellent professor. "I abhor the idea of a mere Gothic lawyer," Jefferson said, meaning a lawyer who was uncouth or unpolished, one who knew nothing out of *Coke upon Littleton*, "who would not be able to associate with his colleagues in conversation, or to utter to enquiring strangers a single academical idea."[24]

Jefferson demanded similar qualifications from all his professors. He wanted Gilmer to recruit men who were experts in their own field but who were knowledgeable in other disciplines. There were practical benefits in having professors with a wide range of knowledge: one professor could take over another's class in a pinch. But Jefferson's motivation was not merely practical—he was forming an intellectual circle, one that he could enjoy the rest of his life but that would survive beyond him and perpetuate itself. Furthermore, he recognized that the professors would be representatives of the university. When they spoke with others outside the school, he wanted them to hold their own in any intellectual conversation.

As he knew he would, Jefferson came under fire for recruiting professors from Great Britain. Many newspaper columnists criticized him for not hiring American professors. Even John Adams criticized his decision to hire professors from abroad. Jefferson's long-standing political animosity toward Great Britain was well known, as was his deep-seated American patriotism. But Jefferson understood that neither politics nor patriotism matters when it comes to hiring quality professors. Seeking to establish a high level of academic rigor, Jefferson looked beyond political borders. When it came to making the best possible university he could, Jefferson saw himself as a citizen of the Republic of Letters, a republic that transcended national boundaries.

Gilmer hesitated to accept the chair in law, but in the spring of 1824, he accepted the responsibility of going to Great Britain to recruit professors for the University of Virginia. Jefferson gave him detailed instructions: Cambridge would be the best place to find experts in the fields of mathematics, natural philosophy, and natural history; Oxford would be better for finding an expert in ancient languages; and Edinburgh would be the best place to recruit a professor in anatomy and medicine. Gilmer was to make inquiries about the temper and sobriety of the candidates. Jefferson considered men with families to be acceptable, perhaps even be preferable—but no clergymen.[25]

The first candidate Gilmer met in London was George Blaettermann, who had already taken the initiative and applied for the chair in modern languages on his own. Born in Saxony, Blaettermann had a remarkable capacity for languages, eventually learning Anglo-Saxon, Danish, Dutch, English, French, Italian, Portuguese, Spanish, and Swedish. He was living in London when Gilmer arrived. He was forty-two, but Gilmer did not see his age as an obstacle. "Finding no specific objection, nor indeed any objection, to Dr. Blaettermann," Gilmer hired him for the chair in modern languages.[26]

Recruiting the remaining professors would be more difficult. In late June he went to Cambridge but was disappointed to learn that students and professors alike had left on vacation. Gilmer dawdled there a few weeks but to no avail. Next he headed north to Edinburgh, where he fared no better. He reached a low point the second week of August, when he wrote Jefferson from Edinburgh that he might not return with any other professors besides Blaettermann. Jefferson had set extremely high standards, and Gilmer was having trouble finding candidates with the necessary qualifications.

He left Edinburgh to give Cambridge another try. Toward the end of August he met Thomas Hewitt Key. At twenty-five, Key was "an intelligent and fine young man, distinguished even at Cambridge for his mathematical genius and attainments, and M.A. of that university." He perfectly suited Jefferson's requirement that the professors be experts in their own fields and qualified in others. Besides being a mathematician, Key had also studied medicine, and he was an expert Latinist—indeed, it was as a Latin scholar that Key ultimately established his lasting reputation. Gilmer hired him to fill the chair of pure mathematics.[27]

From Gilmer's perspective, Key offered another advantage: he promised to help recruit more professors for the University of Virginia. Key introduced Gilmer to his friend George Long, the youngest of Gilmer's recruits. Long was twenty-three and looked even younger than that. Though an excellent classical scholar, Long did not know Hebrew, which Jefferson wanted the professor of ancient languages to teach. Gilmer explained to him, "Oriental literature is very little esteemed in England, and we might seek a whole year, and perhaps not at last find a real scholar in Latin and Greek, who understands Hebrew."[28] The only way he could hire a Hebrew scholar was to violate the "no clergymen" rule. George Long was hired as chair of ancient languages.

By mid-September, Gilmer had also recruited the chair of anatomy and medicine, Dr. Robley Dunglison. At twenty-six, Dunglison already had medical degrees from the Royal College of Surgeons and from the University of Erlangen. In 1824, Dunglison published his first major medical work, *Commentaries of Diseases of the Stomach and Bowels of Children.*[29] Before the month was out, Gilmer had recruited Charles Bonnycastle as professor of natural philosophy. He, too, had expertise in many fields, having studied mathematics at the Royal Military Academy. As professor of natural philosophy, Bonnycastle would become a favorite among University of Virginia students. He emphasized the importance of laboratory work and introduced raised benches in the classroom to let students observe demonstrations.[30]

Gilmer left London for New York in October, having filled five professorships. The chair in chemistry remained unfilled. Though Gilmer contracted a serious illness during the ocean crossing, from which he never fully recovered, he remained in New York to find a professor of chemistry. He eventually hired John Patton Emmett, who also excelled in botany, mathematics, and zoology.[31]

The professor of moral philosophy and the professor of law Jefferson had always planned to hire locally. He found in George Tucker an excellent candidate for the chair in moral philosophy. Tucker, at forty-nine, was the oldest professor and became the first chairman of the faculty. Before joining the university, he had already distinguished himself in terms of both public service and publications. *The Valley of Shenandoah*, his 1824 novel, is considered the precursor to the plantation novels that would flourish in the antebellum South.[32] His *Essays on Various Subjects of Taste, Morals, and National Policy*, published two years before, had more appeal to Jefferson. The chair in law, however, remained unfilled.

By November 1824, the University of Virginia campus was ready to receive its professors. Construction was not completely finished, but it was finished enough that Jefferson would be able to open the university early next year as he had hoped. The dormitories and pavilions were completed. The Rotunda still lacked columns, but the dome itself and its interior were finished. In fact, the first week in November, the Rotunda became the site of a gala affair, a huge banquet in honor of the Marquis de Lafayette.

Having arrived in New York several weeks earlier, Lafayette was on a triumphal tour through the United States. He was fêted wherever he went. The first week of November he reached Albemarle County. Naturally, he stayed with his old friend Thomas Jefferson. Their reunion on Thursday, November 4, proved to be warm and tender-hearted. The following day, an elaborate procession took them from Monticello to the Central Hotel in Charlottesville to the campus of the University of Virginia and up the steps of the Rotunda. Four hundred people gathered beneath the great dome, including many of the most influential men in Virginia. The banquet tables were set up in concentric circles: an appropriate formation. Like a pebble dropped in a pond, Jefferson's mind affected those around him by creating a series of increasingly widening circles.

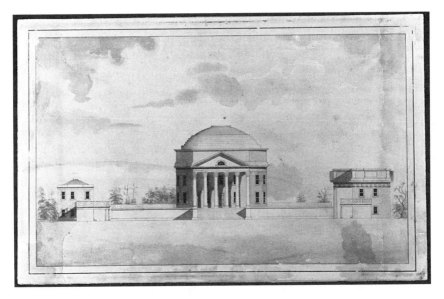

South Elevation of the Rotunda (1823). (MSS 2332, Special Collections, University of Virginia Library)

Once the tablecloths were removed after dinner, the toasts began. The toast to Lafayette, the *Richmond Enquirer* reported, "was received with enthusiastic cheering—the lofty dome of the Rotunda re-echoed back the sound—it rolled in billowy volumes around the spacious Hall, and sunk in the deep stillness of enthusiasm." Jefferson himself was the object of the sixth toast: "Thomas Jefferson and the Declaration of Independence—Alike identified with the cause of liberty."[33]

Jefferson had written a prepared speech, but he did not deliver it himself. Instead, he gave it to the master of ceremonies for him to read. Though the ostensible purpose of this banquet was to honor Lafayette, Jefferson also saw it as a celebration of the opening of the University of Virginia. His speech shows that he was using the occasion to generate additional support for the university. He explained:

My friends I am old, long in the disuse of making speeches, and without voice to utter them. In this feeble state, the exhausted powers of life leave little within my competence for your service. If, with the aid of my younger and abler co-adjutors, I can still contribute any thing to advance the Institution, within whose walls we are now mingling manifestations to this our guest, it will be, as it ever has been, cheerfully and zealously bestowed. And could I live to see it once enjoy the patronage and cherishment of our public authorities with undivided voice, I shall die without a doubt of the future fortunes of my native state, and in the consoling contemplation of the happy influence of this institution on its character, its virtue, its prosperity and safety.[34]

Though the campus itself was ready to welcome the student body, Jefferson knew he could not open the university without professors. As winter approached, he grew anxious about them. By the end of November, Long had reached New York. So had Blaettermann and his family. Dunglison and Key were unmarried when Gilmer first met them, but both had wanted to stay in England to marry English wives before coming to America. ("Tho' if they would take my advice," Gilmer said, "they would prefer Virginians.") Blaettermann called on Gilmer in New York to let him know that Bonnycastle, Dunglison, and Key would be sailing on the *Competitor* directly to Norfolk.[35]

A few days after he arrived, Professor Long walked to Monticello to meet Jefferson. Long remembered the moment all his life.[36] Once he was shown inside, he waited a few minutes before "a tall dignified old man" entered. Before saying anything, Jefferson took a moment to size him up.

"Are you the new professor of antient languages?" Jefferson asked.

Long said that he was.

"You are very young," Jefferson observed.

"I shall grow older," Long responded.

Jefferson smiled.

Despite his youthful appearance, Long greatly impressed Jefferson, who told Senator Cabell that he was "a most amiable man, of fine understanding, well qualified for his department, and acquiring esteem as fast as he becomes known."[37] Blaettermann was less impressive. Jefferson called him "rather a rough looking German, speaking English roughly, but of an excellent mind and high qualifications."[38] As the old year gave way to the new, there was still no sign of the other professors from England. Both Jefferson and Cabell feared the worst. There had been a terrible storm in October, and they worried that the *Competitor* had been lost at sea.

Word had got around that the university would open on February 1. Jefferson was afraid that the students would arrive by then only to be disappointed. The first week of January he detailed their dilemma to Cabell. To send the students back would be discouraging, but to open the university without professors in either mathematics or natural philosophy would be ridiculous.[39] At the end of January, Cabell read an item in the Norfolk press, which he quickly relayed to Jefferson. As of December 5, the *Competitor* was still at Plymouth. A combination of contrary winds, poor equipment, and mismanagement had kept the vessel there for weeks.[40]

Disappointed that they were so far behind schedule, Jefferson was nonetheless relieved that they were alive. His response to Cabell, which incorporates a delightful double entendre, shows that he had retained his sense of humor through these times of uncertainty: "Although our professors were on the 5th of December still in an English port, that they were safe raises me from the dead; for I was almost ready to give up the ship."[41] Upon receiving Cabell's letter the first week of February, Jefferson did some quick calculations and figured that the professors would arrive any day. In fact, Bonnycastle, Dunglison, and Key reached Norfolk on February 10.

The students moved in the first week of March. It rained the whole week, but the weather did little to dampen their spirits. Moving into a university dormitory for the first time, then as now, is a special experience, one simultaneously thrilling yet contemplative. Moving into a brand new university, a university designed, built, and administered by the author of the *Declaration of Independence*, was an unparalleled experience. When the University of Virginia officially opened on March 7, 1825, Jefferson realized his hopes and dreams for higher education.

CHAPTER 42

The Life and Soul of the University

When the University of Virginia officially opened its doors the first week of March 1825, the same week John Quincy Adams was inaugurated president, the school's library remained far from completion—but not from want of trying. Besides giving Francis Walker Gilmer the responsibility of recruiting professors in Great Britain, Jefferson had also assigned him the task of purchasing books for the university while there. He wrote Gilmer a letter of introduction to the distinguished critic and scholar Samuel Parr, asking for his help. And he recommended that Gilmer contact Lackington's, the London bookseller who had supplied numerous books for his personal library in the past. Parr turned out to be a great help. With his advice, Gilmer put together an excellent catalogue of classical books for the university.[1]

Gilmer delayed the purchase of many books until after he had recruited some of the professors, wisely thinking that they could help him choose the best works in the best editions at the best prices. He visited Lackington's but discovered that the original bookshop of that name had long since gone out of business. There was still a shop called Lackington's in Finsbury Square, but it was a shadow of its former self. Parr told Gilmer not to deal with the new Lackington's at all. Bohn, a bookseller in Covent Garden, proved to be much better. He offered to underbid any other bookseller in London. Gilmer accepted the offer and was pleased with the results. Bohn partly filled his order from stock and special ordered many additional titles from the Continent.

By the time he left London for New York, Gilmer was quite pleased with the books he had bought. He had acquired all of the Anglo-Saxon books Jefferson had requested. He may have contacted Anna Gurney, the Anglo-Saxon scholar who had translated the *Saxon Chronicle* in 1819 and issued it in a limited impression for private circulation. Learning about the need for books at the fledgling university, she donated a copy of her edition.[2] The mathematical library, Gilmer boasted, "is superior to any I saw in G. B. and yet it was not expensive." The classics and the works of modern language were the most expensive books.[3]

In his quest for books, Gilmer had worked under a disadvantage. Though Jefferson had supplied him with a list of Anglo-Saxon titles and had suggested some general subject areas, he largely let Gilmer decide what to buy. It was not until after Gilmer went to Great Britain that Jefferson compiled a catalogue of necessary books for the library. The project turned out to be more work than he had anticipated. The second week of August 1824, he wrote James Madison, telling him that the catalogue "has been laborious far beyond my expectation, having already devoted 4. hours a day to it for upwards of two months, and the whole day for some time past and not yet in sight of the end." He asked Madison to help him compile the section on divinity. Later he wrote George Ticknor, asking him to compile a list of important works in German literary history.[4]

Once Jefferson finished compiling the catalogue, it listed nearly seven thousand volumes he wanted to acquire for the university. Like his previous catalogues, this one, too, is divided into three sections according to Francis Bacon's memory-reason-imagination scheme. Each section is divided into different subject areas, each major subject area receiving its own chapter. Altogether, the catalogue contains forty-two chapters.[5]

While working on his catalogue in the summer of 1824, Jefferson received a letter from William Hilliard, a partner in Cummings, Hilliard, and Company, a Boston bookselling firm. Hilliard's letter was not unexpected. Earlier that year, a friend of his, Joseph Coolidge, Jr., had visited Monticello. Speaking with Jefferson about his plans for the university library, Coolidge highly recommended the firm, which had been instrumental in supplying books to Harvard and other schools. Hilliard had numerous correspondents in all the big publishing centers of Europe, from whom he could obtain virtually any book he wished. When Coolidge returned to Boston, he encouraged Hilliard to write Jefferson. Hilliard took his friend's advice and offered to supply the University of Virginia with whatever books it needed. He also informed Jefferson that he had been on an extensive book-buying tour of Europe. With his letter, Hilliard enclosed a recent catalogue to give Jefferson an indication of his stock.[6]

Coolidge was also friends with George Ticknor. In fact, Ticknor was the one who had written Coolidge a letter of introduction allowing him to visit Monticello and make Jefferson's acquaintance. Coolidge could not thank Ticknor enough. He and Jefferson became good friends. In Coolidge, Jefferson found another cultured, intelligent, well-educated young man from Boston. Perhaps there was hope for New England yet. But it was the friendship Coolidge formed with another member of the Jefferson family that made him most grateful. When he visited Monticello in the spring of 1824, he fell in love with Jefferson's granddaughter Ellen. Before leaving Monticello that spring, he made plans to return in the fall. Upon his return, he and Ellen were engaged. Together they began to plan a spring wedding.

Love was in the air at Monticello that year. Nicholas Trist and Ellen's sister Virginia were already engaged, and had been for years. He was back in New Orleans early that year. Virginia's sisters were wondering when Nicholas would ever settle down. Ellen wrote him a charming letter in March, ending it by reminding him that Virginia's "character, temper and understanding as she has advanced to complete womanhood have developed themselves in a way to render her the darling of her family." Ellen explained that in terms of magnanimity, warmth, and purity of heart, Virginia was unsurpassed.[7]

Ellen's words may have had an effect. Trist returned to Monticello that summer, determined now more than ever to get serious about his life. He and Virginia were wed the second Saturday in September. The newly married couple settled down at Monticello. Trist read law under his grandfather-in-law and worked as his personal secretary, an invaluable experience. Trist's notes form an important record of Jefferson's final years. With his grandfather-in-law's guidance, Trist was able to channel his restless energy. He went on to have a distinguished diplomatic career.

The month Nicholas and Virginia were wed, Jefferson wrote Cummings and Hilliard, proposing that the firm establish a bookstore in Charlottesville, where they could sell textbooks to the students. Jefferson was not yet willing to hire them as booksellers to the University of Virginia, but he strongly suggested that if their bookstore went well, they would be able to expand their business significantly.[8] Jefferson could not really make any large-scale acquisitions for the university library until he learned what Gilmer had purchased. He did order a few books from the catalogue Hilliard had sent, including Bryan Walton's *Biblia Sacra Polyglotta*, a six-volume folio edition of the Bible with text in Arabic, Aramaic, Ethiopic, Greek, Hebrew, Latin, Persian, and Syriac. He also ordered Edmund Castell's two-volume *Lexicon Heptaglotton*, a dictionary of Hebrew, Latin, Persian, and the Semitic languages.[9] Jefferson held great hopes for his students. He was ordering books that would let them pursue studies that went far beyond the established curriculum.

In January 1825, eight boxes of books from London reached Charlottesville. The books Bohn ordered from the Continent were being shipped to Virginia directly and would not arrive for months. Comparing what Gilmer had purchased with what he wanted for the library, Jefferson realized that he needed to order many more books and decided to take Hilliard up on his offer. He wrote him a letter, enclosing it with a letter to Coolidge. Jefferson asked Coolidge to deliver the letter in person, so he could answer any questions Hilliard or Cummings may have had.[10]

For the moment, Jefferson's advice to Hilliard mainly concerned the shop they would establish in Charlottesville. He recommended that it stock "respectable books, leaving only novels and poetry to the other bookshops generally." Once the university opened, there would be much demand for schoolbooks. It would also attract business from nearby classical schools. Coolidge called on Hilliard, delivered the letter, and answered all the questions he could. Hilliard still had more questions, but those could wait until either he or a partner reached Charlottesville to ask Jefferson directly. The bookstore Hilliard and Cummings established near campus was only partly successful. Its manager, Mr. Jones, had little knowledge of books. The professors complained that it never stocked enough textbooks for the students.[11]

Almost a member of the family, Coolidge told Jefferson that he wanted to help the University of Virginia any way he could. Jefferson took him up on the offer and sought his help obtaining a clock and a bell for the Rotunda. Coolidge also donated several books from his personal collection to the university library. Some were books he had read in school: a Greek grammar, a Greek reader, a Hebrew grammar, a Hebrew lexicon, a number of scholarly editions of Latin classics, and textbooks treating every major field of mathematics from arithmetic to calculus. Coolidge also donated a variety of other books, including Henry Aldrich's *Elements of Civil Architecture*, a work that had been instrumental in encouraging the Palladian movement, and Andrea Palladio's *I Cinque Ordini di Architettura*. Among the science books he donated were Jacob Bigelow's *Florula Bostoniensis*, the standard manual of New England botany, and Parker Cleaveland's *Elementary Treatise on Mineralogy and Geology*, the first American textbook on the subject.[12]

Not to be outdone by his future brother-in-law, Nicholas Trist donated some books, too: Louis Hennepin's *New Discovery of a Vast Country in America* and William Smith's *History of New York*. Jefferson wanted to assemble a good collection of American history, so both of these books were welcome gifts. He also encouraged others to donate books to the library. In Virginia, donating books became a fashionable way to support the university. Theodore Hansford of King George County donated what he called "some books of rare occurrence and ancient edition." Actually, the books he donated, mainly seventeenth-century editions of classical authors—Epictetus, Isocrates, Plautus, Sophocles—were not as rare as he imagined, but they were useful books for students taking Professor Long's course in ancient languages. Lafayette donated a copy of Augustin Thierry's three-volume *Histoire de la Conquête de l'Angleterre par les Normands*, a forward-thinking work exemplifying the author's belief that the writing of history must be continually reviewed and revised.[13]

J. Evelyn Denison, a Member of Parliament from Newcastle-under-Lyme, was another who donated books to the University of Virginia. His donation, like Lafayette's, was inspired by a visit to Virginia. In April 1825, Denison and some fellow Members of Parliament called at Monticello. They had arrived in New York the previous July and had been traveling around the United States ever since. Announcing their arrival, one American newspaper reporter observed, "If the object of these members be to travel in the new world, they may see many novelties, and learn many wise lessons."[14] While in Virginia, they saw the university and learned about it from its rector. Denison was pleased that Jefferson had recruited professors from England, but he recognized the animosity the imported professors had caused. Throughout his time in America, Denison had read numerous newspaper articles—"puny squibs," in Jefferson's words—snidely criticizing Jefferson's supposed neglect of American intellectuals.

The contract that Jefferson signed with William Hilliard in April stipulated that he supply Hilliard's firm with a catalogue of requested titles. Since Jefferson had prepared a catalogue the previous year, getting it ready for Hilliard did not seem like much work at first, but it was. He had to reconcile the books Bohn had sent with the catalogue and cancel duplicate listings. His granddaughter Virginia helped out considerably. She rewrote the entire catalogue, finishing it in June.[15]

Jefferson could not wait until the catalogue was finished to place some orders. Writing to Hilliard on Sunday, May 22, 1825, he requested three works in particular and asked them to send the books immediately: George Brodie's *History of the British Empire*, John Lingard's *History of England*, and Sharon Turner's *History of the Anglo-Saxons*.[16] Jefferson hated the thought that his students might learn English history solely from reading Hume, and he wanted to counteract that possibility fast: Turner offered an alternate version of early English history that refuted

Hume's; Brodie's history contained a critical examination of Hume's description of the English government; and Lingard's was the first serious, thorough, scholarly English history to appear since Hume's *History of England*. Lingard had set out, unostentatiously and inoffensively, to refute Hume historical era by historical era. Throughout his multivolume *History of England*, Lingard established a reputation for rigorous research and the critical use of original sources.[17]

Henry Tutwiler, a distinguished University of Virginia student who had the pleasure to dine with Jefferson and speak with him on multiple occasions, vividly remembered his comments about Hume: "He used to say that the reading of Hume would make an English Tory, and that the transition to an American Tory was an easy one. He never failed to recommend to the youthful student, as an antidote to Hume, Brodie's *British Empire*; the latter, he said, had 'pulverized' Hume."[18]

Along with these three works of English history, Jefferson also ordered several works of Americana. Hilliard had recently sent him a catalogue of duplicates from Harvard. Jefferson noticed several titles in the catalogue that he wanted for the University of Virginia, but he hesitated to purchase them due to their cost. He found a few that were reasonably priced, including Francisco Alvarez's *Noticia del Establecimiento y Poblacion de las Colonias Inglesas en la America Septentrional*, which surveyed the English colonies from a Spanish perspective, and Henri Joutel's *Journal Historique du Dernier Voyage que Feu M. de LaSale Fit dans le Golfe de Mexique*. The most comprehensive account of La Salle's expedition available, Joutel's *Journal* contained important information regarding the history of Texas and the Mississippi River Valley. American history was not a part of the curriculum, but French and Spanish were. Students could improve their foreign language skills by reading about America.

The week he placed his order to Hilliard, Jefferson took a break from the enormous amount of work he was doing on behalf of the university and its library. On Friday, May 27, all library business, all university business, all everything business was set aside: it was on this day that Ellen Wayles Randolph and Joseph Coolidge were wed. The wedding took place in the drawing room at Monticello. Thomas Jefferson was happy to see his favorite granddaughter marry such a bright and kind young man, but his joy was tinged with sadness as he realized that Ellen would be leaving for her husband's home in faraway Boston. Once she and Joseph left on their honeymoon, a circuitous, thousand-mile journey, her grandfather often gazed wistfully toward her empty chair. Whenever her sisters saw him doing this, one of them would hurry and take her seat. However, none of them could take Ellen's place in her grandfather's heart.[19]

Saddened by her absence, Jefferson was pleased to gain a lively correspondent in the bargain. Some of the best letters he wrote the last year of his life were to Ellen, and some of the best he received that year were by her. After her grandfather, Ellen was the best writer in the family, though Cornelia came a close second. Almost as soon as she reached Boston, Ellen wrote to tell him about their honeymoon. To give her "an idea of the beauty and prosperity of the New England States," Joseph Coolidge had arranged a trip that took them all around New England.[20] Upon reaching New York, they sailed up the Hudson to Albany. From there, they proceeded overland to Saratoga, Lake George, and Lake Champlain, reaching as far north as Burlington, Vermont. They traveled overland from Burlington to the Connecticut River, down which they sailed to Springfield and from there proceeded to Boston.

Ellen went well beyond merely listing the places she visited. She also described the people she met and the sights they saw. A visit to a cotton factory prompted a comparison between factory workers and farmers. Her words suggest that the United States was entering a new era, an era that neither she nor her grandfather was anxious to see:

> I have visited one only of the great cotton factories which are beginning to abound in the country; and, although it was a flourishing establishment, and excited my astonishment by its powers of machinery, and the immense saving of time and labor, yet I could not get reconciled to it. The manufacturer grows rich, whilst the farmer plods on in comparative poverty; but the pure air of heaven, and the liberty of the fields in summer, with a quiet and comfortable fire-side in winter, certainly strikes the imagination more favorably, than the confinement of the large but close, heated, and crowded rooms of a factory; the constant whirl and deafening roar of machinery; and the close, sour and greasy smells emitted by the different ingredients employed in the different processes of manufacturing cotton, and woollen cloths: also, I fancied the farmers and labourers looked more cheerful and healthy than the persons employed in the factories, and their wives and daughters prettier, and neater, than the women and girls I saw before the looms and spinning jennies.[21]

Ellen apparently learned travel writing from her grandfather. In terms of its content, this letter closely resembles his own, yet in a way, Ellen's travel writing goes beyond her grandfather's, for it embodies a keen pictorial sensibility he often excluded from his accounts of travel. Describing the country girls in New England, she said that they "are well looking, healthy and modest, and the cows laden with their milky treasures might, any one of them, serve as a study for a painter who desired to express this sort of abundance."[22] Her idyllic depiction of the farmers' daughters makes it sound like she is describing a Constable painting. Ellen's preference for the farming life over the life of the factory girls also shows that she shared her grandfather's outlook toward the superiority of the agricultural life.

Jefferson received her letter with excitement. Responding to Ellen, he admitted how much he missed her: "We did not know, until you left us, what a void it would make in our family. Imagination had illy sketched its full measure to us: and, at this moment, every thing around serves but to remind us of our past happiness, only consoled by the addition it has made to yours."[23] The details of her itinerary brought back fond memories of the trip he had taken with James Madison in 1791. Recalling the journey to Ellen, Jefferson revealed a twinge of nostalgia, but he had little time to dwell on the past. His eyes were fixed on the future: he foresaw the graduates of the University of Virginia as the new leaders of the nation.

In his letters to Ellen, Jefferson offered an idealized view of the university. She received a different picture from her mother and sisters. Writing in mid-July, Cornelia told her, "The news of the neighborhood is the chit chat and scandal of the University and every thing that passes there."[24] The influx of college students had changed the whole social dynamic of Albemarle County. Initially, the local girls welcomed the college boys, but before long the liberties the boys took offended them. Because of the students' improper behavior, the girls now refused to attend any on-campus barbecues.

In one letter that summer, Cornelia offered Ellen a general survey of the faculty. Ever since he first started building Monticello, their grandfather had imagined it as the center of a tight-knit intellectual circle. Now it had become so. Jefferson frequently invited the professors and their wives to Monticello, and his family came to know them well. Cornelia told Ellen that Professor Key was considered "the finest fellow that ever trod the earth." Professor Bonnycastle was quite amiable, too. Professor Emmett was "warm in his likings and dislikes; fiery, and so impetuous even in lecturing that his students complain his words are too rapid for their apprehension; they cannot follow him quick enough; to which he answers, they must catch his instruction as it goes, he cannot wait for any man's understanding." Professor Blaettermann was a bit gruff at first but had apparently mended his ways and become "very popular among the students."[25] The only person Cornelia could not stand was Mrs. Blaettermann. A "vulgar virago" she called her. To give Ellen an idea of Mrs. Blaettermann, Cornelia quoted from William Shenstone's poem "A Proposal to Advice": "There's not such a b—— in king George's dominion / She's peevish, she's thievish, she's ugly, she's old / And a liar, and a fool and a slut and a scold."[26]

Joseph Coolidge became one of Jefferson's regular correspondents, too. The letters to Joseph and those to Ellen parallel letters Jefferson had written husbands and wives in the past. Men received stories of conflict; women were treated with pictures of harmony. The night of October 1, 1825, a riot broke out on the University of Virginia campus. Jefferson wrote Joseph about it on October 13, shortly after punishment had been meted out. He did not write Ellen about the incident until the following month when the matter had cooled down. Instead of providing any more details to her, her grandfather described the state of the university now that the crisis had subsided: "A perfect subordination has succeeded, entire respect towards the Professors, and industry, order, and quiet the most exemplary, has prevailed ever since."[27]

In his letter to Joseph, on the other hand, Jefferson related the story of the riot. Fourteen students "animated first with wine, masked themselves so as not to be known, and turned out on the lawn of the University, with no intention, it is believed, but of childish noise and uproar." When two professors went to investigate, the students insulted them and even threw stones at them. The two professors each seized an offender. Before they could discern their identities, the students escaped. Ultimately, all fourteen culprits were identified. Three were expelled; the others were reprimanded. Toward the end of his letter, Jefferson mentioned one of the three in more detail, "My dear Ellen may be told that at the head of the expelled, as of the riot, was W. M. C., expelled from two other seminaries before."[28]

This last sentence helps explain the differences between the two letters. Jefferson related the story of the riot to his grandson-in-law but left him to decide how to tell his wife. Jefferson did not forbid Joseph from telling Ellen about the riot, but he did give him the responsibility of mediating the story for her. Even as he told Joseph the story, Jefferson shaped it to soften its details and make it more abstract. He identified one culprit by his initials but kept the others anonymous. The two professors who confronted the students remain anonymous in Jefferson's account. Attributing the riot to general childishness, Jefferson further softened the story. If he had his way, Ellen would receive a twice-filtered version of the story, one that he softened in his letter to Joseph, which Joseph would soften himself as he related it to Ellen.

As things turned out, Ellen received the whole, unfiltered story from her mother, who had written her the same day Jefferson wrote Joseph. Martha named not only the two professors (Tucker and Emmett), but also the three students who were expelled (Ayre, Cary, and Thompson). Furthermore, she mentioned another incident that had occurred the night before the October 1 riot, when "a young Man of the name of Ayre, a rich fool, threw a bottle, with a pack of cards in Mr Long's window [and] cursed the 'European professors.' "[29] In his letter to Joseph, Jefferson did not mention this incident at all. He could not have done so without undermining the general motive of childishness he attributed to the rioters. Martha also wrote that Professors Long and Key, weary of coping with the unruly students, had submitted their resignations. Jefferson had said nothing about this in his letter, either. (Holding them to their contracts, the board of visitors refused to accept their resignations.)

Jefferson was an eternal optimist. He told the story of the riot in as positive a light as possible. He was convinced that everything would turn out fine. Though he respected the intelligence of both Joseph and Ellen, he told the story the way he did not only to protect Ellen's delicate sensibilities but also to emphasize his authority. As both patriarch of the family and rector of the university, he was the one ultimately in charge of maintaining order. Martha, on the other hand, wrote to capture the drama of the moment. She loved and respected her father, but she did not find it necessary to hide facts from her daughter to protect her father's image of authority. In her eyes, his authority was so firmly established that no amount of bad news could tarnish it. Martha saw nothing wrong with depicting him as he was, even down to his frailties. That fall, in fact, he was quite ill, and Martha said so. He had been sick before the riot, which now exacerbated his illness. Martha told Ellen, "Your dear Grand father is not so well. The fatigue of the last week has thrown him back a good deal and obliged me to encrease his nightly dose of laudanum to 100 drops."[30]

Though Jefferson had little respect for physicians in general, he was impressed with Dr. Dunglison, who attended him regularly that fall. By late November, Jefferson health improved considerably. Writing to Ellen again, Martha explained, "My father's health is wonderfully improved but as usual when he gets better he will venture too far and injures him self. He had ridden 5 miles on horse back without inconvenience, and extending it still farther he fatigued him self and passed a bad night, but he is again recovering from it and I hope will be more cautious; the doctor has always protested against exercise on horseback." In a postscript, she informed Ellen that they had just heard that Bernhard, Duke of Saxe-Weimar-Eisenach, had arrived in Charlottesville that day. "Of course," she wrote, we "shall have him for dinner."[31] They dispatched a messenger to town to extend the invitation to him. He happily accepted.

The duke's *Travels through North America* provides a good indication of the state of the university and its rector that November. The duke apparently took a self-guided tour of the campus. The Rotunda remained unfinished, but he recognized its similarity to the Pantheon and could see its potential: "The interior of the library was not yet finished, but according to its plan it will be a beautiful one." He disliked the design of the pavilions: "As for the rest, the ten buildings on the right and left are not at all regularly built, but each of them in a different manner, so that there is no harmony in the whole, which prevents it from having a beautiful and majestic appearance."[32]

Without a guide, the duke had no one to tell him that such irregularity was intentional. The University of Virginia campus was a living museum: each pavilion was different to teach students the different styles of architecture. Though critical, the duke's description shows that the university's architectural style, like so much of Jefferson's creative work, combined elements of classicism and Romanticism. The Pantheon-inspired Rotunda aligned the campus within the classical tradition, but the irregularity of the pavilions, along with other irregular features such as the crooked garden walls, which the duke liked very much, aligned it with Romanticism, the celebration of irregularity being one of its defining characteristics.

By chance, the duke and his party encountered Dr. Dunglison, who introduced himself and showed them the library, currently housed in Pavilion VII. The library "was still inconsiderable," the duke noted, but it was accumulating a good collection of German books. Dunglison showed him several belletristic works, including *Almanach Dramatischer Spiele zur Geselligen Unterhaltung auf dem Lande*, the dramatic yearbook August von Kotzebue founded in 1803 and had continued editing since then. Furthermore, Dunglison informed him that many more books were on their way.

Unable to find transportation from Charlottesville to Monticello, the duke had to walk three miles. He arrived just as dinner was being served. Jefferson rose from the table and came to greet him and his party. The duke was a big, strapping fellow. William Wirt, who had dined with him in Baltimore, called him "brawny, muscular, and of herculean strength." He looked "like a Russian, or one of those gigantic Cossacks." The duke was flattered when Jefferson "ordered dinner to be served up anew" upon his arrival.[33]

The dinner company that evening included Martha, Professor Key, and his wife Sarah. Though Professor Key had tried to resign from the university the previous month, Jefferson, through sheer force of personality, had reconciled him to staying. The duke was thoroughly impressed with the master of Monticello: "In conversation he was very lively, and his spirits, as also his hearing and sight, seemed not to have decreased at all with his advancing age. I found in him a man who retained his faculties remarkably well in his old age, and one would have taken him for a man of sixty."[34]

After dinner, Jefferson invited the duke to stay the night. The evening proved to be absolutely delightful. Sitting by the fire, Jefferson and his guests discussed natural history, the fine arts, and travel. Jefferson "spoke also of his travels in France, and the country on the Rhine, where he was very much pleased."

As the first school year ended in December, Jefferson looked forward to the next one, which would begin in February after a winter break. The University of Virginia had gone without a chair in law for the first year, but that fall Jefferson offered it to Gilmer again, who accepted the position this time. Sadly, he would not live to fill the chair. He died the month the second year began.

One of the most progressive aspects of Jefferson's curriculum concerned the amount of personal choice students had when it came to designing their own course of study. They could choose whatever courses they wished. Edgar Allan Poe, the most famous student who entered the university during its second year, took Professor Long's Ancient Languages and Professor Blaetterman's Modern Languages. Poe greatly appreciated the intellectual life the University of Virginia offered. He joined a club called the Jefferson Literary Society and became its secretary. Members discussed books they had read, made recommendations for reading, and shared writings of their own composition.[35]

Though Jefferson often invited students to dinner at Monticello, there is no direct evidence that Poe dined with him. According to another student who did, Jefferson's dinner invitations were both systematic and insistent. If a student were unable to visit Monticello when invited, Jefferson made sure to invite him again. During these dinners, he would talk books with the students and offer them reading advice. The books Poe read at the University of Virginia provide the most suggestive evidence that he received literary advice from Jefferson and acted upon it: they include John Lingard's *History of England*.[36]

Jefferson turned eighty-three on April 13, 1826. He remained in fairly good health and was still riding every day. Jeff Randolph recalled, "He retained to the last his fondness for riding on horseback; he rode within three weeks of his death, when from disease, debility and age, he mounted with difficulty."[37] In June, he received an invitation from General Weightman, the mayor of Washington, D.C., to attend the fiftieth anniversary celebration of the *Declaration of Independence* on July 4. Jefferson responded on June 24, refusing the invitation but offering some spirited comments on the importance of the event.

Jeff Randolph, Nicholas Trist, and Dr. Dunglison, all of whom attended Jefferson during his last days, each left detailed accounts of the experience, and their accounts closely coincide.[38] To be sure, no one nursed him more during his final days than his daughter Martha, but she could never bring herself to write about her father's death, so her whereabouts during his last illness has escaped history.

Dr. Dunglison wrote that on Sunday, July 2, Jefferson was affected with stupor, experiencing "intervals of wakefulness and consciousness." On Monday, the third, the stupor became almost permanent. About seven o'clock that evening, Jefferson awoke to see Dr. Dunglison at his bedside.

"Ah! Doctor, are you still there?" he asked. The doctor could scarcely make out his words. His voice was husky and indistinct. "Is it the 4th?"

"It soon will be," the doctor replied.

While seated by his bedside around eleven o'clock that evening, Nicholas Trist heard him ask the same question.

"This is the Fourth?"

Trist could tell that Jefferson was just trying to hang on until the Fourth of July. He could not bear to tell him it was not, so he ignored the question.

"This is the Fourth?" Jefferson asked again.

The Fourth remained an hour away, but Trist could no longer bear watching his father-in-law suffer in agony. Trist nodded.

"Ah," Jefferson murmured, "just as I wished."

His family recognized the significance of Jefferson living until the Fourth of July, but with only one hour to go, they were not sure he was going to make it. Jeff Randolph soon entered his room. He remembered, "As twelve o'clock at night approached, we anxiously desired that his death should be hallowed by the Anniversary of Independence. At fifteen minutes before twelve we stood noting the minute hand of the watch, hoping a few minutes of prolonged life." Jefferson lapsed into a stupor once more, but as the sun rose on July 4, 1826, he still lived.

Seated by his bedside later that morning, Nicholas Trist knew it was just a matter of hours. He put pen to paper and wrote a letter to Joseph Coolidge. Dated "His bedside, July 4th, 1826, 9.15, A.M.," Trist's letter begins, "There is no longer any doubt, unless one chance to a hundred thousand, or a million, may be ground for doubt. He has been dying since yesterday morning; and until twelve o'clock last night, we were in momentary fear that he would not live, as he desired, to see his own glorious Fourth. It has come at last; and he is still alive, if we can apply the word to one who is all but dead. He has been to the last, the same, calm, clear-minded, amiable philosopher."

About eleven o'clock, as Jeff Randolph remembered, his grandfather looked toward him and slightly moved his lips. Jeff applied a wet sponge to his mouth, "which he sucked and appeared to relish—this was the last evidence he gave of consciousness." At 12:50 that afternoon, Thomas Jefferson breathed his last.

A parallel scene was taking place simultaneously to the north in Quincy, Massachusetts. This afternoon, John Adams lay on his deathbed, too. He expired at 6:20 that evening.

When the news got out that both Thomas Jefferson and John Adams had died on the same day and that day happened to be July 4, 1826, the fiftieth anniversary of the *Declaration of Independence*, many Americans saw it as a sign from God, a divine blessing of the United States and all that it represented.[39]

God had nothing to do with it. The fact that both Thomas Jefferson and John Adams survived until July 4, 1826, indicates that these were two great men, strong of mind, strong of body, strong of will: both proud of having signed the *Declaration of Independence*, both proud of their contributions to their nation and to the development of democracy, and both with the will, the endurance, the patience, the sheer stubbornness to live long enough to witness the fiftieth anniversary of the founding of the United States of America.

Ever disdainful of ceremony, Jefferson wanted his burial to be "private, without parade." The family did not send out funeral notices, but somehow the word got out. His casket was borne from Monticello to the private cemetery a little way down the hill, where a huge crowd of friends and neighbors had gathered.

Jefferson wrote his own epitaph:

HERE WAS BURIED
THOMAS JEFFERSON
AUTHOR OF THE
DECLARATION
OF
AMERICAN INDEPENDENCE
OF THE
STATUTE OF VIRGINIA
FOR
RELIGIOUS FREEDOM
AND FATHER OF THE
UNIVERSITY OF VIRGINIA

The spare quality of this epitaph has puzzled many people, who cannot understand why he made no mention of the fact that he was president of the United States, vice president, secretary of state, minister plenipotentiary to France, or president of the American Philosophical Society. But his neglect of these roles in his epitaph is consistent with the long-standing discomfort Jefferson experienced when writing about himself. The accomplishments he did list were more important to him and much more fundamental.

Again laying personal claim to the *Declaration of Independence*, Jefferson expressed his pride in creating the document that shook off the yoke of monarchy and tyranny, brought the Enlightenment to politics, and established the world's first modern democracy. The Statute for Religious Freedom he saw as a parallel document to the *Declaration*. Whereas the *Declaration* let man break free from political tyranny, the Statute for Religious Freedom let man break free from religious tyranny. Education offered the best way to ensure and perpetuate democracy. Naming himself the father of the University of Virginia, he conveyed the pride he took in the institution, but he was also depicting himself as a representative of the powers of education. There is continuity to the three accomplishments he listed in his epitaph. The first two establish democracy and freedom from tyranny. The third ensures that democracy and freedom from tyranny will continue into the future.

Sadly, the father of the University of Virginia did not live long enough to witness the completion of the university library. Even in his final illness, he had continued building the collection. From his deathbed, he wrote Joseph Coolidge asking his help obtaining some additional books for the library. At the time of his death, the library was still housed in Pavilion VII. Once the books were finally moved into the Rotunda, they

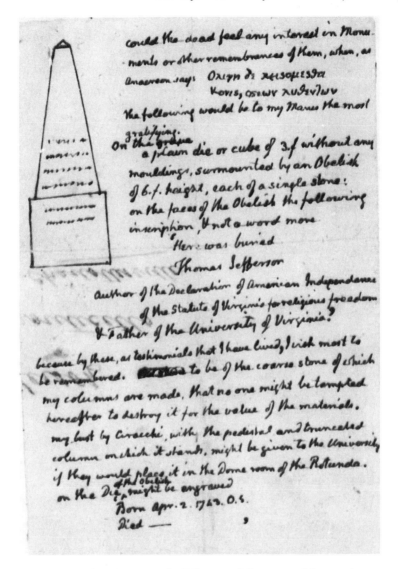

Jefferson's Design for His Epitaph. (Library of Congress, Manuscripts Division)

made an impressive sight. As Edgar Allan Poe observed, "They have nearly finished the Rotunda—The pillars of the Portico are completed and it greatly improves the appearance of the whole—The books are removed into the library—and we have a very fine collection."[40]

Besides Lingard's *History of England*, Poe also read John Marshall's *Life of George Washington*, another work Jefferson talked much about—but not in a good way. Whereas Jefferson recommended that students read Lingard's history, he cautioned them about reading Marshall's biography. Neither of these books was required for Poe's coursework in ancient and modern languages. Reading both, he was doing just what Jefferson wanted students to do: read on their own and think on their own. Though only a first-year student, Poe chose to be examined with the seniors and earned honors in both Latin and French.[41] The time Poe spent at Jefferson's university helped prepare him for a life of writing.

In a short story titled "The Power of Words," Poe suggested that words can exist indefinitely. Once uttered, a phrase can trigger a series of reactions with extraordinary, far-reaching, unimaginable results. Words even have the power to alter the physical universe. The words one character speaks in Poe's story ultimately create a whole new world. Poe was writing fantasy, of course, but it is not difficult to find a real-world equivalent in Thomas Jefferson's life and work. What Jefferson wrote more than two hundred years ago lives on today. His writings continue to influence people across the United States and around the globe. The powerful words of Thomas Jefferson created a nation and pointed the world toward democracy.

ACKNOWLEDGMENTS

The Road to Monticello makes use of a largely unutilized source in Jefferson studies, that is, the marginalia in books that survive from his library. I am grateful to the staff of the Rare Book and Special Collections Reading Room at the Library of Congress for all of their help. Many books formerly in Jefferson's possession also survive at the University of Virginia, and I thank the staff of the Special Collections department there for all of their help, especially since they were in the process of moving to their fine new building during my stay in Charlottesville. The American Philosophical Society also has books in its collections from Jefferson's retirement library that contain his marginalia. I thank Roy Goodman for all of his help at the American Philosophical Society.

I also thank other libraries for their assistance and cordiality: Colonial Williamsburg, Historical Society of Pennsylvania, Huntington Library, Library Company of Philadelphia, and the Virginia Historical Society. A special thanks goes to the Interlibrary Loan department at the Max Chambers Library, University of Central Oklahoma, which was instrumental in obtaining many hard-to-find items.

My wife, Myung-Sook, patiently shared me with "Jeffy" for more than five years.

This book is dedicated to my parents. They did not realize what they were starting when they took me to Colonial Williamsburg as a boy thirty-seven years ago. Or maybe they did.

AN ESSAY ON SOURCES

Eighty years have passed since John Livingston Lowes first published *The Road to Xanadu*, a landmark study of the mind of Samuel Coleridge. Lowes's basic purpose was to study what books Coleridge read in order to determine how they shaped his life and work. *The Road to Monticello* shares a similar purpose: to study what Thomas Jefferson read and what he wrote to show how the written word shaped his life. My title deliberately echoes Lowes's to express my indebtedness to his work. Though *The Road to Xanadu* has helped inspire *The Road to Monticello*, a number of other essential works also deserve mention.

Anyone who has made a cursory study of Jefferson scholarship knows E. Millicent Sowerby's magnificent *Catalogue of the Library of Thomas Jefferson*. Though a scholarly landmark, Sowerby's *Catalogue*, paradoxically, has sometimes proven to be a barrier to further study. It is so detailed that some readers have assumed that it is the last word on Jefferson's library. Nothing could be further from the truth. Despite the length of the completed work, Sowerby's assignment was fairly narrow. The Library of Congress assigned her the task of identifying and cataloguing the books from Jefferson's great library that Congress purchased in 1815. She did not attempt to identify the books Congress did not receive. She did not reconstruct the Shadwell library, which was largely destroyed in the fire of 1770. She did not reconstruct Jefferson's Annapolis library, which he sold to James Monroe. She did not reconstruct his vacation library at Poplar Forest. She did not reconstruct his retirement library. Nor did she consider books belonging to the family members who lived at Monticello.

These comments are meant to explain Sowerby's work, not to diminish her achievement. Her catalogue of Jefferson's library remains the fullest repository of information for understanding the life of his mind.

Furthermore, it has served as a model for the catalogues of several other prominent bookmen in early America. As Edwin Wolf II observed in his preface to a reissue of Sowerby's autobiography, *Rare People and Rare Books*, "She created a monument, a monument flawed... by characteristically Sowerbian impatience with detail, but she had a grand scheme." *The Road to Monticello* makes extensive use of Sowerby's *Catalogue*. To keep the notes to a minimum, I cite Sowerby only when I have taken information or quoted from her annotations to the catalogue.

No one can write about Jefferson without expressing gratitude to Princeton University Press and the editors of *The Papers of Thomas Jefferson*. Begun by Julian P. Boyd with the release of the first volume in 1950, *Papers* is now thirty-two volumes strong, and it has made it only through the year 1800. The papers of Jefferson's presidency are yet to come. In addition, Princeton University Press has issued a number of separate works as part of the Second Series of Jefferson's *Papers*. Each edited by a different editor or set of editors, all are models of scholarship. Douglas L. Wilson's edition, *Jefferson's Literary Commonplace Book*, has been most valuable for the present work, but the other volumes in the Second Series have also been useful. *Memorandum Books*, edited by James A. Bear, Jr., and Lucia C. Stanton, is a magisterial work. In 2004, a new phase in the Jefferson *Papers* was inaugurated with the publication of the first volume of the Retirement Series under the general editorship of J. Jefferson Looney. If the first volume is any indication, the Retirement Series will sustain the high quality of scholarship Julian P. Boyd established more than a half century ago.

Whenever possible, I have cited primary texts from the Princeton edition of Jefferson's *Papers*, but because the Princeton edition, except for the initial volume of the Retirement Series, has yet to cover the last quarter century of Jefferson's life, I cite numerous other sources, too. Four multivolume editions of Jefferson's collected writings preceded *Papers*. In 1829, Jefferson's grandson Thomas Jefferson Randolph published the first collected edition of his writings, the four-volume *Memoir, Correspondence, and Miscellanies, from the Papers of Thomas Jefferson*, the edition Thomas Peacock called "one of the most important publications ever presented to the world" (*Westminster Review* 13 [1830]: 312). In 1859, H. A. Washington published a nine-volume edition, *The Writings of Thomas Jefferson*. In the 1890s, Paul Leicester Ford issued a ten-volume edition, *The Writings of Thomas Jefferson*, which was rereleased in a twelve-volume collector's edition in 1904. In 1903–1905, Andrew A. Lipscomb and Albert E. Bergh issued *The Writings of Thomas Jefferson* in twenty volumes. All of these editions are now available online in fully searchable texts.

A number of other scholarly editions of Jefferson letters are more specific in scope. These include *Family Letters of Thomas Jefferson*, an edition of Jefferson's letters to his daughters and grandchildren and their letters to him edited by Edwin M. Betts and James A. Bear; Lester J. Cappon's *Adams-Jefferson Letters*, which presents the complete correspondence between Thomas Jefferson and Abigail and John Adams; Worthington Chauncey Ford's *Thomas Jefferson Correspondence*, an edition of letters from the collections of William K. Bixby; Donald D. Jackson's *Letters of the Lewis and Clark Expedition*; *Writings*, Merrill D. Peterson's Library of America edition; James Morton Smith's *Republic of Letters*, a three-volume edition of the correspondence between Thomas Jefferson and James Madison; and many, many others.

The protocol I followed for documentation in *The Road to Monticello* was to cite Jefferson's writings from the *Papers* if possible; if a document was unavailable in the *Papers*, then I cited one of the more specific scholarly editions; if a document was unavailable in either the *Papers* or the more specific collections, I then cited one of the older collected editions, in the following priority: Ford, Washington, Randolph, Lipscomb and Bergh. Although the Lipscomb and Bergh edition is the fullest collected edition before the *Papers*, it is quite weak in terms of its editorial standards and generally should be avoided if possible.

With my documentation, I have tried to strike a balance between giving credit where credit is due and telling a good story. In other words, I have avoided placing a note directly after the most dramatic moments in this book, the reconstructed bits of conversation. I never could bring myself to place a note number directly after an exclamation mark, either. In these cases, the documentation is usually tucked into the preceding note. In the quotations themselves, I have silently emended a few of Jefferson's idiosyncrasies: his use of "it's" for "its" and his disuse of capital letters to start sentences—whenever necessary, I have changed Jefferson's lowercase letters to capitals. And sometimes I have silently expanded abbreviations whenever necessary for clarity.

Much of Jefferson's correspondence remains unpublished. The fullest collection of letters survives in the Manuscripts Division of the Library of Congress. I am grateful for the help I received when I visited the Library of Congress in 2004. I am also pleased that so much of Jefferson's unpublished correspondence has been made available online in facsimile as part of the American Memory project. Another extraordinary online collection, the *Family Letters Project*, presents the correspondence of Thomas Jefferson's extended family in facsimile and transcription.

Numerous biographies of Thomas Jefferson have preceded this one. Henry S. Randall's three-volume biography, *The Life of Thomas Jefferson*, which first appeared in 1858, was the fullest biography written to that date. It suffers from the same flaws of most large nineteenth-century biographies: Randall was a powerful writer in his own right, but all too often he let his quotations bear the burden of biography. Still, his work remains useful for those long quotations. He corresponded with Jefferson's grandchildren and many others who knew him and were still alive in the 1850s. Randall's biography largely determined the course of Jefferson biography for the next century. Writing in 1943 in *Jefferson: The Road to Glory, 1743–1776*, the first volume of her multivolume biography, Marie Kimball observed, "The majority of more recent biographies are little more than a paraphrase and condensation of Randall." Kimball released two subsequent volumes but did not live to see her biography to completion. Dumas Malone released the first volume of his multivolume biography, *Jefferson and His Time*, in 1948, five years after Kimball's first volume. Malone did live long enough to see his biography to completion when the sixth and last volume appeared in 1981. Something similar to what Kimball said about biographies since Randall's can now be said about biographies since Malone's. The majority of them are little more than a paraphrase and condensation of Malone.

Though there have been dozens of Jefferson biographies, remarkably, there has never been a literary biography until now. This is not to say that Jefferson's biographers have ignored the place of literature in his life, but literature has typically been treated solely as a means of exploring other aspects of Jefferson's life. In *The Inner Jefferson: Portrait of a Grieving Optimist* (1995), for example, Andrew Burstein examines Jefferson as a letter writer and also takes a look at his reading of Laurence Sterne. In his follow-up study, *Jefferson's Secrets: Death and Desire at Monticello* (2005), Burstein begins by arguing that the medical books in Jefferson's library, few as they were, contributed significantly to his way of thinking. Though Burstein deals with Jefferson as both reader and writer in these two works, his purpose is not to emphasize the importance of literature but rather to use Jefferson's literary interests as a starting point to plumb the depths of his mind or, in Burstein's words, to "crack the shell and find an internal energy, a man both imaginative and emotional, who stands up to dissection" (p. xiii).

The purpose of *The Road to Monticello* is much different. It is based on the fundamental belief that literature is important in and of itself and that a literary life is a life worth living. Jefferson was a multifaceted man whose literary life is significant regardless how it touched other aspects of his life. Literary biography is important for the same reasons literary history is important: it shows the importance of this art form known as literature to the life of man. Some good work has been done previously in this regard, especially by Douglas L. Wilson, who has written on the classical foundations of Jefferson agrarianism, Jefferson's early notebooks, Jefferson's library, the composition of *Notes on the State of Virginia*, Jefferson and the Republic of Letters, and Jefferson and French literature. *The Road to Monticello* combines previous scholarship with new information to tell the detailed story of Jefferson's life of the mind.

Abbreviations

The following abbreviations are used in the documentation to indicate frequently cited sources:

AJL	*The Adams-Jefferson Letters: The Complete Correspondence between Thomas Jefferson and Abigail and John Adams.* Ed. Lester J. Cappon. 1959. Reprint; Chapel Hill: University of North Carolina Press, 1987.
ANB	*American National Biography.* Ed. John A. Garraty and Mark C. Carnes. New York: Oxford University Press, 1999. 24 vols.
Bernard, *Retrospections*	Bernard, John. *Retrospections of America, 1797–1811.* Ed. Mrs. Bayle Bernard. New York: Harper & Bros., 1887.
Cabell	Cabell, Nathaniel Francis, ed. *Early History of the University of Virginia as Contained in the Letters of Thomas Jefferson and Joseph C. Cabell.* Richmond: J. W. Randolph, 1856.
Daybooks	*Virginia Gazette Daybooks, 1750–1752 & 1764–1766.* Ed. Paul P. Hoffman. Charlottesville: University of Virginia Library, 1967.
DLC	Library of Congress.
EG	*Jefferson's Extracts from the Gospels: "The Philosophy of Jesus" and "The Life and Morals of Jesus."* Ed. Dickinson W. Adams and Ruth W. Lester. Princeton, N.J.: Princeton University Press, 1983.
Family Letters	*Family Letters of Thomas Jefferson.* Ed. Edwin M. Betts and James A. Bear, Jr. Columbia: University of Missouri Press, 1966.

First Forty Years	Smith, Margaret Bayard. *The First Forty Years of Washington Society*. Ed. Gaillard Hunt. New York: Charles Scribner's Sons, 1906.
FLP	*Family Letters Project: The Correspondence of Thomas Jefferson's Family Members*. 2006. http://familyletters.dataformat.com.
Ford	Ford, Paul Leicester, ed. *The Writings of Thomas Jefferson*. Federal Edition. New York: G. P. Putnam's Sons, 1904–1905. 12 vols.
Gribbel	Gribbel, John, ed. *Reminiscences of Patrick Henry in the Letters of Thomas Jefferson to William Wirt*. Philadelphia: John Gribbel, 1911.
Jackson	Jackson, Donald D., ed. *Letters of the Lewis and Clark Expedition, with Related Documents, 1783–1854*. Urbana: University of Illinois Press, 1962.
Jefferson at Monticello	*Jefferson at Monticello: Memoirs of a Monticello Slave, as Dictated to Charles Campbell by Isaac... The Private Life of Thomas Jefferson by Rev. Hamilton Wilcox Pierson*. Ed. James A. Bear, Jr. Charlottesville: University Press of Virginia, 1967.
L&B	Lipscomb, Andrew A., and Albert E. Bergh, eds. *The Writings of Thomas Jefferson*. Washington, D.C.: Thomas Jefferson Memorial Association of the United States, 1903–1905. 20 vols.
LCB	*Jefferson's Literary Commonplace Book*. Ed. Douglas L. Wilson. Princeton, N.J.: Princeton University Press, 1989.
LDC	*Letters of Delegates to Congress, 1774–1789*. Ed. Paul Hubert Smith and Ronald M. Gephart. Washington, D.C.: Library of Congress, 1976–2000. 26 vols.
Memorandum Books	*Jefferson's Memorandum Books: Accounts, with Legal Records and Miscellany, 1767–1826*. Ed. James A. Bear, Jr., and Lucia C. Stanton. Princeton, N.J.: Princeton University Press, 1997. 2 vols.
NSV	*Notes on the State of Virginia*. Ed. William Peden. Chapel Hill: University of North Carolina Press, 1955.
ODNB	*Oxford Dictionary of National Biography*. Ed. H. C. G. Matthew and Brian Harrison. New York: Oxford University Press, 2004. 60 vols.

Papers	*The Papers of Thomas Jefferson*. Ed. Julian P. Boyd et al. Princeton, N.J.: Princeton University Press, 1950–. 32 vols. to date.
PTJRS	*The Papers of Thomas Jefferson: Retirement Series*. Ed. J. Jefferson Looney et al. Princeton, N.J.: Princeton University Press, 2004–. 1 vol. to date.
Randall	Randall, Henry S. *The Life of Thomas Jefferson*. New York: Derby & Jackson, 1858. 3 vols.
Sowerby	Sowerby, E. Millicent. *Catalogue of the Library of Thomas Jefferson*. Washington, D.C.: Library of Congress, 1952–1959. 5 vols.
VMHB	*Virginia Magazine of History and Biography*.
Washington	Washington, H. A., ed. *The Writings of Thomas Jefferson: Being His Autobiography, Correspondence, Reports, Messages, Addresses, and Other Writings, Official and Private*. New York: Derby & Jackson, 1859. 9 vols.
Webster, "Notes"	Webster, Daniel. "Notes of Mr. Jefferson's Conversation 1824 at Monticello." *The Papers of Daniel Webster*, Vol. 1: Ed. Charles M. Wiltse et al. Hanover, N.H.: University Press of New England, 1974; pp. 370–378.
WMQ	*William and Mary Quarterly*. Arabic numerals preceding the abbreviation denote the series.

NOTES

Chapter 1: Fire!

1. *Virginia Gazette*, February 22, 1770; Randall, 1: 59.
2. *Memorandum Books*, 1: 158.
3. T.J. to James Ogilvie, February 20, 1771, *Papers*, 1: 63.
4. T.J. to John Page, February 21, 1770, *Papers*, 1: 34–35.
5. T.J. to John Page, December 25, 1762, *Papers*, 1: 3.
6. T.J. to John Page, February 21, 1770, *Papers*, 1: 35.
7. T.J. to George Wythe, January 16, 1796, *Papers*, 28: 583–584.
8. *Thomas Jefferson's Prayer Book*, ed. John Cook Wyllie (Charlottesville, Va.: Meriden Gravure, 1952).
9. T.J. to Thomas Adams, February 20, 1771, *Papers*, 1: 62.
10. *Daybooks*, fol. 191.
11. *LCB*, 182.
12. Laurence Sterne, *The Works of Laurence Sterne*, 5 vols. (London: n.p., 1769), 5: 294.
13. David Pearson, *Provenance Research in Book History: A Handbook* (London: British Library, 1994), 19.
14. James A. Bear, Jr., *Thomas Jefferson's Book-Marks* (Charlottesville, Va.: Alderman Library, 1958), 8.
15. "Life of Thomas Wilson, D.D.," *Christian Journal and Literary Register* 3 (1819): 166.
16. Douglas L. Wilson, *Jefferson's Books* (Charlottesville, Va.: Thomas Jefferson Memorial Foundation, 1996), 19; Bear, *Thomas Jefferson's Book-Marks*, 3.
17. "Books in Colonial Virginia," *VMHB* 10 (1903): 391; *Daybooks, passim*; Perkins, Buchanan & Brown to T.J., October 2, 1768, *Papers*, 1: 34.
18. Kevin J. Hayes, "How Thomas Jefferson Read the Qur'an," *Early American Literature* 39 (2004): 247–261.
19. John Dixon Hunt, *Greater Perfections: The Practice of Garden Theory* (Philadelphia: University of Pennsylvania Press, 2000), 208.

20. Carsten Ruhl, "England," *Architectural Theory from the Renaissance to the Present: 87 Essays on 117 Treatises*, ed. Christof Thoenes (Los Angeles: Taschen, 2003), 422–424.

21. Oliver Macdonagh, "The Origins of Porter," *Economic History Review*, n.s. 16 (1964): 530–535; T.J. to Vine Utley, March 21, 1819, Randall, 3: 450; T.J. to Martha Jefferson Randolph, October 20, 1806, *Family Letters*, 289.

22. Susan Kern, "The Material World of the Jeffersons at Shadwell," *3WMQ* 62 (2005): 213–232.

23. T.J. to John Minor, August 30, 1814, Ford, 11: 421.

24. T.J. to Maria Cosway, October 12, 1786, *Papers*, 10: 447.

25. Martin C. Battestin, *The Providence of Wit: Aspects of Form in Augustan Literature and the Arts* (Charlottesville: University Press of Virginia, 1989), 46–47.

26. Stephen Switzer, *Ichnographia Rustica*, 3 vols. (1718; reprint, New York: Garland, 1982), 3: 13–14.

27. François-Jean Chastellux, *Travels in North America in the Years 1780–81–82* (New York: White, Gallaher, & White, 1827), 227, 229.

28. Quoted in Margaret Bayard Smith, *The First Forty Years of Washington Society*, ed. Gaillard Hunt (New York: Charles Scribner's Sons, 1906), 80–81.

Chapter 2: A Boy and His Books

1. T.J. to Maria Cosway, December 24, 1786, *Papers*, 10: 627.

2. Kevin J. Hayes, *Folklore and Book Culture* (Knoxville: University of Tennessee Press, 1997), 9–10.

3. T.J. to Wilson Miles Cary, August 12, 1787, *Papers*, 12: 23.

4. T.J. to James Madison, December 28, 1794, *Papers*, 28: 229.

5. John Page, "Governor Page," *Virginia Historical Register, and Literary Note Book* 3 (1850): 144.

6. *Memorandum Books*, 1: 12; Nathaniel P. Poor, *Catalogue: President Jefferson's Library* (Washington, D.C.: Gale & Seaton, 1829), lots 800–801; T.J. to James Jay, April 7, 1809, Jefferson Papers (DLC).

7. T.J. to Francis Hopkinson, February 18, 1784, *Papers*, 6: 542.

8. T.J. to William Duane, March 22, 1806, Ford, 10: 242.

9. T.J. to Benjamin Hawkins, August 4, 1787, *Papers*, 11: 684.

10. T.J. to Cornelia Randolph, April 3, 1808, *Family Letters*, 339.

11. William Douglas, *The Douglas Register*, ed. William MacFarlane Jones (1928; reprint, Baltimore: Genealogical Publishing, 1966), 7.

12. Frederick Lewis Weis, *The Colonial Clergy of Virginia, North Carolina and South Carolina* (1955; reprint, Baltimore: Genealogical Publishing, 1976), 15, 20.

13. William Meade, *Old Churches, Ministers and Families of Virginia* (Philadelphia: Lippincott, 1857), 1: 457–459.

14. T.J. to Thomas Law, June 13, 1814, *EG*, 355.

15. James Moore and Michael Silverthorne, "Gershom Carmichael and the Natural Jurisprudence Tradition in Eighteenth-Century Scotland," *Wealth and Virtue: The Shaping of Political Economy in the Scottish Enlightenment*, ed. Istavn Hont and Michael Ignatieff (New York: Cambridge University Press, 1983), 73–87.

16. *Autobiography*, Ford, 1: 5.

17. William Dawson to the Bishop of London, March 1, 1748, "Documents Relating to the Early History of the College of William and Mary and to the History of the Church in Virginia," *2WMQ* 20 (1940): 216.

18. Marie Kimball, *Jefferson: The Road to Glory, 1743–1776* (New York: Coward-McCann, 1943), 31.

19. T.J. to Overton Carr, March 16, 1782, *Papers*, 6: 166.

20. "The Statutes of the College of William and Mary, Codified in 1736," *1WMQ* 22 (1914): 288.

21. *LCB*, 82–89.

22. Kevin J. Hayes, *A Colonial Woman's Bookshelf* (Knoxville: University of Tennessee Press, 1996), 62.

23. Douglas L. Wilson, "Thomas Jefferson's Library and the French Connection," *Eighteenth-Century Studies* 26 (1993): 674.

24. Weis, *The Colonial Clergy of Virginia, North Carolina and South Carolina*, 20; G. McLaren Brydon, "The Virginia Clergy: Governor Gooch's Letters to the Bishop of London, 1727–1749," *VMHB* 32 (1924): 212, 333.

25. Daniel Defoe, "A Relation of the Apparition of Mrs. Veal," *The Book of the Short Story*, ed. Alexander Jessup and Henry Seidel Canby (New York: D. Appleton, 1926), 203.

26. Hayes, *Colonial Woman's Bookshelf*, 56–57.

27. *Autobiography*, Ford, 1: 4; "Notes from the Record of Albemarle County," *VMHB* 26 (1918): 318; "Books in Colonial Virginia," *VMHB* 10 (1903): 391; William Peden, "Some Notes Concerning Thomas Jefferson's Libraries," *3WMQ* 1 (1944): 266.

28. Richard Beale Davis, "Jefferson as Collector of Virginiana," *Studies in Bibliography* 14 (1961): 117–144.

29. H. Trevor Colburn, *The Lamp of Experience: Whig History and the Intellectual Origins of the American Revolution* (1965; reprint, New York: Norton, 1974), 35–36.

30. Gray, *Account*, 71; T.J. to George Washington Lewis, October 25, 1825, Jefferson Papers (DLC).

31. Hayes, *Colonial Woman's Bookshelf*, 116–117.

32. T.J. to the Editor of the *Journal de Paris*, August 29, 1787, *Papers*, 12: 61–62.

33. James Gilreath and Douglas L. Wilson, *Thomas Jefferson's Library: A Catalog with the Entries in His Own Order* (Washington, D.C.: Library of Congress, 1989), 98.

34. T.J. to John Adams, October 12, 1813, *AJL*, 385.

35. Hayes, *Folklore and Book Culture*, 89–102.

Chapter 3: A Correct, Classical Scholar

1. T.J. to Thomas Jefferson Randolph, November 24, 1808, *Family Letters*, 362–363.

2. Marie Kimball, *Jefferson: The Road to Glory, 1743–1776* (New York: Coward-McCann, 1943), 24–25.

3. *Autobiography*, Ford, 1: 5; *LCB*, 202; Richard Beale Davis, *Intellectual Life in the Colonial South, 1585–1763*, 3 vols. (Knoxville: University of Tennessee Press, 1978), 1: 303.

4. Jonathan Boucher, *Reminiscences of an American Loyalist, 1738–1789*, ed. Jonathan Bouchier (Boston: Houghton Mifflin, 1925), 60–61. For Maury's biography, see Homer D. Kemp, "James Maury," *American Colonial Writers, 1735–1781*, ed. Emory Elliot (Detroit: Gale, 1984), 156–158.

5. James Blair to the Bishop of London, February 19, 1742, in Park Rouse, Jr., *James Blair of Virginia* (Chapel Hill: University of North Carolina Press, 1971), 253.

6. James Blair to the Bishop of London, February 19, 1742, in Rouse, *James Blair*, 253.

7. Frederick Lewis Weis, *The Colonial Clergy of Virginia, North Carolina and South Carolina* (1955; reprint, Baltimore: Genealogical Publishing, 1976), 36.

8. "Personal Notices from the *Virginia Gazette*," *1WMQ* (1900): 188.

9. "Letters of the Rev. James Maury," *Memoirs of a Huguenot Family*, ed. Ann Maury (New York: G. P. Putnam, 1872), 379.

10. T.J. to Dabney Carr, Jr., January 19, 1816, *Memoir, Correspondence, and Miscellanies*, ed. Thomas Jefferson Randolph, 4 vols. (Charlottesville, Va.: F. Carr, 1829), 4: 281.

11. T.J. to James Maury, April 25, 1812, Washington, 6: 54.

12. "Letters of the Rev. James Maury," 413.

13. Ibid., 415.

14. T.J. to William Wirt, August 14, 1814, Ford, 11: 402.

15. Kimball, *Jefferson: The Road to Glory*, 35.

16. "Library of Dabney Carr, 1773, with a Notice of the Carr Family," *VMHB* 2 (1894): 221–228.

17. T.J. to Thomas J. Rogers, December 1823, quoted in Sowerby, no. 70.

18. Francis Walker Gilmer, "Sketches of American Statesmen," in Richard Beale Davis, *Francis Walker Gilmer: Life and Learning in Jefferson's Virginia* (Richmond, Va.: Dietz Press, 1939), 350.

19. James Boswell, *The Life of Samuel Johnson*, ed. Claude Rawson (New York: Everyman's Library, 1992), 115.

20. James Maury, "A Dissertation on Education in the Form of the Letter from James Maury to Robert Jackson, July 17, 1762," ed. Helen Duprey Bullock, *Papers of the Albemarle County Historical Society* 3 (1942–1943): 36–60.

21. Carl Bridenbaugh, *Myths and Realities: Societies of the Colonial South* (Baton Rouge: Louisiana State University Press, 1952), 37.

22. Maury, "Dissertation on Education," 40–41.

23. Ibid., 58.

24. Ibid., 47.

25. Ibid., 49, 52.

26. Ibid., 52.

27. Ibid.

28. T.J. to Bernard Moore, ca. 1765, Ford, 11: 421.

29. Maury, "Dissertation on Education," 42.

30. Norman Fiering, "The First American Enlightenment: Tillotson, Leverett, and Philosophical Anglicanism," *New England Quarterly* 54 (1981): 307–344.

31. Maury, "Dissertation on Education," 51; T.J. to John Adams, July 5, 1814, *AJL*, 433.

32. T.J. to John Page, July 15, 1763, *Papers*, 1: 10.

33. Cicero, *Tusculan Disputations*, trans. J. E. King (London: William Heinemann, 1927), 45.

34. Maury, "Dissertation on Education," 47.

35. T.J. to John Waldo, August 16, 1813, Washington, 6: 188.

36. Boucher, *Reminiscences*, 60–61; Davis, *Intellectual Life in the Colonial South*, 2: 741–742.

37. T.J. to John Waldo, August 16, 1813, Washington, 6: 185.

38. "Letters of the Rev. James Maury," 388–389.

39. Ibid., 390.

40. *LCB*, 93.

41. T.J. to unknown correspondent, October 25, 1825, Washington, 7: 413.

42. T.J. to Joseph Priestley, January 27, 1800, *Papers*, 31: 340.

Chapter 4: William and Mary

1. T.J. to William Wirt, August 5, 1815, Gribbel, 24.

2. T.J. to John Harvie, January 14, 1760, *Papers*, 1: 3.

3. Edward Kimber, *Itinerant Observation in America*, ed. Kevin J. Hayes (Newark: University of Delaware Press, 1998), 63.

4. Maria Byrd to an English correspondent, September 6, 1745, quoted in Kevin J. Hayes, *The Library of William Byrd of Westover* (Madison, Wisc.: Madison House, 1997), 90.

5. "Education in Colonial Virginia," *1WMQ* 6 (1898): 172.

6. John Page, "Governor Page," *Virginia Historical Register, and Literary Note Book* 3 (1850): 146.

7. T.J. to Walker Maury, August 19, 1785, *Papers*, 8: 409.

8. T.J. to John Bannister, Jr., October 15, 1785, *Papers*, 8: 636.

9. Ibid., 8: 637.

10. "The Statutes of the College of William and Mary in Virginia [1758]," *1WMQ* 16 (1908): 247.

11. "Journal of a French Traveller in the Colonies, 1765," *American Historical Review* 26 (1921): 741.

12. Andrew Burnaby, *Burnaby's Travels through North America*, ed. Rufus Rockwell Wilson (New York: A. Wessels Company, 1904), 32–36.

13. John Gwilym Jones, *Goronwy Owen's Virginia Adventure* (Williamsburg, Va.: Botetourt Bibliographical Society, 1969), 32–35; Branwen Jarvis, *Goronwy Owen* (Cardiff: University of Wales Press, 1986), 13; Prys Morgan, "From a Death to a View: The Hunt for the Welsh Past in the Romantic Period," *The Invention of Tradition*, ed. Eric Hobsbaum and Terence Ranger (New York: Cambridge University Press, 1983), 44–45.

14. *Autobiography*, Ford, 1: 6.

15. T.J. to Louis Hue Girardin, January 15, 1815, L&B, 14: 231.

16. *Autobiography*, Ford, 1: 6.

17. "The Statutes of the College of William and Mary in Virginia [1758]," *1WMQ* 16 (1908): 248.

18. T.J. to Peter Carr, August 10, 1787, *Papers*, 12: 15.

19. George Alan Daly, "Argumentation and Unified Structure in *Notes on the State of Virginia*," *Eighteenth-Century Studies* 26 (1993): 587; Wilbur Samuel Howell, "The Declaration of Independence and Eighteenth-Century Logic," *3WMQ* 18 (1961): 472; John Stephen Martin, "Jefferson, Democracy, and Commonsense Rhetoric," *Studies on Voltaire* 305 (1992): 1383.

20. Page, "Governor Page," 150–151.

21. T.J. to the Reverend James Madison, December 29, 1811, L&B, 19: 183.

22. T.J. to Robert Patterson, March 30, 1798, *Papers*, 30: 234.

23. I. Bernard Cohen, *Science and the Founding Fathers: Science in the Political Thought of Jefferson, Franklin, Adams, and Madison* (New York: Norton, 1997), 294.

24. Ted Ruddock, "Emerson, William," *A Biographical Dictionary of Civil Engineers in Great Britain and Ireland*, Vol. 1: *1500–1830*, ed. A. W. Skempton et al. (London: Thomas Telford, 2002), 215–216.

25. *Memorandum Books*, 1: 282–283.

26. Erasmus Darwin to William Withering, February 25, 1775, *The Letters of Erasmus Darwin*, ed. Desmond King-Hele (New York: Cambridge University Press, 1981), 68; Keir and Edgeworth are both quoted from Robert E. Schofield, *The Lunar Society of Birmingham: A Social History of Provincial Science and Industry in Eighteenth-Century England* (Oxford: Clarendon Press, 1963), 35–36.

27. *Autobiography*, Ford, 1: 6.

28. Erasmus Darwin to the Royal Society, March 10, 1777, *Letters*, 79; T.J. to Louis Hue Girardin, January 15, 1815, L&B, 14: 231.

29. John M. Jennings, *The Library of the College of William and Mary in Virginia, 1693–1793* (Charlottesville: University Press of Virginia, 1968).

30. T.J. to John Adams, June 11, 1812, *AJL*, 307.

31. T.J. to John Page, December 25, 1762, and T.J. to John Page, July 15, 1763, *Papers*, 1: 6, 11.

32. Page, "Governor Page," 151.

Chapter 5: The Williamsburg Circle

1. Garrett Ward Sheldon, *The Political Philosophy of Thomas Jefferson* (Baltimore: Johns Hopkins University Press, 1991), 123.

2. On February 29, 1764, T.J. purchased a copy of Thomas Sheridan's *Course of Lectures on Elocution*; see *Daybooks*, fol. 17.

3. Andrew Burnaby, *Burnaby's Travels through North America*, ed. Rufus Rockwell Wilson (New York: A. Wessels, 1904), 53.

4. "Notes, for the Biography of George Wythe," *Memoir, Correspondence, and Miscellanies*, ed. Thomas Jefferson Randolph, 4 vols. (Charlottesville, Va.: F. Carr, 1829), 1: 99.

5. T.J. to Thomas Cooper, January 16, 1814, Washington, 6: 292.

6. Albert C. Baugh, "Thomas Jefferson, Linguistic Liberal," *Studies for William A. Read: A Miscellany Presented by Some of His Colleagues and Friends*, ed. Nathaniel M. Caffee and Thomas A. Kirby (Baton Rouge: Louisiana State University Press, 1940), 92.

7. John Fortescue, *The Difference between an Absolute and Limited Monarchy* (London: W. Bowyer for E. Parker and T. Ward, 1714), 4.

8. Richard Terry, *Poetry and the Making of the English Literary Past, 1660–1781* (New York: Oxford University Press, 2001), 172–173.

9. Quoted in Sowerby, no. 4836.

10. *NSV*, 153.

11. Quoted in *The Official Papers of Francis Fauquier, Lieutenant Governor of Virginia, 1758–1768*, ed. George Reese, 3 vols. (Charlottesville: University Press of Virginia, 1980), 1: xxxvi.

12. George H. Reese, "Books in the Palace: The Libraries of Three Virginia Governors," *Virginia Cavalcade* 18, no. 1 (1968): 20–31.

13. William Fauquier, "An Account of an Extraordinary Storm of Hail in Virginia," *Philosophical Transactions* 50 (1757–1758): 796.

14. T.J. to L. H. Giradin, January 15, 1815, L&B, 14: 231–232.

15. Robert E. Schofield, *The Lunar Society of Birmingham: A Social History of Provincial Science and Industry in Eighteenth-Century England* (Oxford: Clarendon Press, 1963), 36–39; Peter Rowland, *The Life and Times of Thomas Day, 1748–1789, English Philanthropist and Author* (Lewiston, N.Y.: Edwin Mellen Press, 1996), 15, 62.

16. Quoted in Schofield, *Lunar Society*, 36.

17. *LCB*, 115.

18. Burnaby, *Travels*, 53.

19. T.J. to John Page, December 25, 1762, *Papers*, 1: 4.

20. Ibid., 1: 6.

21. Ibid., 1: 5; T.J. to Thomas Cooper, January 16, 1814, Washington, 6: 292; T.J. to Judge Tyler, June 17, 1812, *Memoir, Correspondence, and Miscellanies*, 4: 183; "Revisal of the Laws," *Papers*, 2: 495.

22. T.J. to Anne Randolph Bankhead, December 29, 1809, *Family Letters*, 394.

23. T.J. to John Page, December 25, 1762, *Papers*, 1: 5.

24. Ibid.

25. Dr. Alexander Hamilton, *The History of the Ancient and Honorable Tuesday Club*, ed. Robert Micklus, 3 vols. (Chapel Hill: University of North Carolina Press, 1990), 3: 215.

26. Quoted in Schofield, *Lunar Society*, 114; *NSV*, 64.

27. T.J. to John Page, October 7, 1763, *Papers*, 1: 12.

28. Burnaby, *Travels*, 34–35.

29. T.J. to John Page, October 7, 1763, *Papers*, 1: 11.

30. Quoted in Edwin Wolf II, *The Library of James Logan of Philadelphia, 1674–1751* (Philadelphia: Library Company of Philadelphia, 1974).

31. Jon Erklund, "Duhamel du Monceau, Henri-Louis," *Dictionary of Scientific Biography*, ed. Charles Coulston Gillispie, 16 vols. (New York: Scribner, 1970–1980), 4: 223–225.

32. T.J. to Tristram Dalton, May 2, 1817, Jefferson Papers (DLC).

33. T.J. to Thomas Turpin, February 5, 1769, *Papers*, 1: 24.

34. T.J. to Mary Jefferson Eppes, February 12, 1800, *Papers*, 31: 368.

35. *Daybooks*, fol. 55.

36. Ian N. Sneddon, "Stewart, Matthew," *Dictionary of Scientific Biography*, 13: 54–55.

37. *NSV*, 177.

38. *Daybooks*, fol. 94.

39. T.J. to William Small, May 7, 1775, *Papers*, 1: 165–166.

Chapter 6: The Limits of English Law

1. T.J. to Martha Jefferson, March 28, 1787, *Papers*, 11: 251.

2. *Daybooks*, fol. 103.

3. For a good overview, see Howard Jay Graham, "The Rastells and the Printed Law Book of the Renaissance," *Law Library Journal* 47 (1954): 6–25.

4. Alfred Owen Aldridge, "The Eclecticism of Mark Akenside's *The Pleasures of Imagination*," *Journal of the History of Ideas* 5 (1944): 292–314.

5. Francis Fauquier to the Board of Trade, June 5, 1765, *The Official Papers of Francis Fauquier, Lieutenant Governor of Virginia, 1758–1768*, ed. George Reese, 3 vols. (Charlottesville: University Press of Virginia, 1980), 3: 1250.

6. T.J. to William Wirt, August 4, 1805, Gribbel, 6.

7. Quoted in John Finch, *Travels in the United States of America and Canada* (London: Longman, Rees, Orme, Green, & Longman, 1833), 254–255.

8. "Journal of a French Traveler in the Colonies, 1765," *American Historical Review* 26 (1921): 745. Spelling and punctuation have been regularized for clarity.

9. Quoted in William Stevens Perry, *Papers Relating to the History of the Church in Virginia, A.D. 1650–1776* (n.p., 1870), 574.

10. T.J. to William Wirt, August 4, 1805, Gribbel, 3.

11. *Autobiography*, Ford, 1: 8; William Shepard, "Some Buckingham County Letters," *2WMQ* 15 (1935): 409; George Gordon, Lord Byron, "The Age of Bronze," *Poetical Works*, ed. Frederick Page (New York: Oxford University Press, 1970), 174.

12. T.J. to William Wirt, August 4, 1805, Gribbel, 3–6.

13. Webster, "Notes," 372.

14. *Autobiography*, Ford, 1: 15; Webster, "Notes," 372–373.

15. T.J. to William Wirt, August 4, 1805, Gribbel, 10; Nicholas P. Trist, "Notes of Conversations with Jefferson," quoted in Randall, 1: 40.

16. T.J. to William Ludlow, September 6, 1824, Washington, 7: 377–378.

17. T.J. to William Wirt, September 4, 1816, Gribbel, 25.

18. T.J. to William Wirt, August 4, 1805, Gribbel, 28.

19. "Journal of a French Traveler," 745.

20. J. A. Leo Lemay, "John Mercer and the Stamp Act in Virginia, 1764–1765," *VMHB* 91 (1983): 14–17; Edmund S. Morgan and Helen M. Morgan, *The Stamp Act Crisis: Prologue to Revolution* (Chapel Hill: University of North Carolina Press, 1953), 95; Francis Fauquier to the Board of Trade, June 5, 1765, *Official Papers*, 3: 1250; *Autobiography*, Ford, 1: 8; Jefferson to William Wirt, 4 August 1805, Gribbel, 5.

21. Quoted in Henry Mayer, *A Son of Thunder: Patrick Henry and the American Republic* (1986; reprint, New York: Grove Press, 2001), 90; Francis Fauquier to the Board of Trade, June 5, 1765, *Official Papers*, 3: 1250.

22. Quoted in Morgan and Morgan, *Stamp Act Crisis*, 95.

23. Stephen Sayre, *The Englishman Deceived: A Political Piece: Wherein Some Very Important Secrets of State Are Briefly Recited, and Offered to the Consideration of the Public* (London: G. Kearsly, 1768), 19; Benjamin Franklin to John Hughes, August 9, 1765, *The Papers of Benjamin Franklin*, ed. Leonard W. Labaree et al., 37 vols. to date (New Haven, Conn.: Yale University Press, 1959–), 12: 234.

24. *LCB*, 38.

25. Jon Parkin, "Cumberland, Richard," *ODNB*, 14: 615–616.

26. Jeremy Bentham, *An Introduction to the Principles of Morals and Legislation*, ed. J. H. Burns and H. L. A. Hart (Oxford: Clarendon Press, 1996), 298.

27. "Opinion on the Treaties with France," *Papers*, 25: 613.

28. For more on this idea, see Peter S. Onuf and Leonard J. Sadosky, *Jeffersonian America* (Malden, Mass.: Blackwell, 2002), 176–179.

29. "Argument in the Case of Howell vs. Netherland," Ford, 1: 474.

Chapter 7: A Shelf of Notebooks

1. Frank L. Dewey, *Thomas Jefferson, Lawyer* (Charlottesville: University Press of Virginia, 1986), 9–17.

2. "Thoughts on English Prosody," *L&B*, 18: 422.

3. *Memorandum Books*, 1: 247.

4. Quoted in Isaiah Thomas, *The History of Printing in America*, ed. Marcus A. McCorison (New York: Weathervane Books, 1970), 556.

5. Douglas L. Wilson, "Thomas Jefferson: Early Notebooks," *3WMQ* 42 (1985): 444–445.

6. T.J. to John Minor, August 30, 1814, Ford, 11: 424.

7. T.J. to Thomas Jefferson Randolph, December 7, 1808, *Family Letters*, 368–369.

8. Gilbert Chinard, ed., *The Commonplace Book of Thomas Jefferson: A Reportory of His Ideas on Government* (Baltimore: Johns Hopkins Press, 1926), 95–103. Elsewhere in this edition Chinard abbreviates Jefferson's original text significantly. For the complete text, see "Legal Commonplace Book, 1762–1767," Jefferson Papers (DLC).

9. Henry Home, Lord Kames, *Historical Law Tracts*, 2 vols. (Edinburgh: for A. Millar, 1758), 1: 2.

10. *LCB*, 66.

11. Bernard, *Retrospections*, 238.

12. Wilson, "Thomas Jefferson: Early Notebooks," 450.

13. Alastair J. Durie and Stuart Handley, "Home, Henry, Lord Kames," *ODNB*, 27: 879–882.

14. T.J. to Thomas Law, June 13, 1814, *EG*, 358.

15. Douglas L. Wilson, "Thomas Jefferson's Library and the Skipwith List," *Harvard Library Bulletin*, n.s. 3 (1992–1993): 86–88.

16. *Thomas Jefferson's Garden Book, 1766–1824*, ed. Edwin M. Betts (Philadelphia: American Philosophical Society, 1944), 1.

17. *LCB*, 182; Laurence Sterne, *The Life and Opinions of Tristram Shandy, Gentleman* (London: Oxford University Press, 1928), 11.

18. T.J. to John Page, May 25, 1766, *Papers*, 1: 18–19.

19. *Papers*, 1: 18–19.

20. "William Gregory's Journal, from Fredericksburg, Va., to Philadelphia, 30th of September, 1765, to 16th of October, 1765," *1WMQ* 13 (1905): 227.

21. T.J. to Charles Thomson, January 9, 1816, *EG*, 364.

22. *Thomas Jefferson's Garden Book*, 4–5.

23. H. R. Woudhuysen, "Writing-Tables and Table-Books," *Electronic British Library Journal*, 2004, http://www/bl.uk/eblj/2004articles/pdf/article3.pdf (accessed July 25, 2005); Peter Stallybrass, Roger Chartier, J. Franklin Mowery, and Heather Wolfe, "Hamlet's Tables and the Technologies of Writing in Renaissance England," *Shakespeare Quarterly* 55 (2004): 379–419.

24. *Memorandum Books*, 1: 385–386.

25. T.J. to Nicholas Lewis, July 11, 1788, *Papers*, 13: 342.

26. *Memorandum Books*, 1: xvii–xviii.

27. *NSV*, 133.

Chapter 8: Becoming a Burgess

1. "Francis Fauquier's Will," *1WMQ* 8 (1900): 174.

2. *Memorandum Books*, 1: 73; Odai Johnson and William J. Burling, *The Colonial American Stage, 1665–1774: A Documentary Calendar* (Madison, N.J.: Fairleigh Dickinson University Press, 2001), 299; T.J. to John Page, January 20, 1763, *Papers*, 1: 7.

3. Paula R. Backscheider, "John Home," *Restoration and Eighteenth-Century Dramatists* (Detroit: Gale, 1989), 222–223.

4. *Memorandum Books*, 1: 77.

5. Brent Tarter, "Botetourt, Norborne Berkeley, baron de," *Dictionary of Virginia Biography*, ed. John T. Kneebone, J. Jefferson Looney, Brent Tarter, and Sandra Gioia Treadway, 3 vols. to date (Richmond: Library of Virginia, 1998–), 2: 108–109.

6. *Memorandum Books*, 1: 82.

7. Genevieve Yost, "The Reconstruction of the Library of Norborne Berkeley, Baron de Botetourt, Governor of Virginia, 1768–1770," *Publications of the Bibliographical Society of America* 36 (1942): 97–123.

8. John R. Thompson, "Colonial Life of Virginia," *Southern Literary Messenger* 20 (1854): 341.

9. Webster, "Notes," 374.

10. *Memorandum Books*, 1: 141; *NSV*, 57.

11. Jane Carson, *Colonial Virginians at Play* (Williamsburg, Va.: Colonial Williamsburg Foundation, 1989), 99; *Memorandum Books*, 1: 141–142.

12. Daniel Meade, "Autobiography," *1WMQ* 13 (1904): 87; *Journal of the House of Burgesses* (Williamsburg, Va.: William Rind, 1769), 2.

13. "Biographical Sketch of Peyton Randolph," Ford, 12: 31.

14. Ibid.

15. Meade, "Autobiography," 87.

16. *Autobiography*, Ford, 1: 59.

17. T.J. to William Wirt, August 5, 1815, Gribbel, 22.

18. Ibid., 23.

19. *Memorandum Books*, 1: 16.

20. Perkins, Buchanan and Brown to T.J., October 2, 1789, *Papers*, 1: 34.

21. Dumas Malone, *Jefferson the Virginian* (Boston: Little, Brown, 1948), 129–130.

22. *Determinations . . . Concerning Elections*, 3d ed. (London: for W. Owen, 1753), 251–252.

23. H. Trevor Colbourn, *The Lamp of Experience: Whig History and the Intellectual Origins of the American Revolution* (1965; reprint, New York: Norton, 1974), 13.

24. William Hakewill, *Modus Tenendi Parliamentum; or, The Old Manner of Holding Parliaments in England* (London: for Abel Roper, 1671); *NSV*, 125; *Jefferson's Parliamentary Writings: "Parliamentary Pocket-Book" and a Manual of Parliamentary Practice*, ed. Wilbur Samuel Howell (Princeton, N.J.: Princeton University Press, 1988), 5.

25. *Journal of the House of Burgesses*, 21–22.

26. Meade, "Autobiography," 87.

27. *Journal of the House of Burgesses*, 42; Meade, "Autobiography," 88; Webster, "Notes," 374.

28. "Virginia Nonimportation Resolutions, 1769," *Papers*, 1: 28.

29. Jacqueline R. Hill, "Popery and Protestantism, Civil and Religious Liberty: The Disputed Lessons of Irish History, 1690–1812," *Past and Present*, no. 118 (1988): 112–113.

30. Caroline Robbins, "The Strenuous Whig: Thomas Hollis of Lincoln's Inn," *3WMQ* 7 (1950): 449.

Chapter 9: Domestic Life and Literary Pursuits

1. Thomas Nelson, Sr., to T.J., March 6, 1770; Thomas Nelson, Jr., to T.J., March 6, 1770; and George Wythe to T.J., March 9, 1770, *Papers*, 1: 37–38.

2. Quoted in Sowerby, no. 13.

3. Philip Gaskell, *A Bibliography of the Foulis Press*, 2d ed. (London: St. Paul's Bibliographies, 1986), 54.

4. T.J. to Thomas Elder, June 26, 1786, *Papers*, 10: 72.

5. E. Millicent Sowerby, "Thomas Jefferson and His Library," *Publications of the Bibliographical Society of America* 50 (1956): 218; Edwin Wolf II and Kevin J. Hayes, *The Library of Benjamin Franklin* (Philadelphia: American Philosophical Society and the Library Company of Philadelphia, 2006), no. 1684; T.J. to Wells and Lilly, April 1, 1818, *Thomas Jefferson Correspondence: Printed from the Originals in the Collections of William K. Bixby*, ed. Worthington Chauncey Ford (Boston, 1916), 238.

6. T.J. to John Page, February 21, 1770, *Papers*, 1: 35.

7. *Memorandum Books*, 1: 212; T.J. to James Ogilvie, February 20, 1771, *Papers*, 1: 63.

8. Thomas Morton, *New English Canaan*, ed. Charles Francis Adams (1883; reprint, New York: B. Franklin, 1967), 306; Increase Mather, *The Necessity of Reformation* (Boston: John Foster, 1679), 7; William Byrd, *William Byrd's Histories of the Dividing Line betwixt Virginia and North Carolina*, ed. William K. Boyd (New York: Dover, 1967), 5.

9. *Autobiography*, Ford, 1: 7–8.

10. Mrs. Drummond to T.J., March 12, 1771, *Papers*, 1: 65.

11. T.J. to Lucy Chiswell Nelson, October 24, 1777, *Papers*, 2: 36.

12. T.J. to Thomas Adams, June 1, 1771, *Papers*, 1: 71.

13. T.J. to Robert Skipwith, August 3, 1771, *Papers*, 1: 78.

14. Randall, 1: 64–65; *Thomas Jefferson's Garden Book, 1766–1824*, ed. Edwin M. Betts (Philadelphia: American Philosophical Society, 1944), 33.

15. Sarah N. Randolph, *The Domestic Life of Thomas Jefferson* (1871; reprint, Charlottesville: University Press of Virginia, 1994), 45.

16. *Jefferson at Monticello*, 3.

17. T.J. to John Minor, August 30, 1814, Ford, 11: 421; "Course of Study for William G. Munford," December 5, 1798, *Papers*, 30: 594; T.J. to John Walker, *Papers*, 1: 32.

18. Robert Skipwith to T.J., July 17, 1771, *Papers*, 1: 74–75.

19. T.J. to Robert Skipwith, August 3, 1771, *Papers*, 1: 76–80.

20. Douglas L. Wilson, "Thomas Jefferson's Library and the Skipwith List," *Harvard Library Bulletin*, n.s. 3 (1992–93): 86–88.

21. T.J. to Robert Skipwith, August 3, 1771, *Papers*, 1: 76–77.

22. Francis Calley Gray, *Thomas Jefferson in 1814: Being an Account of a Visit to Monticello, Virginia*, ed. Henry S. Rowe and T. Jefferson Coolidge, Jr. (Boston: The Club of Odd Volumes, 1924), 72.

23. T.J. to Robert Skipwith, August 3, 1771, *Papers*, 1: 77.

24. *LCB*, 35.

25. Judith Hawley, "Carter, Elizabeth," *ODNB* 10: 341–345; T.J. to William Short, October 31, 1819, *EG*, 389.

26. T.J. to Robert Skipwith, August 3, 1771, *Papers*, 1: 77.

27. T.J. to Peter Carr, August 10, 1787, *Papers*, 12: 15.

28. *Jefferson at Monticello*, 3–4.

29. T.J. to Robert Skipwith, August 3, 1771, *Papers*, 1: 78.

30. *Memorandum Books*, 1: 248.

31. Richard M. Jellison, "Scientific Enquiry in Eighteenth-Century Virginia," *Historian* 25 (1963): 305.

32. Fraser Neiman, "The Letters of William Gilpin to Samuel Henley," *Huntington Library Quarterly* 35 (1972): 159–169.

33. Quoted in Mellen Chamberlain, "Rev. Samuel Henley, D.D.," *Proceedings of the Massachusetts Historical Society* 15 (1878): 235.

34. T.J. to Samuel Henley, March 3, 1785, *Papers*, 8: 11–14; Arthur Sherbo, *Shakespeare's Midwives: Some Neglected Shakespeareans* (Newark: University of Delaware Press, 1992), 109–131; Bernice W. Kliman, "Cum Notis Variorum: Samuel Henley, Shakespeare Commentator in Bell's *Annotations*," *Shakespeare Newsletter* 48 (1998–99): 91–92, 108, 110.

35. Samuel Henley to T.J., July 18, 1785, *Papers*, 8: 304; Samuel Henley to T.J., November 16, 1785, *Papers*, 9: 39.

36. Quoted in Chamberlain, "Rev. Samuel Henley," 236.

37. *Memorandum Books*, 1: 289, 347.

38. John T. Shawcross, "John Milton and His Spanish and Portuguese Presence," *Milton Quarterly* 32 (1998): 49.

39. A. Owen Aldridge, "The Perception of China in English Literature of the Enlightenment," *Asian Culture Quarterly* 14 (1986): 17.

40. Thomas Percy to Samuel Henley, February 1, 1775, in Chamberlain, "Rev. Samuel Henley," 239.

41. Quoted in J. W. Oliver, *The Life of William Beckford* (London: Oxford University Press, 1932), 97–98.

Chapter 10: Rude Bard of the North

1. T.J. to Charles Macpherson, February 25, 1773, *Papers*, 1: 96.
2. "Library of Col. William Fleming" *1WMQ* 6 (1898): 164; "Books in Williamsburg," *2WMQ* 15 (1906): 105; T.J. to Charles Macpherson, February 25, 1773, *Papers*, 1: 96.
3. *LCB*, 142–143.
4. *Daybooks*, fol. 80.
5. *LCB*, 144.
6. T.J. to Charles Macpherson, February 25, 1773, *Papers*, 1: 96–97.
7. Ibid., 1: 97.
8. *LCB*, 172.
9. Peter Carr to T.J., December 30, 1786, *Papers*, 10: 648.
10. Susan Manning, "Why Does It Matter That Ossian Was Thomas Jefferson's Favourite Poet?" *Symbiosis: A Journal of Anglo-American Literary Relations* 1 (1997): 231.
11. The University of Virginia holds numerous Wayles-Jefferson volumes not in the Sowerby catalogue.
12. T.J. to George Washington Lewis, October 25, 1825, Jefferson Papers (DLC).
13. Sowerby, no. 259.
14. *Memorandum Books*, 1: 341.
15. Kevin J. Hayes, *The Library of William Byrd of Westover* (Madison, Wisc.: Madison House, 1997), 95.
16. *Memorandum Books*, 1: 332.
17. Edmund Randolph, *History of Virginia*, ed. Arthur H. Shaffer (Charlottesville: University Press of Virginia, 1970), 182.
18. Jonathan Gross, ed., *Thomas Jefferson's Scrapbooks: Poems of Nation, Family, and Romantic Love Collected by America's Third President* (Hanover, N.H.: Steerforth Press, 2006), 130.
19. Charles Macpherson to T.J., August 12, 1773, *Papers*, 1: 102.
20. Marquis de Chastellux, *Travels in North America in the Years 1780, 1781 and 1782*, ed. Howard C. Rice, Jr., 2 vols. (Chapel Hill: University of North Carolina Press, 1963), 2: 392.
21. Edward Gibbon, *The History of the Decline and Fall of the Roman Empire*, 6 vols. (London: for W. Strahan, and T. Cadell, 1783), 1: 209.
22. Kevin J. Hayes, "How Thomas Jefferson Read the Qur'an," *Early American Literature* 39 (2004): 254–255.
23. T.J. to John Adams, May 25, 1785, *Papers*, 8: 164.
24. Gross, *Thomas Jefferson's Scrapbooks*, 405.
25. T.J. to Mary Jefferson Eppes, February 7, 1799, *Papers*, 31: 13. Anne Cary Randolph's copy of a two-volume edition of *The Works of Ossian* survives at the University of Virginia. Both volumes are inscribed, "Th. Jefferson to Ann C. Randolph"; Ellen Randolph Coolidge to T.J., December 26, 1825, *Family Letters*, 465.
26. T.J. to Marquis de Lafayette, November 4, 1823, L&B, 15: 493.

Chapter 11: *A Summary View of the Rights of British America*

1. Philip Mazzei, *Memoirs of the Life and Peregrinations of the Florentine Philip Mazzei, 1730–1816*, trans. Howard R. Marraro (New York: Columbia University Press, 1942), 192–204.

2. For the fullest treatment, see John R. Hailman, *Thomas Jefferson on Wine* (Jackson: University Press of Mississippi, 2006).

3. T.J. to William Drayton, July 30, 1787, *Papers*, 11: 648.

4. "On the Instructions Given to the 1st Delegation of Virginia to Congress in August 1774," *Papers*, 1: 670.

5. *Autobiography*, Ford, 1: 12.

6. Webster, "Notes," 374.

7. *Autobiography*, Ford, 1: 12.

8. "Resolution of the House of Burgesses Designating a Day of Fasting and Prayer," *Papers*, 1: 105–106, which includes in its notes the following quotation from Governor Dunmore.

9. *Autobiography*, Ford, 1: 13.

10. Mazzei, *Memoirs*, 205; T.J. to William Wirt, August 5, 1815, Gribbel, 22.

11. T.J. to William Wirt, August 5, 1815, Gribbel, 22.

12. T.J. to William Plumer, January 31, 1815, L&B, 14: 238.

13. Michael Kammen, "The Meaning of Colonization in American Revolutionary Thought," *Journal of the History of Ideas* 31 (1970): 349.

14. "Monthly Catalogue," *Critical Review* 38 (1774): 391; William L. Hedges, "Telling Off the King: Jefferson's *Summary View* as American Fantasy," *Early American Literature* 22 (1987): 170.

15. *A Summary View*, *Papers*, 1: 121.

16. Ibid., 1: 122–123.

17. Captain John Smith, *The Complete Works of Captain John Smith (1580–1631)*, ed. Philip L. Barbour, 3 vols. (Chapel Hill: University of North Carolina Press, 1986), 2: 420.

18. *A Summary View*, *Papers*, 1: 123.

19. Ibid., 1: 125.

20. Ibid.

21. Ibid., 1: 121.

22. Ibid., 1: 125.

23. Ibid., 1: 126.

24. "Association of Members of the Late House of Burgesses," *Papers*, 1: 107–108.

25. *A Summary View*, *Papers*, 1: 127–128.

26. J. A. Leo Lemay, *The American Dream of Captain John Smith* (Charlottesville: University Press of Virginia, 1991), 187.

27. *A Summary View*, *Papers*, 1: 132.

28. Ibid., 1: 135.

29. *Memorandum Books*, 1: 376–377.

30. "On the Instructions Given to the 1st Delegation of Virginia to Congress, in August, 1774," *Papers*, 1: 670.

31. Edmund Randolph, *History of Virginia*, ed. Arthur H. Shaffer (Charlottesville: University Press of Virginia, 1970), 205.

32. "On the Instructions Given to the 1st Delegation of Virginia to Congress, in August, 1774," *Papers*, 1: 671.

33. Thomas Coombe, Jr., to Benjamin Franklin, September 24, 1774, *The Papers of Benjamin Franklin*, ed. Leonard W. Labaree et al., 37 vols. to date (New Haven, Conn.: Yale University Press, 1959–), 21: 315.

Chapter 12: The Pen and the Tomahawk

1. Edmund Randolph, *History of Virginia*, ed. Arthur H. Shaffer (Charlottesville: University Press of Virginia, 1970), 213.

2. "Report of Committee to Prepare a Plan for a Militia," *Papers*, 1: 161.

3. Ibid.

4. William J. Van Schreeven and Robert L. Scribner, eds., *Revolutionary Virginia: The Road to Independence*, Vol. 2: *The Committees and the Second Convention, 1773–1775: A Documentary Record* (Charlottesville: University Press of Virginia, 1975), 376, 385.

5. T.J. to James Bowdoin, July 10, 1807, Ford, 10: 454; T.J. to Dupont de Nemours, July 14, 1807, Washington, 5: 127; T.J. to William Small, May 7, 1775, *Papers*, 1: 165.

6. T.J. to William Wirt, August 5, 1815, Washington, 6: 487.

7. "Virginia Resolutions on Lord North's Conciliatory Proposal," *Papers*, 1: 171.

8. Ibid., 1: 172–173.

9. Quoted in Joseph Towne Wheeler, "Booksellers and Circulating Libraries in Colonial Maryland," *Maryland Historical Magazine* 34 (1939): 117.

10. T.J. to John Wyche, May 19, 1809, Washington, 5: 448–449.

11. Wheeler, "Booksellers and Circulating Libraries," 125–126.

12. *Memorandum Books*, 1: 388.

13. Samuel Ward to Henry Ward, June 22, 1775, *LDC*, 1: 535.

14. "Comments on François Soulés' *Histoire*," *Papers*, 10: 371; John Adams to Timothy Pickering, August 22, 1822, *Jefferson: Political Writings*, ed. Joyce Appleby and Terence Ball (New York: Cambridge University Press, 1999), 609–611.

15. T.J. to S. A. Wells, May 12, 1819, *Memoir, Correspondence, and Miscellanies*, ed. Thomas Jefferson Randolph, 4 vols. (Charlottesville, Va.: F. Carr, 1829), 1: 104; Randall, 1: 182.

16. John Adams, *Diary and Autobiography of John Adams*, ed. L. H. Butterfield et al., 4 vols. (Cambridge, Mass.: Belknap Press of Harvard University Press, 1961), 2: 218.

17. Sowerby, no. 4838, lists no information regarding where or when Jefferson obtained this work, but Robert Aitken's Waste-Book at the Library Company of Philadelphia indicates that he purchased it from Aitken's Philadelphia shop on August 3, 1776.

18. Marie Kimball, *Jefferson: The Road to Glory, 1743 to 1776* (New York: Coward-McCann, 1943), 108–109, prints the two German poems with Jefferson's verse translations but does not identify the poems or their authors.

19. Richard Henry Lee to Robert Carter, *LDC*, 1: 569.

20. Bernard, *Retrospections*, 232–233.

21. Ibid., 232; *Autobiography*, Ford, 1: 19.

22. "Declaration of the Causes and Necessity for Taking Up Arms: Jefferson's Fair Copy for the Committee," *Papers*, 1: 201.

23. "Declaration of the Causes and Necessity for Taking Up Arms: The Declaration as Adopted by Congress," *Papers*, 1: 217–218.

24. Quoted in Elisa P. Douglass, "German Intellectuals and the American Revolution," *3WMQ* 17 (1960): 200–218.

25. John Adams to Timothy Pickering, August 22, 1822, *Jefferson: Political Writings*, 609–611.

26. "Resolutions of Congress on Lord North's Conciliatory Proposal," *Papers*, 1: 232.

27. T.J. to John Randolph, August 25, 1775, *Papers*, 1: 240–243.

Chapter 13: *The Declaration of Independence*

1. T.J. to John Randolph, November 29, 1775, *Papers*, 1: 268; Richard Henry Lee to George Washington, October 22, 1775, *LDC*, 2: 229–230.

2. Francis Lightfoot Lee to Landon Carter, October 21, 1775, and Richard Henry Lee to George Washington, October 22, 1775, *LDC*, 2: 227–230.

3. T.J. to John Randolph, November 29, 1775, *Papers*, 1: 269.

4. See Allen Jayne, *Jefferson's Declaration of Independence: Origins, Philosophy and Theology* (Lexington: University Press of Kentucky, 1998).

5. Quoted in Marie Kimball, *Jefferson: The Road to Glory, 1743–1776* (New York: Coward-McCann, 1943), 282.

6. *NSV*, 122.

7. T.J. to Thomas Nelson, May 16, 1776, *Papers*, 1: 292.

8. T.J. to John Page, May 17, 1776, *Papers*, 1: 293; J. Hector St. John de Crèvecoeur, *Letters from an American Farmer and Sketches of Eighteenth-Century America*, ed. Albert E. Stone (New York: Penguin, 1987), 70.

9. T.J. to Thomas Nelson, May 16, 1776, *Papers*, 1: 292.

10. T.J. to Ellen Randolph Coolidge, November 14, 1825, *Family Letters*, 461–462.

11. "Resolution of Independence Moved by R. H. Lee for the Virginia Delegation," *Papers*, 1: 298.

12. T.J. to Henry Lee, May 8, 1825, Washington, 7: 407.

13. T.J. to James Madison, August 30, 1823, *The Republic of Letters: The Correspondence between Thomas Jefferson and James Madison, 1776–1826*, ed. James Morton Smith, 3 vols. (New York: Norton, 1995), 3: 1876.

14. *Declaration of Independence, Papers*, 1: 429–432. Subsequent references to the *Declaration of Independence* come from this edition and are not cited separately.

15. James MacClurg, *Experiments upon the Human Bile: and Reflections on the Bilary Secretion* (London: for T. Cadell, 1772), vii.

16. "Jefferson's Original Rough Draft of the *Declaration of Independence*," *Papers*, 1: 423.

17. T.J. to Benjamin Rush, September 23, 1800, *EG*, 320.

18. *Papers*, 1: 427–428, suggests that there is no conclusive evidence to attribute this change to Franklin, but Walter Isaacson, *Benjamin Franklin: An American Life* (New York: Simon & Schuster, 2003), 311–312, asserts that Franklin made the change.

19. "Marginalia in *An Inquiry*," *The Papers of Benjamin Franklin*, ed. Leonard W. Labaree et al., 37 vols. to date (New Haven, Conn.: Yale University Press, 1959–), 17: 317–348.

20. George Lyttelton, *Dialogues of the Dead*, 4th ed. (London: for W. Sandby, 1765), 404.

21. Samuel Adams to John Pitts, ca. July 9, 1776, *LDC*, 4: 417.

22. Benjamin Franklin to William Strahan, February 12, 1745, *The Papers of Benjamin Franklin*, 3: 13–14.

23. *LCB*, 184–186.

24. "Jefferson's 'Original Rough Draft' of the *Declaration of Independence*," *Papers*, 1: 427.

25. John Penn to Samuel Johnston, June 28, 1776, *LDC*, 4: 333; John Adams to Archibald Bulloch, July 1, 1776, *LDC*, 4: 345.

26. *Memorandum Books*, 1: 432.

27. Josiah Bartlett to John Langdon, July 1, 1776, *LDC*, 4: 351.

28. Paul M. Zall, *Jefferson on Jefferson* (Lexington: University Press of Kentucky, 2002), 32–33.

29. T.J. to Richard Henry Lee, July 8, 1776, *Papers*, 1: 455–456.

30. *Autobiography*, Ford, 1: 34.

31. Robert B. Sullivan, "Rush, Benjamin," *ANB*, 19: 72–75.

32. Benjamin Rush to John Adams, July 20, 1811, *Letters of Benjamin Rush*, ed. L. H. Butterfield, 2 vols. (Princeton, N.J.: for the American Philosophical Society by Princeton University Press, 1951), 2: 1090.

33. John H. Hazelton, *The Declaration of Independence: Its History* (1906; reprint, New York: Da Capo, 1970), 240–243.

Chapter 14: The Book Culture of Philadelphia and Williamsburg, Contrasted

1. *Memorandum Books*, 1: 421–423; Robert Aitken, Waste-Book, Library Company of Philadelphia.

2. James N. Green, "English Books and Printing in the Age of Franklin," *A History of the Book in America*, Vol. 1: *The Colonial Book in the Atlantic World*, ed. Hugh Amory and David D. Hall (New York: Cambridge University Press, 2000), 283–291.

3. "William McCulloch's Additions to Thomas's *History of Printing*," *Proceedings of the American Antiquarian Society* 31 (1921): 232.

4. Robert Bell, *Bell's Address to Every Free-Man; but Especially to the Free Citizens of Pennsylvania, Concerning a Tyrannical Embargo, Now Laid upon the Free-Sale of Books by Auction* (Philadelphia: Robert Bell, 1784), 5.

5. Robert Bell, *Memorandum* (Philadelphia: Bell, 1774).

6. T.J. to Francis Hopkinson, July 6, 1788, *Papers*, 13: 309.

7. Vincent Freimarck, "Aitken, Robert," *ANB*, 1: 199–200; Willman Spawn and Carol Spawn, "The Aitken Shop: Identification and an Eighteenth-Century Bindery," *Publications of the Bibliographical Society of America* 57 (1963): 422–437; "William McCulloch's Additions," 105; Robert Aitken, Waste-Book, Library Company of Philadelphia.

8. Dwight L. Teeter, Jr., "Dunlap, John," *ANB*, 7: 88.

9. J. A. W. Gunn, *Beyond Liberty and Property: The Process of Self-Recognition in Eighteenth-Century Political Thought* (Montreal: McGill-Queen's University Press, 1983), 244–245.

10. *Benjamin Franklin's Autobiography*, ed. J. A. Leo Lemay and P. M. Zall (New York: Norton, 1986), 57.

11. T.J. to Francis Eppes, October 10, 1775, *Papers*, 1: 246.

12. T.J. to Francis Eppes, October 24, 1775, *Papers*, 1: 249.

13. T.J. to Edmund Pendleton, August 26, 1776, *Papers*, 1: 505.

14. T.J. to Francis Eppes, July 15, 1776, *Papers*, 1: 458–459.

15. T.J. to Francis Eppes, July 23, 1776, *Papers*, 1: 473.

16. T.J. to Richard Henry Lee, July 29, 1776, *Papers*, 1: 477.

17. Ibid.

18. Richard Henry Lee to Patrick Henry, August 20, 1776, in William Wirt Henry, *Patrick Henry: Life, Correspondence and Speeches*, 3 vols. (New York: Charles Scribner's Sons, 1891), 2: 8.

19. Sowerby, nos. 127, 1434, 2930, and 4638. Sowerby no. 309 is a duplicate copy of Pétis's *Histoire du Grand Genghizcan*; Lord Dunmore's inscribed copy, also containing T.J.'s characteristic marks of identification, survives at the University of Virginia. For the significance of this work to Mongol historiography, see David Morgan, *The Mongols* (Oxford: Blackwell, 1986), 27–28.

20. Fraser Neiman, *The Henley-Horrocks Inventory* (Williamsburg, Va.: Botetourt Bibliographical Society and the Earl Gregg Swem Library, 1968).

21. T.J. to Samuel Henley, June 9, 1778, *Papers*, 2: 198.

22. Ibid., 2: 199.

23. Jonathan Gross, ed., *Thomas Jefferson's Scrapbooks: Poems of Nation, Family, and Romantic Love Collected by America's Third President* (Hanover, N.H.: Steerforth Press, 2006), 363.

24. T.J. to Samuel Henley, March 3, 1785, *Papers*, 8: 11–14; Barbara Brandon Schnorrenberg, "Montagu, Elizabeth," *ODNB*, 38: 720–725.

25. Randall, 3: 404.

26. T.J. to Samuel Henley, March 3, 1785, *Papers*, 8: 11–14; *NSV*, 42.

27. Samuel Henley to T.J., September 15, 1785, *Papers*, 8: 523.

28. *Memorandum Books*, 1: 457, 461.

29. T.J. to Hugh P. Taylor, October 4, 1823, Washington, 7: 313.

30. T.J. to George Wythe, January 16, 1796, *Papers*, 28: 583.

31. *Autobiography*, Ford, 1: 62.

32. Sowerby, no. 624; Kevin J. Hayes, "Blackamore, Arthur," *Dictionary of Virginia Biography*, ed. John T. Kneebone, J. Jefferson Looney, Brent Tarter, and Sandra Gioia Treadway, 3 vols. to date (Richmond: Library of Virginia, 1998–), 1: 516–517.

33. D. R. Woolf, "William Fulbecke," *Sixteenth-Century Nondramatic Writers, Fourth Series*, ed. David A. Richardson (Detroit: Gale, 1996), 93–95.

34. *Papers*, 1: 555.

35. T.J. to James Madison, December 16, 1786, *Papers*, 10: 603–604.

Chapter 15: Of Law and Learning

1. *Autobiography*, Ford, 1: 67.

2. Ibid.

3. Ibid., 1: 68.

4. Ibid., 1: 70.

5. T.J. to George Wythe, November 1, 1778, *Papers*, 2: 230.

6. T.J. to Benjamin Franklin, August 13, 1777, *Papers*, 2: 26.

7. T.J. to Silas Deane, August 13, 1777, *Papers*, 2: 25.

8. T.J. to John Adams, May 16, 1777, *Papers*, 2: 18–19.

9. Philip Mazzei to Giovanni Fabbroni, December 25, 1773, *Philip Mazzei: Selected Writings and Correspondence*, ed. Margherita Marchine et al., 3 vols. (Prato, Italy: Edizioni del Palazzo, 1983), 1: 50.

10. T.J. to Giovanni Fabbroni, June 8, 1778, *Papers*, 2: 195–196.

11. Rev. James Madison to T.J., July 26, 1778, *Papers*, 2: 205.

12. *NSV*, 64.

13. T.J. to David Rittenhouse, July 19, 1778, *Papers*, 2: 202.

14. Edmund Pendleton to T.J., May 11, 1779, *Papers*, 2: 266.

15. "Revisal of the Laws," *Papers*, 2: 534n.

16. T.J. to George Wythe, August 13, 1786, *Papers*, 10: 244.

17. "Revisal of the Laws," *Papers*, 2: 577.

18. *NSV*, 147.

19. "Revisal of the Laws," *Papers*, 2: 528.

20. Samuel Stanhope Smith to T.J., March? 1779, *Papers*, 2: 246.

21. *Autobiography*, Ford, 1: 75–76.

22. "Revisal of the Laws," *Papers*, 2: 538–539.

23. Ibid., 2: 540.

24. *NSV*, 101.

25. "Revisal of the Laws," *Papers*, 2: 544.

Chapter 16: Lines of Communication

1. "A Bill for Establishing Cross Posts," *Papers*, 2: 388.
2. T.J. to William Phillips, April? 1779, *Papers*, 2: 261.
3. Johann Ludwig de Unger to T.J., November 13, 1780, *Papers*, 4: 118.
4. T.J. to John Adams, August 15, 1820, *AJL*, 568.
5. T.J. to John Minor, August 30, 1814, Ford, 11: 421.
6. T.J. to Philip Mazzei, April 4, 1780, *Papers*, 3: 342.
7. John Page to T.J., June 2, 1779, *Papers*, 2: 278.
8. T.J. to John Page, June 3, 1779, *Papers*, 2: 279.
9. T.J. to Richard Henry Lee, June 17, 1779, *Papers*, 2: 298; T.J. to Riedesel, July 4, 1779, *Papers*, 3: 24.
10. George Washington to T.J., May 15, 1780, *Papers*, 3: 376.
11. "Instructions to Express Riders between Richmond and Cape Henry," *Papers*, 3: 404.
12. T.J. to George Washington, June 11, 1780, *Papers*, 3: 432.
13. T.J. to James Wood, June 9, 1780, *Papers*, 3: 428–429.
14. T.J. to Col. William Duane, October 1, 1812, L&B, 13: 188.
15. T.J. to George Washington, June 11, 1780, *Papers*, 3: 433.
16. T.J. to d'Anmours, September 9, 1780, *Papers*, 3: 619.
17. T.J. to Horatio Gates, October 15, 1780, *Papers*, 4: 40; Thomas Nelson, Jr., to T.J., October 21, 1780, *Papers*, 4: 54.
18. T.J. to Jacob Wray, January 15, 1781, *Papers*, 4: 377; Thomas Nelson to T.J., January 4, 1781, *Papers*, 4: 307.
19. "Notes and Documents Relating to the British Invasions in 1781," *Papers*, 4: 260.
20. Louis Hue Girardin, *The History of Virginia* (Petersburg: M. W. Dunnavant, 1816), 499.
21. *Jefferson at Monticello*, 8; "Diary of Arnold's Invasion and Notes on Subsequent Events in 1781: The 1796? Version," *Papers*, 4: 265.

Chapter 17: *Notes on the State of Virginia*

1. *NSV*, 2; T.J. to Giovanni Fabbroni, May 23, 1785, *Papers*, 27: 745.
2. *Autobiography*, Ford, 1: 94.
3. T.J. to d'Anmours, November 30, 1780, *Papers*, 4: 168.
4. T.J. to James Monroe, May 20, 1782, *Papers*, 6: 185.
5. Marbois to T.J., April 22, 1782, *Papers*, 6: 177–178.
6. T.J. to G. K. van Hogendorp, October 13, 1785, *Papers*, 8: 632.
7. Douglas L. Wilson, "The Evolution of Jefferson's *Notes on the State of Virginia*," *VMHB* 112 (2004): 109.
8. T.J. to Chastellux, January 16, 1784, *Papers*, 6: 467.
9. *NSV*, 2.
10. "Marbois' Queries Concerning Virginia," *Papers*, 4: 166.
11. *NSV*, 5–16.

12. William Byrd, *William Byrd's Histories of the Dividing Line betwixt Virginia and North Carolina*, ed. William K. Boyd (New York: Dover, 1967), 7.

13. Richard Price to T.J., July 2, 1785, *Papers*, 8: 258.

14. *NSV*, 17.

15. Robert A. Ferguson, " 'Mysterious Obligation': Jefferson's *Notes on the State of Virginia*," *American Literature* 52 (1980): 393.

16. Charles Thomson to T.J., March 6, 1785, *Papers*, 8: 16.

17. Wilson, "The Evolution of Jefferson's *Notes*," 108.

18. T.J. to Charles Thomson, June 21, 1785, *Papers*, 8: 245.

19. Louis Guillaume Otto to T.J., May 28, 1785, *Papers*, 8: 169–170.

20. Francis Hopkinson to T.J., November 18, 1784, *Papers*, 7: 535.

21. John Adams to T.J., May 22, 1785, *Papers*, 8: 160.

22. T.J. to James Monroe, June 17, 1795, *Papers*, 8: 229.

23. *NSV*, 24–25.

24. Ibid., 263–264.

25. John Davis, *Travels of Four Years and a Half in the United States of America; During 1798, 1799, 1800, 1801, and 1802* (London: for R. Edwards, 1803), 167.

Chapter 18: The Narrow House

1. Marquis de Chastellux, *Travels in North America in the Years 1780, 1781 and 1782*, trans. and ed. Howard C. Rice, Jr., 2 vols. (Chapel Hill: University of North Carolina Press, 1963), 1: 134, 2: 388.

2. Ibid., 2: 390.

3. Ibid., 2: 391.

4. Ibid., 2: 392.

5. Quoted in ibid., 1: 7.

6. Ibid., 2: 396.

7. Ibid., 1: 190.

8. Ibid., 1: 68, 186.

9. T.J. to Chastellux, September 2, 1785, *Papers*, 8: 467.

10. Chastellux, *Travels*, 2: 391.

11. T.J. to James Monroe, May 20, 1782, *Papers*, 6: 184.

12. T.J. to Chastellux, November 26, 1782, *Papers*, 6: 203.

13. Chastellux, *Travels*, 2: 396.

14. T.J. to James Monroe, May 20, 1782, *Papers*, 6: 186.

15. Quoted in Randall, 1: 382.

16. "Lines Copied from *Tristram Shandy* by Martha and Thomas Jefferson," *Papers*, 6: 196.

17. Cyrus Hamlin, "The Conscience of Narrative: Toward a Hermeneutics of Transcendence," *New Literary History* 13 (1982): 211–212.

18. Quoted in Randall, 1: 382.

19. Quoted in ibid.

20. Quoted in ibid., 1: 383.

21. Quoted in ibid., 1: 382.

22. T.J. to Elizabeth Wayles Eppes, October 3? 1782, *Papers*, 6: 198.

23. T.J. to Chastellux, November 26, 1782, *Papers*, 6: 203.

24. *Autobiography*, Ford, 1: 80.

25. T.J. to Chastellux, November 26, 1782, *Papers*, 6: 203.

26. T.J. to Joseph C. Cabell, February 2, 1816, Cabell, 52.

27. *NSV*, 159.

28. Kevin J. Hayes, "How Thomas Jefferson Read the Qur'an," *Early American Literature* 39 (2004): 253–254.

Chapter 19: An American Odyssey

1. T.J. to Martha Jefferson Randolph, May 31, 1791, *Papers* 20: 463–464.

2. *NSV*, 22.

3. Ibid.

4. Kevin J. Hayes, *The Library of William Byrd of Westover* (Madison, Wisc.: Madison House, 1997), 98–102.

5. *NSV*, 22.

6. T.J. to Isaac Zane, November 8, 1783, *Papers*, 6: 347.

7. T.J. to Horatio G. Spafford, May 14, 1809, L&B, 12: 280–281.

8. *NSV*, 19.

9. *LCB*, 143.

10. Hayes, *Library of William Byrd*, nos. 15, 356, 393, 574–575, 1711, 1738, 1746–1747, 1780–1781, 1976, 2016, 2504, 5536, B1.

11. *Autobiography*, Ford, 1: 66.

12. T.J. to Francis Eppes, November 10, 1783, *Papers*, 6: 350.

13. T.J. to James Monroe, May 21, 1784, *Papers*, 7: 281.

14. T.J. to Francis Hopkinson, January 4, 1784, *Papers*, 6: 445.

15. T.J. to Marbois, December 5, 1783, *Papers*, 6: 374.

16. *Catalogue des Livres qui se Trouvent chez Boinod & Gaillard* (Philadelphia, 1784).

17. T.J. to George Washington, April 6, 1784, *Papers*, 7: 84.

18. David Howell to Jonathan Arnold, February 21, 1784, *LDC*, 21: 380.

19. T.J. to James Madison, February 20, 1784, *Papers*, 6: 548–549.

20. *Papers*, 7: 82.

21. Isaac Disraeli, *The Calamities and Quarrels of Authors: with Some Inquiries Respecting Their Moral and Literary Characters, and Memoirs for Our Literary History*, ed. Benjamin Disraeli (London: Routledge, Warnes, & Routledge, 1859), 71.

22. *Papers*, 7: 82.

23. T.J. to James Madison, February 20, 1784, *Papers*, 6: 550.

24. Ezra Stiles, *The United States Elevated to Glory and Honor: A Sermon* (New Haven, Conn.: Thomas & Samuel Green, 1783), 46.

25. Quoted in Frank P. King, *America's Nine Greatest Presidents* (Jefferson, N.C.: McFarland, 1997), 174.

26. T.J. to George Washington, March 15, 1784, *Papers*, 7: 26.

27. T.J. to Chastellux, September 2, 1785, *Papers*, 8: 468.

Chapter 20: Bookman in Paris

1. *Memorandum Books*, 1: 555.

2. *Observations on the Whale-Fishery*, in Thomas Jefferson, *Writings*, ed. Merrill D. Peterson (New York: Library of America, 1984), 388.

3. For a fine appreciation of Jefferson's pamphlet, see Monteagle Stearns, *Talking to Strangers: Improving American Diplomacy at Home and Abroad* (Princeton, N.J.: Princeton University Press, 1996), 28–30.

4. John Quincy Adams, *Memoirs*, ed. Charles Francis Adams (Philadelphia: J. B. Lippincott, 1874), 1: 317.

5. T.J. to Peter Carr, August 19, 1785, *Papers*, 8: 408.

6. T.J. to Cabot, July 24, 1784, *Papers*, 27: 739–740.

7. Martha Jefferson to Eliza House Trist, after August 24, 1785, *Papers*, 8: 436.

8. *Memorandum Books*, 1: 556.

9. T.J. to Elizabeth Blair Thompson, January 19, 1787, *Papers*, 11: 57.

10. Elizabeth Blair Thompson to T.J., January 10, 1787, *Papers*, 11: 34.

11. Martha Jefferson to Eliza House Trist, after August 24, 1785, *Papers*, 8: 436–437.

12. Ibid., 8: 437.

13. Ibid.

14. T.J. to Carlo Bellini, September 30, 1785, *Papers*, 8: 568.

15. Benjamin Franklin to Richard Price, August 16, 1784, *The Correspondence of Richard Price*, ed. Bernard Peach and T. O. Thomas, 3 vols. (Cardiff: University of Wales Press, 1983–1994), 2: 225.

16. Jefferson to Abigail Adams, August 22, 1813, *AJL*, 367.

17. Sowerby, no. 4375, questions whether this work was among the books Jefferson sold to the Library of Congress. It was not. The copy at the University of Virginia is inscribed "M. Randolph Monticello."

18. T.J. to James Monroe, May 26, 1795, *Papers*, 28: 360–361.

19. T.J. to Samuel H. Smith, September 21, 1814, Ford, 11: 427–428.

20. T.J. to Ezra Stiles, July 17, 1785, *Papers*, 8: 298.

21. T.J. to Edmund Randolph, September 20, 1785, *Papers*, 8: 537; Adams, quoted in *Memorandum Books*, 1: 569; T.J. to James Madison, September 1, 1785, *Papers*, 8: 461.

22. T.J. to Carlo Bellini, September 30, 1785, *Papers*, 8: 569.

23. T.J. to Peter Carr, August 19, 1785, *Papers*, 8: 407.

24. T.J. to Madame de Tessé, March 20, 1787, *Papers*, 11: 226.

25. *Memorandum Books*, 1: 561.

26. Ibid.

27. David Charleton, "Grétry, André Ernest Modest," *New Grove Dictionary of Music and Musicians*, ed. Stanley Sadie, 29 vols. (New York: Grove, 2001), 10: 385–395.

28. Francis Hopkinson to T.J., March 12, 1784, *Papers*, 7: 20.

29. Abigail Adams to Elizabeth Cranch, December 3, 1784, *Adams Family Correspondence*, ed. Lyman H. Butterfield et al., 8 vols. to date (Cambridge, Mass.: Belknap Press of Harvard University Press, 1963–), 6: 5.

30. Quoted in Sowerby, no. 4444.

31. David Humphreys to George Washington, May 10, 1785, *Papers of George Washington: Confederation Series*, ed. W. W. Abbott and Dorothy Twohig, 6 vols. (Charlottesville: University Press of Virginia, 1992–1997), 2: 545.

32. *Autobiography*, Ford, 1: 96.

33. David Humphreys to George Washington, *Papers of George Washington*, 2: 268.

34. John Quincy Adams to Louisa Catherine Adams, March 5, 1809, *Writings of John Quincy Adams*, ed. Worthington Chauncey Ford, 7 vols. (New York: Macmillan, 1913–1917), 3: 289; John Adams to T.J., January 22, 1825, *AJL*, 606.

35. T.J. to James Monroe, March 18, 1785, *Papers*, 8: 43.

36. John Adams to T.J., May 22, 1785, *Papers*, 8: 160; John Quincy Adams, *Life in a New England Town, 1787, 1788: Diary of John Quincy Adams, While a Student in the Office of Theophilus Parsons at Newburyport* (Boston: Little, Brown, 1903), 23.

37. Kevin J. Hayes, "Portraits of the Mind: Ebenezer Devotion and Ezra Stiles," *New England Quarterly* 70 (1997): 616–630.

Chapter 21: Talking about Literature

1. T.J. to John Jay, June 17, 1785, *Papers*, 8: 226. The following anecdote comes from a letter from T.J. to the Rev. William Smith, February 19, 1791, *Papers*, 19: 113.

2. St. John de Crèvecoeur to T.J., July 15, 1784, *Papers*, 7: 376.

3. "Philip Mazzei's Memoranda Regarding Persons and Affairs in Paris," *Papers*, 7: 386; St. John de Crèvecoeur to T.J., July 15, 1784, *Papers*, 7: 377.

4. T.J. to Geismar, September 6, 1785, *Papers*, 8: 500.

5. Margaret Bayard Smith to Susan B. Smith, March 1809, *First Forty Years*, 59.

6. Quoted in Claude-Anne Lopez, *Mon Cher Papa: Franklin and the Ladies of Paris* (New Haven, Conn.: Yale University Press, 1990), 151.

7. T.J. to Abigail Adams, June 21, 1785, *Papers*, 8: 241.

8. T.J. to Madame d'Houdetot, April 2, 1790, *Papers*, 16: 292.

9. Webster, "Notes," 371; see, e.g., Bernard, *Retrospections*, 233–237.

10. Webster, "Notes," 371.

11. Ibid., 377.

12. Dennis Wood, "Staël, Anne-Louise-Germaine Necker," *New Oxford Companion to Literature in French*, ed. Peter France (Oxford: Clarendon Press, 1995), 777–778; T.J. to Madame de Staël, May 24, 1813, *Memoir,*

Correspondence, and Miscellanies, ed. Thomas Jefferson Randolph, 4 vols. (Charlottesville, Va.: F. Carr, 1829), 4: 190; T.J. to Madame de Staël, July 16, 1807, Washington, 5: 133.

13. Henry Tutwiler, "Thomas Jefferson," *Southern Opinion*, October 17, 1868.

14. T.J. to Madame de Staël, July 3, 1815, Washington, 6: 482.

15. T.J. to Madame de Staël, July 16, 1807, Washington, 5: 133.

16. George A. Leavitt, *Catalogue of a Private Library Comprising a Rich Assortment of Rare and Standard Works . . . Also, the Remaining Portion of the Library of the Late Thomas Jefferson, Comprising many Classical Works and Several Autograph Letters, Offered by his Grandson, Francis Eppes, of Poplar Forest, Va.* (New York: George A. Leavitt & Co., 1873), lot 654.

17. T.J. to James Madison, May 7, 1783, *Papers*, 6: 266; T.J. to John Trumbull, June 1, 1789, *Papers*, 15: 164.

18. *Autobiography*, Ford, 1: 103.

19. Webster, "Notes," 277; T.J. to John Adams, April 8, 1816, *AJL*, 467.

20. "Extract from the Diary of Nathaniel Cutting at Le Havre and Cowes," *Papers*, 15: 492–493.

21. Kevin J. Hayes, *Melville's Folk Roots* (Kent, Ohio: Kent State University Press, 1999), 4–5.

22. John Ledyard to T.J., July 29, 1787, *Papers*, 11: 638.

23. "Philip Mazzei's Memoranda," *Papers*, 7: 387.

24. Philip Mazzei, *Memoirs of the Life and Peregrinations of the Florentine*, trans. Howard Rosario Marraro (New York: Columbia University Press, 1942), 292–293.

25. Webster, "Notes," 377.

26. "Philip Mazzei's Memoranda," *Papers*, 7: 387.

27. T.J. to La Rochefoucauld d'Enville, April 3, 1790, *Papers*, 16: 296.

28. T.J. to Abigail Adams, September 4, 1785, *Papers*, 8: 473.

29. Webster, "Notes," 376.

30. Ibid.

31. "History of the Rise and Fall of the British Empire in America," *Britannic Magazine* 3 (1794–1807): 142.

32. John Finch, *Travels in the United States of America and Canada* (London: Longman, Rees, Orme, Green, & Longman, 1833), 254.

33. T.J. to the Rev. James Madison, July 19, 1788, *Papers*, 13: 381.

34. T.J. to John Minor, August 30, 1814, Ford, 11: 425.

35. *Memorandum Books*, 1: 597.

36. "Thoughts on English Prosody," L&B, 18: 414.

37. Ibid., 18: 415.

38. Ibid., 18: 417–418.

39. Ibid., 18: 428.

40. Ibid., 18: 436; Michael T. Gilmore, "The Literature of the Revolutionary and Early National Periods," *The Cambridge History of American Literature*, Vol. 1: *1590–1820*, ed. Sacvan Bercovitch (New York: Cambridge University Press, 1994), 618.

41. See, e.g., I. A. Richards, *Principles of Literary Criticism* (1924; reprint, New York: Routledge, 2002), 129.

42. "Thoughts on English Prosody," L&B, 18: 446.

Chapter 22: London Town

1. John Adams to T.J., February 17, 1786, *Papers*, 9: 285–287.

2. John Adams to T.J., February 21, 1786, *Papers*, 9: 295.

3. T.J. to James Madison, January 30, 1787, *Papers*, 11: 97.

4. Quoted in *Memorandum Books*, 1: 611.

5. T.J. to John Jay, March 12, 1786, *Papers*, 9: 325.

6. David Humphreys to George Washington, February 11, 1786, *Papers of George Washington: Confederation Series*, ed. W. W. Abbott and Dorothy Twohig, 6 vols. (Charlottesville: University Press of Virginia, 1992–1997), 3: 556.

7. *Autobiography*, Ford, 1: 97.

8. Ibid.

9. *Memorandum Books*, 1: 614.

10. Quoted in Richard D. Altick, *The Shows of London* (Cambridge, Mass.: Belknap Press of Harvard University Press, 1978), 41–42; James Boswell, *Life of Johnson, Together with Journal of a Tour to the Hebrides and Johnson's Diary of a Journey into North Wales*, ed. George Birkbeck Hill, 6 vols. (Oxford: Clarendon Press, 1934), 4: 373–374.

11. *London Unmask'd: or The New Town Spy* (London: for William Adlard, n.d.), 141–142; Abigail Adams II to John Quincy Adams, *Adams Family Correspondence*, ed. Lyman H. Butterfield et al., 8 vols. to date (Cambridge, Mass.: Belknap Press of Harvard University Press, 1963–), 6: 220.

12. Quoted in Altick, *Shows of London*, 41–42.

13. Ezra Pound, *Guide to Kulchur* (1938; reprint, New York: New Directions, 1968), 181.

14. T.J. to Sir Herbert Croft, October 30, 1798, *Papers*, 30: 568.

15. L. T. Rede, *Anecdotes & Biography, Including Many Modern Characters in the Circles of Fashionable and Official Life* (London: J. W. Myers for R. Pitkeathley, 1799), 456.

16. Peter Pindar, *The Lousiad*, in *The Works of Peter Pindar, Esq, Complete*, 2 vols. (Dublin: for J. Williams, 1792), canto 2, lines 7–10; James Boswell, *Boswell's London Journal, 1762–1763*, ed. Frederick A. Pottle (1950; reprint, New Haven, Conn.: Yale University Press, 2004), 86.

17. "An Interlude at Dolly's Chop House," *Papers*, 9: 350.

18. Herman Melville, *Omoo: A Narrative of Adventures in the South Seas*, ed. Harrison Hayford and Walter Blair (New York: Hendricks House, 1969), 73.

19. American Commissioners to John Jay, March 28, 1786, *Papers*, 9: 358.

20. Kevin J. Hayes, "How Thomas Jefferson Read the Qur'an," *Early American Literature* 39 (2004): 256–257.

21. John Adams to T.J., July 3, 1786, *Papers*, 10: 87.

22. T.J. to John Adams, July 11, 1786, *Papers*, 10: 123.

23. Karl Moritz, *Travels, Chiefly on Foot, through Several Parts of England, in 1782* (London: for G. G. and J. Robinson, 1795), 39.

24. T.J. to Madame de Corny, June 30, 1787, *Papers*, 11: 509.

25. "Notes of a Tour of English Gardens," *Papers*, 9: 369.

26. T.J. to John Page, May 4, 1786, *Papers*, 9: 445.

27. John Adams, *Diary and Autobiography of John Adams*, ed. L. H. Butterfield, Leonard C. Faber, and Wendell D. Garrett (Cambridge, Mass.: Belknap Press of Harvard University Press, 1961), 3: 184–186.

28. Moritz, *Travels*, 186–187; Adams, *Diary and Autobiography*, 3: 185.

29. Moritz, *Travels*, 186–187.

30. Adams, *Diary and Autobiography*, 3: 185.

31. Bernice W. Kliman, "Cum Notis Variorum: Samuel Henley, Shakespeare Commentator in Bell's *Annotations*," *Shakespeare Newsletter* 48 (1998–1999): 91–92, 108, 110.

32. "1789 Catalog of Books," *Thomas Jefferson Papers: An Electronic Archive* (Boston: Massachusetts Historical Society, 2003), 46, http://www .thomasjeffersonpapers.org.

33. Andrew Becket, *A Concordance to Shakespeare* (London: for G. G. J. and J. Robinson, 1787), iii.

34. Bernard, *Retrospections*, 238.

35. David Humphreys to George Washington, February 11, 1786, *Papers of George Washington*, 3: 556.

36. Quoted in *The London Stage, 1660–1800: A Calendar of Plays, Entertainments & Afterpieces, Together with Casts, Box-Receipts and Contemporary Comment*, ed. W. Van Lennep et al., 5 vols. (Carbondale: Southern Illinois University Press, 1960–1968), 2: 876.

37. T.J. to George Washington, August 14, 1787, *Papers*, 12: 36.

38. John Trumbull, *The Autobiography of Colonel John Trumbull, Patriot-Artist, 1756–1843*, ed. Theodore Sizer (New Haven, Conn.: Yale University Press, 1953).

39. T.J. to Harry Innes, March 7, 1791, *Papers*, 19: 521.

40. Altick, *The Shows of London*, 28–30.

41. *Memorandum Books*, 1: 624.

42. Abigail Adams to T.J., February 11, 1786, *Papers*, 9: 277–278.

43. T.J. to Robert Skipwith, August 3, 1771, *Papers*, 1: 77.

Chapter 23: Summer of '86

1. David Ramsay to T.J., June 15, 1785, *Papers*, 8: 210.

2. David Ramsay to T.J., August 8, 1785, *Papers*, 8: 360.

3. T.J. to David Ramsay, August 31, 1785, *Papers*, 8: 457.

4. Robert L. Brunhouse, "David Ramsay's Publication Problems, 1784–1808," *Publications of the Bibliographical Society of America* 39 (1945): 56–58.

5. T.J. to William Stephens Smith, July 9, 1786, *Papers*, 10: 117.

6. T.J. to James Madison, August 2, 1787, *Papers*, 11: 667–668.

7. T.J. to Francis Hopkinson, August 14, 1786, *Papers*, 10: 250.

8. T.J. to Ezra Stiles, September 1, 1786, *Papers*, 10: 317.

9. Howard C. Rice, Jr., *Thomas Jefferson's Paris* (Princeton, N.J.: Princeton University Press, 1976), 33–35.

10. T.J. to Maria Cosway, October 12, 1786, *Papers*, 10: 444. The remainder of the quotations from this letter are drawn from this edition, 10: 443–455, and are not separately documented.

11. Arthur Young, *Travels during the Years 1787, 1788, and 1789* (Bury St. Edmund's, England: J. Rackham for W. Richardson, 1792), 63.

12. Ibid.

13. Joseph Townsend, *A Journey through Spain in the Years 1786 and 1787...and Remarks in Passing through a Part of France*, 3 vols. (London: for C. Dilly, 1791), 1: 35.

14. James A. Bear, *Jefferson's Advice to His Children and Grandchildren on Their Reading: An Address Delivered during the Celebration of the 25th Anniversary of the Tracy W. McGregor Library, 1939-1964* (Charlottesville: University of Virginia, Tracy W. McGregor Library, 1967), 16, locates a 1785 copy of Florian's *Galatée* inscribed "A Mademoiselle Jefferson."

15. T.J. to Maria Cosway, October 5, 1786, *Papers*, 10: 432.

16. Ibid., 10: 431–432.

17. Jeanne M. Malloy, *American Secular Prose Dialogues before 1790* (Newark: University of Delaware Press, 1991).

18. Boethius, *The Consolation of Philosophy*, trans. Victor Watts, rev. ed. (New York: Penguin, 1999), 6.

Chapter 24: An Inquisitive Journey through France and Italy

1. T.J. to George Watterston, May 7, 1815, Jefferson Papers (DLC).

2. "Hints to Americans Travelling in Europe," *Papers*, 13: 268.

3. "Notes on the Letter of Christoph Daniel Ebeling," after October 15, 1795, *Papers*, 28: 506.

4. "Hints," *Papers*, 13: 268.

5. Joseph Addison, *Remarks on Several Parts of Italy* (London: J. Tonson, 1705), 301–302.

6. "Hints," *Papers*, 13: 268.

7. Ibid., 13: 269.

8. T.J. to Chastellux, April 4, 1787, *Papers*, 11: 261–262.

9. Laurence Sterne, *A Sentimental Journey through France and Italy*, ed. Virginia Woolf (New York: Oxford University Press, 1948), 91.

10. "Notes of a Tour into the Southern Parts of France, etc.," *Papers*, 11: 415.

11. John Finch, *Travels in the United States of America and Canada* (London: Longman, Rees, Orme, Green, & Longman, 1833), 253.

12. "Notes of a Tour," *Papers*, 11: 417.

13. Ibid., 11: 420.

14. T.J. to William Short, March 15, 1787, *Papers*, 11: 214.

15. Quoted in *Papers*, 10: 158.

16. T.J. to Madame de Tessé, March 20, 1787, *Papers*, 11: 226.

17. Ibid., 11: 226–227.

18. Ibid., 11: 227.

19. T.J. to Madame de Tott, April 5, 1787, *Papers*, 11: 271–272.

20. T.J. to William Short, March 27, 1787, *Papers*, 11: 247–248.

21. T.J. to William Short, March 29, 1787, *Papers*, 11: 254.

22. Ezra Pound, *The Spirit of Romance* (New York: New Directions, 1952), 39.

23. T.J. to Lafayette, April 11, 1787, *Papers*, 11: 283.

24. Ibid., 11: 285.

25. "Notes of a Tour," *Papers*, 11: 432; T.J. to Maria Cosway, July 1, 1787, *Papers*, 11: 519.

26. T.J. to George Wythe, September 16, 1787, *Papers*, 12: 127.

27. T.J. to William Drayton, July 30, 1787, *Papers*, 11: 648.

28. *Jefferson at Monticello*, 5.

29. *Papers*, 11: 464.

30. "Hints," *Papers*, 13: 270.

31. "Notes of a Tour," *Papers*, 11: 441.

32. Ibid., 11: 441–442.

33. "Hints," *Papers*, 13: 271.

34. T.J. to Martha Jefferson, March 28, 1787, *Papers*, 11: 251.

35. Abigail Adams to T.J., July 10, 1787, *Papers*, 11: 573; *The History of Fanny Meadows*, 2 vols. (London: for T. Becket, 1775), 1: 179; *Disinterested Love: or, The History of Sir Charles Royston, and Emily Lessley*, 2 vols. (London: for John Wilkie, 1776), 1: 217.

36. Abigail Adams to T.J., July 10, 1787, *Papers*, 11: 573.

37. T.J. to Martha Jefferson, May 21, 1787, *Papers*, 11: 369–370.

Chapter 25: A Tour through Holland and the Rhine Valley

1. T.J. to John Adams, May 25, 1785, *Papers*, 8: 164.

2. T.J. to Abigail Adams, June 21, 1785, *Papers*, 8: 239.

3. T.J. to Abigail Adams, September 25, 1785, *Papers*, 8: 549.

4. T.J. to Abigail Adams, August 9, 1786, *Papers*, 10: 202–203.

5. T.J. to Abigail Adams, July 1, 1787, *Papers*, 11: 515.

6. T.J. to Abigail Adams, February 2, 1788, *Papers*, 12: 553.

7. Howard C. Rice, Jr., *Thomas Jefferson's Paris* (Princeton, N.J.: Princeton University Press, 1976), 105–107.

8. T.J. to John Adams, March 2, 1788, *Papers*, 12: 637.

9. T.J. to William Short, March 10, 1788, *Papers*, 12: 659.

10. Ibid.

11. *Autobiography*, Ford, 1: 127.

12. "Hints to Americans Travelling in Europe," *Papers*, 13: 264; *Memorandum Books*, 1: 698.

13. T.J. to William Short, March 29, 1788, *Papers*, 12: 697.

14. T.J. to Maria Cosway, April 24, 1788, *Papers*, 13: 103.

15. T.J. to William Short, April 9, 1788, *Papers*, 13: 48–49.

16. T.J. to John Trumbull, March 27, 1788, *Papers*, 12: 694.

17. John Trumbull, *The Autobiography of Colonel John Trumbull Patriot-Artist, 1756–1843*, ed. Theodore Sizer (New Haven, Conn.: Yale University Press, 1953); John Owen, *Travels into Different Parts of Europe, in the Years 1791 and 1792* (London: for T. Cadell, Jun. and W. Davies, 1796), 142; "Notes of a Tour through Holland and the Rhine Valley," *Papers*, 13: 12.

18. T.J. to Maria Cosway, April 24, 1788, *Papers*, 13: 103.

19. Owen, *Travels*, 143.

20. T.J. to Maria Cosway, April 24, 1788, *Papers*, 13: 104.

21. Laurence Sterne, *The Life and Opinions of Tristram Shandy, Gentleman* (New York: Oxford University Press, 1928), 162; T.J. to Maria Cosway, April 24, 1788, *Papers*, 13: 104.

22. T.J. to William Wirt, November 12, 1816, Jefferson Papers (DLC).

23. T.J. to Maria Cosway, April 24, 1788, *Papers*, 13: 103; Owen, *Travels*, 143–144; Trumbull, *Autobiography*, 137.

24. T.J. to Maria Cosway, April 24, 1788, *Papers*, 13: 103.

25. Charles McCorquodale, "Dolci, Carlo," *Dictionary of Art*, ed. Jane Turner, 34 vols. (New York: Grove, 1996), 9: 76–79.

26. "Notes of a Tour," *Papers*, 13: 14.

27. Adam Walker, *Ideas, Suggested on the Spot in a Late Excursion through Flanders, Germany, France, and Italy* (London: for J. Robson, 1790), 66.

28. "Notes of a Tour," *Papers*, 13: 19–20; T.J. to Geismar, July 13, 1788, *Papers*, 13: 357.

29. T.J. to Maria Cosway, April 24, 1788, *Papers*, 13: 104.

30. Maria Cosway to T.J., April 29, 1788, *Papers*, 13: 115.

31. William Howard Adams, *The Paris Years of Thomas Jefferson* (New Haven, Conn.: Yale University Press, 1997), 235–237.

32. T.J. to Angelica Schuyler Church, August 17, 1788, *Papers*, 13: 521.

33. Sterne, *Tristram Shandy, Gentleman*, 66–67.

34. T.J. to John Trumbull, March 27, 1788, *Papers*, 12: 694; "Hints," *Papers*, 13: 267.

35. T.J. to Thomas Payne, October 2, 1788, *Papers*, 13: 650.

36. "Hints," *Papers*, 13: 267.

Chapter 26: Last Days in Paris

1. *Autobiography*, Ford, 1: 132; T.J. to Madame de Bréhan, March 14, 1789, *Papers*, 14: 656.

2. T.J. to John Trumbull, February 15, 1788, *Papers*, 14: 561.

3. Gilbert Chinard, "Introduction," *A Huguenot Exile in Virginia: Or, Voyages of a Frenchman Exiled for His Religion with a Description of Virginia and Maryland*, trans. Gilbert Chinard (New York: Press of the Pioneers, 1934), 10.

4. T.J. to John Adams, June 11, 1812, *AJL*, 306.

5. T.J. to Joseph Willard, March 24, 1789, *Papers*, 14: 697–698.

6. T.J. to Joseph Willard, March 24, 1789, *Papers*, 14: 699.

7. Archer Taylor, *Book Catalogues: Their Varieties and Uses*, revised by William P. Barlow, 2d ed. (London: St. Paul's Biographies, 1986), 97–98.

8. *Bibliotheca Pinelliana: A Catalogue of the Magnificent and Celebrated Library of Maffei Pinelli* (London: Robson & Clarke, 1789), 189.

9. Lucy Ludwell Paradise to T.J., May 26, 1789, *Papers*, 15: 151; T.J. to Lucy Ludwell Paradise, June 1, 1789, *Papers*, 15: 162–163.

10. Myles Davies, *Athenae Britannicae: or, The Critical News, and Parallels of Miscelanies*, vol. 4 (London: Myles Davies, 1715); Isaac Disraeli, *Curiosities of Literature: Consisting of Anecdotes, Characters, Sketches, and Observations, Literary Critical, and Historical* (London: for J. Murray, 1791), 19; Philip Dormer Stanhope, Earl of Chesterfield, *Letters…to His Son*, ed. Eugenia Stanhope (London: J. Dodsley, 1774), 567; Abel Boyer, *Boyer's Royal Dictionary Abridged*, ed. J. C. Prieur, 14th ed. (London, 1777).

11. For a good survey of the situation, see *Memorandum Books*, 1: 730 n47.

12. *Autobiography*, Ford, 1: 127–128.

13. Ibid., 1: 135.

14. "A Fourth of July Tribute to Jefferson," July 4, 1789, *Papers*, 15: 239–240.

15. *Autobiography*, Ford, 1: 144.

16. Ibid., 1: 154.

17. Abigail Adams to T.J., June 6, 1785, *Papers*, 6: 178.

18. *Autobiography*, Ford, 1: 157.

Chapter 27: The Young Idea

1. "Extract from the Diary of Nathaniel Cutting at Le Havre and Cowes," *Papers*, 15: 490–492.

2. Quoted in *Memorandum Books*, 1: 745; T.J. to William Short, October 7, 1789, *Papers*, 15: 509.

3. T.J. to William Short, October 7, 1789, *Papers*, 15: 509.

4. "Revisal of the Laws," *Papers*, 2: 325, 496; Howard I. Kuchner, *American Suicide: A Psychocultural Exploration* (New Brunswick, N.J.: Rutgers University Press, 1991), 30.

5. Quoted in *Memorandum Books*, 1: 745; *Jefferson at Monticello*, 21.

6. "Extract from the Diary of Nathaniel Cutting," *Papers*, 15: 496.

7. George A. Leavitt, *Catalogue of a Private Library Comprising a Rich Assortment of Rare and Standard Works…Also, the Remaining Portion of the Library of the Late Thomas Jefferson, Comprising many Classical Works and Several Autograph Letters, Offered by his Grandson, Francis Eppes, of Poplar Forest, Va.* (New York: George A. Leavitt & Co., 1873), lot 639, lists a copy of La Fontaine inscribed with the autograph of Mary Jefferson.

8. "Extract from the Diary of Nathaniel Cutting," *Papers*, 15: 497.

9. Ibid., 15: 498.

10. T.J. to Madame de Corny, April 2, 1790, *Papers* 16: 289.

11. "Reminiscences of Th.J. by MR," *Papers*, 15: 560.

12. Ibid., 15: 560–561.

13. T.J. to Madame de Corny, April 2, 1790, *Papers*, 16: 289.

14. Quoted in *Papers*, 16: 167–168.

15. Jack McLaughlin, *Jefferson and Monticello: The Biography of a Builder* (New York: Henry Holt, 1988), 240.

16. *Autobiography*, Ford, 1: 159; T.J. to Madame de Corny, April 2, 1790, *Papers*, 16: 290.

17. T.J. to Thomas Mann Randolph, Jr., July 6, 1787, *Papers*, 11: 558; T.J. to Thomas Mann Randolph, Jr., March 8, 1790, *Papers*, 16: 214.

18. T.J. to William Short, December 14, 1789, *Papers*, 16: 26.

19. T.J. to William Fitzhugh, March 11, 1790, *Papers*, 16: 223; T.J. to Thomas Mann Randolph, Jr., March 28, 1790, *Papers*, 16: 278.

20. Kevin J. Hayes, "Introduction," Edwin Wolf II and Kevin J. Hayes, *The Library of Benjamin Franklin* (Philadelphia: American Philosophical Society and the Library Company of Philadelphia, 2006), 19.

21. *Autobiography*, Ford, 1: 159–160; T.J. to Samuel Smith, August 22, 1798, *Papers*, 30: 484; T.J. to Jonathan Williams, July 3, 1796, *Papers*, 29: 140.

22. T.J. to Madame d'Enville, April 2, 1790, *Papers*, 16: 291.

23. T.J. to Lafayette, April 2, 1790, *Papers*, 16: 293.

24. "Explanations of the 3. Volumes Bound in Marbled Paper," Jefferson Papers (DLC).

25. Ibid.

26. Ibid.

27. Ibid.

28. T.J. to David Rittenhouse, June 20, 1790, *Papers* 16: 543.

29. Ezra Stiles to T.J., August 27, 1790, *Papers*, 17: 442–444.

30. T.J. to Mercy Warren, November 25, 1790, *Papers*, 18: 78.

31. Edward Dumbauld, *Thomas Jefferson, American Tourist: Being an Account of His Journeys in the United States of America, England, France, Italy, the Low Countries, and Germany* (Norman: University of Oklahoma Press, 1946), 156–158; *Catalogue of Books Belonging to the Library of Rhode-Island College* (Providence, R.I.: J. Carter, 1793).

32. *Memorandum Books*, 1: 764–765.

33. Thomas Lee Shippen to William Shippen, September 15, 1790, *Papers*, 17: 464.

34. *Memorandum Books*, 1: 770.

35. T.J. to Martha Jefferson Randolph, December 23, 1790, *Papers*, 18: 350.

36. Mary Jefferson to T.J., January 22, 1791, *Papers*, 18: 594.

37. George Chapman, *A Treatise on Education*, 4th ed. (London: for the author, 1790), 85; Mary Jefferson to T.J., January 22, 1791, *Papers*, 18: 594.

38. Martha Jefferson Randolph to T.J., January 16, 1791, *Papers*, 18: 500.

39. T.J. to Mary Jefferson, February 16, 1791, *Papers*, 19: 282.

40. T.J. to Joseph Willard, March 24, 1789, *Papers*, 14: 697.

41. T.J. to Martha Jefferson Randolph, May 31, 1791, *Papers*, 20: 463.

42. T.J. to Mary Jefferson, May 30, 1791, *Papers*, 20: 462–463.

43. Mary Jefferson to T.J., July 16, 1791, *Papers*, 20: 633.

44. T.J. to Thomas Mann Randolph, Jr., June 5, 1791, *Papers*, 20: 464–465.

Chapter 28: *The Anas*

1. Robert Southey, *The Doctor, &c.*, ed. John Wood Warter (London: Longman, Brown, Green, & Longmans, 1848), 623.

2. "Explanations of the 3. Volumes Bound in Marbled Paper," Jefferson Papers (DLC).

3. "The 'Anas': Editorial Note," *Papers*, 22: 33–38.

4. James Boswell, "The Journal of a Tour to the Hebrides," in Samuel Johnson and James Boswell, *A Journey to the Western Islands of Scotland and the Journal of a Tour to the Hebrides*, ed. Peter Levi (New York: Penguin, 1984), 350.

5. "Notes of a Conversation with Alexander Hamilton," *Papers*, 22: 38.

6. Ibid., 22: 38–39.

7. Laurence Sterne, *A Sentimental Journey through France and Italy*, ed. Virginia Woolf (New York: Oxford University Press, 1948), 50; Sterne, *The Life and Opinions of Tristram Shandy, Gentleman* (New York: Oxford University Press, 1928), 507.

8. "Notes on Conversation on Rufus King," *Papers*, 22: 445.

9. Sergei M. Eisenstein, *The Film Sense*, trans. Jay Leyda (San Diego: Harcourt Brace, 1947), 4.

10. "Memoranda of Conversations with the President," *Papers*, 23: 187.

11. "Memorandum on References by Congress to Heads of Departments," *Papers*, 23: 246–247.

12. "Memorandum of Conference with the President on Treaty with Algiers," *Papers*, 23: 256–257.

13. Ibid., 23: 257.

14. T.J. to Thomas Paine, July 11, 1789, *Papers*, 15: 269; T.J. to Monsieur A. Coray, October 31, 1823, L&B, 15: 489.

15. T.J. to Martha Jefferson Randolph, July 7, 1793, *Papers*, 26: 445–446.

16. T.J. to Martha Jefferson Randolph, May 26, 1793, *Papers*, 26: 122.

17. T.J. to Martha Jefferson Randolph, May 12, 1793, *Papers*, 26: 18.

18. Kevin J. Hayes, "Freneau, Philip," *ODNB*, 20: 976–977.

19. "Notes of a Conversation with George Washington," *Papers*, 26: 102.

20. "American Philosophical Society's Instructions to André Michaux," ca. April 30, 1793, *Papers*, 25: 625.

21. "American Philosophical Society's Instructions to André Michaux," ca. April 30, 1793, *Papers*, 25: 625–626.

22. T.J. to Isaac Shelby, June 28, 1793, *Papers*, 26: 393.

23. "Notes of Cabinet Meeting and Conversations with Edmond Charles Genet," *Papers*, 26: 438.

24. Dumas Malone, *Jefferson and the Ordeal of Liberty* (Boston: Little, Brown, 1962), 126, 128.

25. "Notes of Cabinet Meeting on Edmond Charles Genet," *Papers*, 26: 730.

26. Ibid.

27. Ibid.

28. Ibid., 26: 731.

29. Ibid., 26: 731–732.

30. "Notes of a Conversation with John Beckley," *Papers*, 27: 467.

Chapter 29: Letters from a Virginia Farmer

1. T.J. to Mann Page, August 30, 1795, *Papers*, 28: 440.

2. T.J. to Horatio Gates, February 3, 1794, *Papers*, 28: 14; T.J. to Edward Rutledge, November 30, 1795, *Papers*, 28: 541.

3. T.J. to Martha Jefferson Randolph, January 22, 1795, *Papers*, 28: 249; T.J. to Martha Jefferson Randolph, March 6, 1796, *Papers*, 29: 11.

4. T.J. to Pierre Auguste Adet, October 14, 1795, *Papers*, 28: 503–504.

5. John Spurrier, *The Practical Farmer: Being a New and Compendious System of Husbandry, Adapted to the Different Soils and Climates of America* (Wilmington, Del.: Bryneberg & Andrews, 1798), iii.

6. François-Alexandre-Fréderic La Rochefoucauld-Liancourt, *Travels through the United States of North America*, trans. Henry Neuman, 2d ed., 4 vols. (London: for R. Phillips, 1800), 3: 141.

7. T.J. to William Branch Giles, April 27, 1795, *Papers*, 28: 337.

8. T.J. to James Madison, April 3, 1794, *Papers* 28: 50.

9. T.J. to John Adams, April 25, 1794, *Papers*, 28: 57.

10. T.J. to Froullé, May 26, 1795, *Papers*, 28: 357.

11. Ibid.

12. Benjamin Rush, "Excerpts from the Papers of Dr. Benjamin Rush," *Pennsylvania Magazine of History and Biography* 29 (1905): 26.

13. T.J. to Joseph Milligan, March 28, 1815, Jefferson Papers (DLC).

14. T.J. to Archibald Stuart, May 23, 1795, *Papers*, 28: 350–352; *Report of the Curator to the Board of Trustees of the Thomas Jefferson Memorial Foundation for the Year 1974* (Monticello: The Foundation, 1974).

15. T.J. to Wilson Cary Nicholas, December 16, 1809, Jefferson Papers (DLC).

16. The copy at the University of Virginia, which contains T.J.'s characteristic marks of identification, is also inscribed with the autograph of Cornelia Randolph.

17. T.J. to James Monroe, May 26, 1795, *Papers*, 28: 362.

18. Z. A. Pelczynski, "Hegel as a Political Writer," *Hegel's Political Writings*, trans. T. M. Knox (Oxford: Clarendon Press, 1964), 10.

19. T.J. to John Adams, April 25, 1794, *Papers*, 28: 57.

20. T.J. to George Wythe, April 18, 1795, *Papers*, 28: 332.

21. T.J. to George Wythe, October 23, 1794, *Papers*, 28: 181.

22. George Wythe to T.J., November 1, 1794, *Papers*, 28: 185.

23. T.J. to George Wythe, April 18, 1795, *Papers*, 28: 332.

24. T.J. to James Madison, April 3, 1794, *Papers*, 28: 50.

25. T.J. to George Washington, May 14, 1794, *Papers*, 28: 75; T.J. to Edmund Randolph, February 3, 1794, *Papers*, 28: 15.

26. T.J. to the Rev. Isaac Story, December 5, 1801, *EG*, 325.

27. T.J. to Edward Rutledge, November 30, 1795, *Papers*, 28: 541.

28. T.J. to Edmund Randolph, February 3, 1794, *Papers*, 28: 15–16.

29. T.J. to Pierre Auguste Adet, October 14, 1795, *Papers*, 28: 503–504.

30. T.J. to Philip Mazzei, April 24, 1796, *Papers*, 29: 82.

31. S. V. Henkels, *The Extraordinary Library of Hon. Samuel W. Pennypacker*, 2 vols. (Philadelphia, 1905–1909), lot 442 1/2, lists an octavo edition of *Gulliver's Travels* (London, 1727) owned by George Washington.

32. T.J. to Philip Mazzei, April 24, 1796, *Papers*, 29: 82.

33. Bernard, *Retrospections*, 238.

Chapter 30: The Vice President and the Printed Word

1. T.J. to the American Philosophical Society, January 28, 1797, *Papers*, 29: 276.

2. Charles Thomson to T.J., March 9, 1782, *Papers*, 6: 163.

3. T.J. to Charles Thomson, December 20, 1781, *Papers*, 6: 142.

4. T.J. to David Rittenhouse, July 3, 1796, *Papers*, 29: 138.

5. T.J. to Elbridge Gerry, May 13, 1797, *Papers*, 29: 362.

6. Volney to T.J., December 26, 1796, *Papers*, 29: 229; T.J. to Volney, January 8, 1797, *Papers*, 29: 258.

7. T.J. to Benjamin Rush, January 22, 1797, *Papers*, 29: 275.

8. Ibid.

9. "Memoir on the Megalonyx," *Papers*, 29: 295.

10. Ibid.

11. T.J. to James Madison, January 30, 1797, *Papers*, 29: 281.

12. "Address to the Senate [March 4, 1797]," *Papers* 29: 310–311.

13. *NSV*, 275.

14. "Extract and Commentary Printed in the New York *Minerva*," May 2, 1797, *Papers*, 29: 86.

15. T.J. to Samuel Smith, August 22, 1798, *Papers*, 30: 485–486.

16. Kevin J. Hayes, "Freneau, Philip Morin," *ODNB*, 20: 976–977.

17. Michael Durey, "Callender, James Thomson," *ODNB*, 9: 550–551.

18. T.J. to James Monroe, July 15, 1802, *L&B*, 10: 331; T.J. to Abigail Adams, July 22, 1804, *AJL*, 274.

19. *Memorandum Books*, 2: 971–986, *passim*.

20. "The Kentucky Resolutions of 1798," *Papers*, 30: 529–535.

21. "Course of Reading for William G. Munford," *Papers*, 30: 594–595.

22. T.J. to William G. Munford, February 27, 1799, *Papers*, 31: 68.

23. Condorcet, *Outlines of an Historical View of the Progress of the Human Mind* (Philadelphia: for M. Carey, H. and P. Rice & Co., J. Ormond, B. F. Bache, and J. Fellows, 1796), 148.

24. *Papers*, 30: 596–597.

25. T.J. to William G. Munford, June 18, 1799, *Papers*, 31: 128.

26. T.J. to George Wythe, February 28, 1800, *Papers*, 31: 400–401.

27. Condorcet, *Outlines*, 146.

28. George Wythe to T.J., December 7, 1800, *Papers*, 32: 282.

29. Joseph P. McKerns, "Smith, Samuel Harrison," *ANB*, 20: 282–283.

30. *First Forty Years*, 5–8.

Chapter 31: The First Inaugural Address

1. *National Intelligencer and Washington Advertiser*, March 6, 1801; *First Forty Years*, 10, 12.

2. *National Intelligencer and Washington Advertiser*, March 6, 1801.

3. John Davis, *Travels of Four Years and a Half in the United States of America* (London: T. Ostell, 1803), 177.

4. *National Intelligencer and Washington Advertiser*, March 4, 1801; *Philadelphia Gazette*, March 7, 1801; Margaret Bayard Smith to Susan B. Smith, March 4, 1801, *First Forty Years*, 26; *National Intelligencer and Washington Advertiser*, March 6, 1801.

5. "First Inaugural Address," in Thomas Jefferson, *Writings*, ed. Merrill D. Peterson (New York: Library of America, 1984), 492–496. The remaining quotations from this address come from this edition and are not documented separately.

6. Samuel Johnson, *The History of Rasselas, Prince of Abbissinia* (Edinburgh: for William Creech, 1789), 4.

7. T.J. to Ellen Wayles Randolph, June 29, 1807, *Family Letters*, 309.

8. T.J. to John Dickinson, March 6, 1801, Washington, 4: 365–366.

9. William Thornton to James Madison, March 16, 1801, *Papers of William Thornton*, Vol. 1: *1781–1802*, ed. C. M. Harris and Daniel Preston (Charlottesville: University Press of Virginia, 1995), 555.

10. *American Citizen and General Advertiser*, March 20, 1801; John Marshall to Charles Cotesworth Pinckney, March 4, 1801, *The Papers of John Marshall*, ed. Herbert T. Johnson, Charles T. Cullen, and Charles F. Hobson, 11 vols. (Chapel Hill: University of North Carolina Press, 1974–2002), 6: 89–90.

11. Margaret Bayard Smith to Susan B. Smith, March 4, 1801, *First Forty Years*, 25–26.

12. Ibid., 26.

13. Noble E. Cunningham, *The Inaugural Addresses of President Thomas Jefferson, 1801 and 1805* (Columbia: University of Missouri Press, 2001), 17–22, provides a good selection of quotations from the contemporary press. Quotations otherwise undocumented in this chapter come from this work.

14. Allan Kline, "The 'American' Stanzas in Shelley's *Revolt of Islam*: A Source," *Modern Language Notes* 70 (1955): 101–103; Percy Bysshe Shelley,

"The Revolt of Islam," *The Poetical Works of Percy Bysshe Shelley*, ed. Edward Dowden (London: Macmillan, 1895), 198.

15. John Orbell, "Baring, Alexander," *ODNB*, 3: 815–818.

16. *Poulson's American Daily Advertiser*, June 19, 1801; *American Citizen*, February 17, 1801.

17. *National Intelligencer and Washington Advertiser*, March 20, 1801.

18. "On President Jefferson's Speech," *American Mercury*, April 2, 1801.

19. Benjamin Rush to T.J., March 12, 1801, *Letters of Benjamin Rush*, ed. L. H. Butterfield, 2 vols. (Philadelphia: American Philosophical Society, 1951), 2: 831.

20. Ibid.

21. Margaret Bayard Smith to Susan B. Smith, March 4, 1801, *First Forty Years*, 26.

22. Pierre Samuel Du Pont de Nemours to T.J., December 17, 1801, *Correspondence between Thomas Jefferson and Pierre Samuel du Pont de Nemours, 1798–1817*, ed. Dumas Malone, trans. Linwood Lehman (Boston: Houghton Mifflin, 1930), 36.

23. Rush to Thomas Jefferson, March 12, 1801, *Letters of Benjamin Rush*, 2: 831–832.

24. *National Intelligencer and Washington Advertiser*, March 6, 1801.

Chapter 32: The Wall of Separation

1. T.J. to Benjamin Rush, September 23, 1800, *EG*, 320.

2. T.J. to Benjamin Rush, March 24, 1801, Ford, 9: 230–231.

3. T.J. to Moses Robinson, March 23, 1801, *EG*, 324.

4. Ibid., 324–325.

5. T.J. to Elbridge Gerry, March 29, 1801, Ford, 9: 241–242.

6. Quoted in Bernard, *Retrospections*, 238.

7. Robert E. Scofield, "Priestley, Joseph," *ODNB*, 45: 351–359.

8. T.J. to Joseph Priestley, March 21, 1801, L&B, 10: 228–229.

9. "Tunis: Interesting Account of the Tunisians, and Other People Inhabiting the Coast of Barbary," *Courier of New Hampshire*, July 23, 1801.

10. Edwin G. Burrows, "Gallatin, Albert," *ANB*, 8: 639–642.

11. Paul David Nelson, "Lincoln, Levi," *ANB*, 13: 677–678.

12. William M. Fowler, Jr., "Smith, Robert," *ANB*, 20: 276–277.

13. T.J. to William A. Burwell, March 26, 1804, *Thomas Jefferson Correspondence: Printed from the Originals in the Collections of William K. Bixby*, ed. Worthington Chauncey Ford (Boston, 1916), 105.

14. T.J. to Martha Jefferson Randolph, May 28, 1801, *Family Letters*, 202.

15. Margaret Bayard Smith to Maria Bayard, May 28, 1801, *First Forty Years*, 29.

16. *First Forty Years*, 11–12.

17. T.J. to Edmund Bacon, May 13, 1807, *Jefferson at Monticello*, 66.

18. "Dr. Mitchill's Letters from Washington, 1801–1813," *Harper's New Monthly Magazine* 58 (1879): 740–755.

19. Bernard, *Retrospections*, 176–177.

20. Page Life, "Bernard, John," *ODNB*, 5: 431–432; Bernard, *Retrospections*, 190.

21. Bernard, *Retrospections*, 239, 232–233.

22. T.J. to Martha Jefferson Randolph, June 25, 1801, *Family Letters*, 206–207.

23. Samuel Harrison Smith to Mary Ann Smith, July 5, 1801, *First Forty Years*, 30.

24. Ellen Wayles Randolph to T.J., before November 10, 1801, *Family Letters*, 212.

25. T.J. to Ellen Wayles Randolph, November 23, 1801, *Family Letters*, 213–214; Virginia Randolph Trist to an unknown correspondent, May 26, 1839, Randall, 3: 350.

26. Gray, *Account*, 68; T.J. to Cornelia Jefferson Randolph, June 3, 1811, *Family Letters*, 401; Virginia Jefferson Randolph to T.J., February 17, 1809, *Family Letters*, 383; Martha Jefferson Randolph to T.J., November 24, 1808, *Family Letters*, 361; T.J. to Anne Randolph Bankhead, May 26, 1811; *Family Letters*, 400.

27. Adele M. Fasick, "Maria Edgeworth," *British Children's Writers, 1800–1880*, ed. Meena Khorana (Detroit, Mich.: Gale, 1996).

28. Virginia J. Trist to an unknown correspondent, May 26, 1839, Randall, 3: 350.

29. This volume survives at the University of Virginia.

30. William H. Peden, *Thomas Jefferson: Book-Collector* (Charlottesville: University of Virginia, 1942), 134.

31. *Memorandum Books*, 2: 1043, 1227.

32. Ibid., 2: 1064.

33. T.J. to William F. Gray, November 8, 1818, Jefferson Papers (DLC).

34. T.J. to James Madison, November 12, 1801, Ford, 9: 321.

35. T.J. to John Waldo, August 16, 1813, Washington, 6: 184–189.

36. "First Annual Message," Ford, 9: 321–346. The remaining quotations from this message come from this edition and are not cited separately.

37. *Washington National Intelligencer*, January 20, 1802.

38. Daniel L. Dreisbach, *Thomas Jefferson and the Wall of Separation between Church and State* (New York: New York University Press, 2002), 10.

39. "To Messrs. Nehemiah Dodge and Others, a Committee of the Danbury Baptist Association, in the State of Connecticut," in Thomas Jefferson, *Writings*, ed. Merrill D. Peterson (New York: Library of America, 1984), 510.

40. T.J. to Levi Lincoln, January 1, 1802, Dreisbach, *Thomas Jefferson and the Wall*, 43.

41. Samuel Willard, *A Compleat Body of Divinity in Two Hundred and Fifty Expository Lectures on the Assembly's Shorter Catechism* (Boston: for B.

Eliot and D. Henchman, 1726), 308; Madame Le Prince de Beaumont, *Moral Tales* (London: for J. Nourse, 1775), 48; Frederick Schiller, *Don Carlos: A Tragedy* (London: for W. J. and J. Richardson, 1798), 312.

42. Margaret Bayard Smith to Susan Bayard Smith, December 26, 1802, *First Forty Years*, 34–35.

43. T.J. to Benjamin Rush, April 21, 1803, *EG*, 331.

44. T.J. to Joseph Priestley, April 9, 1803, *EG*, 328.

45. "Syllabus of an Estimate of the Merit of the Doctrines of Jesus, Compared with Those of Others," *EG*, 332–333.

Chapter 33: "Life of Captain Lewis"

1. Lester J. Cappon, "Who Is the Author of *History of the Expedition under the Command of Captains Lewis and Clark* (1814)?" *3WMQ* 19 (1962): 257–268.

2. T.J. to Paul Allen, August 5, 1813, Jackson, 584–585.

3. Paul Allen to T.J., August 18, 1813, Jackson, 586.

4. T.J. to Paul Allen, August 18, 1813, Jackson, 586, 593.

5. Nicholas Biddle to T.J., September 28, 1813, Jackson, 594–595.

6. "Life of Captain Lewis," in Paul Allen, ed., *History of the Expedition under the Command of Lewis and Clark, to the Sources of the Missouri, thence Across the Rocky Mountains and down the River Columbia to the Pacific Ocean*, 2 vols. (Philadelphia: Bradford & Inskeep, 1814), 1: vii.

7. Ibid., ix.

8. "Biographical Sketch of Lewis," Jackson, 593.

9. T.J. to Peter Carr, August 19, 1785, *Papers*, 8: 407.

10. Nicholas Biddle to T.J., September 28, 1813, Jackson, 595.

11. William R. Manierre II, "Cotton Mather and the Biographical Parallel," *American Quarterly* 13 (1961): 153–160.

12. "Jefferson's Message to Congress," Jackson, 13.

13. T.J. to Paul Allen, August 18, 1813, Jackson, 590.

14. "Life of Captain Lewis," *Port Folio*, n.s. 3, 4 (1814): 132.

15. "Life of Captain Lewis," *History*, xiv.

16. Benjamin Rush to Meriwether Lewis, May 17, 1803, Jackson, 50.

17. "Life of Captain Lewis," *History*, xvi–xvii.

18. Ibid., xvii–xviii.

19. Ibid., xviii–xix.

20. Dumas Malone, *Jefferson the President: Second Term, 1805–1809* (Boston: Little, Brown, 1974), 180.

21. "Life of Captain Lewis," *History*, xx.

22. Samuel Harrison Smith to Margaret Bayard Smith, July 5, 1803, *First Forty Years*, 38–39.

23. Thomas Jefferson, *An Account of Louisiana: Being an Abstract of Documents, in the Offices of the Departments of State, and of the Treasury* (Washington, 1803).

24. "Jefferson to the Osages [no. 126]," Jackson, 199–200; T.J. to Albert Gallatin, July 12, 1804, Jefferson Papers (DLC); T.J. to Robert Smith, July 13, 1804, Jefferson Papers (DLC).

25. "Jefferson to the Osages [no. 127]," Jackson, 200.

26. Ibid.

27. Steven E. Siry, "Burr, Aaron," *ANB*, 4: 34–36.

28. Malone, *Jefferson the President*, 234–237, 256–259.

29. For the fullest account, see Julian P. Boyd, "The Murder of George Wythe," *3WMQ* 12 (1955): 513–542.

30. R. A. Brock, *Catalogue of the Choice and Extensive Law and Miscellaneous Library of the Lat Hon. William Green* (Richmond: John E. Laughton, Jr., 1880), lot 645.

31. *Catalogue of the Rare, Curious and Valuable Library Collected by the Late Hon. Thos. H. Wynne* (Richmond: J. Thompson Brown, 1875), lot 816½.

32. Sowerby, no. 4700.

33. William H. Gaines, Jr., *Thomas Mann Randolph, Jefferson's Son-in-Law* (Baton Rouge: Louisiana State University Press, 1966), 61–63.

34. "Jefferson Annual Message to Congress: Extract from First Draft," Jackson, 352.

35. "Life of Captain Lewis," *History*, xx.

36. Quoted in Dawson A. Phelps, "The Tragic Death of Meriwether Lewis," *3WMQ* 13 (1956): 312.

37. "Life of Captain Lewis," *History*, xxi–xxii.

Chapter 34: The President as Patron of Literature

1. Jonathan Brunt to T.J., November 30, 1807, Jefferson Papers (DLC).

2. William Peden, "A Book Peddler Invades Monticello," *3WMQ* 6 (1949): 631–636.

3. The following narrative consists of direct quotations from Jonathan Brunt's known writings: *Few Particulars of the Life of Jonathan Brunt, Junior, Printer and Bookseller* (n.p.: Jonathan Brunt, 1797), 2–7; *Extracts from Locke's Essay on the Human Understanding, and Other Writers: Containing a Defence of Natural, Judicial, and Constitutional Rights, on the Principles of Morality, Religion, & Equal Justice, Against the Private and Public Intrigues of Artificial Society* (Frankfort, Ky.: J. Brunt, 1804), 21; *Rush's Extracts: Containing the Evidences of Genuine Patriotism, and the Love of Our Country* (Cooperstown, N.Y.: E. Phinney, for Jonathan Brunt, 1801), 24, 31–33; *The Little Medley: Containing Short Remarks on the Genuine Principles and Exalted Spirit of the Glorious Gospel of the New Testament Also an Account of Some Cases of Personal Domestic Tyranny, Or, Oppression, Properly Called Civil Despotism Likewise, Short Strictures on the Domestic Education of Youth of Both Sexes* (Knoxville, Tenn.: written, printed and sold by the bearer hereof, travelling bookseller, 1809), 10, 14.

4. Brunt, *Extracts from Locke's Essay on the Human Understanding*, 31.

5. Jonathan Brunt to T.J., October 25, 1802, Jefferson Papers (DLC), reminding T.J. of the pamphlet he had sent the previous year.

6. Ibid.

7. Jonathan Brunt to T.J., November 30, 1807, Jefferson Papers (DLC); Brunt, *Little Medley*, 12–13.

8. Arthur H. Shaffer, "Burk, John Daly," *Dictionary of Virginia Biography*, ed. John T. Kneebone, J. Jefferson Looney, Brent Tarter, and Sandra Gioia Treadway, 3 vols. to date (Richmond: Library of Virginia, 1998–), 2: 400–402.

9. See the correspondence between Burk and Jefferson excerpted in Sowerby, no. 464.

10. T.J. to John Burk, June 1, 1805, quoted in Sowerby, no. 464.

11. Ibid.

12. John Burk, *The History of Virginia, from Its First Settlement to the Present Day*, vol. 1 (Petersburg, Va.: for the author, 1804), i.

13. Louis Hue Girardin, "Prefatory Remarks," in Skelton Jones and Louis Hue Girardin, *The History of Virginia* (Petersburg, Va.: M. W. Bunnavant, 1816), vi.

14. T.J. to Abiel Holmes, December 7, 1804, quoted in Sowerby, no. 444.

15. Ibid.

16. T.J. to Abiel Holmes, May 9, 1806, quoted in Sowerby, no. 444.

17. Abiel Holmes to T.J., November 9, 1808, quoted in Sowerby, no. 444.

18. T.J. to Charles Thomson, January 11, 1808, quoted in Sowerby, no. 1474.

19. T.J. to Charles Thomson, December 25, 1808, quoted in Sowerby, no. 1474.

20. John W. Wayland, "The Poetical Tastes of Thomas Jefferson," *Sewanee Review* 18 (1910): 283–299, provides an excellent overview of these scrapbooks. For a modern, selected edition, see Jonathan Gross, ed., *Thomas Jefferson's Scrapbooks: Poems of Nation, Family, and Romantic Love* (Hanover, N.H.: Steerforth Press, 2006).

21. T.J. to Ellen Wayles Randolph, March 4, 1805, *Family Letters*, 269.

22. T.J. to Ellen Wayles Randolph, March 1, 1807, *Family Letters*, 296.

23. Ellen Wayles Randolph to T.J., January 29, 1808, *Family Letters*, 324; T.J. to Ellen Wayles Randolph, February 23, 1808, *Family Letters*, 329.

24. Gross, *Thomas Jefferson's Scrapbooks*, 244.

25. T.J. to John Waldo, August 16, 1813, Washington, 6: 185.

26. Gross, *Thomas Jefferson's Scrapbooks*, 366.

27. Ellen Randolph Coolidge to Henry S. Randall, June 15, 1856, Randall, *Life*, 3: 101.

28. Anne Randolph Bankhead to T.J., November 26, 1808, *Family Letters*, 365–366.

29. T.J. to Charles Willson Peale, March 10, 1809, Horace W. Sellers, ed., "Letters of Thomas Jefferson to Charles Willson Peale, 1796–1825," *Pennsylvania Magazine of History and Biography* 28 (1904): 318.

30. Thomas Jefferson Randolph to Henry S. Randall, undated, Randall, 3: 673.

31. Noble Cunningham, Jr., "The Diary of Frances Few, 1808–1809," *Journal of Southern History* 29 (1963): 351. The punctuation in this quotation has been regularized for clarity.

32. Margaret Bayard Smith to Susan B. Smith, March 1809, *First Forty Years*, 58.

33. Ibid., 61.

34. John Quincy Adams to Louisa Catherine Adams, March 5, 1809, *Writings of John Quincy Adams*, ed. Worthington Chauncey Ford, 7 vols. (New York: Macmillan, 1913–1917), 3: 289.

35. Margaret Bayard Smith to Susan B. Smith, March 1809, *First Forty Years*, 62–63.

36. T.J. to Philip Freneau, May 22, 1809, *PTJRS*, 1: 211.

37. Jonathan Brunt to T.J., July 31, 1809, *PTJRS*, 1: 402–403.

Chapter 35: Return to Monticello

1. T.J. to Edmund Bacon, November 9, 1807, *Jefferson at Monticello*, 67.

2. *Jefferson at Monticello*, 106.

3. *Thomas Jefferson's Garden Book, 1766–1824*, ed. Edwin M. Betts (Philadelphia: American Philosophical Society, 1944), 382; T.J. to Mrs. Samuel Harrison Smith, March 6, 1809, *PTJRS*, 1: 29.

4. *Memorandum Books*, 2: 1243; T.J. to James Madison, March 17, 1809, *PTJRS*, 1: 61.

5. *Jefferson at Monticello*, 106.

6. Ibid., 107.

7. T.J. to Martha Jefferson Randolph, February 27, 1809, *Family Letters*, 385.

8. Martha Jefferson Randolph to T.J., March 2, 1809, *Family Letters*, 388.

9. T.J. to James Madison, March 17, 1809, *PTJRS*, 1: 61.

10. T.J. to Charles Willson Peale, May 5, 1809, *PTJRS*, 1: 187.

11. T.J. to Benjamin Smith Barton, September 21, 1809, *PTJRS*, 1: 555–556.

12. *Jefferson at Monticello*, 113–114.

13. Margaret Bayard Smith, *The First Forty Years of Washington Society*, ed. Gaillard Hunt (New York: Charles Scribner's Sons, 1906), 66–79. The rest of the story of the Smiths' visit to Monticello comes from this source and is not documented separately.

14. Thomas Jefferson Randolph to Henry S. Randall, undated, Randall, 3: 675.

15. Jack McLaughlin, *Jefferson and Monticello: The Biography of a Builder* (New York: Henry Holt, 1988), 25.

16. Sowerby, no. 4502.

17. James Gilreath and Douglas L. Wilson, eds., *Thomas Jefferson's Library: A Catalog with the Entries in His Own Order* (Washington, D.C.: Library of Congress, 1989), 113.

18. Giuseppe Giangrande, "Xenophon Ephesius," *Oxford Classical Dictionary*, 2d ed. (Oxford: Clarendon Press, 1970), 1144.

19. Virginia Randolph Trist to an unknown correspondent, May 26, 1839, Randall, 3: 349.

20. T.J. to Vine Utley, March 21, 1819, Randall, 3: 450; Marie Kimball, *Thomas Jefferson's Cook Book* (Charlottesville: University Press of Virginia, 1976), 43–46.

21. T.J. to Vine Utley, March 21, 1819, Randall, 3: 450.

22. Francis Walker Gilmer, "Sketches of American Statesmen," in Richard Beale Davis, *Francis Walker Gilmer: Life and Learning in Jefferson's Virginia* (Richmond, Va.: Dietz Press, 1939), 351.

23. T.J. to Vine Utley, March 21, 1819, Randall, 3: 450.

24. T.J. to John W. Campbell, September 3, 1809, *PTJRS*, 1: 486–487.

25. Ibid., 1: 487.

26. Wilbur Samuel Howell, "Jefferson's Parliamentary Studies, Activities, and Writings: A Chronology," *Jefferson's Parliamentary Writings: "Parliamentary Pocket-Book and A Manual of Parliamentary Practice*, ed. Wilbur Samuel Howell (Princeton, N.J.: Princeton University Press, 1988), 29–31.

27. T.J. to Joseph Milligan, January 7, 1812, quoted in Howell, "Jefferson's Parliamentary Studies," 32.

28. Ibid.

29. Joseph Milligan to T.J., February 2, 1812, quoted in Howell, Jefferson's Parliamentary Studies," 34; George A. Leavitt, *Catalogue of a Private Library Comprising a Rich Assortment of Rare and Standard Works . . . Also, the Remaining Portion of the Library of the Late Thomas Jefferson, Comprising many Classical Works and Several Autograph Letters, Offered by his Grandson, Francis Eppes, of Poplar Forest, Va.* (New York: George A. Leavitt & Co., 1873), lot 670.

30. For a good discussion of Montesquieu's influence in America, see Nicholas Greenwood Onuf and Peter S. Onuf, *Nations, Markets, and War: Modern History and the American Civil War* (Charlottesville: University of Virginia Press, 2006).

31. T.J. to Colonel William Duane, August 12, 1810, L&B, 12: 407–408.

32. William Wirt to T.J., April 15, 1812, quoted in Sowerby, no. 3501.

33. *The Proceedings of the Government of the United States, in Maintaining the Public Right to the Beach of the Missisipi, Adjacent to New-Orleans, Against the Intrusion of Edward Livingston* (New York: Ezra Sargeant, 1812), 6. For clarity, T.J.'s legal citations have been silently ellipted from this quotation. For an appreciation of the *Proceedings*, see Douglas L. Wilson, "Jefferson and the Republic of Letters," in *Jeffersonian Legacies*, ed. Peter S. Onuf (Charlottesville: University Press of Virginia, 1993), 71–72.

34. *The Proceedings of the Government of the United States*, 23, 58, 75–76, 79.

35. John Tyler to T.J., May 17, 1812, quoted in Sowerby, no. 3501.

Chapter 36: Letters to an Old Friend

1. Benjamin Rush to John Adams, October 17, 1809, *Letters of Benjamin Rush*, ed. L. H. Butterfield, 2 vols. (Philadelphia: American Philosophical Society, 1951), 2: 1021–1022.

2. John Adams to Benjamin Rush, October 25, 1809, quoted in *Letters of Benjamin Rush*, 2: 1023.

3. Benjamin Rush to T.J., January 2, 1811, *Letters of Benjamin Rush*, 2: 1075–1076.

4. *AJL*, 282.

5. Benjamin Rush to T.J., February 1, 1811, *Letters of Benjamin Rush*, 2: 1078.

6. Edward Coles to Henry S. Randall, May 11, 1857, Randall, 3: 640.

7. T.J. to Benjamin Rush, December 5, 1811, Ford, 174–175.

8. Benjamin Rush to John Adams, December 16, 1811, and Benjamin Rush to T.J., December 7, 1811, *Letters of Benjamin Rush*, 2: 1110–1112.

9. John Adams to T.J., January 1, 1812, *AJL*, 290.

10. T.J. to Benjamin Rush, January 21, 1812, Ford, 11: 218.

11. T.J. to John Adams, January 21, 1812, *AJL*, 291.

12. Ibid.

13. T.J. to John Adams, January 21, 1812, *AJL*, 292.

14. Benjamin Rush to T.J., February 11, 1812, *Letters of Benjamin Rush*, 2: 1118; David McCullough, *John Adams* (New York: Simon & Schuster, 2001), 601–602, 613.

15. John Adams to T.J., February 3, 1812, *AJL*, 294.

16. Ibid., 296.

17. Ibid., 295.

18. T.J. to Benjamin Rush, January 21, 1812, Ford, 11: 219.

19. T.J. to John Adams, April 20, 1812, *AJL*, 298.

20. John Adams to T.J., May 1, 1812, *AJL*, 300–301.

21. John Adams to T.J., May 21, 1812, *AJL*, 305.

22. T.J. to John Adams, June 11, 1812, *AJL*, 305–306.

23. Ibid., 306–307.

24. Ibid., 307.

25. John Adams to T.J., October 12, 1812, *AJL*, 312; Abiel Holmes, *American Annals: or, A Chronological History of America* (Cambridge, Mass.: W. Hilliard, 1805), 238.

26. T.J. to John Adams, May 27, 1813, *AJL*, 323.

27. John Adams to T.J., June 11, 1813, *AJL*, 328.

28. Eugene R. Fingerhut, "Floyd, William," *ANB*, 8: 150–151.

29. T.J. to John Adams, June 1, 1822, *AJL*, 577; John Adams to T.J., June 11, 1822, *AJL*, 579.

30. T.J. to John Adams, June 15, 1813, *AJL*, 331.

31. John Adams to T.J., June 25, 1813, *AJL*, 333.

32. T.J. to John Adams, August 22, 1813, *AJL*, 369.

33. T.J. to Abigail Adams, August 22, 1813, *AJL*, 367.

34. John Adams to T.J., August 14?, 1813, *AJL*, 366.

35. Abigail Adams to T.J., September 20, 1812, *AJL*, 378.

36. T.J. to John Adams, October 28, 1813, *AJL*, 388.

37. T.J. to John Adams, July 5, 1814, *AJL*, 431.

38. Ibid.

39. [Thomas Love Peacock,] "Randolph's *Memoirs, &c. of Thomas Jefferson*," *Westminster Review* 13 (1830): 326.

Chapter 37: The Library of Congress

1. Martin K. Gordon, "Patrick Magruder: Citizen, Congressman, Librarian of Congress," *Librarians of Congress* (Washington, D.C.: Library of Congress, 1977), 39–55.

2. Quoted in W. Johnston, *History of the Library of Congress*, Vol. 1: *1800–1864* (Washington, D.C.: GPO, 1904), 68.

3. T.J. to Abraham Baldwin, April 14, 1802, Jefferson Papers (DLC).

4. Ibid.

5. Ibid.

6. Ibid.

7. Edwin Wolf II and Kevin J. Hayes, *The Library of Benjamin Franklin* (Philadelphia: American Philosophical Society and the Library Company of Philadelphia, 2006), *passim*.

8. William Short to T.J., March 11, 1815, "The Jefferson Papers," *Collections of the Massachusetts Historical Society*, 7th ser. 1 (1900): 229.

9. John Adams to T.J., October 28, 1814, *AJL*, 440.

10. T.J. to Samuel Harrison Smith, September 21, 1814, Ford, 11: 427–428.

11. Ibid., 11: 428.

12. *Annals of Congress*, 13th Congress, 3d session, col. 23.

13. Arthur Bestor, "Thomas Jefferson and the Freedom of Books," *Three Presidents and Their Books*, ed. Robert B. Downs (Urbana: University of Illinois Press, 1955), 2.

14. Charles J. Ingersoll, *History of the Second War between the United States of America and Great Britain*, 2 vols. (Philadelphia: Lippincott, Grambo, 1852), 2: 271–272.

15. *New Hampshire Sentinel*, November 5, 1814.

16. T.J. to William Hilliard, August 7, 1825, *Jefferson's Ideas on a University Library: Letters from the Founder of the University of Virginia to a Boston Bookseller*, ed. Elizabeth Cometti (Charlottesville, Va.: Tracy W. McGregor Library, 1950), 30.

17. Quoted in Johnston, *History of the Library of Congress*, 80.

18. Kevin J. Hayes, *A Colonial Woman's Bookshelf* (Knoxville: University of Tennessee Press, 1996), 123–136.

19. *Annals of Congress*, 13th Congress, 3d session, col. 398.

20. Ibid., cols. 410–411.

21. *Alexandria Gazette*, October 22, 1814.

22. William Thornton to T.J., December 11, 1814, Jefferson Papers (DLC); "Mr. Jefferson's Library," *Niles Weekly Register*, December 31, 1814, 285.

23. *National Intelligencer*, November 16, 1814, quoted in Johnston, *History of the Library of Congress*, 91.

24. *Baltimore Patriot and Evening Advertiser*, October 28, 1814.

25. *Annals of Congress*, 13th Congress, 3d session, col. 1105.

26. Ibid.

27. John Adams to T.J., December 20, 1814, *AJL*, 441.

28. George Ticknor, *Life, Letters, and Journals of George Ticknor*, 2 vols. (London: Sampson Low, Marston, Searle, & Rivington, 1876), 1: 34; Francis Calley Gray, *Thomas Jefferson in 1814: Being an Account of a Visit to Monticello, Virginia*, ed. Henry S. Rowe and T. Jefferson Coolidge, Jr. (Boston: The Club of Odd Volumes, 1924), 66–67.

29. Ticknor, *Life, Letters, and Journals*, 1: 34; Henry Fielding, *The History of Tom Jones: A Foundling*, ed. Fredson Bowers (Middletown, Conn.: Wesleyan University Press, 1975), 445–446.

30. Ticknor, *Life, Letters, and Journals*, 1: 34.

31. Gray, *Account*, 67.

32. T.J. to John Adams, June 10, 1815, *AJL*, 443.

33. Gray, *Account*, 72–73.

34. Ticknor, *Life, Letters, and Journals*, 1: 35.

35. T.J. to Madame de Tessé, December 8, 1813, excerpted in Sowerby, no. 271.

36. Sowerby, no. 409, misidentifies the title of this work, but Jefferson's description of it in his letter to Madame de Tessé, December 8, 1813, makes identification clear. He calls it "the memoirs of Mrs Clarke and of her *Darling* prince."

37. T.J. to Madame de Tessé, December 8, 1813, Ford, 11: 361.

38. Ibid.

39. T.J. to Joseph Milligan, October 17, 1814, Jefferson Papers (DLC).

40. Ticknor, *Life, Letters, and Journals*, 1: 36.

41. T.J. to John Vaughan, February 5, 1815, Washington, 6: 417; T.J. to the Marquis de Lafayette, February 14, 1815, Washington, 6: 427.

42. T.J. to Samuel Harrison Smith, February 27, 1815, quoted in Johnston, *History of the Library of Congress*, 99.

43. William Matheson, "George Watterston: Advocate of a National Library," *Librarians of Congress*, 58.

44. Frederick R. Goff, "Freedom of Challenge: The Great Library of Thomas Jefferson," *Thomas Jefferson and the World of Books: A Symposium Held at the Library of Congress, September 21, 1976* (Washington, D.C.: Library of Congress, 1977), 12.

45. T.J. to George Watterston, May 7, 1815, Jefferson Papers (DLC).

46. Ibid.

47. *Jefferson at Monticello*, 109.

48. Quoted in Johnston, *History of the Library of Congress*, 104.

49. T.J. to Joseph C. Cabell, February 2, 1816, Cabell, 52.

50. Randolph G. Adams, "Thomas Jefferson: Librarian," in *Three Americanists* (Philadelphia: University of Pennsylvania Press, 1939), 95.

Chapter 38: The Retirement Library

1. T.J. to John Adams, June 10, 1815, *AJL*, 443.

2. T.J. to George Ticknor, July 4, 1815, Jefferson Papers (DLC).

3. George Ticknor to T.J., November 25, 1815, Jefferson Papers (DLC).

4. T.J. to George Ticknor, February 8, 1816, Jefferson Papers (DLC).

5. T.J. to George Ticknor, June 6, 1817, Jefferson Papers (DLC).

6. T.J. to David B. Warden, February 27, 1815, Jefferson Papers (DLC).

7. T.J. to Thomas J. Rogers, December 1823, quoted in Sowerby, no. 70.

8. R. H. Vetch, revised by Gordon L. Teffeteller, "Wilson, Sir Robert Thomas," *ODNB*, 59: 631–635.

9. Leonard Barkan, "The Beholder's Tale: Ancient Sculpture, Renaissance Narratives," *Representations* 44 (1993): 156–157.

10. Robert C. Winthrop, *Address and Speeches on Various Occasions, from 1878 to 1886* (Boston: Little, Brown, 1886), 499, retells a story he had heard from Daniel Webster, with whom he read law. Webster had heard the story from Jefferson when he visited Monticello in 1824.

11. Randall, 1: 301.

12. T.J. to John Adams, January 14, 1814, *AJL*, 425.

13. Francis Hall, *Travels in Canada and the United States in 1816 and 1817* (Boston: Wells & Lilly, 1818), 229–230.

14. Ibid., 230.

15. T.J. to John Adams, August 10, 1815, and May 5, 1817, *AJL*, 452, 513.

16. Richard Harlan to T.J., June 10, 1825, Jefferson Papers (DLC).

17. Whitfield J. Bell, Jr., "Harlan, Richard," *Dictionary of Scientific Biography* (New York: Charles Scribner's Sons, 1972), 6: 119–121.

18. Kevin J. Hayes, "Introduction," Edwin Wolf II and Kevin J. Hayes, *The Library of Benjamin Franklin* (Philadelphia: American Philosophical Society and the Library Company of Philadelphia, 2006), 30.

19. Samuel X. Radbill, ed., "The Autobiographical Ana of Robley Dunglison," *Transactions of the American Philosophical Society*, n.s. 53 (1963): 26.

20. Quoted in Peter Richmond, *Marketing Modernisms: The Architecture and Influence of Charles Reilly* (Liverpool: Liverpool University Press, 2001), 5.

21. Quoted in Peter J. Hatch, *The Fruits and Fruit Trees of Monticello* (Charlottesville: University Press of Virginia, 1998), 145.

22. T.J. to Robert Patterson, September 11, 1811, Jefferson Papers (DLC).

23. E. D. Lilley, "Stendhal," *The Dictionary of Art*, ed. Jane Turner, 34 vols. (New York: Grove, 1996), 29: 629–630.

24. Ekkehart Krippendorff's parallel biography, *Jefferson und Goethe* (Hamburg: Europäische Verlagsanstalt, 2001), though provocative, ignores Jefferson's knowledge of Goethe's *Faust*.

25. Percy Bysshe Shelley to John Gisborne, April 10, 1822, *The Letters of Percy Bysshe Shelley*, ed. Frederick Jones, 2 vols. (Oxford: Clarendon Press, 1964), 2: 376, 407.

26. T.J. to Nicholas P. Trist, June 14, 1822, *Thomas Jefferson Correspondence: Printed from the Originals in the Collections of William K. Bixby*, ed. Worthington Chauncey Ford (Boston, 1916), 272.

27. Alan Richardson, "Byron and the Theatre," *Cambridge Companion to Byron*, ed. Drummond Bone (New York: Cambridge University Press, 2004), 139–141.

28. Ellen Wayles Randolph to Nicholas P. Trist, March 30, 1824, *FLP*.

29. Charles Brockden Brown to T.J., December 25, 1799, *Papers*, 31: 275.

30. T.J. to Charles Brockden Brown, January 15, 1800, *Papers*, 31: 308.

31. W. Jennings, trans., *The Foundling of Belgrade* (New York: D. Longworth, 1808), 9. The copy at the University of Virginia is inscribed, "to His excellency, Thomas Jefferson."

32. Jonathan Gross, ed., *Thomas Jefferson's Scrapbooks: Poems of Nation, Family, and Romantic Love Collected by America's Third President* (Hanover, N.H.: Steerforth Press, 2006), 414–418.

33. Randall, 3: 448; *Memorandum Books*, 2: 1274; *National Intelligencer*, October 3, 1811; Henry Tutwiler, "Thomas Jefferson," *Southern Opinion*, October 17, 1868.

34. Randall, 1: 28.

35. T.J. to Nathaniel Burwell, March 14, 1817, Washington, 7: 102.

36. T.J. to Baron Lescallier, June 14, 1817, *Thomas Jefferson Correspondence*, 229–230.

37. Ellen Randolph Coolidge to Henry S. Randall, 185?, Randall, 3: 346.

38. Quoted in Randall, 3: 404.

39. T.J. to Joseph Coolidge, Jr., January 15, 1825, *The Jefferson Papers, 1770–1826* (Boston: Massachusetts Historical Society, 1900), 340.

40. For an excellent study of this work, see Stanley R. Hauer, "Thomas Jefferson and the Anglo-Saxon Language," *PMLA* 98 (1983): 879–898.

41. Gross, *Thomas Jefferson's Scrapbooks*, 163.

42. R. S. Maclay, *Life among the Chinese: With Characteristic Sketches and Incidents of Missionary Operations and Prospects in China* (New York: Carlton & Porter, 1861), 23.

Chapter 39: *The Life and Morals of Jesus of Nazareth*

1. T.J. to Thomas Law, June 13, 1814, *EG*, 356.

2. Nathaniel P. Poor, *Catalogue: President Jefferson's Library* (Washington, D.C.: Gale & Seaton, 1829), lot 491.

3. Thomas Jefferson, "On the Writings of the Baron d'Holbach on the Morality of Nature and That of the Christian Religion," *Free Enquirer* 2 (1830): 102–103.

4. "On the Writings of the Baron d'Holbach," 102–103.

5. T.J. to Francis Adrian Van der Kemp, April 25, 1816, *EG*, 369.

6. T.J. to William Short, April 13, 1820, *EG*, 392.

7. T.J. to Charles Thomson, January 9, 1816, *EG*, 364–365.

8. T.J. to Margaret Bayard Smith, August 6, 1816, *EG*, 376.

9. T.J. to Matthew Carey, September 1, 1816, Jefferson Papers (DLC); T.J. to John Adams, October 12, 1813, *AJL*, 386.

10. T.J. to Matthew Carey, November 11, 1816, Jefferson Papers (DLC).

11. Francis Adrian Van der Kemp to T.J., March 24, 1816, *EG*, 366–367.

12. Sheridan, "Introduction," *EG*, 35; T.J. to Francis Adrian Van der Kemp, April 25, 1816, *EG*, 369.

13. T.J. to John Adams, August 1, 1816, and John Adams to T.J., August 9, 1816, *AJL*, 484–485.

14. Eugene R. Sheridan, "Introduction," *EG*, 35.

15. T.J. to Francis Adrian Van der Kemp, July 30, 1816, *EG*, 375.

16. T.J. to William Short, October 31, 1819, *EG*, 388.

17. Ibid., 389.

18. William Short to T.J., December 1, 1819, quoted in *EG*, 391.

19. Sheridan, "Introduction," *EG*, 38.

20. Susan Bryan, "Reauthorizing the Text: Jefferson's Scissor Edit of the Gospels," *Early American Literature* 22 (1987): 19, 38; William S. Burroughs, *Conversations with William S. Burroughs*, ed. Allen Hibbard (Jackson: University Press of Mississippi, 1999), 92.

21. Bryan, "Reauthorizing the Text," 22.

22. T.J. to William Short, August 4, 1820, *EG*, 396.

23. William Peden, "A Book Peddler Invades Monticello," *3WMQ* 6 (1949): 633–634.

Chapter 40: *The Autobiography*

1. William Short to T.J., March 27, 1820, *The Jefferson Papers* (Boston: Massachusetts Historical Society, 1900), 298.

2. "Autobiography Draft Fragment," Jefferson Papers (DLC).

3. *Autobiography*, Ford, 1: 6.

4. T.J. to Chastellux, October 1786, *Papers*, 10: 498.

5. *Autobiography*, Ford, 1: 15.

6. T.J. to George Mason, February 4, 1791, *Papers*, 19: 241.

7. *Autobiography*, Ford, 1: 76.

8. T.J. to Charles Thomson, January 9, 1816, *EG*, 365.

9. T.J. to Francis Wayles Eppes, October 6, 1820, *Family Letters*, 434.

10. T.J. to James Madison, January 13, 1821, *The Republic of Letters: The Correspondence between Thomas Jefferson and James Madison, 1776–1826*, ed. James Morton Smith, 3 vols. (New York: Norton, 1995), 3: 1828.

11. T.J. to Francis Wayles Eppes, January 19, 1821, *Family Letters*, 438.

12. T.J. to Jared Mansfield, February 13, 1821, L&B, 15: 313–314.

13. Robert L. Gale, "Sully, Thomas," *ANB*, 21: 131.

14. Thomas Sully to T.J., April 6, 1821, Jefferson Papers (DLC); *1828 Catalogue of the Library of the University of Virginia*, ed. William Harwood Peden (Charlottesville, Va.: Alderman Library, 1945), 89.

15. Thomas Sully to T.J., April 6, 1821, Jefferson Papers (DLC).

16. Quoted in Alfred L. Bush, *The Life Portraits of Thomas Jefferson: Catalogue of an Exhibition at the University of Virginia Museum of Fine Arts, 12 through 26 April 1962* (Charlottesville, Va.: Thomas Jefferson Memorial Foundation, 1962), 92.

17. James M. Cox, "Jefferson's Autobiography: Recovering Literature's Lost Ground," *Southern Review* 14 (1978): 639.

18. *Autobiography*, Ford, 1: 79.

19. Ibid.

20. Randall, 1: 384.

21. *Autobiography*, Ford, 1: 89–90.

22. Quoted in John Finch, *Travels in the United States of America and Canada* (London: Longman, Rees, Orme, Brown, Green, & Longman, 1833), 254.

23. *Autobiography*, Ford, 1: 89–90.

24. Ellen Randolph Coolidge to Henry S. Randall, February 18, 1856, Randall, 3: 342.

25. Quoted in Randall, 3: 344; *Jefferson at Monticello*, 13.

26. Quoted in Randall, 3: 344; T.J. to Martha Jefferson Randolph, June 3, 1802, *Family Letters*, 227.

27. Ellen Randolph Coolidge to Henry S. Randall, February 18, 1856, Randall, 3: 342–344.

28. Cornelia Jefferson Randolph to Virginia Jefferson Randolph, April 24, 1821, *FLP*.

29. Rosemary Mitchell, "Hutton, Catherine," *ODNB*, 29: 49–51.

30. Ellen Randolph to Martha Jefferson Randolph, April 14, 1818, *FLP*.

31. Cornelia Jefferson Randolph to Virginia Jefferson Randolph, April 24, 1821, *FLP*.

32. Ellen Randolph Coolidge to Henry S. Randall, February 18, 1856, Randall, 3: 342.

33. Cornelia Jefferson Randolph to Virginia Jefferson Randolph, July 18, 1819, *FLP*.

34. Ellen Wayles Randolph to Martha Jefferson Randolph, July 18, 1819, *FLP*.

35. T.J. to Thomas Law, June 13, 1814, *EG*, 355–358.

36. S. Allan Chambers, Jr., *Poplar Forest and Thomas Jefferson* (Forest, Va.: for the Corporation for Jefferson's Poplar Forest, 1993), 86.

37. Cornelia Jefferson Randolph to Ellen Randolph Coolidge, August 3, 1825, *FLP*; "Thoughts on English Prosody," L&B 18: 424.

38. T.J. to Francis Wayles Eppes, September 21, 1820, *Family Letters*, 433.

39. Ellen Randolph Coolidge to Henry S. Randall, 185?, Randall, 3: 346.

40. Dennis Wood, "Staël, Anne-Louise-Germaine Necker," *New Oxford Companion to Literature in French*, ed. Peter France (Oxford: Clarendon Press, 1995), 778.

41. Cornelia Jefferson Randolph to Virginia Jefferson Randolph, August 30, 1817, *FLP.*

42. Ellen Randolph Coolidge to Henry S. Randall, February 18, 1856, Randall, 3: 343.

43. Ibid.

44. T.J. to Martha Jefferson Randolph, August 18, 1817, *Family Letters*, 419.

45. Ellen Randolph Coolidge to Henry S. Randall, February 18, 1856, Randall, 3: 343; *Memorandum Books*, 2: 1218.

46. Cornelia Jefferson Randolph to Virginia Randolph, August 31, 1819, *FLP.*

47. *Autobiography*, Ford, 1: 155–156.

48. Ibid., 1: 159.

Chapter 41: The University of Virginia from Dream to Reality

1. T.J. to William Short, November 24, 1821, L&B, 18: 315.

2. T.J. to Joseph Priestley, January 18, 1800, *Papers*, 31: 320.

3. T.J. to Littleton Waller Tazewell, January 5, 1805, in Thomas Jefferson, *Writings*, ed. Merrill D. Peterson (New York: Library of America, 1984), 1151.

4. Ibid., 1150.

5. T.J. to Trustees for the Lottery of East Tennessee College, May 6, 1810, Washington, 5: 521.

6. T.J. to Peter Carr, September 7, 1814, Cabell, 389.

7. Dumas Malone, *The Sage of Monticello* (Boston: Little, Brown, 1970), 236–237.

8. H. Trevor Colburn, "The Reading of Joseph Carrington Cabell: 'A List of Books on Various Subjects Recommended to a Young Man,' " *Studies in Bibliography* 13 (1960): 179–188.

9. Lynn A. Nelson, "Cabell, Joseph Carrington," *Dictionary of Virginia Biography*, ed. John T. Kneebone, J. Jefferson Looney, Brent Tarter, and Sandra Gioia Treadway, 3 vols. to date (Richmond: Library of Virginia, 1998–), 2: 488–490.

10. T.J. to Joseph C. Cabell, January 5, 1815, Cabell, 37.

11. Ibid.

12. Malone, *Sage of Monticello*, 249.

13. "Proceedings and Report of the Commissioners for the University of Virginia," *Analectic Magazine* 13 (1819): 103–104.

14. "Report on the University," *Niles' Weekly Register*, February 20, 1819, 79.

15. [Edward Everett,] "University of Virginia," *North American Review* 10 (1820): 118.

16. Ibid., 130.

17. Ibid., 124–125.

18. Edgar Allan Poe, "Nathaniel Hawthorne," *Essays and Reviews* (New York: Library of America, 1984), 588.

19. T.J. to John Adams, August 15, 1820, *AJL*, 565.

20. Ibid., 566–567.

21. Stephen L. Newman, "Cooper, Thomas," *ODNB*, 13: 280–283; Orie William Long, *Literary Pioneers: Early American Explorers of European Culture* (Cambridge, Mass.: Harvard University Press, 1935), 36, 45; Kevin J. Hayes, *Melville's Folk Roots* (Kent, Ohio: Kent State University Press, 1999), 68.

22. E. Lee Shepard, "Gilmer, Francis Walker," *ANB*, 9: 64–65; Kevin J. Hayes, *Captain John Smith: A Reference Guide* (Boston: G. K. Hall, 1991), 19–20.

23. T.J. to Francis Walker Gilmer, November 25, 1823, Richard Beale Davis, "A Postscript on Thomas Jefferson and His University Professors," *Journal of Southern History* 12 (1946): 425.

24. T.J. to Francis Walker Gilmer, January 20, 1825, Davis, "Postscript," 429–430.

25. Davis, "Postscript," 427–428.

26. Brent Tarter, "Blaetterman, George, Wilhelm," *Dictionary of Virginia Biography*, 1: 533–534; Francis Walker Gilmer to T.J., June 21, 1824, *Correspondence of Thomas Jefferson and Francis Walker Gilmer, 1814–1826*, ed. Richard Beale Davis (Columbia: University of South Carolina Press, 1946), 86.

27. Francis W. Gilmer to T.J., August 27, 1824, *Correspondence*, 98; Christopher Stray, "Key, Thomas Hewitt," *ODNB*, 31: 471–472.

28. Francis Walker Gilmer to T.J., September 15, 1824, *Correspondence*, 101.

29. Whitfield J. Bell, Jr., "Dunglison, Robley," *ODNB*, 17: 298–299.

30. Karen Hunger Parshall, "Bonnycastle, Charles," *Dictionary of Virginia Biography*, 2: 77–78.

31. Philip Alexander Bruce, *History of the University of Virginia, 1819–1919*, 5 vols. (New York: Macmillan, 1920–1922), 2: 15–16.

32. Malcolm Lester, "Tucker, George," *ANB*, 21: 892–894.

33. "Reception of Gen. Lafayette," *Richmond Enquirer*, November 16, 1824.

34. Ibid.

35. Francis Walker Gilmer to T.J., September 16, 1824, and November 30, 1824, *Correspondence*, 102, 122.

36. George Long to Henry Tutwiler, May 30, 1875, *Letters of George Long*, ed. Thomas Fitzhugh (Charlottesville: The Library, University of Virginia, 1917), 23.

37. T.J. to Joseph C. Cabell, December 22, 1824, Cabell, 323.

38. Quoted in Brent Tarter, "Blaetterman, George, Wilhelm," *Dictionary of Virginia Biography*, 1: 533.

39. T.J. to Joseph C. Cabell, January 11, 1825, Cabell, 330.

40. Joseph C. Cabell to T.J., January 30, 1825, Cabell, 336.

41. T.J. to Joseph C. Cabell, February 3, 1825, Cabell, 339.

Chapter 42: The Life and Soul of the University

1. Francis Walker Gilmer to T.J., July 20, 1824, *Correspondence of Thomas Jefferson and Francis Walker Gilmer, 1814–1826*, ed. Richard Beale Davis (Columbia: University of South Carolina Press, 1946), 92.

2. G. C. Boase, "Gurney, Anna," revised by John D. Haigh, *ODNB*; William Peden, ed., *1828 Catalogue of the Library of the University of Virginia* (Charlottesville: for the Alderman Library of the University of Virginia, 1945), 107.

3. Peden, *1828 Catalogue*, 107; Francis Walker Gilmer to T.J., November 30, 1824, *Correspondence*, 121.

4. T.J. to James Madison, August 8, 1824, *The Republic of Letters: The Correspondence between Thomas Jefferson and James Madison, 1776–1826*, ed. James Morton Smith, 3 vols. (New York: Norton, 1995), 3: 1897; T.J. to George Ticknor, March 23, 1825, Jefferson Papers (DLC).

5. Peden, *1828 Catalogue*, ii–iii.

6. *Jefferson's Ideas on a University Library: Letters from the Founder of the University of Virginia to a Boston Bookseller*, ed. Elizabeth Cometti (Charlottesville, Va.: Tracy W. McGregor Library, 1950), 3.

7. Ellen Wayles Randolph to Nicholas P. Trist, March 30, 1824, *FLP*.

8. T.J. to Cummings, Hilliard, and Company, September 6, 1824, *Jefferson's Ideas*, 17–18.

9. T.J. to Cummings, Hilliard, and Company, October 25, 1824, *Jefferson's Ideas*, 19.

10. T.J. to Joseph Coolidge, Jr., January 15, 1825, *The Jefferson Papers* (Boston: Massachusetts Historical Society, 1900), 340.

11. T.J. to Cummings & Hilliard, January 14, 1825, *Jefferson's Ideas*, 20–21; Joseph Coolidge, Jr., to T.J., February 23, 1825, *Jefferson Papers* (1900), 342.

12. Olivia Walling, "Bigelow, Jacob," *ANB*, 2: 752–753; Kennard B. Bork, "Cleaveland, Parker," *ANB*, 5: 42–44.

13. Douglas Johnson, "Thierry, Augustin," *New Oxford Companion to Literature in French*, ed. Peter France (Oxford: Clarendon Press, 1995), 802.

14. J. Evelyn Denison, July 30, 1825, Jefferson Papers (DLC); "Members of Parliament," *Salem Gazette*, July 27, 1824.

15. *Jefferson's Ideas*, 5–6.

16. T.J. to William Hilliard, May 22, 1825, *Jefferson's Ideas*, 23.

17. A. W. Ward and A. R. Waller, *The Cambridge History of English Literature* (New York: G. P. Putnam's Sons, 1917), 14: 58–61.

18. Henry Tutwiler, "Thomas Jefferson," *Southern Opinion*, October 17, 1868.

19. Virginia Randolph Trist to Ellen Randolph Coolidge, June 27, 1825, *FLP*.

20. Ellen Randolph Coolidge to T.J., August 1, 1825, *Family Letters*, 454.

21. Ibid., 456.

22. Ibid.

23. T.J. to Ellen Randolph Coolidge, August 27, 1825, *Family Letters*, 457.

24. Cornelia Jefferson Randolph to Ellen Randolph Coolidge, July 13, 1825, *FLP*.

25. Cornelia Jefferson Randolph to Ellen Randolph Coolidge, August 3, 1825, *FLP*.

26. Ibid.

27. T.J. to Ellen Randolph Coolidge, November 14, 1825, *Family Letters*, 460.

28. T.J. to Joseph Coolidge, Jr., October 13, 1825, *Jefferson Papers* (1900), 356–359.

29. Martha Jefferson Randolph to Ellen Randolph Coolidge, October 13, 1825, *FLP*.

30. Ibid.

31. Martha Jefferson Randolph to Ellen Randolph Coolidge, November 26, 1825, *FLP*.

32. Bernhard, *Travels through North America, during the Years 1825 and 1826* (New York: G. & C. Carvill, 1828), 196–197.

33. Quoted in Randall, 3: 523; Bernhard, *Travels*, 197.

34. Bernhard, *Travels*, 197–198.

35. Kevin J. Hayes, *Poe and the Printed Word* (New York: Cambridge University Press, 2000), 9.

36. Ibid., 10.

37. Thomas Jefferson Randolph to Henry S. Randall, undated, Randall, 3: 675.

38. Randall, 3: 543–549; Samuel X. Radbill, ed., "The Autobiographical Ana of Robley Dunglison," *Transactions of the American Philosophical Society*, n.s. 53 (1963): 32–33.

39. David McCullough, *John Adams* (New York: Simon & Schuster, 2001), 648.

40. Edgar Allan Poe to John Allan, September 21, 1826, *The Letters of Edgar Allan Poe*, ed. John Ward Ostrom (1948; reprint, with supplement, New York: Gordian Press, 1966), 1: 6.

41. Edgar Allan Poe to John Allan, September 21, 1826, *Letters*, 1: 6, asserts that both classes will be examined together, but as Robley Dunglison's report of the results indicates, *Richmond Enquirer*, December 27, 1826, there were separate examinations for the juniors and seniors. Poe chose to be examined with the seniors and earned honors among the senior class in Latin and French.

INDEX

Abdrahaman, 309, 315–316
Acosta, José d', *Historia Natural y Moral de las Indias*, 330
Adair, James, 539
Adams, Abigail (1744–1818)
  correspondence with Jefferson, 295, 302, 325, 353, 355–357, 440–441, 534, 542–543
  friendship with Jefferson, 290, 310
  life in London, 311
  life in Paris, 287, 379
  life in Washington, 465
  opinion of David Humphreys, 288
  opinion of Mary Jefferson, 352–353
  reads Jefferson's "Syllabus," 585
  views balloon ascension, 287
Adams, Abigail (1765–1813). *See,* Smith, Abigail Adams
Adams, John
  commissions Mather Brown to paint portraits, 322
  conversation with James Duane, 168, 276
  correspondence with Jefferson, 2, 4, 29, 210, 277, 290, 309, 371, 423, 426, 532–545, 564, 551, 571, 580, 584–586, 617, 619–620, 622
  death of, 641
  Defence of the Constitutions of the United States, 328, 393, 401
  diary of, 178
  Discourses on Davila, 393, 401
  elected president, 431
  Federalist policies, 394–395, 403, 422

friendship with Jefferson, 355, 532–545
inauguration of, 434, 436, 449
judicial appointments of, 461–462
life in London, 314
life in Paris, 145
mission to Amsterdam, 356–358
opinion of Jonathan Jackson, 284
owns Voltaire's *Oeuvres*, 553
policy toward the Barbary States, 309, 315–317
presidential administration, 441, 461–462, 465, 468, 472
reads Harrington's *Oceana*, 264
reads Johnson's *Lives of the Poets*, 287, 292
reads *Notes on the State of Virginia*, 243, 292
receives Barton's *Memoirs of David Rittenhouse*, 570
serves in the Continental Congress, 167–168, 171, 178, 187,
serves on commission to negotiate treaties of amity and commerce, 270, 281, 291, 309–310, 315–316
serves as vice president, 394
supports Alien and Sedition Acts, 441, 500
views balloon ascension, 287
visits English gardens with Jefferson, 319–320
writes letters of introduction, 557

Adams, John Quincy
  acquires Johnson's *Lives of the Poets*,
    287
  authors "Publicola" essays, 401
  book buying in Berlin, 539
  conversations with Jefferson,
    276–277, 311, 509–510
  diary of, 145
  enjoyment of poetry, 510
  inauguration, 628
  Lectures on Rhetoric and Oratory, 535,
    537
  reads Jefferson's "Syllabus," 586
  reads *Notes on the State of Virginia*,
    292
  visits Jefferson in Paris, 290
Adams, Samuel, 168, 171
Adams, Thomas, 5–6, 121, 147–148
Addison, Joseph, 8, 251
  "Letter from Italy," 308
  Miscellaneous Works, 26
  Remarks on Several Parts of Italy, 342,
    574
Adet, Pierre Auguste, 420–421, 429
Adlum, John, *Memoir on the Cultivation
    of the Vine*, 573
Aeschylus, 117, 425, 608
Aesop, *Fables*, 17–19, 427, 608
Aikman, William
  bookshop of, 166–167, 172
  circulating library, 166, 172, 218
  leaves Annapolis for Jamaica, 172
Aitken, Robert
  bookbinding skills, 194, 472
  bookshop of, 168, 191, 194
  estimate to print *Notes on the State of
    Virginia*, 265, 270
Akenside, Mark, 9
  Pleasures of Imagination, 73–75, 77, 85
Aldrich, Henry, *Elements of Civil
    Architecture*, 631
Alexandria Gazette, 555
'Ali, Sharaf al-Din, *Histoire de
    Timur-Bec*, 426
Allen, Paul, 478–479, 484
Allen, Thomas, 396
Alvarez, Francisco, *Noticia del
    Establecimiento y Poblacion de les
    Colonias Inglesas en la America
    Septentrional*, 633

Ambler, Jacquelin, 68
*American and British Chronicle of War
    and Politics*, 502–503
American Museum, 400
American Philosophical Society
  elects Jefferson councilor, 432–433
  elects Jefferson president, 432, 436,
    642
  elects John Page to membership, 53
  elects Meriwether Lewis to
    membership, 489
  library of, 580
  meetings, 434, 437
  receives Sully's portrait of Jefferson,
    601
  sponsors literary contest, 446
  supports Michaux's scientific
    exploration, 413–415
Anacreon, 330
Analectic Magazine, 618
Andreani, Paolo, Count, 395
Anmours, Charles François, Chevalier
    d', 229, 234
Annals of Congress, 555–557
Anson, George, *Voyage Round the
    World*, 26–27
Arabian Nights' Entertainment, 554
Ariosto, 608
Aristotle, 139, 179
Arnold, Benedict, 230, 234, 251
Articles of Confederation, 210
Athenaeus, *Dipnosophistarum*, 405–406
Atterbury, Francis, *Sermons and
    Discourses*, 38
Augustine, 222
Aurelius, Marcus, 181
  Commentaries, 9
Aurora, 440
*Authentic and Interesting Memoirs of
    Mrs. Clarke*, 559
Ayre, Mr., 637

Babes in the Wood, 106
Bache, Benjamin F., 440, 572
Bache, William, 391
Bachmair, John James, *Complete
    German Grammar*, 168
Bacon, Edmund, 507, 515–517, 519, 520
Bacon, Francis, 574, 629
  Advancement of Learning, 10, 257, 370

Baldwin, Abraham, 548–551
Baltimore Weekly Magazine, 457
Bancroft, Edward, 329
Bankhead, Anne C. Randolph (TJ's granddaughter), 65, 145, 399, 420, 469, 469, 504, 507
Bankhead, Charles Lewis, 65, 507
Bannister, John, Jr., 46–47
Barbé de Marbois, François, 234–237, 242–243, 256, 267, 433
Barbeyrac, Jean, 492
Baretti, Giuseppe, *Dictionary of the English and Italian Languages*, 68–69
Baring, Alexander, 457
Barlow, Joel, *Vision of Columbus*, 377
Barrow, John, *New and Universal Dictionary of Arts and Sciences*, 71
Barthélemy, *Voyage de Jeune Anacharsis*, 398–399
Bartlett, Josiah, 188
Barton, Benjamin Smith, 433, 518–519
Barton, William, *Memoirs of the Life of David Rittenhouse*, 570
Baxter, Richard, 20
Beauties of the English Stage, 63, 184
Becket, Andrew, *Concordance to Shakespeare*, 321
Beckford, William, 132
    Vathek, 130
Beckley, John, 400, 416, 548
Bede, the Venerable, *Historia Ecclesiastica Gentis Anglolum*, 584
Bell, John
    Bell's Edition of Shakespeare, 321, 608
    edition of English poets, 304–305
Bell, Robert, 191–194, 261
Bellini, Carlo, 149, 280, 284
Belsham, Thomas, *Memoires of the Late Reverend Theophilus Lindsey*, 541–542, 585
Bentham, Jeremy, 83
Bergère, 384, 398
Bernard, John, 92, 321, 431, 468–469
Bernhard, Duke of Saxe-Weimar-Eisenach, 638–639
    Travels through North America, 638

Bezout, Étienne, *Cours de Mathématiques*, 222
Bible, 127, 215, 258–249, 339, 374, 503, 581–594
    Massachuset, *Mamusse Wunneetupanatamwe Up-Biblium God Naneeswe Nukkone Testament Kah Wonk Wusku Testament* (Eliot), 374
    New Testament, 126, 258, 58
        Gaelic, Stuart, *Tiomnadh nuadh*, 142
        Greek, 34, 503
    Old Testament, 258, 482
        Greek, 503
        Psalms, English, Brady and Tate, *New Version of the Psalms of David*, 28–29
    Polyglot, Walton, *Biblia Sacra Polyglotta*, 630
Bibliotheca Pinelliana, 372–373
Biddle, Nicholas, 478–479
Bigelow, Jacob, *Florula Bostoniensis*, 631
"Bill for Amending the Constitution of the College of William and Mary," 213, 216–218, 599, 613
"Bill for Establishing a Public Library," 213, 218
"Bill for Establishing Cross Posts," 220
"Bill for Establishing Religious Freedom," 204, 205–206, 453
"Bill for the More General Diffusion of Knowledge," 213–214, 220, 615
"Bill for Proportioning Crimes and Punishments," 209
"Bill for the Revision of the Laws," 207
Bingham, William, 436
Blackamore, Arthur, 204
Blackstone, William, *Commentaries on the Laws of England*, 193
Blaettermann, George, 622–623, 626, 632, 639
Blaettermann, Mrs. George, 636
Blair, Elizabeth, 278
Blair, Hugh, "Critical Dissertation on the Poems of Ossian," 135
Blair, James, 31–32
    Our Saviour's Divine Sermon on the Mount...Explained, 31

Bland, Richard, 108, 163, 174
  *Inquiry into the Rights of the British
    Colonies*, 153, 155
Bliss, Philip, 7
Boccaccio, Giovanni, *Decameron*, 578
Bodin, Jean, *Six Livres de la République*,
  84
Boethius, 337, 339, 507
  Consolation of Philosophy, 330, 336,
    339
Bohn, Henry George, 628, 631–632
Boileau-Despréaux, Nicholas, 222
Boinod and Galliard, 267
Bolingbroke, Henry St. John, 431, 582,
  600
  Philosophical Works, 82–83, 125–126
Bolling, Mary Jefferson (TJ's sister),
  10–11
Bonaparte, Napoleon, 605
Bonnycastle, Charles, 623–624, 627,
  635
Book, 559
Book of Common Prayer, 4–5, 7, 25,
  27–29
Book of Kings, 559–560
Bordley, John Beale, *Sketches on
  Rotations of Crops*, 422
Boswell, James, 35, 313–314
  Life of Johnson, 312–313, 404
Bosworth, Joseph, *Elements of Anglo-
  Saxon Grammar*, 580
Botetourt, Norborne Berkeley, Baron
  de
  death of, 150
  dissolves the House of Burgesses, 111
  library of, 105
  patronage of William and Mary, 105,
    129
  serves as governor of Virginia,
    104–105, 107–108, 111
Botta, Carlo, *Storia della Guerra
  dell'Indepenza degli Stati Uniti
  d'America*, 570–571
Boucher, Jonathan, 31, 35, 39
Boulton, Matthew, 54, 62, 67
Bowditch, Nathaniel, *New American
  Practical Navigator*, 621
Bower, Archibald, *History of the Popes*,
  140
Boyer, Abel, *Royal Dictionary*, 375

Brackenridge, Hugh Henry, *Rising
  Glory of America*, 451
Bradford, William, 154–155
Brady, Nicholas, *New Version of the
  Psalms of David*, 28–29
Breckinridge, John, 442
Bréhan, Marquise de, 369
Brodie, George, *History of the British
  Empire*, 632–633
Brown, Charles Brockden
  Arthur Mervyn, 458
  correspondence with Jefferson,
    577–578
  Edgar Huntley, 458
  Wieland, 577
Brown, Mather, 292, 322–323, 603
Brunt, Jonathan, 495–499, 510–511
  *Extracts from Locke's Essay on the
    Human Understanding*, 500
  Little Medley, 511
  Rush's Extracts, 499
Brutus, Marcus Junius, 76–77, 79
Buchanan, William, 486
Buffon, Georges Louis Leclerc, Comte de,
  271, 302–304, 395–396, 434, 559
Bulloch, Archibald, 187
Bunyan, Paul, *Pilgrim's Progress*, 532
Burch, Samuel, 546–547
Burgh, James, *Political Disquisitions*, 193
Burgoyne, John, 402
Burk, John Daly, 500
  History of Virginia, 501, 540
Burlamaqui, Jean Jacques, 176
  Principles de Droit Naturel, 83–84
Burnaby, Andrew, 47–48, 58, 64, 67
  Travels, 48, 64
Burnet, Gilbert, *History of the
  Reformation of the Church of
  England*, 204
Burns, Robert, "To Mary in Heaven,"
  506
Burr, Aaron
  duel with Alexander Hamilton,
    490–491
  as vice president, 450, 459
Burwell, Nathaniel, 579
Burwell, Rebecca, 66–68
Butler, Samuel, *Hudibras*, 314
Byrd, Maria Taylor, 45, 141
Byrd, William (1652–1704), 141

Byrd, William (1674–1744), 45, 420
  *History of the Dividing Line Betwixt
    Virginia and North Carolina,*
    119, 156, 238
  library of, 139, 141, 261, 264, 374,
    550–551
  secret diary, 572
Byrd, William (1728–1777), 45, 73,
    140–141
Byron, George Gordon, Lord Byron, 77,
    575
  Island, 576–577
  Marino Faliero, 575

Cabell, Joseph C., 616–617, 621, 626–627
Cabot, George, 417
Cabot, Mr., 276
Caesar, Julius, 76–79
Callender, James Thomson, 440–441,
    534
  History of the United States for 1796,
    440–441
  Political Progress of Britain, 440
  Prospect before US, 441
  Sketches of the History of America, 441
Callimachus, 117
Campbell, John W., 526, 598
Canning, Elizabeth, 139
Capell, Edward, 125
  *Notes and Various Readings to
    Shakespeare,* 321
Caractacus, 232
Carey, Henry, *Honest Yorkshire-Man,* 103
Carey, Matthew, 456, 575–576, 584–585
  American Museum, 400
Carmarthen, Francis Godolphin
    Osborne, Lord, 311
Carmichael, Gershom, 21
Carmichael, William, 330
Carr, Dabney (1743–1773)
  contributions to American
    Revolution, 137, 149, 150
  death of, 22, 137, 140
  education of, 32, 35
  friendship with Jefferson, 32–33
  library of, 35–36
Carr, Dabney (1773–1837), 22, 137, 492
Carr, Jane, 137
Carr, Martha Jefferson, 11, 15, 22, 137,
    254

Carr, Peter
  Albemarle Academy and, 615, 617
  education of, 22, 24
  Jefferson's correspondence with, 51,
    127, 138, 276, 284, 481, 617
  library of, 118
Carr, Samuel, 22
Carroll, Charles, of Carrollton, 540
Cart, Jean Jacques, *Lettres . . . sur le Droit
    Public de ce Pays,* 426
Carter, Charles, 121
Carter, Edward, 221
Carter, Elizabeth, 126
Cary, Archibald, 256
Cary, Wilson Miles, 637
Castell, Edmund, *Lexicon Heptaglotton,*
    630
Castell, Robert, *Villas of the Ancients
    Illustrated,* 521
*Catalogue of the Library of the United
    States,* 563
Catharine II (the Great), 299
Cervantes, Miguel de, *Don Quixote,* 214,
    232, 266–267, 276–277, 389, 398,
    418, 426, 474, 578
Charles I, King of England, 76
Charron, Pierre, *De la Sagesse,* 558
Chastellux, François Jean de Beauvoir,
    Chevalier de
  character sketch of Jefferson,
    251–252, 269
  correspondence with Jefferson,
    255–256, 343
  De la Félicité Publique, 247
  *Essai sur l'Union de la Poésie et de la
    Musique,* 250
  friendship with Jefferson, 271, 280,
    294, 302, 328
  introduces Jefferson to Buffon,
    302–303
  literary conversations with Jefferson,
    304–305
  receives copy of *Notes on the State of
    Virginia,* 236, 242–243
  returns to France, 253
  Travels in North America, 143, 247, 272
  visits Monticello, 13, 247–253, 259
  Voyage de Newport á Philadelphie, 247
  *Voyages . . . dans l'Amérique
    Septentrionale,* 247

Chaucer, Geoffrey
  Canterbury Tales, 523
  Workes, 522, 558
Cheselden, William, *Anatomy of Human
    Body*, 69
Chesterfield, Philip Dormer Stanhope,
    Earl of, *Letters to His Son*, 341, 375
Chiari, Pietro, *La Storia di Tom Jones*, 69
Chipman, Nathaniel, *Sketches of the
    Principles of Government*, 443
Christ, Jesus, 25, 477, 581–594
  "Sermon on the Mount," 31, 182,
    590–592
Cicero, Marcus Tullius, 126, 139, 171,
    179, 182, 195, 379, 586
  De Officiis, 34, 126, 160
  De Philosophia, 608
  De Senectute, 537
  Orationes, 34
  Thoughts of Cicero, 9
  Tusculan Disputations, 38–39, 126
Citizen's and Farmer's Almanac, 457
Clark, William, 413, 478, 479, 482–483,
    486–487, 489, 491, 493–495
Claudius, 232
Clavigero, Francesco Saverio, *History of
    Mexico*, 371
Clayton, John, 129
  Flora Virginica, 201
Cleaveland, Parker, *Elementary Treatise
    on Mineralogy and Geology*, 631
Cleland, John, *Memoirs of a Woman of
    Pleasure*, 140
Clinton, George, 490–491
Cobbett, William (a.k.a. Peter
    Porcupine), 437–439
Coke upon Littleton, 64–65, 425, 621
Cole, John, 232
Coleridge, Samuel T., 113, 569
Coles, Edward, 534–535
Colles, Christopher, *Survey of the Roads
    of the United States*, 390
Collins, Isaac, 327
Collins, William, 306
Complete Collection of the Lords' Protests,
    550
Condorcet, Marquis de, 302, 445, 581
  *Outlines of an Historical View of the
    Progress of the Human Mind*,
    443–444

Confessions (Rousseau), 295, 595
Connecticut Magazine, 457
Connecticut Society of Arts and
    Sciences, 374
Constable, John, 635
Constitution, 264, 283
Conti, Natale, 406
Cook, Captain James, 299
Coolidge, Ellen W. Randolph (TJ's
    granddaughter), 145, 420,
    469–470, 476, 504–507, 524, 562,
    576–577, 579, 601, 605–610, 630,
    633, 634, 635, 636–638
Coolidge, Joseph, 629–631, 633,
    636–637, 641–642
Cooper, James Fenimore, 601
Cooper, Samuel, *First Lines of the
    Practice of Surgery*, 571
Cooper, Thomas, 621
  Institutes of Justinian, 58
Copley, John Singleton, 323
Coquebert, Felix, 502
Cordier, Maturin, *Colloquia*, 22–23
Corneille, Pierre, 608
Cornwallis, Charles, Lord, 231, 251,
    328
Corny, Louis Dominque Ethis de, 378
Corrêa de Serra, Jose Francisco, 621
Correggio, 575
Cortés, Hernando, 389, 521
Coste, Pierre, 385
Cosway, Maria, 12, 15–16, 331–339,
    359–363, 365–366
Cosway, Richard, 333, 335, 337
Courier of New Hampshire, 474
Coutts, William, 121
Cowley, Abraham, *Poetical Works*, 305
Coxe, Daniel, *Description of the English
    Province of Carolana*, 40–41
Cresap, Michael, 437
Cresap, Thomas, 437, 438
Crèvecoeur, J. Hector St. John de, 294
  Letters from an American Farmer, 177,
    294
Cromwell, Oliver, 76, 151
Cumberland, Richard
  Observer, 399
  Treatise of the Laws of Nature, 83
Cummings, Hilliard, and Company,
    629–631

Cunego, Domenico, 608
Cutting, Nathaniel, 383–387

D'Alembert, Jean le Rond, 296–297, 581
Damme, Pieter Bernhard van
    sends Jefferson book auction
        catalogue, 370–371
    special book orders for Jefferson,
        367
Dandridge, Nathaniel West, 43
Dante Alighieri, 608
Dares, Phrygius, 42
Darwin, Erasmus, 54–55, 62
David, Jacques-Louis
    Death of David, 331
    Oath of the Horatii, 331
Davies, John, *Antiquae Linguae
        Britannicae*, 49
Davies, Myles, 375
Davila, Enrico, *Historia delle Guerre
        Civile di Francia*, 68, 70, 124,
        569
Davis, John
    attends Jefferson's inauguration, 450
    *Captain John Smith and Princess
        Pocahontas*, 471
    opinion of *Notes on the State of
        Virginia*, 246
    Travels . . . in the United States, 457
Davis, Thomas, 471
Dawson, William, 22
Day, Thomas, 54, 62
De Bry, Theodor, 371, 538, 539
    Voyages, 556
Deane, Silas, 168, 210
Dearborn, Henry, 465
Declaration of Independence, 96,
        174–190, 195–196, 198, 205, 223,
        264, 268, 271, 311, 366, 376–377,
        379, 451, 453, 526, 532, 598–599,
        611, 625, 627, 640–642
*Declaration of the Causes and Necessity
        for Taking up Arms*, 169–171
Defoe, Daniel
    "Relation of the Apparition of Mrs.
        Veal," 25
    Robinson Crusoe, 17
Demarest, A. G., *Mammologie*, 571
Democritus, *Epistolae Veterum
        Graecorum,* 373

Demosthenes, 77–78, 128, 139, 171
Denison, J. Evelyn, 632
*Determinations of the Honourable House
        of Commons, Concerning
        Elections*, 109–110
Dézallier d'Argenville, Antoine-Joseph,
        *Theory and Practice of
        Gardening*, 9
Dickinson, John, 452
    attitude toward American
        Revolution, 597
    *Declaration of the Causes and
        Necessity for Taking up Arms*,
        169–171
    Letters from a Farmer in Pennsylvania,
        169
Dickinson, William, 527
Dictionnaire de l'Academie Française,
        558
Dictionnaire de Trévoux, 558
Diderot, Denis, 296–297, 581, 608
Dilly, Charles, 328–329
Dinmore, Richard
    circulating library, 471
    Select and Fugitive Poetry, 471
Diogenes, *Epistolae Veterum Graecorum*,
        373–374
Disraeli, Isaac, 269
Dixon, John, 88
Dodd, William, *Beauties of Shakespeare*,
        321
Doddridge, Philip, *Sermons to Young
        Persons*, 20
Dodsley, Robert, *Preceptor*, 35, 36, 52
Dolci, Carlo, 362–363
Douglas, William, 19–23, 25, 31
Dr. Faustus, 15
Drelincourt, Charles, *Consolations*,
        24–25, 137
Drummond, Mrs., 120
Dryden, John, 71, 127
Duane, James, 168, 276–277
Duane, William
    arranges for translation of Tracy's
        Commentary, 528
    as editor of *Aurora*, 440
    opens bookstore in Washington,
        D.C., 471
    publishes Tracy's *Commentary*, 529,
        558

Dufief, Nicolas Gouin
  plan for Library of Congress, 549, 552
  sells Franklin's library, 549
  sends catalogue of Franklin library
      to Jefferson, 550
  supplies books to Jefferson, 471
Dufresnoy, Nicolas Lenglet, *Geography
      for Children*, 35
Duhamel du Monceau, Henri Louis,
      Practical Treatise of Husbandry,
      68, 70
Dumont de Montigny, *Mémoires de la
      Louisiane*, 40
Duncan, William, *Elements of Logick*, 52
Dunglison, Robley, 572, 623, 626–627,
      637–638, 640
  *Commentaries of Diseases of the
      Stomach and Bowels of Children*,
      623
Dunlap, John
  Jefferson considers as publisher of
      Notes on the State of Virginia,
      270
  Jefferson patronizes his bookshop,
      191, 195
  publishes *Declaration of
      Independence*, 195
  publishes *Pennsylvania Packet*, 194
  publishes *Summary View*, 194–195,
      270
Dunmore, John Murray, fourth Earl of
  character of, 150
  convenes House of Burgesses to
      present Lord North's proposal,
      164–165
  dissolves House of Burgesses, 152
  flees Governor's Palace, 199
  gubernatorial responsibilities, 150
  Jefferson's opinion of, 168
  library of, 150, 199
  prorogues House of Burgesses, 150
Dupont de Nemours, Pierre Samuel,
      459
Duport, James, *Metaphrasis Libri
      Psalmorum Graecis Versibus
      Contexta*, 584
Durand, Jean Nicolas Louis, *Recueil et
      Parallèle des Édifices de Tout
      Genre Anciens et Modernes*, 601
Du Roi, August Wilhelm, 221–222

Eaton, Amos, *Geological and
      Agricultural Survey of the District
      Adjoining the Erie Canal*, 573
Edgeworth, Maria, 62
  Modern Griselda, 470
  Moral Tales for Young People, 470
  Parent's Assistant, 470–471
  Rosamond, 470
  Stories for Children, 470
Edgeworth, Richard Lovell, 54–55, 62
Edinburgh Review, 579
Edwards, James, 372, 373
Edwards, Jonathan, *Observations on the
      Language of the Muhhekaneew
      Indians*, 374
Eliot, John, *Mamusse
      Wunneetupanatamwe Up-
      Biblium God Naneeswe Nukkone
      Testament Kah Wonk Wusku
      Testament*, 374
Ellis, William, *London and Country
      Brewer*, 10
Ellys, Anthony, *Tracts of the Liberty,
      Spiritual and Temporal, of
      Protestants in England*, 113
Elmslie, John, 486
Elstob, Elizabeth, *Rudiments of
      Grammar for the English-Saxon
      Tongue*, 60
Emerson, William
  Doctrine of Fluxions, 53
  Principles of Mechanics, 53–54
Emmett, John Patton, 624, 635, 637
Encyclopedie Methodique, 205–206, 310,
      424
Enville, Louise Elisabeth de la
      Rouchefoucauld, 333
Epictetus, 117, 126, 586, 587, 632
Epicurus, 586
Epistolae Veterum Graecorum, 373–374
Eppes, Elizabeth Wayles, 255
Eppes, Francis, 147, 196–197, 265, 389,
      470, 599–600, 608
Eppes, Maria Jefferson (TJ's daughter,
      a.k.a. Mary)
  arrives in Paris, 352
  attends school in Philadelphia,
      411–412
  birth of, 209
  childhood, 253

contracts the whooping cough, 290
correspondence with Jefferson, 145,
    398–399, 402
Cutting's impressions of her,
    386–387
death of, 506
gives birth to Francis, 470
leaves France for Virginia, 383
meets John and Abigail Adams,
    352–353
reads Spanish, 385, 389, 398
receives books, 399
requests books from Jefferson, 398
Erasmus, 23
Espagnol, 357
Ethis de Corny, Louis Dominique,
    378
Euclid, 536
Euripides, 608
    Hecuba, 91–92
Evans, Theophilus, 49
Everett, Edward, 619

Fabbroni, Giovanni, 211–212, 233
Fables of Pilpay, 425
*Famous History of the Seven Champions
    of Christendom*, 15
"Farmer's Letters" (Lincoln), 465
Farneworth, Ellis, 124
Farquhar, George, 222
Faujas de Saint-Fond, Barthélemy,
    *Description des Experience de la
    Machine Aérostatiques*, 286
Fauquier, Francis
    "Account of an Extraordinary Storm
        of Hail," 61
    character of, 60–62
    death of, 102
    library of, 61
    meets Franklin, 66–67
    musical interests, 62, 103–104
    social activities, 60, 62, 81
    Stamp Act and, 75, 80, 82
    weather records of, 48, 64, 187
Félice, Fortuné Barthélemy de, *Leçons
    de Droit de la Nature et des Gens*,
    268
Fénelon, *Adventures of Telemachus*, 24,
    122, 277
Fennel, James, 437

Fenno, John, 412
    Gazette of the United States, 439
Ferguson, Adam, *Essay on the History of
    Civil Society*, 113, 180
Ferguson, James
    Astronomy, 122
    Lectures, 122
Few, Francis, 507–508
Fielding, Henry
    Tom Jones, 69, 278, 557
    Works, 123
Fleming, William, 133
Flood, Henry, 606–608
Florian, Jean-Pierre-Claris de
    Arlequinades, 334
    Deux Billets, 334
    Galatée, 334
Florus, *Rerum Romanorum Epitome*,
    23–24
Floyd, William, 541
Fontaine, Francis, 31
Fontaine, Jean de la, *Fables Choisies*, 385
Fontaine, Mary Anne, 31
Foote, Samuel, 307
Fortescue, John, *Difference between an
    Absolute and Limited Monarchy*,
    59–60
Fortescue-Aland, John, 59–60
Foulis Press, 117–118, 126–127, 567
Foulke, John, 286
Foundling of Belgrade, 577
Foxcroft, Thomas, 67
Franklin, Benjamin
    anecdotes, 188, 390–392, 570, 596,
        598
    appointed commissioner to negotiate
        treaties of amity and commerce,
        270, 356
    Autobiography, 390–392, 595, 596, 611
    Congressional committee work, 169,
        171, 178, 181, 605
    contributions to *Declaration of
        Independence*, 181, 187–188
    correspondence with Jefferson, 210
    death of, 611–612
    "Dialogue between the Gout and Mr.
        Franklin," 332
    efforts to overturn the Stamp Act, 81
    elected president of American
        Philosophical Society, 432

Franklin, Benjamin (*continued*)
  establishes Library Company of
    Philadelphia, 195
  *Experiments and Observations on
    Electricity*, 127
  Fourth of July celebrations, 300
  friendship with Jefferson, 188,
    260–281, 390
  friendship with Mazzei, 147
  friendship with William Small, 54,
    63–64, 66
  honorary degree, 371
  leaves Paris, 291, 293–294
  library of, 424, 427, 549–550, 572
  literary personae, 528
  member of Houdetot's salon, 296
  receives a copy of *Notes on the State of
    Virginia*, 243
  receives a copy of *Summary View*,
    160
  receives volumes of *Encyclopedia
    Methodique*, 310
  "Silence Dogood, No 4," 532
  use of ivory table-book, 98
  visits Williamsburg, 66–67
  Way to Wealth, 158
Franklin, William Temple, 611
Freneau, Philip
  National Gazette, 412–413 440
  Poems, 510
  Rising Glory of America, 451
  Time Piece, 500
Frost, J. T., 546–547
Froullé, Jacques François, 282, 328–329,
  423–426
Fry, Joshua, 40–41
Fulbecke, William, *Parallel of
  Conference of the Civil Law, the
  Canon Law, and the Common
  Law*, 204
Fulton, Robert, *Treatise on the
  Improvement of Canal
  Navigation*, 573

Gage, Thomas, 163
Galileo, 463
Gallatin, Albert
  attitude toward embargo, 505
  correspondence with Jefferson, 489,
    530

Jefferson appoints treasury secretary,
    464
  opposition to Hamilton, 464
  Treatise on Internal Navigation, 573
Galt, John, *Entail; or, The Lairds of
    Grippy*, 576–577
Galvan, William, 225–226, 229
García de la Huerta, Vincente Antonio,
    Obras Poéticas, 330
Garcilaso de la Vega
  Commentarios Reale, 330
  Florida, 330
Gardiner, Peter, 106
Gavin, Anthony, 19, 24–25
  Master Key to Popery, 24–25
Gavin, Rachael, 24
Gay, John, 21, 127
Gazette of the United States, 401, 412
Geismar, Baron von, 221, 365
General Collection of Treaty's, 199
Genet, Edmund Charles, 413, 414–415
Genghis Khan, 426
Genlis, Stéphanie Félicité, Comtesse de
  Tales of the Castle, 399
  Théatre á Usage de Jeunes Personnes,
    304
Geoffrin, Marie-Thérèse, Madame de,
    296
*Geographiae Veteris Scriptores Graeci
    Minores*, 374
Geoponica, 425
George II, King of Great Britain, 26
George III, King of Great Britain, 56,
    81, 104, 108, 153, 157, 183, 311
Gerry, Elbridge
  correspondence with Jefferson, 433,
    462–463
  meets Jefferson in New York,
    96–97
  serves in Continenal Congress, 167
  serves as vice president, 540–541
  signs *Declaration of Independence*,
    189–190
Gessner, Salomon, *Death of Abel*, 9
Gibbon, Edward, *History of the Decline
    and Fall of the Roman Empire*,
    143–144, 398
Gibbs, James, *Rules for Drawing the
    Several Parts of Architecture*, 10
Giles, William Branch, 422

Gilmer, Francis Walker
  accepts chair in law at the University
    of Virginia, 639
  character of, 621
  edits Captain John Smith's *True
    Travels* and *Generall Historie*,
    621
  friendship with Jefferson, 34
  impressions of Monticello, 525
  Sketches of American Orators, 621
  travels to Great Britain on behalf of
    the University of Virginia,
    621–624, 626, 628–629, 631
Girardin, Louis Hue, 502, 540,
    603–604
  History of Virginia, 604
Gleim, Johann Wilhelm Ludwig, "Falle
    doch auf Doris Augenlieder,"
    168
Goethe, *Faust*, 575
Goldsborough, Robert, 552, 556
Goldsmith, Mr., 304
Goldsmith, Oliver, *Hermit*, 476
Gordon, Nathaniel, 517
Graham, Richard, 50, 57
Gravier, Jean, 529–531
Gray, Francis C., 557, 559–560, 602
Gray, Thomas, 129, 306, 363
Green, Jonas, 88
Gregory, John, *Comparative View of the
    State and Faculties of Man*, 399
Gregory, William, 95–96
Grétry, André-Ernest-Modeste
  Aucassin et Nicolette, 285–286
  Richard Coeur de Lion, 334
  Silvain, 285–286
Grimm, Friedrich Melchior, Baron von,
    299
Grindle, Mrs., 493
Grotius, Hugo, 21
  Annales et Historiae de Rebus Belgicis,
    370
  De Jure Belli ac Pacis, 83
  Droit de la Guerre, et de la Paix 83
  *Grounds and Rudiments of Law and
    Equity*, 86
  Rights of War and Peace, 492
Guardian, 26
Guarini, Battista, 608
  Il Pastor Fido, 282

Gudin, Paul Philippe, *L'Astronomie*,
    573–574
Guicciardini, Francesco, *Della Istoria
    d'Italia*, 68, 70
Gunn, James, 408–409
Gurdon, Thornagh, *History of the High
    Court*, 110
Gurney, Anna, *Saxon Chronicle*, 628–
    629
Gwatkin, Thomas, 132

Hafiz, "Persian Song," 201
Hakewill, William, *Modus Tenendi
    Parliamentum*, 110
Hall, Francis, 570–571
Hamilton, Alexander
  affair with Maris Reynolds, 440
  appointed treasury secretary, 392
  character of, 393
  depiction in *The Anas*, 406–409
  duel with Aaron Burr, 490–491
  Jefferson's relationship with,
    393–395, 401, 403, 416–417,
    422, 429
  opposed by Albert Gallatin, 464
  opposition to Genet, 413, 415–416
Hancarville, Pierre Fraçois Hugues d',
    335
Händel, George Frideric, 62
Hanmer, Thomas, 105
Hansford, Theodore, 632
"Happy Fireside," 506
Hargrave, Francis, 425
Hariot, Thomas, *Admiranda Narratio*,
    371
Harlan, Richard, *Fauna Americana*, 571
Harrington, James, *Commonwealth of
    Oceana*, 264
Harrison, Benjamin, 163, 169, 189–190
Harrison, Joseph, *Attorney's Pocket
    Companion*, 70
Hartley, David, *Observations on Man*, 61
Harvey, Edward, *Manual Exercise*,
    162–163
Harvie, John, 30, 34, 44
Harwood, Edward, *Biographia Classica*,
    140
Hatsell, John, *Precedents of Proceedings
    in the House of Commons*, 527
Hawkins, John Isaac, 596

Hay, George, 530
Hegel, Georg Wilhelm Friedrich, 426
Hemings, James, 260, 271, 275, 352, 383,
    389
Hemings, Robert, 389
Hemings, Sally, 352, 383, 441–442
Henings, William Waller, *Statutes at
    Large*, 428, 540
Henley, Samuel
    friendship with Jefferson, 130, 201
    helps found Virginia's Philosophical
        Society for the Advancement of
        Useful Knowledge, 129
    library of, 128–130, 172, 200, 353, 523
    as professor at William and Mary,
        128
    returns to England, 172
    scholarly activities, 129–132, 321
Hennepin, Louis, *New Discovery of a
    Vast Country in America*, 631
Henry IV (King of France), 68, 124
Henry VIII (King of England), 73, 82
Henry, Patrick
    compared to Jesus, 583
    depiction of, in Jefferson's
        Autobiography, 76–77, 597
    elected to Continenetal Congress,
        163
    Jefferson's testament to his
        eloquence, 76–78
    leadership in American Revolution,
        136, 151, 159, 161
    Liberty-or-Death speech, 161–162,
        164
    meets Jefferson, 43
    serves as governor of Virginia, 223
    Stamp Act and, 75, 79–80
Heraclitus, *Epistolae Veterum
    Graecorum*, 373–374
Herculus and Antaeus, 69
Herodotus, 28, 69, 135, 264, 318
Hewes, Thomas, 486
Heyne, Christian Gottlob, 565
Hickes, George, 60
Hidalgo, Juan, *Romances de Germanía*,
    330
Hill, Henry, 174
Hillhouse, Augustus, *Essay on the
    History and Cultivation of the
    European Olive-Tree*, 573

Hilliard, William, 629–633
Hilliard and Cummings, 629–631
Hippocrates, *Epistolae Veterum
    Graecorum*, 373–374
History of Fortunatus, 15–16
History of Parismus, 15
History of Tom Thumb, 15, 16
Hogeboom, Cornelius, 410–411
Hogendorp, Gijbert Karel, Count van,
    236, 267–269
Holbach, Paul Henri Thiry, Baron de,
    581–582
    Bon Sens, 581
    Christianisme Dévoilé, 581–582
    Système de la Nature, 581
    Système Social, 582
    Tableau des Saints, 582
Holmes, Abiel, 503
    American Annals, 502–503, 540
"Home," 506
Home, John, *Douglas*, 102–103
Homer, 42, 77–78, 135, 139, 507, 510
    Iliad, 118, 135, 255, 525, 565–566
    Odyssey, 565
Hoole, John, 201
Hopkins and Earle, 527
Hopkinson, Francis, 17, 194, 242–243,
    266, 286, 310, 331
Hopkinson, Mary Johnson (Mrs.
    Thomas Hopkinson), 266
Horace, 23, 34, 128, 330
    Odes, 23
    Satires, 23
Horrocks, James, library of, 199–200
Houdetot, Elisabeth Françoise Sophie
    de La Live Bellegarde,
    Comtesse d', 295–297, 306, 345
Houdon, Jean Antoine, 322
Howe, Richard, 197
Howell, David, 268
Hudson, John, 374
Hulbert, John, 555
Hume, David, 21, 27, 632–633
    Essays, 78
    History of England, 72, 82–83,
        632–633
Humphreys, David, 287–288, 311, 321
    Poem, on the Happiness of America,
        288
Hunter, Robert, 69

Husayni, Abu Talib, *Instituts Politiques et Militaire de Tamerlan*, 426
Hutcheson, Francis, 9, 21
Hutton, Catherine, *Miser Married*, 607

Inchbald, Elizabeth, 607
Independent Chronicle, 457
Ingersoll, Charles, 553–554
Irving, Washington, 616
Isocrates, 632
Izard, Ralph, 410

Jack the Giant Killer, 15
Jackson, Jonathan, 284
James, John, *Theory and Practice of Gardening*, 9
Jefferson, Anna S. (TJ's sister). *See,* Marks, Anna S. Jefferson
Jefferson, Elizabeth (TJ's sister), 11, 15
Jefferson, Isaac (TJ's slave), 120, 122, 127, 232, 350, 606
Jefferson, Jane (TJ's sister), 10–11, 87, 93, 174
Jefferson, Jane Randolph (1720–1776, TJ's mother), 10–11, 174–175
Jefferson, Jane Randolph (1774–1775, TJ's daughter), 174
Jefferson, Lucy (TJ's sister), 11
Jeferson, Lucy Elizabeth (1780–1781, TJ's daughter), 253
Jefferson, Lucy Elizabeth (1782–1784, TJ's daughter), 253, 290
Jefferson, Martha (TJ's daughter). *See,* Randolph, Martha Jefferson
Jefferson, Martha Wayles Skelton (TJ's wife), 143
  correspondence with Jefferson, 4, 120, 196
  courtship with Jefferson, 119–121
  death, 254–255, 259
  depiction of, in Jefferson's *Autobiography*, 604
  friendship with William Small, 132
  gives birth, 121, 209, 252–253
  illness, 198, 253–254
  reading, 122
  wedding, 121–122
Jefferson, Mary (TJ's daughter). *See* Eppes, Maria Jefferson

Jefferson, Peter (TJ's father), 30, 39
  athleticism, 33
  builds Shadwell, 1
  death of, 25
  education of, 26
  executor for William Randolph, 45
  library of, 4–5, 8, 10–12, 26, 27,
  purchases books for TJ, 22
Jefferson, Randolph (TJ's brother), 11
Jefferson, Thomas (TJ)
  literary life
    almanacs, 2, 37, 53, 88, 98–100, 166–167, 186 283
    Annapolis library, 267–270
    attends the theatre, 102–103, 106, 285–286, 321–322, 334
    attends William and Mary, 43–56
    bibliomania, 375, 425, 566
    biography writing, 478–494, 581–612
    book buying in Europe, 330, 367, 371–374
    book buying in Paris, 282–285
    book buying in Philadelphia, 191–199
    book buying in Williamsburg, 199–204
    bookplates and, 5–7
    chapbooks and, 15–17
    character sketches, 32, 107, 265, 310, 393, 596
    childhood reading, 15–19
    circulating libraries and, 166, 172, 218, 471
    collects Virginiana, 26, 202, 233
    correspondence, 418–431, 532–545. *See* also under names of individual correspondents
    drafts legislation, 108–109, 162–163, 165, 167, 171, 207–209, 213–221, 270
    education, 11, 19–25, 30–60
    educational theory, 213–219
    equity commonplace book, 92
    finds publisher for David Ramsay, 326–330
    great library, 4, 7, 50, 117–118, 122, 138, 140, 173, 183, 257, 443, 546–563, 573–574, 581

Jefferson, Thomas (TJ) (*continued*)
    impressions of the French
       Revolution, 375–376, 377, 378,
       393, 426, 611
    joins Small's Williamsburg circle,
       57–72
    legal commonplace book, 49, 86,
       89, 90, 92, 290
    Library Company of Philadelphia
       and, 192, 195–196, 218, 550
    Library of Congress and, 4, 24, 27,
       35, 72, 84, 443, 550, 546–563,
       571, 577
    library organization, 10, 126, 126,
       257–259, 561–563, 567–576
    literary commonplace book, 23,
       39, 41, 63, 82, 83, 86, 135, 184;
       86–87, 89, 91, 92, 134, 135, 139
    literary criticism of, 304–308
    literary patronage, 495–511
    memorandum books, 2, 86,
       97–101, 106, 109, 245, 264, 275,
       282, 285, 298–299, 312, 340, 383,
       441
    opinion of Patrick Henry, 75–80,
       161
    ownership inscriptions, 4–8,
       24–25, 27–29, 35, 69–70, 84, 140,
       144
    poetry of, 314–315
    Poplar Forest Library, 544,
       554–555
    public libraries, proposal for,
       218–219
    reads law under Wythe, 57–60
    received honorary degree, 371
    recommends books to others, 122,
       130–131, 221–222
    retirement library, 7, 39, 564–580,
       581, 582, 588
    salons of Paris and, 294–298
    scientific writings, 432–436
    scrapbooks, 504–505
    Shadwell library, 1–14, 22, 26, 34,
       70, 104
    table-books, 98–99
    travel writing, 93–96, 318–321,
       340–368
    University of Virginia and,
       613–627

    University of Virginia library and,
       601, 628–644
    visits library of Rhode Island
       College, 396
  writings
    Account of Louisiana, 487–489
    *Act for Establishing Religious
       Freedom*, 297, 526
    Anas, 404–417, 479, 484, 504, 612
    "Appendix to the Notes on
       Virginia Relative to the Murder
       of Logan's Family," 438
    Autobiography, 17, 50, 55, 76, 78,
       189, 203, 374–379, 484, 588,
       595–612
    "Bill for Amending the
       Constitution of the College of
       William and Mary," 213,
       216–218, 599, 613
    "Bill for Establishing a Public
       Library," 213, 218
    "Bill for Establishing Cross Posts,"
       220
    "Bill for Establishing Religious
       Freedom," 204–206, 453
    "Bill for Proportioning Crimes
       and Punishments," 209
    "Bill for the More General
       Diffusion of Knowledge,"
       213–214, 220, 615
    "Bill for the Revision of the
       Laws," 207
    Declaration of Independence, 96,
       174–190, 195–196, 198, 205, 223,
       264, 268, 311, 366, 376, 377, 379,
       451, 453, 526, 532, 598–599, 611,
       625, 627, 640
    *Declaration of the Causes and
       Necessity for Taking up Arms*,
       composed, 169–171
    "Dialogue between My Head and
       My Heart," 12, 332, 335–339,
       453
    *Essay on the Anglo-Saxon
       Language*, 580
    "Explanations of the 3 Volumes
       Bound in Marbled Paper," 404–
       405, 612
    Farm Book, 86
    "First Annual Message," 472–474

Garden Book, 86, 93, 97, 212, 253, 345, 408, 423
"Hints to Americans Traveling in Europe," 340–343, 348, 354, 359, 367, 396, 485
"Instructions to Express Riders between Richmond and Cape Henry," 226
"Instructions to Lewis," 484–486
"Kentucky Resolutions," 442
Life and Morals of Jesus of Nazareth, 581–594, 587, 588, 619
"Life of Captain Lewis," 478–494
Manual of Parliamentary Practice, 95, 110, 444–448, 526–527, 528, 588
"Mazzei letter," 429–431, 439, 544–545
"Memoir on the Megalonyx," 434–437, 448
Message . . . Communicating Discoveries Made in Exploring the Missouri, Red River, and Washita, 491
"Notes and Proceedings on Discontinuing the Establishment of the Church of England," 204
"Notes of a Conversation between A. Hamilton and Th:J.", 406
"Notes of a Tour into the Southern Parts of France," 340–341, 344–345, 349, 350, 354
"Notes of a Tour of English Gardens," 318, 320, 366
"Notes of a Tour through Holland and the Rhine Valley," 358–359, 363–368
"Notes of Proceedings in the Continental Congress," 178
"Notes on Commerce of the North States," 271, 275–276
Notes on the State of Virginia, 40, 72, 96, 99, 106, 110, 176–177, 201, 212, 215, 253, 259, 260, 262, 264, 265, 268, 270, 271, 282, 292, 296, 302, 303, 318, 322, 327, 405, 433, 434, 437, 457–458, 467, 468, 526, 587, 611

Observations on the Whale-Fishery, 276, 369
"On the Writings of the Baron d'Holbach on the Morality of Nature and That of the Christian Religion," 582–583
"Parliamentary Pocket-Book," 444
"Philosophy of Jesus," 583, 585–587
Proceedings and Report of the Commissioners for the University of Virginia, 618, 619, 620
Proceedings of the Government of the United States, in Maintaining the Public Right to the Beach of the Missisipi, 530–531, 537, 538
"Report of Committee to Prepare a Plan for a Militia," 161
"Report on Commerce," 526
"Report on Copper Coinage," 526
"Report on Desalination of Sea Water," 526
"Report on Fisheries," 526
Report . . . on the Subject of Establishing a Uniformity in the Weights, Measures and Coins, 395, 526
"Resolutions of Congress on Lord North's Conciliatory Proposal," 171
Summary View of the Rights of British America, 153–160, 162, 167, 185, 194–195, 526–527
"Syllabus of an Estimate of the Merit of the Doctrines of Jesus," 477, 542, 583, 585–586, 619
"Thoughts on English Prosody," 29, 87, 304–308, 580, 608
"Virginia Resolutions on Lord North's Conciliatory Proposal," 165, 167, 171
Jefferson Literary Society, 639
Jesus, of Nazareth, 25, 477, 581–594
"Sermon on the Mount," 31, 182, 590, 591
Jodrell, Richard, *Persian Heroine*, 318
Johnson, Benjamin, 503
Johnson, Edward, *Wonder-Working Providence*, 539

Johnson, Samuel, 201, 306, 312, 313, 406
　Dictionary of the English Language,
　　313
　Lives of the Poets, 287, 292
　Rasselas, 451
Jones, Joseph, 234
Jones, Mr., 631
Jones, Thomas, *British Language in Its
　　Lustre*, 49–50
Jones, William, 399
　Poeseos Asiaticae Commentariorum,
　　200–201
　Sacontalá, 399–400
　"Very Ancient Chinese Ode," 580
Jonson, Ben, *Every Man in His Humour*,
　　607
Jouett, John, Jr., 231
Journal of the House of Commons, 550
Journals of the House of Burgesses, 80
Joutel, Henri, *Journal Historique du
　　Dernier Voyage que Feu M. de
　　LaSale*, 633
Judith, 580
Jupiter (TJ's slave), 18, 70–71, 159
Justinian, *Institutes*, 58, 64
Juvenal, 565

Kalidasa, *Sacontalá*, 399–400
Kames, Henry Home, Lord, 176
　Elements of Criticism, 92, 123, 609
　*Essays on the Principles of Morality
　　and Natural Religion*, 92
　Historical Law Tracts, 90–92
　Principles of Equity, 92
Karamanli Ali Pasha, Bey of Tripoli,
　　464
Keats, John, 568
Keir, James, 54, 62
Kennett, Basil, *Antiquities of Rome*, 8
Kennett, White, *Bibliothecae
　　Americanae Primordia*, 502, 540
Key, Sarah, 638
Key, Thomas Hewitt, 623, 626–627,
　　635, 637–638
Kimber, Edward, 44
King, Cyrus, 555, 556
King, Rufus, 408, 410
Knox, Henry, 392, 416
Koenig, Armand, 367
Kohle, Pastor, 221–222

Koran, 9, 258, 315
Kotzebue, August von, *Almanach
　　Dramatischer Spiele*, 636
Krumpholtz, Johann Baptiste, 334
Kuster, Ludolf, *De Vero Usu Verborum
　　Mediorum apud Grecos*, 427

Lackington, James, 318, 628
Laclos, Choderlos de, *Les Liasons
　　Dangereuses*, 295
Lafayette, Marie Joseph Paul Yves Roch
　　Gilbert du Motier, Marquis de,
　　345
　banquet at the University of
　　Virginia, 624–625
　correspondence with Jefferson,
　　348–349, 392, 528
　French Revolution and, 376–377, 379
　presents books, 145, 632
　triumphal tour through the United
　　States, 624
　writes letters of introduction for
　　Jefferson, 294
Lafitau, Joseph-François, *Moeurs des
　　Sauvages Amériquains*, 538–539
Lagrange, Joseph-Louis, *Mechanique
　　Analitique*, 371
La Motte, Jeanne de Saint-Rémy de
　　Valois, Comtesse, *Mémoires
　　Justificatifs*, 559
Lampredi, Giovanni Maria, 68
Langdon, John, 417
Langland, William, *Vision of Pierce
　　Plowman*, 129, 201, 522–523, 532
La Rochefoucauld (-d'Enville), Louis
　　Alexandre, Duc de la Roche-
　　Guyon et de 294, 302
　*Constitutions des Treize États-Unis de
　　l'Amérique*, 281
La Rochefoucauld-Liancourt, François
　　Alexandre, Duc de, 422
Laval, Antoine François, *Voyage de la
　　Lousiane*, 371
Lavoisier, Antoine-Laurent de, 302
Law, Thomas, *Second Thoughts on
　　Instinctive Impulses*, 581, 582, 608
Laws of Virginia, 26
Lazarillo de Tormes, 398
Lear, Tobias, 416–417
Learned Pig, 312–313

Ledyard, John, 298–300, 384, 414, 482, 484
Lee, Francis Lightfoot, 174
Lee, Henry, *Memoirs of the War in the Southern Department of the United States*, 570
Lee, Richard Henry, 108, 151, 163, 168, 171, 178, 189, 195, 198, 224
Lee, Thomas Ludwell, 207–208
Lee, William, 444
Legrand, Jacques-Guillaume, 601
Leland, John, 474
Lemprière, John, *Classical Dictionary*, 568
Lenclos, Ninon de, 608
Le Prince de Beaumont, Madame de, *Moral Tales*, 476
Lesage, Alain René
    Diable Boiteux, 397–398
    Gil Blas, 266–267, 609
Lescallier, Daniel, Baron, *Enchanted Throne*, 579
Lettice, John, 129
Lever, Ashton, 324
Lewis, Meriwether
    character of, 481
    expedition of, 478–493
    Indian vocabulary of, 518
    Jefferson's biography of, 478–495
    Jefferson's instructions to, 413, 484–487
    returns to Washington, 493
    serves as governor of upper Louisiana Territory, 493
    serves as presidential secretary, 465, 472, 483
    suicide of, 493
Lewis, Monk, *Tales of Wonder*, 554
Lincoln, Levi, 464–465, 475
    "Farmer's Letters," 465
    Letters to the People, by a Farmer, 465
Lingard, John, *History of England*, 632–633, 640, 643, 644
Littleton, Thomas, *Tenures*, 64–65
Liverpool Royal Institution, 572
Livingston, Edward, 530, 531, 538
Livingston, Robert, 178
Livingston, William, 598
    Review of the Military Operations in North America, 41

Livy, 127, 139, 472, 599
    History, 352
Lloyd, Robert, 95
Locke, John, 9, 10, 21, 176, 179, 370, 386, 500, 554
    Extracts from Locke's Essay on the Human Understanding, 500
    "Letter Concerning Toleration," 204
    Two Treatises of Government, 113, 179
Logan, Chief, 99–100, 131, 146, 186, 437–438
Logan, George, 421–422
Logan, James, 68, 550
Loganian Library, 550
Lomax, Judith
    Notes of an American Lyre, 145
    "Written at Monticello," 145–146
London Sporting Magazine, 504
Long, George, 623, 626, 632, 637, 639
Longinus, *De Sublimitate*, 492
López de Gómara, Francisco, 389
López de Sedano, Juan José, *Parnaso Español*, 330
Lord's Prayer in above a Hundred Languages, 584
Lorenzana, Francisco Antonio, *Historia de Nueva España*, 521
Louis, Antoine, 335
Louis XVI, King of France, 293
Lubin, Eilhard, 374
Ludwell, Philip, 104
Luzac, Elie, 83–84
Lydgate, John, 523
Lyly, John, "No Place Commends the Man Unworthy Praise," 506
Lyric Harmony, 139
Lyttelton, George Lyttelton, Baron, 319
    Dialogues of the Dead, 181

MacDonald, Alexander, *Galick and English Vocabulary*, 142
Machiavelli, *Opere Inedite in Prosa e in Verso*, 68, 70
Macpherson, Charles, 135–136, 142–143, 146
Macpherson, James, 133–135, 142–144
    "Conlath and Cuthona," 135, 143
    Fingal, An Ancient Epic, 133–135
    Fragments of Ancient Poetry, 133

Macpherson, James (*continued*)
  Poems, 133
  Temora, 133, 135, 137
Madison, Dolley, 465, 509, 561
Madison, James (1749–1812), 35, 53, 128,
    200–201, 212, 303, 432, 444
Madison, James (1751–1836)
  acquires books and papers for
    Jefferson, 422, 424, 428
  acquires books from the Byrd
    library, 261
  advice to Jefferson regarding the
    "First Inaugural Address," 472
  appoints George Watterson
    Librarian of Congress, 561
  character of, 265
  correspondence with Jefferson, 205,
    256, 267, 268, 269, 310, 267, 330,
    401, 423, 436, 530, 599
  drafts U.S. Constitution, 283
  embargo and, 505
  elected president, 503
  friendship with Jefferson, 265–266
  inaugurated president, 509–510
  library of, 282–283, 573
  loans Jefferson a copy of Paine's
    Rights of Man, 400
  opposition to Hamilton, 395
  receives copy of *Notes on the State of
    Virginia*, 241
  serves as secretary of state, 464–465,
    505
  serves in U.S. House of
    Representatives, 394
  serves in Virginia House of
    Delegates, 204
  serves on University of Virginia
    Board of Visitors, 617–618, 629
  travels with Jefferson to New York,
    401–402, 635
  travels with Jefferson to Virginia,
    396–398
  writes letters of introduction, 534
Magruder, George, 546
Magruder, Patrick, 546, 548, 561
Mahomet II, 144
Main, Thomas, 516
Malesherbe, Chrétien Guillaume de
    Lamoignon de, 356
Mansfield, Jared, 600

March, John
  bookbinding skills, 472
  Jefferson patronizes his bookstore,
    471–472
Marius, 323
Marks, Anna Scott Jefferson (TJ's
    sister), 11, 517–518
Marmontel, Jean-François, 250, 300–302
  Contes Moreaux, 222
  Fausse Magie, 285–286
  Memoires, 595–596
  Moral Tales, 301
  Oeuvres Posthume, 596
  Silvain, 285
  Zemire et Azor, 285–286
Marmontel, Marie Adélaide Lerein de
    Montigny, Madame de, 302
Marshall, John, 455, 459, 644
  Life of Washington, 404, 417, 597, 643
Martens, Georg Friedrich de, 84
Martin, Benjamin, *Philosophical
    Grammar*, 35
Martin, Luther, 437–438
Martyn, Thomas, 129
Maryland Gazette, 81, 88
Mason, George, 207–208, 214
Mather, Cotton, *Magnalia Christi
    America*, 482
Mather, Increase, 119
Matthieu, J. D., *Dialogue Rustiques*, 35
Maury, James (1718–1769), 30–42, 46,
    47, 101, 267, 389
  "Dissertation on Education," 35–36,
    38
Maury, James (1746–1840), 32, 33
Maury, Matthew, 31
Maury, Walker, 46
Mazzei, Marie Hauteville "Petronilla"
    Martin (Mrs. Philip Mazzei),
    148
Mazzei, Philip, 147–149, 153, 211, 222,
    294, 300–302, 377, 429, 438, 573
McClurg, James, 128–129, 179
  Experiments upon the Human Bile,
    140
McCulloch, William, 192, 194
Mclane, Mrs., 410
Meik, Thomas, 278
Meikleham, Septimia A. Randolph, 420
Memoires de l'Amerique, 502

Mémoires de les Expèriences Aerostatiques, 287

Mercer, John Francis, 604

Metastasio, Pietro
  Adriano in Siria, 544–545, 608
  Opere, 544

Michael (Wythe's slave), 491

Michaux, André, 413–415, 484

Michelangelo, 575

Middleton, Conyers, 204

Miller, Philip, *Gardener's Dictionary*, 97

Milligan, Joseph
  bookbinding skills, 472, 560
  inventories Jefferson's great library, 555
  packs Jefferson's great library for shipment, 562
  publishes *Manual of Parliamentary Practice*, 527–528
  publishes *Treatise on Political Economy*, 529
  takes over John March's store, 472

Milton, John, 49, 120, 251, 307
  Comus, 130
  Of Reformation in England, 204
  Paradise Lost, 41–42, 91–92, 129, 130, 201, 308, 558, 594
  Paradise Regain'd, 130
  Reason of Church-Government, 204
  Samson Agonistes, 130
  Works, 9

Minerva, 438–439

Miscellaneous Poetry, 471

Mitchill, Samuel, 467–468

Molière, Jean Baptiste Poquelin, 105, 608

Molini, Jean Claude, 282

Monboddo, James Burnet, Lord, 324

Moncacht-Apé, 40–41

Monroe, James
  character of, 227–229, 310
  correspondence with Jefferson, 235, 243, 252–253, 278, 282, 290, 440
  friendship with Jefferson, 227, 266, 269
  inauguration, 618
  library of, 270
  serves as U.S. minister to France, 426
  serves in Congress, 266

Montagu, Edward, 129

Montagu, Elizabeth, *Essay on the Writings and Genius of Shakespeare*, 201

Montaigne, Michel de, 279, 428
  Essais, 429
  "Of Experience," 429

Montesquieu, Charles de Secondat, Baron de, 113, 279, 608
  Spirit of Laws, 239, 528

Monthly Repository of Theology, 586

Moreli, Jacopo, 372

Morellet, André, 244, 302

Morgan, John, 96

Morison, Robert
  Dialogues and Detached Sentences in the Chinese Language, 580
  View of China for Philological Purposes, 580

Moritz, Karl, 317, 319–320

Morris, Gouverneur, 415

Morris, Robert, 410

Morton, Nathaniel, *New-England's Memorial*, 540

Morton, Thomas, *New English Canaan*, 119, 539–540

Moulson, John, 498, 499

Muhammad, 258

Munford, William G. (a.k.a. W. G. Monfort), 442–444

Murray, John, fourth earl of Dunmore, 150, 152, 164–165, 168, 199

Napoleon Bonaparte, 544, 545, 605

National Gazette, 412, 440

National Intelligencer, 446, 456

Necker, Jacques, 297

Neely, James, 493

Nelson, Lucy Chiswell, 120

Nelson, Robert, *Companion for the Festivals and Fasts of the Church of England*, 71

Nelson, Thomas (1715–1787), 117

Nelson, Thomas (1738–1789), 117, 176, 223, 230, 231, 429

Nepos, Cornelius, 379, 567–568, 569
  De Vita Excellentium, 34

New York Daily Advertiser, 412

Newton, Isaac, 10, 21, 53, 213, 347, 370, 536, 537

Nicholas, Robert Carter, 108–109,
    151–152, 165
Niles' Weekly Register, 618
Norris Isaac, Jr., 110
North, Frederick, second Earl of
    Guilford, 163, 165, 167
North American Review, 618–619

Ode to the Mammoth Cheese, 474–475
Ogilby, John, *America*, 26
Ogilvie, James, 2, 119, 621
Origen
    Against Celsus, 222
    Hexapla, 222
Osborne, Henrietta, 103
Ossian, 77, 103, 133–138, 139, 142–146,
    176, 182, 250, 264, 363, 492, 578,
    609
Ostenaco, 55–56
Otis, Sameul, 547
Otto, Guillaume, 242
Ovid, 23, 507
    Epistolae, 34
    Heroides, 23
Owen, Goronwy, 49–50
Owen, John, 360
Oyré, François Ignace, Chevalier d',
    247–248

Page, John
    boyhood reading, 16
    correspondence with Jefferson, 2–4,
        10, 16–17, 23, 64–68, 93–95, 118,
        319, 336
    education of, 45–46, 49, 52–54
    friendship with Jefferson, 2, 56, 224
    runs for governor of Virginia, 223–224
    scientific activities, 53, 129, 212
    serves as governor of Virginia, 501
Page, Mann, 418
Paine, Robert Treat, 541
Paine, Thomas, 401, 411, 600
    Common Sense, 176–177, 193
    Rights of Man, 400, 446
Palladio, Andrea, *I Cinque Ordini di
    Architettura*, 631
Pantchatantra, 425
Paradise, John, 373, 377
Paradise, Lucy Ludwell, 372–375
Parker, Richard, 214

Parliamentary Register, 550
Parr, Samuel, 628
Pasteur, William, 103–104
Payne, Thomas, 367
Peacock, Thomas Love, 545
Peale, Charles Wilson, 507, 518, 596
Pendleton, Edmund, 108, 163, 168, 198,
    207–208, 214, 220
Penn, John, 176, 187
Pennsylvania Packet, 194
Percy, Thomas
    Five Pieces of Runic Poetry, 131
    Hau Kiou Choaan, 130
    Key to the New Testament, 131
    *Miscellaneous Pieces Relating to the
        Chinese*, 130
    Reliques of Ancient English Poetry,
        125, 130
Peters, Richard, 313
Petersburg Courier, 553–554
Pétis, François, *Histoire du Grand
    Genghizcan*, 199, 42
Petrarch, 608
    Il Petrarca, 353
Petty, William, *Political Survey of
    Ireland*, 112
Petyt, William, *Jus Parliamentarium*, 110
Peyrou, Pierre Alexandre, 298, 554
Philadelphia Repository, 457
Philidor, F. D., *Chess Rendered Familiar*,
    609
Phillips, William, 221, 251
Philosophical Transactions, 61
"Philosophy of Jesus" (Jefferson), 583
Pickering, Timothy, 463
*Pièces Diverses et Correspondance
    Relatives aux Opérations de
    l'Armée d' Orient en Égypte*, 569
Pierres, Philippe-Denys, 240, 281–282,
    292
Pigalle, Jean-Baptiste, 600
Pignotti, Lorenzo, *Favole e Novelle*, 282
Pike, Zebulon, *Account of Expeditions to
    the Sources of the Mississippi*, 574
Pindar, Peter, *Lousiad*, 314
Pinelli, Maffeo, 372, 373, 374
Pinto de Sousa Coutinho, Luis,
    Chevalier de, 317
Pissot, Laurent Noel, 194
Plato, 139, 379, 586

Plautus, 632
"Pleasures of Retirement," 506
Plutarch's Lives, 140
Poe, Edgar Allan, 639–640, 643–644
    "Power of Words," 644
Pohlman, J. G., 609
Pollexfen, Henry, *Of Trade*, 139
Pope, Alexander, 42, 135, 319, 321, 362
    "Epitaph; On Himself," 306
    Selecta Poemata Italorum, 69, 74
    Works, 122
Porcupine's Gazette, 437–439
*Posthumous Works of Frederic II, King of
    Prussia*, 371
Potter, John, *Antiquities of Greece*, 8
Potter, Nathaniel, *Memoir on Contagion*,
    572
Potter, Suky, 66
Price, Richard, 239, 281
    *Observations of the Nature of Civil
    Liberty*, 195
Priestley, Joseph, 42, 462–463, 541–524,
    585, 614–615
    Harmony of the Evangelists, 584
    Socrates and Jesus Compared, 477
Prior, Matthew, 127
Pritchard, William, 261, 264
Ptolemy, *L'Etat des Etoiles Fixes au
    Second Siecle*, 371
"Publicola" (J.Q. Adams), 401, 406
Pufendorf, Samuel
    De Officio Hominis et Civis, 21
    Droit de la Nature et des Gens, 83
    Of the Law of Nature and Nations, 83
Purchas, Samuel, *Purchas His
    Pilgrimage*, 556
Purdie, Alexander, 88
Purvis, John, *Complete Collection of All
    the Laws of Virginia*, 139

Quevedo, Francisco de, 330
Quintilian, 34
Qur'an, 9, 130, 201, 258, 259, 316

Rabelais, François
    Gargantua and Pantagruel, 578
    Oeuvres, 578
Ramsay, David, *History of the
    Revolution in South Carolina*,
    326–331

Randolph, Anne C. (TJ's
    granddaughter). *See* Bankhead,
    Anne C. Randolph
Randolph, Benjamin F. (TJ's grandson),
    177, 420
Randolph, Cornelia J. (TJ's
    granddaughter), 19, 420, 426,
    504, 562, 606, 607–611, 634, 635,
    636
Randolph, Edmund, 142, 159, 166, 283,
    392, 424, 428, 429
Randolph, Ellen W. (TJ's
    granddaughter). *See* Coolidge,
    Ellen W. Randolph
Randolph, George W. (TJ's grandson),
    420
Randolph, James M. (TJ's grandson),
    420
Randolph, John, 172, 173, 492
Randolph, Martha Jefferson (TJ's
    daughter), 640
    birth of, 121
    childhood, 196
    correspondence with Ellen Coolidge,
    637
    correspondence with Jefferson, 341,
    352–354, 398, 402, 411–412,
    469, 517
    education of, 266–267, 280, 375, 403
    encourages Jefferson to read *Ivanhoe*,
    578
    gives birth, 399, 470
    hospitality of, 518–519, 525, 638
    Jefferson presents books to, 266, 282,
    304, 471, 399–400, 577, 608
    meets Margaret Bayard Smith,
    476
    memories of her mother's death,
    253–255
    returns to America, 383–388
    sits for Sully, 601–602
    teaches French, 621
    travels in America, 260, 271
    travels to Paris, 275–280
    wedding of, 389
Randolph, Mary J. (TJ's
    granddaughter), 420
Randolph, Meriwether L. (TJ's
    grandson), 420
Randolph, Peter, 30, 43–44, 80

Randolph, Peyton, 167, 172
  death of, 174–175, 196
  elected to Continental Congress, 163
  library of, 202, 204, 425
  serves in House of Burgesses, 107,
    111, 164–165
  serves in Virginia Convention, 159,
    161
  Stamp Act and, 80
Randolph, Sir John, 202
Randolph, Thomas J. (TJ's grandson,
    ak.a. Jeff), 30, 89, 420, 507, 640,
    641
Randolph, Thomas Mann (1741–1793),
    45, 492
Randolph, Thomas Mann (1768–1828),
    388–389
Randolph, Virginia J. (TJ's
    granddaughter). *See* Trist,
    Virginia J. Randolph
Randolph, William, 11, 45
Rapin, René, *Critical Works*, 139
Rapin-Thoyras, Paul de, *History of
    England*, 26–27
Rastell, William, *Collection in English of
    the Statutes Now in Force*, 73–74
Ravaillac, François, 68, 124
Rawle, R. T., 457
Raymond, Robert
  Reports of Cases Argued and Adjudged,
    49
  *Reports of Cases of King's Bench and
    Common Pleas*, 492
Raynal, Abbé, 570
Real Academia Española, 426
Reed, John, 555
Reibelt, J. P., 471
Reni, Guido, *Herodias Bearing the Head
    of St. John*, 590
Report of the Committee of Revisors,
    213
Retzsch, Moritz, 575
Revere, Paul, 163
Reynard the Fox, 15
Reynolds, Maria, 440
Richardson, Robert
  *Attorney's Practice in the Court of
    Common Pleas*, 70
  *Attorney's Practice in the Court of
    King's Bench*, 70

Richardson, Samuel, 251
  Clarissa, 123
  Pamela, 123
  Sir Charles Grandison, 123
Richmond Enquirer, 617, 625
Riedesel, Frederika, Baroness von,
    221–222
Riedesel, Friedrich Adolphus, Baron
    von, 221, 224
Rind, Clementina, 160
Rind, William, 88
Rittenhouse, David, 212–213, 395, 432,
    433
Rivington, James, 271, 276
Roberts brothers, *Mémoires de les
    Expèriences Aerostatiques*, 287
Robertson, William
  History of America, 398
  History of Scotland, 72
  History of the Reign of Charles V,
    193
Robespierre, Maximilien, 529
Robinson, Moses, 462
Robinson, William, 76, 79–80
Robson, James, 373
Rochambeau, Jean-Baptiste-Donatien
    de Vimeur, Count de, 247
Rodney, Caesar, 529, 530
Roebuck, John, 54
Rogers, Thomas, *A New American
    Biographical Dictionary*,
    567–469
Rollin, Charles
  *De la Manière d'Enseigner et d'Étudier
    les Belles-Lettres*, 35
  Histoire Ancienne, 199
Roscoe, William, *On the Origin and
    Vicissitudes of Literature*, 572
Rose, Hugh, 232
Rousseau, Jean-Jacques
  Confessions, 295, 595
  Letters on the Elements of Botany,
    554
  Nouvelle Héloïse, 295, 298
  Oeuvres Completes, 298, 554
Rowe, Jacob, 50
Royal Society of London, 61, 67
Royez, Jean François, *L'Itinéraire et
    Guide des Postes d'Italie*, 342
Royle, Joseph, 68, 88

Rubens, Peter Paul
  Adoration of the Shepherds, 360
  Death of Seneca, 360
  Last Judgment, 360
Ruperti, Georg Alexander, 565
Rush, Benjamin, 525
  advice for Lewis and Clark, 485
  appreciation of "First Inaugural
    Address," 458–459
  correspondence with Jefferson, 434,
    458, 461–462, 477, 532–537,
    545
  death of, 540–541
  efforts to reconcile Adams and
    Jefferson, 532–537
  Jefferson's anecdote concerning, 469
  *Observations on the Origin of the
    Malignant Bilious*, 572
  suggests changing American place
    names, 180
  *Syllabus of a Course of Lectures in
    Chemistry*, 189
Rush, Jacob, 499
Rush, Richard, 532
Rushworth, John, *Historical Collections*,
  150
Russell, Gilbert, 493
Rutledge, Edmund, 419, 429
Rutledge, John, Jr., 169, 340–341, 351,
  354, 358, 419

Saint-Lambert, Jean-François, Marquis
  de, 295–297, 301
Sale, George, *Koran*, 9, 258, 315
Sallust, 89, 472
Sargeant, Ezra, 530
Sarsfield, Guy Claude, Comte de, 356
Saunderson, John, 596
Scapula, Johann, *Lexicon Graeco-
  Latinum*, 68–69
Schiller, Frederick, *Don Carlos*, 476
Schütz, Christian Gottfried, 425
Scott, John, *Christian Life*, 20
Scott, Walter
  Ballads and Lyrical Pieces, 578
  Ivanhoe, 578
  Lady of the Lake, 578
  Lay of the Last Minstrel, 578
  Marmion, 578
  Vision of Don Roderick, 578

Sedaine, Michel Jean
  Aucassin et Nicolette, 285
  Richard Coeur de Lion, 334
Selden, John
  Opera Omnia, 406
  Table-Talk, 406
Seneca, 126, 586
  Morals, 126
Shaaf, Mr., 396–397
Shackelford, Benjamin, 517
Shaftesbury, Anthony Ashley Cooper,
  Earl of, "Letter Concerning
  Enthusiasm," 204
Shakespeare, William, 30, 105, 125, 129,
  201, 317, 320, 366, 610
  Beauties of Shakespeare, 321
  Coriolanus, 607
  Hamlet, 91, 98
  Henry IV, Part I, 531
  King Lear, 125
  Love's Labour's Lost, 125
  Macbeth, 124, 321, 610
  Measure for Measure, 125, 543
  Merchant of Venice, 63
  Merry Wives of Windsor, 125
  Much Ado about Nothing, 125
  Othello, 607, 609, 610
  Plays, 610
  Taming of the Shrew, 611
  Tempest, 607
  Twelfth Night, 607
Sharp, Joshua, 457
Sharpe, John, *Plays of William
  Shakespeare*, 610
Shelby, Isaac, 414–415
Shelley, Percy Bysshe, 568, 575
  Revolt of Islam, 457
Shenstone, William, 306, 308, 318–319
  Poetical Works, 608
  "Princess Elizabeth," 87
  "Proposal to Advice," 636
  "Unconnected Thoughts on
    Gardening," 87
  Works, 87, 319
Sheridan, Richard Brinsley, *Rivals*, 577
Sherlock, William, 38, 176
  *Practical Discourse Concerning a
    Future Judgment*, 126
  Practical Discourse Concerning Death,
    25, 38, 126, 137

Sherman, Roger, 178
Shippen, Thomas Lee, 340–341, 351, 354, 358, 396–398
Short, William, 269, 298, 341, 345, 347, 357–359, 390, 426, 551, 586–587, 595, 601, 613
Siddons, Sarah, 321–322
Sidney, Algernon, *Discourses Concerning Government*, 179
"Simple Susan," 471
Skelton, Bathurst, 119, 122
Skelton, Reuben, 120, 140
Skipwith, Robert, 122–127, 130–131, 577
Skipwith, Tabitha, 122
Sloan, James, *Rambles in Italy*, 574
Slodtz, Michaelangelo, *Diana*, 346
Small, William, 50–55, 56, 60, 62, 64, 67–68, 71–72, 122, 128, 132, 298
Smith, Abigail Adams, 287, 290, 309, 311, 536, 543
Smith, Captain John, 154, 190, 238, 435
  Description of New England, 155
  Generall Historie of Virginia, 155, 556, 621
  Map of Virginia, 158
  True Travels, 621
Smith, Jonathan Bayard, 400
Smith, Margaret Bayard, 446–447, 450, 455–456, 459, 467, 469, 476, 509–510, 516, 520–524, 584
Smith, Robert, 465
Smith, Samuel, 439, 440, 465
Smith, Samuel Harrison, 400–401, 446–448, 456, 467, 487, 509, 520–523, 552–553, 555, 562
  Remarks on Education, 446
Smith, Samuel Stanhope, 215–216
Smith, William, *History of New York*, 631
Smith, William Loughton, 410–411
Smith, William Stephens, 309–311, 313, 326, 329
Smollett, Tobias
  Peregrine Pickle, 123
  Roderick Random, 123
Society in Scotland for Propagating Christian Knowledge, 142
Socrates, 586

Solís, Antonio de, *Historia de la Conquista de México*, 385
Sophocles, 608, 632
South-Carolina Society for Promoting and Improving Agriculture, 350
Southey, Robert, 404, 569
  Life of Nelson, 569
Spaight, Richard Dobbs, 268
Spectator, 26, 122
Spurrier, John, *Practical Farmer*, 421, 422
Staël de Holstein, Anne Louise Necker Germaine, Baronne de, 297, 298
  Corinne, ou l'Italie, 298
  De la Littérature Considérée dans ses Rapports avec les Institutions Sociales, 609
  Lettres sur les Ouvrages et le Caractere de J.-J. Rousseau, 298
Staël de Holstein, Eric Magnus, Baron de, 297
Stanley, Thomas, *History of Philosophy*, 140
Staphorst, Jacob Van, 438
Statius, 135
Stendhal, *Histoire de la Peinture en Italie*, 575–576
Sterett, Samuel, 410
Sterne, Laurence, 5, 526
  Life and Opinions of Tristram Shandy, 5–6, 94, 123, 239, 254, 360–361, 365, 366, 407
  Political Romance, 6
  Sentimental Journey through France and Italy, 6, 324–325, 343–344, 366, 407
  Sermons of Mr. Yorick, 5, 126
  Works, 6, 9, 609
Sternhold, Thomas, 28
Stewart, Matthew, *Tracts, Physical and Mathematical*, 71
Stiles, Ezra, 271, 283, 331, 395
Stith, William, 238
  History of Virginia, 72, 79
Stockdale, John, 318
Stoer, Jacques, 569
Stuart, Archibald, 425
Stuart, Gilbert, 292, 601
Stuart, James, *Tiomnadh nuadh*, 142
Sully, Thomas, 600–603

Sweeney, George Wythe, 491
Swift, Jonathan, 30, 60, 431
  Gulliver's Travels, 430–431, 463
  "To Mr. Sheridan, Upon His Verses
    Written in Circles," 306
Switzer, Stephen, *Ichnographia Rustica*,
  12–13

Tacitus, 89, 127, 472, 536, 599
  Annals, 232
Tarleton, Banastre, 231, 328
Tarquin, 76
Tasso, Torquato
  Aminta, 282, 608
  Jerusalem Delivered, 201, 433
Tate, Nahum, *New Version of the Psalms
  of David*, 28–29
Tatler, 26
Tazewell, Littleton Waller, 530,
  614–615
Tencin, Claudine-Alexandrine Guérin,
  Marquise de, 296
Tessé, Adrienne Catherine de Noailles,
  Comtesse de, 345–346, 354, 362,
  559–560
Teutsche Merkur, 171
Themistocles, 380
Théodore, Gaspar, *Le Gras*, 286
Thierry, Augustin, *Histoire de la
  Conquête de l'Angleterre par les
  Normands*, 632
Thomas, Isaiah, 88
Thompson, Mr., 637
Thompson, Mrs., 279
Thompson, Samuel, 278–279
Thomson, Charles
  advice regarding *Notes on the State of
    Virginia*, 240, 246, 292, 324, 433
  friendship with Jefferson, 96, 167,
    599
  Jefferson's advice regarding his
    translation of the Bible,
    503–504
  illness of, 584
  longevity of, 541
  serves as councilor for American
    Philosophical Society, 432–433
  Synopsis of the Four Evangelists, 583
Thomson, James, 319, 363
  Seasons, 183–184

Spring, 386
Tancred and Sigismunda, 184
Works of James Thomson, 183–184
Thornton, William, 453, 555–556
Thucydides, 139, 536
Thwaites, Edward, *Heptateuchus*, 580
Tibullus, 130
Ticknor, George, 557–560, 564–566,
  621, 629
Tillotson, John, 20, 38
  Works, 38
Time Piece, 500
Tindal, Nicolas, 26
Tissot, S. A. D.
  Advice to the People, 269
  De la Santé des Gens de Lettres,
    268–269
"To My Armchair," 506
Toland, John, *Militia Reformed*, 104
Torquemada, Juan de, *La Monarchia
  Indiana*, 330
Tott, Sophie Ernestine, 345–347
Townshend, Charles, 110–111
Tracy, Antoine Louis Claude Destutt,
  Comte de,
  *Commentary and Review of
    Montesquieu's Spirit of Laws*,
    528–529, 558–559
  Treatise on Political Economy, 529
Tracy, Nathaniel, 271, 276
Trist, Eliza, 278, 279
Trist, Hore Browse, 572
Trist, Nicholas P., 562–563, 575, 576,
  630, 631, 640–641
Trist, Virginia J. Randolph (TJ's
  granddaughter), 420, 470, 524,
  562, 563, 606, 610, 630, 632
Trumbull, John (1750–1831)
  Elegy for the Times, 185
  McFingal, 288
Trumbull, John (1756–1843)
  correspondence with Jefferson, 367,
    370
  *Death of General Montgomery in the
    Attack on Quebec*, 324, 331
  *Death of General Warren at the Battle
    of Bunker Hill*, 324, 331
  European travels, 358–360
  friendship with Jefferson, 323–324,
    326, 387

Trumbull, John (1756–1843) (*continued*)
  introduces Jefferson to Maria
    Cosway, 333
  life in Paris, 330–331
Tucker, George, 637
  Essays, 624
  Valley of Shenandoah, 624
Tucker, Josiah, *True Interest of Britain,
    Set Forth in Regard to the
    Colonies*, 192
Tull, Jethro, *Horse-Hoeing Husbandry*,
    70, 424
Tullius, Jacob, 492
Tullius, Servis, 181
Turner, Dawson, 130
Turner, Sharon, *History of the Anglo-
    Saxons*, 632
Tutwiler, Henry, 633
Tyler, Henry, 106
Tyler, John, 531
Tyler, Royall, "Versification of Ossian's
    Description," 145

Unger, Johann Ludwig de, 221–222
Universal Gazette, 446
Universal History, 140
Ursula (TJ's slave), 122

Valentin and Orson, 15
Van der Kemp, Francis Adrian,
    585–587
Vattel, Emmerich de
  Le Droit des Gens, 83–84
  Questions de Droit Natural, 268
Vergennes, Charles Gravier, Comte de,
    293, 310, 316
Verling, William, 102–103, 106
Vikramacarita, 579
Villegas, Esteban Manuel de, *La
    Eroticas*, 330
Villoison, Jean Baptiste d'Angge,
    565
Virgil, 22, 23, 135, 139, 507, 510, 565
  Aeneid, 40, 130, 168
  Opera, 34
Virginia Almanack, 53, 88, 99, 128, 166,
    167, 186
Virginia Gazette, 1, 8, 32, 68, 70–71, 72,
    73, 86, 87, 88, 101, 133, 199, 202,
    501

Virginia Society for the Promotion of
    Useful Knowledge (a.k.a.
    Philosophical Society for the
    Advancement of Useful
    Knowledge) 53, 129, 140
Voiture, Vincent, *Oeuvres*, 199
Volney, Constantin François
    Chaseboeuf, Comte de, 433–434
Voltaire, 201, 553, 600, 603, 608
  Candide, 222
  History of Charles XII, 140
  Ignorant Philosopher, 105
  Oeuvres, 553
*Voyage d'un François Exile pour la
    Religion*, 370

Walker, Adam, 364
Walker, Mary, 32
Walker, Thomas, 25, 30, 32, 236
Walthoe, Nathaniel, 107, 111
Walton, Bryan, *Biblia Sacra Polyglotta*,
    630
Ward, Samuel, 167, 174
Warner, Ferdinando, *History of the
    Rebellion and Civil Wars in
    Ireland*, 112
Warren, Mercy Otis, *Poems, Dramatic
    and Miscellaneous*, 395
Washington, George, 174, 287
  agricultural ideas of, 421
  appoints Jefferson secretary of state,
    388–389
  Battle of Princeton and, 208
  befriends Priestley, 463
  British forces drive from New York,
    198
  correspondence with Humphreys,
    288, 311, 21
  correspondence with Jefferson, 84,
    272, 322, 401, 428, 449, 472, 549
  Declaration of Causes and, 169–170
  drives British forces across New
    Jersey, 208
  elected to Continental Congress, 163
  Freneau and, 412
  Genet and, 413, 415
  marches forces from Boston to New
    York, 197
  "Mazzei letter" and, 438
  orders maps prepared, 390

portrayal in *The Anas*, 404–405, 409,
    415–417
presidential administration of,
    392–395, 416–417
reads *Gulliver's Travels*, 430
serves in House of Burgesses, 605
serves in Virginia Convention,
    162–163
visits Rhode Island with Jefferson,
    396
Waterland, Daniel, 204
Watson, Elkanah, *History of the Rise,*
    Progress, and Existing Condition
    of the Western Canals in the State
    of New York, 573
Watt, James, 54, 62
Watterston, George, 562–563
    Wanderer in Jamaica, 561
Watts, Isaac, 20
    Logick, 35
Wayles, Elizabeth, 119–120
Wayles, John, 119–120, 138, 140, 425,
    605
    library of, 120, 138–139, 140, 141
Wayne, Anthony, 486
Webster, Daniel, 76–77, 296, 301, 303,
    569–570
Webster, Noah, 438
Wedgwood, Josiah, 54, 62
Weekly Museum, 457
Weightman, General, 640
Weightman, Roger C., 578
Weisse, Christian Felix, "Ohn Lieb und
    ohne Wein," 168
Werff, Adrian van der, 361–363
    Children Playing before a Statue of
    Hercules, 361–362
    Sarah Presenting Hagar to Abraham,
    362
West, Benjamin, 292, 323–324
Wharton, Joseph, 458
Whately, Thomas, *Observations on*
    Modern Gardening, 318
Wheatcroft family, 383
Whitcomb, Samuel, 495–496, 593
White, Thomas, *Little Book for Little*
    Children, 19
White Hairs, 489–491
Whitman, Walt, "Passage to India," 486
Wieland, Christoph M., 171

Wilkes, John, 313
Willard, Joseph, 371–371
Willard, Samuel, 476–477
William V, Prince of Orange, 357
Willie, William, 202, 501
Wilson, Robert, *History of the British*
    Expedition to Egypt, 569
Wilson, Thomas, *Short and Plain*
    Instruction for the Better
    Understanding of the Lord's
    Supper, 7–8
Wirt, William
    appreciation of *Proceedings of the*
    Government, 530–531
    correspondence with Jefferson,
    76–77, 79
    dines with Duke of Saxe-Weimar-
    Eisenach, 638–639
    as Jefferson's attorney, 530
    Letters of the British Spy, 527, 530
    Sketches of the Life and Character of
    Patrick Henry, 76, 161, 569–570,
    597
Wise Men of Gotham, 15
Wistar, Caspar, *System of Anatomy*, 571
Wolff, Christian, *Institutions du Droit de*
    la Nature et des Gens, 83–84
Wollaston, William, *Religion of Nature*
    Delineated, 20–21
Wood, James, 227
Wood, Robert, *Ruins of Balbec*, 521
Wood, William, *New Englands Prospect*,
    539
Worrall, John, *Bibliotheca Legum*, 425
Wren, Christopher, 10
Wright, Captain, 383–384
Wright, Frances, *Few Days in Athens*,
    145
Wythe, George
    classical learning, 58, 64
    correspondence with Jefferson, 349,
    428, 445, 586
    Decisions of Cases in Virginia, by the
    High Court of Chancery,
    427–428
    encourages Jefferson's *Manual of*
    Parliamentary Practice, 445, 448
    founder of Virginia Philosophical
    Society for the Advancement of
    Useful Knowledge, 129

Wythe, George (*continued*)
    friendship with Fauquier, 60
    friendship with Small, 71
    as Jefferson's teacher, 57–58, 73, 75,
        596
    legal abilities, 57–58
    library of, 235, 491, 492
    murder, 491–492
    receives Jefferson's *Report on
        Establishing a Uniformity,*
        395
    revises Virginia laws, 207–208,
        220–221
    sends Jefferson Foulis catalogues,
        117, 127
    as William Short's teacher, 298

Xanthus, 17–18
Xenophon, of Ephesus, 379, 524
    De Amoribus Anthiae et Abrocomae, 374

Young, Edward, 9, 176, 306
    Night Thoughts, 135
    Works, 135

Zane, Isaac, 261–262